Lecture Notes in Computer Science
Edited by G. Goos, J. Hartmanis and J. van Leeuv

Springer
Berlin
Heidelberg
New York
Barcelona
Hong Kong
London
Milan
Paris
Singapore
Tokyo

Jerzy Tiuryn (Ed.)

Foundations of Software Science and Computation Structures

Third International Conference, FOSSACS 2000
Held as Part of the Joint European Conferences on Theory and Practice of Software, ETAPS 2000
Berlin, Germany, March 25 – April 2, 2000
Proceedings

Springer

Volume Editor

Jerzy Tiuryn
Warsaw University
Institute of Informatics
Banacha 2, 02-097 Warsaw, Poland
E-mail: tiuryn@mimuw.edu.pl

Cataloging-in-Publication Data applied for

Die Deutsche Bibliothek - CIP-Einheitsaufnahme

Foundations of software science and computation structures : third international conference ; proceedings / FOSSACS 2000, held as part of the Joint European Conferences on Theory and Practice of Software, ETAPS 2000, Berlin, Germany, March 25 - April 2, 2000. Jerzy Tiuryn (ed.). - Berlin ; Heidelberg ; New York ; Barcelona ; Hong Kong ; London ; Milan ; Paris ; Singapore ; Tokyo : Springer, 2000
(Lecture notes in computer science ; Vol. 1784)
ISBN 3-540-67257-5

CR Subject Classification (1991): F.3, F.4.2, F.1.1, D.3.3-4, D.2.1

ISSN 0302-9743
ISBN 3-540-67257-5 Springer-Verlag Berlin Heidelberg New York

Typesetting: Camera-ready by author, data conversion by Boller Mediendesign
Printed on acid-free paper SPIN 10719960 06/3142 5 4 3 2 1 0

Foreword

ETAPS 2000 was the third instance of the European Joint Conferences on Theory and Practice of Software. ETAPS is an annual federated conference that was established in 1998 by combining a number of existing and new conferences. This year it comprised five conferences (FOSSACS, FASE, ESOP, CC, TACAS), five satellite workshops (CBS, CMCS, CoFI, GRATRA, INT), seven invited lectures, a panel discussion, and ten tutorials.

The events that comprise ETAPS address various aspects of the system development process, including specification, design, implementation, analysis, and improvement. The languages, methodologies, and tools which support these activities are all well within its scope. Different blends of theory and practice are represented, with an inclination towards theory with a practical motivation on one hand and soundly-based practice on the other. Many of the issues involved in software design apply to systems in general, including hardware systems, and the emphasis on software is not intended to be exclusive.

ETAPS is a loose confederation in which each event retains its own identity, with a separate program committee and independent proceedings. Its format is open-ended, allowing it to grow and evolve as time goes by. Contributed talks and system demonstrations are in synchronized parallel sessions, with invited lectures in plenary sessions. Two of the invited lectures are reserved for "unifying" talks on topics of interest to the whole range of ETAPS attendees. The aim of cramming all this activity into a single one-week meeting is to create a strong magnet for academic and industrial researchers working on topics within its scope, giving them the opportunity to learn about research in related areas, and thereby to foster new and existing links between work in areas that were formerly addressed in separate meetings. The program of ETAPS 2000 included a public business meeting where participants had the opportunity to learn about the present and future organization of ETAPS and to express their opinions about what is bad, what is good, and what might be improved.

ETAPS 2000 was hosted by the Technical University of Berlin and was efficiently organized by the following team:

Bernd Mahr (General Chair)
Hartmut Ehrig (Program Coordination)
Peter Pepper (Organization)
Stefan Jähnichen (Finances)
Radu Popescu-Zeletin (Industrial Relations)

with the assistance of BWO Marketing Service GmbH. The publicity was superbly handled by Doris Fähndrich of the TU Berlin with assistance from the ETAPS publicity chair, Andreas Podelski. Overall planning for ETAPS conferences is the responsibility of the ETAPS steering committee, whose current membership is:

Egidio Astesiano (Genova), Jan Bergstra (Amsterdam), Pierpaolo Degano (Pisa), Hartmut Ehrig (Berlin), José Fiadeiro (Lisbon), Marie-Claude Gaudel (Paris), Susanne Graf (Grenoble), Furio Honsell (Udine), Heinrich Hußmann (Dresden), Stefan Jähnichen (Berlin), Paul Klint (Amsterdam), Tom Maibaum (London), Tiziana Margaria (Dortmund), Ugo Montanari (Pisa), Hanne Riis Nielson (Aarhus), Fernando Orejas (Barcelona), Andreas Podelski (Saarbrücken), David Sands (Göteborg), Don Sannella (Edinburgh), Gert Smolka (Saarbrücken), Bernhard Steffen (Dortmund), Wolfgang Thomas (Aachen), Jerzy Tiuryn (Warsaw), David Watt (Glasgow), Reinhard Wilhelm (Saarbrücken)

ETAPS 2000 received generous sponsorship from:

the Institute for Communication and Software Technology of TU Berlin
the European Association for Programming Languages and Systems
the European Association for Theoretical Computer Science
the European Association for Software Science and Technology
the "High-Level Scientific Conferences" component of the European Commission's Fifth Framework Programme

I would like to express my sincere gratitude to all of these people and organizations, the program committee members of the ETAPS conferences, the organizers of the satellite events, the speakers themselves, and finally Springer-Verlag for agreeing to publish the ETAPS proceedings.

January 2000 — Donald Sannella
ETAPS Steering Committee chairman

Preface

This volume contains the proceedings of the international conference Foundations of Software Science and Computation Structures (FOSSACS 2000), held in Berlin, March 27–31, 2000. FOSSACS is a constituent event of the Joint European Conferences on Theory and Practice of Software (ETAPS). This was the third meeting of ETAPS. The previous two meetings took place in Lisbon (1998) and Amsterdam (1999).

FOSSACS seeks papers which offer progress in foundational research with a clear significance for software science. A central issue is theories and methods which support the specification, transformation, verification, and analysis of programs and software systems. The articles contained in the proceedings represent various aspects of the scope of the conference described above. In addition to the invited lectures of ETAPS 2000, FOSSACS 2000 had one invited lecture by Abbas Edalat (Imperial College, London) "A Data Type for Computational Geometry and Solid Modelling".

These proceedings contain 25 contributed papers, selected out of a total of 68 submissions. This has been the largest number of submissions to FOSSACS to date. The selection procedure was done through a virtual meeting of the program committee. Each paper was thoroughly evaluated by the members of the program committee and their subreferees. I would like to sincerely thank all of them for the excellent job they did during the very difficult process of selecting the papers. Special thanks go to Robert Maron for his help in organizing the WWW page for the selection process and for his continuous efforts in maintaining and processing large data files.

January 2000 Jerzy Tiuryn

FOSSACS 2000 Program Committee

Andre Arnold (Bordeaux)
Mariangiola Dezani (Torino)
Harald Ganzinger (Saarbrücken)
Georg Gottlob (Vienna)
Fritz Henglein (Copenhagen)
Jean-Pierre Jouannaud (Orsay)
Dexter Kozen (Ithaca, NY)
Marta Kwiatkowska (Birmingham)
Giuseppe Longo (Paris)
Andrew Pitts (Cambridge)
Wolfgang Thomas (Aachen)
Glynn Winskel (Aarhus)
Moshe Y. Vardi (Houston, TX)
Jerzy Tiuryn (Warsaw, chair)

Referees

S. Abramsky
L. Aceto
L. de Alfaro
T. Altenkirch
H.R. Andersen
R. Back
S. van Bakel
F. Barbanera
D. Beauquier
M. Benke
J. Berstel
G.M. Bierman
E. Bihler
F. Blanqui
V. Bono
A. Boudet
M. Bozzano
M. Bravetti
A.C. Caron
D. Caucal
G. Chen
M. Coppo
R. Di Cosmo
J.-M. Couvreur
P.R. D'Argenio
F. Damiani
G. Delzanno
A. Dicky
U. H. Engberg
J. Esparza
M. Fernandez
A. Filinski
J.-C. Filliatre
W. Fokkink
C. Fournet
R. Freund
P. Gardner
S. Gay
G. Ghelli
P. Di Gianantonio
D. Giannakopoulou
P. Giannini
H. Goguen
A. Gordon
B. Gramlich
M. Griebl
S. Guerrini
R. Heckel
R. Heckmann
N. Heintze
J. G. Henriksen
H. Hermanns
T. T. Hildebrandt
C.A.R. Hoare
F. Honsell
H. Hosoya
M. Huth
H. Huttel
D. Janin
M. Kegelmann
D. Kesner
L. J. Khalil
U. Kohlenbach
T. Kurata
A. Kuvcera
C. Laneve
R. Langerak
G. Lenzi
M. Leucker
F. Levi
U. de' Liguoro
L. Liquori
P. Madhusudan
P. Maier
L. Maranget
R. Mayr
P.-A. Mellies
J. Meseguer
M. Mohnen
B. Monate
Ch. Morvan
A. Muscholl
P. Møller Neergaard
M. Nielsen
A. Nonnengart
G. Norman
I. Ogata
F. Otto
C. Palamidessi
L. Palopoli
F. Pfenning
B. Pierce
A. Piperno
A. Podelski
E. Polonovski
F. Pottier
F. Prost
L. Puel
R. Pugliese
F. Ranzato
L. Regnier
J. Rehof
J.H. Rety
E. Ritter
S. Ronchi
D. Rosenzweig
L. Roversi
M. Ryan
D. Sands
C. Schröter
R. Segala
S. Seibert
H. Seidl
G. Senizergues
P. Sewell
A. Skou
L. Staiger
B. Steffen
R. Strandh
M. Stumptner
R. Treinen
J. Tyszkiewicz
P. Urzyczyn
T. Valkevych
H. Veith
W. Vogler
D. Volpano
B. Werner
J. Wiedermann
W. Zielonka
P. Zimmer
J. Zwanenburg

Table of Contents

Norm Functions for Probabilistic Bisimulations with Delays 1
Christel Baier, Mariëlle Stoelinga

Constructor Subtyping in the Calculus of Inductive Constructions 17
Gilles Barthe, Femke van Raamsdonk

Verifying Performance Equivalence for Timed Basic Parallel Processes ... 35
Beatrice Bérard, Anne Labroue, Philippe Schnoebelen

On Word Rewriting Systems Having a Rational Derivation 48
Didier Caucal

Proof Nets and Explicit Substitutions 63
Roberto Di Cosmo, Delia Kesner, Emmanuel Polonovski

Typing Local Definitions and Conditional Expressions with Rank 2 Intersection 82
Ferruccio Damiani

Hierarchical Graph Transformation 98
Frank Drewes, Berthold Hoffmann, Detlef Plump

A Program Refinement Framework Supporting Reasoning about Knowledge and Time 114
Kai Engelhardt, Ron van der Meyden, Yoram Moses

A Higher-Order Simulation Relation for System F 130
Jo Erskine Hannay

Probabilistic Asynchronous π-Calculus 146
Oltea Mihaela Herescu, Catuscia Palamidessi

Constructive Data Refinement in Typed Lambda Calculus 161
Furio Honsell, John Longley, Donald Sannella, Andrzej Tarlecki

On Recognizable Stable Trace Languages 177
Jean-François Husson, Rémi Morin

The State Explosion Problem from Trace to Bisimulation Equivalence 192
François Laroussinie, Philippe Schnoebelen

A Proof System for Timed Automata 208
Huimin Lin, Wang Yi

Categorical Models for Intuitionistic and Linear Type Theory 223
Maria Emilia Maietti, Valeria de Paiva, Eike Ritter

Locality and Polyadicity in Asynchronous Name-Passing Calculi 238
Massimo Merro

On Rational Graphs 252
Christophe Morvan

Sequential and Concurrent Abstract Machines for Interaction Nets 267
Jorge Sousa Pinto

On Synchronous and Asynchronous Mobile Processes 283
Paola Quaglia, David Walker

Type Inference for First-Order Logic 297
Aleksy Schubert

An Algebraic Foundation for Adaptive Programming 314
Peter Thiemann

Predicate Logic and Tree Automata with Tests 329
Ralf Treinen

Compositional Verification in Linear-Time Temporal Logic 344
Yih-Kuen Tsay

On the Semantics of Refinement Calculi 359
Hongseok Yang, Uday S. Reddy

Subtyping and Typing Algorithms for Mobile Ambients 375
Pascal Zimmer

Author Index 391

Norm Functions for Probabilistic Bisimulations with Delays

Christel Baier[1] and Mariëlle Stoelinga[2]

[1] Institut für Informatik I, Universität Bonn
Römerstraße 164, D-53117 Bonn, Germany
baier@cs.uni-bonn.de

[2] Computing Science Institute, University of Nijmegen
P.O.Box 9010, 6500 GL Nijmegen,The Netherlands
marielle@cs.kun.nl

Abstract. We consider action-labelled systems with non-deterministic and probabilistic choice. Using the concept of norm functions [17], we introduce two types of bisimulations (called *(strict) normed bisimulation equivalence*) that allow for delays when simulating a transition and are strictly between strong and weak bisimulation equivalence à la [26,36,37]. Using a suitable modification of the prominent splitter/partitioning technique [25,30], we present polynomial-time algorithms that constructs the quotient space of the (strict) normed bisimulation equivalence classes.

1 Introduction

Probabilistic aspects play a crucial role for a quantitative analysis of various types of parallel systems, such as systems that are designed on the basis of a randomized algorithms or computer systems with unreliable components. In the former case, probabilities can be used to specify the frequencies of the possible outcomes of an explicit probabilistic choice ("tossing a fair coin"); in the latter case, probabilities might express failure rates. Besides the probabilistic choices, the (transition) systems we consider allow for nondeterministic choices. These can be used for modelling probabilistic systems with asynchronous parallelism [41,19,18,34,5] where the non-determinism is used to describe the *interleaving* of the subprocesses. Moreover, as observed by several authors [21,23,34], the non-determinism can also be used to represent *underspecification* or *incomplete information* about the environment. Due to the combination of non-determinism and probability, the design and analysis of such systems (with both types of choices) can be hard.

Like for any kind of computer systems, the use of implementation relations (which compare two systems; thus yielding a formal definition of when a program $\mathcal{P}$ implements correctly another one $\mathcal{P}'$) have turned out to be useful for the design and the system analysis. In this paper, we restrict to the equivalences that yield a notion of *process equality.* There are several highly desirable conditions that any reasonable process equivalence $\approx$ should fulfill, including e.g. the soundness for establishing quantitative linear time properties and congruence

J. Tiuryn (Ed.): FOSSACS 2000, LNCS 1784, pp. 1–16, 2000.

properties w.r.t. certain composition operators of a process calculus (such as parallel composition). A further crucial aspect is the development of methods that support the proof of the equivalence of two processes (i.e. deductive or algorithmic techniques to show $\mathcal{P} \approx \mathcal{P}'$). The algorithmic methods are of great importance for automatic verification tools that take as their input a system $\mathcal{P}$ and its specification $\mathcal{P}'$ and decides whether $\mathcal{P}$ correctly implements $\mathcal{P}'$. Moreover, algorithms for computing the quotient space yield an abstraction technique which is highly relevant for the system analysis. For this, one replaces the states by their equivalence classes and then establishes the desired properties for the quotient space $S/\approx$ rather than the original state space S. Especially when we deal with *weak equivalences* (that abstract from internal computations) the switch from the original system S to the quotient space $S/\approx$ might lead to a much smaller equivalent system; and hence can be viewed as a technique to combat the state explosion problem.

Several (strong and weak) equivalences for various types of probabilistic systems have been proposed in the literature. They range over the full linear and branching time spectrum and are extensions of the corresponding relations on LTSs. While in the fully probabilistic setting, the equivalences are studied under several aspects (compositionality, axiomatization, decidability, logical characterizations, etc.), see e.g. [24,10,22,20,27,9,4], the treatment of equivalences for probabilistic systems with non-determinism is less well-understood. Most of the standard relations that have proven to be useful in the non-probabilistic setting have been extended for the probabilistic case; see e.g. [35] for a trace-based relation, [42,23] for testing equivalences and [26,19,18,36,43,37,35,38,39] for several types of (bi-)simulations. However, due to the combination of non-determinism and probability, the definitions are more complicated than the corresponding notions for non-probabilistic or fully probabilistic systems. Even though some important issues (like compositionality and axiomatization) have been addressed in the above mentioned literature, research on algorithmic methods to decide the equivalence of two systems or to compute the quotient space are rare. For strong bisimulation [26] and strong simulation [36], polynomial-time algorithms have been presented in [3]. To the best of our knowledge, the forthcoming work [32] is the first attempt to formulate an algorithmic method that deals with a weak equivalence for probabilistic processes with non-determinism. We are not aware of any complexity (or even decidability) result for weak bisimulation à la [36,37] or any linear time relation on probabilistic systems with non-determinism, e.g. trace distribution equivalence [35].[1]

Our contribution: We deal with probabilistic systems with non-determinism and action labels modelled by a probabilistic extension of LTSs where the (action-labelled) transitions are augmented with probabilities for the possible target states. Our model essentially agrees with the *simple probabilistic automata* of

[1] As (non-probabilistic) LTSs are special instances of probabilistic systems with non-determinism and the trace distribution preorder à la Segala is a conservative extension of usual trace containment, the PSPACE-completeness for LTSs [25] yields the PSPACE-hardness for the trace distribution relation à la [35].

[36,34]). Our main contribution is the presentation of novel notions of bisimulation equivalence which (in some sense) are insensitive with respect to internal transitions. More precisely, our equivalences are conservative extensions of *delay bisimulation* equivalence [40,14] which relies on the assumption that the simulation of a step of a process $\mathcal{P}$ by another process $\mathcal{P}'$ might happen with a certain delay (i.e. after a sequence of internal transitions). The formal definition of our equivalences is provided by a probabilistic variant of *norm functions* in the style of [17]. Intuitively, the norm functions specify bounds for the delays (i.e. the number of internal transitions that might be performed before a "proper" transition of a process $\mathcal{P}$ is simulated by a corresponding transition of an equivalent process $\mathcal{P}'$). In the probabilistic setting where the combination of internal transitions leads to a tree rather than a linear chain, the norm functions yield conditions on the length of the paths in the trees corresponding to a "delayed transition". Using a modification of the traditional splitter/partioning technique [25,30], we present polynomial time algorithms for computing the quotient spaces. Moreover, we briefly discuss some other aspects (compositionality w.r.t. parallel composition and preservation of linear time properties).
Organization of the paper: Section 2 introduces our model for probabilistic labelled transition systems. The definitions of norm functions and normed bisimulations are presented in Section 3. In Section 4, we present our algorithm for computing the bisimulation equivalence classes. Section 5 concludes the paper.

Because of space restrictions, we present our main results without proofs. We refer the interested reader to [6] where the proofs and other details (including results about various types of bisimulations and simulations) can be found.

2 Probabilistic Labelled Transition Systems

In (ordinary) LTSs, the transitions $s \xrightarrow{a} t$ specify the possibility that the system in state s moves via the action a to state t. In this paper, we deal with a probabilistic variant of LTSs where any transition is augmented with a probabilistic choice for the possible target states (rather than a unique target state t as it is the case in LTSs). That is, in the probabilistic setting, the transitions are of the form $s \xrightarrow{a} \mu$ where s is the starting state, a an action label and μ a distribution on the state space which specifies the probabilities $\mu(t)$ for any possible successor state t. Non-determinism is present in our model since we allow several (possibly equally action-labelled) outgoing transitions of a state s.

Notation 1 Let S be a finite set. A *distribution* on S is a function $\mu : S \to [0,1]$ such that $\sum_{s \in S} \mu(s) = 1$. Let $Supp(\mu) = \{s \in S : \mu(s) > 0\}$ denote the *support* of μ; $\mu[A] = \sum_{s \in A} \mu(s)$ for $\emptyset \neq A \subseteq S$ and $\mu[\emptyset] = 0$. For $s \in S$, μ_s^1 denotes the unique distribution on S with $\mu_s^1(s) = 1$. $Distr(S)$ denotes the collection of all distributions on S. If R is an equivalence relation on S then S/R to denotes the quotient space of S with respect to R. The induced equivalence $\equiv_R$ on $Distr(S)$ is given by $\mu \equiv_R \mu'$ iff $\mu[A] = \mu'[A]$ for all $A \in S/R$. We write $[\mu]_R$ for the equivalence class $\{\mu' : \mu \equiv_R \mu\}$ of μ with respect to $\equiv_R$.

Definition 1. A *probabilistic labelled transition system* (PLTS for short) is a tuple $(S, Act, \longrightarrow)$ where S is a finite set of states, Act a finite set of actions (containing a special symbol τ)[2] and $\longrightarrow \subseteq S \times Act \times Distr(S)$ a transition relation such that for all $s \in S$ and $a \in Act$, $Steps_a(s) = \{\mu : s \xrightarrow{a} \mu\}$ is finite.[3] A *probabilistic program* is a tuple $\mathcal{P} = (S, Act, \longrightarrow, s_{init})$ consisting of a PLTS $(S, Act, \longrightarrow)$ and an initial state $s_{init} \in S$.

Example 1. We consider a simple communication protocol consisting of a sender (that produces certain messages and tries to submit the messages along an unreliable medium) and a receiver (that acknowledges the receipt and consumes the received messages). For simplicity, we assume that both the sender and the receiver work with mailing boxes that cannot hold more than one message at any time. The failure rate of the medium is 1%; i.e., with probability 1/100 the medium looses the messages and the sender retries to submit the message. In state s_{init}, the sender produces a message and passes the message to the medium which leads to the state s_{del} (where the medium tries to deliver the message via an internal action). When the message is delivered correctly, the state s_{ok} is reached. In state s_{ok}, the sender and the receiver can work in parallel (modelled by interleaving): the sender may produce the next message while the receiver may consume the last message.

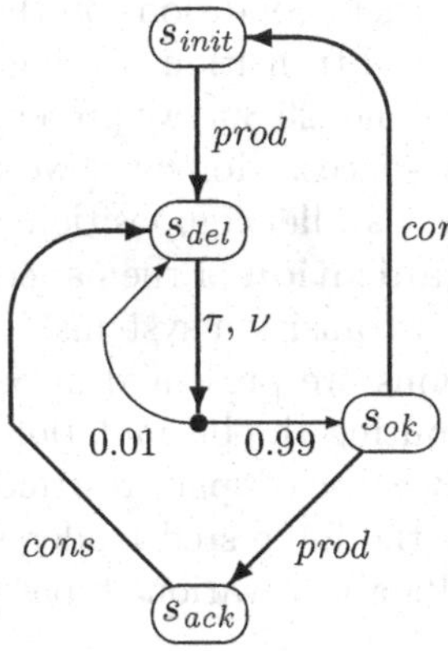

The executions of a PLTS are given by the paths in the underlying directed graph. They arise through the resolution of both the non-deterministic and probabilistic choices.[4] Typically, one assumes that the resolution of the non-deterministic choices are not under the control of the system itself. The entity that resolves the non-determinism (the "environment") can be formalized by a *scheduler* [41] (also called *adversary* [34] or *policy* in the theory of MDPs [33]). Given a scheduler A, the system behaviour under A can be described by a Markov chain which yields a Borel field and probability measure on the paths that can be obtained by A. The details are not of importance for this paper and are omitted here. They can be found e.g. in the above mentioned references.

3 Normed Bisimulation

In ordinary LTSs, the several types of bisimulations (e.g. strong, weak branching or delay bisimulation [28,31,29,16,40,14]) establish a correspondence between the

[2] We refer to τ as the *internal* action. All other actions are called *visible*.

[3] Any finite LTS $(S, Act, \longrightarrow)$ (where $\longrightarrow \subseteq S \times Act \times S$) can be viewed as a PLTS. For this, we identify any transition $s \xrightarrow{a} t$ with its probabilistic counterpart $s \xrightarrow{a} \mu_t^1$.

[4] Formally, a *path* is a "sequence" $s_0 \xrightarrow{a_1,\mu_1} s_1 \xrightarrow{a_2,\mu_2} s_2 \xrightarrow{a_2,\mu_2} \ldots$ where $s_{i-1} \xrightarrow{a_i} \mu_i$, $s_i \in Supp(\mu_i)$.

states and their stepwise behaviour. Intuitively, they identify those states s and s' where any outgoing transition from s can be simulated by s' and vice versa. Most types of bisimulation equivalences on a LTS $(S, Act, \longrightarrow)$ can be characterized as the coarsest equivalence R on the state space S such that

(Bis) If $(s, s') \in R$, $C \in S/R$ and $s \xrightarrow{a} C$ then $s' \in Pre^*(a, C)$.

Here, we write $s \xrightarrow{a} C$ if $s \xrightarrow{a} t$ for some $t \in C$. $Pre^*(a, C)$ denotes a certain *predecessor predicate*. Intuitively, $s' \in Pre^*(a, C)$ asserts that s' can "simulate" the transition $s \xrightarrow{a} C$. The formal definition of $Pre^*(a, C)$ depends on the concrete type of equivalence. E.g., *strong bisimulation* is obtained by using the predicate $Pre^{sbis}(a, C) = \{s' : s' \xrightarrow{a} C\}$ while *delay bisimulation* equivalence [40,14] focuses on the idea that the simulation of a transition $s \xrightarrow{a} t$ might happen with a certain delay (i.e. after a finite number of internal moves) and uses the predicates $Pre^{del}(\cdot)$ which are given by the following three conditions.[5]

(D0) $C \subseteq Pre^{del}(\tau, C)$

(D1) If $s \xrightarrow{a} C$ then $s \in Pre^{del}(a, C)$.

(D2) If $s \xrightarrow{\tau} t$ and $t \in Pre^{del}(a, C)$ then $s \in Pre^{del}(a, C)$.

[26] presented an elegant reformulation of strong bisimulation for a variant of PLTSs which takes the probabilistic effect of the transitions into account. Formally, strong bisimulation equivalence $\approx_{sbis}$ in a PLTSs is the coarsest equivalence R on the state space S such that for all $(s, s') \in R$ and transitions $s \xrightarrow{a} \mu$ there is a transition $s' \xrightarrow{a} \mu'$ where μ and μ' return the same probabilities for all equivalence classes under R (i.e. $\mu \equiv_R \mu'$, cf. Notation 1). [36,37] presented notions of weak and branching bisimulations for PLTSs. All these notions of bisimulation equivalences on a PLTS $(S, Act, \longrightarrow)$ can be characterized as the coarsest equivalence R on S such that

(PBis) If $(s, s') \in R$, $M \in Distr(S)/\equiv_R$ and $s \xrightarrow{a} M$ then $s' \in Pre^*(a, M)$.

Here, $s \xrightarrow{a} M$ iff $s \xrightarrow{a} \mu$ for some $\mu \in M$. E.g., strong bisimulation equivalence is given by (PBis) using the predecessor predicate $Pre^{sbis}(a, M) = \{s' : s' \xrightarrow{a} M\}$.

We now propose novel notions of bisimulation equivalence for PLTSs which are conservative extensions of delay bisimulation equivalence [40,14]. Intuitively, two states s, s' are identified iff any transition $s \xrightarrow{a} \mu$ can be simulated by s' by first performing finitely many internal moves and then performing an a-labelled transition for which the outcome of the associated probabilistic choice agrees with μ.[6] Thus, we aim at an appropriate definition of the predecessor predicate $Pre^{del}(a, M)$ where (for $a \neq \tau$ or $\mu^1_{s'} \notin M$) $s' \in Pre^{del}(a, M)$ states the possibility for s' to perform the action a (possibly with a certain delay) such that the associated distribution μ' of the a-labelled transition belongs to $M = [\mu]_R$. Conditions (D0) and (D1) for $Pre^{del}(a, C)$ can easily be lifted to the probabilistic case (see conditions (BD0) and (BD1) below).

---

[5] Thus, $Pre^{del}(a, C) = \{s' : s' \xrightarrow{\tau^* a} C\}$ for $a \neq \tau$ and $Pre^{del}(\tau, C) = \{s' : s' \xrightarrow{\tau^*} C\}$.

[6] This informal explanation assumes that $s \xrightarrow{a} \mu$ is a "proper" transition, i.e. either $a \neq \tau$ or $\mu^1_s \notin M$. Transitions of the form $s \xrightarrow{\tau} \mu$ where all possible target states $t \in Supp(\mu)$ are equivalent to s can be viewed as "silent moves" and are not taken account when dealing with equivalences that abstract from internal computations.

(BD0) If $\mu_s^1 \in M$ then $s \in Pre^{del}(\tau, M)$.

(BD1) If $s \xrightarrow{a} M$ then $s \in Pre^{del}(a, M)$.

To adapt condition (D2) for the probabilistic setting, we have two possibilities depending on whether or not we allow for unbounded delays. For the simpler case, we require *bounded delays* which leads to condition (BD2).

(BD2) If $s \xrightarrow{\tau} \nu$ and $Supp(\nu) \subseteq Pre^{del}(a, M)$ then $s \in Pre^{del}(a, M)$.

The resulting bisimulation equivalence only abstracts from the combination of finitely many internal moves (corresponding to a bounded delay) but cannot involve the effect of infinite τ-paths (*unbounded delays*). In the communication protocol of Example 1, one might argue that the states s_{del} and s_{ok} have the same observable behaviour as s_{del} moves via τ-transitions to s_{ok} with probability 1. To formalize the effect of infinite τ-loops, we use the concept of *norm functions* which was introduced in [17] to reason about simulation-like relations in non-probabilistic systems. We slightly depart from the notations of [17] and define norm functions in LTSs as partial functions with three arguments (a state s, an action label a and a set C of target states) and whose range are the natural numbers. If the value $n(s, a, C)$ is defined then $s \in Pre^{del}(a, C)$ in which case there is a τ^*-labelled path of length $\leq n(s, a, C)$ from s to a state t where either $t \xrightarrow{a} C$ or $a = \tau$ and $t \in C$. If $s \notin Pre^{del}(a, C)$ then $n(s, a, C)$ is undefined (denoted $n(s, a, C) = \perp$). The formal definition of norm functions in LTSs arises by "refining" the above mentioned three conditions for $Pre^{del}(a, C)$ in the sense that we involve the length of a delayed transition. Formally, norm functions in LTSs are partial functions satisfying the following three conditions.

(N0) $n(s, a, C) = 0$ implies $a = \tau$ and $s \in C$

(N1) $n(s, a, C) = 1$ implies $s \xrightarrow{a} C$

(N2) If $n(s, a, C) \geq 2$ then there is a transition $s \xrightarrow{\tau} t$ where $n(t, a, C) < n(s, a, C)$.

To adapt these three conditions to the probabilistic setting, we deal with a set $M \subseteq Distr(S)$ as the third argument of a norm function. The modifications of (N0) and (N1) are straightforward. In (N2) we require that $n(s, a, M) \geq 2$ implies the existence of a transition $s \xrightarrow{\tau} \nu$ satisfying a certain condition. When we aim at bounded delays then we deal with the constraint $n(t, a, M) < n(s, a, M)$ for *all* $t \in Supp(\nu)$. For unbounded delays, we require that $n(t, a, M)$ is defined for all $t \in Supp(\nu)$ and $n(t, a, M) < n(s, a, M)$ for *some* $t \in Supp(\nu)$.[7]

Definition 2. A *norm function* for a PLTS $(S, Act, \longrightarrow)$ is a partial function $n : S \times Act \times 2^{Distr(S)} \to \mathbb{N}$ which satisfies the following conditions.

(PN0) $n(s, a, M) = 0$ implies $a = \tau$ and $\mu_s^1 \in M$.

(PN1) $n(s, a, M) = 1$ implies $s \xrightarrow{a} M$ (i.e. $s \xrightarrow{a} \mu$ for some $\mu \in M$).

[7] These two conditions about $Supp(\nu)$ guarantee the existence of a scheduler where, for any state s for which $n(s, a, M)$ is defined, almost all paths starting in s lead via τ's to a state t where $n(t, a, M) \in \{0, 1\}$. Thus, in this scheduler, with probability 1, s performs finitely many τ's followed by a transitions $t \xrightarrow{a} \mu'$ where $\mu' \in M$. However, for this scheduler, there might be no upper bound for the number of τ's that will be performed before the action a.

(PN2) If $n(s, a, M) \geq 2$ then there is a transition $s \xrightarrow{\tau} \nu$ where
(i) $n(t, a, M) \neq \bot$ for all $t \in Supp(\nu)$
(ii) $n(t, a, M) < n(s, a, M)$ for some $t \in Supp(\nu)$

n is *strict* iff, in (ii), $n(t, a, M) < n(s, a, M)$ for all $t \in Supp(\nu)$.

Example 2. Consider the system on the right. Let M be the set of distributions μ that return probability 1 for the x-states (i.e. $M = \{\mu : \mu(x_1) + \mu(x_2) = 1\}$). Then, $\mu^1_{x_1}, \mu^1_{x_2} \in M$ and $s_1 \xrightarrow{a} M$, $s_2 \xrightarrow{a} M$. Thus, the partial function n with $n(s_0, a, M) = 2$, $n(s_1, a, M) = n(s_2, a, M) = 1$ and $n(\cdot) = \bot$ in all other cases is a strict norm function.

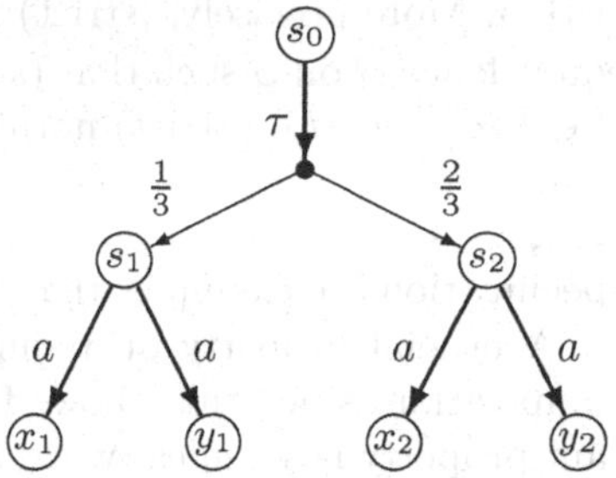

Definition 3. Let $(S, Act, \longrightarrow)$ be a PLTS and R an equivalence on S. R is called a *(strict) normed bisimulation* iff there exists a (strict) norm function n such that for all $a \in Act$ and $M \in Distr(S)/\equiv_R$: if $(s, s') \in R$ and $s \xrightarrow{a} M$ then $n(s', a, M) \neq \bot$. Two states s and s' are called *(strictly) normed bisimilar* (denoted $s \approx_n s'$ resp. $s \approx_{sn} s'$) iff there exists a (strict) normed bisimulation R such that $(s, s') \in R$. The equivalences $\approx_n$ and $\approx_{sn}$ are adapted for probabilistic programs in the obvious way.[8]

Example 3. It is easy to see that the states s_0, s_1 and s_2 in Example 7 are strictly normed bisimilar. For the simple communication protocol of Example 1 and the smallest equivalence relation R that identifies s_{del} and s_{ok}, there is a norm function with $n(s_{ok}, \tau, [\nu]_R,) = 0$ and $n(s_{del}, cons, [s_{init}]_R) = 2$ but no strict norm function. Thus, $s_{ok} \approx_n s_{del}$ but $s_{ok} \not\approx_{sn} s_{del}$. The quotient system that we get when we identify the states by their normed bisimulation equivalence classes can be viewed as a failure-free specification (see the picture on the right).

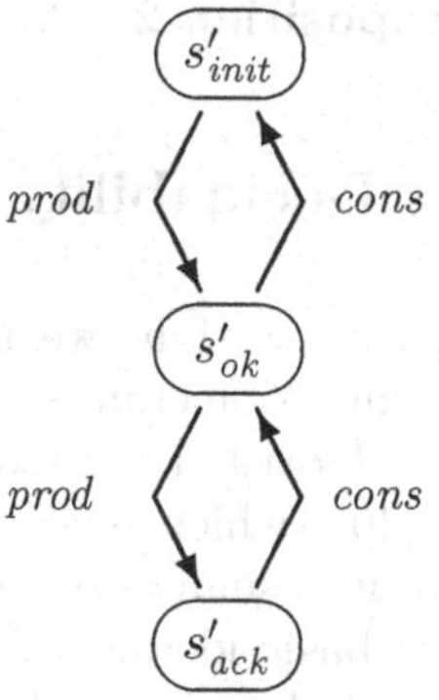

$\approx_n$ and $\approx_{sn}$ can be characterized by condition (PBis) with suitable defined predecessor predicates. The unbounded delay predecessor predicate $Pre^{del}_{ub}(a, M)$ is the set of states s where $n(s, a, M) \neq \bot$ for some norm function n. The bounded predecessor predicate $Pre^{del}_{b}(a, M)$ is the set of states s such that $n(s, a, M) \neq \bot$ for some strict norm function n.[9] Then, $Pre^{del}_{b}(a, M)$ is the least set satisfying the three conditions (BD0), (BD1), (BD2). In what follows,

---

[8] Recall that a probabilistic program is a PLTS with an initial state (Def. 1). Let $\mathcal{P}_i$ be probabilistic programs with initial states s_i, $i = 1, 2$. We define $\mathcal{P}_1 \approx_* \mathcal{P}_2$ iff $s_1 \approx_* s_2$ where s_1, s_2 are viewed as states in the composed system $\mathcal{P}_1 \uplus \mathcal{P}_2$ which arises from the disjoint union of the state spaces of $\mathcal{P}_1$ and $\mathcal{P}_2$.

[9] For a LTS, viewed as a PLTS, the unbounded and bounded predecessor predicates coincide. More precisely, $Pre^{del}(a, C) = Pre^{del}_{ub}(a, M_C) = Pre^{del}_{b}(a, M_C)$ for any set C of states and $M_C = \{\mu^1_t : t \in C\}$.

we simply write $Pre^{del}(a,M)$ to denote $Pre_b^{del}(a,M)$ or $Pre_{ub}^{del}(a,M)$ depending on whether we deal with strict normed bisimulation or normed bisimulation equivalence. It is easy to see that (strict) normed bisimulation equivalence meets the general characterization of bisimulation equivalences in PLTSs via condition (PBis). More precisely, (strict) normed bisimulation equivalence is the coarsest equivalence R on S such that $(s,s') \in R$, $M \in Distr(S)/\equiv_R$ and $s \xrightarrow{a} M$ implies $s' \in Pre^{del}(a,M)$. (Strict) normed bisimulation equivalence lies strictly between strong ($\approx_{sbis}$) and weak ($\approx_{wbis}$) bisimulation equivalence à la [26,36,37], i.e. $\approx_{sbis} \subset \approx_{sn} \subset \approx_n \subset \approx_{wbis}$. The communication protocol and its failure free specification are examples that demonstrate the difference between $\approx_{sn}$ and $\approx_n$.

A crucial property of a simulation equivalence is soundness w.r.t. parallel composition, since this allows for compositional analysis. Another very important property is soundess w.r.t. a specification logic. For divergent-free processes (processes without τ-loops), our equivalences are sound for quantitive linear time properties. These express that, independent how the nondeterminism is resolved, the probability on a certain set of traces is larger than some number p.

Proposition 1. *If $\mathcal{P}_1$ and $\mathcal{P}_2$ are divergence free and $\mathcal{P}_1 \approx_n \mathcal{P}_2$, then $\mathcal{P}_1$ and $\mathcal{P}_2$ satisfy exactly the same quantative lineair time properties.*

Proposition 2. *$\mathcal{P}_1 \approx_n \mathcal{P}_2$ implies $\mathcal{P}_1 \| \mathcal{Q} \approx_n \mathcal{P}_2 \| \mathcal{Q}$ and similarly for $\approx_{sn}$.*

4 Decidability

In this section, we present an algorithm that computes the (strict) normed bisimulation equivalence classes in polynomial time and space. The main idea of our algorithm is a modification of the prominent splitter/partitioning technique [25,30] (which is sketched in Figure 1) that was proposed for computing the strong bisimulation equivalence classes in a non-probabilistic transition system. The basic idea is to start with the trivial partition $\chi = \{S\}$ of the state space S and then successively refine χ by splitting the blocks B of χ into subblocks according to a refinement operator $Ref(\chi,a,C)$ that depends on a *splitter*, i.e. an action/block pair $\langle a,C\rangle$. More precisely, $Ref(\chi,a,C)$ divides each block $B \in \chi$ into the subblocks $B \cap Pre^{str}(a,C)$ and its complement $B \setminus Pre^{str}(a,C)$. [10] Using an appropriate organization of the splitters (resp. splitter candidates), this method can be implemented in time $\mathcal{O}(m \log n)$ where n is the number of states and m the number of transitions (i.e. the size of $\longrightarrow$) [30]. The above sketched technique can easily be modified to compute several other types of bisimulation equivalence classes, such as the strong [20] or weak [4] bisimulation equivalence classes in fully probabilistic systems, but fails for strong (and hence for normed) bisimulation in PLTSs when action/block pairs are used as splitters [3].

[10] $Ref(\chi,a,C)$ yields the partition $\bigcup_{B\in\chi} Ref(B,a,C)$ where $Ref(B,a,C) = \{B \cap Pre^{str}(a,C), B \setminus Pre^{str}(a,C)\} \setminus \{\emptyset\}$.

```
χ := {S};
While χ can be refined do
    choose some splitter ⟨a, C⟩ of χ and put χ := Ref(χ, a, C);
Return χ.
```

Fig. 1. Schema for computing the bisimulation equivalence classes in LTSs

In the remainder of this section, we explain how the splitter/partitioning technique can be modified to get a polynomial-time algorithm for computing the (strict) normed bisimulation equivalence classes in a PLTS.

Notation 2 We fix a PLTS $(S, Act, \longrightarrow)$. Let $M_a = \bigcup_{s \in S} Steps_a(s)$. For Z to be a finite set, we write $|Z|$ to denote the number of elements in Z. Let $n = |S|$ the number of states, $m = |\longrightarrow|$ the total number of transitions and $m_\tau = \sum_{s \in S} |Steps_\tau(s)|$ the number of τ-transitions. We assume that Act does not contain redundant actions, i.e. we require that $M_a \neq \emptyset$ for all actions a.

We use similar ideas as suggested in [3] where an algorithm for computing the strong bisimulation equivalence classes of a PLTS in time $\mathcal{O}(mn(\log m + \log n))$ is presented. The key idea is to refine the current state partition has be according to splitters of the form $\langle a, M \rangle$ where a is an action and M a subset of M_a. That is, we successively replace the current state partition χ by

$$Ref(\chi, a, M) \;=\; \bigcup_{B \in \chi} Ref(B, a, M)$$

where $Ref(B, a, M) = \{B \cap Pre^{del}(a, M), B \setminus Pre^{del}(a, M)\} \setminus \{\emptyset\}$.

Notation 3 A *step partition* is a set $\mathcal{M}$ consisting of pairs $\langle a, M \rangle$ where $M \subseteq M_a$ and such that, for any action a, $\{M : \langle a, M \rangle \in \mathcal{M}\}$ is a partition of M_a. We refer to the pairs $\langle a, M \rangle$ as *step classes*. Given a state partition χ, the induced step partition $\mathcal{M}_\chi$ consists of the step classes $\langle a, M \rangle$ where $M \in M_a / \equiv_\chi$ and $\mu \equiv_\chi \mu'$ iff $\mu[C] = \mu'[C]$ for all $C \in \chi$.

```
χ := {S};
While χ can be refined do
    choose some step class ⟨a, M⟩ of M_χ and put χ := Ref(χ, a, M);
Return χ.
```

Fig. 2. Schema for computing the bisimulation equivalence classes in PLTSs

The rough ideas behind our algorithm are sketched in Figure 2. To keep book about the splitter candidates $\langle a, M \rangle$ we use a step partition $\mathcal{M}$ (that agrees with $\mathcal{M}_\chi$ after any iteration) and a set *SplCnd* (e.g. organized as a queue) which contains the step classes that will serve as splitter candidates. Initially,

SplCnd consists of the "trivial" step classes $\langle a, M_a \rangle$. In each iteration, we first refine the state partition χ according to a step class $\langle a, M \rangle \in$ *SplCnd* which yields the new state partition $\chi_{new} = Ref(\chi, a, M)$. Then, we adjust $\mathcal{M}$ to χ_{new}, i.e. calculate $\mathcal{M}_{new} = \mathcal{M}_{\chi_{new}}$. All new step classes $\langle b, N' \rangle \in \mathcal{M}_{new} \setminus \mathcal{M}$ are viewed as splitter candidates and are inserted into *SplCnd*. To derive $\mathcal{M}_{new}$ from $\mathcal{M}$ we have to replace any step class $\langle b, N \rangle$ in $\mathcal{M}$ by the step classes $\langle b, N' \rangle$ where $N' \in N/\equiv_\chi$. At the beginning of any iteration we have $\mathcal{M} = \mathcal{M}_\chi$. Thus, for $\langle b, N \rangle \in \mathcal{M}$ and ν, $\nu' \in N$ we have $\nu[B] = \nu'[B]$ for all $B \in \chi$. Let $B \in \chi$ and $B' = B \cap Pre^{del}(a, M)$, $B'' = B \setminus B'$ and $C' \in \{B', B''\}$, $\langle b, N \rangle \in \mathcal{M}$ and ν, $\nu' \in N$. Then, $\nu[C'] = \nu'[C']$ iff $\nu[B'] = \nu'[B']$ and $\nu[B''] = \nu'[B'']$. These observations motivate the use of a set *NewBl* which contains only those blocks $C' \in \chi_{new}$ that are relevant for the computation of $\mathcal{M}_{new}$. More precisely, for any block $B \in \chi$ where $|Ref(B, a, M)| = 2$, we choose a block $C'_B \in Ref(B, a, M)$ such that $|C'_B| \leq |B|/2$ and define $NewBl = \{C'_B : B \in \chi, |Ref(B, a, M)| = 2\}$. Then, $\mathcal{M}_{new}$ can be derived from $\mathcal{M}$ by replacing any $\langle b, N \rangle$ in $\mathcal{M}$ by the step classes in $Split(\langle b, N \rangle, NewBl)$ which we compute as follows. We start with $\mathcal{N} = \{\langle b, N \rangle\}$; Then, for all $C' \in NewBl$ we replace any $\langle b, N' \rangle$ in $\mathcal{N}$ by $Split(\langle b, N' \rangle, C')$ where the operator $Split(\langle b, N' \rangle, C')$ divides $\langle b, N' \rangle$ into the step classes $\langle b, N'_1 \rangle, \ldots, \langle b, N'_r \rangle$ where $N'_1, \ldots, N'_r$ is the splitting of N' according to the probabilities for C'.[11] These ideas lead to the algorithm sketched in Figure 3.

Theorem 1. *The (strict) normed bisimulation equivalence classes can be computed in time $\mathcal{O}(mn(\log m + \log n) + m_\tau n^2)$ and space $\mathcal{O}(mn)$.*

The remainder of this section is concerned with the proof of Theorem 1. It follows from Prop. 3 and Prop. 4 We put $\chi_0 = \{S\}$ and write χ_i to denote the state partition χ after the i-th iteration. Similarly, we use the notations $\mathcal{M}_i$, $SplCnd_i$ and $NewBl_i$ with the obvious meaning. Let $AllSplCnd = \bigcup_{i \geq 0} SplCnd_i$ the set of all step classes $\langle a, M \rangle$ that once serve as splitters for the state partition χ and let $AllNewBl = \bigcup_i NewBl_i$ the set of all blocks C' that once are used in a splitting operation $Split(\cdot, C')$. Using set-theoretic arguments, we get:

(i) $|AllSplCnd| \leq |\mathcal{M}_0 \cup \mathcal{M}_1 \cup \ldots| \leq 2(m-1)$
(ii) $|AllNewBl| \leq |\chi_0 \cup \chi_1 \cup \ldots| \leq 2(n-1)$
(iii) $\sum_{C' \in AllNewBl} |C'| \leq n \log n$.

Proposition 3. *The operations $Ref(\chi, a, M)$ in step (2) of the algorithm in Fig. 3 can be implemented in time $\mathcal{O}(m_\tau n^2)$ (where we range over all iterations).*

Proof. Clearly, given the predecessor predicate $Pre^{del}(a, M)$ for a fixed step class $\langle a, M \rangle$, $Ref(\chi, a, M)$ can be performed in time $\mathcal{O}(n)$ when appropriate data structures are used. Combining (i) and the following Lemmatas 1 and 2 we get the desired bound for the time complexity.

[11] $Split(\langle b, N \rangle, NewBl)$ returns the set of step classes $\langle b, N' \rangle$ where $N' \in N/\equiv$ and $\nu \equiv \nu'$ iff $\nu[C'] = \nu'[C']$ for all $C' \in NewBl$. As $N \in M_b/\equiv_\chi$ yields that $\equiv$ and $\equiv_{\chi_{new}}$ coincide, we get $\mathcal{M}_{\chi_{new}} = \bigcup_{\langle b, N \rangle \in \mathcal{M}} Split(\langle b, N \rangle, NewBl)$.

$\chi := \{S\}$; $\mathcal{M} := \{\langle a, M_a\rangle : a \in Act\}$; $SplCnd := \mathcal{M}$;
While $SplCnd \neq \emptyset$ do
  (1) choose some step class $\langle a, M\rangle$ of $SplCnd$ and remove $\langle a, M\rangle$ from $SplCnd$;
  (2) (* Computation of $\chi_{new} := Ref(\chi, a, M)$ *)
      $P := Pre^{del}(a, M)$; $\chi_{new} := \emptyset$; $NewBl := \emptyset$
      For all $B \in \chi$ do
        $B' := B \cap P$; $B'' := B \setminus B'$; $\chi_{new} := \chi_{new} \cup \{B', B''\} \setminus \{\emptyset\}$;
        If $\emptyset \neq B' \neq B$ then
          If $|B'| \leq |B''|$ then $C' := B'$ else $C' := B''$;
          $NewBl := NewBl \cup \{C'\}$;
  (3) (* Computation of $\mathcal{M}_{new} := \mathcal{M}_{\chi_{new}}$ *)
      $\mathcal{M}_{new} := \emptyset$;
      For all $\langle b, N\rangle \in \mathcal{M}$ do
        $\mathcal{N} := Split(\langle b, N\rangle, NewBl)$; $\mathcal{M}_{new} := \mathcal{M}_{new} \cup \mathcal{N}$;
        If $|\mathcal{N}| \geq 2$ then $SplCnd := SplCnd \cup \mathcal{N}$;
  (4) $\chi := \chi_{new}$; $\mathcal{M} := \mathcal{M}_{new}$;
Return χ.

Fig. 3. Algorithm for the (strict) normed bisimulation equivalence classes

Lemma 1. *$Pre_b^{del}(a, M)$ can be computed in time $\mathcal{O}(m_\tau n)$.*

Proof. $Pre_b^{del}(a, M)$ is the least subset of S satisfying the conditions (BD0), (BD1) and (BD2). The standard iterative method for computing the least fixed point of a monotonic set-valued operator leads to the following method for computing $Pre_b^{del}(a, M)$. We consider the directed graph $G_b^{del}(a, M) = (V, E)$ with the vertex set $V = S \cup M_\tau$ and the edge set $E = \{(\nu, s) \in M_\tau \times S : s \xrightarrow{\tau} \nu\} \cup \{(s, \nu) \in S \times M_\tau : s \in Supp(\nu)\}$. We assume a representation of $G_b^{del}(a, M)$ by adjacency lists and write $E(\cdot)$ to denote the adjacency list of $(\cdot)$. We use the algorithm shown in Fig. 4 to compute the set $Pre_b^{del}(a, M)$. For any $\nu \in N$, we use a counter $c(\nu)$ for the number of states $t \in Supp(\nu)$ where the condition $t \in Pre_b^{del}(a, M)$ is not yet verified. N_0 collects all ν where $c(\nu) = 0$, i.e. $Supp(\nu) \subseteq Pre_b^{del}(a, M)$. Hence, if $\nu_0 \in N_0$ and $s \xrightarrow{\tau} \nu_0$ then we may insert s into $Pre_b^{del}(a, M)$. Clearly, this method can be implemented in time $\mathcal{O}(m_\tau n)$.

Lemma 2. *$Pre_{ub}^{del}(a, M)$ can be computed in time $\mathcal{O}(m_\tau n)$.*

Proof. To compute $Pre_{ub}^{del}(a, M)$ we suggest a graph-theoretical method which is based on the following observation. $Pre_{ub}^{del}(a, M)$ is the least subset of S which contains $Pre^{\leq 1}(a, M) = Pre^0(a, M) \cup Pre^1(a, M)$ (where $Pre^0(\tau, M) = \{s : \mu_s^1 \in M\}$, $Pre^0(a, M) = \emptyset$ if a is visible and $Pre^1(a, M) = \{s : s \xrightarrow{a} M\}$) and

Compute the adjacency lists $E(\cdot)$ of the graph $G_b^{del}(a, M)$;
If $a = \tau$ then $Pre_b^{del}(a, M) := \{s : \mu_s^1 \in M\}$ else $Pre_b^{del}(a, M) := \emptyset$;
$N_0 := \emptyset$ and $c(\nu) := |Supp(\nu)|$ for all $\nu \in N$;
For all $s \in S$ where $s \xrightarrow{a} \mu$ for some $\mu \in M$ do:
    $Pre_b^{del}(a, M) := Pre_b^{del}(a, M) \cup \{s\}$;
    For all $\nu \in E(s)$ do
        $c(\nu) := c(\nu) - 1$;
        If $c(\nu) = 0$ then $N_0 := N_0 \cup \{\nu\}$;
While $N_0 \neq \emptyset$ do
    choose some $\nu_0 \in N_0$ and put $N_0 := N_0 \setminus \{\nu_0\}$;
    For all $s \in E(\nu_0) \setminus Pre_b^{del}(a, M)$ do
        $Pre_b^{del}(a, M) := Pre_b^{del}(a, M) \cup \{s\}$;
        For all $\nu \in E(s) \setminus N_0$ do
            $c(\nu) := c(\nu) - 1$;
            If $c(\nu) = 0$ then $N_0 := N_0 \cup \{\nu\}$;
Return $Pre_b^{del}(a, M)$.

Fig. 4. Algorithm for computing $Pre_b^{del}(a, M)$

satisfies the following condition. Whenever $C \subseteq S$ such that for any $s \in C$ there is a finite path $s = s_0 \xrightarrow{\tau,\nu_0} s_1 \xrightarrow{\tau,\nu_1} \dots \xrightarrow{\tau,\nu_{l-1}} s_l \xrightarrow{\tau,\nu_l} t$ where $s_1, \dots, s_l \in C$, $s_i \xrightarrow{\tau} \nu_i$ with $Supp(\nu_i) \subseteq C \cup Pre_{ub}^{del}(a, M)$, $i = 0, 1, \dots, l$, and $t \in Pre_{ub}^{del}(a, M)$ then $C \subseteq Pre_{ub}^{del}(a, M)$. On the basis of this characterization, we compute $Pre_{ub}^{del}(a, M)$ as follows. We start with $Pre_{ub}^{del}(a, M) = Pre^{\leq 1}(a, M)$ Then, we successively add all states of a set C satisfying the above condition which can be reformulated by means of the strongly connected components (SCCs) in a certain directed graph. We consider the directed graph $G_{ub}^{del}(a, M) = (V, E)$ where the vertex set V is given by $V = \{(s, \nu) : \nu \in Steps_\tau(s), s \notin Pre^{\leq 1}(a, M)\} \cup Pre^{\leq 1}(a, M)$ and the edge set is $E = \{\langle (s, \nu), (s', \nu') \rangle : s \in Supp(\nu')\} \cup \{\langle u, (s', \nu') \rangle : u \in Pre^{\leq 1}(a, M) \cap Supp(\nu')\}$. First we compute the SCCs of $G = G_{ub}^{del}(a, M)$ and a topological sorting $C_1, \dots, C_r$ on them. The singleton sets $\{u\}$ where $u \in Pre^{\leq 1}(a, M)$ are bottom SCCs (BSCCs) in G. Thus, we may assume that there is some h such that $Pre^{\leq 1}(a, M) = C_1 \cup \dots \cup C_h$ and $C_i \subseteq V \setminus Pre^{\leq 1}(a, M)$, $i = h+1, \dots, r$. We start with $Pre_{ub}^{del}(a, M) = Pre^{\leq 1}(a, M)$. For $i = h+1, \dots, r$, if C_i is not a BSCC (i.e. $\{j : C_j \rightarrow_G C_i\} \neq \emptyset$) and all states of a predecessor SCC C_j of C_i belong to $Pre_{ub}^{del}(a, M)$ then we insert the states of C_i into $Pre_{ub}^{del}(a, M)$. Clearly, $G = G_{ub}^{del}(a, M)$ has $\mathcal{O}(m_\tau + n)$ vertices and $\mathcal{O}(m_\tau n)$ edges. Hence, this method can be implemented in time and space $\mathcal{O}(m_\tau n)$.

Proposition 4. *Ranging over all iterations, the computation of the step partitions $\mathcal{M}_{new}$ in step (3) of Figure 3 takes $\mathcal{O}(mn(\log m + \log n))$ time.*

Proof. For calculating $Split(\langle b, N'\rangle, C')$ we may apply a technique (similar to the one suggested in [3]) which generates an ordered balanced tree (e.g. AVL tree) by successively inserting the values $\nu[C']$, $\nu \in N'$, possibly creating new nodes and performing the necessary rebalancing steps. Any node v in this tree is labelled by a key value $v.key$ (which is one of the probabilities $\nu[C']$ for one or more $\nu \in N'$) and a subset $v.distr$ of N'. Then, $Split(\langle b, N'\rangle, C')$ is the set of pairs $\langle b, v.distr\rangle$ where v is a node in the final tree. The construction of the tree causes the cost $\mathcal{O}(|N'| \log |N'|)$ as for any $\nu \in N'$ we traverse a tree of height $\leq \log |N'|$. For fixed ν and C', the computation of the values $\nu[C']$ can be implemented in time $\mathcal{O}(|C'|)$. Thus, for any call of the procedure $Split(\langle b, N'\rangle, C')$ the time spent for computing the values $\nu[C']$ is $\mathcal{O}(|N'| \cdot |C'|)$ where we range over all $\nu \in N'$. Summing up over all step classes $\langle b, N\rangle$ in the current step partition $\mathcal{M}$, any $C' \in AllNewBl$ causes the cost $\mathcal{O}(m \log m + m|C'|)$. (ii) and (iii) yield the time complexity $\mathcal{O}(mn(\log m + \log n))$ for all $Split(\cdot)$ operations together.

5 Conclusion

We introduced two notions of bisimulation equivalence in probabilistic systems (with non-determinism) that abstract from internal computations. We presented polynomial-time algorithms that compute the quotient spaces and briefly discussed other important issues (soundness for establishing linear time properties and compositionality). Thus, our notion of bisimulation equivalence yields an alternative to the weak and branching bisimulations of [36,37]. Although the equivalences à la [36,37] are the natural probabilistic counterpart to weak/branching bisimulation equivalence in LTSs [28,31,16], their definitions are rather complicated and the decidability is still an open problem. We argue that the definitions of our equivalences – which rely on the rather intuitive concept of norm functions à la [17] – are comparatively simple. Moreover, the use of norm functions in the definition of our equivalences allows for a characterization of the equivalence classes by means of graph-theoretical criteria which served as basis for our algorithm that computes the equivalence classes. In particular, the characterization of the delay predecessor predicates that we used in the proofs of Lemmatas 1 and 2 can easily be rewritten as terms of the relational mu-calculus. It would be interesting if our ideas can be combined with the techniques of [8,12] for computing the bisimulation equivalence in LTSs with a BDD-based model checking algorithm for the relational mu-calculus seems to get a symbolic technique that might combat the state explosion problem for PLTSs.

In this paper (where we mainly treated the issue of decidability) we restrict our attention to finite systems. However, norm functions and the derived notions of bisimulations can also be defined for infinite systems.[12] We believe that, as in

[12] For our purposes, it was sufficient to consider the natural numbers as range of the norm functions. The framework of [17] also covers infinite, possibly uncountable,

the non-probabilistic case, in many applications, it is quite simple to "guess" a norm function and then to check (e.g. by hand) whether it fulfills the necessary conditions. Further on, the concept of norm functions can also serve as basis for simulation preorders that abstracts from internal moves and is computable in finite systems. Further details about normed simulations can be found in [6] and the forthcoming work [39].

Acknowledgements: The authors would like to thank Frits Vaandrager and Holger Hermanns for many helpful comments.

References

1. P. d'Argenio, H. Hermanns, J. Katoen: On Generative Parallel Composition, Proc. PROBMIV'98, ENTCS, Vol. 21, 1999.
2. J. Baeten, J. Bergstra, S. Smolka: Axiomatizing Probabilistic Processes: ACP with Generative Probabilities, *Inf. and Comp.*, Vol. 122, pp 234-255, 1995.
3. C. Baier, B. Engelen, M. Majster-Cederbaum: Deciding Bisimilarity and Similarity for Probabilistic Systems, to appear in *Journ. of Computer and System Sc.*, 2000.
4. C. Baier, H. Hermanns: Weak Bisimulation for Fully Probabilistic Processes, Proc. CAV'97, LNCS 1254, pp 119-130, 1997.
5. C. Baier, M. Kwiatkowska: Domain Equations for Probabilistic Processes, to appear in *Mathematical Structures in Computer Science*, 2000.
6. C. Baier, M. Stoelinga: Probabilistic Bisimulation and Simulation: Decidability, Complexity and Compositionality, Techn. Report, University Nijmegen, 1999.
7. T. Bolognesi, S. Smolka: Fundamental Results for the Verification of Observational Equivalence: a Survey, Proc. Protocol Specification, Testing and Verification, Elsevier Science Publishers, IFIP, pp 165-179, 1987.
8. J. Burch, E. Clarke, K. McMillan, D. Dill, L. Hwang: Symbolic Model Checking: 10^{20} States and Beyond, *Inform. and Computation*, Vol. 98 (2), pp 142-170, 1992.
9. L. Christoff: Specification and Verification Methods for Probabilistic Processes, Ph. D. Thesis, Uppsala University, 1993.
10. L. Christoff, I. Christoff: Efficient Algorithms for Verification of Equivalences for Probabilistic Processes, Proc. CAV'91, LNCS 575, pp 310-321,1991.
11. T. Cormen, C. Leiserson, R. Rivest: Introd. to Algorithms, McGraw Hill, 1996.
12. R. Enders, T. Filkorn, D. Taubner: Generating BDDs for Symbolic Model checking in CCS, *Distributed Computing*, Vol. 6, pp 155-164, 1993.
13. A. Giacalone, C. Jou, S. Smolka: Algebraic Reasoning for Probabilistic Concurrent Systems, Proc. IFIP TC2 Working Conf. on Prog. Concepts and Methods, 1990.
14. R. van Glabbeek: The Linear Time - Branching Time Spectrum II: The Semantics of Sequential Systems with Silent Moves, extended abstract, Proc. CONCUR'93, LNCS 715, pp 66-81, 1993.
15. R. van Glabbeek, S. Smolka, B. Steffen, C. Tofts: Reactive, Generative, and Stratified Models for Probabilistic Processes, Proc. LICS'90, pp 130-141, 1990.

---

state spaces and allows for arbitrary well-founded sets as range of norm functions. We argue that these ideas can also be used to handle PLTSs of arbitrary size.

16. R. van Glabbeek, W. Weijland: Branching Time and Abstraction in Bisimulation Semantics, *Journal of the ACM*, Vol. 43(3), pp 555-600,1996.
17. D. Griffioen, F. Vaandrager: Normed Simulations, Proc. CAV'98, LNCS 1427, pp 332-344, 1998.
18. H. Hansson: Time and Probability in Formal Design of Distributed Systems, in *Real-Time Safety Ciritical Systems*, Vol. 1, Elsevier, 1994.
19. H. Hansson, B. Jonsson: A Calculus for Communicating Systems with Time and Probabilities, Proc. IEEE Real-Time Systems Symposium, IEEE Computer Society Press, pp 278-287, 1990.
20. T. Huynh, L. Tian: On some Equivalence Relations for Probabilistic Processes, Fundamenta Informaticae, Vol. 17, pp 211-234, 1992.
21. B. Jonsson, C. Ho-Stuart, W. Yi: Testing and Refinement for Nondeterministic and Probabilistic Processes, Proc. FTRTFT'94, LNCS 863, pp 418-430, 1994.
22. B. Jonsson, K.G. Larsen: Specification and Refinement of Probabilistic Processes, Proc. LICS'91, pp 266-277, 1991.
23. B. Jonsson, W. Yi: Compositional Testing Preorders for Probabilistic Processes, Proc. LICS'95, pp 431-443, 1995.
24. C. Jou, S. Smolka: Equivalences, Congruences and Complete Axiomatizations for Probabilistic Processes, Proc. CONCUR'90, LNCS 458, pp 367-383, 1990.
25. P. Kannelakis, S. Smolka: CCS Expressions, Finite State Processes and Three Problems of Equivalence, *Information and Computation*, Vol. 86, pp 43-68, 1990.
26. K. Larsen, A. Skou: Bisimulation through Probabilistic Testing, *Information and Computation*, Vol. 94, pp 1-28, 1991.
27. K. Larsen, A. Skou: Compositional Verification of Probabilistic Processes, Proc. CONCUR'92, LNCS 630, pp 456-471, 1992.
28. R. Milner: A Calculus of Communicating Systems, LNCS 92, 1980.
29. R. Milner: Communication and Concurrency, Prentice Hall, 1989.
30. R. Paige, R. Tarjan: Three Partition Refinement Algorithms, *SIAM Journal of Computing*, Vol. 16, No. 6, pp 973-989, 1987.
31. D. Park: Concurrency and Automata on Infinite Sequences, Proc. 5th GI Conference, LNCS 104, pp 167-183, 1981.
32. A. Philippou, O. Sokolsky, I. Lee: Weak Bisimulation for Probabilistic Systems, submitted for publication.
33. M. Puterman: Markov Decision Processes, John Wiley and Sons, 1994.
34. R. Segala: Modeling and Verification of Randomized Distributed Real-Time Systems, Ph.D.Thesis, Massachusetts Institute of Technology, 1995.
35. R. Segala: A Compositional Trace-Based Semantics for Probabilistic Automata, Proc. CONCUR'95, LNCS 962, pp 234-248, 1995.
36. R. Segala, N. Lynch: Probabilistic Simulations for Probabilistic Processes, Proc. CONCUR'94, LNCS 836, pp 481-496, 1994.
37. R. Segala, N. Lynch: Probabilistic Simulations for Probabilistic Processes, *Nordic Journal of Computing*, Vol. 2 (2), pp 250-273, 1995.
38. M. Stoelinga, F. Vaandrager: Root Contention in IEEE 1394, Proc. ARTS'99, LNCS 1601, pp 53-74, 1999.
39. M. Stoelinga: Hypernorms for Probabilistic Systems, in preparation, 2000.

40. W. Weijland: Synchrony and Asynchrony in Process Algebra, Ph.D.Thesis, Univesity of Amsterdam, 1989.
41. M. Vardi: Automatic Verification of Probabilistic Concurrent Finite-State Programs, Proc. FOCS'85, pp 327-338, 1985.
42. W. Yi, K. Larsen: Testing Probabilistic and Nondeterministic Processes, Proc. Protocol, Specification, Testing, Verification XII, pp 47-61, 1992.
43. W. Yi: Algebraic Reasoning for Real-Time Probabilistic Processes with Uncertain Information, Proc. FTRTFT'94, LNCS 863, pp 680-693, 1994.

Constructor Subtyping in the Calculus of Inductive Constructions

Gilles Barthe[1,2] and Femke van Raamsdonk[3,4]

[1] INRIA Sophia-Antipolis, France,
Gilles.Barthe@inria.fr
[2] Departamento de Informática, Universidade do Minho, Portugal
[3] Division of Mathematics and Computer Science, Faculty of Sciences,
Vrije Universiteit, Amsterdam, The Netherlands,
femke@cs.vu.nl
[4] CWI, Amsterdam, The Netherlands

Abstract. The Calculus of Inductive Constructions (CIC) is a powerful type system, featuring dependent types and inductive definitions, that forms the basis of proof-assistant systems such as Coq and Lego. We extend CIC with constructor subtyping, a basic form of subtyping in which an inductive type σ is viewed as a subtype of another inductive type τ if τ has more elements than σ. It is shown that the calculus is well-behaved and provides a suitable basis for formalizing natural semantics in proof-development systems.

1 Introduction

Proof-development systems like Coq [4], Hol [21], Isabelle [28] and PVS [32] rely on powerful type systems featuring (co-)inductive types. The latter, which capture in a type-theoretical framework the notions of initial algebra or final coalgebra, are extensively used in the formalization of programming languages, reactive and embedded systems, communication and cryptographic protocols... While such works witness that formal verification has reached a certain maturity, users' efforts are often hindered by the rigidity of the existing tools. Thus providing type-theoretical tools for increasing the usability of proof-development systems remains an important objective.

Subtyping is a relation on types that expresses that one type is at least as general as another one and is embedded in the type system via the subsumption rule, stating that a term of type a is also of type b whenever a is a subtype of b. While subtyping has long been perceived as a tool which could significantly improve the usability of proof-development systems, many of the existing approaches to subtyping are inappropriate for the (co-)inductive approach to formalization (see Section 5).

Constructor subtyping [7,8] is a basic form of subtyping in which an inductive type σ is viewed as a subtype of another inductive type τ if τ has more inhabitants than σ. It is fully compatible with the (co-)inductive approach to

J. Tiuryn (Ed.): FOSSACS 2000, LNCS 1784, pp. 17–34, 2000.

formalization and may be used to specify most of the examples arising in natural semantics [23]. For example, constructor subtyping may be used to formalize the expressions of the call-by-value λ-calculus and of the ς-calculus, or the set of Harrop formulae [7,8]. It may also be used to formalize the datatype of lists/non-empty lists:

Parameters:	X
Sorts:	list, nelist
Subsort relation:	nelist $\leq$ list
Declarations:	nil : $X \rightarrow$ list
	cons : $X \rightarrow$ list $\rightarrow$ nelist

The salient feature of constructor subtyping is to impose suitable *coherence* conditions on constructor overloading: roughly speaking, constructor declarations are supposed to be monotonic, i.e. if $c : A \rightarrow \sigma$ and $c : B \rightarrow \tau$ are constructor declarations with $\sigma \sqsubseteq \tau$, then one must have $A \sqsubseteq B$. This is trivially satisfied in the case of the lists/non-empty lists, as constructors are declared only once, and in most datatypes with overloaded constructors such as the one of odd/even/natural numbers:

Parameters:	
Sorts:	even, odd, nat
Subsort relation:	even, odd $\leq$ nat
Declarations:	0 : even
	S : even $\rightarrow$ odd
	S : odd $\rightarrow$ even
	S : nat $\rightarrow$ nat

The immediate benefit of coherence is that the above definitions may be viewed as deterministic rule sets in the sense of [1]—see Section 2 for the difficulties with datatypes that do not yield deterministic rule sets. Therefore they support recursive definitions and may be integrated safely to typed λ-calculi [7,8].

In the present paper, we study constructor subtyping in the context of the Calculus of Inductive Constructions (CIC) [35], a dependently typed λ-calculus that forms the basis of several proof-assistants, including Coq [4] and Lego [25]. In particular, we show that adding constructor subtyping preserves some fundamental properties of CIC, including confluence, subject reduction, strong normalization and decidability of type-checking. These results scale up to dependent types those of previous papers [7,8], and open the road for an integration of constructor subtyping in proof-development systems such as Coq and Lego.

The remaining of the paper is organized as follows: in Section 2, we present an extension of the Calculus of Inductive Constructions with Constructor Subtyping. As we shall explain, our presentation is slightly different from the one of [7,8] so as to scale up to dependent types. In Section 3, we prove that the main meta-theoretical properties of the Calculus of Inductive Constructions are preserved. While the confluence and strong normalization proofs rely on standard techniques, both Subject Reduction and decidability of type-checking do pose some interesting difficulties that are pervasive in all calculi which combine parametric inductive types and subtyping. In Section 4, we extend the type system with unbounded recursion, leaving aside the somewhat intrinsic problem of guarded recursive definitions. We show the calculus remains confluent and enjoys the subject reduction property—strong normalization obviously fails and hence so does decidability of type-checking. Finally, Section 5 concludes with related work and directions for further research. Most proofs are only sketched.

2 Syntax

A countably infinite set $\mathcal{V}$ of *variables*, written as $x, y, z, \ldots$ is assumed. We assume further a set $\mathcal{D}$ of *datatypes* and a set $\mathcal{C}$ of *constructors*. Datatypes are written as $\sigma, \ldots$, and constructors are written as $f, \ldots$. Every datatype σ and every constructor f comes equipped with a fixed *arity*, which is a natural number indicating the number of parameters it is supposed to have. The arity of a symbol s is denoted by $\mathsf{ar}(s)$. In addition, every datatype σ comes equipped with a set of constructors, denoted by $\mathsf{C}(\sigma)$. Finally, two *sorts* are assumed: the sort of *types*, written as $\star$, and the sort of *kinds*, written as $\Box$. The set $\{\star, \Box\}$ is denoted by $\mathcal{S}$.

In the remainder of the paper, we will make use the following two examples. The first one is the datatype nat of natural numbers, with $\mathsf{ar}(\mathsf{nat}) = 0$ and $\mathsf{C}(\mathsf{nat}) = \{\mathsf{0}, \mathsf{S}\}$. We further assume $\mathsf{ar}(\mathsf{0}) = 0$ and $\mathsf{ar}(\mathsf{S}) = 1$. The second one is the datatype list of polymorphic lists, with $\mathsf{ar}(\mathsf{list}) = 1$ and $\mathsf{C}(\mathsf{list}) = \{\mathsf{nil}, \mathsf{cons}\}$. The argument of list is meant to specify the type of the elements of the list; for instance $\mathsf{list\,nat}$ represents the type of lists of natural numbers. We further assume $\mathsf{ar}(\mathsf{nil}) = 1$ and $\mathsf{ar}(\mathsf{cons}) = 3$.

Pseudo-Terms. Pseudo-terms are built from the standard constructions for dependent types, datatypes and constructors, and case-expressions. The latter are annotated by their type (superscript) and by the type of the expression being matched (subscript). The purpose of both annotations is to guide type-inference; see Section 3. Finally, note that at this point no constructor for fixpoints is present. The introduction of such a constructor is postponed until Section 4.

Definition 1. The set $\mathcal{T}$ of *pseudo-terms* is defined inductively as follows:

1. $\mathcal{S} \cup \mathcal{V} \subseteq \mathcal{T}$;
2. if $x \in \mathcal{V}$ and $A, B \in \mathcal{T}$, then $\Pi x : A.\, B,\ \lambda x : A.\, B,\ A\, B \in \mathcal{T}$;
3. if $\sigma \in \mathcal{D}$ with $\mathsf{ar}(\sigma) = n$, and $M_1, \ldots, M_n \in \mathcal{T}$, then $\sigma\ M_1\ \ldots\ M_n \in \mathcal{T}$;
4. if $f \in \mathcal{C}$ with $\mathsf{ar}(f) = n$, and $M_1, \ldots, M_n \in \mathcal{T}$, then $f M_1 \ldots M_n \in \mathcal{T}$;
5. if $\sigma \in \mathcal{D}$ with $\mathsf{ar}(\sigma) = n$, and $\mathsf{C}(\sigma) = \{f_1, \ldots, f_k\}$, and further $M, M_1, \ldots, M_k$, $P_1, \ldots, P_n, Q \in \mathcal{T}$, then $\mathsf{case}^{Q}_{\sigma P_1 \ldots P_n}\ M\ \mathsf{of}\ \{f_1 \to M_1, \ldots, f_k \to M_k\} \in \mathcal{T}$.

The notions of free and bound variable, α-conversion and substitution are defined as usual. We write $M[x := N]$ for the result of substituting all free occurrences of x in M by N. Further, we write $A \to B$ for $\Pi x : A.\, B$ if x does not occur free in B. The set of closed pseudo-terms (i.e. without free variables) is denoted by $\mathcal{T}_0$. Finally, $P_1 \ldots P_n$ is sometimes abbreviated as $\boldsymbol{P}$. We then use the notation $\#\boldsymbol{P}$ to denote the length of such a vector.

Rewriting. We consider three reduction rules on pseudo-terms, for β-reduction, ι-reduction, and κ-reduction respectively:

1. $(\lambda x : A.\, M)\, N \to_\beta M[x := N]$;
2. $\mathsf{case}^{Q}_{\sigma \boldsymbol{P}}\ (f_i\ \boldsymbol{P'}\ N_1\ \ldots\ N_m)\ \mathsf{of}\ \{f_1 \to M_1, \ldots, f_k \to M_k\} \to_\iota M_i\ N_1\ \ldots\ N_m$ with $\#\boldsymbol{P} = \#\boldsymbol{P'} = \mathsf{ar}(\sigma)$ and $\mathsf{ar}(f_i) = \mathsf{ar}(\sigma) + m$;
3. $f\ \boldsymbol{P}\ \boldsymbol{N} \to_\kappa f\ \overbrace{\Box\ \ldots\ \Box}^{\#\boldsymbol{P}\text{ times}}\ \boldsymbol{N}$ where $f \in \mathsf{C}(\sigma)$ with $\mathsf{ar}(\sigma) = \#\boldsymbol{P}$, and $\mathsf{ar}(f) = \#\boldsymbol{P} + \#\boldsymbol{N}$.

As usual, the reduction relation $\to_R$ is defined as the smallest compatible closure of $\to_R$. The definitions of β- and ι-reduction are standard. The κ-reduction relation is less standard; it is there to enforce subject reduction to hold, and is only used in the type conversion rule (see below). We write $\to_{\beta\iota}$ for the reduction relation $\to_\beta \cup \to_\iota$, and $\to_{\beta\iota\kappa}$ for the reduction relation $\to_\beta \cup \to_\iota \cup \to_\kappa$.

Note that in the ι-reduction rule, $\boldsymbol{P}$ and $\boldsymbol{P'}$ are not required to be identical, the idea being that $\boldsymbol{P'}$ may be a subtype of $\boldsymbol{P}$ (pointwise). Note further that κ-reduction does not affect the number of arguments of f.

Subtyping. We assume given a binary subtyping relation $\sqsubseteq_d$ over $\mathcal{D}$ that is reflexive and transitive, and that in addition satisfies the following two requirements for every $\sigma, \tau \in \mathcal{D}$:

1. if $\sigma \sqsubseteq_d \tau$, then $\mathsf{C}(\sigma) \subseteq \mathsf{C}(\tau)$;
2. if $\mathsf{C}(\sigma) \cap \mathsf{C}(\tau) \neq \emptyset$, then $\mathsf{ar}(\sigma) = \mathsf{ar}(\tau)$.

An example also used in the remainder of the paper is that of odd and even natural numbers. Those are represented by datatypes odd and even with $\mathsf{ar}(\mathsf{odd}) = \mathsf{ar}(\mathsf{even}) = 0$, and $\mathsf{C}(\mathsf{odd}) = \{\mathsf{S}\}$, and $\mathsf{C}(\mathsf{even}) = \{0, \mathsf{S}\}$. We assume given the subtyping relation $\mathsf{odd} \sqsubseteq \mathsf{nat}$ and $\mathsf{even} \sqsubseteq \mathsf{nat}$.

The relation $\sqsubseteq_d$ is used in the definition of the subtyping relation $\sqsubseteq$. In the presence of dependent types, the subtyping relation needs to encompass the convertibility relation, and is therefore undecidable. For some purposes, in particular for the notion of strict overloading to be decidable, it is convenient to consider in addition a restricted notion of subtyping $\sqsubseteq_s$ which does not account for convertibility. The two subtyping relations are defined as follows.

Definition 2.

1. The *subtyping relation* $\sqsubseteq$ is defined by the following rules:

$$\text{(refl)}\ \frac{}{A \sqsubseteq A} \qquad \text{(trans)}\ \frac{A \sqsubseteq A' \quad A' \sqsubseteq A''}{A \sqsubseteq A''} \qquad \text{(prod)}\ \frac{A' \sqsubseteq A \qquad B \sqsubseteq B'}{\Pi x : A.B \sqsubseteq \Pi x : A'.B'}$$

$$\text{(conv)}\ \frac{A =_{\beta\iota\kappa} B}{A \sqsubseteq B} \qquad \text{(data)}\ \frac{\sigma \sqsubseteq_d \tau \quad A_1 \sqsubseteq B_1 \quad \ldots \quad A_{\mathsf{ar}(\sigma)} \sqsubseteq B_{\mathsf{ar}(\sigma)}}{\sigma\ A_1\ \ldots\ A_{\mathsf{ar}(\sigma)} \sqsubseteq \tau\ B_1\ \ldots\ B_{\mathsf{ar}(\sigma)}}$$

2. The *conversion-free subtyping relation* $\sqsubseteq_s$ is defined by all the rules above except (conv).

A major design decision is that subtyping is defined independently of typing by defining it on pesudo-terms as in [10,36]. This allows to break the circularity between typing and subtyping found in [2], where subtyping is only defined on legal terms and thereby depends on typing.

The unusual rule (data) requires that inductive types are monotonic in their parameters. It is used for instance to derive list odd $\sqsubseteq$ list nat. An alternative is to consider a polarized calculus as e.g. in [33] but most datatypes of interest are monotonic in their parameters, so we feel the complications are not justified here.

Finally, note that the example of odd and even natural numbers illustrates that it is not possible to use set-theoretic inclusion on the set of constructors to define subtyping on datatypes; this would yield odd $\sqsubseteq$ even which is undesirable.

Typing constructors. A next question is how to provide types for the datatypes and constructors. In order to do this, we assume given two mappings $\mathsf{K} : \mathcal{D} \to \mathcal{T}_0$ and $\mathsf{D} : \prod \sigma \in \mathcal{D}.\mathsf{C}(\sigma) \to \mathcal{T}_0$ such that for every datatype $\sigma \in \mathcal{D}$ and for every constructor $c \in \mathsf{C}(\sigma)$ we have the following:

1. $\mathsf{K}(\sigma)$ is of the form $\Pi \boldsymbol{x} : \boldsymbol{A}. \star$ where $\#\boldsymbol{x} = \mathsf{ar}(\sigma)$,
2. $\mathsf{D}(\sigma, f)$ is of the form $\Pi \boldsymbol{x} : \boldsymbol{A}. \Pi \boldsymbol{y} : \boldsymbol{B}. \sigma\, \boldsymbol{x}$ where $\mathsf{K}(\sigma) = \Pi \boldsymbol{x} : \boldsymbol{A}. \star$ and $\#\boldsymbol{x} + \#\boldsymbol{y} = \mathsf{ar}(f)$.

If $\mathsf{D}(\sigma, f) = \Pi \boldsymbol{x} : \boldsymbol{A}. \Pi \boldsymbol{y} : \boldsymbol{B}. \sigma\, \boldsymbol{x}$, we write $\mathsf{D}^{\Box}(\sigma, f)$ for $\Pi \boldsymbol{x} : \boldsymbol{A}. \Pi \boldsymbol{y} : \boldsymbol{B}. \Box$.

Before proceeding with an example, let us emphasize that we do not consider inductive families since the codomain of $\mathsf{D}(\sigma, f)$ is of the form $\sigma\, \boldsymbol{x}$. It is straightforward to add inductive families to our calculus, but more difficult to adapt the notion of constructor subtyping to inductive families, see Section 5 for a discussion.

To illustrate the intended use of K and D, we consider the datatype list of polymorphic lists. Natural mappings K and D are defined by the following:

$$\begin{array}{ll} \mathsf{K}\,(\mathsf{list}) & = \star \to \star \\ \mathsf{D}\,(\mathsf{list}, \mathsf{nil}) & = \Pi x : \star.\, \mathsf{list}\, x \\ \mathsf{D}\,(\mathsf{list}, \mathsf{cons}) & = \Pi x : \star.\, x \to \mathsf{list}\, x \to \mathsf{list}\, x \end{array}$$

Using the typing system defined below, we have, with n : nat and $l \in$ list nat:

$$\begin{array}{ll} \mathsf{list\ nat} & : \star \\ \mathsf{nil\ nat} & : \mathsf{list\ nat} \\ \mathsf{cons\ nat}\, n\, l & : \mathsf{list\ nat} \end{array}$$

Overloading. In contrast with the Calculus of Inductive Constructions, constructors may be overloaded. This is crucial to the applicability of constructor subtyping, as most examples require constructors to be overloaded. However, in presence of subsumption, overloading leads to difficulties with subject reduction.

To illustrate the problem, we consider two sorts: $\bot$ and $\top$, with $\bot \sqsubseteq_d \top$. We assume the following constructors for these sorts: the constructor of $\bot$ is $f : \top \to \bot$, and the constructors of $\top$ are $f : \bot \to \top$ and $t : \top$. Note that the function f is overloaded. Further, some type A is assumed, and two terms $g : \bot \to A$ and $a : A$. We have (we omit sub- and superscripts in the case-expression)

$$\mathsf{case}^A_\top\ (f\ t)\ \mathsf{of}\ \{f \to g, t \to a\} : A$$

This term reduces to $g\,t$, which is not typable. So subject reduction fails.

Hence overloading must be constrained in some way. The solution advocated in [7,8] is to require the following:

1. $\mathsf{D}^\square$ is anti-monotonic in its first argument: if f is a constructor for σ and τ with $\sigma \sqsubseteq_d \tau$, then the domain of f w.r.t. τ must be a subtype of the domain of f w.r.t. σ;
2. if f is a constructor for σ and τ, then σ and τ must be parameterized over the same types.

Here we follow a similar approach but, in order to enforce decidability, we rely on $\sqsubseteq_s$ rather than on $\sqsubseteq$ to compare domains.

Definition 3 (Strict overloading). A constructor f is *strictly overloaded* if for every $\sigma, \tau \in \mathcal{D}$ and $f \in \mathsf{C}(\sigma) \cap \mathsf{C}(\tau)$ we have the following:

1. if $\sigma \sqsubseteq_d \tau$ then $\mathsf{D}^\square(\tau, f) \sqsubseteq_s \mathsf{D}^\square(\sigma, f)$,
2. $\mathsf{K}(\sigma) = \mathsf{K}(\tau)$.

The constructor S for successor of the datatype for odd and even and natural numbers is strictly overloaded. Indeed, we have:

$$\mathsf{K}(\mathsf{even}) = \mathsf{K}(\mathsf{odd}) = \mathsf{K}(\mathsf{nat}) = \star$$

and:

$$\begin{array}{llll} \mathsf{D}(\mathsf{even},\mathsf{S}) = \mathsf{odd} \to \mathsf{even} & & \mathsf{D}^\square(\mathsf{even},\mathsf{S}) = \mathsf{odd} \to \square \\ \mathsf{D}(\mathsf{odd},\mathsf{S}) \ = \mathsf{even} \to \mathsf{odd} & & \mathsf{D}^\square(\mathsf{odd},\mathsf{S}) \ = \mathsf{even} \to \square \\ \mathsf{D}(\mathsf{nat},\mathsf{S}) \ \ = \mathsf{nat} \to \mathsf{nat} & & \mathsf{D}^\square(\mathsf{nat},\mathsf{S}) \ = \mathsf{nat} \to \square \end{array}$$

So:

$$\mathsf{D}^\square(\mathsf{nat},\mathsf{S}) \sqsubseteq_s \mathsf{D}^\square(\mathsf{even},\mathsf{S})$$
$$\mathsf{D}^\square(\mathsf{nat},\mathsf{S}) \sqsubseteq_s \mathsf{D}^\square(\mathsf{odd},\mathsf{S})$$

From now on, we assume all constructors to be strictly overloaded.

Typing System. The typing system features the standard rules for the Calculus of Inductive Constructions, with the exception of the conversion rule which is replaced by the more general subsumption rule. Note that, in order for datatypes and constructors to be fully applied, the typing relation $\vdash$ is defined via some auxiliary relations $\vdash_n$ where $n \in \mathbb{N}$. We adopt the conventions $\vdash_0 = \vdash$ and $0 - 1 = 0$.

Definition 4. The typing relation $\Gamma \vdash M : A$ is defined by the rules of figure 1, where in the (case) rule it is assumed that:

1. $\mathsf{C}(\sigma) = \{f_1, \ \dots \ , f_k\}$;
2. $\mathsf{K}(\sigma) = \Pi \boldsymbol{x} : \boldsymbol{A}. \star$;
3. $\mathsf{D}(\sigma, f_i) = \Pi \boldsymbol{x} : \boldsymbol{A}. \Pi \boldsymbol{y_i} : \boldsymbol{B_i}. \sigma\ \boldsymbol{x}$ for all i with $1 \leq i \leq k$;
4. $C_i = \Pi \boldsymbol{y_i} : \boldsymbol{B_i}[\boldsymbol{x} := \boldsymbol{E}]. Q\ (f_i\ \boldsymbol{E}\ \boldsymbol{y_i})$ for all i with $1 \leq i \leq k$;
5. $Q\, M \twoheadrightarrow_{\beta\iota} M'$.

The premises in the (datatype) and (constructor) rules are meant to ensure that the types of datatypes and constructors are well-formed. Indeed, not every datatype will be legal: e.g. the datatype σ with $\mathsf{K}(\sigma) = \Pi x : \Box . \Box$ is not legal.

(axiom) $$\frac{}{\vdash \star : \Box}$$

(start) $$\frac{\Gamma \vdash A : s}{\Gamma, x : A \vdash x : A}$$

(weakening) $$\frac{\Gamma \vdash A : s \qquad \Gamma \vdash M : B}{\Gamma, x : A \vdash M : B}$$

(product) $$\frac{\Gamma \vdash A : s \qquad \Gamma, x : A \vdash B : s'}{\Gamma \vdash \Pi x : A.B : s'}$$

(abstraction) $$\frac{\Gamma, x : A \vdash M : B \qquad \Gamma \vdash \Pi x : A.B : s}{\Gamma \vdash \lambda x : A.M : \Pi x : A.B}$$

(application) $$\frac{\Gamma \vdash_n M : \Pi x : A.B \qquad \Gamma \vdash N : A}{\Gamma \vdash_{(n-1)} MN : B[x := N]}$$

(datatype) $$\frac{\vdash \mathsf{K}(\sigma) : K}{\vdash_{\mathsf{ar}(\sigma)} \sigma : \mathsf{K}(\sigma)}$$

(constructor) $$\frac{\vdash \mathsf{D}(\sigma, c) : C}{\vdash_{\mathsf{ar}(c)} c : \mathsf{D}(\sigma, c)}$$

(case) $$\frac{\Gamma \vdash M : \sigma\ \boldsymbol{E} \quad \Gamma \vdash Q : \sigma\ \boldsymbol{E} \to \star \quad \Gamma \vdash N_i : C_i \quad (1 \leq i \leq k)}{\Gamma \vdash \mathsf{case}^{M'}_{\sigma\ \boldsymbol{E}}\ M \ \mathsf{of}\ \{f_1 \to N_1, \dots, f_k \to N_k\} : Q\ M}$$

(subsumption) $$\frac{\Gamma \vdash M : A \qquad \Gamma \vdash B : s \qquad A \sqsubseteq B}{\Gamma \vdash M : B}$$

Fig. 1. Typing rules

To illiustrate the use of case-expressions, we consider a definition of the predecessor function on natural numbers. We have:

$$\begin{array}{ll} \mathsf{C}(\mathsf{nat}) & = \{0, s\} \\ \mathsf{K}(\mathsf{nat}) & = \star \\ \mathsf{D}(\mathsf{nat}, 0) & = \mathsf{nat} \\ \mathsf{D}(\mathsf{nat}, \mathsf{S}) & = \mathsf{nat} \to \mathsf{nat} \end{array}$$

Further, we use:

$$\begin{array}{ll} \lambda x : \mathsf{nat}.\, \mathsf{nat} : \mathsf{nat} \to \star & \\ 0 & : \mathsf{nat} \\ \lambda x : \mathsf{nat}.\, x & : \mathsf{nat} \to \mathsf{nat} \end{array}$$

as Q, N_1, and N_2 in the (case) typing rule. Note that indeed $(\lambda x : \mathsf{nat}.\, \mathsf{nat})\, 0 \to_\beta \mathsf{nat}$ and $\Pi y : \mathsf{nat}.\, (\lambda x : \mathsf{nat}.\, \mathsf{nat})\, (\mathsf{S}\, y) \to_\beta (\mathsf{nat} \to \mathsf{nat})$. Then we have:

$$\mathsf{case}^{\mathsf{nat}}_{\mathsf{nat}}\ M \ \mathsf{of}\ \{0 \to 0, \mathsf{S} \to \lambda x : \mathsf{nat}.\, x\} : \mathsf{nat}$$

with $M : \mathsf{nat}$. The rewrite rules yield that we have

$$\begin{array}{ll} \mathsf{case}^{\mathsf{nat}}_{\mathsf{nat}}\ 0\ \mathsf{of}\ \{0 \to 0, \mathsf{S} \to \lambda x : \mathsf{nat}.\, x\} & \to 0 \\ \mathsf{case}^{\mathsf{nat}}_{\mathsf{nat}}\ (\mathsf{S}\, n)\ \mathsf{of}\ \{0 \to 0, \mathsf{S} \to \lambda x : \mathsf{nat}.\, x\} & \to (\lambda x : \mathsf{nat}.\, x)\, n \to n \end{array}$$

3 Metatheory

Confluence. The first part of the following proposition follows because $\to_{\beta\iota}$ is orthogonal.

Proposition 1.

1. *$\to_{\beta\iota}$ is confluent on the set of pseudo-terms.*
2. *$\to_{\beta\iota\kappa}$ is confluent on the set of pseudo-terms.*

Subtyping. We present an alternative definition of subtyping, denoted by $\sqsubseteq_{int}$, that is shown to be equivalent to the original one. The subtyping relation $\sqsubseteq_{int}$ is used to prove subject reduction.

Definition 5. *The relation $\sqsubseteq_{int}$ is defined by the following rules:*

$$(prod)\ \frac{C =_{\beta\iota\kappa} \Pi x : A.\, B \quad C' =_{\beta\iota\kappa} \Pi x : A'.\, B' \quad A' \sqsubseteq_{int} A \qquad B \sqsubseteq_{int} B'}{C \sqsubseteq_{int} C'}$$

$$(data)\ \frac{C =_{\beta\iota\kappa} \sigma\, \boldsymbol{A} \quad C' =_{\beta\iota\kappa} \tau\, \boldsymbol{B} \quad \sigma \sqsubseteq_d \tau \quad A_i \sqsubseteq_{int} B_i \quad (1 \leq i \leq \mathsf{ar}(\sigma))}{C \sqsubseteq_{int} C'}$$

$$(conv)\ \frac{C =_{\beta\iota\kappa} C'}{C \sqsubseteq_{int} C'}$$

Here the reflexivity and transitivity rules are eliminated, and the conversion rule is distributed over the remaining ones. Note the system is not syntax-directed because of the (conv) rule.

Proposition 2. *$A \sqsubseteq_{int} B$ if and only if $A \sqsubseteq B$.*

Proof. It follows by induction on the definition of $\sqsubseteq_{int}$ that $A \sqsubseteq_{int} B$ implies $A \sqsubseteq B$.

Suppose that $A \sqsubseteq B$. We proceed by induction on the definition of $\sqsubseteq$. The problematic case is if $A \sqsubseteq B$ is the conclusion of the rule (trans). First it can be shown by induction on the derivation of $A \sqsubseteq_{int} B$ that if $A =_{\beta\iota\kappa} A'$, $B =_{\beta\iota\kappa} B'$ and $A \sqsubseteq_{int} B$, then $A' \sqsubseteq_{int} B'$ and moreover the derivation of both judgments have the same length. Then it can be shown that if $A \sqsubseteq_{int} B$ and $B \sqsubseteq_{int} C$,then $A \sqsubseteq_{int} C$ by induction on the derivation of $A \sqsubseteq_{int} B$.

Subject Reduction. The intermediate presentation of subtyping is used to prove the following lemma, which is crucial to prove subject reduction.

Lemma 1. *If $\Pi x : A. B \sqsubseteq \Pi x : A'. B'$ then $A' \sqsubseteq A$ and $B \sqsubseteq B'$.*

Using this lemma, subject reduction can be proved by adapting the standard proof for pure type systems (see for example [15]) to the case of pure type systems with subtying, as also done in [36].

Note however that the use of κ-reduction in the (conv) rule is crucial. Indeed, consider the term $M = \mathsf{cons\ even\ 0\ (nil\ even)}$ which has type $\mathsf{list\ even}$. We have (using notation as in the definition of the typing rules) $N_1 : C_1$ and $N_2 : C_2$ with $N_2 = \lambda n : \mathsf{nat}. \lambda l : \mathsf{list\ nat}. N_2'$, $C_1 = Q\ (\mathsf{nil\ nat})$, $C_2 = \Pi h : \mathsf{nat}. \Pi t : \mathsf{list\ nat}. Q\ (\mathsf{cons\ nat}\ h\ t)$, for some suitably typed N_1 and N_2', and some $Q : \mathsf{list\ nat} \to \star$. Now we have:

$$\mathsf{case}\ M\ \mathsf{of}\ \{\mathsf{nil} \to N_1, \mathsf{cons} \to N_2\} : Q\ (\mathsf{cons\ even\ 0\ (nil\ even)})$$

This term reduces to:

$$N_2\ 0\ (\mathsf{nil\ even}) : Q\ (\mathsf{cons\ nat\ 0\ (nil\ even)})$$

We have the conversion: $Q\ (\mathsf{cons\ even\ 0\ (nil\ even)}) =_\kappa Q\ (\mathsf{cons\ nat\ 0\ (nil\ even)})$ and hence by the conversion rule we have

$$N_2\ 0\ (\mathsf{nil\ even}) : Q\ (\mathsf{cons\ even\ 0\ (nil\ even)}).$$

Proposition 3 (Subject Reduction). *If $\Gamma \vdash M : A$ and $M \to_{\beta\iota} M'$ then $\Gamma \vdash M' : A$.*

Proof. The proof proceeds as in [15] by induction on the structure of derivations, proving simultaneously the following two implications: if $\Gamma \vdash M : A$ and $M \to_{\beta\iota} M'$, then $\Gamma \vdash M' : A$, and if $\Gamma \vdash M : A$ and $\Gamma \to_{\beta\iota} \Gamma'$ then $\Gamma' \vdash M : A$.

Here we only consider the case where the last typing rule is (case) rule. Let $M = \mathsf{case}^{M''}_{\sigma\,E}\ M'\ \mathsf{of}\ \{f_1 \to N_1, \ldots, f_n \to N_k\} : Q\ M'$ with $M' = f_i\ E'\ P$ and $M \twoheadrightarrow_{\beta\iota} M''$. For simplicity we restrict our attention to the case where the constructor f_i has just one argument, and the type σ has just one parameter. Let the last rule of the derivation be the (case) rule, as follows:

$$\frac{\Gamma \vdash M' : \sigma\, E \quad \Gamma \vdash Q : \sigma\, E \to \star \quad \Gamma \vdash N_i : C_i \quad (1 \leq i \leq k)}{\Gamma \vdash \mathsf{case}^{M''}_{\sigma\,E}\ M'\ \mathsf{of}\ \{f_1 \to N_1, \ldots, f_n \to N_k\} : Q\ M'}$$

We have $M \to_{\beta\iota} N_i\, P$. By generation, we have: $E \sqsubseteq E'$, $\Gamma \vdash N_l : \Pi y : B[x := E].\,Q\ (f_l\ E\ y)$, and $\Gamma \vdash E' : A$.

Moreover, there exists $\tau \sqsubseteq_d \sigma$ such that $\mathsf{D}_\tau(f_l) = \Pi x : A.\,\Pi y : B'.\,\tau\ H$, and $\Gamma \vdash P : B'[x := E']$. By strict overloading we have $B' \sqsubseteq B$. Because parameters occur positively in constructor declarations, we have $B'[x := E'] \sqsubseteq B[x := E]$. Subsumption yields that $\Gamma \vdash P : B[x := E]$, and the rule for application that $\Gamma \vdash N_l P : Q\ (f_l\ E\ P)$. Finally, by convertibility we have $\Gamma \vdash N_l P : Q\ (f_l\ E'\ P)$.

Termination. Thus far, we have not imposed any restriction on D and as a consequence the calculus is not terminating; in fact, it is possible to encode Girard's system U into our calculus, see [12, page 113].

In order to ensure termination, we must impose some conditions on D: constructors must be monotonic w.r.t. parameters and datatypes. In order to handle mutual recursion, we introduce a *precedence relation* $\blacktriangleleft$ on $\mathcal{D}$, which is supposed to be a pre-order. Below we let $\blacktriangleright$ be defined by $\tau \blacktriangleright \sigma$ iff $\sigma \blacktriangleleft \tau$, $\blacktriangleleft\!\blacktriangleright$ be defined as $\blacktriangleleft \cap \blacktriangleright$ and $\blacktriangleleft\!\blacktriangleleft\!\blacktriangleright$ be defined as $\blacktriangleleft \setminus \blacktriangleright$. Moreover we require:

1. $\blacktriangleleft\!\blacktriangleleft\!\blacktriangleright$ is well-founded;
2. the precedence relation is respected, i.e. if $\tau \boldsymbol{z}$ occurs in $\mathsf{D}(\sigma, c)$ then $\tau \blacktriangleleft \sigma$;
3. parameters must occur positively in the body of the declarations, i.e. if $\mathsf{D}(\sigma, c)$ is of the form $\Pi \boldsymbol{x} : \boldsymbol{A}.\,\Pi \boldsymbol{y} : \boldsymbol{B}.\,\sigma\ \boldsymbol{x}$, then every $x \in \boldsymbol{x}$ occurs positively in $\Pi \boldsymbol{y} : \boldsymbol{B}.\,\sigma\ \boldsymbol{x}$ (the precise definition of positivity may be found e.g. in [19]);
4. datatypes must occur positively in the body of their declarations, i.e. if $\mathsf{D}(\sigma, c)$ is of the form $\Pi \boldsymbol{x} : \boldsymbol{A}.\,\Pi \boldsymbol{y} : \boldsymbol{B}.\,\sigma\ \boldsymbol{x}$, then for every $\tau \blacktriangleleft\!\blacktriangleright \sigma$ every instance of $\tau\ \boldsymbol{z}$ occurs positively in $\Pi \boldsymbol{y} : \boldsymbol{B}.\,\sigma\ \boldsymbol{x}$.

Under these hypotheses, it is possible to show termination of our calculus by the well-known technique due to Tait and Girard, see e.g. [14,34] for an application to the Calculus of Constructions.

Theorem 1 (Termination). *If $\Gamma \vdash M : A$ then M is $\beta\iota$-terminating.*

It is then easy to conclude that legal terms are $\beta\iota\kappa$-normalizing and hence that convertibility between legal terms is decidable.

Decidability. As usual, the type-checking algorithm is decomposed into:

1. a type-inference algorithm which computes, if it exists, the minimal type of a term in a given context;
2. a subtype-checking algorithm (SCA) based on $\sqsubseteq_{int}$.

There are two problems with the existence of minimal types. We briefly explain what they are and how to solve them.

1. The first problem has to do with the existence of least upper bounds and is independent of constructor subtyping. Consider a if ... then ... else statement: if b is a boolean, $a : A$ and $a' : A'$ then for every B such that $A, A' \sqsubseteq B$, one has $\mathsf{if}\ b\ \mathsf{then}\ a\ \mathsf{else}\ a' : B$. In order for the above expression (which is of course a case-expression in disguise) to have a minimal type, A and A' must have a least upper bound. This needs not be the case in general, since we do not require $\sqsubseteq_d$ to be an upper semi-lattice. To solve this problem, we require case-expressions to be tagged by their type.
2. The second problem with minimal types is caused by constructor overloading. Suppose $\clubsuit, \spadesuit \in \mathcal{D}$ with arity 0 and $f \in \mathsf{C}(\clubsuit), \mathsf{C}(\spadesuit)$ with $\mathsf{D}(\clubsuit, f) = \mathsf{nat} \to \clubsuit$ and $\mathsf{D}(\spadesuit, f) = \mathsf{nat} \to \spadesuit$. Then we can derive $x : \mathsf{nat} \vdash f\ x : \clubsuit$ and $x : \mathsf{nat} \vdash f\ x : \spadesuit$. If $\clubsuit$ and $\spadesuit$ are unrelated by subtyping, then $f\ x$ does not have a minimal type. To solve this problem, we require constructors to be *regular*—a notion derived from order-sorted algebra, see e.g. [20].

First we introduce a notation. Let $f \in \mathsf{C}(\sigma)$ for some datatype σ, and suppose that $\mathsf{D}(\sigma, f) = \Pi \boldsymbol{x} : \boldsymbol{A}. \Pi \boldsymbol{y} : \boldsymbol{B}. \sigma\ \boldsymbol{x}$ with $\#\boldsymbol{A} = \mathsf{ar}(\sigma)$. Recall that $\mathsf{D}^{\square}(\sigma, f)$ denotes $\Pi \boldsymbol{x} : \boldsymbol{A}. \Pi \boldsymbol{y} : \boldsymbol{B}. \square$. We will use $\mathsf{D}^{\square}_{[\boldsymbol{x}:=\boldsymbol{E}]}(\sigma, c)$ to denote $\Pi \boldsymbol{y} : \boldsymbol{B}[\boldsymbol{x} := \boldsymbol{E}]. \square$. Regularity is then defined as follows.

Definition 6. *A constructor f is said to be* regular *if for every datatype σ, and for all terms $P, \boldsymbol{E}$ such that $P \sqsubseteq \mathsf{D}^{\square}_{[\boldsymbol{x}:=\boldsymbol{E}]}(\sigma, c)$, we have that the set*

$$\{\tau \in \mathcal{D} \mid F \sqsubseteq \mathsf{D}^{\square}_{[\boldsymbol{x}:=\boldsymbol{E}]}(\tau, c)\}$$

contains a minimum element.

Under the assumption of regularity, minimal types exist.

Proposition 4. *If all constructors are regular, then the calculus has minimal types, i.e. if $\Gamma \vdash M : A$, then there exists $A' \in \mathcal{T}$ such that $\Gamma \vdash M : A'$ and $A' \sqsubseteq A''$ for every $A'' \in \mathcal{T}$ such that $\Gamma \vdash M : A''$.*

Proof. By induction on the structure of terms. We only consider the case of a constructor term with one parameter and one argument, so suppose $M = f\ E\ P$ and $\Gamma \vdash M : \sigma\ E$. By the induction hypothesis, the term P has a minimal type, say C, with $\Gamma \vdash P : C$. By generation, we have $C \sqsubseteq \mathsf{D}^{\square}_{[x:=E]}(\sigma, f)$. By regularity there exists a minimal ρ such that $C \sqsubseteq \mathsf{D}^{\square}_{[x:=E]}(\rho, f)$. It is easy to verify that the minimal type of M is $\rho\ E$.

Note that the notion of regularity is based on $\sqsubseteq$ and is therefore undecidable. However, we cannot rely on $\sqsubseteq_s$ instead since conversion may lead to new conflicts. Consider for instance a slight modification of the example above, where $\mathsf{D}(\spadesuit, f)$ is now defined by the equation $\mathsf{D}(\spadesuit, f) = ((\lambda \alpha : \star. \alpha)\ \mathsf{nat}) \to \spadesuit$. As before, $f\ x$ does not have a minimal type.

Also note that we need to consider *instances* of constructors, as instantiating constructors may lead to new conflicts. Consider for example $\clubsuit, \spadesuit \in \mathcal{D}$ with arity 1 and $f \in \mathsf{C}(\clubsuit), \mathsf{C}(\spadesuit)$ with $\mathsf{D}(\clubsuit, f) = \Pi\alpha : \star. \mathsf{nat} \to \clubsuit\, \alpha$ and $\mathsf{D}(\spadesuit, f) = \Pi\alpha : \star. \alpha \to \spadesuit\alpha$. Then we can derive $x : \mathsf{nat} \vdash i\mathsf{nat}x : \clubsuit\mathsf{nat}$ and $x : \mathsf{nat} \vdash i\mathsf{nat}x : \spadesuit\mathsf{nat}$. If $\clubsuit$ and $\spadesuit$ are unrelated by subtyping, then $f\ x$ does not have a minimal type.

The notion of regularity being undecidable, it is of some interest to provide some decidable sufficient condition for constructors to be regular. We present such a criterion. It is not the most general one possible, but it is relatively simple.

The idea is to distinguish for each constructor a set of inductive positions and require overloaded declarations only to vary in these inductive positions. So for each constructor $f \in \mathcal{C}$, we assume given a set $\mathsf{ip}(f) \subseteq \{1, \ldots, \mathsf{ar}(f)\}$ and only allow constructor declarations to vary on these positions.

Definition 7.

1. A constructor f is *safe* if for every $\sigma, \tau \in \mathcal{D}$ such that $f \in \mathsf{C}(\sigma) \cap \mathsf{C}(\tau)$ with $\mathsf{ar}(\sigma) = \mathsf{ar}(\tau) = n$ and
$$\mathsf{D}(\sigma, f) = \Pi\boldsymbol{x} : \boldsymbol{A}. \Pi\boldsymbol{y} : \boldsymbol{B}. \sigma\boldsymbol{x}$$
$$\mathsf{D}(\tau, c) = \Pi\boldsymbol{x} : \boldsymbol{A}. \Pi\boldsymbol{y} : \boldsymbol{B'}. \tau\boldsymbol{x}$$
one has the following:
   (a) for every $i \in \mathsf{ip}(f)$, B_i is of the form $\sigma_i\, \boldsymbol{x}$;
   (b) for every $i \notin \mathsf{ip}(f)$, $B_i = B'_i$.
2. Let $i_1, \ldots, i_k$ is an increasing enumeration of $\mathsf{ip}(f)$. We let f_σ denote $\Pi y_{i_1} : B_{i_1}. \ \ldots\ \Pi y_{i_k} : B_{i_k}. \Box$, and for $\rho_1, \ldots, \rho_k \in \mathcal{D}$ we let $f\{\rho_1, \ldots, \rho_k\}$ denote $\Pi y_{i_1} : \rho_1\, \boldsymbol{x}. \ \ldots\ \Pi y_{i_k} : \rho_k\, \boldsymbol{x}. \Box$.

The following proposition gives a sufficient condition

Proposition 5. *If f is a safe constructor and for every $\sigma \in \mathcal{D}$ such that $f \in \mathsf{C}(\sigma)$ and $\boldsymbol{\rho} \in \mathcal{D}$ such that $f\{\boldsymbol{\rho}\} \sqsubseteq_s c_\sigma$ the set*
$$\{\tau \mid f\{\boldsymbol{\rho}\} \sqsubseteq_s f_\tau\}$$
has a minimal element, then f is regular.

Proof. Assume $\mathsf{D}(c, \sigma) = \Pi\boldsymbol{x} : \boldsymbol{A}. \Pi\boldsymbol{y} : \boldsymbol{B}. \sigma\boldsymbol{x}$ and let $F, \boldsymbol{E} \in \mathcal{T}$ such that $F \sqsubseteq \mathsf{D}^{\Box}_{[\boldsymbol{x}:=\boldsymbol{E}]}(\sigma, c)$. Without loss of generality, one can assume $F = \Pi\boldsymbol{y} : \boldsymbol{C}. \Box$ with $C_i = B_i[\boldsymbol{x} := \boldsymbol{E}]$ if $i \notin \mathsf{ip}(c)$ and $C_i = \rho_i\ \boldsymbol{E}$. Let $c\{F\} = \Pi y_{i_1} : \rho_1\, \boldsymbol{x}. \ \ldots\ \Pi y_{i_k} : \rho_k\, \boldsymbol{x}. \Box$. It is then easy to check that for every $\tau \in \mathcal{D}$ such that $c \in \mathsf{C}(\tau)$, $c\{F\} \sqsubseteq_s c_\tau$ iff $F \sqsubseteq \mathsf{D}^{\Box}_{[\boldsymbol{x}:=\boldsymbol{E}]}(\tau, c)$.

We now turn to the SCA algorithm. It is obtained by specifying a reduction strategy for convertibility and by eliminating redundancies caused by the (conv) rule. Here we use the fact that legal types are either syntactically equal to a sort or weak-head reduce to a product $\Pi x : A. B$, a base term $x\,\boldsymbol{P}$ or a datatype $\sigma\,\boldsymbol{A}$.

Definition 8.

1. *Weak-head reduction* $\to_{wh}$ is the smallest relation such that for every $x \in \mathcal{V}$ and $A, P, Q, \boldsymbol{R} \in \mathcal{T}$ we have:

$$(\lambda x : A.\, P)\, Q\, \boldsymbol{R} \quad \to_{wh} \quad P[x := Q]\, \boldsymbol{R}$$

(Weak-head reduction differs from β-reduction by applying only at the top-level.) The reflexive-transitive closure of $\to_{wh}$ is denoted by $\twoheadrightarrow_{wh}$.

2. The SCA is given by the following rules:

$$\text{(prod)}\ \frac{C \twoheadrightarrow_{wh} \Pi x : A.B \quad C' \twoheadrightarrow_{wh} \Pi x : A'.B' \quad A' \sqsubseteq_{alg} A \qquad B \sqsubseteq_{alg} B'}{C \sqsubseteq_{alg} C'}$$

$$\text{(data)}\ \frac{C \twoheadrightarrow_{wh} \sigma\, \boldsymbol{A} \quad C' \twoheadrightarrow_{wh} \tau\, \boldsymbol{B} \quad \sigma \sqsubseteq_{d} \tau \quad A_i \sqsubseteq_{alg} B_i \quad (1 \leq i \leq \mathsf{ar}(\sigma))}{C \sqsubseteq_{alg} C'}$$

$$\text{(var)}\ \frac{C \twoheadrightarrow_{wh} x\, \boldsymbol{A} \quad C' \twoheadrightarrow_{wh} x\, \boldsymbol{B} \quad A_i =_{\beta\iota} B_i \quad (1 \leq i \leq n)}{C \sqsubseteq_{alg} C'}$$

$$\text{(sort)}\ \frac{}{\star \sqsubseteq_{alg} \star}$$

In order to complete the description of our algorithm, one needs to specify how to test convertibility between expressions. This may be done in exactly the same way as in [13], although one has to take care not to compare the types of arguments in constructors (so as to handle κ-conversion). The SCA algorithm is sound and complete w.r.t. $\sqsubseteq$ on legal types.

Proposition 6. *Assume* $\Gamma \vdash A : s$ *and* $\Gamma' \vdash B : s'$. *Then* $A \sqsubseteq_{alg} B$ *iff* $A \sqsubseteq B$.

Proof. We use the fact that $A \sqsubseteq_{int} B$ iff $A \sqsubseteq B$. Soundness is trivial. Completeness is proved by induction over the derivation of $A \sqsubseteq_{int} B$.

Now decidability of type-checking follows from the existence of minimal types and the decidability of subtyping on legal terms. Hence we have the following result.

Theorem 2 (Decidability of type-checking). *If all constructors are regular, then* $\Gamma \vdash M : A$ *is decidable.*

4 Fixpoints

In this section we indicate how the somewhat limited computational power of the calculus can be increased by adding mutually dependent fixpoints. This is done as follows:

1. The set $\mathcal{T}$ of *pseudo-terms* is extended with the clause: if $x_1, \ldots, x_n \in \mathcal{V}$ are distinct variables and $\tau_1, \ldots, \tau_n, a_1, \ldots, a_n \in \mathcal{T}$, then $\mathsf{letrec}_i(x_1 : \tau_1 = a_1, \ldots, x_n : \tau_n = a_n) \in \mathcal{T}$;
2. The typing relation is extended with the rule

$$\frac{\Gamma\, f_1 : \tau_1, \ldots, f_n : \tau_n \vdash a_i : \tau_i \qquad (1 \leq i \leq n)}{\Gamma \vdash \mathsf{letrec}_j(f_1 : \tau_1 = a_1, \ldots, f_n : \tau_n = a_n) : \tau_j}$$

with $1 \leq j \leq n$.
3. Fixpoint reduction $\rightarrow_\mu$ is defined as the compatible closure of the rule:

$$\begin{array}{l} \mathsf{letrec}_i(\boldsymbol{x} : \boldsymbol{\tau} =_{\boldsymbol{k}} \boldsymbol{a}) \quad \rightarrow_\mu \\ \quad a_i[x_1 := \mathsf{letrec}_1(\boldsymbol{x} : \boldsymbol{\tau} =_{\boldsymbol{k}} \boldsymbol{a}), \ldots, x_n := \mathsf{letrec}_n(\boldsymbol{x} : \boldsymbol{\tau} =_{\boldsymbol{k}} \boldsymbol{a})] \end{array}$$

While fixpoints are crucial for the expressivity of the calculus, their introduction leads to non-termination and undecidable type-checking. However, confluence, subject reduction and minimal types are preserved, as stated in the following proposition. The proof is omitted.

Proposition 7.

1. $\rightarrow_{\beta\iota\mu}$ *is confluent;*
2. *If* $\Gamma \vdash M : A$ *and* $M \rightarrow_{\beta\iota\mu} N$ *then* $\Gamma \vdash N : A$*;*
3. *If all constructors are regular and* $\Gamma \vdash M : A$ *then there exists* $A' \in \mathcal{T}$ *such that* $\Gamma \vdash M : A'$ *and* $A' \sqsubseteq A''$ *for every* $A'' \in \mathcal{T}$ *such that* $\Gamma \vdash M : A''$.

5 Concluding Remarks

We have defined constructor subtyping for the Calculus Inductive of Constructions, a powerful type system that forms the basis of proof-development systems as Coq and Lego, and shown the resulting calculus to be well-behaved. A side-effect of our work is to provide a general approach to enforce subject reduction in calculi which combine parametric inductive types, dependent types and subtyping [3,18].

Related work. Subtyping in dependent type systems is an active research area, with some main trends to be distinguished:

- *name inequivalence based subtyping* assumes a subtyping relation on ground types; this relation is then extended to all types. Nordlander [26,27] has been developing such a theory of subtyping for Haskell; his approach allows to capture those instances of constructor subtyping which do not involve overloading, such as the datatype of lists/non-empty lists, but fails to capture those instances of constructor subtyping involving overloading, as even/odd/natural numbers.
  On a more theoretical level, Poll has been investigating subtyping between (co-)inductive types [30,31]. His approach, which is framed in a categorical setting, captures both constructor subtyping and its dual, destructor subtyping, whose prime example is record subtyping. However, Poll does not focus on the syntactic aspects of this form of subtyping;

- *declarative subtyping* allows to declare $X \sqsubseteq A : \star$ in contexts and was originally used in conjunction with related ideas, most notably bounded quantification [9], in order to provide a type-theoretical semantics of object-oriented languages, see e.g. [22]. However, declarative subtyping may also be used to represent formal languages in logical frameworks, see [29] for motivations, examples and a dependent type system based on refinement types. The interaction between dependent types and declarative subtyping has been studied by Aspinall and Compagnoni [2] for the logical frameworks, by Chen [11] for the Calculus of Constructions and by Zwanenburg [36] for Pure Type Systems. One major difference between [2] and [11,36] is that the former lets subtyping depend on typing, which leads to substantial complications in the theoretical study of the system. In order to avoid those, we have followed [11,36] and defined subtyping independently of typing. More recently, Castagna and Chen [10] have extended Chen's variant of Aspinall and Compagnoni's $\lambda P_{\leq}$ with late-binding. Their calculus is a significant improvement over $\lambda P_{\leq}$ and allows to formalize the examples of [29]. However, declarative subtyping, even combined with late-binding, is not appropriate for the inductive approach to formalization;
- *implicit coercions* [5,24] allow to view a term a of type A as a term of type B whenever there is a previously agreed upon function, called coercion, from A to B. This approach, which leads to extremely powerful type systems, is implemented in several proof-development systems, including Coq and Lego, and has proved useful in several efforts to formalize mathematics in type theory. However, implicit coercions also yield intricate coherence problems: one would like to make sure that every two coercions from A to B are extensionally equal, a property which is undecidable in presence of parametric coercions. Moreover, implicit coercions do not capture constructor subtyping.

Further work Much work remains to be done. We indicate some topics that deserve further investigation:

- *inductive families*: it is straightforward to extend our calculus with inductive families. It is however more difficult to define constructor subtyping for inductive families. Such a form of subtyping is useful for formalizing type systems with subtyping. For example, consider a type system with a set of types $\mathsf{object\text{-}types}$ and a subtyping relation $\prec$ on $\mathsf{object\text{-}types}$; one would like to be able to define inductive families of the form $el : \mathsf{Object} - \mathsf{Types} \to \star$ such that $el\ \alpha \sqsubseteq el\ \alpha'$ whenever $\alpha \prec \alpha'$, where $\mathsf{Object\text{-}Types}$ is the datatype describing $\mathsf{object\text{-}types}$. A possible approach to integrate constructor subtyping to inductive families is to replace the (data) rule by

$$\frac{\sigma \sqsubseteq_d \tau \quad (A_1, \ldots, A_{\mathsf{ar}(\sigma)}) \sqsubseteq_\sigma (B_1, \ldots, B_{\mathsf{ar}(\sigma)})}{\sigma\ A_1\ \ldots\ A_{\mathsf{ar}(\sigma)} \sqsubseteq \tau\ B_1\ \ldots\ B_{\mathsf{ar}(\sigma)}}$$

where $\sqsubseteq_\sigma$ is a relation on tuples of pseudo-terms defined for each datatype σ. This approach is currently under investigation;

– *guarded recursive definitions*: while fixpoints are crucial for the expressivity of the calculus, their introduction leads to non-termination and undecidable type-checking. In order to recover both properties, one needs to restrict the typing rule for fixpoints, for example by using a suitable notion of *guard*, see e.g. [17], or a suitable type system based on subtyping, see e.g. [3,18]. We feel the latter approach provides an appealing alternative for our purpose but the technical details remain to be unveiled;
– *canonical inhabitants*: as pointed out in [7], the system is not well-behaved with respect to canonical inhabitants: e.g. both nil even and nil nat are closed normal inhabitants of list nat. This example illustrates how the equational theory is too weak. In [8], we show that an η-expansion rule for datatypes solves the problem in the simply typed case.[1] It should be possible to adopt the same solution for the Calculus of Constructions, although the combination of η-expansion with dependent types is somewhat intricate [6,16].

Addressing these issues should bring us closer to our overall objective, namely to integrate constructor subtyping as a primitive in proof-development systems.

Acknowledgments The authors are grateful to M.J. Frade and to the anonymous referees for their constructive comments on the paper. The first author is partially supported by the Portuguese Science Foundation (FCT) under the project FACS (PRAXIS P/EEI/14172/1998).

References

1. P. Aczel. An introduction to inductive definitions. In J. Barwise, editor, *Handbook of mathematical logic*, volume 90 of *Studies in Logic and the Foundations of Mathematics*, pages 739–782. North-Holland, 1977.
2. D. Aspinall and A. Compagnoni. Subtyping dependent types. In *Proceedings of LICS'96*, pages 86–97. IEEE Computer Society Press, 1996.
3. B. Barras. *Auto-validation d'un système de preuves avec familles inductives.* PhD thesis, Université Paris 7, 1999.
4. B. Barras *et. al. The Coq Proof Assistant User's Guide. Version 6.2*, May 1998.
5. G. Barthe. Implicit coercions in type systems. In S. Berardi and M. Coppo, editors, *Proceedings of TYPES'95*, volume 1158 of *Lecture Notes in Computer Science*, pages 16–35. Springer-Verlag, 1996.
6. G. Barthe. Expanding the cube. In W. Thomas, editor, *Proceedings of FOSSACS'99*, volume 1578 of *Lecture Notes in Computer Science*, pages 90–103. Springer-Verlag, 1999.
7. G. Barthe. Order-sorted inductive types. *Information and Computation*, 149(1):42–76, February 1999.
8. G. Barthe and M.J. Frade. Constructor subtyping. In D. Swiestra, editor, *Proceedings of ESOP'99*, volume 1576 of *Lecture Notes in Computer Science*, pages 109–127. Springer-Verlag, 1999.
9. L. Cardelli and P. Wegner. On understanding types, data abstraction and polymorphism. *ACM Computing Surveys*, 17(4):471–522, December 1985.

[1] It also eliminates the need for κ-conversion.

10. G. Castagna and G. Chen. Dependent types with subtyping and late-bound overloading. *Information and Computation*, 1999. To appear.
11. G. Chen. Subtyping calculus of constructions. In I. Prívara and P. Ruzicka, editors, *Proceedings of MFCS'97*, volume 1295 of *Lecture Notes in Computer Science*, pages 189–198. Springer-Verlag, 1997.
12. T. Coquand. Metamathematical investigations of a calculus of constructions. In P. Odifreddi, editor, *Logic and Computer Science*, pages 91–122. Academic Press, 1990.
13. T. Coquand. An algorithm for type-checking dependent types. *Science of Computer Programming*, 26(1–3):167–177, May 1996.
14. H. Geuvers. A short and flexible proof of strong normalisation for the Calculus of Constructions. In P. Dybjer, B. Nordström, and J. Smith, editors, *Proceedings of TYPES'94*, volume 996 of *Lecture Notes in Computer Science*, pages 14–38. Springer-Verlag, 1995.
15. H. Geuvers and M.J. Nederhof. A modular proof of strong normalisation for the Calculus of Constructions. *Journal of Functional Programming*, 1(2):155–189, April 1991.
16. N. Ghani. Eta-expansions in dependent type theory—the calculus of constructions. In P. de Groote and J. Hindley, editors, *Proceedings of TLCA'97*, volume 1210 of *Lecture Notes in Computer Science*, pages 164–180. Springer-Verlag, 1997.
17. E. Giménez. *Un calcul de constructions infinies et son application à la vérification de systèmes communicants*. PhD thesis, Ecole Normale Superieure de Lyon, 1996.
18. E. Giménez. Structural recursive definitions in Type Theory. In K.G. Larsen, S. Skyum, and G. Winskel, editors, *Proceedings of ICALP'98*, volume 1443 of *Lecture Notes in Computer Science*, pages 397–408. Springer-Verlag, 1998.
19. E. Giménez. A tutorial on recursive types in coq. Technical Report RT-0221, INRIA, 1998.
20. J. Goguen and J. Meseguer. Order-sorted algebra I: Equational deduction for multiple inheritance, overloading, exceptions and partial operations. *Theoretical Computer Science*, 105(2):216–273, 1992.
21. M.J.C. Gordon and T.F. Melham, editors. *Introduction to HOL: A theorem proving environment for higher-order logic*. Cambridge University Press, 1993.
22. C.A. Gunter and J.C. Mitchell. *Theoretical Aspects of Object-Oriented Programming: Types, Semantics and Language Design*. The MIT Press, 1994.
23. G. Kahn. Natural semantics. In *Proceedings of the Symposium on Theoretical Aspects of Computer Science*, volume 247 of *Lecture Notes in Computer Science*, pages 22–39. Springer-Verlag, 1987.
24. Z. Luo. Coercive subtyping. *Journal of Logic and Computation*, 9:105–130, February 1999.
25. Z. Luo and R. Pollack. LEGO proof development system: User's manual. Technical Report ECS-LFCS-92-211, LFCS, University of Edinburgh, May 1992.
26. J. Nordlander. Pragmatic subtyping in polymorphic languages. In *Proceedings of ICFP'98*. ACM Press, 1998.
27. J. Norlander. *Reactive Objects and Functional Programming*. PhD thesis, Chalmers Tekniska Högskola, 1999.
28. L. Paulson. *Isabelle: a generic theorem prover*, volume 828 of *Lecture Notes in Computer Science*. Springer-Verlag, 1994.
29. F. Pfenning. Refinement types for logical frameworks. In H. Geuvers, editor, *Informal Proceedings of TYPES'93*, pages 285–299, 1993.

30. E. Poll. Subtyping and Inheritance for Inductive Types. In *Proceedings of TYPES'97 Workshop on Subtyping, inheritance and modular development of proofs, Durham, UK*, 1997.
31. E. Poll. Subtyping and Inheritance for Categorical Datatypes. In *Proceedings of Theories of Types and Proofs (TTP) - Kyoto*, RIMS Lecture Notes 1023, pages 112–125. Kyoto University Research Insitute for Mathematical Sciences, 1998.
32. N. Shankar, S. Owre, and J.M. Rushby. *The PVS Proof Checker: A Reference Manual.* Computer Science Laboratory, SRI International, February 1993. Supplemented with the PVS2 Quick Reference Manual, 1997.
33. M. Steffen. *Polarized Higher-order Subtyping.* PhD thesis, Department of Computer Science, University of Erlangen, 1997.
34. J. Terlouw. Strong normalization in type systems: a model theoretic approach. *Annals of Pure and Applied Logic*, 73(1):53–78, May 1995.
35. B. Werner. *Méta-théorie du Calcul des Constructions Inductives.* PhD thesis, Université Paris 7, 1994.
36. J. Zwanenburg. Pure type systems with subtyping. In J.-Y. Girard, editor, *Proceedings of TLCA'99*, volume 1581 of *Lecture Notes in Computer Science*, pages 381–396. Springer-Verlag, 1999.

Verifying Performance Equivalence for Timed Basic Parallel Processes

Beatrice Bérard, Anne Labroue, and Philippe Schnoebelen

Lab. Spécification & Vérification
ENS de Cachan & CNRS UMR 8643
61, av. Pdt. Wilson, 94235 Cachan Cedex France
{berard,labroue,phs}@lsv.ens-cachan.fr

Abstract. We address the problem of deciding performance equivalence for a timed process algebra in which actions are urgent and durational, and where parallel components have independent local clocks. This process algebra can be seen as a timed extension of BPP, a process algebra giving rise to infinite-state processes. While bisimulation was known to be decidable for BPP with a non elementary complexity, our main and surprising result is that, for the timed extension, performance equivalence is decidable in polynomial time.

1 Introduction

Performance of processes. In the field of concurrency semantics, there exists a well-developed and widely accepted approach based on equivalences that relate processes having the same behaviour [Mil89, Gla90]. This framework has been extended in many directions in order to take various aspects into consideration: timing, causality, probability, locality, etc.

In the timed framework, some efforts have been directed toward defining a robust notion of *"performance"*, that would allow comparing the efficiency of systems that have the same functional behaviour (what they do) but different speeds (how fast they do it). See, e.g., [MT91, AH92, FM95, GRS95, CGR97, Cor98].

Durational urgent actions. The efficiency preorders and equivalences considered in [GRS95, AM96, CGR97, Cor98] apply to process algebras where parallel components have their own independent local clocks, where actions have a *duration* and are *urgent*. Urgent actions take place as soon as possible and can only be delayed when one process must wait until synchronization with another process becomes possible. When the process algebra does not allow synchronization, this gives rise to a nice theory where performance equivalence is a congruence for all process constructors [CGR97].

Verification. These earlier works mainly focused on semantics. However, verification issues have been addressed in this framework:

J. Tiuryn (Ed.): FOSSACS 2000, LNCS 1784, pp. 35–47, 2000.

(1) In [CP96], *lazy performance equivalence* is shown decidable over a class of systems having only finite control but allowing for an infinite number of configurations when taking into account the values of the local clocks.
(2) In [CC97], a model checking problem for TAL (a modal logic with time) is shown decidable over another class of systems with finite control.
In both cases, the decision method relies on building a *finite* approximation of the system, on which the original problem can be solved with standard finite-state methods. This induces algorithms with exponential running time since the finite approximation has exponential size [1]. These results can probably be implemented with only polynomial-space requirements, but the issue is not addressed and no lower bounds for the structural complexity of the problems are given.

Removing the finite control assumption. To the best of our knowledge, when systems have a potentially infinite number of control states (disregarding clock values), nothing is known about verification issues for these processes algebra with urgent actions and local clocks [2]. This is probably because the problem combines two difficulties as it lies at the intersection of two recent fields: verification of timed systems and verification of infinite untimed systems.

Our contribution. In this paper we investigate the decidability of the *performance equivalence* introduced in [CGR97] when no finite-state restriction is made. Because no synchronization is considered in this framework, the resulting systems have a "BPP + Time" flavor [3], in a setting with local clocks. Hence our use of "TBPP" to denote this algebra.

Decidability of bisimulation for (untimed) BPP is known, via an elegant algorithm (alas with non-elementary complexity) [CHM93]. The connection with BPP is what motivated our study: we wanted to see whether local clocks could be dealt with.

Our main result is that performance equivalence is decidable for TBPP, and can be decided in polynomial-time (it is in fact PTIME-complete). Surprisingly, the addition of local clocks does not make the problem harder: they allow decomposing systems in a way not unlike what happens for normed processes [HJM96].

This is good news since algorithms for the analysis of well-behaved infinite-state systems have important applications, ranging from static analysis [EK99] to modeling and verification of communication protocols [CFP95]. This also justifies our view that negative results about basic process algebra are not always the last word, and that the field still contains many unexplored paths.

---

[1] Since the approximation is based on the idea that exact clock values (or differences between then) can be forgotten when they are large enough, this has similarities with the region graph technique of [ACD93].

[2] In the better known global clock framework, we are aware of [AJ98] where the systems may have infinitely many distinct states. In addition, there exists a large body of literature on Timed Petri Nets, but most of these works do not offer decidability results for unbounded nets.

[3] BPP is the algebra of Basic Parallel Processes [Chr93].

Plan of the paper. Section 2 introduces our notation for TBPP, and the operational semantics while Section 3 introduces the performance equivalences we consider. The main technical part starts with the introduction of the syntactic congruence (Section 4) and the cancellation lemmas (Section 5) that allow us to prove the main result in Section 6.

Our presentation of TBPP is mostly orientated towards the proof of the main result: we refer to [CGR97] for motivations, examples, and further discussion of this process algebra.

2 Timed Basic Parallel Processes

In this section, we define the timed process algebra TBPP as a timed extension of BPP. This definition is based on the features proposed in [GRS95, AM96, CGR97]:

- The time domain is the set $\mathbb{N}$ of natural numbers.
- We consider urgent and *durational* actions: a duration function associates its duration (number of time units taken for execution) with each action. This mapping is external to the syntax.
- Parallel components have independent clocks and executions are asynchronous and *ill-timed but well-caused.*

[AM96] showed the technical advantages of the "ill-timed but well-caused" viewpoint (which admits an intuitive understanding in terms of external observation). In this framework, time is not used to enforce a synchronous view of the system.

We mainly deviate from [GRS95, CGR97] by two technical points that do not bring any real semantical change:

- The date n in a step $u \xrightarrow{a,n} v$ denotes the beginning time for a, not the completing time.
- Instead of defining processes through recursive equations (as is traditional in process algebra), we adopt Moller's approach where behaviour is defined via a set of rewrite rules [Mol96]. This is for technical convenience only.

2.1 Syntax

We consider a set of *action names* Act ranged over by $a, b, \ldots$ and a set of *process variables* $\mathcal{X}$ ranged over by $X, Y, \ldots$.

Definition 2.1. *The set* $\mathcal{T}$ *of* TBPP-terms *is given by the following abstract syntax:*

$$t, u ::= Nil \mid X \mid t \parallel u \mid 1 \rhd t.$$

As usual, *Nil* denotes the empty process which cannot proceed with any action, and $t \parallel u$ is the parallel combination of t and u (no synchronization is possible). $1 \triangleright t$ denotes the process which behaves like t, but with a one time unit delay.

We write $n \triangleright t$ for $\overbrace{1 \triangleright (1 \triangleright (\cdots (1 \triangleright}^{n} t) \cdots))$ and X^n for $\overbrace{X \parallel X \parallel \cdots \parallel X}^{n}$. By convention, $0 \triangleright t$ stands for t and X^0 stands for *Nil*.

For a term t, we denote by $Var(t)$ the set of process variables occurring in t, e.g., $Var(X \parallel 1 \triangleright (X \parallel Y)) = \{X, Y\}$.

Definition 2.2. *A* TBPP declaration *is a finite set* $\Delta \subseteq \mathcal{X} \times Act \times \mathcal{T}$ *of process rewrite rules, written* $\{X_i \xrightarrow{a}_\Delta t_i \mid i = 1, \ldots, n\}$*, such that* $Var(t_i) \subseteq \{X_1, \ldots, X_n\}$ *for any* i.

Note that the X_i's need not be distinct. Additionally, we require that any variable X_i used in Δ appears in the left-hand side of at least one rule from Δ (this is for technical convenience only).

In the examples, we often use the convenient CCS-like notations with action-prefixing, non-deterministic choice (denoted by +) and guarded recursion. E.g., the definition

$$X_1 \stackrel{\text{def}}{=} a.(1 \triangleright (a \parallel a \parallel a)) + a.(1 \triangleright (a.a.a)),$$
$$X_2 \stackrel{\text{def}}{=} a.(1 \triangleright (a \parallel a \parallel a)) + a.(1 \triangleright (a.a) \parallel 1 \triangleright a) + a.(1 \triangleright (a.a.a))$$

is just a shorthand for

$$\Delta \stackrel{\text{def}}{=} \left\{ \begin{array}{l} X_1 \xrightarrow{a} 1 \triangleright (Z_a \parallel Z_a \parallel Z_a),\ X_1 \xrightarrow{a} 1 \triangleright Z_{a.a.a}, \\ X_2 \xrightarrow{a} 1 \triangleright (Z_a \parallel Z_a \parallel Z_a),\ X_2 \xrightarrow{a} 1 \triangleright (Z_{a.a} \parallel 1 \triangleright Z_a),\ X_2 \xrightarrow{a} 1 \triangleright Z_{a.a.a}, \\ Z_a \xrightarrow{a} Nil,\ Z_{a.a} \xrightarrow{a} Z_a,\ Z_{a.a.a} \xrightarrow{a} Z_{a.a}. \end{array} \right\}$$

2.2 Operational Semantics

The evolution of a TBPP process is represented by a transition system where the steps carry visible labels of the form (a, n), where $a \in Act$ is an action and $n \in \mathbb{N}$ is the time at which the step occurs. Actually, n is the time at which the step starts, and knowing when it finishes requires knowing the duration of a (the time it takes to perform an a).

Definition 2.3. *A* duration function f *is a mapping from* Act *to* $\mathbb{N} \setminus \{0\}$.
$\mathbf{1}$ *is the constant duration function s.t.* $\mathbf{1}(a) \stackrel{def}{=} 1$ *for any* a.

Having $f(a) = 3$ means that a takes 3 time units. Here a duration function may represent for instance the performance of a particular machine. Thus this framework makes it possible to clearly distinguish the *functional* definition Δ and the *performance* definition f.

Remark 2.4. It is possible to generalise duration "functions" so that (possibly infinite) *sets* of values are associated with actions. Our main decidability result is still valid in this framework (assuming that f is given effectively, for example by having $f(a)$ be a recognizable set of natural numbers) but the complexity measures are affected. □

A pair (Δ, f) where Δ is a TBPP declaration and f a duration function defines a labeled transition relation $\rightarrow_f \subseteq \mathcal{T} \times (Act \times \mathbb{N}) \times \mathcal{T}$, where $\rightarrow_f$ is given inductively via the following SOS rules:

$$\frac{}{X \xrightarrow{a,0}_f f(a) \rhd t} \; (X \xrightarrow{a}_\Delta t) \in \Delta \qquad \frac{t \xrightarrow{a,n}_f t'}{t \parallel u \xrightarrow{a,n}_f t' \parallel u}$$

$$\frac{t \xrightarrow{a,n}_f t'}{1 \rhd t \xrightarrow{a,n+1}_f 1 \rhd t'} \qquad \frac{t \xrightarrow{a,n}_f t'}{u \parallel t \xrightarrow{a,n}_f u \parallel t'}$$

We use the usual standard abbreviations: $t \xrightarrow{w} t'$ (with $w \in (Act \times \mathbb{N})^*$), $t \xrightarrow{*} t'$, ... and omit the f subscript when it is clear from the context.

A *run* of t is a finite or infinite sequence $(t =)\, t_0 \xrightarrow{a_1,n_1} t_1 \xrightarrow{a_2,n_2} t_2 \cdots \xrightarrow{a_k,n_k} t_k \cdots$. The *trace* of such a run is the sequence $w = (a_1, n_1)(a_2, n_2) \ldots (a_k, n_k) \ldots$

A run is *ill-timed* if there are two positions $i > j$ s.t. $n_i < n_j$. TBPP allows ill-timed runs, but [AM96] argues convincingly that (1) this brings no semantical problem since "the ill-timed runs are well-caused" (i.e. local, causaly related, clock values do increase along a run), and (2) this greatly simplifies the technical treatment (see also [CGR97]).

Example 2.5. Consider $f = \mathbf{1}$ and the term X given by $X \stackrel{\text{def}}{=} a(bb \parallel c) + ac(b \parallel b)$. The maximal traces of X are $(a, 0)(b, 1)(b, 2)(c, 1)$, $(a, 0)(b, 1)(c, 1)(b, 2)$, $(a, 0)(c, 1)(b, 1)(b, 2)$ and $(a, 0)(c, 1)(b, 2)(b, 2)$. The first one is ill-timed.

2.3 Timing Measures

Two structural measures can be associated with a term: $minclock(u) \in \mathbb{N} \cup \{\infty\}$ is the earliest time at which u can start an action, while $maxclock(u) \in \mathbb{N} \cup \{-\infty\}$ is the latest time.

We assume ordering and addition over $\mathbb{N}$ are extended in the obvious way to ∞ and $-\infty$, and we define the two measures by structural induction over terms:

$$\begin{aligned} minclock(Nil) &\stackrel{\text{def}}{=} \infty & maxclock(Nil) &\stackrel{\text{def}}{=} -\infty \\ minclock(X) &\stackrel{\text{def}}{=} 0 & maxclock(X) &\stackrel{\text{def}}{=} 0 \\ minclock(1 \rhd u) &\stackrel{\text{def}}{=} 1 + minclock(u) & maxclock(1 \rhd u) &\stackrel{\text{def}}{=} 1 + maxclock(u) \end{aligned}$$

$$minclock(u \parallel v) \stackrel{\text{def}}{=} \min(minclock(u), minclock(v))$$

$$maxclock(u \parallel v) \stackrel{\text{def}}{=} \max(maxclock(u), maxclock(v))$$

Example 2.6. For $u = 1 \rhd (X \parallel 2 \rhd X)$ we have $minclock(u) = 1$ and $maxclock(u) = 3$, and indeed if Δ contains $X \xrightarrow{a} t$, then $u \xrightarrow{a,1} \dots$ and $u \xrightarrow{a,3} \dots$
More generally:

Lemma 2.7. *For any u, $u \xrightarrow{a,n} v$ implies $minclock(u) \leq n \leq maxclock(u)$ and $minclock(u) \leq minclock(v)$.*
In the other direction, if u can make a move, then there exists a move $u \xrightarrow{a,n} v$ with $n = minclock(u)$ and a $u \xrightarrow{a',n'} v'$ with $n' = maxclock(u)$.

Proof. Easy induction on u. □

More fundamental is the following lemma, stating that *minclock* can be made arbitrarily large:

Lemma 2.8. *For any u and any $n \in \mathbb{N}$ there is a $u \xrightarrow{*} v$ s.t. $minclock(v) > n$.*

Proof. An easy induction on u shows that if $minclock(u) < \infty$ then that $u \xrightarrow{*} v$ for some v s.t. $minclock(v) > minclock(u)$. □

3 Performance Equivalences

In this section, we recall the definition of performance equivalence introduced in [GRS95, CGR97]: "*f-performance equivalence*" is associated with a duration function f while "*independent-performance equivalence*" abstracts from the particular duration function.

f-performance equivalence corresponds to strong bisimulation [Mil89] on TBPP transitions, taking timing information into account.

Definition 3.1. *A relation $\mathcal{R} \subseteq \mathcal{T} \times \mathcal{T}$ is called a* f-performance relation *if $u\mathcal{R}v$ implies that*

1. *for any $u \xrightarrow{a,n}_f u'$ there is a move $v \xrightarrow{a,n}_f v'$ s.t. $u'\mathcal{R}v'$,*
2. *and vice versa: for any $v \xrightarrow{a,n}_f v'$ there is a $u \xrightarrow{a,n}_f u'$ with $u'\mathcal{R}v'$.*

Definition 3.2. *Two TBPP terms u and v are* f-performance equivalent *(written $u \sim_f v$) if there is a f-performance relation $\mathcal{R}$ such that $u\mathcal{R}v$.*

Example 3.3. Assume $f(a) = 1$ and consider $X \stackrel{\text{def}}{=} a.(X \parallel X)$ and $Y \stackrel{\text{def}}{=} a.Y$. Then $X \not\sim_f Y$ because the steps $X \xrightarrow{a,0} 1 \rhd (X \parallel X) \xrightarrow{a,1} 1 \rhd (X \parallel 1 \rhd (X \parallel X)) \xrightarrow{a,1} 1 \rhd (1 \rhd (X \parallel X) \parallel 1 \rhd (X \parallel X))$ cannot be imitated by Y. (However X and Y are bisimilar when timing is not taken into account: they both behave as a^ω.)

As expected, $\sim_f$ is the largest f-performance relation, it is an equivalence, and a congruence for the $\|$ and $1\rhd$ operators:

Proposition 3.4. *If $u \sim_f v$ and $u' \sim_f v'$ then $1\rhd u \sim_f 1\rhd v$ and $u \parallel u' \sim_f v \parallel v'$.*

Proof. A consequence of the fact that the SOS rules for $\rightarrow_f$ are in *tyft/tyxt*, or even De Simone's, format [GV92]. □

Additionally, $u \sim_f v$ entails $minclock(u) = minclock(v)$ and $maxclock(u) = maxclock(v)$, as a consequence of Lemma 2.7.

f-performance equivalence enjoys the usual associativity, commutativity and nilpotence laws. The distributivity law, (Eq4), is called a *clock distribution equation* in [CGR97]:

Proposition 3.5. *For any terms t, u, v*

$$u \parallel t \sim_f t \parallel u \quad \text{(Eq1)}$$
$$(u \parallel t) \parallel v \sim_f u \parallel (t \parallel v) \quad \text{(Eq2)}$$
$$t \parallel Nil \sim_f t \quad \text{(Eq3)}$$
$$1 \rhd (u \parallel v) \sim_f (1 \rhd u) \parallel (1 \rhd v) \quad \text{(Eq4)}$$
$$1 \rhd Nil \sim_f Nil \quad \text{(Eq5)}$$

3.1 Performance Not Depending from f.

Our definitions followed [CGR97] in that we did not mix functional definitions (the rules in Δ, the program, ...) and timing definitions (the duration function f, the hardware, ...).

We may now define a notion of performance equivalence that does not depend on f:

Definition 3.6. *Two terms u and v are* independent-performance equivalent *(written $u \sim_{\mathrm{i}} v$) if $u \sim_f v$ for any duration function f.*

$\sim_{\mathrm{i}}$ is a congruence since it is an intersection of congruences.

Remark 3.7. A byproduct of our study is a proof that $\sim_f$ and $\sim_{\mathrm{i}}$ coincide for any f (Corollary 5.8), which we see as the reason why [CGR97] introduced both an f-performance and an independent-performance preorder (these two preorders do not coincide) but only one performance equivalence, and did not comment about this. However, since we cannot prove Corollary 5.8 without the technical developments of the next sections, we shall keep writing $\sim_f$ as long as necessary. □

4 Structural Congruence

Here we introduce a structural congruence for TBPP. It allows us to exhibit a normal form for the terms that generalizes the usual normal form for BPP [CHM93].

Definition 4.1. *We denote by $\equiv$ the smallest congruence induced by the five equations of Proposition 3.5.*

Clearly $u \equiv v$ implies $u \sim_f v$ since $\sim_f$ is a congruence and it satisfies the five equations. Also, since $\equiv$ does not depend on f, $u \equiv v$ entails $u \sim_\mathrm{i} v$.

Definition 4.2. *A term $u \in \mathcal{T}$ is in* normal form *if it is some $n_1 \rhd X_1 \parallel \ldots \parallel n_k \rhd X_k$ (where the X_i's need not be distinct, and where we allow $n_i = 0$ or $k = 0$).*

Using Proposition 3.5, any term can be rewritten to a structurally equivalent normal form. Moreover, this normal form is unique (modulo associativity and commutativity of $\parallel$). Sometimes we are only interested in the subterms "$0 \rhd X_i$" in a normal form and write it $X_1 \parallel \ldots \parallel X_n \parallel 1 \rhd u$.

The normal form of a term u displays all dates for which u can make an immediate step. A consequence is the very useful Lemma:

Lemma 4.3. *$u \sim_f Nil$ iff $u \equiv Nil$ iff $minclock(u) = +\infty$ iff $maxclock(u) = -\infty$.*

5 Cancellation for Performance Equivalence

In this section, we prove the surprising result that performance equivalence can be reduced to a notion of equality of normal forms. For this, we use a decomposition approach along the lines that have been pioneered by [MM93] and which often work nicely in timed or normed settings (see Prop. 30 in [AM96] or Prop. 2.2.8 in [Hen88]).

The following lemma is the converse of Proposition 3.4. It emphasizes the link between the behaviours of the terms u and $1 \rhd u$.

Lemma 5.1. *$1 \rhd u \sim_f 1 \rhd v$ entails $u \sim_f v$.*

Proof. Standard: one checks that $\mathcal{R} \stackrel{\text{def}}{=} \{(u_1, u_2) \mid 1 \rhd u_1 \sim_f 1 \rhd u_2\}$ is an f-performance equivalence. □

Given two TBPP terms u and v, we say that *u is earlier than v* if $maxclock(u) < minclock(v)$ and $v \not\sim_f Nil$. A *separated product* is some $u \parallel v$ with u earlier than v. This syntactic notion is useful because when $u \parallel v$ makes a move at time n, it is possible to assign the move to u or v on the basis of n only.

Lemma 5.2. *Assume $u_1 \parallel u_2$ and $v_1 \parallel v_2$ are separated products s.t. u_1 and v_1 have same maxclock. Then $u_1 \parallel u_2 \sim_f v_1 \parallel v_2$ entails (1) $u_2 \sim_f v_2$ and (2) $u_1 \sim_f v_1$.*

Proof. (1) is easy to see with the separation hypothesis. Let $\mathcal{R}$ be the set of all pairs (u, v) s.t. $u_1 \parallel u \sim_f v_1 \parallel v$ and both $u_1 \parallel u$ and $v_1 \parallel v$ are separated. We show that $\mathcal{R} \cup \sim_f$ is an f-performance equivalence. Indeed, if $u \xrightarrow{a,n} u'$ then $u_1 \parallel u \xrightarrow{a,n} u_1 \parallel u'$ which is still separated (or $u' \sim_f Nil$). Now there is a $v \parallel v_1 \xrightarrow{a,n} t$ with $u_1 \parallel u' \sim_f t$ but this step can only come from v, so that t is some separated $v_1 \parallel v'$ (or $v' \sim_f Nil$). Since u_1 and v_1 have same *maxclock*, $u' \sim_f Nil$ iff $v' \sim_f Nil$ and we have $(u', v') \in \mathcal{R} \cup \sim_f$.

(2) We now prove $u_1 \sim_f v_1$. Let $\mathcal{R}$ be the set of all pairs (u, v) s.t. u and v have same *maxclock*, and there exists a t s.t. $u \parallel t \sim_f v \parallel t$ and $u \parallel t$ and $v \parallel t$ are separated. We show $\mathcal{R} \cup \sim_f$ is an f-performance equivalence. Consider a pair $(u, v) \in \mathcal{R}$ (via some t) and let K be the largest *maxclock* for all immediate successors of u and v. K is finite because TBPP has finite branching. Thanks to Lemma 2.8, there is a sequence w s.t. $t \xrightarrow{w} t'$ and $minclock(t') > K$.

Consider a step $u \xrightarrow{a,n} u'$. Now $u \parallel t \xrightarrow{w} u \parallel t' \xrightarrow{a,n} u' \parallel t'$. Then there must exist a $v \parallel t \xrightarrow{w} v \parallel t'' \xrightarrow{a,n} v' \parallel t''$ with $u \parallel t' \sim_f v \parallel t''$ and $u' \parallel t' \sim_f v' \parallel t''$. We have $t' \sim_f Nil$ iff $t'' \sim_f Nil$ (because they have same *maxclock*) so that (1) gives us $t' \sim_f t''$. Thanks to $minclock(t') > K$, we have $u' \sim_f Nil$ iff $v' \sim_f Nil$ (because $u' \parallel t'$ and $v' \parallel t'$ have same *minclock*). If $u' \not\sim_f Nil$ then both $u' \parallel t'$ and $v' \parallel t''$ are separated, so that $(u', v') \in \mathcal{R}$. Otherwise $u' \sim_f Nil \sim_f v'$. □

Of course, normal forms are separated in an obvious way. Hence:

Lemma 5.3. *Assume $X_1 \parallel \ldots \parallel X_m \sim_f X'_1 \parallel \ldots \parallel X'_{m'}$. Then $m = m'$ and to any X_i we can associate a X'_j s.t. $X_i \sim_f X'_j$.*

Proof. Obviously $m = m'$ since any maximal execution of $X_1 \parallel \ldots \parallel X_m$ has exactly m steps with date 0. Now pick actions a_i's s.t. $X_i \xrightarrow{a_i,0} u_i$. We have $X_1 \parallel \ldots \parallel X_m \xrightarrow{a_2,0}\xrightarrow{a_3,0} \cdots \xrightarrow{a_m,0} X_1 \parallel 1 \triangleright u$. Then there is $X'_1 \parallel \ldots \parallel X'_m \xrightarrow{a_2,0}\xrightarrow{a_3,0} \cdots \xrightarrow{a_m,0} v$ with $X_1 \parallel 1 \triangleright u \sim_f v$. But v is reached by $m-1$ steps at date 0 from $X'_1 \parallel \ldots \parallel X'_m$, hence it has the form $X'_j \parallel 1 \triangleright u'$. The previous lemmas entail $X_1 \sim_f X'_j$ (and $u \sim_f u'$), which conclude the proof. □

Lemma 5.4. *Assume $X_1 \parallel \ldots \parallel X_m \sim_f X'_1 \parallel \ldots \parallel X'_m$. Then there is a bijective $h : [1..m] \to [1..m]$ s.t. $X_i \sim_f X'_{h(i)}$ for all i.*

Proof. We split the multiset $\{X_1, \ldots, X_m, X'_1, \ldots, X'_m\}$ into the equivalence classes induced by $\sim_f$. If every class contains exactly as many X_i's as X'_j's, then h is easy to build. Otherwise we can assume w.l.o.g. that one class is $\{X_1, X_2, \ldots, X_p, X'_1, X'_2, \ldots, X'_q\}$ with $p < q$. Assume $X_i \xrightarrow{a_i,0}$ for all i's, and consider $w = (a_1, 0) \ldots (a_p, 0)$. We have a move $X_1 \parallel \ldots \parallel X_m \xrightarrow{w} 1 \triangleright u \parallel X_{p+1} \parallel \ldots \parallel X_m$. This is imitated by $X'_1 \parallel \ldots \parallel X'_m \xrightarrow{w} 1 \triangleright u' \parallel X'_{i_{p+1}} \parallel \ldots \parallel X'_{i_m}$. Lemma 5.2 entails that $X_{p+1} \parallel \ldots \parallel X_m \sim_f X'_{i_{p+1}} \parallel \ldots \parallel X'_{i_m}$. Now one index (say j) in $\{i_{p+1}, \ldots, i_m\}$ must belong to $\{1, \ldots, q\}$. This contradicts Lemma 5.3 because we assumed X'_j has no match in $X_{p+1}, \ldots, X_m$. □

As a consequence, we now have the following important result, reducing $\sim_f$ to "equality" of normal forms:

Theorem 5.5. *Assume* $u \equiv n_1 \triangleright X_1 \parallel \ldots \parallel n_m \triangleright X_m$ *and* $v \equiv n'_1 \triangleright X'_1 \parallel \ldots \parallel n'_{m'} \triangleright X'_{m'}$. *Then* $u \sim_f v$ *iff there is a bijective* $h : [1..m] \to [1..m']$ *s.t.* $n_i = n'_{h(i)}$ *and* $X_i \sim_f X'_{h(i)}$ *for all* i.

Hence f-performance equivalence of u and v can be reduced to a combination of f-performance equivalence of variables.

An equivalence relation $\approx$ between variables of $\mathcal{X}$ can be extended to terms: we say $u \approx v$ when the normal forms $n_1 \triangleright X_1 \parallel \ldots$ and $n'_1 \triangleright X'_1 \parallel \ldots$ of u and v can be related by a bijective h s.t. $n_i = n'_{h(i)}$ and $X_i \approx X'_{h(i)}$.

Definition 5.6. *An equivalence relation* $\approx$ *between variables of* $\mathcal{X}$ *has the* transfer property *if for any* $X \approx Y$ *and for any* $X \xrightarrow{a}_\Delta u$ *there is a* $Y \xrightarrow{a}_\Delta v$ *s.t.* $u \approx v$.

Clearly, if $\approx$ has the transfer property, then its extension to terms is an f-performance equivalence. Conversely, Theorem 5.5 implies that $\sim_f \cap (\mathcal{X} \times \mathcal{X})$ has the transfer property. But the transfer property for some $\approx$ does not depend on f. Hence

Lemma 5.7. *Let* f *and* g *be two duration functions. Then* $\sim_f$ *and* $\sim_g$ *coincide.*

Corollary 5.8. $u \sim_{\mathrm{i}} v$ *iff there is a duration function* f *such* $u \sim_f v$ *iff* $u \sim_{\mathbf{1}} v$.

Remark 5.9. Corollary 5.8 calls for comments. It is not a paradox and can be compared, e.g., with Prop. 13 from [AM96]. Still, we see no easy way to prove it without going through the analysis required for our Theorem 5.5.

Observe that it does not hold if we allow duration functions taking the value zero (which is rather meaningless in our framework). E.g., the terms from Example 3.3 become performance equivalent when $f(a) = 0$.

Similarly, it does not hold in a framework where we associate several values to a same action (cf. Remark 2.4). E.g., with

$$\Delta = \{X \xrightarrow{a} X, X \xrightarrow{a} 2 \triangleright X, \quad Y \xrightarrow{a} X, Y \xrightarrow{a} 1 \triangleright X, Y \xrightarrow{a} 2 \triangleright X\}$$

we have $X \not\sim_{\mathrm{i}} Y$ but $X \sim_f Y$ when $f(a) = \{1, 2\}$. □

As a consequence, we may write indistinctly $\sim$ for any $\sim_f$ (and for $\sim_{\mathrm{i}}$). We do that in the rest of the paper, where we assume additionally that f is the constant duration function $\mathbf{1}$.

6 Decidability of Performance Equivalence

With the results from Section 5, deciding performance equivalence is simple since it amounts to computing the largest equivalence on variables that has the transfer property.

Proposition 6.1. *Computing* $\sim \cap (\mathcal{X} \times \mathcal{X})$ *can be done in time polynomial in* $|\Delta|$.

(Where $|\Delta|$ is the number of rules plus the sum of the sizes of the left-hand sides.)

Proof. Given Δ we partition the set $\mathcal{X}$ of variables into equivalence classes. This is done in the usual way, starting with $\approx_0 = \mathcal{X} \times \mathcal{X}$ and refining $\approx_i$ into $\approx_{i+1}$ until stabilization. The refinement step removes a pair (X, Y) from $\approx_i$ whenever there is a $X \xrightarrow{a} u$ in Δ s.t. no $Y \xrightarrow{a} v$ has $u \approx_i v$ (which can be checked easily by a sorting algorithm when u and v are in normal form). Stabilization is reached after at most $|\mathcal{X}| - 1$ refinement steps. □

Hence deciding whether $u \sim v$ can be done in time polynomial in $|u| + |v| + |\Delta|$. Finally we have

Theorem 6.2. *Deciding performance equivalence over TBPP is P-complete.*

Proof. We already know membership in *P* and only prove *P*-hardness.

When no parallel composition is involved, TBPP terms behave like finite-state processes where the single local clock just records the length of the history of the computation. Hence performance equivalence of these sequential terms reduces to strong untimed bisimilarity of the underlying unfolded trees, which is just strong bisimilarity of untimed finite state processes, entailing *P*-hardness [BGS92]. □

7 Conclusion

In this paper we investigated TBPP, a timed extension of the BPP. TBPP is essentially equivalent to the algebra of [CGR97], itself obtained by forbidding synchronization in earlier process algebra with urgent durational actions.

In this framework, [CGR97] introduced *performance equivalence* as a way to relate processes having the same behaviour and the same efficiency.

Our main result is a polynomial-time method for deciding performance equivalence over this class where systems can have an infinite number of different states (even disregarding time). Thus, BPP + Time turns out to be simpler than plain BPP, which is a surprising result. This suggests that timed extensions of related infinite-state algebra should be investigated and could well turn out to be simpler than their better-known untimed counterpart. Let us suggests some directions:

1. Bisimulation of normed PA processes is decidable [HJ99] but appears quite complex. What about performance equivalence for PA+Time?

2. Decidability of observational equivalence (a.k.a. τ-bisimulation) of BPP processes is an important open problem [Esp97, KM99]. What about observational performance equivalence? (Adding τ's to TBPP can be done in several ways: e.g., they can model internal actions with null duration instead of abstracted-away actions with positive duration.)
3. Most behavioural equivalences are undecidable on BPP processes [Hüt94]. What about BPP+Time?

References

[ACD93] R. Alur, C. Courcoubetis, and D. Dill. Model-checking in dense real-time. *Information and Computation*, 104(1):2–34, 1993.

[AH92] S. Arun-Kumar and M. Hennessy. An efficiency preorder for processes. *Acta Informatica*, 29(8):737–760, 1992.

[AJ98] P. A. Abdulla and B. Jonsson. Verifying networks of timed processes. In *Proc. Int. Conf. Tools and Algorithms for the Construction and Analysis of Systems (TACAS'98), Lisbon, Portugal, March 1998*, volume 1384 of *Lecture Notes in Computer Science*, pages 298–312. Springer, 1998.

[AM96] L. Aceto and D. Murphy. Timing and causality in process algebra. *Acta Informatica*, 33(4):317–350, 1996.

[BGS92] J. Balcázar, J. Gabarró, and M. Sántha. Deciding bisimilarity is P-Complete. *Formal Aspects of Computing*, 4(6A):638–648, 1992.

[CC97] Xiao Jun Chen and F. Corradini. On the specification and verification of performance properties for a timed process algebra. In *Proc. 6th Int. Conf. Algebraic Methodology and Software Technology (AMAST'97), Sydney, Australia, Dec. 1997*, volume 1349 of *Lecture Notes in Computer Science*, pages 123–137, 1997.

[CFP95] G. Cécé, A. Finkel, and S. Purushothaman Iyer. Unreliable channels are easier to verify than perfect channels. *Information and Computation*, 124(1):20–31, 1995.

[CGR97] F. Corradini, R. Gorrieri, and M. Roccetti. Performance preorder and competitive equivalence. *Acta Informatica*, 34(11):805–835, 1997.

[CHM93] S. Christensen, Y. Hirshfeld, and F. Moller. Bisimulation equivalence is decidable for basic parallel processes. In *Proc. 4th Int. Conf. Concurrency Theory (CONCUR'93), Hildesheim, Germany, Aug. 1993*, volume 715 of *Lecture Notes in Computer Science*, pages 143–157. Springer, 1993.

[Chr93] S. Christensen. Decidability and decomposition in process algebras. PhD thesis CST-105-93, Dept. of Computer Science, University of Edinburgh, UK, 1993.

[Cor98] F. Corradini. On performance congruences for process algebras. *Information and Computation*, 145(2):191–230, 1998.

[CP96] F. Corradini and M. Pistore. Specification and verification of timed lazy systems. In *Proc. 21st Int. Symp. Math. Found. Comp. Sci. (MFCS'96), Cracow, Poland, Sep. 1996*, volume 1113 of *Lecture Notes in Computer Science*, pages 279–290, 1996.

[EK99] J. Esparza and J. Knoop. An automata-theoretic approach to interprocedural data-flow analysis. In *Proc. Conf. Foundations of Software Science and Computation Structures (FOSSACS'99), Amsterdam, The Netherlands, Mar. 1999*, volume 1578 of *Lecture Notes in Computer Science*, pages 14–30. Springer, 1999.

[Esp97] J. Esparza. Petri nets, commutative context-free grammars, and basic parallel processes. *Fundamenta Informaticae*, 31(1):13–25, 1997.

[FM95] G. Ferrari and U. Montanari. Dynamic matrices and the cost analysis of concurrent programs. In *Proc. 4th Int. Conf. Algebraic Methodology and Software Technology (AMAST'95), Montreal, Canada, July 1995*, volume 936 of *Lecture Notes in Computer Science*, pages 307–321, 1995.

[Gla90] R. J. van Glabbeek. The linear time - branching time spectrum. In *Proc. Theories of Concurrency (CONCUR'90), Amsterdam, NL, Aug. 1990*, volume 458 of *Lecture Notes in Computer Science*, pages 278–297. Springer, 1990.

[GRS95] R. Gorrieri, M. Roccetti, and E. Stancampiano. A theory of processes with durational actions. *Theoretical Computer Science*, 140(1):73–94, 1995.

[GV92] J. F. Groote and F. W. Vaandrager. Structured operational semantics and bisimulation as a congruence. *Information and Computation*, 100(2):202–260, 1992.

[Hen88] M. Hennessy. Axiomatising finite concurrent processes. *SIAM J. Comput.*, 17(5):997–1017, 1988.

[HJ99] Y. Hirshfeld and M. Jerrum. Bisimulation equivalence is decidable for normed process algebra. In *Proc. 26th Int. Coll. Automata, Languages, and Programming (ICALP'99), Prague, Czech Republic, July 1999*, volume 1644 of *Lecture Notes in Computer Science*, pages 412–421. Springer, 1999.

[HJM96] Y. Hirshfeld, M. Jerrum, and F. Moller. A polynomial-time algorithm for deciding bisimulation equivalence of normed Basic Parallel Processes. *Math. Struct. in Comp. Science*, 6(3):251–259, 1996.

[Hüt94] H. Hüttel. Undecidable equivalences for Basic Parallel Processes. In *Proc. Int. Symp. Theoretical Aspects of Computer Software (TACS'94), Sendai, Japan, Apr. 1994*, volume 789 of *Lecture Notes in Computer Science*, pages 454–464. Springer, 1994.

[KM99] A. Kučera and R. Mayr. Weak bisimilarity with infinite-state systems can be decided in polynomial time. In *Proc. 10th Int. Conf. Concurrency Theory (CONCUR'99), Eindhoven, The Netherlands, Aug. 1999*, volume 1664 of *Lecture Notes in Computer Science*, pages 368–382. Springer, 1999.

[Mil89] R. Milner. *Communication and Concurrency.* Prentice Hall Int., 1989.

[MM93] R. Milner and F. Moller. Unique decomposition of processes. *Theoretical Computer Science*, 107(2):357–363, 1993.

[Mol96] F. Moller. Infinite results. In *Proc. 7th Int. Conf. Concurrency Theory (CONCUR'96), Pisa, Italy, Aug. 1996*, volume 1119 of *Lecture Notes in Computer Science*, pages 195–216. Springer, 1996.

[MT91] F. Moller and C. Tofts. Relating processes with respect to speed. In *Proc. 2nd Int. Conf. Theory of Concurrency (CONCUR'91), Amsterdam, NL, Aug. 1991*, volume 527 of *Lecture Notes in Computer Science*, pages 424–438. Springer, 1991.

On Word Rewriting Systems Having a Rational Derivation

Didier Caucal

IRISA–CNRS, Campus de Beaulieu,
35042 Rennes, France
caucal@irisa.fr

Abstract. We define four families of word-rewriting systems: the prefix/suffix systems and the left/right systems. The rewriting of prefix systems generalizes the prefix rewriting of systems: a system is prefix (suffix) if a left hand side and a right hand side are overlapping only by prefix (suffix). The rewriting of right systems generalizes the mechanism of transducers: a system is right (left) if a left hand side overlaps a right hand side only on the right (left).
We show that these systems have a rational derivation even if they are not only finite but recognizable. Besides these four families, we give simple systems having a non rational derivation.

1 Introduction

A general approach to verify properties for systems is to decide whether formulas are verified by their transition graphs: systems with isomorphic transition graphs have the same properties. These graphs are in general infinite but we have a hierarchy of graph families: finite graphs, regular graphs, prefix-recognizable graphs, rational graphs. A family of infinite graphs has been defined in [MS 85] : the connected regular graphs of finite degree meaning that they have a finite number of non isomorphic connected components by decomposition by distance from any vertex. The regular graphs of finite degree are the transition graphs of pushdown automata (restricted to a rational configuration set) and are also the prefix transition graphs of finite word-rewriting systems [Ca 90] : finite unions of elementary graphs of the form $(u \xrightarrow{a} v).W = \{uw \xrightarrow{a} vw \mid w \in W\}$ where u, v are words and W is a rational language. This family has been extended in [Co 90] to all the regular graphs (or equational graphs): the graphs generated by the deterministic graph grammars. A larger family is composed of the prefix-recognizable graphs [Ca 96] which are the prefix transition graphs of the recognizable word-rewriting systems: finite union of elementary graphs of the form $(U \xrightarrow{a} V).W$ where U, V, W are rational languages. Finally, an even larger family of graphs is the set of rational graphs studied in [Mo 00] : the graphs recognized by transducers with labelled outputs. Clearly, all these representations are heterogeneous and a central question is to find a simple and uniform specification for all these graphs.

J. Tiuryn (Ed.): FOSSACS 2000, LNCS 1784, pp. 48–62, 2000.

A solution has been proposed in [CK 98] which considers the 'Cayley graph' of any word-rewriting system: the set of transitions $u \xrightarrow{a} v$ if u, v are irreducible words, a is a letter and ua derives into v. To represent as Cayley graphs the regular graphs and the prefix-recognizable graphs, we translate the prefix (resp. suffix) rewriting of systems [Bü 64] into the rewriting of particular systems, called prefix (resp. suffix) systems. A system is called prefix (resp. suffix) if a left hand side and a right hand side are overlapping only by prefix (resp. suffix). To represent as Cayley graphs the rational graphs, we translate the mechanism of transducers into the rewriting of particular systems, called right systems. A system is called right (resp. left) if a left hand side overlaps a right hand side only on the right (resp. left). These systems yield a uniform characterization of all the previous families of graphs.

In this paper, we show that these systems have a rational derivation: derivation relation itself (the reflexive and transitive closure by composition of the rewriting) is recognizable by a transducer (a finite automaton where each label is a couple of words), and we can construct such a transducer in polynomial time. Such a result is general: a rational relation preserves rational and context-free languages, and the composition of rational relations remains rational. Many others properties are well known [Be 79], [AB 88]. Furthermore the derivation is rational when the systems (left, right, prefix, suffix) are not only finite but recognizable (and false for rational systems). Finally, it appears that we can have a non rational derivation for the remaining families of rewriting systems, defined by overlapping between the left hand sides and the right hand sides.

2 Rational and Recognizable Relations

We present notations and basic properties for rational relations and recognizable relations.

For any set E, we denote by $\#E$ its cardinal and by 2^E its powerset. Let $\mathbb{N}$ be the set of nonnegative integers and for any $n \in \mathbb{N}$, let $[n] = \{1, \ldots, n\}$ with $[0] = \emptyset$.

A binary (total) *operation* $\cdot$ on a set E is a mapping from $E \times E$ into E and we write $a{\cdot}b$ instead of $\cdot(a, b)$. A set M with a binary operation $\cdot$ on M is a *monoid* if $\cdot$ is *associative*: $(a{\cdot}b){\cdot}c = a{\cdot}(b{\cdot}c)$ for every $a, b, c \in M$, and has a (unique) neutral element $1 : a{\cdot}1 = 1{\cdot}a = a$ for every $a \in M$. The powerset 2^M of M is a monoid for operation $\cdot$ extended by union to subsets: $P{\cdot}Q = \{a{\cdot}b \mid a \in P \wedge b \in Q\}$ for every $P, Q \subseteq M$; $\{1\}$ is the neutral element. A subset P of a monoid M is a *submonoid* of M if P is a monoid for $\cdot$ of M: $P{\cdot}P \subseteq P$ and $1 \in P$. The smallest (for inclusion) submonoid of M containing P and called the *submonoid generated* by P, is the following subset $P^* = \bigcup_{n \geq 0} P^n$ with $P^0 = \{1\}$ and $P^{n+1} = P^n{\cdot}P$ for every n. The subset P^* is also called the *reflexive and transitive closure* by $\cdot$ of P. Note that $(P^*)^* = P^*$ and $\emptyset^* = \{1\}$.

We say that M is *finitely generated* if $M = P^*$ for some finite P. We say that M is *free* if $M = P^*$ for some *code* P: there is no two factorizations in P^* of a same element *i.e.* if $a_1 \ldots a_m = b_1 \ldots b_n$ for $a_1, \ldots, a_m, b_1, \ldots, b_n \in P$ then $m = n$ and $u_i = v_i$ for all i.
We say that M is free finitely generated if $M = P^*$ for some finite code P.
The set $Rat(M)$ of the *rational subsets* of M is the smallest subset of 2^M containing the finite subsets of M and closed by the three operations $\cup, \cdot, *$.
We can also recognize the rational subsets by finite automata.
Let P be a subset of M. A (simple oriented labelled) *P-graph* G is a subset of $V{\times}P{\times}V$ where V is an arbitrary set. Any (s,a,t) of G is a *labelled arc* of *source* s, of *target* t, with *label* a, and is identified with the *labelled transition* $s \xrightarrow[G]{a} t$ or directly $s \xrightarrow{a} t$ if G is understood. We denote by $V_G := \{ s \mid \exists\, a\ \exists\, t,\ s \xrightarrow{a} t \vee t \xrightarrow{a} s \}$ the set of *vertices* of G. A graph is *deterministic* if $\xrightarrow{a}$ is a function for every $a \in P$ *i.e.* distinct arcs with the same source have distinct labels: $r \xrightarrow{a} s \wedge r \xrightarrow{a} t \implies s = t$. The set $2^{V\times P^*\times V}$ of P^*-graphs with vertices in V is a monoid for the *composition*: $G \circ H := \{ r \xrightarrow{a\cdot b} t \mid \exists\, s,\ r \xrightarrow[G]{a} s \wedge s \xrightarrow[H]{b} t \}$ for any $G, H \subseteq V{\times}P^*{\times}V$; its neutral element is $\{ s \xrightarrow{1} s \mid s \in V \}$ (in fact $2^{V\times P^*\times V}$ is the powerset monoid of the partial semigroup $V{\times}P^*{\times}V$ with the partial operation $(r,a,s) \circ (s,b,t) = (r, a{\cdot}b, t)$).
The relation $\xrightarrow[G^*]{u}$ denoted by $\overset{u}{\underset{G}{\Longrightarrow}}$ or simply by $\overset{u}{\Longrightarrow}$ if G is understood, is the existence of a *path* in G labelled $u \in P^*$. The labels $L(G,E,F)$ of paths from a set E to a set F is the following subset of P^*: $L(G,E,F) := \{ u \in M \mid \exists\, s \in E,\ \exists\, t \in F,\ s \overset{u}{\underset{G}{\Longrightarrow}} t \}$; in particular $1 \in L(G,E,F)$ when $E \cap F \neq \emptyset$.
A *P-automaton* A is a P-graph G whose vertices are called *states*, with a subset I of *initial states* and a subset F of *final states*; the automaton recognizes the subset $L(A) = L(G,I,F)$ of P^*. An automaton is finite if its graph is finite. An automaton is deterministic if its graph is deterministic and there is a unique initial state. This permits to express a standard result on rational subsets:
Given a subset P of a monoid M, $Rat(P^*)$ is equivalently

- the smallest subset of 2^M containing $\emptyset$ and $\{a\}$ for each $a \in P$, and closed by $\cup$, $\cdot$, $*$
- the set of subsets recognized by the finite P-automata
- the set of subsets recognized by the finite deterministic P-automata.

Given monoids M and N, the *cartesian product* $M{\times}N = \{ (m,n) \mid m \in M \wedge n \in N \}$ is a monoid for the operation defined by $(m,n){\cdot}(m',n') = (m \cdot_M m', n \cdot_N n')$ for every $m, m' \in M$ and every $n, n' \in N$. A *relation* R from M into N is a subset of $M{\times}N$ and we write also $u\ R\ v$ for $(u,v) \in R$. In particular R is a *rational relation* if R belongs to $Rat(M{\times}N)$ *i.e.* R is recognized by a finite (and deterministic) $M{\times}N$-automaton: any transition $\xrightarrow{(u,v)}$ is written simply $\xrightarrow{u/v}$. For any relations R, S from M into N, we have $R{\cdot}S = \{ (m{\cdot}m', n{\cdot}n') \mid m\ R\ m' \wedge n\ S\ n' \}$ and R^* is the reflexive and transitive closure by $\cdot$ of R. As usual, we denote by $R^{-1} = \{ (v,u) \mid u\ R\ v \}$ the *inverse* of R

and $R(P) = \{ v \mid \exists\, u \in P,\ u\, R\, v \}$ is the *image* by R of $P \subseteq M$. In particular $Dom(R) = R^{-1}(N)$ is the *domain* of R and $Im(R) = R(M)$ is the *image* of R. Note that for $R \in Rat(M{\times}N)$, we have $R^{-1} \in Rat(N{\times}M)$, $Dom(R) \in Rat(M)$ and $Im(R) \in Rat(N)$.
Note that the family $2^{M\times M}$ of binary relations on M coincides with the set $2^{M\times\{1\}\times M}$ of (unlabelled) $\emptyset^*$-graphs: (u, v) coincides with the transition $u \xrightarrow{1} v$. So $2^{M\times M}$ is a monoid for the *relational composition* $R \circ S = \{ (u, w) \mid \exists\, v,\ u\, R\, v \wedge v\, S\, w \}$ for every $R, S \subseteq M{\times}M$ with the neutral element $Id_M = \{ (u, u) \mid u \in M \}$. Furthermore for every $R \subseteq M{\times}M$, $R^\star = \bigcup_{n\geq 0} R^{(n)}$ is the reflexive and transitive closure of R for $\circ$: $R^{(0)} = Id_M$ and $R^{(n+1)} = R^{(n)} \circ R$.

Another family of subsets of a monoid M are defined by inverse morphism. A mapping h from M into a monoid N is a (monoid) *morphism* if $h(1) = 1$ and $h(a{\cdot}b) = h(a){\cdot}h(b)$ for every $a, b \in M$. A subset P of M is *recognizable* if there exists a morphism h from M into a finite monoid N such that $P = h^{-1}(h(P))$; we denote by $Rec(M)$ the family of recognizable subsets of M.
Recognizable subsets are also recognizable by automata. We say that a P-graph G is (source) *complete* if for every $a \in P$, every vertex $s \in V_G$ is source of an arc labelled a: $\exists\, t,\ s \xrightarrow{a} t$. We say also that G is *path-deterministic* if G^* is deterministic: $\overset{u}{\Longrightarrow}$ is a function for every $u \in P^*$ *i.e.* if $r \overset{u}{\Longrightarrow} s$ and $r \overset{u}{\Longrightarrow} t$ then $s = t$. Given a subset P of a monoid M, $Rec(P^*)$ is the set of subsets recognized by the path-deterministic and complete P-automata having a finite set of states.
Another way to characterize a recognizable subset is by residual:

$$P \in Rec(M) \iff \{ u^{-1}P \mid u \in M \} \text{ is finite}$$

where the set $Q^{-1}P = \{ v \mid \exists\, u \in Q,\ u{\cdot}v \in P \}$ is the *left residual* of P by $Q \subseteq M$. We denote also by $PQ^{-1} = \{ u \mid \exists\, v \in Q,\ u{\cdot}v \in P \}$ the *right residual* of P by Q. The characterizations of the rational and recognizable subsets by automata permit to deduce usual facts:

— $Rec(M)$ is a boolean algebra
— $P \cap Q \in Rat(M)$ for every $P \in Rat(M)$ and $Q \in Rec(M)$
— $R(P) \in Rat(N)$ for every $R \in Rat(M{\times}N)$ and $P \in Rec(M)$
— $Rec(M) \subseteq Rat(M)$ if M is finitely generated (McKnight theorem)
— $Rec(M) = Rat(M)$ if M is free finitely generated (Kleene theorem)
— $R \in Rec(M{\times}N) \iff R = \bigcup_{i\in I} P_i{\times}Q_i$ for I finite
with $P_i \in Rec(M)$, $Q_i \in Rec(N)$ (Mezei theorem)

We restrict now to rational and recognizable relations on words. Henceforth N is an *alphabet* *i.e.* a finite set of symbols called *letters*.
The set $N^* = \{ (a_1, \ldots, a_n) \mid n \geq 0 \wedge a_1, \ldots, a_n \in N \}$ is a monoid for the *concatenation* operator: $(a_1, \ldots, a_m).(b_1, \ldots, b_n) = (a_1, \ldots, a_m, b_1, \ldots, b_n)$. Any element $(a_1, \ldots, a_n)$ is written simply $a_1 \ldots a_n$ and called a *word*, and the neutral element $()$ is denoted by ε and called the *empty word*. Note that a word u over N of length $|u| \in \mathbb{N}$ is a mapping from $[|u|]$ into N represented by $u(1) \ldots u(|u|) = u$. The *mirror* of any word u is the word $\widetilde{u} = u(|u|) \ldots u(1)$. A *language* L is a set of words: $L \subseteq N^*$. Let $\widetilde{L} = \{ \widetilde{u} \mid u \in L \}$ the mirror of any language L, and let $\widetilde{R} = \{ (\widetilde{u}, \widetilde{v}) \mid u\, R\, v \}$ the mirror of any binary

relation R on N^*. When L and R are finite, we denote by $|L| = \sum_{u\in L}|u|$ the length of L and by $|R| = \sum_{(u,v)\in R}|u|+|v|$ the length of R; in particular $|Dom(R)|+|Im(R)| \leq |R|$. Furthermore we denote by $N_L = \{\, u(i) \mid u \in L \wedge i \in [|u|] \,\}$ the alphabet of letters in L, and by $N_R = N_{Dom(R)} \cup N_{Im(R)}$ the alphabet of R. As N^* is the free monoid generated by N, $Rec(N^*) = Rat(N^*)$ is the set of languages recognized by the (deterministic and/or complete) N-automata. A rational relation on N^*, *i.e.* an element of $Rat(N^*{\times}N^*)$, is a relation recognized by a finite $N^*{\times}N^*$-automaton called a *transducer*. Furthermore $R \in Rec(N^*{\times}N^*)$ if and only if $R = \bigcup_{i\in I} P_i{\times}Q_i$ for some finite I with $P_i, Q_i \in Rat(N^*)$; in particular $Id_{N^*} \in Rat(N^*{\times}N^*) - Rec(N^*{\times}N^*)$. Another remark is that $R(P) \in Rat(N^*)$ for every $R \in Rat(N^*{\times}N^*)$ and $P \in Rat(N^*)$. A crucial property which is not true for any monoid product is the Elgot-Mezei theorem: $Rat(N^*{\times}N^*)$ is closed by composition. The family $Rec(N^*{\times}N^*)$ is also closed by composition, and more generally $R \circ S$, $S \circ R \in Rec(N^*{\times}N^*)$ for every $R \in Rat(N^*{\times}N^*)$ and $S \in Rec(N^*{\times}N^*)$. Obviously $Rec(N^*{\times}N^*)$ is closed by mirror, and $Rat(N^*{\times}N^*)$ is also closed by mirror: for any $N^*{\times}N^*$-graph G, we have $L(G,E,F)^{\sim} = L(\widetilde{G},F,E)$ with $\widetilde{G} = \{\, q \xrightarrow{\widetilde{u}/\widetilde{v}} p \mid p \xrightarrow[G]{u/v} q \,\}$.

3 Rational Derivation

We consider the word-rewriting systems (see for instance the survey [DJ 90] and [BO 93]) associated with a language of admissible words such that any derivation between admissible words contains only admissible words. Like in [Sé 93], we define several subclasses of rewriting systems by considering the overlappings between the left hand sides (of the rules) and the right hand sides, inside of the admissible words. We extract two families of systems, the right systems and the prefix systems, having a rational derivation even if the systems are recognizable (Theorems 3.8 and 3.11). By mirror, we obtain two others families of systems, the left systems and the suffix systems. Besides these four families, we give simple systems having a non rational derivation.

A (word) *rewriting system* (R,C) is a binary relation R on N^* and a language $C \subseteq N^*$ of *configurations* (or *admissible words*). A system (R,C) is respectively *finite*, *recognizable*, *rational* if C is rational, and if R is respectively finite, recognizable, rational. The *rewriting* $\underset{R,\,C}{\longrightarrow}$ according to any system (R,C) is

$$\underset{R,\,C}{\longrightarrow} \;:=\; \{\, (xuy, xvy) \in C{\times}C \mid u\; R\; v \;\wedge\; x,y \in N^* \,\}$$

the application of R under any left and right contexts, but restricted to configurations. Furthermore the *derivation* $\underset{R,\,C}{\overset{\star}{\longrightarrow}}$ according to (R,C) is

$$\underset{R,\,C}{\overset{\star}{\longrightarrow}} \;:=\; \{\, (u_0,u_n) \in C{\times}C \mid n \geq 0 \wedge \exists\, u_1,\ldots,u_{n-1},\; u_0 \underset{R,\,C}{\longrightarrow} u_1 \ldots u_{n-1} \underset{R,\,C}{\longrightarrow} u_n \,\}$$

the reflexive (restricted to C) and transitive closure of $\underset{R,\,C}{\longrightarrow}$ by composition *i.e.*

$$\underset{R,\,C}{\overset{\star}{\longrightarrow}} \;=\; \bigcup_n \underset{R,\,C}{\overset{n}{\longrightarrow}} \quad \text{where} \quad \underset{R,\,C}{\overset{0}{\longrightarrow}} \;=\; Id_C \quad \text{and} \quad \underset{R,\,C}{\overset{n+1}{\longrightarrow}} \;=\; \underset{R,\,C}{\overset{n}{\longrightarrow}} \circ \underset{R,\,C}{\longrightarrow} \quad \forall\, n \geq 0.$$

Note that for any system (R,C),

$$\underset{\tilde{R},\tilde{C}}{\longrightarrow} = (\underset{R,C}{\longrightarrow})^{\sim} \text{ and } \underset{R^{-1},C}{\longrightarrow} = (\underset{R,C}{\longrightarrow})^{-1}$$

$$\text{hence } \xrightarrow[\tilde{R},\tilde{C}]{\star} = (\xrightarrow[R,C]{\star})^{\sim} \text{ and } \xrightarrow[R^{-1},C]{\star} = (\xrightarrow[R,C]{\star})^{-1}.$$

When the configuration set $C = N^*$, it can be omitted: we usually say that the relation R is a rewriting system and we denote by $\underset{R}{\longrightarrow}$ its rewriting (instead of $\underset{R,N^*}{\longrightarrow}$) and by $\xrightarrow[R]{\star}$ its derivation. Note that $\underset{R,C}{\longrightarrow} = \underset{R}{\longrightarrow} \cap\, C{\times}C$.
Even if the configuration set C is rational, it is possible by restriction to C to control the rewriting of simple finite relations in order to get a non rational derivation. This is shown in the following example.

Example 3.1 Consider the finite relation $R = \{(a,bd)\,,(b,c)\,,(c,a)\}$ and the rational configuration set $C = \bigcup_{p\neq q\,\in\{a,b,c\}} pd^*qd^*$. This finite system has a non rational derivation $\xrightarrow[R,C]{\star}$ because the language $\xrightarrow[R,C]{\star}(ab) \cap ad^*bd^* = \{\, ad^nbd^n \mid n \geq 0 \,\}$ is not rational.
However such a relation R is prefix and is left ($\widetilde{R}$ is right) as defined below (cf. Theorems 3.8 and 3.11), and in particular its derivation $\xrightarrow[R]{\star}$ is rational; it is recognized by the following transducer:

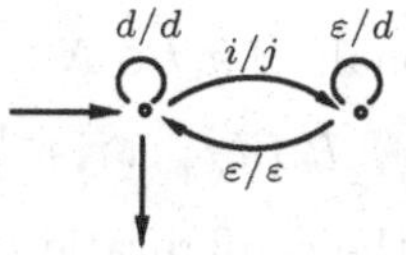

with $(i,j) \in \{(a,a)\,,(a,bd)\,,(a,cd)\,,(b,a)\,,(b,b)\,,(b,c)\,,(c,a)\,,(c,bd)\,,(c,c)\}$.

Thus we introduce a general condition on the systems to be study. A system (R,C) is *stable* if it satisfies the following condition:

$$s \xrightarrow[R]{\star} r \xrightarrow[R]{\star} t \;\wedge\; s,t \in C \implies r \in C$$

Such a general condition is undecidable but there exists decidable sufficient conditions like the closure of C by rewriting: $\underset{R}{\longrightarrow}(C) \subseteq C$. In particular any relation R (on N^*) is stable. A basic property of any stable system is that its derivation is the restriction to the configurations of the derivation of its relation.

Lemma 3.2 *For any stable system* (R,C), $\xrightarrow[R,C]{\star} = \xrightarrow[R]{\star} \cap\, C{\times}C$.

For C rational, $C{\times}C$ is a recognizable relation, and Lemma 3.2 implies that if $\xrightarrow[R]{\star}$ is a rational (resp. recognizable) relation then $\xrightarrow[R,C]{\star}$ is a rational (resp. recognizable) relation. However we will give general families of systems (R,C) such that $\xrightarrow[R,C]{\star}$ is rational, but not containing (R,N^*) in general.

To study the rationality of derivation $\xrightarrow[R,\,C]{\star}$ we consider the composition $\xrightarrow[R,\,C]{} \circ \xrightarrow[R,\,C]{}$ of two rewritings, and we examine the possible overlappings between the right hand side of the rule applied in the first rewriting, with the left hand side of the rule applied in the second rewriting. We extricate families of systems having a rational derivation by discarding the undesirable overlapping rules.
It is easy to find simple finite relations having a non rational derivation.

Example 3.3 For $R = \{(ab, aabb)\}$, $\xrightarrow[R]{\star}(ab) = \{ a^n b^n \mid n \geq 1 \} \notin Rat(\{a,b\}^*)$ hence $\xrightarrow[R]{\star}$ is not rational. Similarly the derivation of $R^{-1} = \{(aabb, ab)\}$ is not rational because $\xrightarrow[R^{-1}]{\star} = (\xrightarrow[R]{\star})^{-1}$. These relations are strict-internals as defined below.

We say that a system (R, C) is *domain-strict-internal* if

$$\exists\ s,t \in N^* \quad \exists\ (w, xuy),\ (u,v)\ \in R,\ x,y \neq \varepsilon\ \wedge\ swt, sxuyt, sxvyt\ \in C$$

meaning that the following representation is allowed:

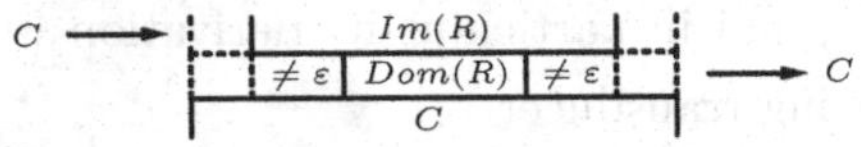

which is decidable for (R, C) rational: $\exists\ s,t \in N^*$,

$$(R \cap s^{-1}Ct^{-1} \times s^{-1}Ct^{-1}) \circ (Id_{N+}.R.Id_{N+} \cap s^{-1}Ct^{-1} \times s^{-1}Ct^{-1}) \neq \emptyset$$

Let us illustrate the significance of the configuration set C for this definition.

Example 3.4 The relation $R = \{(\varepsilon, ab)\}$ is domain-strict-internal and its derivation is not rational because the language $\xrightarrow[R]{\star}(\varepsilon) \cap a^*b^* = \{ a^n b^n \mid n \geq 0 \}$ is not rational. On the other hand $(R, (ab)^*)$ is not domain-strict-internal (and is stable) and $\xrightarrow[R,\,(ab)^*]{\star} = Id_{(ab)^*}.(\{\varepsilon\} \times (ab)^*)$ is rational.

Similarly a system (R, C) is *image-strict-internal* if (R^{-1}, C) is domain-strict-internal, meaning that the following representation is allowed:

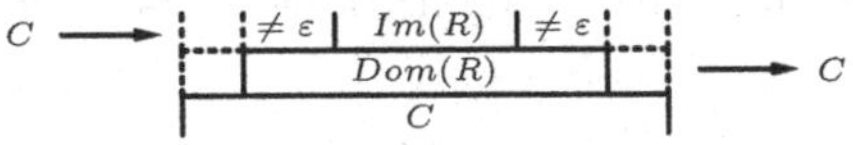

Finally a system is *strict-internal* if it is domain-strict-internal or image-strict-internal.
Another notions of internal systems can be obtained by prefixity and suffixity.
A system (R, C) is *domain-prefix-internal* if

$$\exists\ s,t \in N^* \quad \exists\ (w, uy),\ (u,v)\ \in R,\ y \neq \varepsilon\ \wedge\ swt, suyt, svyt\ \in C$$

meaning that the following representation is allowed:

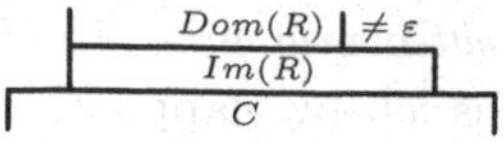

which is decidable for (R, C) rational:

$$\exists\, s,t \in N^*,\ (R \cap s^{-1}Ct^{-1} \times s^{-1}Ct^{-1}) \circ (R.Id_{N+} \cap s^{-1}Ct^{-1} \times s^{-1}Ct^{-1}) \neq \emptyset$$

Similarly we say that (R, C) is

image-prefix-internal if (R^{-1}, C) is domain-prefix-internal,
domain-suffix-internal if $(\widetilde{R}, \widetilde{C})$ is domain-prefix-internal,
image-suffix-internal if $(\widetilde{R}^{-1}, \widetilde{C})$ is domain-prefix-internal.

Finally a system is *prefix-internal* if it is domain-prefix-internal or image-prefix-internal. Similarly a system is *suffix-internal* if it is domain-suffix-internal or image-suffix-internal. Furthermore a system is *domain-internal* if it is domain-strict-internal or domain-prefix-internal or domain-suffix-internal. Similarly a system is *image-internal* if it is image-strict-internal or image-prefix-internal or image-suffix-internal.
Note that it is again easy to find non-internal relations having a non rational derivation.

Example 3.5 For $R = \{(ba, ab)\}$, the language $\xrightarrow[R]{*}((ab)^*) \cap a^*b^*$ is equal to $\{\ a^nb^n \mid n \geq 0\ \}$ hence $\xrightarrow[R]{*}$ is not rational. Such a relation is together left-overlapping and right-overlapping as defined below.

We say that a system (R, C) is *left-overlapping* if

$$\exists\ s,t \in N^* \quad \exists\ (u, yz), (xy, v) \in R,\ x, y, z \neq \varepsilon \ \wedge\ sxut, sxyzt, svzt \in C$$

meaning that the following representation is allowed:

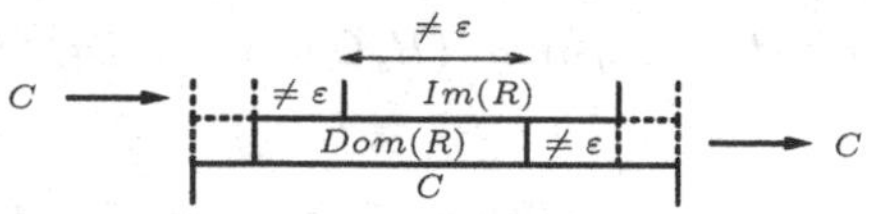

Let us verify that we can decide whether a rational system (R, C) is left-overlapping. Let \$ be a new symbol (not in N). So

$$C_\$ = \{\ u\$v \mid uv \in C\ \} = Id_{N^*}.\{(\varepsilon, \$)\}.Id_{N^*}(C)$$
$$\text{and } R_\$ = \{\ (u\$v, w) \mid uv\ R\ w\ \wedge\ v \neq \varepsilon\ \} = Id_{N^*}.\{(\$, \varepsilon)\}.Id_{N+} \circ R$$

are rational: $C_\$ \in Rat((N \cup \{\$\})^*)$ and $R_\$ \in Rat((N \cup \{\$\})^* \times N^*)$.
Then (R, C) is left-overlapping if and only if it satisfies the following decidable property: $\exists\ s,t \in N^*$,

$$(Id_{N+}.(\varepsilon, \$).R \cap s^{-1}Ct^{-1} \times s^{-1}C_\$t^{-1}) \circ (R_\$.Id_{N+} \cap s^{-1}C_\$t^{-1} \times s^{-1}Ct^{-1}) \neq \emptyset$$

Similarly a system (R, C) is *right-overlapping* if (R^{-1}, C) is left-overlapping (which is equivalent to $(\widetilde{R}, \widetilde{C})$ is left-overlapping), meaning that the following representation is allowed:

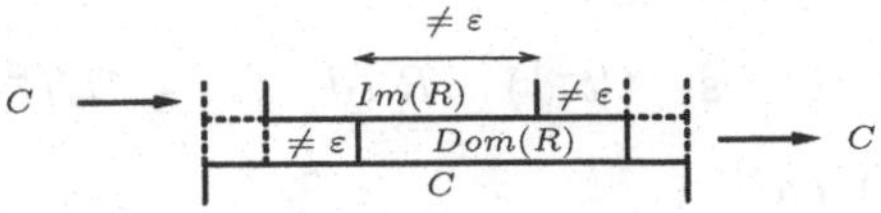

Finally a system is *overlapping* if it is left-overlapping or right-overlapping.

We are ready to give stable systems such that the derivation can be done increasingly.
Precisely, we denote by $\underset{R,\,C}{\longrightarrow}_n$ the rewriting of (R, C) at letter position $n+1$:

$$xuy \underset{R,\,C}{\longrightarrow}_n xvy \quad \text{for every } u \; R \; v \text{ and } xuy, xvy \in C \text{ with } |x| = n\,.$$

This permits to define the following *increasing derivation* :

$$\underset{R,\,C}{\overset{\star}{\hookrightarrow}} \;=\; \bigcup_{n \geq 0} \underset{R,\,C}{\overset{n}{\hookrightarrow}}$$

where $\underset{R,\,C}{\overset{0}{\hookrightarrow}} = Id_C$

and $\underset{R,\,C}{\overset{n}{\hookrightarrow}} = \bigcup_{\ell_1 \leq \ldots \leq \ell_n} \underset{R,\,C}{\longrightarrow}_{\ell_1} \circ \ldots \circ \underset{R,\,C}{\longrightarrow}_{\ell_n}$ for every $n > 0$

with $l_{i-1} = l_i \implies \underset{R,\,C}{\longrightarrow}_{\ell_i}$ is only according to $R - \{\varepsilon\} \times N^*$.

This last condition means that the following derivation:

$$xuy \underset{R}{\longrightarrow}_{|x|} xvy \underset{R}{\longrightarrow}_{|x|} xwvy \quad \text{with } u \; R \; v \text{ and } \varepsilon \; R \; w$$

is not increasing. In fact in this derivation, the rule $\varepsilon \longrightarrow w$ is on the 'left' of the rule $u \longrightarrow v$ and must be applied before to give the following increasing derivation:

$$xuy \underset{R}{\longrightarrow}_{|x|} xwuy \underset{R}{\longrightarrow}_{|xw|} xwvy \quad \text{(assuming that } w \neq \varepsilon).$$

Lemma 3.2 remains true for increasing derivations.

Lemma 3.6 *For any stable system* (R, C), $\underset{R,\,C}{\overset{\star}{\hookrightarrow}} \;=\; \underset{R}{\overset{\star}{\hookrightarrow}} \cap C \times C\,.$

The increasing derivation coincides with the derivation for stable systems having no overlapping configurations where the domain begins before the image.

Lemma 3.7 *For any stable system* (R, C) *which is not left-overlapping, not image-strict-internal and not image-suffix-internal, we have* $\underset{R,\,C}{\overset{\star}{\longrightarrow}} \;=\; \underset{R,\,C}{\overset{\star}{\hookrightarrow}}\,.$

Proof.
By definition, we have $\underset{R,\,C}{\overset{\star}{\hookrightarrow}} \subseteq \underset{R,\,C}{\overset{\star}{\longrightarrow}}\,.$

Let us prove the converse. As $\underset{R,\,C}{\overset{\star}{\longrightarrow}} \;=\; \underset{R - \{\varepsilon,\,\varepsilon\},\,C}{\overset{\star}{\longrightarrow}}$, we may assume that $(\varepsilon, \varepsilon) \notin R$.

We show the following four inclusions:

$$\underset{u,\,v,\,C}{\longrightarrow}^{\geq n} \circ \underset{\varepsilon,\,v',\,C}{\longrightarrow}^{n} \subseteq \underset{\varepsilon,\,v',\,C}{\longrightarrow}^{n} \circ \underset{u,\,v,\,C}{\longrightarrow}^{> n}$$

$$\underset{u,\,v,\,C}{\longrightarrow}^{> n} \circ \underset{u',\,v',\,C}{\longrightarrow}^{n} \subseteq \underset{u',\,v',\,C}{\longrightarrow}^{n} \circ \underset{u,\,v,\,C}{\longrightarrow}^{\geq n} \quad \text{with } u, u' \neq \varepsilon$$

$$\underset{\varepsilon,\,v,\,C}{\longrightarrow}^{> n} \circ \underset{u',\,v',\,C}{\longrightarrow}^{n} \subseteq \underset{u',\,v',\,C}{\longrightarrow}^{n} \circ \underset{\varepsilon,\,v,\,C}{\longrightarrow}^{> n} \quad \text{with } u', v' \neq \varepsilon$$

$$\underset{\varepsilon,\,v,\,C}{\longrightarrow}^{> n} \circ \underset{u',\,\varepsilon,\,C}{\longrightarrow}^{n} \subseteq \underset{u',\,\varepsilon,\,C}{\longrightarrow}^{n} \circ \underset{\varepsilon,\,v,\,C}{\longrightarrow}^{> n} \cup \underset{\varepsilon,\,v,\,C}{\longrightarrow}^{n} \circ \underset{u',\,\varepsilon,\,C}{\longrightarrow}^{> n}$$

where $\underset{u,\,v,\,C}{\longrightarrow}^{P} = \bigcup_{n \in P} \underset{\{(u,\,v)\},\,C}{\longrightarrow}^{n}$ for any integer subset P and with $(u,v) \in R$.

Using these inclusions, we sort increasingly any derivation by applying the bubble sort.
□

A first class of rewriting systems with a decidable rational derivation is obtained by generalizing the mechanism of a transducer. Let (G,E,F) be a transducer: G is a finite $N^* {\times} N^*$-automaton and we assume that its vertex set V_G is disjoint of N. We convert G into the following relation:

$$R_G = \{ (pu, vq) \mid p \overset{u/v}{\underset{G}{\longrightarrow}} q \}$$

in such a way that the language recognized by the transducer is obtained by derivation of R_G as follows:

$$L(G,E,F) = \{ (u,v) \mid pu \overset{\star}{\underset{R_G}{\longrightarrow}} vq \wedge p \in E \wedge q \in F \}$$

Such a system $(R_G, N^*V_GN^*)$ is *right* meaning that it is not strict-internal, not domain-prefix-internal, not image-suffix-internal, and not left-overlapping. So a right system (R,C) is a system where the overlapping configurations have only the following form:

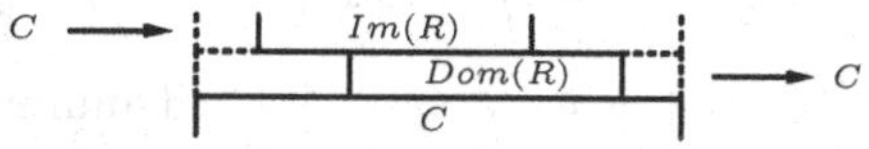

It is important to remark that relation R_G (on $(N \cup V_G)^*$) is not right: we may have the overlapping configuration $puwvq$ with $puw \in Dom(R_G)$ and $wvq \in Im(R_G)$.

The derivation $\overset{\star}{\underset{R,\,C}{\longrightarrow}}$ of any finite right stable system (R,C) can be always recognized by a transducer that we can construct from (R,C), and this can be generalized to any recognizable right stable system.

Theorem 3.8 *For any recognizable right stable system (R,C), the derivation $\overset{\star}{\underset{R,\,C}{\longrightarrow}}$ is an effective rational relation.*

Proof.
i) Let us reduce the proof of this theorem to $C = N^*$.
Let (R,C) be a recognizable system: R is recognizable and C is rational.

Furthermore we assume that (R, C) is stable and is right: it is not left-overlapping, not strict-internal, not domain-prefix-internal and not image-suffix-internal.
Let $\$, \# $ be two new symbols: $\$, \# \notin N$. We consider the following system:

$$S = \{ (x\#y, \$v) \mid xy\ R\ v \}$$

So $S = \{(\varepsilon, \$)\}.(Id_{N^*}.\{(\#, \varepsilon)\}).Id_{N^*} \circ R)$ is recognizable.
As $S \subseteq N^*\#N^* \times \$N^*$, S is a right relation (on $(N \cup \{\$, \#\})^*$).
We verify that

$$\underset{R,\,C}{\overset{\star}{\longrightarrow}} = \{ (h_{\#}(s), h_{\$}(t)) \in C{\times}C \mid s \underset{S}{\overset{\star}{\longrightarrow}} t \}$$

with for $\& \in \{\#, \$\}$, $h_{\&}$ is the morphism from $(N \cup \{\&\})^*$ to N^* erasing $\&$: $h(\&) = \varepsilon$ and $h(a) = a$ for every $a \in N$.
Thus

$$\underset{R,\,C}{\overset{\star}{\longrightarrow}} = \Big((\{(\varepsilon, \#)\} \cup Id_N)^* \circ \underset{S}{\overset{\star}{\longrightarrow}} \circ (\{(\$, \varepsilon)\} \cup Id_N)^* \Big) \cap C{\times}C$$

implying that $\underset{R,\,C}{\overset{\star}{\longrightarrow}}$ is rational if $\underset{S}{\overset{\star}{\longrightarrow}}$ is rational for the recognizable right relation S.

ii) Let R be a finite right relation.
Let us construct from R a transducer to recognize $\underset{R}{\overset{\star}{\longrightarrow}}$.
Its finite set of states Q is

$$Q = \{ w \mid \exists\, x, y \in N^*,\ xw \in Im(R) \wedge wy \in Dom(R) \}$$

which contains ε. Its finite graph G is

$$G = H \cup I$$

where $H = \{ w \overset{x/y}{\longrightarrow} z \mid w, z \in Q \wedge wx\ R\ yz \wedge |x|, |y| \text{ minimal} \}$

and $I = \{ w \overset{x/\varepsilon}{\longrightarrow} wx \mid w, wx \in Q \wedge |x| \geq 1 \text{ minimal} \}$

$\cup \{ yz \overset{\varepsilon/y}{\longrightarrow} z \mid z, yz \in Q \wedge |y| \geq 1 \text{ minimal} \}$

$\cup \{ \varepsilon \overset{a/a}{\longrightarrow} \varepsilon \mid a \in N \}$

We take ε as the initial state and as the unique final state. We show that the transducer $(G, \{\varepsilon\}, \{\varepsilon\})$ recognizes $\underset{R}{\overset{\star}{\longrightarrow}}$.
To implement I and as $\#N$ can be large, we use a new symbol $\bullet$ to designate any letter in N and the label $\bullet/\bullet$ means any couple a/a for $a \in N$.
The minimality of $|x|$ and $|y|$ in H and I is useless but it permits to construct a graph isomorphic to G with a (worst case) complexity $O(|R|)$ in space and $O(|R|^2 \# N_R)$ in time *i.e.* linear in space and quadratic in time if we assume that the number of letters is a constant.

iii) Let us extend (*ii*) to any recognizable right relation R. As R is recognizable,

$$R = \bigcup_{i=1}^{p} L(G_i, r_i, F_i) {\times} L(G'_i, r'_i, F'_i)$$

where $(G_i, r_i, F_i)_{1 \leq i \leq p}$ and $(G'_i, r'_i, F'_i)_{1 \leq i \leq p}$ are finite automata such that their vertex sets $V_{G_1}, V_{G'_1}, \ldots, V_{G_p}, V_{G'_p}$ are pairwise disjoint.
Let us construct from R a transducer to recognize $\xrightarrow[R]{\star}$.
Let r be a new symbol. We define the following finite graph:

$$G = H \cup I$$

$$\text{with } I = \{\, r \xrightarrow{a/a} r \mid a \in N \,\} \cup$$

$$\{\, r \xrightarrow{\varepsilon/\varepsilon} r_i \mid i \in [p] \,\} \cup \{\, s' \xrightarrow{\varepsilon/\varepsilon} r \mid \exists\, i \in [p],\ s' \in F'_i \,\} \cup$$

$$\{\, s \xrightarrow{a/\varepsilon} t \mid \exists\, i \in [p],\ s \xrightarrow[G_i]{a} t \,\} \cup \{\, s' \xrightarrow{\varepsilon/a} t' \mid \exists\, i \in [p],\ s' \xrightarrow[G'_i]{a} t' \,\}$$

$$\text{and } H = \{\, s \xrightarrow{\varepsilon/\varepsilon} r'_i \mid i \in [p] \wedge s \in F_i \,\} \cup$$

$$\{\, t' \xrightarrow{\varepsilon/\varepsilon} s \mid \exists\, i, j \in [p],\ \exists\, u \neq \varepsilon,\ u \in L(G'_i, t', F'_i) \cap L(G_j, r_j, s) \,\}$$

We take r as the initial state and as the unique final state. We show that the transducer (G, r, r) recognizes $\xrightarrow[R]{\star}$.
□

Similarly a system (R, C) is *left* if $(\widetilde{R}, \widetilde{C})$ is right: (R, C) is not strict-internal, not domain-suffix-internal, not image-prefix-internal, and not right-overlapping. Note that (R, C) is left if and only if (R^{-1}, C) is right. By Theorem 3.8 and as the rational relations are preserved by mirror (or by inverse), the derivation of any recognizable left stable system is also an effective rational relation. Note that the condition for a right system to be not domain-prefix-internal is necessary to have a rational derivation.

Example 3.9 For $R = \{(\$, a\&), (\&, \$b)\}$, $\xrightarrow[R]{\star}(\$) \cap \{a, b, \$\}^* = \{\, a^n \$ b^n \mid n \geq 0 \,\}$ hence $\xrightarrow[R]{\star}$ is not rational. This relation R is not overlapping (not left-overlapping and not right-overlapping), is not strict-internal (not domain-strict-internal and not image-strict-internal), and is not image-internal (not image-strict-internal, not image-prefix-internal and not image-suffix-internal). In particular, its derivation is increasing but the system is not right because it is domain-prefix-internal (and domain-suffix-internal).

A second class of rewriting systems follows from the relation of prefix rewriting. The *prefix rewriting* $\underset{R}{\longmapsto}$ of a system R is the restriction of the rewriting $\xrightarrow[R]{}$ obtained by applying the rules only by prefix:

$$uw \underset{R}{\longmapsto} vw \quad \text{for every } u\ R\ v \text{ and } w \in N^*$$

meaning that the prefix rewriting $\underset{R}{\longmapsto}$ is the relation $R.Id_{N^*}$. The *prefix derivation* $\overset{\star}{\underset{R}{\longmapsto}}$ is the reflexive and transitive closure for the composition of the prefix rewriting. Büchi has shown that the prefix derivation $\overset{\star}{\underset{R}{\longmapsto}}(u)$ of any finite relation from any word u is a rational language which can be constructed in exponential time [Bü 64]. Boasson and Nivat have extended this result: the prefix derivation $\underset{R}{\overset{\star}{\longmapsto}}$ of any recognizable relation R is a rational relation [BN 84] and a transducer can be constructed in polynomial time [Ca 90]. To adapt this result for rewriting systems, let us remark that for any system R, we have

$$x \underset{R}{\overset{\star}{\longmapsto}} y \iff \$x \underset{\$R}{\overset{\star}{\longrightarrow}} \$y$$

where $\$R = \{ (\$u, \$v) \mid u \; R \; v \}$ with $\$$ a new symbol.
We say that a rewriting system (R, C) is *prefix* if (R, C) is not overlapping (not left-overlapping and not right-overlapping), not strict-internal (not domain-strict-internal and not image-strict-internal), and not suffix-internal (it is not domain-suffix-internal and not image-suffix-internal). So a prefix system is a system where the overlapping configurations have only the following form:

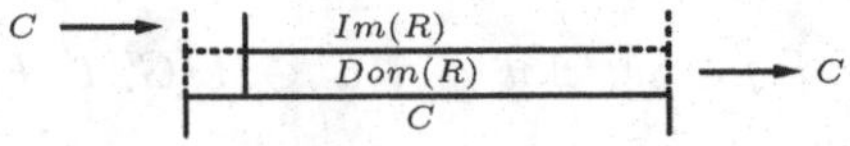

Note that (R, C) is prefix is equivalent to (R^{-1}, C) is prefix.
A usual finite prefix system is a (unlabelled) *pushdown automaton i.e.* a finite $R \subset Q.P^{*} \times Q.P^{*}$ with the language $C = Q.P^{*}$ of configurations, where $P + Q = N$ (N is partitionned into the stack alphabet P and the state alphabet Q); note that such a R (with $C = N^{*}$) is also a prefix relation.
The derivation of any prefix stable system is the restriction to the admissible configurations of the concatenation closure of the prefix derivation of its relation.

Proposition 3.10 *For any prefix stable system* (R, C), *we have*

$$\underset{R,\,C}{\overset{\star}{\longrightarrow}} \;=\; (\underset{R}{\overset{\star}{\longmapsto}})^{*} \cap C \times C\,.$$

Proposition 3.10 permits to extend the rationality of the prefix derivation of any recognizable relation to the derivation of any recognizable prefix stable system.

Theorem 3.11 *For any recognizable prefix stable system* (R, C), *the derivation* $\underset{R,\,C}{\overset{\star}{\longrightarrow}}$ *is an effective rational relation.*

Proof.
By Proposition 3.10, it remains to show that $\underset{R}{\overset{\star}{\longmapsto}}$ is a rational relation for any recognizable relation R. This has been proved in [BN 84]. A short proof is due to J.-M. Autebert and follows from Corollary 3.3 of [Ca 96] :

$$\underset{R}{\overset{\star}{\longmapsto}} \;=\; \underset{S}{\longmapsto} \;=\; S{\cdot}Id_{N^{*}} \quad \text{for a recognizable relation } S \;=\; \bigcup_{i=1}^{q} U_i \times V_i$$

such that for $\overline{N}$ a new alphabet in bijection to N, we have

$$\bigcup_{i=1}^{q} \overline{U}_i \widetilde{V}_i \;=\; \underset{P}{\overset{\star}{\longrightarrow}}(\{ \overline{u}\widetilde{v} \mid u \; R \; v \}^{*}) \cap \overline{N}^{*} N^{*}$$

where $P = \{ (x\overline{x}, \varepsilon) \mid x \in N \}$.

Note that we can specify directly S from R :

$$S \;=\; \{(\varepsilon,\varepsilon)\} \cup \bigcup \{ \underset{R^{-1}}{\overset{\star}{\longmapsto}}(U) \times \underset{R}{\overset{\star}{\longmapsto}}(V) \mid (U,V) \in R \}$$

The construction of S hence of $S.Id_{N^*}$ can be done in polynomial time. But we do not give a precise majoration of the order like for Theorem 3.11 (*ii*).
□

Similarly a system (R, C) is *suffix* if $(\widetilde{R}, \widetilde{C})$ is prefix: (R, C) is not overlapping, not strict-internal and not prefix-internal. By Theorem 3.11 and as the rational relations are preserved by mirror, the derivation of any suffix recognizable stable system is also an effective rational relation.

Example 3.9 shows that we have non rational derivations for prefix finite systems which can be domain-suffix-internal or image-suffix-internal (systems which are not overlapping, not strict-internal, and not domain-suffix-internal or not image-suffix-internal). This includes the basic systems [Sé 93] even if they are not strict-internal, where a *basic* system is a not overlapping and not domain-internal system (the inverse of the system defined in Example 3.9 is basic and not strict-internal).
Furthermore we cannot combine our two theorems as shown below by modifying slighty Example 3.9.

Example 3.12 The overlapping configurations of $R = \{(\$, a\&)\,,\,(\&b, \$bb)\}$ are only prefix $(N^*\$bbN^*)$ and right $(N^*a\&bN^*)$ but $\underset{R}{\overset{\star}{\longrightarrow}}$ is not rational because the language $\underset{R}{\overset{\star}{\longrightarrow}}(\$b) \cap \{a, b, \&\}^* \;=\; \{\, a^n\&b^n \mid n \geq 1 \,\}$ is not rational.

Finally Theorems 3.8 and 3.11 cannot be extended to respectively any rational right stable system and any rational prefix stable system as shown in the following example.

Example 3.13 The relation $R = \{\; (\$xu\$, \$u\$x) \mid u \in \{a,b\}^* \;\wedge\; x \in \{a,b\} \;\}$ is rational and taking $C = \$\{a,b\}^*\$\{a,b\}^*$, the rational system (R, C) has only domain-prefix-internal overlapping configurations. So (R, C) is prefix and is left but

$$\underset{R,\,C}{\overset{\star}{\longrightarrow}} \cap\; (\$\{a,b\}^*\$) \times (\$\$\{a,b\}^*) \;=\; \{\; (\$u\$, \$\$\widetilde{u}) \mid u \in \{a,b\}^* \;\}$$

is not a rational relation, hence $\underset{R,\,C}{\overset{\star}{\longrightarrow}}$ is not rational.

Acknowledgements

Many thanks to Teodor Knapik for the definition of a right relation and the fact that it preserves the rationality, and for the notion of increasing derivation.

References

[AB 88] J.-M. AUTEBERT and L. BOASSON *Transductions rationnelles*, Ed. Masson, pp 1-133, 1988.

[Be 79] J. BERSTEL *Transductions and context-free languages*, Ed. Teubner, pp. 1–278, 1979.

[BN 84] L. BOASSON and M. NIVAT *Centers of context-free languages*, LITP report 84-44, 1984.

[BO 93] R. BOOK and F. OTTO *String-rewriting systems*, Text and monographs in computer science, Springer Verlag, 189 pages, 1993.

[Bü 64] R. BÜCHI *Regular canonical systems*, Archiv für Mathematische Logik und Grundlagenforschung 6, pp. 91–111, 1964
or in *The collected works of J. Richard Büchi*, edited by S. Mac Lane and D. Siefkes, Springer-Verlag, New York, pp. 317–337, 1990.

[CK 98] H. CALBRIX and T. KNAPIK *A string-rewriting characterization of Muller and Schupp's context-free graphs*, FSTTCS 98, LNCS 1530, pp. 331–342, 1998.

[Ca 90] D. CAUCAL *On the regular structure of prefix rewriting*, CAAP 90, LNCS 431, pp. 87–102, 1990, selected in TCS 106, pp. 61–86, 1992.

[Ca 96] D. CAUCAL *On infinite transition graphs having a decidable monadic theory*, ICALP 96, LNCS 1099, pp. 194–205, 1996.

[Co 90] B. COURCELLE *Graph rewriting: an algebraic and logic approach*, Handbook of TCS, Vol. B, Elsevier, pp. 193–242, 1990.

[DJ 90] N. DERSHOWITZ and J.-P. JOUANNAUD *Rewrite systems*, Handbook of TCS, Vol. B, Elsevier, pp. 243–320, 1990.

[Mo 00] C. MORVAN *On rational graphs*, FOSSACS 2000, in this volume.

[MS 85] D. MULLER and P. SCHUPP *The theory of ends, pushdown automata, and second-order logic*, TCS 37, pp. 51–75, 1985.

[Sé 93] G. SÉNIZERGUES *Formal languages and word-rewriting*, LNCS 909, pp. 75–94, 1993.

Proof Nets and Explicit Substitutions

Roberto Di Cosmo[1], Delia Kesner[2], and Emmanuel Polonovski[1]

[1] PPS, Université de Paris VII
Case 7014 - 2 place Jussieu
75251 Paris France
{dicosmo,polonovs}@ens.fr

[2] LRI, Université de Paris-Sud
Bât 490
91405 Orsay Cedex, France
kesner@lri.fr

Abstract. We refine the simulation technique introduced in [10] to show strong normalization of λ-calculi with explicit substitutions via termination of cut elimination in proof nets [13]. We first propose a notion of equivalence relation for proof nets that extends the one in [9], and we show that cut elimination modulo this equivalence relation is terminating. We then show strong normalization of the typed version of the λ_l-calculus with de Bruijn indices (a calculus with full composition defined in [8]) using a translation from typed λ_l to proof nets. Finally, we propose a version of typed λ_l with named variables which helps to better understand the complex mechanism of the explicit weakening notation introduced in the λ_l-calculus with de Bruijn indices [8].

1 Introduction

This paper uses linear logic's proof nets, equipped with an extended notion of reduction, to provide several new results in the field of explicit substitutions. It is also an important step forward in clarifying the connection between explicit substitutions and proof nets, two well established formalisms that have been used to gain a better understanding of the λ-calculus over the past decade. On one side, explicit substitutions provide an intermediate formalism that - by decomposing the β rule into more atomic steps - allows a better understanding of the execution models. On the other side, linear logic decomposes the intuitionistic logical connectives, like the arrow, into more atomic, resource-aware connectives, like the linear arrow and the explicit erasure and duplication operators given by the exponentials: this decomposition is reflected in proof nets, which are the computational side of linear logic, and provides a more refined computational model than the one given by the λ-calculus, which is the computational side of intuitionistic logic[1].

[1] Using various translations of the λ-calculus into proof nets, new abstract machines have been proposed, exploiting the Geometry of Interaction and the Dynamic Algebras [14, 2, 5], leading to the works on optimal reduction [15, 17].

J. Tiuryn (Ed.): FOSSACS 2000, LNCS 1784, pp. 63–81, 2000.

The pioneer calculus with explicit substitutions, λ_σ, was introduced in [1] as a bridge between the classical λ-calculus and concrete implementations of functional programming languages. An important property of calculi with explicit substitutions is nowadays known as PSN, which stands for "Preservation of Strong Normalization": a calculus with explicit substitutions has PSN when all λ-terms that are strongly normalizing using the traditional β-reduction rule are also strongly normalizing w.r.t. the more refined reduction system defined using explicit substitutions. But λ_σ does *not* preserve β-strong normalization as shown by Mellies, who exhibited a well-typed term which, due to the substitution composition rules in λ_σ, is not λ_σ-strongly normalizing [18].
Since then, a quest was started to find an "optimal" calculus having all of a wide range of desired properties: it should preserve strong normalization, but also be confluent (in a very large sense that implies the ability to compose substitutions), and its typed version should be strongly normalizing.
Meanwhile, in the linear logic community, many studies focused of the connection between λ-calculus (without explicit substitutions) and proof nets, trying to find the proper variant or extension of proof nets that could be used to cleanly simulate β-reduction, like in [7].
Finally, in [10], the first two authors of this work showed for the first time that explicit substitutions could be tightly related to linear logic's proof nets, by providing a translation into a variant of proof nets from λ_x [19, 4], a simple calculus with explicit substitutions and named variables, but no composition.
This connection was promising because proof nets seem to have many of the properties which are required of a "good" calculus of explicit substitutions, and especially the strong normalization in the presence of a reduction rule which is reminiscent of the composition rule at the heart of Mellies' counterexample. But [10] only dealt with a calculus without composition, and the translation was complex and obscure enough to make the task of extending it to the case of a calculus with composition quite a daunting one.
In this paper, we can finally present a notion of reduction for Girard's proof nets which is flexible enough to allow a natural and simple translation from David and Guillaume's λ_l, a complex calculus of explicit substitution with de Bruijn indices and full composition [8]. This translation allows us to prove that typed λ_l is strongly normalizing, which is a new result confirming a conjecture in [8]. Also, the fact that in the translation all information about variable order is lost suggests a version of typed λ_l with named variables which is immediately proved to be strongly normalizing. This is due to the fact that only the type information is used in the translation of both calculi. Also, the typed named version of λ_l gives a better understanding of the mechanisms of labels existing in the calculus. In particular, names allow to understand the fine manipulation of explicit weakenings in λ_l without entering into the complicate details of renaming used in a de Bruijn setting.

The paper is organized as follows: we first recall the basic definitions of linear logic and proof nets and we introduce our refined reduction system for proof nets

(Section 2), then prove that it is strongly normalizing (Section 3). In Section 4 we recall the definition of the λ_l calculus with its type system, present the translation into proof nets, and show strong normalization of typed λ_l. Finally, we introduce a version of typed λ_l with named variables (Section 5), enjoying the same good properties, and we conclude with some remarks and directions for future work (Section 6).

2 Linear Logic, Proof Nets, and Extended Reduction

We recall here some classical notions from linear logic, namely the linear sequent calculus and proof nets, and some basic results concerning confluence and normalization.

MELL: Multiplicative Exponential linear logic Let $\mathcal{A}$ be a set of *atomic formulae*. We suppose that $\mathcal{A}$ is partitioned in two disjoint subsets representing *positive* and *negative* atoms respectively.
The set of formulae of the Multiplicative Exponential fragment of linear logic (called MELL) is defined by the following grammar, where $a \in \mathcal{A}$:

$$\mathcal{F} ::= a \mid \mathcal{F} \otimes \mathcal{F} \text{ (tensor)} \mid \mathcal{F} \mathbin{⅋} \mathcal{F} \text{ (par)} \mid !\mathcal{F} \text{ (of course)} \mid ?\mathcal{F} \text{ (why not)}$$

For every $p \in \mathcal{A}$, we assume that there is $p' \in \mathcal{A}$, called the *linear negation of the atom* p. Linear negation of formulae is *defined* as follows

$$p^{\perp} = p' \quad p'^{\perp} = p \quad A^{\perp\perp} = A \quad (?A)^{\perp} = !(A^{\perp}) \quad (A \otimes B)^{\perp} = A^{\perp} \mathbin{⅋} B^{\perp}$$

The name MELL comes from the connectors $\otimes$ and $⅋$ which are called "multiplicatives", while ! and ? are called "exponentials". We say that a formula is exponential if it starts with an exponential connector. While we refer the interested reader to [13] for more details on linear logic, we give here a one-sided presentation of the sequent calculus for MELL:

$$\frac{}{\vdash A, A^{\perp}}\ \textit{Axiom} \qquad \frac{\vdash \Gamma, A \quad \vdash A^{\perp}, \Delta}{\vdash \Gamma, \Delta}\ \textit{Cut} \qquad \frac{\vdash \Gamma, A}{\vdash \Gamma, ?A}\ \textit{Dereliction} \qquad \frac{\vdash \Gamma, ?A, ?A}{\vdash \Gamma, ?A}\ \textit{Contraction}$$

$$\frac{\vdash \Gamma, A, B}{\vdash \Gamma, A ⅋ B}\ \textit{Par} \qquad \frac{\vdash \Gamma, A \quad \vdash B, \Gamma'}{\vdash \Gamma, A \otimes B, \Gamma'}\ \textit{Times} \qquad \frac{\vdash \Gamma}{\vdash \Gamma, ?A}\ \textit{Weakening} \qquad \frac{\vdash A, ?\Gamma}{\vdash !A, ?\Gamma}\ \textit{Box}$$

MELL proof nets To all sequent derivations in MELL it is possible to associate an object called a "proof net", which allows to abstract from many inessential details in a derivation, like the order of application of independent logical rules: for example, there are many inessentially different ways to obtain $\vdash A_1 ⅋ A_2, \ldots, A_{n-1} ⅋ A_n$ from $\vdash A_1, \ldots A_n$, while there is only one proof net representing all these derivations.

Proof nets are defined inductively by rules that follow closely the ones of the one-sided sequent calculus, and the set of proof nets is denoted PN. To simplify the drawing of a proof net, we use the following notation: a conclusion with a capital greek letter $\Gamma, \Delta, \ldots$ really stands for a set of conclusions, each one with its own wire.

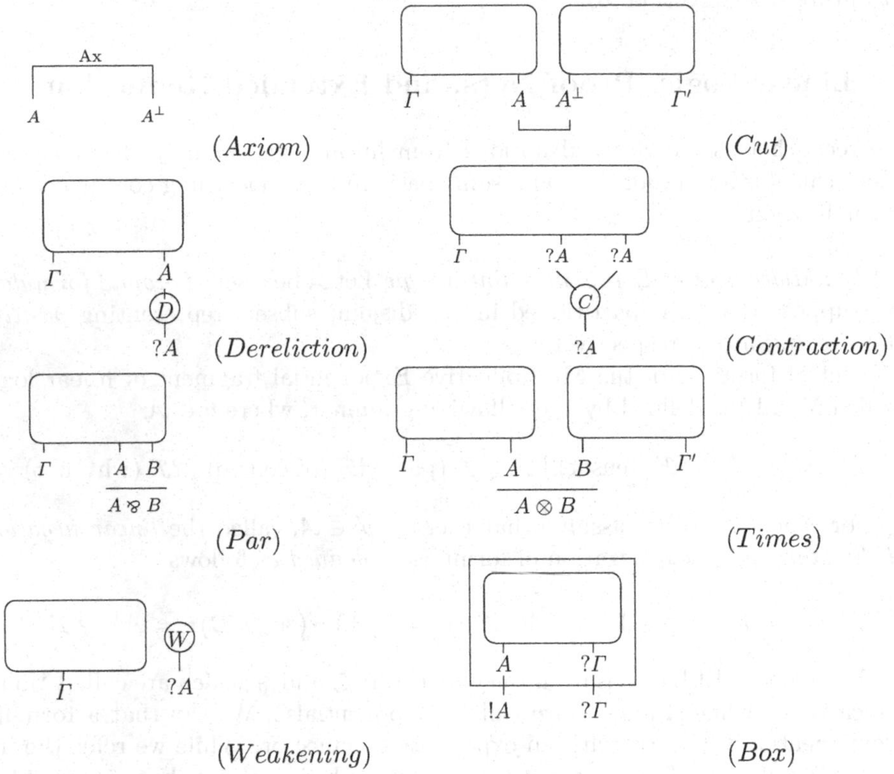

Each box has exactly one conclusion preceded by a !, which is named "principal" port (or formula), while the other conclusions are named "auxiliary" ports (or formulae). In what follows, we will sometimes write an axiom link as $\overline{A \quad A^{\perp}}$.

Reduction of proof nets Proof nets are the "computational object" behind linear logic, because there is a notion of reduction on them (called also "cut elimination") that corresponds to the cut-elimination procedure on sequent derivations. The traditional reduction system for MELL is recalled in Appendix A.

Extended reduction modulo an equivalence relation Unfortunately, the original notion of reduction on PN is not well adapted to simulate neither the β rule of λ-calculus, nor the rules dealing with propagation of substitution in explicit substitution calculi: too many inessential details on the order of application of the rules are still present, and to make abstraction from them, one is naturally led to define an equivalence relation on PN, as is done in [9], where the following two equivalences are introduced:

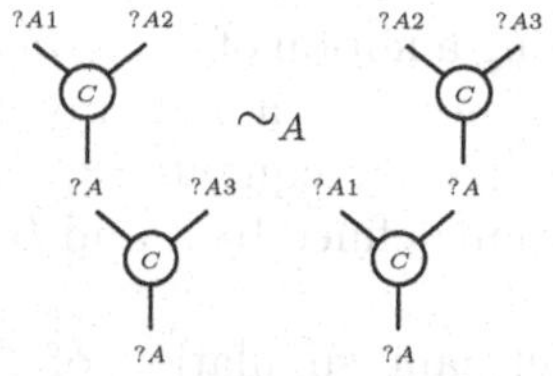

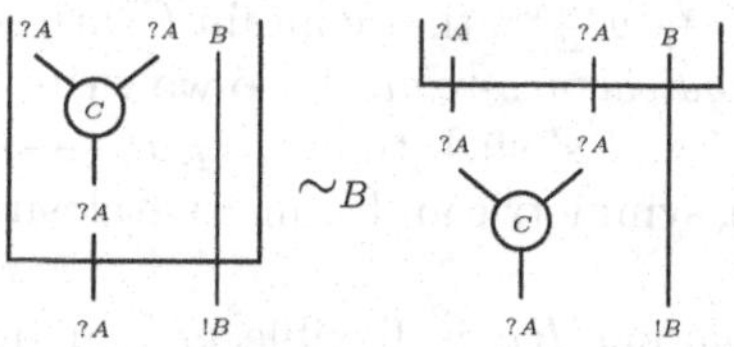

Equivalence A turns contraction into an associative operator, and corresponds to forgetting the order in which the contraction rule is used to build, for example, the derivation:

$$\dfrac{\dfrac{\vdash ?A, ?A, ?A}{\vdash ?A, ?A}\ \mathit{Contraction}}{\vdash ?A}\ \mathit{Contraction}$$

Equivalence B abstracts away the relative order of application of the rules of box-formation and contraction on the premises of a box, like in the following example.

$$\dfrac{\dfrac{\vdash ?A, ?A, B}{\vdash ?A, B}\ \mathit{Contraction}}{\vdash ?A, !B}\ \mathit{Box} \qquad \dfrac{\dfrac{\vdash ?A, ?A, B}{\vdash ?A, ?A, !B}\ \mathit{Box}}{\vdash ?A, !B}\ \mathit{Contraction}$$

Finally, besides the equivalence relation defined in [9], we will also need an extra reduction rule allowing to remove unneeded weakening links when simulating explicit substitutions:

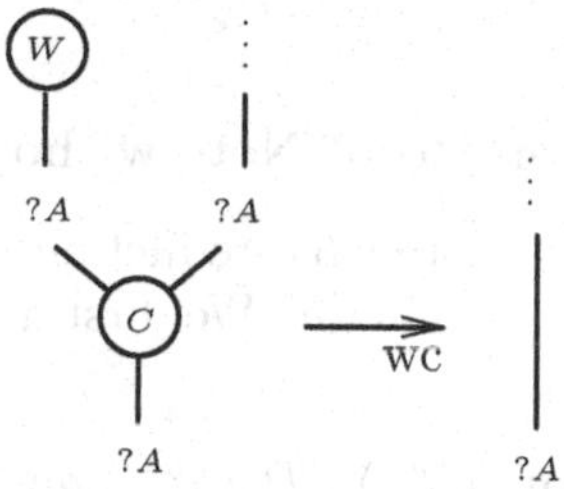

This rule allows to simplify the proof below on the left into the proof on the right

$$\dfrac{\dfrac{\dfrac{\pi}{\vdash ?A}}{\vdash ?A, ?A}\ \mathit{Weakening}}{\vdash ?A}\ \mathit{Contraction} \qquad \dfrac{\pi}{\vdash ?A}$$

Notation We will call in the following R the system made of rules $Ax - cut$, $⅋ - \otimes$, $w - b$, $d - b$, $c - b$, $b - b$ and wc; we will name E the relation induced on PN by the contextual closure of axioms A and B; we will write R_E for the system made of the rules in R and the equivalences in E; finally, $R_E^{\neg wc}$ will stand for system R_E *without* rule wc.

Systems R_E and $R_E^{\neg wc}$, that contain E, are actually defining a notion of *reduction modulo an equivalence relation*, so we write for example $t \longrightarrow_{R_E} s$ if and only if there exist r' and s' such that $r =_E r' \longrightarrow_R s' =_E s$, where the equality $=_E$ is the reflexive, symmetric and transitive closure of the relation defined by A and B.

The reduction R_E is flexible enough to allow an elegant simulation of β reduction and of explicit substitutions, but for that, we first need to establish that R_E is strongly normalizing. Let us see this property in the next section.

3 Termination of R_E

We know from [9] that $R_E^{\neg wc}$ is terminating, and we can show easily that wc is terminating too, so if we could show that the wc-rule can be postponed with respect to all the other rules of $R_E^{\neg wc}$, we would be easily done using a well-known abstract lemma. Unfortunately, there is precisely one case in which we cannot postpone the wc-rule: when a wc reduction creates an axiom-cut redex, which in turn can only happen if the axiom link in question introduces an exponential formula. So we are forced to proceed in two steps: first, we prove by postponement that R_E is terminating on the set of proof nets *without exponential axioms* (Theorem 1). Then, we show that termination of R_E on all proof nets of PN is a consequence of termination of R_E on proof nets without exponential axioms (Theorem 2). To obtain this last result, we show how to translate a proof net R with exponential axioms into a proof net R' without exponential axioms in such a way that a reduction out of R can be simulated by a longer or equal reduction out of R'.

3.1 Termination of R_E on Proof Nets without Exponential Axioms

We show in this section that all the R_E-reduction sequences from a proof net without exponential axioms terminate. We first remind the following result from [9]:

Lemma 1 (Termination of $R_E^{\neg wc}$). *The relation $\longrightarrow_{R_E^{\neg wc}}$ is terminating on PN.*

Then, we establish the termination of wc.

Lemma 2 (Termination of wc). *The relation $\longrightarrow_{wc}$ is terminating on PN.*

Proof. The wc-rule strictly decreases the number of nodes in a proof net so no infinite wc-reduction sequence is possible.

Finally, we show that given any proof net without exponential axioms, the wc-rule can be postponed with respect to any rule of $R_E^{\neg wc}$.

Lemma 3 (Postponement of wc w.r.t $R_E^{\neg wc}$). *Let t be a proof net without exponential axioms. If $t \longrightarrow_{wc} \longrightarrow_{R_E^{\neg wc}} t'$, then, there is a sequence $t \longrightarrow^+_{R_E^{\neg wc}} \longrightarrow^*_{wc} t'$.*

Proof. By analyzing all the possible cases. See [11] for details.

We can now put together the previous results to prove termination of R_E on the set of proof nets without exponential axioms.

Lemma 4 (Extraction of $R_E^{\neg wc}$). *Let S be an infinite sequence of R_E-reductions starting at a proof net t without exponential axioms. Then, there is a sequence of R_E-reductions from the same proof net t which starts by $t \longrightarrow_{R_E^{\neg wc}} t'$, where t' is also a proof net without exponential axioms, and which continues with an infinite sequence S'. We write this sequence as $(t \longrightarrow_{R_E^{\neg wc}} t') \cdot S'$.*

Now it is easy to establish the fundamental theorem of this section:

Theorem 1 (Termination of R_E on proof nets without exponential axioms). *The reduction relation R_E is terminating on the set of proof nets without exponential axioms.*

Proof. We show it by contradiction. Let us suppose that R_E is not terminating on those nets. Then, there exist a proof net without exponential axioms t and an infinite sequence S of R_E starting at t. By applying Lemma 4 to this sequence S, we obtain a sequence $(t \longrightarrow_{R_E^{\neg wc}} t') \cdot S'$ such that S' is infinite again. If we iterate this procedure an arbitrary number times, we obtain a sequence of $R_E^{\neg wc}$-reduction steps arbitrary long. This contradicts the fact that $R_E^{\neg wc}$ is terminating.

3.2 Termination of R_E on Proof Nets with Exponential Axioms

We know now that R_E is terminating on every proof net without exponential axioms, but we want now to show even more: termination of R_E on *all* the proof nets. To achieve this result, we show in this section how to associate to a proof net t, which can eventually contain some exponential axioms, another proof net $E(t)$ without exponential axioms, and such that every reduction from t of length n can be "simulated" on $E(t)$ by another reduction of length at least n. This property will be enough to reduce termination of R_E on proof nets with exponential axioms to termination of R_E on proof nets without exponential axioms.

We define in what follows a notion of complete expansion on axiom links that is able to replace all exponential axiom by a correct net with the same conclusions, but containing no exponential axiom, and then extend it to a full proof net in the natural way (replace each exponential axiom by its complete expansion).

Definition 1 (Complete expansion of an axiom link). *For each axiom link $\overline{A \quad A^{\perp}}$ we can associate a net $exp(\overline{A \quad A^{\perp}})$ with same conclusions, defined by induction on the complexity of the formula A as follows:*

– $exp(\overline{A \quad A^{\perp}}) = \overline{A \quad A^{\perp}}$, if A is not an exponential formula

– $exp(\overline{!A \quad ?A^{\perp}}) =$

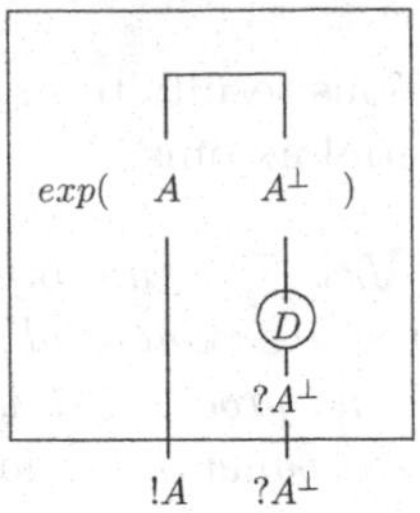

which is well defined, because the formula A is smaller than $!A$.

We can associate a complexity measure rk to a complete expansion.

Definition 2 (Measure of a complete expansion). *We define the measure rk of a complete expansion of an axiom by cases:*

– $rk(exp(\overline{A \quad A^{\perp}})) = 0$, if A is not an exponential formula
– $rk(exp(\overline{?A^{\perp} \quad !A})) = 1 + rk(exp(\overline{A \quad A^{\perp}}))$

We can now define the notion of expanded net $E(t)$ for every net t:

Definition 3 (Expanded net). *The* expanded net *of a net t, written $E(t)$, is the proof net obtained from t by replacing each occurrence of an exponential axiom a by $exp(a)$.*

Remark 1. The only difference between a proof net t and its expanded net $E(t)$ is on the set of their axioms. So, for every reduction $t \longrightarrow_{R_E} t'$ which does not affect the axioms of t, there is a reduction $E(t) \longrightarrow_{R_E} E(t')$.

We have now to show that there is no problem for the axioms either, and to do so we need the following measure:

Definition 4 (Maximal distance of a cut). *Given a proof net t and a cut link on a completely expanded axiom a in t, the measure $d(a,t)$ is the maximal distance, in the proof net t, between this cut and the first weakening or dereliction node encountered in the way which leaves the cut, by the opposite extremity from the expanded axiom a, and go throw the nodes from down to up (here up and down are used formally for the orientation of the nodes presented in the introduction). More precisely, each node encountered and each box passed on the way values 1, including the final dereliction or weakening node. This measure is always finite on a finite proof net because there are no arbitrary long ascendant ways.*

Example 1. In the following net, the maximal distance of the cut is 4.

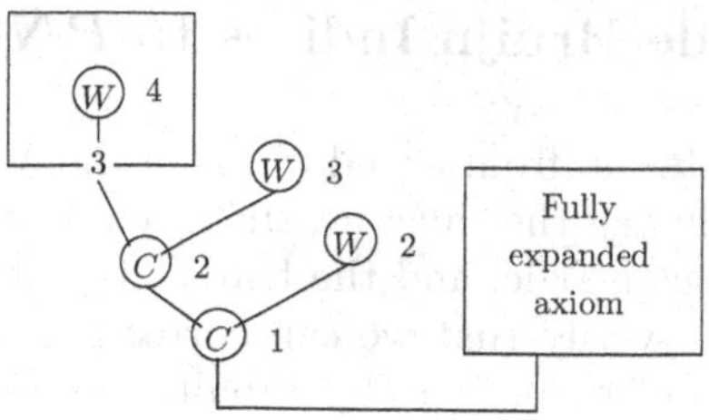

Lemma 5 (Cut elimination on an expanded net). *Let t be an expanded net. A cut in t with a completely expanded axiom exp(a) reduces in t like in an ordinary axiom cut. In other words,*

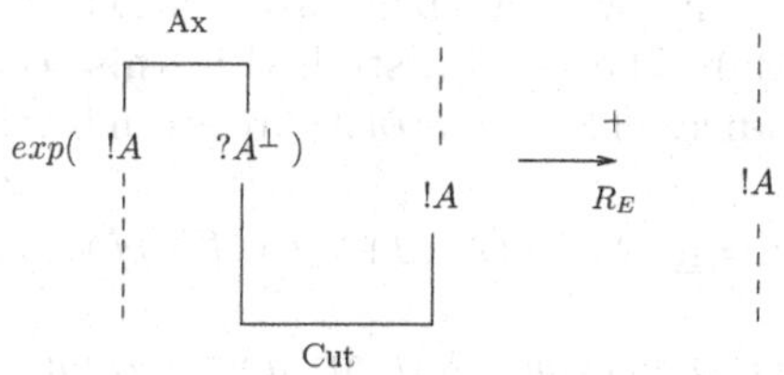

Proof. We prove the property by induction on the lexicographic order $(rk(exp(a)), d(exp(a), t))$ where $exp(a)$ is the completely expanded axiom in the proof net t.

All the cases such that $rk(exp(a)) = 0$ (including the base case) correspond to a proof net in which $exp(a)$ is an axiom link, so the same reduction rule applies and the property then trivially holds. For the cases with $rk(exp(a)) > 0$, we refer the interested reader to [11].

This allows us to establish the final result of this section :

Theorem 2 (Termination of R_E). *The reduction R_E is terminating on all proof nets.*

Proof. We establish this result by proving that each reduction step $t \longrightarrow_{R_E} t'$ can be simulated by at least one reduction step $E(t) \longrightarrow^{+}_{R_E} E(t')$.

If the reduction step $t \longrightarrow_{R_E} t'$ does not reduce any exponential axiom with a cut, then we obtain the result immediately because the only difference between t and $E(t)$ is on their axioms. Indeed, we can reproduce the same reduction on $E(t)$ in order to obtain $E(t')$ and this concludes this case.

Otherwise, if $t \longrightarrow_{R_E} t'$ reduces an exponential axiom a with a cut then by Lemma 5 there exist a non-empty sequence of reductions starting at $E(t)$ which eliminates the complete expansion of the axiom a, and gives the proof net $E(t')$.

Now, to conclude the proof, suppose that there is a proof net t such that the reduction R_E is not terminating on t, that is, there is an infinite R_E-reduction sequence starting at t. By the previous remark we can simulate this infinite reduction sequence by another R_E-reduction sequence on expanded proof nets not containing exponential axioms. This leads to a contradiction with Theorem 1 so that we can conclude that R_E is terminating on the set of all proof nets.

4 From λ_l with de Bruijn Indices to PN

We now study the translation from typed terms of the λ_l-calculus [8] into proof nets. We start by introducing the calculus, then we give the translation of types of λ_l into formulae of linear logic, and the translation of terms of λ_l into linear logic proof nets PN. We verify that we can correctly simulate every reduction step of λ_l via the notion of reduction R_E. Finally, we use this simulation result to show strong normalization of the λ_l-calculus.

4.1 The λ_l-Calculus

The λ_l-calculus is a calculus with explicit substitutions where substitutions are unary (and not multiple). The version studied in this section has variables encoded with de Bruijn indices. The terms of λ_l are given by the following grammar:

$$M ::= \underline{n} \mid \lambda M \mid (MM) \mid \langle k \rangle M \mid [i/M, j]M$$

The term $\underline{n}$ is called a *variable*, λM an *abstraction*, (MM) an *application*, $\langle k \rangle M$ a *labeled term* and $[i/M, j]M$ a *substitution*.

Intuitively, the term $\langle k \rangle M$ means that the $k-1$ first indices in M are not "free" (in the sense of free variables of calculus with indices). The term $[i/N, j]M$ means that the $i-1$ first indices are not free in N and the $j-1$ following indices are not free in M. Those indices are used to split the typing environment of $[i/N, j]M$ in three parts: the first (resp. second) one for free variables of M (resp. N), the third one for the free variables in M and N.

The reduction rules of λ_l are given in Figure 1 and the typing rules of λ_l are given in Figure 2, where we suppose that $|\Gamma| = i$ and $|\Delta| = j$.

$$\begin{array}{llcll}
(b_1) & (\lambda M N) & \longrightarrow & [0/N, 0]M & \\
(b_2) & ((\langle k \rangle(\lambda M) N) & \longrightarrow & [0/N, k]M & \\
(f) & [i/N, j](\lambda M) & \longrightarrow & \lambda[i+1/N, j]M & \\
(a) & [i/N, j](MP) & \longrightarrow & ([i/N, j]M)([i/N, j]P) & \\
(e_1) & [i/N, j]\langle k \rangle M & \longrightarrow & \langle j+k-1 \rangle M & if\ i < k \\
(e_2) & [i/N, j]\langle k \rangle M & \longrightarrow & \langle k \rangle [i-k/N, j]M & if\ i \geq k \\
(n_1) & [i/N, j]\underline{k} & \longrightarrow & \underline{k} & if\ i > k \\
(n_2) & [i/N, j]\underline{i} & \longrightarrow & \langle i \rangle N & \\
(n_3) & [i/N, j]\underline{k} & \longrightarrow & \underline{\text{j+k-1}} & if\ i < k \\
(c_1) & [i/N, j][k/P, l]M & \longrightarrow & [k/[i-k/N, j]P, j+l-1]M & if\ k \leq i < k+l \\
(c_2) & [i/N, j][k/P, l]M & \longrightarrow & [k/[i-k/N, j]P, l][i-l+1/N, j]M & if\ i \geq k+l \\
(d) & \langle i \rangle \langle j \rangle M & \longrightarrow & \langle i+j \rangle M &
\end{array}$$

Fig. 1. Reduction rules of λ_l with de Bruijn indices

$$\frac{}{\Gamma, A, \Delta \vdash \underline{i} : A}\ Axiom \qquad \frac{\Delta, \Pi \vdash N : A \quad \Gamma, A, \Pi \vdash M : B}{\Gamma, \Delta, \Pi \vdash [i/N, j]M : B}\ Subst$$

$$\frac{\Delta \vdash M : B}{\Gamma, \Delta \vdash \langle i \rangle M : B}\ Weak \qquad \frac{\Gamma \vdash M : B \to A \quad \Gamma \vdash N : B}{\Gamma \vdash (MN) : A}\ App \qquad \frac{B, \Gamma \vdash M : C}{\Gamma \vdash \lambda M : B \to C}\ Lambda$$

Fig. 2. Typing rules for λ_l with de Bruijn indices

We notice that for each well-typed term of the λ_l-calculus, there is only one possible typing judgment. This will simplify the proof of simulation of λ_l by easily considering the unique typing judgment of terms.

As expected the λ_l-calculus enjoys the subject reduction property [16].

Theorem 3 (Subject Reduction). *If* $\Psi \vdash M : C$ *and* $M \longrightarrow M'$, *then* $\Psi \vdash M' : C$.

4.2 Translation of Types and Terms of λ_l

We use the translation of types introduced in [6] given by :

$$\begin{array}{lll} A^* & = A & \text{if } A \text{ is an atomic type} \\ (A \to B)^* & = ?((A^*)^\perp) \,\wp\, !B^* & (\text{that is, } !A^* \multimap !B^*) \text{ otherwise} \end{array}$$

Since wires are commutative in proof nets, we feel free to exchange them when we define the translation of a term. The translation associates to every typed term M of λ_l, whose type judgment ends with the conclusion written below on the left, a proof net having the shape sketched below on the right:

$$\frac{}{\Gamma \vdash M : A}$$

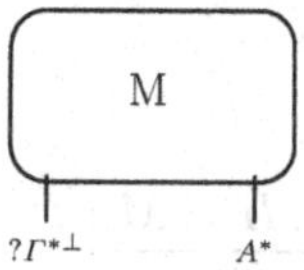

Here is the formal definition of the translation T from λ_l-terms into proof nets.

- If the term is a variable and its type judgment ends with the rule written below on the left, then its translation is the proof net on the right

$$\frac{}{\Gamma, A, \Delta \vdash \underline{i} : A}\ Axiome$$

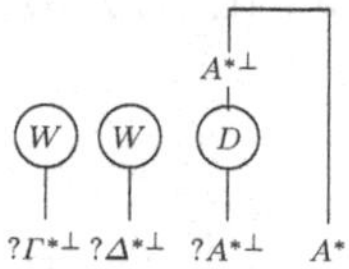

  where i is the position of A in the typing environment,
- If the term is a λ-abstraction and its type judgment ends with the rule written below on the left, then its translation is the proof net on the right

$$\frac{B, \Gamma \vdash M : C}{\Gamma \vdash \lambda M : B \to C} \; Lambda$$

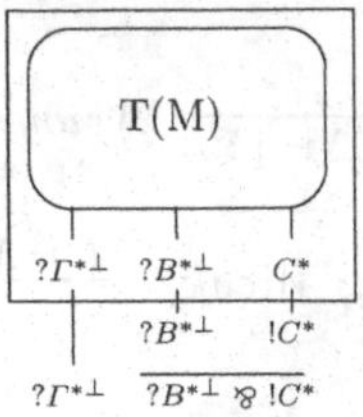

– If the term is an application and its type judgment ends with the rule written below on the left, then its translation is the proof net on the right

$$\frac{\Gamma \vdash M : B \to A \quad \Gamma \vdash N : B}{\Gamma \vdash (MN) : A} \; App$$

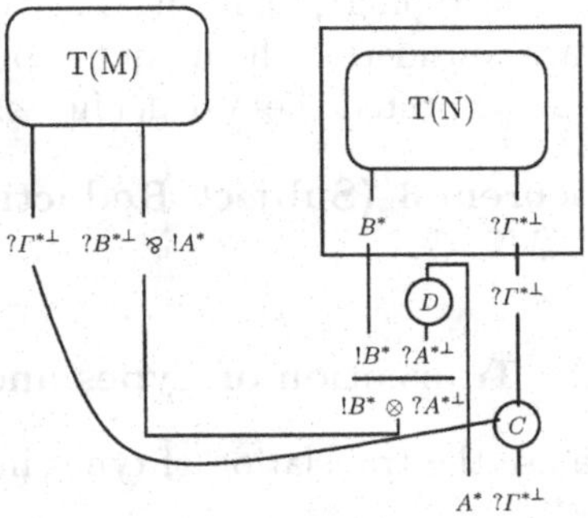

– If the term is a substitution and its type judgment ends with the rule written below on the left, then its translation is the proof net on the right

$$\frac{\Delta, \Pi \vdash N : A \quad \Gamma, A, \Pi \vdash M : B}{\Gamma, \Delta, \Pi \vdash [i/N, j]M : B} \; Subst$$

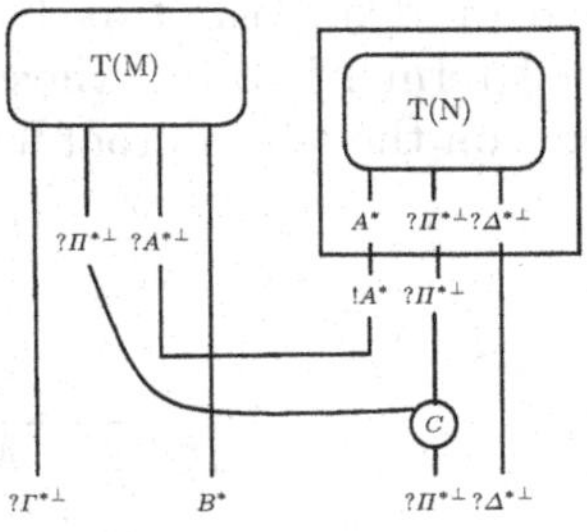

where i is the length of the list Γ and j is the length of the list Δ, then its translation is the proof net

– Finally, if the term is a label and its type judgment ends with the rule written below on the left, then its translation is the proof net on the right

$$\frac{\Delta \vdash M : B}{\Gamma, \Delta \vdash \langle i \rangle M : B} \; Weak$$

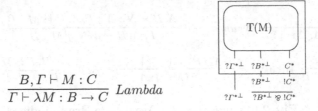

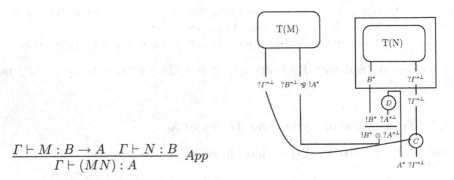

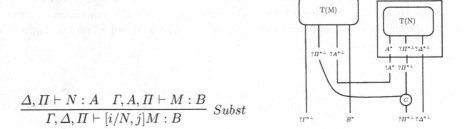

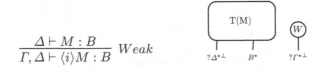

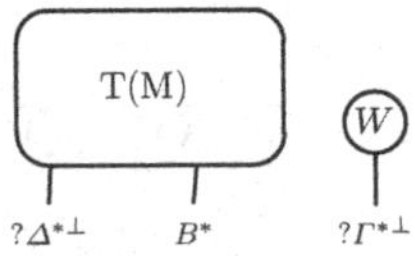

where i is the length of the list Γ, then its translation is the proof net

4.3 Simulating λ_l-Reduction

We now verify that our notion of reduction R_E on PN simulates the λ_l-reduction on typed λ_l-terms. It is in this proof that we find the motivation for our choice of translation from λ-terms into proof nets: with the more traditional translation sending the intuitionistic type $A \to B$ into the linear $!A \multimap B$, the simulation of the rewrite rule f would give rise to an equality, not to a reduction step like in this paper.

Lemma 6 (Simulation of λ_l). *The relation R_E simulates the λ_l-reduction on typed terms: if $t \longrightarrow_{\lambda_l} t'$, then $T(t) \longrightarrow^{+}{}_{R_E} T(t')$, excepted for the rules e_2 and d for which we have $T(t) = T(t')$.*

Proof. The proof proceeds by cases on the reduction rule applied in the step $t \longrightarrow_{\lambda_l} t'$. Since reductions λ_l and R_E are closed under all contexts, we only need to study the cases where reduction takes place at the head position of t. In the proof, rule wc is used to simulate b_2, e_1, n_1, n_2, n_3, equivalence A is used to simulate a, c_1, c_2, and equivalence B is used to simulate f, a, c_1, c_2.

Due to space limitations, we cannot give here the full proof, which is fully developed in [11], but we show anyway the case of rule c_1, one of the composition rules:

$$[i/N, j][k/P, l]M \longrightarrow [k/[i-k/N, j]P, j+l-1]M \text{ if } k \leq i < k+l$$

Here, the typing judgment of $[i/N, j][k/P, l]M$ must end with

$$\dfrac{\Delta, \Pi, \Pi' \vdash N : B \qquad \dfrac{\Gamma', B, \Pi, \Pi' \vdash P : C \quad \Gamma, C, \Pi' \vdash M : A}{\Gamma, \Gamma', B, \Pi, \Pi' \vdash [k/P, l]M : A}\,Subst}{\Gamma, \Gamma', \Delta, \Pi, \Pi' \vdash [i/N, j][k/P, l]M : A}\,Subst$$

while the typing judgment of $[k/[i-k/N, j]P, j+l-1]M$ must end with

$$\dfrac{\dfrac{\Delta, \Pi, \Pi' \vdash N : B \quad \Gamma', B, \Pi, \Pi' \vdash P : C}{\Gamma', \Delta, \Pi, \Pi' \vdash [i-k/N, j]P : C}\,Subst \qquad \Gamma, C, \Pi' \vdash M : A}{\Gamma, \Gamma', \Delta, \Pi, \Pi' \vdash [k/[i-k/N, j]P, j+l-1]M : A}\,Subst$$

So, the translation of the type derivation of the first term is

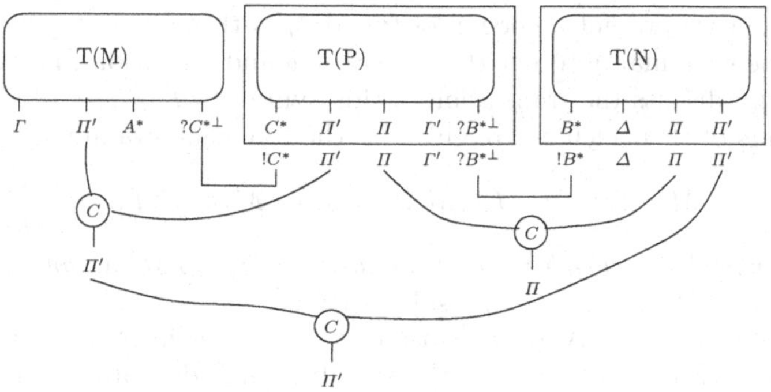

while the translation of the second derivation is

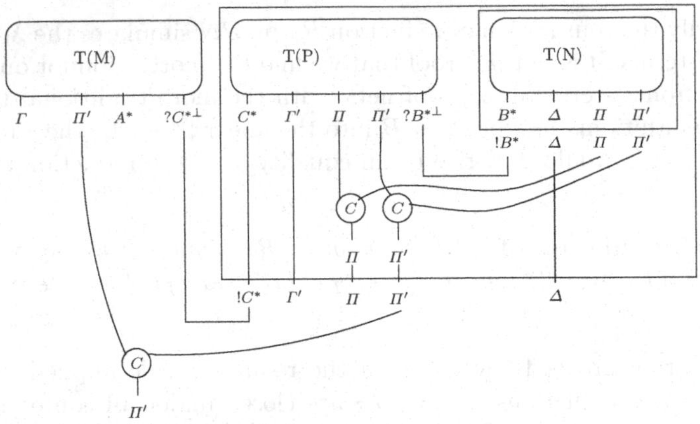

To reduce the first proof net into the second one, we must eliminate the $b - b$ cut, then apply the equivalence relations A and B.

We are now able to show strong normalization of λ_l. To achieve this result, we use the following abstract theorem (see for example [12]) :

Theorem 4. *Let $R = \langle \mathcal{O}, R_1 \cup R_2 \rangle$ be an abstract reduction system such that R_2 is strongly normalizing and there exist a reduction system $S = \langle \mathcal{O}', R' \rangle$, with a translation T of $\mathcal{O}$ into $\mathcal{O}'$ such that $a \longrightarrow_{R_1} b$ implies $T(a) {\longrightarrow^+}_{R'} T(b)$; $a \longrightarrow_{R_2} b$ implies $T(a) = T(b)$. Then if R' is strongly normalizing, $R_1 \cup R_2$ is also strongly normalizing.*

If we take $\mathcal{O}$ as the set of typed λ_l-terms, R_1 as $\lambda_l - \{e_2, d\}$, R_2 as $\{e_2, d\}$, $\mathcal{O}'$ as the set of proof nets and R' as the reduction R_E, then, by the Theorem 4 and the fact that the system including the rules $\{e_2, d\}$ is strongly normalizing [8], we can conclude :

Theorem 5 (Strong normalization of λ_l). *The typed λ_l-calculus is strongly normalizing.*

5 The λ_l-Calculus with Names

In this section we present a version of typed λ_l with named variables. We first introduce the grammar of terms, then the typing and reduction rules, and finally, we will briefly discuss the translation of this syntax to PN.

The terms of this calculus are given by the following grammar:

$$M ::= x \mid \lambda x.M \mid (MM) \mid \Delta M \mid M[x, M, \Gamma, \Delta]$$

The term x is called a *variable*, $\lambda x.M$ an *abstraction*, (MM) an *application*, ΔM a *labeled term* and $M[x, M, \Gamma, \Delta]$ a substitution.

Intuitively, the term ΔM means that the variables in Δ are not in M, and the term $M[x, N, \Gamma, \Delta]$ means that the variables in Γ do not appear in N (they only belong to the type environment of M) and the variables Δ do not appear in M (they only belong to the type environment of N).

Variables are bound by the abstraction and substitution operators, so that for example x is bound in $\lambda x.x$ and in $x[x, N, \Gamma, \Delta]$.

Terms are identified modulo α-conversion so that bound variables can be systematically renamed. Indeed, we have $\lambda y.y[x, z, \emptyset, \emptyset] =_\alpha \lambda y'.y'[x, z, \emptyset, \emptyset]$ and $\lambda y.y[x, z, \emptyset, \emptyset] =_\alpha \lambda y.y[x', z, \emptyset, \emptyset]$ and $\lambda l.y[x, z, \{l\}, \emptyset] =_\alpha \lambda l'.y[x, z, \{l'\}, \emptyset]$. We remark that the conditions on indices used in the typing rules given in Section 4.1 are now conditions on sets of variables. The typing rules are given in Figure 3.

$$\frac{}{\Gamma, x : A \vdash x : A}\ Axiom \qquad \frac{\Gamma \vdash M : A \quad \Gamma \cap \Delta = \emptyset}{\Gamma, \Delta \vdash \Delta M : A}\ Weak$$

$$\frac{\Gamma \vdash M : B \to A \quad \Gamma \vdash N : B}{\Gamma \vdash (MN) : A}\ App \qquad \frac{\Gamma, x : A \vdash M : B}{\Gamma \vdash \lambda x : A.M : B \to A}\ Lambda$$

$$\frac{\Delta, \Pi \vdash N : A \quad \Gamma, x : A, \Pi \vdash M : B \quad (\Gamma, x : A) \cap \Delta = \emptyset}{\Delta, \Gamma, \Pi \vdash M[x, N, \Gamma, \Delta] : B}\ Subst$$

Fig. 3. Typing rules for the λ_l-calculus with named variables

We remark that whenever $\Gamma \vdash M[x, N, \Delta, \Pi]$ is derivable, then Γ necessarily contains Δ and Π.

As expected the λ_l-calculus with names enjoys the subject reduction property (See [11] for a detailed proof).

Theorem 6 (Subject Reduction). *If $\Psi \vdash M : C$ and $M \longrightarrow M'$, then $\Psi \vdash M' : C$.*

We define the reduction rules only on typed terms, since we are focusing here on a named version of the *typed* λ_l calculus with indices. These rules already give the flavor of what a general notion of reduction for non-typed terms with names should be, but a precise formalization of the untyped case is left for further work.

The reduction rules of the typed λ_l-calculus with names are given in Figure 4 (notice that rule b_1 is a particular case of rule b_2 with $\Delta = \emptyset$).

As customary in explicit substitutions calculi with names [3], we work modulo α-conversion, so that we can suppose that in the rule $Weak$ the set Δ does not contain variables that are bound in M. Also, this allows us to restrict rule f, without loss of generality, to the case where no variable capture arise.

In order to translate a term of λ_l into a proof net, we use exactly the same translation of types that we used in Section 4.2 and we then define the translation of a term M using the type derivation of M.

$$
\begin{array}{llll}
(b_1) & (\lambda x : A.M)N & \longrightarrow & M[x, N, \emptyset, \emptyset] \\
(b_2) & (\Delta(\lambda x : A.M))N & \longrightarrow & M[x, N, \emptyset, \Delta] \\
(f) & (\lambda y : A.M)[x, N, \Gamma, \Delta] & \longrightarrow & \lambda y : A.M[x, N, \Gamma + y, \Delta] \quad \text{if } y \notin FV(N) \\
(a) & (MP)[x, N, \Gamma, \Delta] & \longrightarrow & (M[x, P, \Gamma, \Delta]P[x, N, \Gamma, \Delta]) \\
(e_1) & \Lambda M[x, N, \Gamma, \Delta] & \longrightarrow & (\Delta \cup (\Lambda \setminus x))M \quad x \in \Lambda \\
(e_2) & \Lambda M[x, N, \Gamma, \Delta] & \longrightarrow & (\Gamma \cap \Lambda)M[x, N, \Gamma \setminus \Lambda, \Delta \cup (\Lambda \setminus \Gamma)] \quad x \notin \Lambda \\
(n_1) & y[x, N, \Gamma, \Delta] & \longrightarrow & y \quad y \neq x \\
(n_2) & x[x, N, \Gamma, \Delta] & \longrightarrow & \Gamma N \\
(c_1) & M[y, P, \Lambda, \Phi][x, N, \Gamma, \Delta] & \longrightarrow & M[y, P[x, N, \Gamma \setminus \Lambda, \Delta], \Lambda, \Delta \cup (\Phi \setminus x)] \quad x \in \Phi \setminus \Lambda \\
(c_2) & M[y, P, \Lambda, \Phi][x, N, \Gamma, \Delta] & \longrightarrow & M[x, N, (\Gamma \setminus \Phi) + y, \Delta] \\
 & & & [y, P[x, N, \Gamma \setminus \Lambda, \Delta], \Lambda, \Gamma \cap \Phi] \quad x \notin \Phi \cup \Lambda \\
(d) & \Gamma \Delta M & \longrightarrow & (\Gamma \cup \Delta)M
\end{array}
$$

Fig. 4. Reduction Rules of the λ_l-calculus with named variables

Since in proof nets there is no trace left of the order which is implicit in the formalism of de Bruijn indices, it comes as no surprise that the translation of λ_l with names into the nets is really the same than the one for λ_l (see [11] for full details).

The simulation of the reduction rules of the λ_l-calculus with names by the reduction R_E is identical to that given in Section 4.2 for the λ_l-calculus with indices. We just remark that rule n_3 has no sense in the formalism with names so that the proof has one less case. We just state the result without repeating a boring verification:

Lemma 7 (Simulation of λ_l with names). *If t λ_l-reduces to t' in the formalism with names, then $T(t) \longrightarrow^{+}_{R_E} T(t')$, except for the rules e_2 and d for which we have $T(t) = T(t')$.*

We can then conclude the following:

Theorem 7 (Strong Normalization of λ_l with names). *The typed λ_l-calculus with names is strongly normalizing.*

6 Conclusion and Future Works

In this paper we enriched the standard notion of cut elimination in proof nets in order to obtain a system R_E which is flexible enough to provide an interpretation of λ-calculi with explicit substitutions and which is much simpler than the one proposed in [10]. We have proved that this system is strongly normalizing.

We have then proposed a natural translation from λ_l into proof nets that immediately provides strong normalization of the typed version of λ_l, a calculus featuring full composition of substitutions. The proof is extremely simple w.r.t the proof of PSN of λ_l given in [8] and shows in some sense that λ_l, which was designed independently of proof nets, is really tightly related to reduction in proof nets.

Finally, the fact that the relative order of variables is lost in the proof-net representation of a term lead us to discover a version of typed λ_l with named variables, instead of de Bruijn indices. This typed named version of λ_l gives a better understanding of the mechanisms of the calculus. In particular, names allow to understand the manipulation of explicit weakenings in λ_l without entering into the details of renaming of de Bruijn indices. However, the definition of a general notion of reduction for non-typed terms with names remains as further work.

This work suggests several interesting directions for future investigation: on the linear logic side, one should wonder whether R_E is the definitive system able to interpret β reduction, or whether we need some more equivalences to be added. Indeed, there are still a few cases in which the details of a sequent calculus derivation are inessential, even if we did not need to consider them for the purpose of our work, like for example

$$\dfrac{\dfrac{\vdash \Gamma, B}{\vdash ?A, \Gamma, B}\ Weakening}{\vdash ?A, \Gamma, !B}\ Box \qquad \dfrac{\dfrac{\vdash \Gamma, B}{\vdash \Gamma, !B}\ Box}{\vdash ?A, \Gamma, !B}\ Weakening$$

On the explicit substitutions side, we look forward to the discovery of a calculus with multiple substitutions with the same properties as λ_l, in the spirit of λ_σ.

Acknowledgments

We would like to thank Bruno Guillaume and Pierre-Louis Curien for their interesting remarks.

References

[1] M. Abadi, L. Cardelli, P. L. Curien, and J.-J. Lévy. Explicit substitutions. *Journal of Functional Programming*, 4(1):375–416, 1991.

[2] S. Abramsky and R. Jagadeesan. New foundations for the geometry of interaction. In *Proc. of LICS*, pages 211–222, 1992.

[3] R. Bloo. *Preservation of Termination for Explicit Substitution.* PhD thesis, Eindhoven University of Technology, 1997.

[4] R. Bloo and K. Rose. Preservation of strong normalization in named lambda calculi with explicit substitution and garbage collection. In *Computing Science in the Netherlands*, pages 62–72. Netherlands Computer Science Research Foundation, 1995.

[5] V. Danos. *La logique linéaire appliquée à l'étude de divers processus de normalisation (et principalement du λ-calcul).* PhD thesis, Université de Paris VII, 1990. Thèse de doctorat de mathématiques.

[6] V. Danos, J.-B. Joinet, and H. Schellinx. Sequent calculi for second order logic. In J.-Y. Girard, Y. Lafont, and L. Regnier, editors, *Advances in Linear Logic.* Cambridge University Press, 1995.

[7] V. Danos and L. Regnier. Proof-nets and the Hilbert space. In J.-Y. Girard, Y. Lafont, and L. Regnier, editors, *Advances in Linear Logic*, pages 307–328. Cambridge University Press, London Mathematical Society Lecture Notes, 1995.
[8] R. David and B. Guillaume. The λ_l-calculus. In *Proceedigs of WESTAPP*, pages 2–13, Trento, Italy, 1999.
[9] R. Di Cosmo and S. Guerrini. Strong normalization of proof nets modulo structural congruences. In P. Narendran and M. Rusinowitch, editors, *Proc of RTA*, volume 1631 of *LNCS*, pages 75–89, Trento, Italy, 1999. Springer Verlag.
[10] R. Di Cosmo and D. Kesner. Strong normalization of explicit substitutions via cut elimination in proof nets. In *Proc of LICS*, pages 35–46, Warsaw, Poland, 1997.
[11] R. Di Cosmo, D. Kesner, and E. Polonovski. Proof nets and explicit substitutions. Technical report, LRI, Université Paris-Sud, 2000. Available as `ftp://ftp.lri.fr/LRI/articles/kesner/es-pn.ps.gz`.
[12] M. C. Ferreira, D. Kesner, and L. Puel. Lambda-calculi with explicit substitutions preserving strong normalization. *Applicable Algebra in Engineering Communication and Computing*, 9(4):333–371, 1999.
[13] J.-Y. Girard. Linear logic. *Theoretical Computer Science*, 50(1):1–101, 1987.
[14] J.-Y. Girard. Geometry of interaction I: interpretation of system F. In R. Ferro, C. Bonotto, S. Valentini, and A. Zanardo, editors, *Logic colloquium 1988*, pages 221–260. North Holland, 1989.
[15] G. Gonthier, M. Abadi, and J.-J. Lévy. The geometry of optimal lambda reduction. In *Proc. of POPL*, pages 15–26, Albuquerque, New Mexico, 1992. ACM Press.
[16] B. Guillaume. *Un calcul de substitution avec Étiquettes.* PhD thesis, Université de Savoie, 1999.
[17] J. Lamping. An algorithm for optimal lambda calculus reduction. In *Proc. of POPL*, pages 16–30, San Francisco, California, 1990. ACM Press.
[18] P.-A. Melliès. Typed λ-calculi with explicit substitutions may not terminate. In M. Dezani-Ciancaglini and G. Plotkin, editors, *Proc of TLCA*, volume 902 of *LNCS*, April 1995.
[19] K. Rose. Explicit cyclic substitutions. In Rusinowitch and Rémy, editors, *Proc. of CTRS*, number 656 in LNCS, pages 36–50, 1992.

A Reduction of Proof Nets

Reduction acting on a cut $Ax - cut$, removing an axiom :

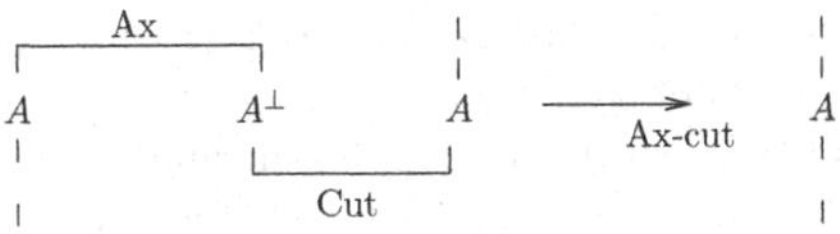

Reduction acting on a cut $\wp - \otimes$:

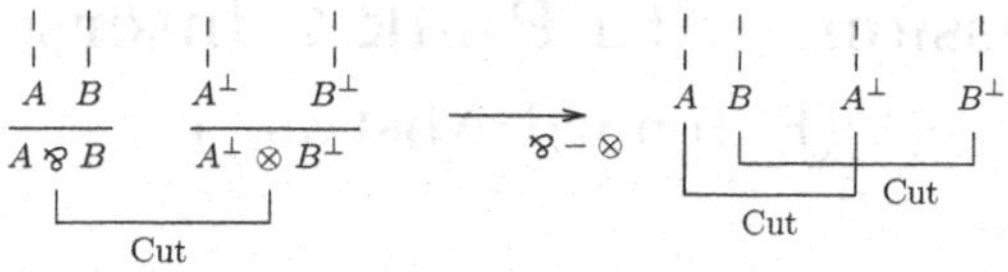

Reduction acting on a cut $w - b$, erasing a box :

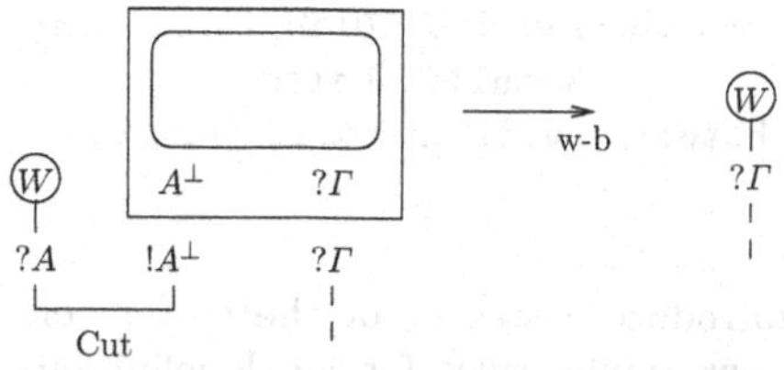

Reduction acting on a cut $d - b$, opening a box :

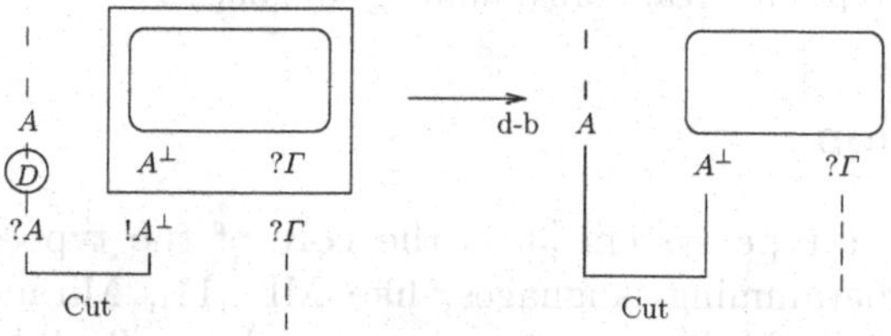

Reduction acting on a cut $c - b$, duplicating a box :

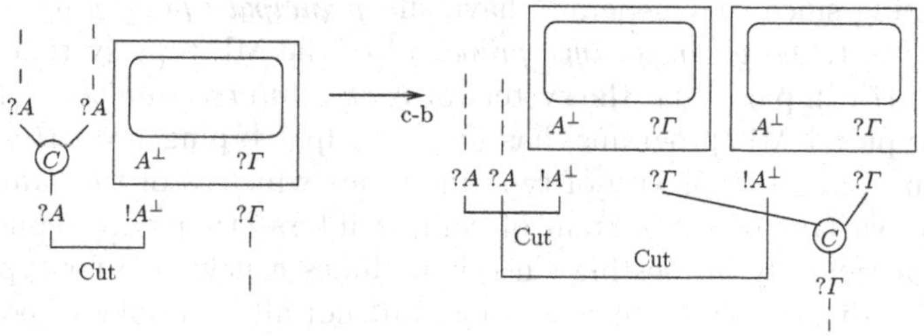

Reduction acting on a cut $b - b$, absorbing a box into another :

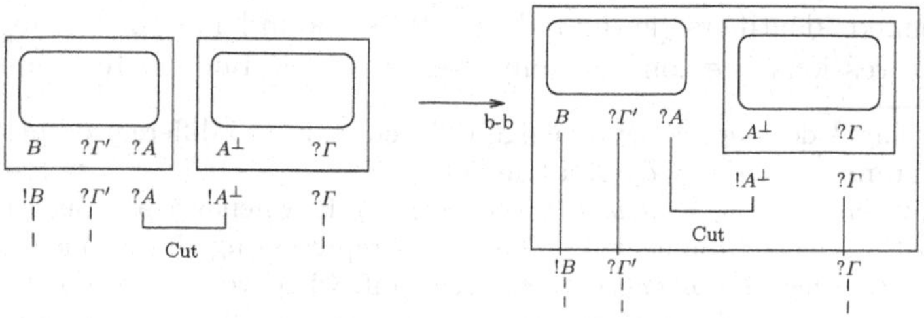

Typing Local Definitions and Conditional Expressions with Rank 2 Intersection
(Extended Abstract)

Ferruccio Damiani

Dipartimento di Informatica, Università di Torino,
Corso Svizzera 185, 10149 Torino, Italy
damiani@di.unito.it
http://www.di.unito.it/~damiani

Abstract. We introduce a variant of the system of rank 2 intersection types with new typing rules for local definitions (let-expressions and letrec-expressions) and conditional expressions (if-expressions and case-expressions). These extensions are a further step towards the use of intersection types in "real" programming languages.

1 Introduction

The Hindley-Milner type system [3] is the core of the type systems of modern functional programming languages, like ML [11], Miranda, Haskell, and Clean. The fact that this type system is somewhat inflexible[1] has motivated the search for more expressive, but still decidable, type systems (see, for instance, [10,14,4,2,8,7,9]). The extensions based on intersection types are particular interesting since they generally have the *principal typing property*[2], whose advantages w.r.t. the *principal type property*[3] of the ML type system have been described in [7]. In particular the system of *rank 2 intersection types* [10,14,15,7] is able to type all ML programs, has the principal typing property, decidable type inference, and complexity of type inference which is of the same order as in ML. The variant of the system of rank 2 intersection types considered by Jim [7] is particularly interesting since it includes a new rule for typing recursive definitions which allows to type some, but not all, examples of polymorphic recursion [12].

In this paper we build on Jim's work [7] and present a new system of rank 2 intersection types, $\vdash_{\wedge_2}^{\mathrm{If,Let,Rec}}$, which allows to give more expressive typings to locally defined identifiers (let-bound and letrec-bound identifiers) and to conditional expressions (we consider only if-expressions, but the technique can be

[1] In particular it does not allow to assign different types to different occurrences of a formal parameter in the body of a function.

[2] A type system has the *principal typing property* if, whenever a term e is typable, there exist a type environment A and a type v representing all possible typings of e.

[3] A type system has the *principal type property* if, whenever a term e is typable in a type environment A, there exists a type v representing all possible types of e in A.

J. Tiuryn (Ed.): FOSSACS 2000, LNCS 1784, pp. 82–97, 2000.

straightforwardly applied to case-expressions). These extensions are a further step towards the use of intersection types in "real" programming languages.

Better Typings for Local Definitions. The system of simple types [5] assigns the same type to all the uses of an identifier. To overcome this limitation the Hindley-Milner type system [3] considers a special rule to type local definitions, in this way locally defined identifiers (let-bound identifiers) are handled in a different way from the formal parameters of the functions (λ-bound identifiers).

In practice let-polymorphism is also used to allow polymorphic use of globally defined identifiers. The key idea is that of handling an expression e which uses globally defined identifiers $x_1, \ldots, x_n$ like the expression $\mathsf{let}\, x_1 = e_1 \mathsf{~in} \cdots \mathsf{let}\, x_n = e_n \mathsf{~in}\, e$, in which the definitions of $x_1, \ldots, x_n$ are local (and therefore available). This use of let-polymorphism to deal with global definitions has often been described as an odd feature, since it does not allow to typecheck global definitions in isolation. The problem can be identified with the fact that algorithm $\mathcal{W}$ requires as necessary inputs the type assumptions for the free identifiers of the expression being typed. Some solutions to overcome this limitation have been proposed in the literature (see for instance [1,13]).

Systems with rank 2 intersection types can provide an elegant solution to this problem by relying on the principal typing property, see [7], and handling let-expressions "$\mathsf{let}\, x = e_0 \mathsf{~in}\, e$" as syntactic sugar for "$(\lambda\, x.e)e_0$". In this way both locally defined and globally defined identifiers are handled as function formal parameters. However this strategy has a drawback: it forces to assign simple types to the uses of locally defined identifiers. For instance, the expression

$$\mathsf{let} \quad g = \lambda\, f.\mathsf{pair}\,(f\,2)\,(f\,\mathsf{true}) \quad \mathsf{in} \quad g(\lambda\, y.\mathsf{cons}\, y\, \mathsf{nil}) \tag{1}$$

cannot be typed, since to type (1) it is necessary to assign the rank 2 type $((\mathsf{int} \to \mathsf{int\, list}) \wedge (\mathsf{bool} \to \mathsf{bool\, list})) \to (\mathsf{int\, list} \times \mathsf{bool\, list})$ to the locally defined identifier g.

In this paper we present a technique that, while preserving the benefits of the principal typing property of the system of rank 2 intersection types, allows to assign rank 2 intersection types to the uses of locally defined identifiers, by exploiting the fact that their definition is indeed available. As we will see, typing let-expressions $\mathsf{let}\ x = e_0 \ \mathsf{in}\ e$ by associating to the identifier x the *principal type scheme* of e_0 (which is a formula $\forall\overrightarrow{\alpha}.v_0$, where v_0 is a rank 2 type and $\overrightarrow{\alpha}$ are *some* of the type variables of v_0) is not a good solution, since, when e_0 contains free identifies, it may happen that replacing a subexpression $(\lambda\, x.e)e_0$ with $\mathsf{let}\, x = e_0 \mathsf{~in}\, e$ does not preserve typability. To avoid this problem we will associate to x the *principal pair scheme* of e_0 (which is a formula $\forall\overrightarrow{\alpha}.\langle A_0, v_0\rangle$, where A_0 is a type environment, v_0 is a rank 2 type, and $\overrightarrow{\alpha}$ are *all* the type variables of A_0 and v_0).

Better Typings for Conditional Expressions. The ML type system handles an if-expression "$\mathsf{if}\ e \mathsf{~then}\ e_1 \mathsf{~else}\ e_2$" like the application "$\mathsf{ifc}\ e\ e_1\ e_2$", where ifc is a special constant of principal type scheme $\forall\alpha.\mathsf{bool} \rightarrow \alpha \rightarrow \alpha \rightarrow \alpha$. If we apply this strategy to a system with rank 2 intersection types we are forced to assign simple types to the conditional expression and to its branches, e_1 and e_2, and so the additional type information provided by intersection is lost.

In this paper we present a technique that allows to overcome this limitation and to assign rank 2 intersection types to conditional expressions. For simplicity we consider only if-expressions, but the technique can be straightforwardly applied to case-expressions and functions defined by cases. As we will see, allowing to assign to an if-expression $\mathsf{if}\ e\ \mathsf{then}\ e_1\ \mathsf{else}\ e_2$ any rank 2 type v that can be assigned to both e_1 and e_2 will destroy the principal typing (and type) property of the rank 2 intersection type system. So, to preserve the principal typing property, we will introduce a condition that limits the use of intersection in the type v assigned to the branches e_1 and e_2 of the if-expression.

Organization of the Paper. In Section 2 of this paper we describe a simple programming language, that we call mini-ML, which can be considered the kernel of functional programming languages like ML, Miranda, Haskell, and Clean (the evaluation mechanism, call-by-name or call-by-value, is not relevant for the purpose of typechecking). Section 3 introduces the syntax of our rank 2 intersection types, together with other basic definitions. Section 4 presents the $\vdash^{\mathrm{Rec}}_{\wedge_2}$ type system, which is essentially the extension to mini-ML of the type system $\vdash_{\mathbf{P}^{\mathrm{R}}_{2}}$ of [7]. In Sections 5 and 6 we describe two new type systems for mini-ML: $\vdash^{\mathrm{Let,Rec}}_{\wedge_2}$, which extends the system $\vdash^{\mathrm{Rec}}_{\wedge_2}$ with more powerful rules for typing local definitions (let-expressions and letrec-expressions), and $\vdash^{\mathrm{If,Let,Rec}}_{\wedge_2}$, which extends the system $\vdash^{\mathrm{Let,Rec}}_{\wedge_2}$ with a more powerful rule for typing if-expressions.

2 The Language Mini-ML

We consider two classes of *constants*: *constructors* for denoting base values (integer, booleans) and building data structures, and *base functions* for denoting operations on base values and for inspecting and decomposing data structures. The base functions include some arithmetic operators, and the functions for decomposing pairs (prj_1 and prj_2) and for decomposing and inspecting lists (hd, tl, and null). The constructors include the unique element of type unit, the booleans, the integer numbers, and the constructors for pairs and lists. Let *bf* range over base functions (all unary) and *cs* range over constructors. The syntax of constants (ranged over by c) is as follows

$$\begin{array}{lcl} c & ::= & bf \mid cs \\ bf & ::= & \mathsf{not} \mid \mathsf{and} \mid \mathsf{or} \mid + \mid - \mid * \mid / \mid = \mid \cdots \mid \mathsf{prj}_1 \mid \mathsf{prj}_2 \mid \mathsf{hd} \mid \mathsf{tl} \mid \mathsf{null} \\ cs & ::= & () \mid \mathsf{true} \mid \mathsf{false} \mid \cdots \mid -1 \mid 0 \mid 1 \mid \cdots \mid \mathsf{nil} \mid \mathsf{pair} \mid \mathsf{cons} \end{array}$$

Expressions (ranged over by e) have the following syntax

$$\begin{array}{lcl} e & ::= & x \mid c \mid \lambda x.e \mid e_1 e_2 \mid \mathsf{if}\ e\ \mathsf{then}\ e_1\ \mathsf{else}\ e_2 \\ & \mid & \mathsf{let}\ x = e_1\ \mathsf{in}\ e_2 \mid \mathsf{letrec}\ \{x_1 = e_1, \ldots, x_n = e_n\}\ \mathsf{in}\ e \end{array}$$

where x, x_1, ..., x_n range over identifiers. The construct letrec allows mutually recursive expression definitions. Let $\mathrm{FV}(e)$ denote the set of free identifiers of the expression e. Expressions are considered syntactically equal modulo renaming of the bound identifiers. In order to simplify the presentation we assume that, in every expression, different bound identifiers have different names and that the names of bound identifiers cannot occur free in the expression (this can be always enforced by suitable renaming of bound identifiers).

3 Types, Schemes, and Environments

In this section we introduce the syntax of our rank 2 intersection types, together with other basic definitions that will be used in the rest of the paper.

Types and Schemes. The language of *simple types* ($\mathbf{T}_0$), ranged over by u, is defined by the grammar: $u ::= \alpha \mid \mathsf{unit} \mid \mathsf{bool} \mid \mathsf{int} \mid u \to u \mid u \times u \mid u\,\mathsf{list}$. We have type variables (ranged over by α) and a selection of *ground* types and *composite* types. The *ground* types are unit (the singleton type), bool (the set of booleans), and int (the set of integers). The composite types are product and list types.

The language of *rank 1 intersection types* ($\mathbf{T}_1$), ranged over by ui, the language of *rank 2 intersection types* ($\mathbf{T}_2$), ranged over by v, and the language of *rank 2 intersection schemes* ($\mathbf{T}_{\forall 2}$), ranged over by vs, are defined as follows

$ui ::= u_1 \wedge \cdots \wedge u_n$	(rank 1 types, i.e. intersections of simple types)
$v ::= u \mid ui \to v$	(rank 2 types)
$vs ::= \forall \overrightarrow{\alpha}.v$	(rank 2 schemes)

where u ranges over the set of simple types $\mathbf{T}_0$, $n \geq 1$, and $\overrightarrow{\alpha}$ is a finite (possibly empty) sequence of type variables $\alpha_1 \cdots \alpha_m$ ($m \geq 0$). Note that $\mathbf{T}_0 = \mathbf{T}_1 \cap \mathbf{T}_2$. Let ϵ denote the empty sequence. We consider $\forall \epsilon.v \neq v$, so $\mathbf{T}_2 \cap \mathbf{T}_{\forall 2} = \emptyset$.

Free and *bound* type variables are defined as usual. For every type $t \in \mathbf{T}_1 \cup \mathbf{T}_2 \cup \mathbf{T}_{\forall 2}$ let $\mathrm{FTV}(t)$ denote the set of free type variables of t. We say that a scheme vs is *closed* if $\mathrm{FTV}(vs) = \emptyset$.

To simplify the presentation we adopt the following syntactic convention: we consider $\wedge$ to be associative, commutative, and idempotent. Modulo this convention any type in $\mathbf{T}_1$ can be considered as a set of types in $\mathbf{T}_0$. We also assume that for every scheme $\forall \overrightarrow{\alpha}.v$ we have that $\{\overrightarrow{\alpha}\} \subseteq \mathrm{FTV}(v)$.

A *substitution* $\mathbf{s}$ is a mapping from type variables to simple types which is the identity on all but a finite number of type variables. The domain, $\mathrm{Dom}(\mathbf{s})$, of a substitution $\mathbf{s}$ is the set of type variables $\{\alpha \mid \mathbf{s}(\alpha) \neq \alpha\}$. We use $\mathbf{s}_{\{\overrightarrow{\alpha}\}}$ to range over substitutions whose domain is a subset of $\{\overrightarrow{\alpha}\}$. Note that, since substitutions replace free variables by simple types, we have that $\mathbf{T}_0$, $\mathbf{T}_1$, $\mathbf{T}_2$, and $\mathbf{T}_{\forall 2}$ are closed under substitution.

The following definition are fairly standard. Note that we keep a clear distinction between *subtyping* and *instantiation* relations, and we do not introduce a subtyping relation between rank 2 schemes.

Definition 1 (Subtyping relations $\leq_1$ and $\leq_2$). *The subtyping relations* $\leq_1$ ($\subseteq \mathbf{T}_1 \times \mathbf{T}_1$) *and* $\leq_2$ ($\subseteq \mathbf{T}_2 \times \mathbf{T}_2$) *are inductively defined as follows*

- $u \leq_2 u$, *if* $u \in \mathbf{T}_0$
- $u_1 \wedge \cdots \wedge u_n \leq_1 u'_1 \wedge \cdots \wedge u'_m$, *if* $\{u_1, \ldots, u_n\} \supseteq \{u'_1, \ldots, u'_m\}$
- $ui \rightarrow v \leq_2 ui' \rightarrow v'$, *if* $ui' \leq_1 ui$ *and* $v \leq_2 v'$.

Definition 2 (Instantiation relations $\leq_{\forall 2,0}$, $\leq_{\forall 2,1}$ and $\leq_{\forall 2,2}$). *The instantiation relations* $\leq_{\forall 2,0}$ ($\subseteq \mathbf{T}_{\forall 2} \times \mathbf{T}_0$), $\leq_{\forall 2,1}$ ($\subseteq \mathbf{T}_{\forall 2} \times \mathbf{T}_1$), *and* $\leq_{\forall 2,2}$ ($\subseteq \mathbf{T}_{\forall 2} \times \mathbf{T}_2$) *are defined as follows. For every scheme* $\forall \overrightarrow{\alpha}.v \in \mathbf{T}_{\forall 2}$ *and for every type*

0. $u \in \mathbf{T}_0$, *we write* $\forall \overrightarrow{\alpha}.v \leq_{\forall 2,0} u$ *if* $u = \mathbf{s}_{\{\overrightarrow{\alpha}\}}(v)$, *for some substitution* $\mathbf{s}_{\{\overrightarrow{\alpha}\}}$;
1. $u_1 \wedge \cdots \wedge u_n \in \mathbf{T}_1$, *we write* $\forall \overrightarrow{\alpha}.v \leq_{\forall 2,1} u_1 \wedge \cdots \wedge u_n$ *if* $\forall \overrightarrow{\alpha}.v \leq_{\forall 2,0} u_i$, *for every* $i \in \{1, \ldots, n\}$;
2. $v' \in \mathbf{T}_2$, *we say that* v' is an instance of $\forall \overrightarrow{\alpha}.v$, *and write* $\forall \overrightarrow{\alpha}.v \leq_{\forall 2,2} v'$, *if* $\mathbf{s}_{\{\overrightarrow{\alpha}\}}(v) \leq_2 v'$, *for some substitution* $\mathbf{s}_{\{\overrightarrow{\alpha}\}}$.

For example, for $vs = \forall \alpha_1\alpha_2\alpha_3.((\alpha_1 \rightarrow \alpha_3) \wedge (\alpha_2 \rightarrow \alpha_3)) \rightarrow \alpha_3$, we have (remember that $\wedge$ is idempotent) $vs \leq_{\forall 2,0} (\mathsf{int} \rightarrow \mathsf{int}) \rightarrow \mathsf{int}$ (by using the substitution $\mathbf{s}_1 = [\alpha_1, \alpha_2, \alpha_3 := \mathsf{int}]$) and $vs \leq_{\forall 2,1} ((\mathsf{int} \rightarrow \mathsf{int}) \rightarrow \mathsf{int}) \wedge ((\mathsf{bool} \rightarrow \mathsf{bool}) \rightarrow \mathsf{bool})$ (by $\mathbf{s}_1$ as above, and $\mathbf{s}_2 = [\alpha_1, \alpha_2, \alpha_3 := \mathsf{bool}]$). We also have $\forall \alpha.\alpha \rightarrow \alpha \leq_{\forall 2,2} (\alpha_1 \wedge \alpha_2) \rightarrow \alpha_1$ (by $\mathbf{s} = [\alpha := \alpha_1]$ and $\leq_2$).

Type Environments. A *type environment* T is a set $\{x_1 : t_1, \ldots, x_n : t_n\}$ of type assumptions for identifiers such that every identifier x can occur at most once in T. We write $\mathrm{Dom}(T)$ for $\{x_1, \ldots, x_n\}$ and $T, x : t$ for the environment $T \cup \{x : t\}$ where it is assumed that $x \notin \mathrm{Dom}(T)$. In particular:

- a *rank 1 type environment* A is an environment $\{x_1 : ui_1, \ldots, x_n : ui_n\}$ of rank 1 type assumptions for identifiers, and
- a *rank 2 scheme environment* B is an environment $\{x_1 : vs_1, \ldots, x_n : vs_n\}$ of *closed* rank 2 schemes assumptions for identifiers.

For every type $v \in \mathbf{T}_2$ and type environment T we write $\mathrm{Gen}(T, v)$ for the $\forall$*-closure of* v *in* T, i.e. for the scheme $\forall \overrightarrow{\alpha}.v$ where $\{\overrightarrow{\alpha}\} = \mathrm{FTV}(v) - \mathrm{FTV}(T)$.

Given two rank 1 environments A_1 and A_2 we write $A_1 + A_2$ to denote the rank 1 environment

$$\{x : ui_1 \wedge ui_2 \mid x : ui_1 \in A_1 \text{ and } x : ui_2 \in A_2\}$$
$$\cup \{x : ui_1 \in A_1 \mid x \notin \mathrm{Dom}(A_2)\} \cup \{x : ui_2 \in A_2 \mid x \notin \mathrm{Dom}(A_1)\} ,$$

and write $A_1 \leq_1 A_2$ to mean that $\mathrm{Dom}(A_1) = \mathrm{Dom}(A_2)$ and for every assumption $x : ui_2 \in A_2$ there is an assumption $x : ui_1 \in A_1$ such that $ui_1 \leq_1 ui_2$.

4 System $\vdash^{\mathrm{Rec}}_{\wedge_2}$: Jim's $\vdash_{\mathbf{P}^{\mathbf{R}}_{\mathbf{2}}}$ Type System Revised

In this section we introduce the $\vdash^{\mathrm{Rec}}_{\wedge_2}$ type system for mini-ML. System $\vdash^{\mathrm{Rec}}_{\wedge_2}$ is essentially an extension to mini-ML of the type system $\vdash_{\mathbf{P}^{\mathbf{R}}_{\mathbf{2}}}$ of [7] (the language considered in [7] is a λ-calculus without constants enriched with letrec-expressions). Then, in Sections 5 and 6, we will extend $\vdash^{\mathrm{Rec}}_{\wedge_2}$ with new typing rules for local definitions and conditional expressions.

The Type Inference Rules. The type inference system $\vdash^{\mathrm{Rec}}_{\wedge_2}$ has judgements of the form $A; B \vdash^{\mathrm{Rec}}_{\wedge_2} e : v$, where B is a rank 2 environment specifying closed $\mathbf{T}_{\forall 2}$ types for library identifiers[4], and A is a rank 1 environment containing the type assumptions for the remaining free identifiers of e. So $\mathrm{FV}(e) \subseteq \mathrm{Dom}(A \cup B)$, $\mathrm{Dom}(A) \cap \mathrm{Dom}(B) = \emptyset$, and $\mathrm{Dom}(A) = \mathrm{FV}(e) - \mathrm{Dom}(B)$[5]. Note that (by definition of rank 2 scheme environment) $\mathrm{FTV}(B) = \emptyset$.

We say that e *is typable in* $\vdash^{\mathrm{Rec}}_{\wedge_2}$ *w.r.t. the library environment* B if there exist a typing $A; B \vdash^{\mathrm{Rec}}_{\wedge_2} e : v$, for some A and v.

The type inference rules are presented in Fig. 2. The rule for typing constants uses the function Typeof (tabulated in Fig. 1) which assigns a closed scheme to each constant. Since, by definition, $\mathrm{Dom}(A)$ contains exactly the assumptions for the free non-library identifiers of the expression e being typed, we have two rules for typing an abstraction $\lambda x.e$, corresponding to the two cases $x \in \mathrm{FV}(e)$ and $x \notin \mathrm{FV}(e)$. The rule for typing function application, (App), allows to use a different typing for each expected type of the argument. The rule for typing if-expressions handles an expression $\mathsf{if}\ e\ \mathsf{then}\ e_1\ \mathsf{else}\ e_2$ like the application $\mathsf{ifc}\ e\ e_1\ e_2$, where ifc is a special constant of type $\forall\alpha.\mathsf{bool} \to \alpha \to \alpha \to \alpha$. A let-expression, $\mathsf{let}\, x = e_0 \,\mathsf{in}\, e$, is considered as syntactic sugar for the application $(\lambda x.e)e_0$.

The rule for typing letrec-expressions, $\mathsf{letrec}\,\{x_1 = e_1, \ldots, x_n = e_n\}\,\mathsf{in}\, e$, introduces auxiliary expressions of the form $\mathsf{rec}_i\,\{x_1 = e_1, \ldots, x_n = e_n\}$, for $1 \le i \le n$. These auxiliary expressions are introduced just for convenience in presenting the type system ($\mathsf{rec}_i\,\{x_1 = e_1, \ldots, x_n = e_n\}$ is simply a short for $\mathsf{letrec}\,\{x_1 = e_1, \ldots, x_n = e_n\}\,\mathsf{in}\, x_i$).

The only non-structural rule is (Sub), which allows to assume less specific types for the free non-library identifiers and to assign more specific types to expressions (for instance, without rule (Sub) it would not be possible to assign type $(\alpha_1 \wedge \alpha_2) \to \alpha_1$ to the identity function $\lambda x.x$). The operations of $\forall$-introduction and $\forall$-elimination are embedded in the structural rules.

Comparison with the System $\vdash_{\mathbf{P}^{\mathbf{R}}_{\mathbf{2}}}$. Besides the presence of constants, if-expressions, and let-expressions, the main differences between $\vdash^{\mathrm{Rec}}_{\wedge_2}$ and $\vdash_{\mathbf{P}^{\mathbf{R}}_{\mathbf{2}}}$ are the presence of the library environment B (which is not present in $\vdash_{\mathbf{P}^{\mathbf{R}}_{\mathbf{2}}}$, although its use has been suggested in [7]) and the improved typing rules for recursive

---

[4] I.e. for the identifiers defined in the libraries available to the programmer.

[5] The fact that the environment A is *relevant* (i.e., $x \in \mathrm{Dom}(A)$ implies $x \in \mathrm{FV}(e)$) is used in rule (Rec) of Fig. 2 (as explained at the end of Section 4).

c	Typeof(c)	c	Typeof(c)
()	$\forall\epsilon.\mathsf{unit}$	pair	$\forall\alpha_1\alpha_2.\alpha_1 \to \alpha_2 \to (\alpha_1 \times \alpha_2)$
true, false	$\forall\epsilon.\mathsf{bool}$	prj_i	$\forall\alpha_1\alpha_2.(\alpha_1 \times \alpha_2) \to \alpha_i$
not	$\forall\epsilon.\mathsf{bool} \to \mathsf{bool}$	nil	$\forall\alpha.\alpha\ \mathsf{list}$
and, or	$\forall\epsilon.\mathsf{bool} \times \mathsf{bool} \to \mathsf{bool}$	cons	$\forall\alpha.\alpha \to \alpha\ \mathsf{list} \to \alpha\ \mathsf{list}$
$\cdots -1, 0, 1, \cdots$	$\forall\epsilon.\mathsf{int}$	hd	$\forall\alpha.\alpha\ \mathsf{list} \to \alpha$
$+, -, *, /$	$\forall\epsilon.\mathsf{int} \times \mathsf{int} \to \mathsf{int}$	tl	$\forall\alpha.\alpha\ \mathsf{list} \to \alpha\ \mathsf{list}$
$=, <, \cdots$	$\forall\epsilon.\mathsf{int} \times \mathsf{int} \to \mathsf{bool}$	null	$\forall\alpha.\alpha\ \mathsf{list} \to \mathsf{bool}$

Fig. 1. Types for constants

definitions. For instance we have that $\mathsf{rec}_1\,\{x_1 = \lambda y.yy\}$ can be typed in $\vdash^{\mathrm{Rec}}_{\wedge_2}$: $\emptyset;\emptyset \vdash^{\mathrm{Rec}}_{\wedge_2} \mathsf{rec}_1\,\{x_1 = \lambda y.yy\} : ((\alpha_1 \to \alpha_2) \wedge \alpha_1) \to \alpha_2$, while it is not typable in $\vdash_{\mathbf{P}^{\mathrm{R}}_2}$. This is due to the fact that, when typing a (possibly mutually) recursive definition $\mathsf{rec}_{i_0}\,\{x_1 = e_1, \ldots, x_n = e_n\}$, the rules of $\vdash_{\mathbf{P}^{\mathrm{R}}_2}$ require that (also for those $i \in \{1,\ldots,n\}$ such that $x_i \notin \cup_{j\in\{1,\ldots,n\}}\mathrm{FV}(e_j)$) the rank two type v_i assigned to e_i must be such that $\mathrm{Gen}(A, v_i) \leq_{\forall 2,1} u_i$, for some simple type u_i. This anomaly has been pointed out in [6] where it is also described a solution to the problem in the case of a single recursive definition ($\mathsf{rec}_1\{x_1 = e_1\}$): if $x_1 \notin \mathrm{FV}(e_1)$ then do not require that $\mathrm{Gen}(A, v_1) \leq_{\forall 2,1} u_1$. System $\vdash^{\mathrm{Rec}}_{\wedge_2}$ generalizes this idea to mutually recursive definitions: the constraint $\mathrm{Gen}(A, v_i) \leq_{\forall 2,1} ui_i$ is enforced only for those i such that $x_i \in \cup_{j\in\{1,\ldots,n\}}\mathrm{FV}(e_j)$.

Principal Typings for $\vdash^{\mathrm{Rec}}_{\wedge_2}$. The type system $\vdash^{\mathrm{Rec}}_{\wedge_2}$ has the principal typing property. The following definition and theorem are a formulation for $\vdash^{\mathrm{Rec}}_{\wedge_2}$ (keeping in account the presence of the library environment B) of an analogous result for $\vdash_{\mathbf{P}^{\mathrm{R}}_2}$ presented in [7].

Definition 3 (Principal typings for $\vdash^{\mathrm{Rec}}_{\wedge_2}$). *A typing $A'; B \vdash^{\mathrm{Rec}}_{\wedge_2} e : v'$ is an* instance *of a typing $A; B \vdash^{\mathrm{Rec}}_{\wedge_2} e : v$ if there is a substitution* $\mathbf{s}$ *such that* $\mathrm{Dom}(\mathbf{s}) = \mathrm{FTV}(A) \cup \mathrm{FTV}(v)$*,* $\mathbf{s}(v) \leq_2 v'$ *and* $A' \leq_1 \mathbf{s}(A)$*.*
A typing $A; B \vdash^{\mathrm{Rec}}_{\wedge_2} e : v$ is a principal typing *for e* w.r.t. *B if any other typing of e w.r.t. B is an instance of it.*

Theorem 1 (Principal typing property for $\vdash^{\mathrm{Rec}}_{\wedge_2}$). *If e is typable in $\vdash^{\mathrm{Rec}}_{\wedge_2}$ w.r.t. B, then it has a principal typing w.r.t. B.*

5 The System $\vdash^{\mathrm{Let,Rec}}_{\wedge_2}$: Better Typings for Local Definitions

Rule (LETSUGAR) of $\vdash^{\mathrm{Rec}}_{\wedge_2}$ prevents us to assign rank 2 types to the uses of local definitions. The following rule, which allows to store the rank 2 type schemes

$$(\text{ID}_1)\ \{x:u\};B\vdash x:u \quad x\notin \mathrm{Dom}(B) \qquad (\text{ID}_2)\ \emptyset;B,\,x:\forall\overrightarrow{\alpha}.v\vdash x:\mathbf{s}_{\{\overrightarrow{\alpha}\}}(v)$$

$$(\text{CON})\ \emptyset;B\vdash c:\mathbf{s}_{\{\overrightarrow{\alpha}\}}(v) \quad \mathrm{Typeof}(c)=\forall\overrightarrow{\alpha}.v$$

$$(\text{ABS})\ \frac{A,\,x:ui;B\vdash e:v}{A;B\vdash\lambda x.e:ui\to v} \qquad (\text{ABSVAC})\ \frac{A;B\vdash e:v}{A;B\vdash\lambda x.e:u\to v}\ x\notin\mathrm{Dom}(A\cup B)$$

$$(\text{APP})\ \frac{A;B\vdash e:u_1\wedge\cdots\wedge u_n\to v \quad (\forall i\in\{1,\ldots,n\})\ A_i;B\vdash e_0:v_i\ \mathrm{Gen}(A_i,v_i)\leq_{\forall 2,0}u_i}{A+A_1+\cdots+A_n;B\vdash ee_0:v}$$

$$(\text{IFSIMPLE})\ \frac{A;B\vdash e:\mathsf{bool} \quad A_1;B\vdash e_1:u \quad A_2;B\vdash e_2:u}{A+A_1+A_2;B\vdash \mathsf{if}\ e\ \mathsf{then}\ e_1\ \mathsf{else}\ e_2:u}$$

$$(\text{LETSUGAR})\ \frac{A;B\vdash(\lambda x.e)e_0:v}{A;B\vdash \mathsf{let}\,x=e_0\ \mathsf{in}\ e:v}$$

$$(\text{LETREC})\ \frac{A;B\vdash(\lambda x_1.\cdots.\lambda x_n.e)e'_1\cdots e'_n:v}{A;B\vdash \mathsf{letrec}\,\{x_1=e_1,\ldots,x_n=e_n\}\ \mathsf{in}\ e:v}$$
where, for $i\in\{1,\ldots,n\}$, $e'_i=\mathsf{rec}_i\,\{x_1=e_1,\ldots,x_n=e_n\}$

$$(\text{REC})\ \frac{(\forall i\in\{1,\ldots,n\})\ A_i;B\vdash e_i:v_i \quad (\forall j\in\{j_1,\ldots,j_m\})\ \mathrm{Gen}(A,v_j)\leq_{\forall 2,1}ui_j}{A_0;B\vdash \mathsf{rec}_{i_0}\,\{x_1=e_1,\ldots,x_n=e_n\}:v_{i_0}}$$
where $\{x_{j_1},\ldots,x_{j_m}\}=\{x_1,\ldots,x_n\}\cap(\cup_{1\leq i\leq n}\mathrm{FV}(e_i))$,
$A=A_0,\,x_{j_1}:ui_{j_1},\ldots,x_{j_m}:ui_{j_m}=A_1+\cdots+A_n,$ and $i_0\in\{1,\ldots,n\}$

$$(\text{SUB})\ \frac{A_1;B\vdash e:v_1 \quad A_2\leq_1 A_1 \quad v_1\leq_2 v_2}{A_2;B\vdash e:v_2}$$

Fig. 2. Type assignment rules (system $\vdash^{\mathrm{Rec}}_{\wedge_2}$)

inferred for local definitions in the environment B, has been suggested in [7] to overcome this limitation.

$$(\text{LETWEAK})\ \frac{A_0;B\vdash e_0:v_0 \quad A;B,\,x:\mathrm{Gen}(A_0\cup B,v_0)\vdash e':v}{A_0+A;B\vdash \mathsf{let}\,x=e_0\ \mathsf{in}\ e:v}$$

However the system $\vdash^{\mathrm{LetWeak}}_{\wedge_2}$ which uses such a rule to type let-expressions[6] has an unpleasant feature: for some e_0 and e such that $\mathrm{FV}(e_0)\neq\emptyset$, replacing $(\lambda x.e)e_0$ with $\mathsf{let}\,x=e_0\ \mathsf{in}\ e$ may not preserve typability, as the following example shows.

Example 1. We have that $\{y:(\alpha_1\to\alpha_2)\wedge\alpha_1\};\emptyset\vdash^{\mathrm{LetWeak}}_{\wedge_2}(\lambda x.xx)y:\alpha_2$ and so $\emptyset;\emptyset\vdash^{\mathrm{LetWeak}}_{\wedge_2}\lambda y.((\lambda x.xx)y):((\alpha_1\to\alpha_2)\wedge\alpha_1)\to\alpha_2$.
Instead $\lambda y.(\mathsf{let}\,x=y\ \mathsf{in}\ xx)$ cannot be typed in $\vdash^{\mathrm{LetWeak}}_{\wedge_2}$.

[6] The rank 2 type v_0 may contain free type variables (which are not allowed to occur in the library environment in the judgements of $\vdash^{\mathrm{Rec}}_{\wedge_2}$). So, if we want to use rule (LETWEAK) instead of (LETSUGAR), we have to replace, in the type inference rules of Fig. 2, every occurrence of $\mathrm{Gen}(A,v)$ by $\mathrm{Gen}(A\cup B,v)$.

This problem is due to the fact that, like the ML type system does, rule (LETWEAK) associates to each let-bound identifier a *type scheme* which, in general, cannot express the principal typing of the body, e_0, of the local definition. To overcome this limitation we introduce the notions of *pair scheme* and *pair environment*.

Definition 4 (Pair schemes and pair environments). *A* pair scheme p *is a formula* $\forall\overrightarrow{\alpha}.\langle A, v\rangle$ *where* A *is a rank 1 environment,* v *is a rank 2 type, and* $\overrightarrow{\alpha} = \mathrm{FTV}(A) \cup \mathrm{FTV}(v)$.
A pair environment L *is an environment* $\{x_1 : \forall\overrightarrow{\alpha}^1.\langle A_1, v_1\rangle, \ldots, x_n : \forall\overrightarrow{\alpha}^n.\langle A_n, v_n\rangle\}$ *of pair scheme assumptions for identifiers.*

The New Typing Rules. The new typing rules for local definitions allow to associate to each locally defined identifier a pair scheme representing the principal typing of its definition. The new type system uses an additional pair environment for locally defined identifiers (let-bound and letrec-bound identifiers), i.e. it has judgements of the form $A; B; L \vdash^{\mathrm{Let,Rec}}_{\wedge_2} e : v$, where $\mathrm{FV}(e) \subseteq \mathrm{Dom}(A \cup B \cup L)$, the domains of the three environments A, B, L, are pairwise disjoint, and $\mathrm{Dom}(A) = \mathrm{FV}(e) - \mathrm{Dom}(B \cup L)$.

We say that e *is typable in* $\vdash^{\mathrm{Let,Rec}}_{\wedge_2}$ *w.r.t. the library environment* B *and the local environment* L if there exist a typing $A; B; L \vdash^{\mathrm{Let,Rec}}_{\wedge_2} e : v$, for some A and v.

The type inference rules for system $\vdash^{\mathrm{Let,Rec}}_{\wedge_2}$ are in Fig. 3. There are two rules for typing a let-expression, $\mathsf{let}\, x = e_0 \,\mathsf{in}\, e$, corresponding to the two cases $x \in \mathrm{FV}(e)$ and $x \notin \mathrm{FV}(e)$. The key rule is the first one, (LETNEW), which uses the local environment L to store a pair scheme ($\forall\overrightarrow{\alpha}.\langle A_0, v_0\rangle$) representing the typings of the local definition $x = e_0$. Then the rule (ID_3) allows to associate a new typing to each use of a locally defined identifier. The new rule for typing letrec-expressions, (LETRECNEW), simply relies on rule (LETNEW). All the remaining rules ignore the local environment L and behave as the corresponding rules of system $\vdash^{\mathrm{Rec}}_{\wedge_2}$.

The system $\vdash^{\mathrm{Let,Rec}}_{\wedge_2}$ extends both $\vdash^{\mathrm{Rec}}_{\wedge_2}$ and $\vdash^{\mathrm{LetWeak}}_{\wedge_2}$, and is such that $A; B; L \vdash^{\mathrm{Let,Rec}}_{\wedge_2} (\lambda x.e)e_0 : v$ implies $A; B; L \vdash^{\mathrm{Let,Rec}}_{\wedge_2} \mathsf{let}\, x = e_0 \,\mathsf{in}\, e : v$, for all expressions e_0 and e. For instance (considering the expression in Example 1) we have

1. $\{y : \alpha\}; \emptyset; \emptyset \vdash^{\mathrm{Let,Rec}}_{\wedge_2} y : \alpha$, by rule ($\mathrm{ID}_1$),
2. $\{y : \alpha_1 \to \alpha_2\}; \emptyset; \{x : \forall\alpha.\langle\{y : \alpha\}, \alpha\rangle\} \vdash^{\mathrm{Let,Rec}}_{\wedge_2} x : \alpha_1 \to \alpha_2$, by rule ($\mathrm{ID}_3$), with $\mathbf{s} = [\alpha := \alpha_1 \to \alpha_2]$,
3. $\{y : \alpha_1\}; \emptyset; \{x : \forall\alpha.\langle\{y : \alpha\}, \alpha\rangle\} \vdash^{\mathrm{Let,Rec}}_{\wedge_2} x : \alpha_1$, by rule ($\mathrm{ID}_3$), with $\mathbf{s} = [\alpha := \alpha_1]$,
4. $\{y : (\alpha_1 \to \alpha_2) \wedge \alpha_1\}; \emptyset; \{x : \forall\alpha.\langle\{y : \alpha\}, \alpha\rangle\} \vdash^{\mathrm{Let,Rec}}_{\wedge_2} xx : \alpha_2$, from hypotheses (2) and (3), by rule (APP),
5. $\{y : (\alpha_1 \to \alpha_2) \wedge \alpha_1\}; \emptyset; \emptyset \vdash^{\mathrm{Let,Rec}}_{\wedge_2} (\mathsf{let}\, x = y \,\mathsf{in}\, xx) : \alpha_2$, from hypotheses (1) and (4), by rule (LETNEW),

$(\text{ID}_1)\ \{x : u\}; B; L \vdash x : u \qquad \text{where } x \notin \text{Dom}(B \cup L) \text{ and } \text{Dom}(B) \cap \text{Dom}(L) = \emptyset$

$(\text{ID}_2)\ \emptyset; B, x : \forall\overrightarrow{\alpha}.v; L \vdash x : \mathbf{s}_{\{\overrightarrow{\alpha}\}}(v) \qquad \text{where } (\text{Dom}(B) \cup \{x\}) \cap \text{Dom}(L) = \emptyset$

$(\text{ID}_3)\ \mathbf{s}_{\{\overrightarrow{\alpha}\}}(A); B; L, x : \forall\overrightarrow{\alpha}.\langle A, v\rangle \vdash x : \mathbf{s}_{\{\overrightarrow{\alpha}\}}(v) \text{ where } \text{Dom}(B) \cap (\text{Dom}(L) \cup \{x\}) = \emptyset$

$(\text{CON})\ \emptyset; B; L \vdash c : \mathbf{s}_{\{\overrightarrow{\alpha}\}}(v) \qquad \text{where } \text{Dom}(B) \cap \text{Dom}(L) = \emptyset \text{ and } \text{Typeof}(c) = \forall\overrightarrow{\alpha}.v$

$$(\text{ABS})\ \frac{A, x : ui; B; L \vdash e : v}{A; B; L \vdash \lambda x.e : ui \to v} \qquad (\text{ABSVAC})\ \frac{A; B; L \vdash e : v}{A; B; L \vdash \lambda x.e : u \to v}\ x \notin \text{Dom}(A \cup B)$$

$$(\text{APP})\ \frac{A;B;L \vdash e : u_1 \wedge \cdots \wedge u_n \to v \quad (\forall i \in \{1,\ldots,n\})\ A_i;B;L \vdash e_0 : v_i \quad \text{Gen}(A_i, v_i) \leq_{\forall 2,0} u_i}{A + A_1 + \cdots + A_n; B; L \vdash ee_0 : v}$$

$$(\text{IFSIMPLE})\ \frac{A; B; L \vdash e : \mathsf{bool} \quad A_1; B; L \vdash e_1 : u \quad A_2; B; L \vdash e_2 : u}{A + A_1 + A_2; B; L \vdash \mathsf{if}\ e\ \mathsf{then}\ e_1\ \mathsf{else}\ e_2 : u}$$

$$(\text{LETNEW})\ \frac{A_0; B; L \vdash e_0 : v_0 \quad A; B; L, x : \forall\overrightarrow{\alpha}.\langle A_0, v_0\rangle \vdash e : v}{A; B; L \vdash \mathsf{let}\ x = e_0\ \mathsf{in}\ e : v}\ x \in \text{FV}(e)$$
where $\{\overrightarrow{\alpha}\} = \text{FTV}(A_0) \cup \text{FTV}(v_0)$

$$(\text{LETVAC})\ \frac{A_0; B; L \vdash e_0 : v_0 \quad A; B; L \vdash e : v}{A_0 + A; B; L \vdash \mathsf{let}\ x = e_0\ \mathsf{in}\ e : v}\ x \notin \text{FV}(e)$$

$$(\text{LETRECNEW})\ \frac{A; B; L \vdash \mathsf{let}\ x_1 = e_1'\ \mathsf{in}\ \cdots \mathsf{let}\ x_n = e_n'\ \mathsf{in}\ e : v}{A; B; L \vdash \mathsf{letrec}\ \{x_1 = e_1, \ldots, x_n = e_n\}\ \mathsf{in}\ e : v}$$
where, for $i \in \{1, \ldots, n\}$, $e_i' = \mathsf{rec}_i\ \{x_1 = e_1, \ldots, x_n = e_n\}$

$$(\text{REC})\ \frac{(\forall i \in \{1, \ldots, n\})\ A_i; B; L \vdash e_i : v_i \quad (\forall j \in \{j_1, \ldots, j_m\})\ \text{Gen}(A, v_j) \leq_{\forall 2,1} ui_j}{A_0; B; L \vdash \mathsf{rec}_{i_0}\ \{x_1 = e_1, \ldots, x_n = e_n\} : v_{i_0}}$$
where $\{x_{j_1}, \ldots, x_{j_m}\} = \{x_1, \ldots, x_n\} \cap (\cup_{1 \leq i \leq n} \text{FV}(e_i))$,
$A = A_0, x_{j_1} : ui_{j_1}, \ldots, x_{j_m} : ui_{j_m} = A_1 + \cdots + A_n$, and $i_0 \in \{1, \ldots, n\}$

$$(\text{SUB})\ \frac{A_1; B; L \vdash e : v_1 \quad A_2 \leq_1 A_1 \quad v_1 \leq_2 v_2}{A_2; B; L \vdash e : v_2}$$

Fig. 3. Type assignment rules (system $\vdash_{\wedge_2}^{\text{Let,Rec}}$)

6. $\emptyset; \emptyset; \emptyset \vdash_{\wedge_2}^{\text{Let,Rec}} \lambda y.(\mathsf{let}\ x = y\ \mathsf{in}\ xx) : ((\alpha_1 \to \alpha_2) \wedge \alpha_1) \to \alpha_2$, from hypothesis (5), by rule (ABS).

The following example shows another application of rule (LETNEW).

Example 2. The expression $e = (\ \mathsf{let}\ g = \lambda f\,x.f(fx)\ \mathsf{in}\ g(\lambda y.\mathsf{cons}\,y\,\mathsf{nil})\ )$ cannot be typed neither in ML nor by system $\vdash_{\wedge_2}^{\text{Rec}}$. With system $\vdash_{\wedge_2}^{\text{Let,Rec}}$, instead, we have

1. $\emptyset; \emptyset; \emptyset \vdash_{\wedge_2}^{\text{Let,Rec}} \lambda f\,x.f(fx) : ((\alpha_1 \to \alpha_2) \wedge (\alpha_2 \to \alpha_3)) \to \alpha_1 \to \alpha_3$,
2. $\emptyset; \emptyset; \emptyset \vdash_{\wedge_2}^{\text{Let,Rec}} \lambda y.\mathsf{cons}\,y\,\mathsf{nil} : \alpha \to (\alpha\ \mathsf{list})$,

3. $\emptyset; \emptyset; \{g : \forall\alpha_1\alpha_2\alpha_3.\langle\emptyset, ((\alpha_1 \to \alpha_2) \wedge (\alpha_2 \to \alpha_3)) \to \alpha_1 \to \alpha_3\rangle\} \vdash_{\wedge_2}^{\mathrm{Let,Rec}} g : ((\alpha' \to (\alpha' \,\mathsf{list})) \wedge ((\alpha' \,\mathsf{list}) \to (\alpha' \,\mathsf{list}\,\mathsf{list}))) \to \alpha' \to (\alpha' \,\mathsf{list}\,\mathsf{list})$, by rule (ID3), with $\mathbf{s} = [\alpha_1 := \alpha', \ \alpha_2 := \alpha' \,\mathsf{list}, \ \alpha_3 := \alpha' \,\mathsf{list}\,\mathsf{list}]$,
4. $\emptyset; \emptyset; \{g : \forall\alpha_1\alpha_2\alpha_3.\langle\emptyset, ((\alpha_1 \to \alpha_2) \wedge (\alpha_2 \to \alpha_3)) \to \alpha_1 \to \alpha_3\rangle\} \vdash_{\wedge_2}^{\mathrm{Let,Rec}} g(\lambda y.\mathsf{cons}\, y \,\mathsf{nil}) : \alpha' \to (\alpha' \,\mathsf{list}\,\mathsf{list})$, from hypotheses (2) and (3), by rule (APP),
5. $\emptyset; \emptyset; \emptyset \vdash_{\wedge_2}^{\mathrm{Let,Rec}} e : \alpha' \to (\alpha' \,\mathsf{list}\,\mathsf{list})$, from hypotheses (1) and (4), by rule (LETNEW).

Also the expression (1) of Section 1 can be typed with $\vdash_{\wedge_2}^{\mathrm{Let,Rec}}$.

Principal Typings for $\vdash_{\wedge_2}^{\mathrm{Let,Rec}}$. The following definition and theorem generalize the corresponding result of Section 5 by keeping in account the presence of the local environment L.

Definition 5 (Principal typings for $\vdash_{\wedge_2}^{\mathrm{Let,Rec}}$). *A typing $A'; B; L \vdash_{\wedge_2}^{\mathrm{Let,Rec}} e : v'$ is an* instance *of a typing $A; B; L \vdash_{\wedge_2}^{\mathrm{Let,Rec}} e : v$ if there is a substitution $\mathbf{s}$ such that $\mathrm{Dom}(\mathbf{s}) = \mathrm{FTV}(A) \cup \mathrm{FTV}(v)$, $\mathbf{s}(v) \le_2 v'$ and $A' \le_1 \mathbf{s}(A)$.*
A typing $A; B; L \vdash_{\wedge_2}^{\mathrm{Let,Rec}} e : v$ is a principal typing *for e w.r.t. B and L if any other typing of e w.r.t. B and L is an instance of it. When $L = \emptyset$ we say that $A; B; \emptyset \vdash_{\wedge_2}^{\mathrm{Let,Rec}} : v$ is a* principal typing *for e w.r.t. B.*

Theorem 2 (Principal typing property for $\vdash_{\wedge_2}^{\mathrm{Let,Rec}}$). *If e is typable in $\vdash_{\wedge_2}^{\mathrm{Let,Rec}}$ w.r.t. B and L, then it has a principal typing w.r.t. B and L.*

6 The System $\vdash_{\wedge_2}^{\mathrm{If,Let,Rec}}$: Better Typings for if-Expressions

The rule (IFSIMPLE) of $\vdash_{\wedge_2}^{\mathrm{Rec}}$ and $\vdash_{\wedge_2}^{\mathrm{Let,Rec}}$ seems overly restrictive: it does not allow to assign rank 2 types to the branches of if-expressions. We may think to replace that rule by the following rule

$$(\textsc{IfStrong}) \ \frac{A; B; L \vdash e : \mathsf{bool} \quad A_1; B; L \vdash e_1 : v \quad A_2; B; L \vdash e_2 : v}{A + A_1 + A_2; B; L \vdash \mathsf{if}\, e \,\mathsf{then}\, e_1 \,\mathsf{else}\, e_2 : v}$$

which allows to assign a rank 2 type to the branches of an if-expression. However the resulting system, $\vdash_{\wedge_2}^{\mathrm{IfStrong}}$, does not have neither the principal typing property nor the principal type property, as the following example shows.

Example 3. Take the expressions $e_1 = \lambda f.f3$, $e_2 = \lambda g.\mathsf{prj}_1(g(\mathsf{pair}\,1\,4))$, and $e_0 = \mathsf{if}\, z \,\mathsf{then}\, e_1 \,\mathsf{else}\, e_2$. We have

- $\emptyset; \emptyset; \emptyset \vdash_{\wedge_2}^{\mathrm{Let,Rec}} e_1 : v_1$, *where* $v_1 = (\mathsf{int} \to \mathsf{int}) \to \mathsf{int}$, *and*
- $\emptyset; \emptyset; \emptyset \vdash_{\wedge_2}^{\mathrm{Let,Rec}} e_2 : v_2$, *where* $v_2 = ((\mathsf{int} \times \mathsf{int}) \to (\mathsf{int} \times \mathsf{int})) \to \mathsf{int}$,

but the expression e_0 cannot be typed by using $\vdash_{\wedge_2}^{\mathrm{Let,Rec}}$. Instead with system $\vdash_{\wedge_2}^{\mathrm{IfStrong}}$ we have: $\{z : \mathsf{bool}\}; \emptyset; \emptyset \vdash_{\wedge_2}^{\mathrm{IfStrong}} e_0 : v_0$, where $v_0 = ((\mathsf{int} \to \mathsf{int}) \wedge ((\mathsf{int} \times \mathsf{int}) \to (\mathsf{int} \times \mathsf{int}))) \to \mathsf{int}$ is the least upper bound of v_1 and v_2 w.r.t. $\leq_2$. Also the expressions $e_0' e_2$ and $e_0'' e_1 e_2$, where $e_0' = \lambda x.\mathsf{if}\ z\ \mathsf{then}\ e_1\ \mathsf{else}\ x$ and $e_0'' = \lambda x_1\, x_2.\mathsf{if}\ z\ \mathsf{then}\ x_1\ \mathsf{else}\ x_2$, are not typable by $\vdash_{\wedge_2}^{\mathrm{Let,Rec}}$ and typable by $\vdash_{\wedge_2}^{\mathrm{IfStrong}}$. For instance we have

- $\{z : \mathsf{bool}\}; \emptyset; \emptyset \vdash_{\wedge_2}^{\mathrm{IfStrong}} e_0' : v_0'$, where $v_0' = (\alpha \to \mathsf{int}) \to ((\mathsf{int} \to \mathsf{int}) \wedge \alpha) \to \mathsf{int}$ (and also $\{z : \mathsf{bool}\}; \emptyset; \emptyset \vdash_{\wedge_2}^{\mathrm{IfStrong}} e_0' : v_1 \to v_2 \to v_0$, so $\{z : \mathsf{bool}\}; \emptyset; \emptyset \vdash_{\wedge_2}^{\mathrm{IfStrong}} e_0' e_2 : v_0$), and
- $\{z : \mathsf{bool}\}; \emptyset; \emptyset \vdash_{\wedge_2}^{\mathrm{IfStrong}} e_0'' : v_1 \to v_2 \to v_0$, (so $\{x : \mathsf{bool}\}; \emptyset; \emptyset \vdash_{\wedge_2}^{\mathrm{IfStrong}} e_0''\, e_1\, e_2 : v_0$).

Note that in $\vdash_{\wedge_2}^{\mathrm{IfStrong}}$ there is no principal type for e_0'' (the "natural candidate" is $u = \alpha \to \alpha \to \alpha$, but there exists no substitution $\mathbf{s}$ such that $\mathbf{s}(u) \leq_2 v_1 \to v_2 \to v_0$). This problem is due to the fact that the rank 2 schemes cannot express the fact that, because of rules (SUB) and (IFSTRONG), a type v can be assigned to an if-expression $\mathsf{if}\ e\ \mathsf{then}\ e_1\ \mathsf{else}\ e_2$ if and only if it is the upper bound w.r.t. $\leq_2$ of a pair of types v_1 and v_2 that can be inferred for e_1 and e_2, respectively.

In order to preserve the principal typing property of $\vdash_{\wedge_2}^{\mathrm{Let,Rec}}$ we restrict rule (IFSTRONG) by limiting the use of intersection in the type assigned to the branches of an if-expression. The condition that we will use to restrict rule (IFSTRONG) is based on the notions of *$\wedge$-index and $\to$-index of a type* and of *index of an expression.*

Definition 6 ($\wedge$-index and $\to$-index of a type). *For every type $v \in \mathbf{T}_2$ the* $\wedge$-index of v, $\mathbf{Ind}^\wedge(v)$, *and the* $\to$-index of v, $\mathbf{Ind}^\to(v)$, *are the natural numbers defined in Fig. 4 (note that $\mathbf{Ind}^\wedge(v) \leq \mathbf{Ind}^\to(v)$).*

The fundamental properties of the metrics $\mathbf{Ind}^\wedge$ and $\mathbf{Ind}^\to$ are expressed by the following proposition[7].

Proposition 1. *1. If $\mathbf{Ind}^\wedge(v) = p$ and $\mathbf{Ind}^\to(v) = p + q$ ($p, q \geq 0$), then v is of the form $v = ui_1 \to \cdots \to ui_p \to u_1 \to \cdots \to u_q \to u$ for some $ui_1, \cdots, ui_p \in \mathbf{T}_1$, $u_1, \cdots, u_q, u \in \mathbf{T}_0$, $ui_p \notin \mathbf{T}_0$, and u not of the form $u' \to u''$.*
2. For every substitution $\mathbf{s}$, $\mathbf{Ind}^\wedge(v) \geq \mathbf{Ind}^\wedge(\mathbf{s}(v))$ and $\mathbf{Ind}^\to(v) \leq \mathbf{Ind}^\to(\mathbf{s}(v))$.
3. If $v \leq_2 v'$ then $\mathbf{Ind}^\wedge(v) \leq \mathbf{Ind}^\wedge(v')$ and $\mathbf{Ind}^\to(v) = \mathbf{Ind}^\to(v')$.

Definition 7 (Index of an expression). *An* index environment I *is an environment $\{x_1 : i_1, \ldots, x_n : i_n\}$ of natural number (index) assumptions for identifiers. For every expression e and index environment* I *such that* $\mathrm{FV}(e) \subseteq \mathrm{Dom}(\mathrm{I})$, *the* index of e in I, $\mathbf{Ind}(e, \mathrm{I})$, *is the natural number defined by the clauses in Fig. 5.*

[7] Remember that $\wedge$ is idempotent, so, for any $u \in \mathbf{T}_0$, the type $u \wedge u$ is considered to be an element of $\mathbf{T}_0$.

$\mathbf{Ind}^{\wedge}(u) = 0$, for $u \in \mathbf{T}_0$
$\mathbf{Ind}^{\wedge}(ui \to v) = 1 + \mathbf{Ind}^{\wedge}(v)$, for $ui \to v \in \mathbf{T}_1 - \mathbf{T}_0$

$\mathbf{Ind}^{\to}(\mathsf{unit}) = \mathbf{Ind}^{\to}(\mathsf{bool}) = \mathbf{Ind}^{\to}(\mathsf{int}) = \mathbf{Ind}^{\to}(u_1 \times u_2) = \mathbf{Ind}^{\to}(u\,\mathsf{list}) = 0$
$\mathbf{Ind}^{\to}(ui \to v) = 1 + \mathbf{Ind}^{\to}(v)$

Fig. 4. The functions $\mathbf{Ind}^{\wedge}(v)$ and $\mathbf{Ind}^{\to}(v)$

The fundamental property of the metric **Ind** is given by the following proposition (the proof is by structural induction on e, the only non-trivial case is the computation of the index of the auxiliary expressions $\mathsf{rec}_i\,\{x_1 = e_1, \ldots, x_n = e_n\}$).

Proposition 2. *If* $A; B; L \vdash_{\wedge_2}^{\mathrm{Let,Rec}} e : v$ *then* $\mathbf{Ind}(e, \{x : 0 \mid x \in \mathrm{FV}(e)\}) \leq \mathbf{Ind}^{\to}(v)$.

This implies that every $\vdash_{\wedge_2}^{\mathrm{Let,Rec}}$-typable expressions e has an index and, if $\mathbf{Ind}(e, \{x : 0 \mid x \in \mathrm{FV}(e)\}) = i$, then e is a function that can accept at least i arguments[8]. The indexes of the *open* subexpressions of a *closed* expression e are computed by associating index 0 to formal parameters of functions, and the index of the corresponding definition to locally defined identifiers. For instance: $\mathbf{Ind}(y, \{y : 0\}) = 0$, $\mathbf{Ind}(\lambda y.y, \emptyset) = 1$, and $\mathbf{Ind}(g, \{g : 1\}) = 1$, so $\mathbf{Ind}(\mathsf{let}\, g = (\lambda y.y)\,\mathsf{in}\, g, \emptyset) = 1$. For an example involving mutually recursive definitions, take the auxiliary expression $e = \mathsf{rec}_1\,\{x_1 = \lambda w.x_2(w+1),\ x_2 = \lambda yz.\mathsf{if}\,(y > z)\,\mathsf{then}\,1\,\mathsf{else}\,z * (x_1 yz)$. We have $\mathbf{Ind}(e, \emptyset) = 2$ (note that this requires two iterations of the while-loop in Fig. 5). We remark that the clauses in Fig. 5 are just a specification, and do not represent an efficient algorithm for computing the index of an expression.

The New Typing Rules. Let (IFNEW) be the restriction of rule (IFSTRONG) requiring that the rank 2 type, say v, assigned to the branches of an if-expression, $\mathsf{if}\ e\ \mathsf{then}\ e_1\ \mathsf{else}\ e_2$, must satisfy the condition

$$\mathbf{Ind}^{\wedge}(v) \leq \mathbf{Ind}(\mathsf{if}\ e\ \mathsf{then}\ e_1\ \mathsf{else}\ e_2, \{x : 0 \mid x \in \mathrm{FV}(\mathsf{if}\ e\ \mathsf{then}\ e_1\ \mathsf{else}\ e_2)\}).$$

By using rule (IFNEW) instead of (IFSIMPLE), it is possible to assign types v_0, v' and v_0 to the expressions e_0, e'_0 and $e'_0 e_2$ of Example 3, respectively. Instead, it is not possible to assign type $v_1 \to v_2 \to v_0$ to the expression e''_0, so the expression $e''_0\ e_1\ e_2$ cannot be typed.

In order to compute more accurate indexes for expressions involving free library and local identifiers we introduce indexed environments, which allow to store the indexes of library and local definitions.

[8] This does not hold for non-$\vdash_{\wedge_2}^{\mathrm{Let,Rec}}$-typable expressions (unless we restrict to expressions not containing conditionals). Take for instance $e = \lambda x\,.\mathsf{if}\ x\ \mathsf{then}\ 0\ \mathsf{else}\ \lambda y\,.y$. We have $\mathbf{Ind}(e, \emptyset) = 2$, but $e\ \mathsf{true}$ is not a function.

$$
\begin{aligned}
\mathbf{Ind}(c,\mathrm{I}) &= \mathbf{Ind}^{\rightarrow}(\mathrm{Typeof}(c))\\
\mathbf{Ind}(x,\mathrm{I}) &= i \text{ if } x : i \in \mathrm{I}\\
\mathbf{Ind}(\lambda x.e,\mathrm{I}) &= \mathbf{Ind}(e,\mathrm{I}\cup\{x:0\})+1\\
\mathbf{Ind}(e_1\,e_2,\mathrm{I}) &= \begin{cases} 0 & \text{if } \mathbf{Ind}(e_1,\mathrm{I})=0\\ \mathbf{Ind}(e_1,\mathrm{I})-1 & \text{if } \mathbf{Ind}(e_1,\mathrm{I})\geq 1\end{cases}\\
\mathbf{Ind}(\mathsf{if}\ e\ \mathsf{then}\ e_1\ \mathsf{else}\ e_2,\mathrm{I}) &= \mathrm{Max}(\mathbf{Ind}(e_1,\mathrm{I}),\mathbf{Ind}(e_2,\mathrm{I}))\\
\mathbf{Ind}(\mathsf{let}\, x = e_0 \ \mathsf{in}\ e,\mathrm{I}) &= \mathbf{Ind}(e,\mathrm{I}\cup\{x:\mathbf{Ind}(e_0,\mathrm{I})\})\\
\mathbf{Ind}(\mathsf{letrec}\,\{x_1\!=\!e_1,\ldots,x_n\!=\!e_n\}\ \mathsf{in}\ e,\mathrm{I}) &= \mathbf{Ind}(e,\mathrm{I}\cup\{x_1\!:\!\mathbf{Ind}(e_1',\mathrm{I}),\ldots,x_n\!:\!\mathbf{Ind}(e_n',\mathrm{I})\})\\
&\quad \text{where, for } i\in\{1,\ldots,n\},\ e_i' = \mathsf{rec}_i\,\{x_1=e_1,\ldots,x_n=e_n\}\\
\mathbf{Ind}(\mathsf{rec}_i\,\{x_1=e_1,\ldots,x_n=e_n\},\mathrm{I}) &= \text{begin}\\
&\quad (k_1,\ldots,k_n) := (0,\ldots,0);\\
&\quad (j_1,\ldots,j_n) := (\mathbf{Ind}(e_1,\mathrm{I}),\ldots,\mathbf{Ind}(e_n,\mathrm{I}));\\
&\quad \text{while } (j_1,\ldots,j_n)\neq(k_1,\ldots,k_n) \text{ do begin}\\
&\quad\quad (k_1,\ldots,k_n) := (j_1,\ldots,j_n);\\
&\quad\quad \mathrm{I}' := \mathrm{I}\cup\{x_1:j_1,\ldots,x_n:j_n\};\\
&\quad\quad (j_1,\ldots,j_n) :=\\
&\quad\quad (\mathbf{Ind}(e_1,\mathrm{I}'),\ldots,\mathbf{Ind}(e_n,\mathrm{I}')) \text{ end}\\
&\quad \text{return } j_i\\
&\quad \text{end}
\end{aligned}
$$

Fig. 5. The function $\mathbf{Ind}(e,\mathrm{I})$

Definition 8 (Indexed environments). *An indexed rank 2 scheme environment B is an environment $\{x_1 : (i_1, \forall\overrightarrow{\alpha}^1.v_1), \ldots, x_n : (i_n, \forall\overrightarrow{\alpha}^n.v_n)\}$ of index and closed rank 2 scheme assumptions for identifiers such that, for every $j \in \{1,\ldots,n\}$, $i_j \leq \mathbf{Ind}^{\rightarrow}(v_j)$.*
An indexed pair environment L is an environment $\{x_1 : (i_1, \forall\overrightarrow{\alpha}^1.\langle A_1, v_1\rangle), \ldots, x_n : (i_n, \forall\overrightarrow{\alpha}^n.\langle A_n, v_n\rangle)\}$ of index and pair scheme assumptions for identifiers such that, for every $j \in \{1,\ldots,n\}$, $i_j \leq \mathbf{Ind}^{\rightarrow}(v_j)$.

For every environment T containing rank 1, indexed rank 2, and indexed pair assumptions define $\mathbf{Ind}(T) = \{x : 0 \mid x : ui \in T\} \cup \{x : i \mid x : (i,v) \in T\} \cup \{x : i \mid x : (i,p) \in T\}$. Let $\vdash^{\mathrm{If,Let,Rec}}_{\wedge_2}$ be the extension of $\vdash^{\mathrm{Let,Rec}}_{\wedge_2}$ which uses (in the typing judgements of Fig. 3) library indexed environments and local indexed environments, uses (see Fig. 6) rule (IFNEW′) instead of (IFSIMPLE) and rules (LETNEW′), (ID_2'), and (ID_3') instead of the corresponding rules of $\vdash^{\mathrm{Let,Rec}}_{\wedge_2}$. Rule (LETNEW′) computes and stores the indexes of local definitions in the local environment in order to allow to compute more accurate indexes, while rules (ID_2') and (ID_3') simply ignore the indexes and behave as the corresponding rules of $\vdash^{\mathrm{Let,Rec}}_{\wedge_2}$. Rephrase of Proposition 2 holds also for system $\vdash^{\mathrm{If,Let,Rec}}_{\wedge_2}$.

Proposition 3. *If $A; B; L \vdash^{\mathrm{If,Let,Rec}}_{\wedge_2} e : v$ then $\mathbf{Ind}(e, \mathbf{Ind}(A \cup B \cup L)) \leq \mathbf{Ind}^{\rightarrow}(v)$.*

This guarantees that the indexes required in rules (IFNEW′) and (LETNEW′) in Fig. 6 (which involve only typable expressions) are always defined.

$$(\textsc{IfNew}')\ \frac{A;B;L\vdash e:\mathsf{bool}\quad A_1;B;L\vdash e_1:v\quad A_2;B;L\vdash e_2:v\quad \mathbf{Ind}^\wedge(v)\le\mathbf{Ind}(\mathsf{if}\ e\ \mathsf{then}\ e_1\ \mathsf{else}\ e_2,\mathbf{Ind}((A+A_1+A_2)\cup B\cup L))}{A+A_1+A_2;B;L\vdash \mathsf{if}\ e\ \mathsf{then}\ e_1\ \mathsf{else}\ e_2:v}$$

$$(\textsc{LetNew}')\ \frac{A_0;B;L\vdash e_0:v_0\quad A;B;L,x:(i_0,\forall\overrightarrow{\alpha}.\langle A_0,v_0\rangle)\vdash e:v}{A;B;L\vdash \mathsf{let}\ x=e_0\ \mathsf{in}\ e:v}\ x\in\mathrm{FV}(e)$$

where $i_0=\mathbf{Ind}(e_0,\mathbf{Ind}(A_0\cup B\cup L))$ and $\{\overrightarrow{\alpha}\}=\mathrm{FTV}(A_0)\cup\mathrm{FTV}(v_0)$

$(\textsc{Id}_2')\ \emptyset;B,x:(i,\forall\overrightarrow{\alpha}.v);L\vdash x:\mathbf{s}_{\{\overrightarrow{\alpha}\}}(v)$ where $(\mathrm{Dom}(B)\cup\{x\})\cap\mathrm{Dom}(L)=\emptyset$

$(\textsc{Id}_3')\ \mathbf{s}_{\{\overrightarrow{\alpha}\}}(A);B;L,x:(i,\forall\overrightarrow{\alpha}.\langle A,v\rangle)\vdash x:\mathbf{s}\{\overrightarrow{\alpha}\}(v)$ where $\mathrm{Dom}(B)\cap(\mathrm{Dom}(L)\cup\{x\})=\emptyset$

Fig. 6. Typing rules for if-expressions and indexes manipulation (system $\vdash^{\mathrm{If,Let,Rec}}_{\wedge_2}$)

Principal Typings and Type Inference for $\vdash^{\mathrm{If,Let,Rec}}_{\wedge_2}$. Principal typings w.r.t. a library environment B and a local environment L are defined as for $\vdash^{\mathrm{Let,Rec}}_{\wedge_2}$ (see Definition 5). The following result holds.

Theorem 3 (Principal typing property for $\vdash^{\mathrm{If,Let,Rec}}_{\wedge_2}$). *If e is typable in $\vdash^{\mathrm{If,Let,Rec}}_{\wedge_2}$ w.r.t. B and L, then it has a principal typing w.r.t. B and L.*

System $\vdash^{\mathrm{If,Let,Rec}}_{\wedge_2}$ admits a complete inference algorithm (not included in this paper) that, for any expression e, library environment B, and local environment L such that $\mathrm{Dom}(B)\cap\mathrm{Dom}(L)=\emptyset$, computes a principal typing for e w.r.t. B and L.

Acknowledgements. I thank Mario Coppo, Paola Giannini, and the referees of earlier versions on this paper, for suggestions to improve the presentation.

References

1. S. Aditya and R. Nikhil. Incremental polymorphism. In *POPL'93*, LNCS 523, pages 379–405. Springer–Verlag, 1991.
2. M. Coppo and P. Giannini. Principal Types and Unification for Simple Intersection Types Systems. *Information and Computation*, 122(1):70–96, 1995.
3. L. M. M. Damas and R. Milner. Principal type schemas for functional programs. In *POPL'82*, pages 207–212. ACM, 1982.
4. F. Damiani and P. Giannini. A Decidable Intersection Type System based on Relevance. In *TACS'94*, LNCS 789, pages 707–725. Springer–Verlag, 1994.
5. R. Hindley. *Basic Simple Type Theory.* Number 42 in Cambridge Tracts in Theoretical Computer Science. Cambridge University Press, London, 1997.
6. T. Jim. Rank 2 type systems and recursive definitions. Technical Report MIT/LCS/TM-531, LCS, Massachusetts Institute of Technology, 1995.
7. T. Jim. What are principal typings and what are they good for? In *POPL'96*, pages 42–53. ACM, 1996.

8. A. J. Kfoury and J. B. Wells. A direct algorithm for type inference in the rank-2 fragment of the second-order lambda -calculus. In *LISP and Functional Programming '94*. ACM, 1994.
9. A. J. Kfoury and J. B. Wells. Principality and Decidable Type Inference for Finite-Rank Intersection Types. In *POPL'99*. ACM, 1999.
10. D. Leivant. Polymorphic Type Inference. In *POPL'83*. ACM, 1983.
11. R. Milner, M. Tofte, R. Harper, and D. MacQueen. *The Definition of Standard ML - Revised.* MIT press, 1997.
12. A. Mycroft. Polymorphic Type Schemes and Recursive Definitions. In *International Symposium on Programming*, LNCS 167, pages 217–228. Springer–Verlag, 1984.
13. Z. Shao and A. W. Appel. Smartest recompilation. In *POPL'93*, pages 439–450. ACM, 1993.
14. S. van Bakel. *Intersection Type Disciplines in Lambda Calculus and Applicative Term Rewriting Systems.* PhD thesis, Katholieke Universiteit Nijmegen, 1993.
15. H. Yokouchi. Embedding a Second-Order Type System into an Intersection Type System. *Information and Computation*, 117:206–220, 1995.

Hierarchical Graph Transformation*

Frank Drewes[1], Berthold Hoffmann[1], and Detlef Plump[2]**

[1] Fachbereich Mathematik/Informatik, Universität Bremen
Postfach 33 04 40, D-28334 Bremen, Germany
{drewes, hof}@informatik.uni-bremen.de

[2] Department of Computing and Electrical Engineering
Heriot-Watt University, Edinburgh EH14 4AS, Scotland
det@cee.hw.ac.uk

Abstract. We present an approach for the rule-based transformation of hierarchically structured (hyper)graphs. In these graphs, distinguished hyperedges contain graphs that can be hierarchical again. Our framework extends the double-pushout approach from flat to hierarchical graphs. In particular, we show how to construct recursively pushouts and pushout complements of hierarchical graphs and graph morphisms. To further enhance the expressiveness of the approach, we also introduce rule schemata with variables which allow to copy and to remove hierarchical subgraphs.

1 Introduction

Recently, the idea of using rule-based graph transformation as a framework for specification and programming has received some attention, and several researchers have proposed structuring mechanisms for graph transformation systems to make progress towards this goal (see for example [2, 8, 10]). Structuring mechanisms will be indispensable to manage large numbers of rules and to develop complex systems from small components that are easy to comprehend. Moreover, we believe that it will be necessary to structure the graphs that are subject to transformation, too, in order to cope with applications of a realistic size. A mechanism for hiding (or abstracting from) subgraphs in large graphs will facilitate both the control of rule applications and the visualization of graphs.

In this paper we introduce hierarchical hypergraphs in which certain hyperedges, called frames, contain hypergraphs that can be hierarchical again, with an arbitrary depth of nesting. We show that the well-known double-pushout approach to graph transformation [5, 3] extends smoothly to these hierarchical (hyper)graphs, by giving recursive constructions for pushouts and pushout complements in the category of hierarchical graphs. Hierarchical transformation rules consist of hierarchical graphs and can be applied at all levels of the hierarchy, where the "dangling condition" known from the transformation of flat graphs is adapted in a natural way.

* This work has been partially supported by the ESPRIT Working Group *Applications of Graph Transformation* (APPLIGRAPH) and by the TMR Research Network GETGRATS through the University of Bremen.

** On leave from Universität Bremen.

J. Tiuryn (Ed.): FOSSACS 2000, LNCS 1784, pp. 98–113, 2000.

To further enhance the expressiveness of hierarchical graph transformation for programming purposes (without damaging the theory), we also introduce rule schemata containing frame variables. These variables can be instantiated with frames containing hierarchical graphs, and can be used to copy or remove frames without looking at their contents. Our running example of a queue implementation indicates that this concept is useful, as it allows to delete and to duplicate queue entries regardless of their structure and size.

Finally, we relate hierarchical graph transformation to the conventional transformation of flat graphs by introducing a flattening operation. Flattening recursively replaces each frame in a hierarchical graph by its contents, yielding a flat graph without frames. Every transformation step on hierarchical graphs—under a mild assumption on the transformed graph—gives rise to a conventional step on the flattened graphs by using the flattened rule.

2 Graph Transformation

If S is a set, the set of all finite sequences over S, including the empty sequence λ, is denoted by S^*. The ith element of a sequence s is denoted by $s(i)$, and its length by $|s|$. If $f\colon S \to T$ is a function then the canonical extensions of f to the powerset of S and to S^* are also denoted by f. The composition $g \circ f$ of functions $f\colon S \to T$ and $g\colon T \to U$ is defined by $(g \circ f)(s) = g(f(s))$ for $s \in S$.

A *pushout* in a category $\mathbb{C}$ (see, e.g., [1]) is a tuple (m_1, m_2, n_1, n_2) of morphisms $m_i\colon O \to O_i$ and $n_i\colon O_i \to O'$ with $n_1 \circ m_1 = n_2 \circ m_2$, such that for all morphisms $n'_i\colon O_i \to P$ $(i \in \{1,2\})$ with $n'_1 \circ m_1 = n'_2 \circ m_2$ there is a unique morphism $n\colon O' \to P$ satisfying $n \circ n_1 = n'_1$ and $n \circ n_2 = n'_2$.

Let L be an arbitrary but fixed set of labels. A *hypergraph* H is a quintuple $(V_H, E_H, att_H, lab_H, p_H)$ such that

- V_H and E_H are finite sets of *nodes* and *hyperedges*, respectively,
- $att_H\colon E_H \to V_H^*$ is the *attachment function*,
- $lab_H\colon E_H \to L$ is the *labelling function*, and
- $p_H \in V_H^*$ is a sequence of nodes, called the *points* of H.

In the following, we will simply say *graph* instead of hypergraph and *edge* instead of hyperedge. We denote by A_H the set $V_H \cup E_H$ of *atoms* of H. In order to make this a useful notation, we shall always assume without loss of generality that V_H and E_H are disjoint, for every graph H.

A *morphism* $m\colon G \to H$ between graphs G and H is a pair (m_V, m_E) of mappings $m_V\colon V_G \to V_H$ and $m_E\colon E_G \to E_H$ such that $m_V(p_G) = p_H$ and, for all $e \in E_G$, $lab_H(m_E(e)) = lab_G(e)$ and $att_H(m_E(e)) = m_V(att_G(e))$. Such a morphism is *injective* (*surjective*, *bijective*) if both m_V and m_E are injective (respectively surjective or bijective). If there is a bijective morphism $m\colon G \to H$ then G and H are *isomorphic*, which is denoted by $G \cong H$. For a morphism $m\colon G \to H$ and $a \in A_G$ we let $m(a)$ denote $m_V(a)$ if $a \in V_G$ and $m_E(a)$ if $a \in E_G$. The composition of morphisms is defined componentwise.

For graphs G and H such that $A_G \cap A_H = \emptyset$, the *disjoint union* $G+H$ yields the graph $(V_G \cup V_H, E_G \cup E_H, att, lab, p_G)$, where

$$att(e) = \begin{cases} att_G(e) \text{ if } e \in E_G \\ att_H(e) \text{ otherwise} \end{cases} \quad \text{and} \quad lab(e) = \begin{cases} lab_G(e) \text{ if } e \in E_G \\ lab_H(e) \text{ otherwise} \end{cases}$$

for all edges $e \in E_G \cup E_H$. (If $A_G \cap A_H \neq \emptyset$, we assume that some implicit renaming of atoms takes place.) Notice that this operation is associative but does *not* commute since $G + H$ inherits its points from the first argument.

We recall the following well-known facts about pushouts and pushout complements in the category of graphs and graph morphisms (see [5]). Let $m_1\colon G \to H_1$ and $m_2\colon G \to H_2$ be morphisms. Then there is a graph H and there are morphisms $n_1\colon H_1 \to H$ and $n_2\colon H_2 \to H$ such that (m_1, m_2, n_1, n_2) is a pushout. Furthermore, H and the n_i are determined as follows. Let H' be the disjoint union of H_1 and H_2, and let $\sim$ be the equivalence relation on $A_{H'}$ generated by the set of all pairs $(m_1(a), m_2(a))$ such that $a \in A_G$. Then H is the graph obtained from H' by identifying all atoms a, a' such that $a \sim a'$ (i.e., H is the quotiont graph $H'/{\sim}$). Moreover, for $i \in \{1, 2\}$ and $a \in A_{H_i}$, $n_i(a) = [a]_\sim$, where $[a]_\sim$ denotes the equivalence class of a according to $\sim$.

In order to ensure the existence and uniqueness of pushout complements (i.e., the existence and uniqueness of m_2 and n_2 if m_1 and n_1 are given), additional conditions must be satisfied. Below, we only need the case where both of the given morphisms are injective. In this case it is sufficient to assume that the *dangling condition* is satisfied. Two morphisms $m_1\colon G \to H_1$ and $n_1\colon H_1 \to H$ satisfy the dangling condition if no edge $e \in E_H \setminus n_1(E_{H_1})$ is attached to a node in $n_1(V_{H_1}) \setminus n_1(m_1(V_G))$. It is well-known that, if m_1 and n_1 are injective, then there are m_2 and n_2 such that (m_1, m_2, n_1, n_2) is a pushout, if and only if m_1 and n_1 satisfy the dangling condition. Furthermore, if they exist, then m_2 and n_2 are uniquely determined (up to isomorphism).

A *transformation rule* (*rule*, for short) is a pair $t\colon L \overset{l}{\leftarrow} I \overset{r}{\rightarrow} R$ of morphisms $l\colon I \to L$ and $r\colon I \to R$ such that l is injective. L, I, and R are the *left-hand side*, *interface*, and *right-hand side* of t. A graph G can be transformed into a graph H by an application of t, denoted by $G \Rightarrow_t H$, if there is an injective morphism $o\colon L \to G$, called an occurrence morphism, such that two pushouts

$$\begin{array}{ccccc} L & \xleftarrow{\;l\;} & I & \xrightarrow{\;r\;} & R \\ {\scriptstyle o}\downarrow & & \downarrow & & \downarrow \\ G & \longleftarrow & K & \longrightarrow & H \end{array}$$

exist. It follows from the facts about pushouts and pushout complements recalled above that such a diagram exists if and only if l and o satisfy the dangling condition, and in this case H is uniquely determined up to isomorphism. Notice that we only consider injective occurrence morphisms, which is done in order to avoid additional difficulties when considering the hierarchical case. On the other hand, the morphism r of a rule $t\colon L \overset{l}{\leftarrow} I \overset{r}{\rightarrow} R$ is allowed to be non-injective.

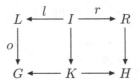

3 Hierarchical Graphs

Graphs as defined in the previous section are flat. If someone wished to implement, say, some complicated abstract data type by means of graph transformation, there would be no structuring mechanisms available, except for the possibilities the graphs themselves provide. Thus, any structural information would have to be coded into the graphs, a solution which is usually inappropriate and error-prone. To overcome this limitation, we introduce graphs with an arbitrarily deep hierarchical structure. This is achieved by means of special edges, called frames, which may contain hierarchical graphs again. In fact, it turns out to be useful to be even more general by allowing some frames to contain variables instead of graphs. These structures will be called hierarchical graphs.

Let $\mathcal{X}$ be a set of symbols called *variables*. The class $\mathcal{H}(\mathcal{X})$ of *hierarchical graphs with variables in* $\mathcal{X}$ consists of triples $H = \langle G, F, cts \rangle$ such that G is a graph (the root of the hierarchy), $F \subseteq E_G$ is the set of *frame edges* (or just *frames*), and $cts\colon F \to \mathcal{H}(\mathcal{X}) \cup \mathcal{X}$ assigns to each frame $f \in F$ its *contents* $cts(f) \in \mathcal{H}(\mathcal{X}) \cup \mathcal{X}$. Formally, $\mathcal{H}(\mathcal{X})$ is defined inductively over the depth of frame nesting, as follows. A triple $H = \langle G, F, cts \rangle$ as above is in $\mathcal{H}_0(\mathcal{X})$ if $F = \emptyset$. In this case, H may be identified with the graph G. For $i > 0$, $H \in \mathcal{H}_i(\mathcal{X})$ if $cts(f) \in \mathcal{H}_{i-1}(\mathcal{X}) \cup \mathcal{X}$ for every frame $f \in F$. Finally, $\mathcal{H}(\mathcal{X})$ denotes the union of all these classes: $\mathcal{H}(\mathcal{X}) = \bigcup_{i \geq 0} \mathcal{H}_i(\mathcal{X})$. (Notice that $\mathcal{H}_i(\mathcal{X}) \subseteq \mathcal{H}_{i+1}(\mathcal{X})$ for all $i \geq 0$. We have $\mathcal{H}_0(\mathcal{X}) \subseteq \mathcal{H}_1(\mathcal{X})$ because an empty set of frames trivially satisfies the requirement; using this, $\mathcal{H}_i(\mathcal{X}) \subseteq \mathcal{H}_{i+1}(\mathcal{X})$ follows by an obvious induction on $i \geq 0$.) The sets $\mathcal{H}(\emptyset)$ and $H_i(\emptyset)$ ($i \geq 0$) are briefly denoted by $\mathcal{H}$ and $\mathcal{H}_i$, respectively. These *variable-free* hierarchical graphs are those in which we are mainly interested.

Notice that, to avoid unnecessary restrictions, the definition of a hierarchical graph $H = \langle G, F, cts \rangle$ does not impose any relation between the nodes and edges of G and those of $cts(f)$, $f \in F$. Restrictions of this kind may be added for specific application areas, but the results of this paper hold in general.

Example 1 (Queue graphs). As a running example, we show how queues and their typical operations can be implemented using hierarchical graph transformation. Two kinds of frames are used to represent queues as hierarchical graphs: Unary *item frames* contain the graphs stored in the queue; binary *queue frames* contain a *queue graph*, which is a chain of edges connecting their *begin* point to their *end* point, every node in between carrying an item frame.

Figure 1 shows two queue frames. Nodes are drawn as circles, and filled if

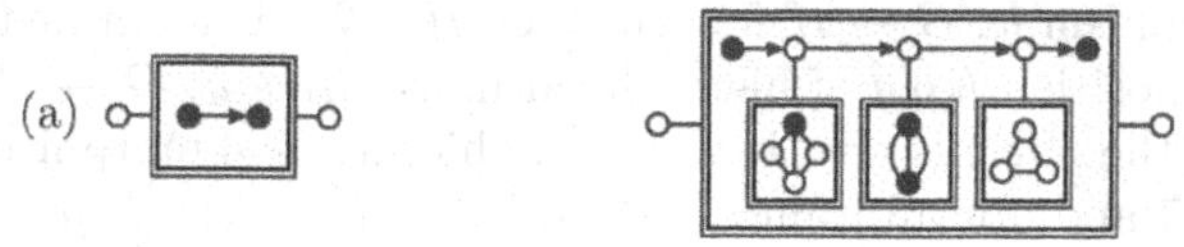

Fig. 1. Two queue frames representing (a) an empty queue (b) a queue of length 3

they are points. Edges are drawn as boxes, and connected to their attachments by lines that are ordered counter-clockwise, starting at noon. Frames have double lines, and their contents is drawn inside.Plain binary edges are drawn as arrows from their first to their second attachment (as in simple graphs). In our examples, their labels do not matter, and are omitted. (In the item graphs, the arrowheads are omitted too.) Frame labels are not drawn either, as queue and item frames can be distinguished by their arity.

Note that item frames may contain graphs of any arity; in Figure 1 (b), they have 1, 2, and no points, respectively.

Unless they are explicitly named, the three components of a hierarchical graph H are denoted by $\overline{H}$, F_H, and cts_H, respectively. The notations V_H, E_H, att_H, lab_H, p_H, and A_H are used as abbreviations denoting $V_{\overline{H}}$, $E_{\overline{H}}$, $att_{\overline{H}}$, $lab_{\overline{H}}$, $p_{\overline{H}}$, and $A_{\overline{H}}$, respectively. Furthermore, we denote by X_H the set $\{f \in F_H \mid cts_H(f) \in \mathcal{X}\}$ of *variable frames* of H and by

$$var(H) = cts_H(X_H) \cup \bigcup_{f \in F_H \setminus X_H} var(cts_H(f))$$

the set of variables occurring in H.

Let G and H be hierarchical graphs such that $A_G \cap A_H = \emptyset$. The *disjoint union* of G and H is denoted by $G + H$ and yields the hierarchical graph K such that $\overline{K} = \overline{G} + \overline{H}$, $F_K = F_G \cup F_H$, and $cts_K(f)$ equals $cts_G(f)$ if $f \in F_G$ and $cts_H(f)$ if $f \in F_H$. For a hierarchical graph G and a set $S = \{H_1, \ldots, H_n\}$ of hierarchical graphs, we denote $G + H_1 + \cdots + H_n$ by $G + \sum_{H \in S} H$. (Notice that, although the disjoint union of hierarchical graphs does not commute, this is well defined as it does not depend on the order of $H_1, \ldots, H_n$).

We will now generalize the concept of morphisms to the hierarchical case. The definition is quite straightforward. Such a hierarchical morphism $h\colon G \to H$ consists of an ordinary morphism on the topmost level and, recursively, hierarchical morphisms from the contents of non-variable frames to the contents of their images. Naturally, only variable frames can be mapped to variable frames, but they can also be mapped to any other frame carrying the right label.

Formally, let $G, H \in \mathcal{H}(\mathcal{X})$. A *hierarchical morphism* $h\colon G \to H$ is a pair $h = \langle \overline{h}, (h^f)_{f \in F_G \setminus X_G} \rangle$ where

- $\overline{h}\colon \overline{G} \to \overline{H}$ is a morphism,
- $\overline{h}(f) \in F_H$ for all frames $f \in F_G$, where $\overline{h}(f) \in X_H$ implies $f \in X_G$, and
- $h^f\colon cts_G(f) \to cts_H(\overline{h}(f))$ is a hierarchical morphism for every $f \in F_G \setminus X_G$.

For atoms $a \in A_G$, we usually write $h(a)$ instead of $\overline{h}(a)$. Furthermore, a hierarchical morphism $h\colon G \to H$ for which $G, H \in \mathcal{H}_0$ is identified with $\overline{h}$.

The composition $h \circ g$ of hierarchical morphisms $g\colon G \to H$ and $h\colon H \to L$ is defined in the obvious way. It yields the hierarchical morphism $l\colon G \to L$ such that $\overline{l} = \overline{h} \circ \overline{g}$ and, for all frames $f \in F_G \setminus X_G$, $l^f = h^{g(f)} \circ g^f$. The hierarchical morphism g is *injective* if $\overline{g}$ is injective and, for all $f \in F_G \setminus X_G$, g^f is injective. It is *surjective up to variables* if $\overline{g}$ is surjective and, for all $f \in F_G \setminus X_G$, g^f is surjective up to variables. Finally, g is *bijective up to variables* if it is surjective up to variables and injective. If G does not contain variables, we speak of surjective and bijective hierarchical morphisms. A bijective hierarchical morphism is also called an *isomorphism*, and $G, H \in \mathcal{H}$ are said to be *isomorphic*, $G \cong H$, if there is an isomorphism $m: G \to H$.

Let $\mathbb{H}$ be the category whose objects are variable-free hierarchical graphs and whose morphisms are the hierarchical morphisms $h: G \to H$ with $G, H \in \mathcal{H}$ (which is indeed a category, as one can easily verify). The main result we are going to establish in order to obtain a notion of hierarchical graph transformation is that $\mathbb{H}$ has pushouts. For this, looking at the inductive definition of hierarchical graphs and their morphisms, it is a rather obvious idea to proceed by induction on the depth of the frame nesting. The induction basis is then provided by the non-hierarchical case recalled in Section 2. In order to use the induction hypothesis, we have to reduce the depth of a hierarchical graph in some way. This can be done on the basis of a rather simple construction. Given a hierarchical graph $H \in \mathcal{H}_i$, we take the contents of its frames out of these frames (which, thereby, become ordinary edges) and add them disjointly to $\overline{H}$, thus obtaining a hierarchical graph in $\mathcal{H}_{i-1}$ (provided that $i > 0$). Denoting this mapping by φ, we get the desired theorem, which is the main result of this section. It states that the category $\mathbb{H}$ has pushouts, and the proof shows how to construct them effectively.

Theorem 1. *For every pair $m_1: G \to H_1$ and $m_2: G \to H_2$ of morphisms in $\mathbb{H}$ there are morphisms $n_1: H_1 \to H$ and $n_2: H_2 \to H$ in $\mathbb{H}$ (for some hierarchical graph H) such that (m_1, m_2, n_1, n_2) is a pushout. Furthermore, $(\overline{m_1}, \overline{m_2}, \overline{n_1}, \overline{n_2})$ is a pushout in the category of graphs.*

Proof sketch. The proof works by induction on i, where $H_1, H_2 \in \mathcal{H}_i$. The case $i = 0$ is the non-hierarchical one, and it is easy to see that every pushout in the category of non-hierarchical graphs and morphisms is a pushout in $\mathbb{H}$ as well. Thus, let $i > 0$. Extending φ to morphisms in the canonical way, one obtains $\varphi(m_1) = (m_1': G' \to H_1')$ and $\varphi(m_2) = (m_2': G' \to H_2')$ where $H_1', H_2' \in \mathcal{H}_{i-1}$. By the induction hypothesis, this yields a pushout (m_1', m_2', n_1', n_2') for some $n_j': H_j' \to H'$ $(j \in \{1, 2\})$. Now, it can be shown that $n_j' = \varphi(n_j)$ for hierarchical morphisms $n_j: H_j \to H$, yielding a commuting square (m_1, m_2, n_1, n_2). Intuitively, the parts of H' which stem from the contents of a frame f in H_j can be stored in $n_j'(f)$, turning this edge into a frame of the hierarchical graph H constructed. The main part of the proof is to show that H and the hierarchical morphisms n_j obtained in this way are well defined.

Finally, one has to verify the universal pushout property of (m_1, m_2, n_1, n_2). Let $l_1: H_1 \to L$ and $l_2: H_2 \to L$ be such that (m_1, m_2, l_1, l_2) commutes and let $\varphi(l_j) = (l_j': H' \to L')$ for $j \in \{1, 2\}$. Then (m_1', m_2', l_1', l_2') commutes as well. Therefore, the pushout property of (m_1', m_2', n_1', n_2') yields a unique morphism $l': H' \to L'$ such that $l_j' = l' \circ n_j'$. Again, l' can be turned into $l: H \to L$ with $l' = \varphi(l)$ and $l_j = l \circ n_j$ for $j \in \{1, 2\}$. Furthermore, for $k: H \to L$ with $k \neq l$ we have $\varphi(k) \neq \varphi(l)$, which shows that l is unique, by the uniqueness of l'. □

Notice that the proof of Theorem 1 yields a recursive procedure to construct pushouts in $\mathbb{H}$, based on the construction of pushouts in the case of ordinary graph morphisms.

The construction in the proof of the theorem yields a corollary for the special case where m_1 and m_2 are injective. Obviously, in this case the hierarchical morphisms m'_1 and m'_2 in the proof are also injective. As a consequence, it follows that $(m_1^f, m_2^f, n_1^{m_1(f)}, n_2^{m_2(f)})$ is a pushout for every frame $f \in F_G$. This yields the following specialization of Theorem 1.

Corollary 1. *Let $m_1: G \to H_1$ and $m_2: G \to H_2$ be injective hierarchical morphisms in $\mathbb{H}$. Then, one can construct hierarchical morphisms $n_1: H_1 \to H$ and $n_2: H_2 \to H$ such that (m_1, m_2, n_1, n_2) is a pushout, as follows:*

- *$\overline{n_1}$ and $\overline{n_2}$ are such that $(\overline{m_1}, \overline{m_2}, \overline{n_1}, \overline{n_2})$ is a pushout,*
- *for every frame $f \in F_G$, $n_1^{m_1(f)}$ and $n_2^{m_2(f)}$ are constructed recursively in such a way that $(m_1^f, m_2^f, n_1^{m_1(f)}, n_2^{m_2(f)})$ is a pushout, and*
- *for every frame $f \in F_{H_i} \setminus m_i(F_G)$ $(i \in \{1,2\})$, n_i^f is an isomorphism.*

Next, we shall see how pushout complements can be obtained. For simplicity, we consider only the case where the two given hierarchical morphisms are *both* injective. This enables us to make use of Corollary 1 in an easy way, whereas the more general case would be unreasonably complicated as it required a hierarchical version of the so-called identification condition [5].

Clearly, in order to ensure the existence of pushout complements, a hierarchical version of the dangling condition must be satisfied. However, for the hierarchical case it must also be required that, intuitively, no frame is deleted unless its contents is deleted as well. Let $H_1 \in \mathcal{H}(\mathcal{X})$ and $G, H \in \mathcal{H}$ (right below, we shall only use the following definition for $H_1 \in \mathcal{H}$, but later on the more general case $H_1 \in \mathcal{H}(\mathcal{X})$ will turn out to be valuable, too). Two hierarchical morphisms $m: I \to L$ and $n: L \to G$ satisfy the *hierarchical dangling condition* (*dangling condition*, for short) if

- $\overline{m}$ and $\overline{n}$ satisfy the (non-hierarchical) dangling condition,
- for every frame $f \in F_L \setminus (m(F_I) \cup X_L)$, n^f is bijective up to variables, and
- for every frame $f \in F_I \setminus X_I$, m^f and $n^{m(f)}$ satisfy the dangling condition.

Notice that this condition coincides with the usual one in the special case where m and n are ordinary graph morphisms, because in this case only the first requirement is relevant as there are no frames. Intuitively, the second part of the condition states that, as mentioned above, a frame can be deleted only if its contents is deleted as well (at least in the case where $L \in \mathcal{H}$; the more general case is not yet our concern). As the proof below shows, this corresponds to the last item in Corollary 1 (and is thus indeed necessary).

Theorem 2. *Let $m_1: G \to H_1$ and $n_1: H_1 \to H$ be injective hierarchical morphisms in $\mathbb{H}$. Then there are hierarchical morphisms $m_2: G \to H_2$ and $n_2: H_2 \to H$ such that (m_1, m_2, n_1, n_2) is a pushout, if and only if m_1 and n_1 satisfy the dangling condition. In this case m_2 and n_2 are uniquely determined.*

Proof. Let $G \in \mathcal{H}_i$. Again, we proceed by induction on i. Clearly, if m_2 and n_2 exist, then m_2 must be injective since $n_1 \circ m_1 = n_2 \circ m_2$ is injective. By Corollary 1 this means that m_2 and n_2 exist if and only if they can be constructed in such a way that the following are satisfied:

(1) $\overline{m_2}$ and $\overline{n_2}$ are such that $(\overline{m_1}, \overline{m_2}, \overline{n_1}, \overline{n_2})$ is a pushout,
(2) for every frame $f \in F_G$, the hierarchical morphisms m_2^f and $n_2^{m_2(f)}$ are constructed recursively, so that $(m_1^f, m_2^f, n_1^{m_1(f)}, n_2^{m_2(f)})$ is a pushout, and
(3) for every frame $f \in F_{H_i} \setminus m_i(F_G)$ ($i \in \{1,2\}$), n_i^f is an isomorphism.

As m_1 and n_1 satisfy the dangling condition, $\overline{m_2}$ and $\overline{n_2}$ exist and are uniquely determined (since $\overline{m_1}$ and $\overline{n_1}$ satisfy the dangling condition for non-hierarchical morphisms), and (3) is satisfied for $i = 1$ (because of the second part of the dangling condition). Furthermore, the induction hypothesis yields the required hierarchical morphisms m_2^f and $n_2^{m_2(f)}$ satisfying (2), for every frame $f \in F_G$. Together with the remaining requirement in (3) (i.e., the case where $i = 2$) this determines m_2 and n_2 up to isomorphism, thus finishing the proof. □

4 Hierarchical Graph Transformation

Based on the results presented in the previous section we are now able to define rules and their application in the style of the double-pushout approach. From now on, a *rule* $t\colon L \overset{l}{\leftarrow} I \overset{r}{\rightarrow} R$ is assumed to consist of two hierarchical morphisms $l\colon I \to L$ and $r\colon I \to R$, where $L, I, R \in \mathcal{H}$ and l is injective. The hierarchical graphs L, I, and R are called the *left-hand side*, *interface*, and *right-hand side*.

The application of rules is defined by means of the usual double-pushout construction, with one essential difference. In order to make sure that transformations can take place on an arbitrary level in the hierarchy of frames (rather than only on top level) one has to employ recursion.

Definition 1 (*Transformation of hierarchical graphs*). Let $t\colon L \overset{l}{\leftarrow} I \overset{r}{\rightarrow} R$ be a rule. A hierarchical graph $G \in \mathcal{H}$ is transformed into a hierarchical graph $H \in \mathcal{H}$ by means of t, denoted by $G \Rightarrow_t H$, if one of the following holds:

(1) There is an injective hierarchical morphism $o\colon L \to G$, called an *occurrence morphism*, such that there are two pushouts

$$\begin{array}{ccccc} L & \xleftarrow{\;l\;} & I & \xrightarrow{\;r\;} & R \\ {\scriptstyle o}\downarrow & & \downarrow & & \downarrow \\ G & \longleftarrow & K & \longrightarrow & H \end{array}$$

in $\mathbb{H}$, or
(2) $\overline{H} \cong \overline{G}$ via some isomorphism $m\colon \overline{G} \to \overline{H}$, and there is a frame $f \in F_G$ such that $cts_G(f) \Rightarrow_t cts_H(m(f))$ and $cts_H(m(f')) \cong cts_G(f')$ for all $f' \in F_G \setminus \{f\}$.

For a set T of rules, we write $G \Rightarrow_T H$ if $G \Rightarrow_t H$ for some $t \in T$.

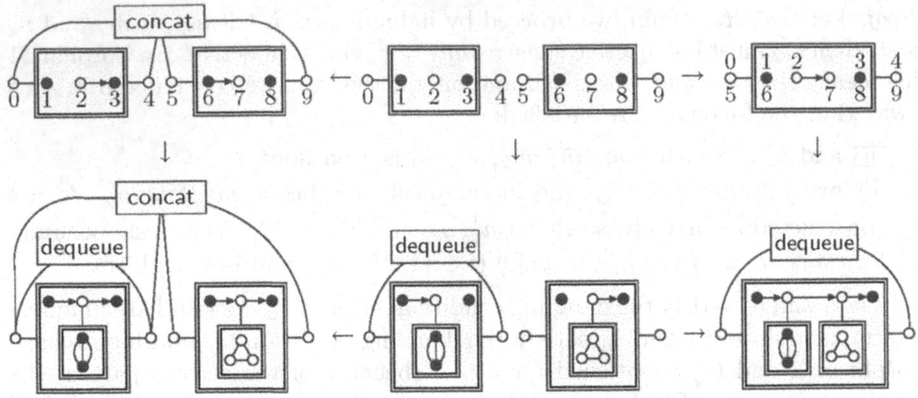

Fig. 2. The concatenation rule and its application

Example 2 (Concatenation of queues). In Figure 2, we show a concatenation rule for queues that identifies two queue frames and concatenates their contents, and a transformation with this rule. The digits in the rule indicate how the nodes of the graphs have to be mapped onto each other.

It should be noticed that the definition of transformation steps requires occurrence morphisms to be injective. Therefore, we need three variants of this rule where node 1 is identified with node 2, or 7 with 8, or both 1 with 2 and 7 with 8. (Similar variants are needed for the rules in the subsequent examples.)

Since occurrence morphisms are injective, we get the following theorem as a consequence of Theorems 1 and 2.

Theorem 3. *Let* $t\colon L \overset{l}{\leftarrow} I \overset{r}{\rightarrow} R$ *be a rule,* $G \in \mathcal{H}$*, and* $o\colon L \rightarrow G$ *an occurrence morphism. Then the two pushouts in Definition 1(1) exist if and only if o satisfies the dangling condition.*[1] *Furthermore, in this case the pushouts are uniquely determined up to isomorphism.*

Proof. By Theorem 2 the pushout on the left exists if and only if the dangling condition is satisfied, and if it exists then it is uniquely determined up to isomorphism. Finally, by Theorem 1 the pushout on the right always exists, and it is a general fact known from category theory that a pushout (m_1, m_2, n_1, n_2) is uniquely determined (up to isomorphism) by the morphisms m_1 and m_2. □

The reader should also notice that, as a consequence of the effectiveness of the results presented in Section 3, given a tranformation rule, a hierarchical graph, and an occurrence morphism satisfying the dangling condition, one can effectively construct the required pushouts.

[1] If the rule $t\colon L \overset{l}{\leftarrow} I \overset{r}{\rightarrow} R$ in question is clear we say that o satisfies the dangling condition if l and o do.

Unfortunately, the notion of transformation of hierarchical graphs is not yet expressive enough to be satisfactory for certain programming purposes. There are some natural effects that one would certainly like to be able to implement as single transformation steps, but which cannot be expressed by rules. Consider the example of queues, for instance. It should be possible to design a rule *dequeue* which removes the first item in a queue, *regardless of its contents.* However, this is not possible as the dangling condition requires the occurrence morphism to be bijective on the contents of deleted frames. Conversely, another rule *enqueue* should take an *item* frame, again regardless of its contents, and add it to the queue—preferably without affecting the original *item* frame. In order to implement this, one has to circumvent two obstacles. First, hierarchical morphisms preserve the frame hierarchy, which implies that, intuitively, rules cannot move frames across frame boundaries. Second, by now it is simply not possible to duplicate frames together with their contents.

This is where variables start to play an important role. The idea is to turn from rules to rule schemata and to transform hierarchical graphs by applying instances of these rule schemata. In order to make sure that an occurrence morphism satisfying the dangling condition always yields a well-defined transformation, we restrict ourselves to left-linear rule schemata. For this, a hierarchical graph H is called *linear* if no variable occurs twice in H.

A *variable instantiation for* $H \in \mathcal{H}(\mathcal{X})$ is a mapping $\imath\colon var(H) \to \mathcal{H}$. The application of $\imath$ to H is denoted by $H\imath$. It turns every variable frame $f \in X_H$ into a frame whose contents is $\imath(cts_H(f))$. By the definition of hierarchical morphisms, for every hierarchical morphism $h\colon G \to H$ such that $G \in \mathcal{H}$ and every variable instantiation $\imath$ for H, h can as well be understood as a hierarchical morphism from G to $H\imath$. In the following, this hierarchical morphism will be denoted by $h\imath$. Based on this observation, rule schemata and their application can be defined.

Definition 2 (*Transformation by rule schemata*). A *rule schema*, denoted by $t\colon L \overset{l}{\leftarrow} I \overset{r}{\rightarrow} R$, is a pair consisting of hierarchical morphisms $l\colon I \to L$ and $r\colon I \to R$, where $L, R \in \mathcal{H}(\mathcal{X})$, $I \in \mathcal{H}$, L is linear, and $var(R) \subseteq var(L)$. If $\imath$ is a variable instantiation for L then the rule $t'\colon L\imath \overset{l\imath}{\leftarrow} I \overset{r\imath}{\rightarrow} R\imath$ is an *instance* of t.

A rule schema t transforms $G \in \mathcal{H}$ into $H \in \mathcal{H}$, denoted by $G \Rrightarrow_t H$, if $G \Rightarrow_{t'} H$ for some instance t' of t. For a set T of rule schemata we write $G \Rrightarrow_T H$ if $G \Rrightarrow_t H$ for some $t \in T$.

Example 3 (The rule schemata enqueue *and* dequeue*).* In Figure 3, we show a rule schema that inserts a framed item graph at the tail of a queue graph, and a transformation with that rule. The item frame contains the variable x. Otherwise, it would not be possible to duplicate the item graph, and to move it into the queue frame.

In Figure 4, we show a rule schema that removes the first item frame in a queue graph. The item graph is denoted by the variable x so that it can be removed entirely.

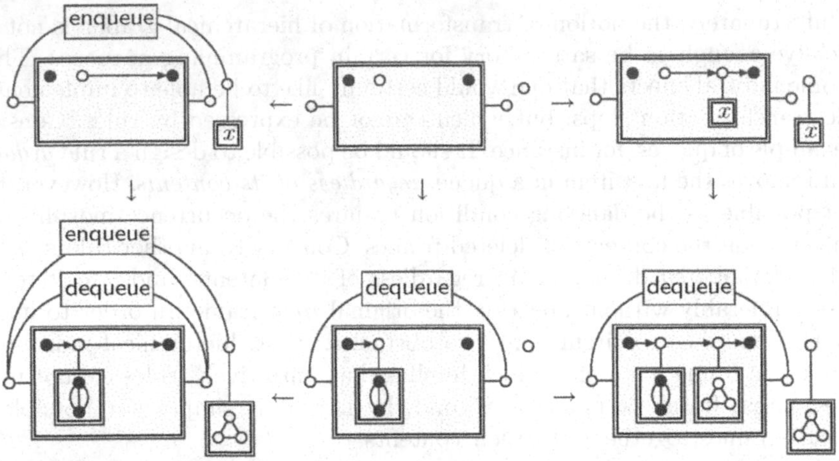

Fig. 3. The rule schema enqueue and its application

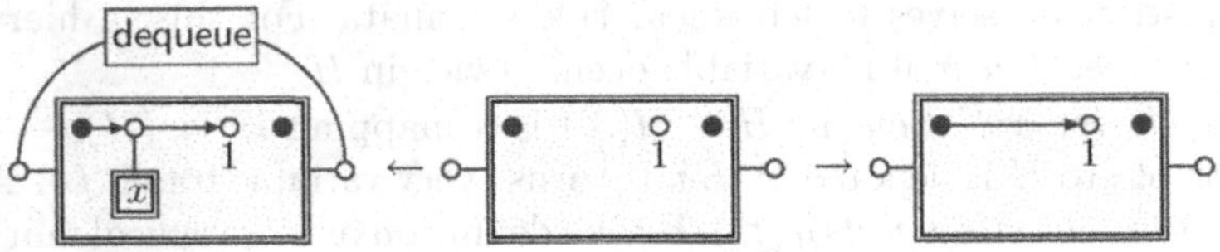

Fig. 4. The rule schema dequeue

For practical purposes Definition 2 is not very convenient because there are infinitely many instances of a rule schema as soon as it contains at least one variable. Therefore, the naive approach to implement $\Rrightarrow_t$ by constructing all its instances and then testing each of them for applicability does not work. However, there is quite an obvious way how one can do better than that. Consider some linear hierarchical graph $L \in \mathcal{H}(\mathcal{X})$ and a hierarchical graph $G \in \mathcal{H}$, and let $o\colon L \to G$ be a hierarchical morphism. Then, due to the linearity of L, o induces a variable instantiation $\imath_o\colon var(L) \to \mathcal{H}$ and an occurrence morphism $inst(o)\colon L\imath_o \to G$, as follows. For all $x \in var(L)$, if there is some $f \in X_L$ such that $cts_L(f) = x$ then $\imath_o(x) = cts_G(o(f))$. Otherwise, $\imath_o(x) = \imath_{o^f}(x)$, where $f \in F_L \setminus X_L$ is the unique frame such that $x \in var(cts_L(f))$. Furthermore, $\overline{inst(o)} = \overline{o}$ and for all $f \in F_L$, $inst(o)^f$ is the identity on $cts_G(o(f))$ if $f \in X_L$ and $inst(o)^f = inst(o^f)$ otherwise.

The theorem below states that the transformations given by a rule schema $t\colon L \overset{l}{\leftarrow} I \overset{r}{\rightarrow} R$ can be obtained by considering occurrence morphisms $o\colon L \to G$ that satisfy the dangling condition.

Theorem 4. *Let* $t\colon L \overset{l}{\leftarrow} I \overset{r}{\rightarrow} R$ *be a rule schema and* $G \in \mathcal{H}$.

1. *If* $o\colon L \to G$ *is an occurrence morphism satisfying the dangling condition, then* $inst(o)$ *is an occurrence morphism for* $L\imath_o$ *satisfying the dangling condition.*
2. *If* $\imath\colon var(L) \to \mathcal{H}$ *is a variable instantiation and* $q\colon L\imath \to G$ *is an occurrence morphism satisfying the dangling condition, then* $\imath = \imath_o$ *and* $q = inst(o)$ *(up to isomorphism) for some occurrence morphism* $o\colon L \to G$ *satisfying the dangling condition.*

The proof by induction on i, where $L \in \mathcal{H}_i(\mathcal{X})$, is rather straightforward and is therefore skipped in this short version.

5 Flattening

A natural operation on hierarchical graphs is the *flattening operation* which removes the hierarchy by recursively replacing every frame with its contents. For this, we use the well-known concept of hyperedge replacement (see [9, 4]) in a slightly generalized form. Flattening is similar to (a recursive version of) the operation φ considered in Section 3, but it removes all frames and identifies their attached nodes with the corresponding points of their contents. If the numbers of attached nodes and points differ, the additional nodes of the longer sequence are treated like ordinary nodes. In addition, flattening forgets about the points of its argument, so that the resulting graph is "unpointed".

It will be shown in this section that, under modest assumptions, hierarchical graph transformation is compatible with the flattening operation: A transformation $G \Rightarrow_t H$ induces a corresponding transformation $G' \Rightarrow_{t'} H'$, where G', H', and t' are the flattened versions of G, H, and t, respectively.

In order to proceed, we first need to define hyperedge replacement on hierarchical graphs. Let H be a hierarchical graph and consider a mapping $\sigma\colon E \to \mathcal{H}$ such that $E \subseteq E_H$, called a *hyperedge substitution for* H. Hyperedge replacement yields the hierarchical graph $H[\sigma]$ obtained from $H + \sum_{e\in E} \sigma(e)$ by deleting the edges in E and identifying, for all $e \in E$, the ith node of $att_H(e)$ with the ith point of $p_{\sigma(e)}$, for all i such that both these nodes exist.

Finally, for all $H \in \mathcal{H}$, let $\mathit{fl}(H) = H[\sigma]$ where $\sigma\colon F_H \to \mathcal{H}$ is given inductively by $\sigma(f) = \mathit{fl}(cts_H(f))$ for all $f \in F_H$. Then, the *flattening* of H yields the graph $\mathit{flat}(H) = \langle V_{\mathit{fl}(H)}, E_{\mathit{fl}(H)}, att_{\mathit{fl}(H)}, lab_{\mathit{fl}(H)}, \lambda\rangle$. For most of the considerations below, it is sufficient to study the mapping fl, which removes the hierarchy without forgetting points, instead of flat.

We can flatten morphisms as well. Consider a hierarchical morphism $h\colon G \to H$ with $G, H \in \mathcal{H}$ and let $\sigma = \mathit{fl} \circ cts_G$ and $\tau = \mathit{fl} \circ cts_H$. Then, $\mathit{fl}(h)$ is the morphism $m\colon \mathit{fl}(G) \to \mathit{fl}(H)$ defined inductively, as follows. For all $a \in A_{\mathit{fl}(G)}$, if $a \in A_G$ then $m(a) = h(a)$, and if $a \in A_{\sigma(f)}$ for some $f \in F_G$ then $m(a) = \mathit{fl}(h^f)(a)$. Furthermore, $\mathit{flat}(h) = (m'\colon \mathit{flat}(G) \to \mathit{flat}(H))$ is given by $m'(a) = m(a)$ for all $a \in A_{\mathit{flat}(G)}$. (Notice that, although the two cases in the definition of $m(a)$ above intersect, they are consistent with each other.)

Above, it was mentioned that the main result of this section holds only under a certain assumption. The reason for this is that a morphism *flat*(h) may be non-injective although $h\colon G \to H$ itself is injective. This is caused by the fact that building *fl*(G) may identify some nodes in V_G because they are incident with a frame whose contents has repetitions in its point sequence. If the attached nodes of the frame are distinct, hyperedge replacement identifies them (by identifying each with the same point of the contents). Thus, flattening may turn an occurrence morphism into a non-injective morphism, making it impossible to apply the corresponding flattened rule. In fact, the dual situation where there are identical attached nodes of a frame while the corresponding points of its contents are distinct, must also be avoided. The reason lies in the recursive part of the definition of $\Rightarrow_t$. If a rule is applied to the contents of some frame, but the replacement of the frame identifies two distinct points of the contents because the corresponding attached points of the frame are identical, the flattened rule cannot be applied either.

For this, call a hierarchical graph $H \in \mathcal{H}$ *identification consistent* if every frame $f \in F_H$ satisfies the following:

(1) For all $i, j \in [\min(|att_H(f)|, |p_{cts_H(f)}|)]$, $att_H(f)(i) = att_H(f)(j)$ if and only if $p_{cts_H(f)}(i) = p_{cts_H(f)}(j)$, and
(2) $cts_H(f)$ is identification consistent.

The reader ought to notice that identification consistency is preserved by the application of a rule $t\colon L \overset{l}{\leftarrow} I \overset{r}{\rightarrow} R$ if R is identification consistent and r is injective. Thus, if we restrict ourselves to systems with rules of this kind then all derivable hierarchical graphs are identification consistent (provided that the initial ones are).

It is not very difficult to verify the following two lemmas.

Lemma 1. *For every injective hierarchical morphism* $h\colon G \to H$ $(G, H \in \mathcal{H})$ *such that* H *is identification consistent,* *fl*(h) *is injective.*

Lemma 2. *If* (m_1, m_2, n_1, n_2) *is a pushout in* $\mathbb{H}$*, then* (*flat*(m_1), *flat*(m_2), *flat*(n_1), *flat*(n_2)) *is a pushout as well.*

As a consequence, one obtains the main theorem of this section: If a rule can be applied to an identification consistent hierarchical graph, then the flattened rule can be applied to the flattened graph, with the expected result.

Theorem 5. *Let* $t\colon L \overset{l}{\leftarrow} I \overset{r}{\rightarrow} R$ *be a rule and let* $t'\colon L' \overset{l'}{\leftarrow} I' \overset{r'}{\rightarrow} R'$ *be the rule given by* $l' =$ *flat*(l) *and* $r' =$ *flat*(r)*. For every transformation* $G \Rightarrow_t H$ *such that* G *is identification consistent, there is a transformation* *flat*$(G) \Rightarrow_{t'}$ *flat*(H).

Proof sketch. Consider a transformation step $G \Rightarrow_t H$. Due to the definition of $\Rightarrow_t$ there are two cases to be distinguished. If there is a double-pushout diagram as in the first case of Definition 1, Lemmas 1 and 2 yield a corresponding "flattened" diagram. The second case to be considered is the recursive one, i.e., the transformation takes place inside a frame f. In this case it may be assumed inductively that the diagram corresponding to a transformation of the flattened contents of f exists. Due to the assumed identification consistency the flattened contents of f is injectively embedded in $\mathit{flat}(G)$. Therefore, the given diagram can be extended to a larger pushout diagram in the required way, retaining the injectivity of the occurrence morphism. □

It should be noticed that the flattening process implies a loss of crucial structural information so that there is no chance to prove the converse of the theorem.

6 Conclusion

We conclude this paper by briefly mentioning some related work and possible directions for future research.

Pratt [15] was probably the first to consider a concept of hierarchical graph transformation, where he used a certain kind of node replacement to define the semantics of programming languages. His graph concept was extended in [6] by allowing edges between subgraphs contained in different nodes, but without defining transformation.

A different concept of graph nesting is given by the abstraction mechanisms of the (old) graph transformation system AGG [12] and the multi-level graph grammars of [13], providing flat graphs with several views which are related by a rigid layering and a partial inclusion ordering, respectively.

An indirect nesting concept can be found in the framework of [16] and the new AGG system [7], where nesting is realized by labels and attributes, respectively.

The idea of using variables to extend the double-pushout approach with non-local effects, like copying and removal of subgraphs, is also followed in the so-called substitution-based approach to graph transformation [14] (working on flat hypergraphs).

One direction for future work on hierarchical graph transformation is to lift to the hierarchical setting the classical results of the double-pushout approach, like sequential and parallel commutativity, results on parallelism, concurrency and amalgamation, etc. Another important task is to combine hierarchical graph transformation in an orthogonal way with concepts for structuring and controlling systems of rules. As mentioned in the introduction, several such concepts (mainly for flat graphs) have recently been proposed in the literature.

A further topic of research is to develop hierarchical graph transformation towards object-oriented graph transformation, as outlined in [11]. There the idea is to restrict the visibility of frames so that only rules designated to some frame type may inspect or update the contents of frames of this type. Such frame types come close to "classes", and the designated rules correspond to "methods". In this way frames can be seen as objects of their types that can only be manipulated by invoking the methods of the class.

Acknowledgement We thank the referees for their helpful comments.

References

[1] J. Adámek, H. Herrlich, and G. Strecker. *Abstract and Concrete Categories.* John Wiley, New York, 1990.

[2] M. Andries, G. Engels, A. Habel, B. Hoffmann, H.-J. Kreowski, S. Kuske, D. Plump, A. Schürr, and G. Taentzer. Graph transformation for specification and programming. *Science of Computer Programming*, 34:1–54, 1999.

[3] A. Corradini, U. Montanari, F. Rossi, H. Ehrig, R. Heckel, and M. Löwe. Algebraic approaches to graph transformation — Part I: Basic concepts and double pushout approach. In G. Rozenberg, editor, *Handbook of Graph Grammars and Computing by Graph Transformation*, volume 1, chapter 3, pages 163–245. World Scientific, 1997.

[4] F. Drewes, A. Habel, and H.-J. Kreowski. Hyperedge replacement graph grammars. In G. Rozenberg, editor, *Handbook of Graph Grammars and Computing by Graph Transformation*, volume 1, chapter 2, pages 95–162. World Scientific, Singapore, 1997.

[5] H. Ehrig. Introduction to the algebraic theory of graph grammars. In *Proc. Graph-Grammars and Their Application to Computer Science and Biology*, volume 73 of *Lecture Notes in Computer Science*, pages 1–69. Springer-Verlag, 1979.

[6] G. Engels and A. Schürr. Encapsulated hierachical graphs, graph types, and meta types. In A. Corradini and U. Montanari, editors, *Proc. Joint COMPUGRAPH/SEMAGRAPH Workshop on Graph Rewriting and Computation*, volume 2 of *Electronic Notes in Theoretical Computer Science.* Elsevier, 1995.

[7] C. Ermel, M. Rudolf, and G. Taentzer. The AGG approach: Language and environment. In H. Ehrig, G. Engels, H.-J. Kreowski, and G. Rozenberg, editors, *Handbook of Graph Grammars and Computing by Graph Transformation*, volume 2, pages 551–603. World Scientific, 1999.

[8] P. Fradet and D. L. Métayer. Structured Gamma. *Science of Computer Programming*, 31(2/3):263–289, 1998.

[9] A. Habel. *Hyperedge Replacement: Grammars and Languages*, volume 643 of *Lecture Notes in Computer Science.* Springer-Verlag, Berlin, 1992.

[10] R. Heckel, H. Ehrig, and G. Taentzer. Classification and comparison of module concepts for graph transformation systems. In H. Ehrig, G. Engels, H.-J. Kreowski, and G. Rozenberg, editors, *Handbook of Graph Grammars and Computing by Graph Transformation*, volume 2, chapter 17, pages 669–689. World Scientific, 1999.

[11] B. Hoffmann. From graph transformation to rule-based programming with diagrams. In M. Nagl and A. Schürr, editors, *Proc. Int'l Workshop on Applications of Graph Transformations with Industrial Relevance (AGTIVE'99)*, Lecture Notes in Computer Science, 1999. To appear.

[12] M. Löwe and M. Beyer. AGG — an implementation of algebraic graph rewriting. In C. Kirchner, editor, *Proc. Rewriting Techniques and Applications*, volume 690 of *Lecture Notes in Computer Science*, pages 451–456, 1993.

[13] F. Parisi-Presicce and G. Piersanti. Multi-level graph grammars. In E. W. Mayr, G. Schmidt, and G. Tinhofer, editors, *Graph-Theoretical Concepts in Computer Science (WG '94)*, volume 903 of *Lecture Notes in Computer Science*, pages 51–64, 1995.

[14] D. Plump and A. Habel. Graph unification and matching. In *Proc. Graph Grammars and Their Application to Computer Science*, volume 1073 of *Lecture Notes in Computer Science*, pages 75–89. Springer-Verlag, 1996.

[15] T. W. Pratt. Pair grammars, graph languages and string-to-graph translations. *Journal of Computer and System Sciences*, 5:560–595, 1971.

[16] H.-J. Schneider. On categorical graph grammars integrating structural transformations and operations on labels. *Theoretical Computer Science*, 109:257–274, 1993.

A Program Refinement Framework Supporting Reasoning about Knowledge and Time (Preliminary Report)

Kai Engelhardt[1], Ron van der Meyden[1], and Yoram Moses[2]

[1] School of Computer Science and Engineering
The University of New South Wales, Sydney 2052, Australia
[kaie|meyden]@cse.unsw.edu.au
[2] Department of Electrical Engineering
Technion, Haifa, Israel
moses@ee.technion.ac.il

Abstract. This paper develops a highly expressive semantic framework for program refinement that supports both temporal reasoning and reasoning about the knowledge of a single agent. The framework generalizes a previously developed temporal refinement framework by amalgamating it with a logic of quantified local propositions, a generalization of the logic of knowledge. The combined framework provides a formal setting for development of knowledge-based programs, and addresses two problems of existing theories of such programs: lack of compositionality and the fact that such programs often have only implementations of high computational complexity. Use of the framework is illustrated by a control theoretic example concerning a robot operating with an imprecise position sensor.

1 Introduction

The *knowledge-based* approach to the design and analysis of distributed systems, introduced by Halpern and Moses [6] involves the use of modal logics of knowledge. One of the key contributions of this approach is the notion of *knowledge-based programs* [5,4], which generalize standard programs by allowing the tests in conditional constructs to be formulas in the logic of knowledge. Such programs contain statements of the form "if you know that X then do A else B". This provides a high level abstraction of distributed programs that allows for perspicuous descriptions of how an agent's actions are related to its state of information (which, in a distributed system, is typically incomplete) about its environment.

In its current state of development, the knowledge-based approach has a number of limitations, among them that:

1. The formal methodology for developing and reasoning about knowledge-based programs is at present only weakly developed.

J. Tiuryn (Ed.): FOSSACS 2000, LNCS 1784, pp. 114–129, 2000.

2. The existing semantics for knowledge-based programs is based on a particular interpretation of knowledge that requires a complete description of the implementing program. This prevents the compositional development of program fragments.
3. Knowledge-based programs often have only implementations of unacceptably high computational complexity.

This paper is a step in the direction of the formulation of the knowledge-based approach that addresses these limitations.

One of the starting points for our work is the observation that knowledge-based programs are in one respect more like specifications than like standard programs. They cannot be directly executed — instead, their meaning is defined by a relation of "implementation" between knowledge based programs and standard programs: a given knowledge-based program may have no, one, or many concrete programs as its implementations. As a specification formalism, however, knowledge-based programs are unbalanced, abstracting only the tests performed by agents, but providing no abstraction mechanism for their actions [11].

Action abstraction is handled much better in *refinement calculi* [1,9,10], also known as "broad spectrum" languages. Such calculi view programs and specifications as having the same semantic type, and support a formal methodology for the development of programs that are "correct by design", where one begins with a specification and transforms it to an implementation by means of a sequence of correctness preserving refinement steps. The focus in this area has been on sequential programs and atemporal assertions but recently some approaches to refinement admitting the expressive power of temporal logics have been developed [14,7].

A first step in the direction of a refinement calculus suited to the knowledge-based development of programs was taken in van der Meyden and Moses [17,16], where it is shown how to develop a refinement approach capturing certain types of temporal reasoning that will be critical in knowledge-based program development. We further develop these ideas in the present paper, by showing how they may be extended to accommodate knowledge-based reasoning. Significantly, the framework we define admits compositional program development.

In developing the extension, we also seek to address the final limitation of knowledge-based programs alluded to above. To implement the statement "if you know that X then do A else B", a concrete program must do A exactly when it is in a local state (captured by the values of the variables and storage it maintains locally) that carries the information that X is true. The difficulty with this is that computing whether a local state bears the information that X may have very high computational complexity [12,15,18]. As argued by Sanders [13] and us [3], in practice, it may often be sufficient to use conditions on the agent's state of information that are sound, but not complete, tests of its knowledge. Such tests may be expressed in the *Logic of Local Propositions* (LLP) [3].

The present paper integrates the temporal refinement framework of van der Meyden and Moses [16] with the logic of local propositions. Although our ultimate aim is a framework for the development of distributed systems, we deal in this paper with a single agent operating synchronously with its environment: asynchrony and multiple agents introduce complexities that we plan to address in the future. The main novelty is the introduction of a programming/specification construct that resembles a quantification over local propositions. This construct makes it possible to write specifications stating that the agent conditions its behaviour on a *local* test for some property of interest, without stating explicitly what test is used. The introduction of this construct necessitates an adaptation of the semantics of the temporal refinement of [16].

The paper is structured as follows. Section 2 defines an assertion language that adapts the LLP semantics to the richer temporal setting required for reasoning about programs. Section 3 defines the syntax and semantics of our broad spectrum programming and specification language that incorporates the assertion language from Sect. 2. Section 4 defines the semantic refinement relation we use for this class of programs and develops a number of refinement rules valid for this relation. Section 5 illustrates the use of the framework by presenting a formal development of a control theoretic example previously treated informally in the literature on knowledge-based programs.

2 A Semantics for Reasoning about Knowledge and Time

We begin by presenting a semantic framework for a single agent and its environment, inspired by [4], to which we refer the reader for motivation.

Let L_e be a set of possible states for the environment and let L_1 be a set of possible local states for agent 1. We take $\mathcal{G} = L_e \times L_1$ to be the set of *global states*. Let A_1 and A_e be nonvoid sets of *actions* for agent 1 and for the environment, respectively. (These sets usually contain a special *null action* Λ.) A *joint action* is a pair $(a_e, a_1) \in \mathcal{A} = A_e \times A_1$. A *run* over $\mathcal{G}$ and $\mathcal{A}$ is a pair $r = (h, \alpha)$ of infinite sequences: a *state history* $h : \mathbb{N} \longrightarrow \mathcal{G}$, and an *action history* $\alpha : \mathbb{N} \longrightarrow \mathcal{A}$. Intuitively, for $c \in \mathbb{N}$, $h(c)$ is the global state of the system at time c and $\alpha(c)$ is the joint action occurring at time c. (We say more about the transition relation connecting states and actions later.) A *system* over $\mathcal{G}$ and $\mathcal{A}$ is a set of runs over $\mathcal{G}$ and $\mathcal{A}$, intuitively representing all possible histories. A pair (r, c) consisting of a run r (in system S) and a time $c \in \mathbb{N}$ is called a *point (in S)*. We write $\mathrm{Points}(S)$ for the set of points of S. Let *Prop* be a set of propositional variables. An *interpretation* of a system S is a mapping $\pi : \mathit{Prop} \longrightarrow 2^{\mathrm{Points}(S)}$ associating a set of points with each propositional variable. Intuitively, proposition $p \in \mathit{Prop}$ is true exactly at the points contained in $\pi(p)$. An *interpreted system (over $\mathcal{G}$ and $\mathcal{A}$)* is a pair $\mathfrak{I} = (S, \pi)$ where S is a system over $\mathcal{G}$ and $\mathcal{A}$ and π is an interpretation of S.

The structure in the above definitions supports the following notions used to define the agent's knowledge. We say two points $(r, c), (r', c')$ in a system S are 1-*indistinguishable*, denoted $(r, c) \sim_1 (r', c')$, if the local components of the global states at these points are equal, i.e., if there exists a local state $s_1 \in L_1$ and states of the environment s_e, s'_e such that $h(c) = (s_e, s_1)$ and $h'(c') = (s'_e, s_1)$, where $r = (h, \alpha)$ and $r' = (h', \alpha')$. A set P of points of S is 1-*local* if it is closed under $\sim_1$, in other words, when for all points $(r,c),(r',c')$ of S, if $(r,c) \in P$ and $(r,c) \sim_1 (r',c')$ then $(r',c') \in P$. Intuitively, 1-local sets of points correspond to properties that the agent is able to determine entirely on the basis of its local state. If π and π' are interpretations and $p \in \mathit{Prop}$, then π' is said to be a 1-*local* p-*variant* of π, denoted $\pi \simeq^1_p \pi'$, if π and π' differ at most in the value of p and $\pi'(p)$ is 1-local. If $\mathfrak{I} = (S,\pi)$ and $\mathfrak{I} = (S',\pi')$ are two interpreted systems over $\mathcal{G}$ and $\mathcal{A}$, then $\mathfrak{I}'$ is said to be 1-*local* p-*variant* of $\mathfrak{I}$, denoted $\mathfrak{I} \simeq^1_p \mathfrak{I}'$, if $S = S'$ and $\pi \simeq^1_p \pi'$.

The logical language $\mathfrak{L}$ we use in this paper resembles a restricted monadic second order logic with two additions: (a) an S5-modality for necessity and (b) operators from the linear time temporal logic LTL [8]. Its syntax is given by:

$$\mathfrak{L} \ni \phi ::= p \mid \neg\phi \mid \phi \wedge \phi \mid \mathsf{Nec}\,\phi \mid \forall_1 p\,(\phi) \mid \bigcirc\phi \mid \phi\,\mathsf{U}\,\phi \mid \ominus\phi \mid \phi\,\mathsf{S}\,\phi$$

where $p \in \mathit{Prop}$. Intuitively, $\mathsf{Nec}\,\phi$ says that ϕ is true at all points in the interpreted system, and its dual $\mathsf{Poss}\,\phi = \neg\,\mathsf{Nec}\,\neg\phi$ states that ϕ is true at some point. The formula $\forall_1 p\,(\phi)$ says that ϕ is true for all assignments of a 1-local proposition (set of points) to the propositional variable p. We write $\exists_1 p\,(\phi)$ for its dual $\neg\forall_1 p\,(\neg\phi)$. The remaining connectives have their standard interpretations from linear time temporal logic: $\bigcirc$ ("next"), U ("until"), $\ominus$ ("previously") and S ("since"). We employ parenthesis to indicate aggregation and use standard abbreviations such as *true*, *false*, $\vee$, and definable future time operators like $\Box$ ("henceforth") and $\Diamond$ ("eventually"), as well as their past time counterparts $\boxminus$ ("until now") and $\diamondminus$ ("once").

Formulae of $\mathfrak{L}$ are interpreted at a point (r,c) of an interpreted system $\mathfrak{I} = (S,\pi)$ by means of the satisfaction relation $\models$, defined inductively by:

- $\mathfrak{I},(r,c) \models p$ iff $(r,c) \in \pi(p)$;
- $\mathfrak{I},(r,c) \models \neg\phi$ iff $\mathfrak{I},(r,c) \not\models \phi$;
- $\mathfrak{I},(r,c) \models \phi \wedge \psi$ iff $\mathfrak{I},(r,c) \models \phi$ and $\mathfrak{I},(r,c) \models \psi$;
- $\mathfrak{I},(r,c) \models \mathsf{Nec}\,\phi$ iff $\mathfrak{I},(r',c') \models \phi$, for all $(r',c') \in \mathrm{Points}(S)$;
- $\mathfrak{I},(r,c) \models \forall_1 p\,(\phi)$ iff $\mathfrak{I}',(r,c) \models \phi$ for all $\mathfrak{I}'$ such that $\mathfrak{I} \simeq^1_p \mathfrak{I}'$;
- $\mathfrak{I},(r,c) \models \bigcirc\phi$ iff $\mathfrak{I},(r,c+1) \models \phi$;
- $\mathfrak{I},(r,c) \models \phi\mathsf{U}\psi$ iff there exists a $d \geq c$ such that $\mathfrak{I},(r,d) \models \psi$ and $\mathfrak{I},(r,e) \models \phi$ for all e with $c \leq e < d$;
- $\mathfrak{I},(r,c) \models \ominus\phi$ iff $c > 0$ and $\mathfrak{I},(r,c-1) \models \phi$;
- $\mathfrak{I},(r,c) \models \phi\mathsf{S}\psi$ iff there exists a $d \leq c$ such that $\mathfrak{I},(r,d) \models \psi$ and $\mathfrak{I},(r,e) \models \phi$ for all e with $d < e \leq c$.

Given these constructs, it is possible to express many operators from the literature on reasoning about knowledge. For example, consider the standard knowledge operator K_1, defined by $\mathfrak{I},(r,c) \models K_1\phi$ if $\mathfrak{I},(r',c') \models \phi$ for all points (r',c') of $\mathfrak{I}$ such that $(r,c) \sim_1 (r',c')$. This is expressible as $\exists_1 p\,(p \wedge \mathsf{Nec}(p \to \phi))$. We refer to [3] for further examples and discussion.

3 Sequential Programs with Quantification over Local Propositions

In this section we define our wide spectrum programming language, and discuss its semantics. We also define a refinement relation on programs.

3.1 Syntax

The programming language describes the structure of segments of runs. Let CV be a set of *constraint variables* and PV a set of *program variables.* Define the syntactic category *Prg* of *programs* by

$$Prg \ni P ::= \epsilon \mid Z \mid a \mid P * P \mid P + P \mid P^{\omega} \mid \exists_1 p\,(P) \mid [\phi, \psi]^X \mid [\phi]^X \mid \{\phi\}_C$$

where $Z \in PV$, $a \in A_1$, $p \in Prop$, $\phi, \psi \in \mathfrak{L}$, $X \in CV$, and $C \subseteq CV$. The intuitive meaning of these constructs is as follows. The symbol ϵ denotes the *empty program,* which takes no time to execute, and has no effects. Program variables Z are placeholders used to allow substitution of programs. Note that a program may refer directly to actions a of the agent, but the actions of the environment are left implicit. The operation $*$ represents *sequential composition.* The symbol $+$ denotes nondeterministic choice, while P^{ω} denotes zero or more (possibly infinitely many) repetitions of P. The construct $\exists_1 p\,(P)$ can also be understood as a kind of nondeterministic choice: it states that P runs with respect to some assignment of a 1-local proposition to the propositional variable p. The last three constructs are like certain constructs found in refinement calculi. Intuitively, the *specification* $[\phi, \psi]^X$ states that some program runs in this location that has the property that, if started at a point satisfying ϕ, eventually terminates at a point satisfying ψ.[1] The *coercion* $[\phi]^X$ is a program that takes no time to execute, but expresses a constraint on the surrounding program context: this must guarantee that ϕ holds at this location. The constraint variable X in specifications and coercions acts as a label that allows references by other pieces of program text. Specifically, this is done in the *assertions* $\{\phi\}_C$, which act like program annotations: such a statement takes no time to execute, and, intuitively, asserts that ϕ can be proved to hold at this program location, with the proof depending only on concrete program fragments and on specification and coercion statements whose labels are in C. We may omit the constraint variables when it is not necessary to make such references.

In programs "$*$" binds tighter than "$+$". We employ parentheses to indicate aggregation wherever necessary and tend to omit $*$ near coercions and assertions. Moreover, we use the following abbreviations: **if** ^{X} ϕ **then** P **else** Q **fi** $= [\phi]^X\ P + [\neg\phi]^X\ Q$ and **while** ^{X} ϕ **do** P **od** $= ([\phi]^X\ P)^{\omega}\ [\neg\phi]^X$. Our programming

[1] In refinement calculi, such statements are typically associated with *frame variables,* representing the variables allowed to change during the execution — we could add these, but omit them for brevity.

language can express some programs closely related to the knowledge-based programs of [4]. These are program such as:

case of
  if $K_1\phi$ **do** a_1
  if $\neg K_1\psi$ **do** a_2
end case

A program closely related to this is $([K_1\phi]\, a_1 + [\neg K_1\psi]\, a_2 + [\neg(K_1\phi \vee \neg K_1\psi)]\, \Lambda)^\omega$. The precise relationship is subtle and deferred to the full version of this paper.

3.2 Semantics

Our semantics will treat programs like specifications of certain sets of run segments in a system, intuitively, the sets of run segments that can be viewed as having been generated by executing the program. We note that the semantics presented in this section treats assertions $\{\phi\}_C$ as equivalent to the null program ϵ — the role of assertions in the framework will be explained later.

We first define execution trees, which represent unfoldings of the nondeterminism in a program. It is convenient to represent these trees as follows. A *binary tree domain* is a prefix-closed subset of the set $\{0,1\}^* \cup \{0,1\}^\omega$. So, each nonvoid tree domain contains the empty sequence λ. Let A be a set. An *A-labelled binary tree* is a function T from a binary tree domain D to A. The *nodes* of T are the elements of D. The node λ is called the *root* of T. If $n \in D$ we call $T(n)$ the *label* at node n. If $n \in D$ then the *children of* n *in* T are the nodes of T (if any) of the form $n \cdot i$ where $i \in \{0,1\}$. Finite maxima in the prefix order on D are called *leaves* of T.

An *execution tree* is a *Prg*-labelled binary tree, subject to the following constraints on the nodes n:

1. If n is labelled by ϵ, a program variable $Z \in PV$, a basic action a, a specification $[\phi,\psi]^X$, a coercion $[\phi]^X$, or an assertion $\{\phi\}_C$, then n is a leaf.
2. If n is labelled by $\exists_1 p\,(P)$ then n has exactly one child $n \cdot 0$, labelled by P.
3. If n is labelled by $P * Q$ or $P + Q$ then n has exactly two children $n \cdot 0$, $n \cdot 1$, labelled by P and Q respectively.
4. If n is labelled by P^ω then n has exactly two children, $n \cdot 0$, $n \cdot 1$, labelled by ϵ and $P * (P^\omega)$, respectively.

With each program P we associate a particular execution tree, T_P, namely the unique execution tree labelled with P at the root λ.

We now define the semantic constructs specified by programs. An *interval in a system* S is a triple $r[c,d]$ consisting of a run r of S and two elements c and d of $\mathbb{N}_+ = \mathbb{N} \cup \{\infty\}$ such that $c \leq d$. We say that the interval is *finite* if $d < \infty$. A set I of intervals is *run-unique* if $r[c,d], r[c',d'] \in I$ implies $c = c'$ and $d = d'$. An *interpreted interval set over* S (or *iis* for short) is a pair (π, I) consisting of an interpretation π of S and a run-unique set I of intervals over S.

We will view programs as specifying, or executing over, interpreted interval sets, by means of certain mappings from execution trees to interpreted interval sets. To facilitate the definition in the case of sequential composition, we introduce a shorthand for the two sets obtained by splitting each interval in a given set I of intervals of S in two. Say that $f : I \longrightarrow \mathbb{N}_+$ *divides* I whenever $c \leq f(r[c,d]) \leq d$ holds for all $r[c,d] \in I$. Given some f dividing I, we write $f_\blacktriangleleft(I)$ for the set of intervals $r[f(r[c,d]),d]$ such that $r[c,d] \in I$. Analogously, we write $f_\blacktriangleright(I)$ for $\{\, r[c,f(r[c,d])] \mid r[c,d] \in I \,\}$.

Let S be a system, let (π, I) be an iis w.r.t. S, and let P be a program. A function θ mapping each node n of T_P to an iis $(\pi_\theta(n), I_\theta(n))$, respectively, is an *embedding* of T_P in (π, I) w.r.t. S whenever the following conditions are satisfied:

1. $\theta(\lambda) = (\pi, I)$.
2. If n is labelled ϵ or $\{\phi\}_C$, then $c = d$ for all $r[c,d] \in I_\theta(n)$.
3. If n is labelled a then, for all $(h,\alpha)[c,d] \in I_\theta(n)$, if $c < \infty$ then both $d = 1+c$ and $a = a_1$, where $\alpha(c) = (a_e, a_1)$.
4. If n is labelled $[\phi, \psi]$, then, for all $r[c,d] \in I_\theta(n)$, whenever $c < \infty$ and $(S, \pi_\theta(n)), (r,c) \models \phi$, then both $d < \infty$ and $(S, \pi_\theta(n)), (r,d) \models \psi$.
5. If n is labelled $[\phi]$, then $c < \infty$ implies that $c = d$ and $(S, \pi_\theta(n)), (r,c) \models \phi$, for all $r[c,d] \in I_\theta(n)$.
6. If n is labelled $\exists_1 p\,(Q)$ then $\pi_\theta(n) \simeq^1_p \pi_\theta(n \cdot 0)$ and $I_\theta(n \cdot 0) = I_\theta(n)$.
7. If n is labelled $Q_1 + Q_2$, then $\pi_\theta(n \cdot 0) = \pi_\theta(n \cdot 1) = \pi_\theta(n)$ and $I_\theta(n)$ is the disjoint union of $I_\theta(n \cdot 0)$ and $I_\theta(n \cdot 1)$.
8. If n is labelled $Q_1 * Q_2$, then $\pi_\theta(n \cdot 0) = \pi_\theta(n \cdot 1) = \pi_\theta(n)$ and there is an f dividing $I_\theta(n)$ such that $I_\theta(n \cdot 0) = f_\blacktriangleright(I_\theta(n))$ and $I_\theta(n \cdot 1) = f_\blacktriangleleft(I_\theta(n))$.
9. If n is labelled Q^ω then $\pi_\theta(n \cdot 0) = \pi_\theta(n \cdot 1) = \pi_\theta(n)$ and $I_\theta(n)$ is the disjoint union of $I_\theta(n \cdot 0)$ and $I_\theta(n \cdot 1)$ (as in case 7) and, for all $r[c,d] \in I_\theta(n)$: $d = \bigsqcup\{\, d' \mid r[c',d'] \in I_\theta(n \cdot m)$ for some leaf $n \cdot m$ of T_P below $n \,\}$.

We write $S, (\pi, I) \Vdash_\theta P$ whenever θ is an embedding of T_P in (π, I) w.r.t. S. Say that P *occurs over* (π, I) *w.r.t.* S if there exists a θ such that $S, (\pi, I) \Vdash_\theta P$.

Clauses 1 to 8 formalize the intuitive understanding given above for each of the program constructs. Concerning clause 9 of this definition, we remark that, by run-uniqueness and the other clauses, if $n \cdot m_0, n \cdot m_1 \ldots$ are the leaves $n \cdot m$ below n for which $I_\theta(n \cdot m)$ contains an interval on r, in left to right order, and these intervals are $r[c_0, d_0], r[c_1, d_1], \ldots$, respectively, then we have $d_i = c_{i+1}$ for each index i in the sequence. (We may have $c_i = d_i$.) Intuitively, if d were not the least upper bound d' of the d_i, then this sequence of intervals would amount to an execution of Q^ω over $r[c,d']$ rather than over $r[c,d]$. (See [16] for further motivation.)

3.3 Refinement

The semantics just presented can be shown to be a generalization of the semantics of [16] for a similar language without the local propositional quantifier. That semantics, however, dealt with *single* intervals where we have used a set of intervals. The motivation for the change is that certain undesirable refinement rules involving the local propositional quantifier would be valid under the earlier semantic approach. We now present two definitions of refinement and an example that motivates the richer semantics.

Intuitively, a program P refines Q if, whenever P executes, so does Q. A refinement relation of this type, when transitive and preserved under program composition, allows us to start with a high level specification and derive a concrete implementation through a sequence of refinement steps.

One refinement relation definable using our semantics as is follows: P refines Q, denoted $P \sqsubseteq Q$ when for all systems S, and interpreted interval sets (π, I) over S, if $S, (\pi, I) \Vdash P$ then $S, (\pi, I) \Vdash Q$. For the semantics using single intervals, the corresponding relation would be defined by $P \sqsubseteq^* Q$ when for all systems S, interpretations π and intervals $r[c,d]$ of S, if $S, (\pi, \{r[c,d]\}) \Vdash P$ then $S, (\pi, \{r[c,d]\}) \Vdash Q$. Clearly, if $P \sqsubseteq Q$ then $P \sqsubseteq^* Q$. As the following example demonstrates, the converse is false.

Example 1. Let $\phi \in \mathcal{L}$ be any formula and consider the following two programs.

$$P = \textbf{if } \phi \textbf{ then } a \textbf{ else } a * a \textbf{ fi} \qquad\qquad Q = \exists_1 p\, (\textbf{if } p \textbf{ then } a \textbf{ else } a * a \textbf{ fi})$$

We shall first show that $P \sqsubseteq^* Q$ and then argue that this is not desirable. Suppose $S, (\pi, \{r[c,d]\}) \Vdash P$. Recall that an **if** statement abbreviates a nondeterministic choice. Thus, there are two cases to be considered:

Case 1: $S, (\pi, \{r[c,d]\}) \Vdash [\phi]\, a$. Define the 1-local p-variant π' of π by $\pi'(p) = \text{Points}(S)$, that is, p is everywhere true under π'. It follows that $S, (\pi', \{r[c,d]\}) \Vdash [p]\, a$, and thus, $S, (\pi', \{r[c,d]\}) \Vdash \textbf{if } p \textbf{ then } a \textbf{ else } a * a \textbf{ fi}$. By definition, $S, (\pi, \{r[c,d]\}) \Vdash Q$.

Case 2: $S, (\pi, \{r[c,d]\}) \Vdash [\neg\phi]\, a * a$. This is handled analogously by defining $\pi'(p) = \emptyset$.

To see that it is not the case that $P \sqsubseteq Q$, take ϕ to be a propositional variable q. It is straightforward to construct a system S, finite intervals $i = r[c,d]$ and $i' = r'[c', d']$, and interpretation π such that $S, (\pi, \{i\}) \Vdash [q]\, a$ and $S, (\pi, \{i'\}) \Vdash [\neg q]\, a * a$. Hence $S, (\pi, \{i, i'\}) \Vdash \textbf{if } q \textbf{ then } a \textbf{ else } a * a \textbf{ fi}$), but (r, c) and (r', c') are 1-indistinguishable. If we were to have $S, (\pi, \{i, i'\}) \Vdash \exists_1 p\, (\textbf{if } p \textbf{ then } a \textbf{ else } a * a \textbf{ fi})$, then we would have a 1-local p-variant π' of π such that $S, (\pi', \{i, i'\}) \Vdash \textbf{if } p \textbf{ then } a \textbf{ else } a * a \textbf{ fi}$. But by assumption $(r, c) \in \pi'(p)$ iff $(r', c') \in \pi'(p)$, so we have either $S, (\pi', \{i, i'\}) \Vdash a$ or $S, (\pi', \{i, i'\}) \Vdash a * a$. But neither of these is possible, since one or the other interval has the wrong length.

Our intuition in writing Q is that it specifies a program that chooses to do either a or $a * a$ on the basis of some locally computable test p. The refinement $P \sqsubseteq^* Q$ is contrary to this intuition: it states that Q may be implemented by using in place of p *any* test, even one not locally computable. Intuitively, this result is obtained by using a different 1-local test in different executions of the program. Our semantics has been designed so as to avoid this: it ensures that a *uniform* test p is used in every execution of the program. Thereby, the undesirable refinement is blocked.

We remark that a slight variant of the example is a valid, and desired refinement: $[\exists_1 p\, (\mathsf{Nec}(p \equiv \phi))]\ P \sqsubseteq Q$. Here, the coercion states that ϕ is in fact equivalent to a 1-local proposition. We will use this rule below. □

4 Validity and Valid Refinement

We now briefly discuss the role of assertions $\{\phi\}_C$ in the framework and define the associated semantic notions. The reader is referred to [16] for a more detailed explanation of these ideas in a simpler setting.

Intuitively, an assertion $\{\phi\}_C$ is like an annotation at a program location stating that ϕ is guaranteed to hold whenever the program execution reaches this location. Moreover, such an assertion states that this fact "depends" only on constraints in the program (specifications and coercions) labelled with constraint variables in the set C, as well as on concrete program fragments. (We do not include labels for these because they cannot be "refined away".) The reason we include the justification C for the assertion is that it proves to be necessary to track such information in order to be able to formulate a number of desirable refinement rules. These rules refine a program fragment in ways that depend upon the larger program context within which the fragment occurs.

One typical example of this is a rule concerning the elimination of coercions. Suppose a coercion $[\phi]$ occurs at a program location where ϕ is guaranteed to hold. Intuitively, we would like to say that the coercion can be eliminated (replaced by ϵ) in such circumstances. However, the attempt to formulate this by the refinement rule $\epsilon \leq \{\phi\}\ [\phi]$ is not quite correct, for the reason the assertion holds could be the very coercion we seek to eliminate. (It may seem a little odd at first to say that the justification for the assertion is some part of the program text that follows, but consider the case of $\phi = \Diamond\psi$. See [16] for an example that makes essential use of assertions justified by later pieces of program text.) The use of justifications enables us to formulate the rule as $\epsilon \leq \{\phi\}_C\, [\phi]^X$, *provided* X is not in C, i.e., provided the assertion does not rely upon the coercion. This blocks the circular reasoning.

The semantics of assertions is formalized as follows. In order to capture constraint dependencies, we first define for each program P and constraint set $C \subseteq CV$ a program relax(P, C) that is like P, except that only constraints whose labels are in C are enforced: all other constraints are relaxed. Formally, we obtain relax(P, C) from P by replacing each occurrence of a coercion $[\phi]^X$ where $X \notin C$ by ϵ, and also replacing each occurrence of a specification $[\phi, \psi]^X$ where $X \notin C$ by $[\mathit{false}, \mathit{true}]^X$ in P^C.

We may now define a program P to be *valid* with respect to a set of interpreted systems $\mathcal{S}$ when for all assertions $\{\phi\}_C$ in P, all interpreted systems $(S, \pi) \in \mathcal{S}$ and all intervals sets I over S, all embeddings θ of $T_{\mathsf{relax}(P,C)}$ into $S, (I, \pi)$ have the property that for all nodes n of $T_{\mathsf{relax}(P,C)}$ labelled with $\{\phi\}_C$, we have $S, \theta(n) \Vdash [\phi]$. Intuitively, the embedding represents an execution of P

in which only constraints in C are enforced, and we check that the associated assertions hold at the appropriate points in the execution. Note that when n is labelled by an assertion, $I_\theta(n)$ must be a set of intervals of length 0. Moreover, the semantics of $S, (I, \pi) \Vdash [\phi]$ checks ϕ only at finite points in this set. Thus, validity can be understood as a kind of generalized partial correctness. We define validity with respect to a set of interpreted systems $\mathcal{S}$ to allow assumptions concerning the environment to be modelled: e.g., $\mathcal{S}$ might be the set of all interpreted systems in which actions have specific intended interpretations. We give an example of this in the next section.

Clearly, we want to avoid programs that are not valid (such as $[p]^X \{\neg p\}_{\{X\}}$). Thus, we would now like a notion of refinement that preserves validity, so that we derive only valid programs from valid programs by refinement. The refinement relation $\sqsubseteq$ defined above does not have this property. However, we may use it to define a notion that does. In order to do so, we first need to define a technical notion. A *justification transformation* is a mapping $\eta : 2^{CV} \longrightarrow 2^{CV}$ that is increasing, i.e., satisfies $C \subseteq \eta(C)$ for all $C \subseteq CV$. The result of applying a justification transformation η to a program P is the program $P\eta$ obtained by replacing each instance of an assertion $\{\phi\}_C$ in P by the assertion $\{\phi\}_{\eta(C)}$. When $R(Z)$ is a program containing a program variable Z and P is a program, we write $R\eta(P)$ for the result of first applying η to $R(Z)$ and then substituting P for Z. We need such transformations for refinements such as replacing $\{\phi\}_C[\phi]^X$ by ϵ when $X \notin C$ within some large program context. Intuitively, when we do this, any assertion in the larger context that depended on the coercion labelled X is still valid, but its justification should now include C in place of X.

The identity justification transformation is denoted by ι. We will also represent justification transformations using expressions of the form $X \hookrightarrow D$, where $X \in CV$ and $D \subseteq CV$. Such an expression denotes the justification transformation η such that $\eta(C) = C \cup D$ if $X \in C$ and $\eta(C) = C$ otherwise.

Let $\mathcal{S}$ be a set of interpreted systems, let η be a justification transformation and let P and Q be programs. Say that P *validly refines* Q *in* $\mathcal{S}$ *under* η, and write $P \leq_\eta^{\mathcal{S}} Q$, if for all programs $R(Z)$ with Z a program variable, if $R(Q)$ is valid with respect to $\mathcal{S}$ then $R\eta(P)$ is valid with respect to $\mathcal{S}$, and for all $(S, \pi) \in \mathcal{S}$ and interval sets I over S, if $S, (I, \pi) \Vdash R\eta(P)$ then $S, (I, \pi) \Vdash R(Q)$.

We remark that other definitions of valid refinement are possible. While intuitive, the definition above is very sensitive to the syntax of the programming language. We will consider some closely related semantic alternatives elsewhere.

4.1 Valid Refinement Rules

We now present a number of rules concerning valid refinement that are sound with respect to the semantics just presented, making no attempt at completeness. We focus on rules concerning the existential quantifiers, and refer to [16] for additional rules concerning the other constructs, which are also sound in the framework of the present paper.

The following rules make it possible for refinement to broken down into a sequence of steps that operate on small program fragments. (Only justification transformation operate globally, but this can also be managed locally by means of appropriate data structures.)

$$\frac{P \leq^{\mathbb{S}}_{\eta} Q,\ Q \leq^{\mathbb{S}}_{\eta'} R}{P \leq^{\mathbb{S}}_{\eta\circ\eta'} R} \qquad \frac{P \leq^{\mathbb{S}}_{\eta} Q}{R\eta(P) \leq^{\mathbb{S}}_{\eta} R(Q)}$$

Reducing the amount of nondeterminism and introducing a coercion are sound refinement steps.

$$P \leq^{\mathbb{S}}_{\iota} P + Q \qquad [\phi] \leq^{\mathbb{S}}_{\iota} \epsilon$$

Quantification over local propositional variables can be introduced, extracted from a coercion, and lifted to contexts.

$$\exists_1 p\,(P) \leq^{\mathbb{S}}_{\iota} P \quad \textit{if } p \textit{ not free in } P \qquad \textbf{i-lq}$$

$$\exists_1 p\,([\phi]) \leq^{\mathbb{S}}_{\iota} [\exists_1 p\,(\phi)] \qquad \textbf{ext-lq}$$

$$\exists_1 p\,(R(P)) \leq^{\mathbb{S}}_{\iota} R(\exists_1 p\,(P)) \quad \textit{if } p \textit{ not free in } R(Z) \qquad \textbf{lift-lq}$$

Let P_ϕ denote the program obtained from P by substituting formula ϕ for all free occurrences of p in P, while taking the usual care of free variables in ϕ by renaming clashing bound variables in P.

$$[\exists_1 p\,(\mathsf{Nec}(\phi \equiv p))]\ P_\phi \leq^{\mathbb{S}}_{\iota} \exists_1 p\,(P) \qquad \textbf{inst-lp}$$

4.2 Single-Stepping Programs and Loops

Reasoning about termination of a loop, say, **while** g **do** P **od** becomes easier when strict bounds on the running time of P are known. We present here a simple example of this phenomenon that is useful for the example we present in Sect. 5. More general rules can be formulated than the one we develop here.

Say that program P is *single-stepping*, if $S, (\pi, I) \Vdash P$ and $r[c,d] \in I$ and $c < \infty$ imply that $d = 1 + c$, for all S, π, and I. In a slightly broader syntax with existential quantification over arbitrary propositions, not just local ones, the fact that P is single-stepping could be expressed by:

$$P \leq^{\mathbb{S}}_{\eta} \exists p\,([\bigcirc\, \mathsf{first}\, p]\ [\mathit{true}, \mathsf{first}\, p]) \ .$$

where $\mathsf{first}\,\phi$ is an abbreviation for $\phi \wedge \neg\ominus\diamondminus\phi$, which holds exactly at the first point in a run that makes ϕ true. This notion can be combined with the usual pre/post-condition style of specifying P's behaviour to specify that P is single-stepping and terminates in points satisfying ψ when started in points satisfying ϕ:

$$P \leq^{\mathbb{S}}_{\eta} \exists p \left([\bigcirc\, \mathsf{first}\, p]^X\ [\mathit{true}, \mathsf{first}\, p \wedge (\ominus\phi \rightarrow \psi)]^X \right)$$

Denote the RHS of the above by $\mathbf{ss}[\phi,\psi]^X$. So $S,(\pi,I) \Vdash \mathbf{ss}[\phi,\psi]^X$ if for all $r[c,d] \in I$, whenever $c < \infty$ and $(S,\pi),(r,c) \models \phi$, then both $d = c+1$ and $(S,\pi),(r,d) \models \psi$. Observe that $\mathbf{ss}[\phi,\psi]^X$ takes a single step regardless of whether ϕ holds initially. Consequently, $\mathbf{ss}[\phi,\psi]^X$ is indeed single-stepping. Adding the single-stepping requirement yields a valid refinement: $\mathbf{ss}[\phi,\psi]^X \leq_\iota^{\mathbb{S}} [\phi,\psi]^X$. The following rule for single-stepping loop bodies will be used in Section 5.

$$[\phi \to \psi]^X \, \exists_1 p \begin{pmatrix} [\psi \to \Diamond p]^X * \\ \mathbf{while}^X \, \neg p \, \mathbf{do} \, \mathbf{ss}[\psi \wedge \neg p, \psi]^X \, \mathbf{od} * \\ [\psi \wedge p \to \phi']^X \end{pmatrix} \leq_\iota^{\mathbb{S}} [\phi,\phi']^X \qquad \textbf{i-ss-loop}$$

To apply this rule, one has to invent a (not necessarily local) loop invariant ψ. Finding a concrete local guard is postponed via use of the existential quantification. Just as for ordinary sequential programs, the first and last coercion link the invariant to the pre- and postcondition of the specification that is to be implemented. The second coercion, $[\psi \to \Diamond p]^X$ ensures termination of the loop.

5 Example: Autonomous Robot

In this section we discuss an example that closely resembles Example 7.2.2 in [4] which in turn has been inspired by the 1994 conference version of [2].

A robot travels along an endless corridor, which in this example is identified with the natural numbers. The robot starts at 0 and has the goal of stopping in the goal region $\{2,3,4\}$. To judge when to stop the robot has a sensor that reads the current position. (See Fig. 1.) Unfortunately, this sensor is inaccurate;

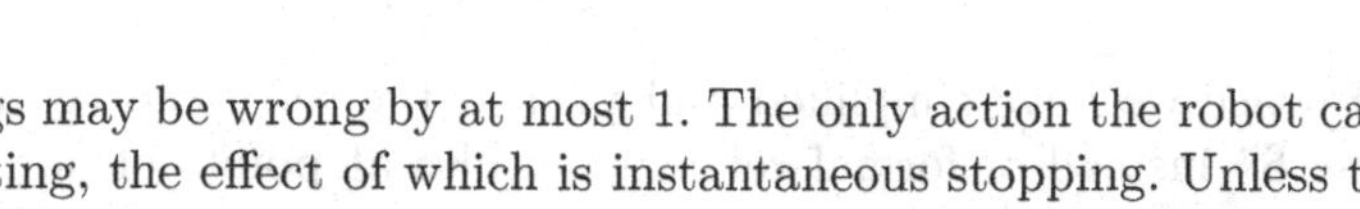

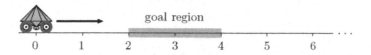

Fig. 1. Autonomous Robot

the readings may be wrong by at most 1. The only action the robot can actively take is halting, the effect of which is instantaneous stopping. Unless this action is taken, the robot may move by steps of length 1 to higher numbers. Unless it has taken its halting action, it is beyond its control whether it moves in a step. Our task is now to design a control program for the robot such that:

(safety) The robot only stops in the goal region.

(liveness) The robot is guaranteed to stop eventually.

A modest assumption about the environment is needed for the latter to be achievable. We insist that it is not the case that the robot sits still forever without moving forward or taking the halting action.

To model these assumptions we introduce a system constraint reflecting the following conditions. Strictly speaking, our specification language $\mathcal{L}$ only contains variables that are interpreted as Boolean values but none for natural numbers. It is possible to present this example only using propositions by sacrificing legibility. An extension of our framework to typed variables is straightforward and omitted here for brevity. Let $\mathcal{S}$ be the set of interpreted systems satisfying the following constraints.

1. Initially, the robot's position x is zero: $\mathit{init} \to x = 0$, where *init* abbreviates the formula $\neg\ominus \mathit{true}$, which holds exactly in the initial points of runs.
2. Proposition h is initially false and it is becomes true once the robot has halted. Halting is an irreversible action ($h \to \bigcirc h$) and means that the robot does not move anymore: $h \to x = \bigcirc x$.
3. Proposition m is true iff the robot moves in the current step. Moving means that the robot's position is increased by one, otherwise it is unchanged: $(m \to x + 1 = \bigcirc x) \wedge \neg m \to x = \bigcirc x$.
4. If the robot has not halted it should move eventually: $(\neg h) \mathsf{U} (h \vee m)$.
5. The robot's sensor reading is s (an integer) and off by at most one from x, the actual position: $x - 1 \leq s \leq x + 1$.
6. Only the robot's basic action *halt* immediately halts the robot.

The variables and propositions mentioned in the constraints are *reserved* in the sense that quantification over them is is not allowed. Thus they essentially "behave" the same in each $(S, \pi) \in \mathcal{S}$. In the full paper we introduce a syntactic representation for such system constraints, give a formal semantics, and introduce valid refinement rules that exploit these constraints. These rules fall into two classes: assertion introduction rules and rules for specification implementation by basic actions. A typical assertion introduction rule for this particular $\mathcal{S}$ is

$$\{\mathit{init} \to x = 0 \wedge \neg h\}_{\emptyset} \leq_{\iota}^{\mathcal{S}} \epsilon \tag{1}$$

allowing one to assert a property of initial states in interpreted systems contained in $\mathcal{S}$. For the halting action we would have

$$\mathit{halt} \leq_{\iota}^{\mathcal{S}} \mathbf{ss}[\mathit{true}, h \wedge x = \ominus x] \ . \tag{2}$$

For lack of space we have simplified and pruned the set-up to the above. We refer to "use $\mathcal{S}$" instead of formal refinement rules at points of our derivation that refer to the rules omitted.

In [4] a run-based specification of the system is given by a temporal logic formula equivalent to $\Box(h \to g) \wedge \Diamond h$, where g abbreviates being in the goal region, i.e., $2 \leq x \leq 4$. The two conjuncts respectively formalize the safety and liveness property from above. The main problem in finding the robot's protocol is to derive a suitable local condition for halting.

We formally derive a protocol for the robot from as abstract as possible a specification of the protocol. The point of departure of our derivation below merely states that the robot must eventually halt in the goal region when started in an initial state.

$$[\mathit{init}, g \wedge h]^X$$

$\geq_\iota^{\mathcal{S}}$ (sequential composition [16])

$$[\mathit{init}, g]^X * [g, g \wedge h]^X$$

$\geq_\iota^{\mathcal{S}}$ (use $\mathcal{S}$ to establish $\mathit{halt} \leq_\iota^{\mathcal{S}} [g, g \wedge h]$, cf. (2))

$$[\mathit{init}, g \wedge \neg h]^X * \mathit{halt}$$

$\geq_\iota^{\mathcal{S}}$ (**i-ss-loop** with loop invariant $x \leq 4$ to prevent exiting the goal region) ♣

$$[\mathit{init} \rightarrow x \leq 4]^X *$$
$$\exists_1 p \left([x{\leq}4{\rightarrow}\Diamond p]^X \,\mathbf{while}^X \neg p \,\mathbf{do}\, \mathbf{ss}[x{\leq}4{\wedge}p, x{\leq}4]^X \mathbf{od}\, [x \leq 4 \wedge p \rightarrow g]^X \right) *$$
$$\mathit{halt}$$

$\geq_\iota^{\mathcal{S}}$ (use $\mathcal{S}$ as in (1) to assert $\mathit{init} \rightarrow x \leq 4$, eliminate coercion)

$$\exists_1 p \left([x{\leq}4{\rightarrow}\Diamond p]^X \,\mathbf{while}^X \neg p \,\mathbf{do}\, \mathbf{ss}[x{\leq}4{\wedge}p, x{\leq}4]^X \mathbf{od}\, [x \leq 4 \wedge p \rightarrow g]^X \right) *$$
$$\mathit{halt}$$

At this point we select the local test p. The need to satisfy coercion $x \leq 4 \wedge p \rightarrow g$ together with the fact that the sensor reading differs from the position x by at most 1, leads naturally to the choice $p = s > 2$.

$\geq_\iota^{\mathcal{S}}$ (**inst-lp**)

$$[\exists_1 p\, (\mathsf{Nec}(p \equiv (s > 2)))]^Y * [x \leq 4 \rightarrow \Diamond s > 2]^X *$$
$$\mathbf{while}^X\ s \leq 2\ \mathbf{do}\ \mathbf{ss}[x \leq 4 \wedge s \leq 2, x \leq 4]^X\ \mathbf{od} * [x \leq 4 \wedge s > 2 \rightarrow g]^X * \mathit{halt}$$

$\geq_\iota^{\mathcal{S}}$ (eliminate two coercions using $\mathcal{S}$)

$$[x \leq 4 \rightarrow \Diamond s > 2]^X * \mathbf{while}^X\ s \leq 2\ \mathbf{do}\ \mathbf{ss}[x \leq 4 \wedge s \leq 2, x \leq 4]^X\ \mathbf{od} * \mathit{halt}$$

$\geq_\iota^{\mathcal{S}}$ (use $\mathcal{S}$ for $\Lambda \leq_\eta^{\mathcal{S}} \mathbf{ss}[x \leq 4 \wedge s \leq 2, x \leq 4]^X$)

$$[x \leq 4 \rightarrow \Diamond s > 2]^X * \mathbf{while}^X\ s \leq 2\ \mathbf{do}\ \Lambda\ \mathbf{od} * \mathit{halt}$$

$\geq_\iota^{\mathcal{S}}$ (introduce coercion and strengthen coercion [16])

$$[\mathit{init}]^Y * [\Diamond s > 2]^X * \mathbf{while}^X\ s \leq 2\ \mathbf{do}\ \Lambda\ \mathbf{od} * \mathit{halt}$$

The coercion $\Diamond s > 2$ can be eliminated by reasoning about both the program and $\mathcal{S}$. From the initial state predicate it follows that the loop begins in a state satisfying $\neg h$. The only action executed in the loop is Λ, which in $\mathcal{S}$ preserves the value of h. On termination of the loop the guard must be false, i.e., $s > 2$. In (the purely hypothetical) case the loop diverges the run satisfies $\Box \neg h$, which together with point 4, $(\neg h)\,\mathsf{U}\,(h \vee m)$, allows us to conclude that the robot moves infinitely often. But this also implies that eventually $s > 2$.

$\geq^{\mathcal{S}}_{\iota}$ (use $\mathcal{S}$ and the loop)

$$[init]^Y * \{\Diamond(s > 2)\}_Y * [\Diamond(s > 2)]^X \, \textbf{while}^X \; s \leq 2 \; \textbf{do} \; \Lambda \; \textbf{od} * halt$$

$\geq^{\mathcal{S}}_{X \hookrightarrow \{Y\}}$ (eliminate coercion)

$$[init]^Y \, \textbf{while}^X \; s \leq 2 \; \textbf{do} \; \Lambda \; \textbf{od} * halt$$

Finally, the rule

$$\frac{[\phi] \, P \leq^{\mathcal{S}}_{\eta} [\phi, \psi]^X}{P \leq^{\mathcal{S}}_{\eta} [\phi, \psi]^X}$$

proves $\textbf{while}^X \; s \leq 2 \; \textbf{do} \; \Lambda \; \textbf{od} * halt \leq^{\mathcal{S}}_{X \hookrightarrow \{Y\}} [init, g \wedge h]^X$, yielding a concrete implementation.

An alternative derivation from point ♣ onwards indicates how the knowledge-based approach could be modeled in our framework. Firstly we would choose just *true* as loop invariant. Secondly, instead of guessing the appropriate local exit condition $s > 2$ we would let the robot execute the loop until it *knows* that it is in the goal region, i.e., instantiate p with $K_1 g$. The derivation then proceeds as before till reaching the stage before eliminating the last coercion concerning completeness of the test:

$$[init]^Y * [\Diamond(K_1 g)]^Y \, \textbf{while}^X \; \neg K_1 g \; \textbf{do} \; \Lambda \; \textbf{od} * halt$$

To develop this to an implementation, that is, eliminate $[\Diamond(K_1 g)]^Y$, requires additional features to be introduced into the framework, so we will not pursue this here.

6 Conclusion and Future Work

We have sketched the main features of the first compositional refinement calculus incorporating an assertion language strong enough to express temporal and epistemic notions. While, as we have noted, some further features are required to give a complete treatment of knowledge-based programs in the sense of [4], we already have enough expressiveness in the framework to be able to view knowledge-based programs as special cases of our more general programs using quantified local propositions. Moreover, the derivation we have presented at length is very much in the spirit of the knowledge-based approach. (Indeed, precisely the same implementation is derived in [2].) In contrast to tests for knowledge, tests for local predicates satisfying some extra conditions are more likely, in general, to admit efficient implementations. In future work, we plan to extend the framework of this paper to multiple agents and asynchrony. Ultimately, we hope to achieve a highly expressive, flexible and abstract framework supporting the knowledge-based development of distributed systems.

References

1. R.-J. Back and J. von Wright. *Refinement Calculus: A Systematic Introduction.* Graduate Texts in Computer Science. Springer-Verlag, 1998.
2. R. I. Brafman, J.-C. Latombe, Y. Moses, and Y. Shoham. Applications of a logic of knowledge to motion planning under uncertainty. *Journal of the ACM*, 44(5):633–668, Sept. 1997.
3. K. Engelhardt, R. van der Meyden, and Y. Moses. Knowledge and the logic of local propositions. In I. Gilboa, editor, *Theoretical Aspects of Rationality and Knowledge, Proceedings of the Seventh Conference (TARK 1998)*, pages 29–41. Morgan Kaufmann, July 1998.
4. R. Fagin, J. Y. Halpern, Y. Moses, and M. Y. Vardi. *Reasoning About Knowledge.* MIT-Press, 1995.
5. R. Fagin, J. Y. Halpern, Y. Moses, and M. Y. Vardi. Knowledge-based programs. *Distributed Computing*, 10(4):199–225, 1997.
6. J. Y. Halpern and Y. Moses. Knowledge and common knowledge in a distributed environment. *Journal of the ACM*, 37(3):549–587, July 1990.
7. I. Hayes. Separating timing and calculation in real-time refinement. In J. Grundy, M. Schwenke, and T. Vickers, editors, *International Refinement Workshop and Formal Methods Pacific 1998*, Discrete Mathematics and Theoretical Computer Science, pages 1–16. Springer-Verlag, 1998.
8. Z. Manna and A. Pnueli. *The Temporal Logic of Reactive and Concurrent Systems: Specification.* Springer-Verlag, 1992.
9. C. C. Morgan. *Programming from Specifications.* Prentice Hall, 1990.
10. J. M. Morris. A theoretical basis for stepwise refinement and the programming calculus. *Science of Computer Programming*, 9(3):287–306, Dec. 1987.
11. Y. Moses and O. Kislev. Knowledge-oriented programming. In *Proceeding of the 12th Annual ACM Symposium on Principles of Distributed Computing (PODC 93)*, pages 261–270, New York, USA, Aug. 1993. ACM Press.
12. Y. Moses and M. R. Tuttle. Programming simultaneous actions using common knowledge. *Algorithmica*, 3:121–169, 1988.
13. B. Sanders. A predicate transformer approach to knowledge and knowledge-based protocols. In *Proceeding of the 10th Annual ACM Symposium on Principles of Distributed Computing (PODC 91)*, pages 217–230, 19–21 Aug. 1991.
14. M. Utting and C. Fidge. A real-time refinement calculus that changes only time. In H. Jifeng, J. Cooke, and P. Wallis, editors, *BCS-FACS Seventh Refinement Workshop.* Springer-Verlag, 1996.
15. R. van der Meyden. Knowledge based programs: On the complexity of perfect recall in finite environments. In Y. Shoham, editor, *Proceedings of the Sixth Conference on Theoretical Aspects of Rationality and Knowledge*, pages 31–50. Morgan Kaufmann, Mar. 17–20 1996.
16. R. van der Meyden and Y. Moses. On refinement and temporal annotations. `http://www.cse.unsw.edu.au/~{}meyden/research/temprefine.ps`.
17. R. van der Meyden and Y. Moses. Top-down considerations on distributed systems. In *Proceedings 12th International Symposium on Distributed Computing, DISC'98*, volume 1499 of *LNCS*, pages 16–19, Sept. 1998. Springer-Verlag.
18. M. Y. Vardi. Implementing knowledge-basd programs. In Y. Shoham, editor, *Proceedings of the Sixth Conference on Theoretical Aspects of Rationality and Knowledge*, pages 15–30. Morgan Kaufmann, Mar. 17–20 1996.

A Higher-Order Simulation Relation for System F

Jo Erskine Hannay

LFCS, Division of Informatics, University of Edinburgh
joh@dcs.ed.ac.uk

Abstract. The notion of data type specification refinement is discussed in a setting of System F and the logic for parametric polymorphism of Plotkin and Abadi. At first order, one gets a notion of specification refinement up to observational equivalence in the logic simply by using Luo's formalism. This paper generalises this notion to abstract data types whose signatures contain higher-order and polymorphic functions. At higher order, the tight connection in the logic between the existence of a simulation relation and observational equivalence ostensibly breaks down. We show that an alternative notion of simulation relation is suitable. This also gives a simulation relation in the logic that composes at higher order, thus giving a syntactic logical counterpart to recent advances on the semantic level.

1 Introduction

The idea behind formal specification refinement is that a program is the end-product of a step-wise refinement process starting from an abstract high-level specification. At each refinement step some design decisions and implementation issues are resolved, and if each refinement step can be proven correct, the resulting program is guaranteed to satisfy the initial specification.

There are several frameworks in which to do this and several ideas of what it is for one specification to be a refinement of another. A prominent framework is that of algebraic specification; see [9] for a survey and comprehensive bibliography. But there has been substantial development in other fields as well, notably in type theory, where also ideas from algebraic specification have been expressed.

This paper investigates specification refinement in a setting consisting of System F and relational parametricity in Reynolds' sense [35,23] as expressed in Plotkin and Abadi's logic for parametric polymorphism [31]. This setting allows an elegant formalisation of abstract data types as existential types [27]. Moreover, the relational parametricity axiom enables one to derive in the logic that two concrete data types, *i.e.* inhabitants of existential type, are equal if and only if there exists a simulation relation [16] between their implementation parts. Together with the fact that at first order, equality at existential type is derivably equivalent to a notion of observational equivalence, this formalises the semantic proof principle of Mitchell [25]. This lifts the type-theoretic formalism

J. Tiuryn (Ed.): FOSSACS 2000, LNCS 1784, pp. 130–145, 2000.

of refinement due to Luo [22] to a notion in the logic of specification refinement up to observational equivalence; a key issue in program development.

In this paper, we discuss the above type-theoretic notion of specification refinement in more generality, *i.e.* we treat data types whose operations may be higher order and polymorphic. At higher order, the formal link between the existence of a simulation relation and observational equivalence breaks down. Our solution in the logic is to use an alternative notion of simulation relation based on a weaker arrow-type relation. This notion composes at higher-order, thus relating the syntactic level to recent and on-going work on the semantic level remedying the fact that logical relations traditionally used to describe refinement do not compose at higher order [17,18,21,20,32].

In [12] an account of algebraic specification refinement [38,37] is mapped to the first-order type-theoretic refinement notion, and the two accounts of refinement are shown to coincide. Important issues in algebraic specification refinement, such as the choice of input sorts [36] and the stability of constructors [39,37,10], are automatically resolved in the type-theoretic setting. Other work linking algebraic specification and type theory includes [28,34,2,41,40]. Relevant work using System F and parametricity includes [29,30] showing that the introduction of non-terminating recursion also breaks down the tight correspondence between the existence of a simulation relation and observational equivalence.

In [12] a proof method from algebraic specification for proving observational refinements [5,4,6] is imported into the type-theory logic by adding axioms postulating the existence of quotients and sub-objects. Work related to this is [33,42]. The higher-order generalisation of this is to be found in [13].

Section 2 outlines the type theory. In Sect. 3 refinement is introduced in a first-order setting, and Sect. 4 generalises to higher-order and polymorphism.

2 System F and the Logic for Parametric Polymorphism

We briefly recall the parametric λ-calculus System F, and sketch the accompanying logic of [31,24] for relational parametricity on System F. It is this accompanying logic that bears a relational extension rather than the λ-calculus. See [1] for a more internalised approach. System F has types and terms as follows:

$$T ::= X \mid T \to T \mid \forall X.T \qquad\qquad t ::= x \mid \lambda x{:}T.t \mid tt \mid \Lambda X.t \mid tT$$

where X and x range over type and term variables resp. However, formulae are now built using the usual connectives from equations *and* relation symbols:

$$\phi ::= (t =_A u) \mid R(t,u) \mid \cdots \mid \forall R \subset A \times B.\phi \mid \exists R \subset A \times B.\phi$$

where R ranges over relation symbols. We write $\alpha[R, X, x]$ to indicate *possible* and *all* occurrences of R, X and x in α, and may write $\alpha[\rho, A, t]$ for the result of substitution, following the appropriate rules concerning capture.

A second-order environment consists of a type environment Δ and a term-environment Γ depending on Δ as usual. For notational convenience we will amalgamate environments into a single environment Γ. Judgements for type and term formation are as usual. However, formula formation now involves relation symbols, and we therefore employ relation environments, *viz.* a finite sequence Υ of relational typings $R \subset A \times B$ of relation variables, depending on Δ, and obeying standard conventions for environments. The formation rules for atomic formulae consists of the usual one for equations, and now also one for relations:

$$\frac{\Gamma \vdash t{:}A, \quad \Gamma \vdash u{:}B, \quad \Gamma \vdash \Upsilon, \quad \Upsilon \vdash R \subset A \times B}{\Gamma, \Upsilon \vdash R(t,u)\ \mathit{Prop} \qquad (\textit{also written } tRu)}$$

The other formation rules for formulae are as one would expect. Relation environments will also be amalgamated into Γ. Relation definition is accommodated:

$$\frac{\Gamma, x{:}A, y{:}B \ \vdash\ \phi\ \mathit{Prop}}{\Gamma\ \vdash\ (x{:}A, y{:}B)\ .\ \phi\quad \subset A \times B}$$

For example $\mathsf{eq}_A \stackrel{\mathit{def}}{=} (x{:}A, y{:}A).(x =_A y)$.

If $\rho \subset A \times B$, $\rho' \subset A' \times B'$ and $\rho''[R] \subset A[Y] \times B[Z]$, then complex relations are built by $\rho \to \rho' \subset (A \to A') \times (B \to B')$ where

$$(\rho \to \rho') \stackrel{\mathit{def}}{=} (f{:}A \to A', g{:}B \to B').(\forall x{:}A \forall x'{:}B.(x\rho x' \ \Rightarrow\ (fx)\rho'(gx')))$$

and $\forall(Y, Z, R \subset Y \times Z)\rho''[R] \subset (\forall Y.A[Y]) \times (\forall Z.B[Z])$ where

$$\forall(Y, Z, R \subset Y{\times}Z)\rho'' \stackrel{\mathit{def}}{=} (y{:}\forall Y.A[Y], z{:}\forall Z.B[Z]).(\forall Y \forall Z \forall R \subset Y{\times}Z.((yY)\rho''[R](zZ)))$$

One can now acquire further definable relations by substituting definable relations for type variables in types. For $\boldsymbol{X} = X_1, \ldots, X_n$, $\boldsymbol{B} = B_1, \ldots, B_n$, $\boldsymbol{C} = C_1, \ldots, C_n$ and $\boldsymbol{\rho} = \rho_1, \ldots, \rho_n$, where $\rho_i \subset B_i{\times}C_i$, we get $T[\boldsymbol{\rho}] \subset T[\boldsymbol{B}]{\times}T[\boldsymbol{C}]$, the action of $T[\boldsymbol{X}]$ on $\boldsymbol{\rho}$, defined by cases on $T[\boldsymbol{X}]$ as follows:

$$\begin{array}{ll} T[\boldsymbol{X}] = X_i : & T[\boldsymbol{\rho}] = \rho_i \\ T[\boldsymbol{X}] = T'[\boldsymbol{X}] \to T''[\boldsymbol{X}] : & T[\boldsymbol{\rho}] = T'[\boldsymbol{\rho}] \to T''[\boldsymbol{\rho}] \\ T[\boldsymbol{X}] = \forall X'.T'[\boldsymbol{X}, X'] : & T[\boldsymbol{\rho}] = \forall(Y, Z, R \subset Y \times Z).T'[\boldsymbol{\rho}, R] \end{array}$$

The proof system giving the consequence relation of the logic is natural deduction over formulae now involving relation symbols, and is hence augmented with inference rules for relation symbols, for example we have for Φ a finite set of formulae:

$$\frac{\Phi \vdash_{\Gamma, R \subset A \times B} \phi[R]}{\Phi \vdash_{\Gamma} \forall R \subset A \times B\ .\ \phi[R]} \qquad \frac{\Phi \vdash_{\Gamma} \forall R \subset A \times B.\phi[R], \quad \Gamma \vdash \rho \subset A \times B}{\Phi \vdash_{\Gamma} \phi[\rho]}$$

We will usually conveniently omit the sequent symbol $\vdash_\Gamma$ henceforth. One also has axioms for equational reasoning and $\beta\eta$ equalities. Finally, the following parametricity axiom schema is asserted:

$$\textsc{Param}:\ \forall Y_1, \ldots, \forall Y_n \forall u{:}(\forall X.T[X, Y_1, \ldots, Y_n])\ .\ u(\forall X.T[X, \mathsf{eq}_{Y_1}, \ldots, \mathsf{eq}_{Y_n}])u$$

To understand, it helps to ignore the parameters Y_i and expand the definition to get $\forall u{:}(\forall X.T[X])\ .\forall Y \forall Z \forall R \subset Y \times Z\ .\ u(Y)\ T[R]\ u(Z)$ *i.e.* if one instantiates a polymorphic inhabitant at two related types then the results are also related. This logic is sound w.r.t. to the parametric PER-model of [3] and the syntactic parametric models of [14]. Crucially, we have the following link to equality:

Fact 1 (Identity Extension Lemma [31]**).** *For any $T[Z]$, the following sequent is derivable using* PARAM.

$$\forall \boldsymbol{Z}.\forall u, v{:}T\ .\ (u\ T[\mathbf{eq}_{\boldsymbol{Z}}]\ v \ \Leftrightarrow\ (u =_T v))$$

Encapsulation is provided by the following encoding of existential types and the following pack and unpack combinators.

$$\exists X.T[X] \stackrel{def}{=} \forall Y.(\forall X.(T[X] \to Y) \to Y)$$

$$\begin{aligned}&\mathsf{pack}_{T[X]}{:}\forall X.(T[X] \to \exists X.T[X])\\ &\mathsf{pack}_{T[X]}(A)(impl) \stackrel{def}{=} \Lambda Y.\lambda f{:}\forall X.(T[X] \to Y).f(A)(impl)\end{aligned}$$

$$\begin{aligned}&\mathsf{unpack}_{T[X]}{:}(\exists X.T[X]) \to \forall Y.(\forall X.(T[X] \to Y) \to Y)\\ &\mathsf{unpack}_{T[X]}(package)(B)(client) \stackrel{def}{=} package(B)(client)\end{aligned}$$

We omit subscripts to pack and unpack as much as possible. Operationally, pack packages a data representation and an implementation of operators on that data representation. The resulting package is a polymorphic functional that given a client and its result domain, instantiates the client with the particular elements of the package. And unpack is the application operator for pack.

Fact 2 (Characterisation by Simulation Relation [31]**).** *The following sequent schema is derivable using* PARAM.

$$\begin{aligned}&\forall \boldsymbol{Z}.\forall u, v{:}\exists X.T[X, \boldsymbol{Z}]\ .\\ &\quad u =_{\exists X.T[X,\boldsymbol{Z}]} v \quad\Leftrightarrow\quad \exists A, B.\exists \mathfrak{a}{:}T[A, \boldsymbol{Z}], \mathfrak{b}{:}T[B, \boldsymbol{Z}].\exists R \subset A \times B\ .\\ &\qquad\qquad u = (\mathsf{pack} A \mathfrak{a})\ \wedge\ v = (\mathsf{pack} B \mathfrak{b})\ \wedge\ \mathfrak{a}(T[R, \mathbf{eq}_{\boldsymbol{Z}}])\mathfrak{b}\end{aligned}$$

The sequent in Fact 2 states the equivalence of equality at existential type with the existence of a simulation relation in the sense of [25]. From this we also get

$$\forall \boldsymbol{Z}.\forall u{:}\exists X.T[X, \boldsymbol{Z}].\exists A.\exists \mathfrak{a}{:}T[A, \boldsymbol{Z}]\ .\ u = (\mathsf{pack} A\, \mathfrak{a})$$

Weak versions of standard constructs such as products, initial and final (co-)algebras are encodable in System F [7]. With PARAM, these constructs are provably universal constructions. We can *e.g.* freely use product types. Given $\rho \subset A \times B$ and $\rho' \subset A' \times B'$, $(\rho \times \rho)$ is defined as the action $(X \times X')[\rho, \rho']$. One derives $\forall u{:}A \times A', v{:}B \times B'\ .\ u(\rho \times \rho')v \ \Leftrightarrow\ (\mathsf{fst}(u)\ \rho\ \mathsf{fst}(v) \wedge \mathsf{snd}(u)\ \rho\ \mathsf{snd}(v))$. We use the abbreviations $\mathsf{bool} \stackrel{def}{=} \forall X.X \to X \to X$, $\mathsf{nat} \stackrel{def}{=} \forall X.X \to (X \to X) \to X$, and $\mathsf{list}(A) \stackrel{def}{=} \forall X.X \to (A \to X \to X) \to X$. These inductive types are provably initial constructs.

3 Data Type Specification and First-Order Results

Existential types provide a nice way of specifying abstract data types [27]. In System F and the accompanying logic of [31], this mode of specification leads to specification up to observational equivalence, where the latter is defined w.r.t. some given finite set *Obs* of closed inductive types for which the Identity Extension Lemma (Fact 1) gives $x\,(C[\rho])\,y \;\Leftrightarrow\; x =_C y$. Examples are bool and nat. In the following we shall use record type notation as a notational convenience.

Definition 1 (Abstract Data Type Specification). *An* abstract data type specification *SP is a tuple*

$$\langle\langle Sig_{SP}, \Theta_{SP}\rangle, Obs\rangle$$

where $Sig_{SP} = \exists X.\mathfrak{T}_{SP}[X]$, *for* $\mathfrak{T}_{SP}[X] = Record(f_1{:}T_1, \ \ldots\ , f_k{:}T_k)$, *and where* $\Theta_{SP}(u) = \exists X.\exists \mathfrak{x}{:}\mathfrak{T}_{SP}[X]\ .\ u = (\mathsf{pack} X \mathfrak{x}) \ \wedge\ \Phi_{SP}[X, \mathfrak{x}]$.

If $\Theta_{SP}(u)$ *is derivable, then u is said to be a* realisation *of SP.*

Example 1. For example Stack $\stackrel{def}{=} \langle\langle Sig_{\mathsf{Stack}}, \Theta_{\mathsf{Stack}}\rangle, \{\mathsf{nat}\}\rangle$, where
$Sig_{\mathsf{Stack}} = \exists X.\mathfrak{T}_{\mathsf{Stack}}[X]$,
$\mathfrak{T}_{\mathsf{Stack}}[X] = Record(\mathsf{empty}{:}\,X, \mathsf{push}{:}\,\mathsf{nat}\times X \to X, \mathsf{pop}{:}\,X \to X, \mathsf{top}{:}\,X \to \mathsf{nat})$,
$\Theta_{\mathsf{Stack}}(u) = \exists X.\exists \mathfrak{x}{:}\mathfrak{T}_{\mathsf{Stack}}[X]\ .\ u = (\mathsf{pack} X \mathfrak{x}) \ \wedge$
$\forall x{:}\,\mathsf{nat}, s{:}\,X\ .\ \mathfrak{x}.\mathsf{pop}(\mathfrak{x}.\mathsf{push}(x, s)) = s \ \wedge$
$\forall x{:}\,\mathsf{nat}, s{:}\,X\ .\ \mathfrak{x}.\mathsf{top}(\mathfrak{x}.\mathsf{push}(x, s)) = x$ ○

We reserve $\mathfrak{T}[X]$ for the function-profile part of abstract data types $\exists X.\mathfrak{T}[X]$. For brevity, in this paper we do not consider parameterised specifications and so assume X to be the only free type variable in $\mathfrak{T}[X]$.

The notion of specification of Def. 1 resembles that of [22]. However, as we are about to see, the important difference is that here equality of data-type inhabitants is inherently behavioural, and implementation is up to observational equivalence. In analogy to the meta-level notion in [25], we define observational equivalence in terms of observable computations in the logic as follows.

Definition 2 (Observational Equivalence (ObsEq)). *Define* observational equivalence ObsEq w.r.t. *Obs in the logic by*

$$\begin{aligned}&\mathsf{ObsEq} \stackrel{def}{=} (u{:}\,\exists X.\mathfrak{T}[X], v{:}\,\exists X.\mathfrak{T}[X]).\\ &(\exists A, B.\exists \mathfrak{a}{:}\,\mathfrak{T}[A], \mathfrak{b}{:}\,\mathfrak{T}[B]\ .\ u = (\mathsf{pack} A\mathfrak{a}) \ \wedge\ v = (\mathsf{pack} B \mathfrak{b}) \ \wedge\\ &\qquad \textstyle\bigwedge_{C \in Obs} \forall f{:}\,\forall X.(\mathfrak{T}[X] \to C)\ .\ (f A\, \mathfrak{a}) = (f B\, \mathfrak{b}))\end{aligned}$$

The first result is essential to understanding the notion of specification in Def. 1. It is a syntactic counterpart to a semantic result in [25,26].

Theorem 3 ([12])**.** *Suppose* $\langle\langle \exists X.\mathfrak{T}[X], \Theta\rangle, Obs\rangle$ *is an abstract data type specification such that* $\mathfrak{T}[X]$ *only contains first-order function profiles. Then, assuming* PARAM, *equality at existential type is derivably equivalent to observational equivalence, i.e. the following is derivable in the logic.*

$$\forall u, v{:}\,\exists X.\mathfrak{T}[X]\ .\ u =_{\exists X.\mathfrak{T}[X]} v \quad\Leftrightarrow\quad u\ \mathsf{ObsEq}\ v$$

Proof: This follows from Fact 2 and Theorem 4 below. □

Theorem 4 ([12]). *Let $\exists X.\mathfrak{T}[X]$ be as in Theorem 3. Then, assuming* PARAM, *the existence of a simulation relation is derivably equivalent to observational equivalence, i.e. the following is derivable.*

$$\begin{array}{l}\forall A, B.\forall \mathfrak{a}{:}\mathfrak{T}[A], \mathfrak{b}{:}\mathfrak{T}[B] \,. \\ \quad \exists R\subset A\times B \,.\, \mathfrak{a}(\mathfrak{T}[R])\mathfrak{b} \quad \Leftrightarrow \quad \bigwedge_{C\in Obs} \forall f{:}\forall X.(\mathfrak{T}[X] \to C) \,.\, (f A\, \mathfrak{a}) = (f B\, \mathfrak{b})\end{array}$$

Proof: $\Rightarrow$: This follows from PARAM.

$\Leftarrow$: We must exhibit an R such that $\mathfrak{a}(\mathfrak{T}[R])\mathfrak{b}$. Semantically, [25,26,39] relate elements iff they are denotable by some common term. We mimic this: For R give $\mathsf{Dfnbl} \stackrel{def}{=} (a{:}A, b{:}B).(\exists f{:}\forall X.(\mathfrak{T}[X] \to X).(f A\, \mathfrak{a}) = a \ \wedge\ (f B\, \mathfrak{b}) = b)$. □

Given Theorem 3, $\Theta_{SP}(u)$ of Def. 1 expresses "u is observationally equivalent to a package $(\mathsf{pack} X \mathfrak{x})$ that satisfies the axioms Φ_{SP}". Hence specification according to Def. 1 is up to observational equivalence.

Notice that there is nothing hindering having free variables in an observable computation $f{:}\forall X.(\mathfrak{T}[X] \to C)$. Importantly, though, these free variables can not be of the existentially bound type.

Example 2 ([15]). Consider specification Set $\stackrel{def}{=} \langle\langle Sig_{\mathsf{Set}}, \Theta_{\mathsf{Set}}\rangle, \{\mathsf{bool}, \mathsf{nat}\}\rangle$, for
$Sig_{\mathsf{Set}} = \exists X.\mathfrak{T}_{\mathsf{Set}}[X]$,
$\mathfrak{T}_{\mathsf{Set}}[X] = Record(\mathsf{empty}{:}\, X, \mathsf{add}{:}\, \mathsf{nat}{\times}X{\to}X, \mathsf{remove}{:}\, \mathsf{nat}{\times}X{\to}X, \mathsf{in}{:}\, \mathsf{nat}{\times}X{\to}\mathsf{bool})$,

$$\begin{array}{l}\Theta_{\mathsf{Set}}(u) = \exists X.\exists \mathfrak{x}{:}\mathfrak{T}_{\mathsf{Set}}[X] \,.\, u = (\mathsf{pack} X \mathfrak{x}) \ \wedge \\ \qquad \forall x{:}\,\mathsf{nat}, s{:}\,X \,.\, \mathfrak{x}.\mathsf{add}(x, \mathfrak{x}.\mathsf{add}(x, s)) = \mathfrak{x}.\mathsf{add}(x, s) \ \wedge \\ \qquad \forall x, y{:}\,\mathsf{nat}, s{:}\,X \,.\, \mathfrak{x}.\mathsf{add}(x, \mathfrak{x}.\mathsf{add}(y, s)) = \mathfrak{x}.\mathsf{add}(y, \mathfrak{x}.\mathsf{add}(x, s)) \ \wedge \\ \qquad \forall x{:}\,\mathsf{nat} \,.\, \mathfrak{x}.\mathsf{in}(x, \mathfrak{x}.\mathsf{empty}) = \mathsf{false} \ \wedge \\ \qquad \forall x, y{:}\,\mathsf{nat}, s{:}\,X \,.\, \mathfrak{x}.\mathsf{in}(x, \mathfrak{x}.\mathsf{add}(y, s)) = \mathsf{if}\ x =_{\mathsf{nat}} y\ \mathsf{then\ true\ else}\ \mathfrak{x}.\mathsf{in}(x, s) \ \wedge \\ \qquad \forall x{:}\,\mathsf{nat}, s{:}\,X \,.\, \mathfrak{x}.\mathsf{in}(x, \mathfrak{x}.\mathsf{remove}(x, s)) = \mathsf{false}\end{array}$$

Consider the data type $LI \stackrel{def}{=} (\mathsf{pack\ list(nat)}\ \mathfrak{l}){:}\ Sig_{\mathsf{Set}}$, where $\mathfrak{l}.\mathsf{empty}$ gives the empty list, $\mathfrak{l}.\mathsf{add}$ adds a given element to the end of a list only if the element does not occur in the list, $\mathfrak{l}.\mathsf{in}$ is the occurrence function, and $\mathfrak{l}.\mathsf{remove}$ removes the first occurrence of a given element. Typing allows users of LI to only build lists using $\mathfrak{l}.\mathsf{empty}$ and $\mathfrak{l}.\mathsf{add}$, and on such lists the efficient $\mathfrak{l}.\mathsf{remove}$ gives the intended result. Crucially, any closed observation $f{:}\forall X.(\mathfrak{T}_{\mathsf{Set}}[X] \to C)$, $C \in Obs$ can only refer to lists built using $\mathfrak{l}.\mathsf{empty}$ and $\mathfrak{l}.\mathsf{add}$. For example, in the observable computation $\Lambda X.\lambda\mathfrak{x}{:}\,\mathfrak{T}_{\mathsf{Set}}[X] \,.\, \mathfrak{x}.\mathsf{in}(x, \mathfrak{x}.\mathsf{remove}(x, g))$, where g is a term of the bound type X, the typing rules insist that g can only be of the form $\mathfrak{x}.\mathsf{add}(\cdots \mathfrak{x}.\mathsf{add}(\mathfrak{x}.\mathsf{empty}) \cdots)$ and not a free variable. This implies through Theorem 3 that LI is a realisation of Set according to Def. 1.

In the world of algebraic specification, there is no formal restriction on the set In of so-called input-sorts. Thus, if one chooses the set of input sorts to be $In = \{\mathsf{set}, \mathsf{bool}, \mathsf{nat}\}$, then $\mathsf{in}(x, \mathsf{remove}(x, s))$ where s is a variable, is an observable computation. This computation might give true, since s ranges over all lists. In algebraic specification one has to explicitly restrict input sorts to not include the abstract sort, in this case set, when defining observational equivalence [36], whereas the type-theoretic formalism deals with this automatically. ○

The idea of specification refinement up to observational equivalence can now be expressed straight-forwardly by simply using the notion of refinement in [22].

Definition 3 (Type Theory Specification Refinement). *A specification SP' is a* refinement *of specification SP, via* constructor $F\colon Sig_{SP'} \to Sig_{SP}$ *if*

$$\forall u{:}\, Sig_{SP'} \,.\, \Theta_{SP'}(u) \;\Rightarrow\; \Theta_{SP}(Fu)$$

is derivable. We write $SP \underset{F}{\rightsquigarrow} SP'$ for this fact.

The notion of constructor $F\colon Sig_{SP'} \to Sig_{SP}$ in Def. 3 is based on the notion of parameterised program [10]. Given a program P that is a realisation of SP', the instantiation $F(P)$ is then a realisation of SP. Constructors correspond to refinement maps in [22]. It is evident that the refinement relation of Def. 3 is in a sense transitive, *i.e.* we have *vertical composability* [11]:

$$SP \underset{F}{\rightsquigarrow} SP' \text{ and } SP' \underset{F'}{\rightsquigarrow} SP'' \;\Rightarrow\; SP \underset{F\circ F'}{\rightsquigarrow} SP''$$

where $F \circ F' \stackrel{def}{=} \lambda u{:}\, Sig_{SP''} . F(F'u)$. In terms of algebraic-specification, any constructor $F\colon Sig_{SP'} \to Sig_{SP}$ is by Theorem 3 inherently stable under parametricity: Congruence gives $\forall u, v\colon Sig_{SP'} \,.\, u =_{Sig_{SP'}} v \;\Rightarrow\; F(u) =_{Sig_{SP}} F(v)$. And equality at existential type is of course observational equivalence.

Relating data types by simulation relations is often called *data refinement.* There are thus two refinement dimensions; one concerning specifications, and within each stage of this refinement process, a second dimension concerning observational equivalence, *i.e.* simulation relations, *i.e.* data refinement. At first order, theorems 3 and 4 give the essential property that the existence of simulation relations is transitive, but we can actually give a more constructive result:

Theorem 5 (Composability of Simulation Relations). *Suppose $\mathfrak{T}[X]$ only contains first-order function profiles. Then we can derive*

$$\forall A, B, G, R \subset A \times B, S \subset B \times G, \mathfrak{a}{:}\,\mathfrak{T}[A], \mathfrak{b}{:}\,\mathfrak{T}[B], \mathfrak{g}{:}\,\mathfrak{T}[G].$$
$$\mathfrak{a}(\mathfrak{T}[R])\mathfrak{b} \;\wedge\; \mathfrak{b}(\mathfrak{T}[S])\mathfrak{g} \;\Rightarrow\; \mathfrak{a}(\mathfrak{T}[S \circ R])\mathfrak{g}$$

4 Higher Order

If $\mathfrak{T}[X]$ has higher-order function profiles, Theorem 4 fails due to Dfnbl not extending to a logical relation. Theorem 5 fails as well, and indeed we cannot even derive that the existence of simulation relations is transitive.

The solution we present here is based on an alternative notion of simulation relation, and is motivated as follows. Consider the higher-order signature $\exists X. Record(f : (X \to X) \to \mathsf{nat}, g : X \to X)$. One requirement for an $R \subset A \times B$ to be respected in the standard sense by two implementations $\mathfrak{a}$ and $\mathfrak{b}$, is that $\forall \delta\colon A \to A, \forall \gamma\colon B \to B \,.\, \delta(R \to R)\gamma \;\Rightarrow\; \mathfrak{a}.f(\delta) =_{\mathsf{nat}} \mathfrak{b}.f(\gamma)$.

But since f is defined within a package, f should be specific to that package, and f's behaviour on elements outside the package should be irrelevant. Therefore the proof obligation should not have to consider the behaviour of $\mathfrak{a}.f$ and $\mathfrak{b}.f$ on arbitrary operators $\delta: A \to A$ and $\gamma: B \to B$ as long as their behaviour satisfies the requirement for operators defined in terms of $\mathfrak{a}.g$ and $\mathfrak{b}.g$ and operators of globally accessible types. This view is partly what the type system promotes through existential types: Operationally, the only way two concrete data types $(\mathsf{pack} A \mathfrak{a})$ and $(\mathsf{pack} B \mathfrak{b})$ can be used is in clients of the form $\Lambda X.\lambda \mathfrak{x}: \mathit{Record}(f: (X \to X) \to \mathsf{nat}, g: X \to X) \ . \ t$. Such a client can incite the application of $\mathfrak{a}.f$ and $\mathfrak{b}.f$ to $\mathfrak{a}.g$ and $\mathfrak{b}.g$ resp., but not to arbitrary $\delta: A \to A$ and $\gamma: B \to B$. Existential types therefore provide an abstraction barrier to which the standard definition of type relations is in a certain sense oblivious, and we suggest altering the relational proof criteria accordingly.

As before $\mathfrak{T}[X]$ denotes the body of an abstract data type $\exists X.\mathfrak{T}[X]$, now possibly with higher-order and polymorphic profiles. We shall assume that

***adt*:** $\mathfrak{T}[X] = \mathit{Record}(f_1: T_1[X], \ldots, f_k: T_k[X])$, where each $f_i: T_i[X]$ is in uncurried form, *i.e.* $T_i[X]$ is of the form $T_{i1}[X] \times \cdots \times T_{n_i}[X] \to T_{c_i}[X]$, where $T_{c_i}[X]$ is not an arrow type. If $T_{c_i}[X]$ is a universal type, then $T_{c_i}[X] \in \mathit{Obs}$.

4.1 The Alternative Simulation Relation

For brevity we will abuse vector notation. For a k-ary vector $\boldsymbol{Y}$, we write *e.g.* $\forall \boldsymbol{Y}$ for the string $\forall Y_1.\forall Y_2.\ldots\forall Y_k$, and similarly for $\boldsymbol{\Lambda Y}$. If $k = 0$ then the above all denote the empty string. The first l components of $\boldsymbol{Y}$ are denoted by $\boldsymbol{Y}|_l$.

Definition 4 (Data Type Relation). *For $\mathfrak{T}[X]$, for k-ary $\boldsymbol{Y}$, l-ary, $l \geq k$, $\boldsymbol{E}$, $\boldsymbol{F}$, $\boldsymbol{\rho} \subset \boldsymbol{E} \times \boldsymbol{F}$, A, B, $R \subset A \times B$, $\mathfrak{a}: \mathfrak{T}[A]$, $\mathfrak{b}: \mathfrak{T}[B]$, we define the* data type relation *$U[\boldsymbol{\rho}, R]^\star$ inductively by*

$$
\begin{array}{ll}
U = X & : U[\boldsymbol{\rho}, R]^\star \stackrel{def}{=} R \\
U = Y_i & : U[\boldsymbol{\rho}, R]^\star \stackrel{def}{=} \rho_i \\
U = \forall X'.U'[\boldsymbol{Y}, X', X] & : U[\boldsymbol{\rho}, R]^\star \stackrel{def}{=} \\
& \quad \forall (E_{l+1}, F_{l+1}, \rho_{l+1} \subset E_{l+1} \times F_{l+1})(U'[\boldsymbol{\rho}, \rho_{l+1}, R]^\star) \\
U = U' \to U'' & : U[\boldsymbol{\rho}, R]^\star \stackrel{def}{=}
\end{array}
$$

$$
\begin{array}{l}
(g{:}\, U'[\boldsymbol{E}, A] \to U''[\boldsymbol{E}, A],\ h{:}\, U'[\boldsymbol{F}, B] \to U''[\boldsymbol{F}, B]) \ . \ (\forall x{:}\, U'[\boldsymbol{E}, A], \forall y{:}\, U'[\boldsymbol{F}, B] \ . \\
\qquad (x \ U'[\boldsymbol{\rho}, R]^\star \ y \ \wedge \ \mathsf{Dfnbl}^\star_{U'[\boldsymbol{Y}, X]}(x, y)) \ \Rightarrow \ (gx) \ U''[\boldsymbol{\rho}, R]^\star \ (hy))
\end{array}
$$

where

$$
\begin{array}{l}
\mathsf{Dfnbl}^\star_{U'[\boldsymbol{Y}, X]}(x, y) \stackrel{def}{=} \\
\qquad \exists f{:}\forall \boldsymbol{Y}.\forall X.(\mathfrak{T}[X] \to U'[\boldsymbol{Y}, X]) \ . \ (f \boldsymbol{E}|_k A \, \mathfrak{a}) = x \ \wedge \ (f \boldsymbol{F}|_k B \, \mathfrak{b}) = y
\end{array}
$$

We usually omit the type subscript to the $\mathsf{Dfnbl}^\star$ *clause.*

The essence of Def. 4 is that the arrow type relation is weakened with the $\mathsf{Dfnbl}^\star$ clause. This clause is an extension of the relation exhibited for the proof of Theorem 4. We have conveniently:

Lemma 6. *For $\mathfrak{T}[X]$ satisfying* **adt**, *we can derive*

$$\mathfrak{a}(\mathfrak{T}[R]^\star)\mathfrak{b} \;\Leftrightarrow\; \wedge_{1\leq i\leq k}\ \mathfrak{a}.f_i\ (T_i[R]^\star)\ \mathfrak{b}.f_i$$

We also want the data type relation of Def. 4 to retain the property of being the equality over types in *Obs*. This is not derivable, but since *Obs* contains only inductive types, we get a semantic justification for this property.

Lemma 7. *With respect to the parametric PER-model of [3] it is sound to assert the following axiom schema for $C \in Obs$.*

$$\textsc{Ident}:\ \forall x,y{:}C\ .\ x =_C y \ \Leftrightarrow\ x(C[\rho]^\star)y$$

Now with the alternative notion of simulation relation $\mathfrak{T}[R]^\star$ obtained from Def. 4, we obtain variants of Theorem 4 valid also for higher-order function profiles (theorems 9 and 15). However, this comes at a price, since we here choose not to alter the parametricity axiom schema. Consequently, we loose proof power when considering the alternative simulation relation in universal type relations, and we can no longer rely directly on parametricity, as in Lemma 4, when deriving observational equivalence from the existence of a simulation relation.

4.2 Special Parametricity

Our solutions to this is to validate semantically special instances of alternative parametricity sufficient to reinstate the necessary proof power.

The special instances come in two variants, both based on the notion of closed observations. In shifting attention from general observable computations as proclaimed in Def. 2, to a notion of closed observations, we must now specify the collection *In* of input types in observations. (Compare this to the discussion around Example 2.) A sensible choice is to regard all types in *Obs* as input types, and henceforth *In* is assumed to contain this.

In the following we write for instance $(\forall X.\mathfrak{T}[X]^\star \to U[X]^\star)$, meaning the relation $\forall(A,B,R\subset A\times B)(\mathfrak{T}[R]^\star \to U[R]^\star)$.

Lemma 8. *For $\mathfrak{T}[X]$ adhering to* **adt**, *for $f{:}\forall X.(\mathfrak{T}[X] \to U[X])$, for any $U[X]$, and where free term variables of f are of types in In, we can derive*

$$f\ (\forall X.\mathfrak{T}[X]^\star \to U[X]^\star)\ f$$

By Lemma 8, the following axiom schema is sound w.r.t. any model whose interpretations of all $f{:}\forall X.(\mathfrak{T}[X] \to U[X])$ are denotable by terms whose only free variables are of types in *In*. For $\mathfrak{T}[X]$ adhering to **adt**, for any $U[X]$,

$$\textsc{spParam}:\ \forall f{:}\forall X.(\mathfrak{T}[X] \to U[X])\ .\ f\ (\forall X.\mathfrak{T}[X]^\star \to U[X]^\star)\ f$$

And then using SPPARAM we get a general version of Theorem 4:

Theorem 9. *Given* SPPARAM, *for* $\mathfrak{T}[X]$ *adhering to* ***adt***, *the existence of a simulation relation coincides with observational equivalence, i.e. we can derive*

$$\forall A, B. \forall \mathfrak{a}{:}\mathfrak{T}[A], \mathfrak{b}{:}\mathfrak{T}[B] \;.$$
$$\exists R \subset A \times B \;.\; \mathfrak{a}(\mathfrak{T}[R]^\star)\mathfrak{b} \;\Leftrightarrow\; \bigwedge_{C \in Obs} \forall f{:}\forall X.(\mathfrak{T}[X] \to C) \;.\; (f A\, \mathfrak{a}) = (f B\, \mathfrak{b})$$

Proof: $\Rightarrow$: This follows from SPPARAM and IDENT.

$\Leftarrow$: We have to show that $\exists R \subset A \times B \;.\; \mathfrak{a}(\mathfrak{T}[R]^\star)\mathfrak{b}$ is derivable. We exhibit $R \stackrel{def}{=} (a : A, b : B).(\mathsf{Dfnbl}^\star(a, b))$. Due to the assumption ***adt***, it suffices by Lemma 6 to show for every component $g{:}U \to V$ in $\mathfrak{T}[X]$ the derivability of

$$\forall x{:}U[A], \forall y{:}U[B] \;.\; (x\; U[R]^\star\; y \;\wedge\; \mathsf{Dfnbl}^\star(x, y)) \;\Rightarrow\; (\mathfrak{a}.g\, x)\; V[R]^\star\; (\mathfrak{b}.g\, y)$$

where $V[X]$ is either some $C \in Obs$, whence we recall IDENT, or the variable X. Now $\mathsf{Dfnbl}^\star(x, y)$ gives $\exists f_U{:}\forall X.(\mathfrak{T}[X] \to U[X]) \;.\; (f_U A\, \mathfrak{a}) = x \;\wedge\; (f_U B\, \mathfrak{b}) = y$. Let $f \stackrel{def}{=} \Lambda X.\lambda \mathfrak{x}{:}\mathfrak{T}[X] \;.\; (\mathfrak{x}.g(f_U X \mathfrak{x}))$.

$V[X] = C \in Obs$: We may show that $\mathfrak{a}.g\, x =_C \mathfrak{b}.g\, y$ is derivable. The assumption gives $(f A\, \mathfrak{a}) =_C (f B\, \mathfrak{b})$ which by β-reduction gives the desired result.

$V[X] = X$: We must derive $\exists f : \forall X.(\mathfrak{T}[X] \to V[X]) \;.\; (f A\, \mathfrak{a}) = (\mathfrak{a}.g\, x) \;\wedge\; (f B\, \mathfrak{b}) = (\mathfrak{b}.g\, y)$. For this we display f above. □

We also regain not only transitivity of the existence of simulation relations, but also composability of simulation relations. This relates the syntactic level to recent and on-going work on the semantic level, namely the *pre-logical relations* of [17,18], the *lax logical relations* of [32,21], and the *L-relations* of [20].

Theorem 10 (Composability of Simulation Relations). *Given* SPPARAM, *for* $\mathfrak{T}[X]$ *adhering to* ***adt***, *we can derive*

$$\forall A, B, G, R \subset A \times B, S \subset B \times G, \mathfrak{a}{:}\mathfrak{T}[A], \mathfrak{b}{:}\mathfrak{T}[B], \mathfrak{g}{:}\mathfrak{T}[G].$$
$$\mathfrak{a}(\mathfrak{T}[R]^\star)\mathfrak{b} \;\wedge\; \mathfrak{b}(\mathfrak{T}[S]^\star)\mathfrak{g} \;\Rightarrow\; \mathfrak{a}(\mathfrak{T}[S \circ R]^\star)\mathfrak{g}$$

Proof: Assuming $\mathfrak{a}(\mathfrak{T}[R]^\star)\mathfrak{b} \;\wedge\; \mathfrak{b}(\mathfrak{T}[S]^\star)\mathfrak{g}$, the goal is to derive for every component $g{:}U \to V$ in $\mathfrak{T}[X]$

$$\forall x{:}U[A], \forall z{:}U[G] \;.\; (x\; U[S \circ R]^\star\; z \;\wedge\; \mathsf{Dfnbl}^\star(x, z)) \;\Rightarrow\; (\mathfrak{a}.g\, x)\; V[S \circ R]^\star\; (\mathfrak{g}.g\, z)$$

By $\mathsf{Dfnbl}^\star(x, z)$ we construct $f \stackrel{def}{=} \Lambda X.\lambda \mathfrak{x}{:}\mathfrak{T}[X] \;.\; (\mathfrak{x}.g(f_U X \mathfrak{x}))$.

$V[X] = C \in Obs$: By assumption and Theorem 9 $(f A\, \mathfrak{a}) = (f B\, \mathfrak{b}) = (f G \mathfrak{g})$, and $\mathfrak{a}.g\, x = (f A\, \mathfrak{a})$ and $(f G \mathfrak{g}) = \mathfrak{g}.g\, z$

$V[X] = X$: We must show $\exists b : U[B] \;.\; (\mathfrak{a}.g\, x)\; R\; b \;\wedge\; b\; S\; (\mathfrak{g}.g\, z)$. Exhibit $f B\, \mathfrak{b} = (\mathfrak{b}.g(f_U B \mathfrak{b}))$ for b. To show *e.g.* $(\mathfrak{a}.g\, x)\; R\; (\mathfrak{b}.g(f_U B \mathfrak{b}))$ it suffices by assumption to show $x\; U[R]^\star\; (f_U B \mathfrak{b}) \;\wedge\; \mathsf{Dfnbl}^\star(x, (f_U B \mathfrak{b}))$. But $x = (f_U A \mathfrak{a})$, so $\mathsf{Dfnbl}^\star(x, (f_U B \mathfrak{b}))$ is trivial and $(f_U A \mathfrak{a})\; U[R]^\star\; (f_U B \mathfrak{b})$ follows by SPPARAM. □

As far as we know, it is not known whether or not the parametric PER-model of [3] satisfies SPPARAM, even for $U[X] = C$, $C \in Obs$. We can however validate SPPARAM in the polymorphic extensionally collapsed syntactic models of [8] or the parametric term models of [14].

4.3 Sticking to the Parametric PER-Model

However, in this paper our preference is to continue to seek validation under the non-syntactic parametric PER-model of [3]. Semantically, observational equivalence is usually defined w.r.t. contexts that when filled, are closed terms. Thus a reasonable alternative definition in the logic of observational equivalence is the following.

Definition 5 (Closed Context Observational Equivalence (ObsEqC)**).** *Define* closed context observational equivalence ObsEqC w.r.t. *Obs in the logic by*

$$\begin{aligned}&\mathsf{ObsEqC} \stackrel{\text{def}}{=} (u{:}\exists X.\mathfrak{T}[X], v{:}\exists X.\mathfrak{T}[X]).\\ &(\exists A, B.\exists \mathfrak{a}{:}\mathfrak{T}[A], \mathfrak{b}{:}\mathfrak{T}[B]\ .\ u = (\mathsf{pack} A\mathfrak{a})\ \wedge\ v = (\mathsf{pack} B\mathfrak{b})\ \wedge\\ &\qquad \textstyle\bigwedge_{C\in Obs} \forall f{:}\forall X.(\mathfrak{T}[X] \to C)\ .\ \mathsf{Closed}_{\Gamma^{In}}(f)\ \Rightarrow\ (fA\,\mathfrak{a}) = (fB\,\mathfrak{b}))\end{aligned}$$

where $\mathsf{Closed}_{\Gamma^{In}}(f)$ *is derivable iff* $\Gamma^{In} \vdash f$.

The idea is that closedness is qualified by a given context Γ^{In} so as to allow for variables of input types in observable computations. Note that this was automatically taken care of in the notion of observational computations of Def 2.

The task is now to determine what the predicate $\mathsf{Closed}_{\Gamma^{In}}(f)$ should be. This is intractable in the existing logic, but we can easily circumvent this problem by introducing $\mathsf{Closed}_{\Gamma^{In}}$ as a family of new basic predicates together with a predefined semantics as follows.

Definition 6. *The logical language is extended with families of basic predicates* $\mathsf{Closed}_{\hat{\Gamma}}(T)$ *ranging over types* T, *and* $\mathsf{Closed}_{\hat{\Gamma}}(t, T)$ *ranging over terms* $t{:}\,T$, *both relative to a given environment* $\hat{\Gamma}$. *This new syntax is given a predefined semantics as follows. For any type* $\Gamma \vdash T$, *term* $\Gamma \vdash t{:}T$, *and evaluation* $\gamma \in [\![\Gamma]\!]$,

$$\models_{\Gamma,\gamma} \mathsf{Closed}_{\hat{\Gamma}}(T) \stackrel{\text{def}}{\Leftrightarrow} \text{exists some type } \hat{\Gamma} \vdash A, \text{ some } \hat{\gamma} \in [\![\hat{\Gamma}]\!] \quad \text{s.t. } [\![\Gamma \vdash T]\!]_\gamma = [\![\hat{\Gamma} \vdash A]\!]_{\hat{\gamma}}$$

$$\models_{\Gamma,\gamma} \mathsf{Closed}_{\hat{\Gamma}}(t, T) \stackrel{\text{def}}{\Leftrightarrow} \text{exists some type } \hat{\Gamma} \vdash A, \text{ term } \hat{\Gamma} \vdash a{:}A, \text{ some } \hat{\gamma} \in [\![\hat{\Gamma}]\!] \quad \text{s.t. } [\![\Gamma \vdash T]\!]_\gamma = [\![\hat{\Gamma} \vdash A]\!]_{\hat{\gamma}} \text{ and } [\![\Gamma \vdash t{:}T]\!]_\gamma = [\![\hat{\Gamma} \vdash a{:}A]\!]_{\hat{\gamma}}$$

Lemma 11. *It is easily seen that the following axiom schemata are sound.*

1. $\vdash_\Gamma \mathsf{Closed}_{\hat{\Gamma},X}(X)$
2. $\vdash_\Gamma \mathsf{Closed}_{\hat{\Gamma}}(U)\ \wedge\ \mathsf{Closed}_{\hat{\Gamma}}(V)\ \Rightarrow\ \mathsf{Closed}_{\hat{\Gamma}}(U \to V)$
3. $\vdash_\Gamma \mathsf{Closed}_{\hat{\Gamma},X}(U)\ \Rightarrow\ \mathsf{Closed}_{\hat{\Gamma}}(\forall X.U)$

4. $\vdash_\Gamma \mathsf{Closed}_{\hat{\Gamma},x:U}(x, U)$
5. $\vdash_\Gamma \mathsf{Closed}_{\hat{\Gamma},x:U}(t, V)\ \Rightarrow\ \mathsf{Closed}_{\hat{\Gamma}}(\lambda x{:}U.t, U \to V)$
6. $\vdash_\Gamma \mathsf{Closed}_{\hat{\Gamma}}(g, U \to V)\ \wedge\ \mathsf{Closed}_{\hat{\Gamma}}(t, U)\ \Rightarrow\ \mathsf{Closed}_{\hat{\Gamma}}(gt, V)$
7. $\vdash_\Gamma \mathsf{Closed}_{\hat{\Gamma},X}(t, U)\ \Rightarrow\ \mathsf{Closed}_{\hat{\Gamma}}(\Lambda X.t, \forall X.U)$
8. $\vdash_\Gamma \mathsf{Closed}_{\hat{\Gamma}}(f, \forall X.U[X])\ \wedge\ \mathsf{Closed}_{\hat{\Gamma}}(A)\ \Rightarrow\ \mathsf{Closed}_{\hat{\Gamma}}(fA, U[A])$

9. $\vdash_\Gamma \mathsf{Closed}_{\hat\Gamma}(T) \;\Rightarrow\; \mathsf{Closed}_{\hat\Gamma'}(T),\;\; \hat\Gamma \subseteq \hat\Gamma'$
10. $\vdash_\Gamma \mathsf{Closed}_{\hat\Gamma}(t,T) \;\Rightarrow\; \mathsf{Closed}_{\hat\Gamma'}(t,T),\;\; \hat\Gamma \subseteq \hat\Gamma'$

We will usually omit the type argument in the term family of Closed. Intuitively, we should now be able to use Lemma 8 to show the necessary special parametricity instance. However, to make the induction spiral work, we have to strengthen lemmas 8 and 6, by incorporating Closed into the $\mathsf{Dfnbl}^\star$ clause.

Definition 7 (Data Type Relation by Closed Observers). *Define the* data type relation by closed observers $U[\boldsymbol{\rho}, R]^\star_{\mathsf{C}}$ *as the data type relation* $U[\boldsymbol{\rho}, R]^\star$ *of Def. 4, but where we use*

$$\mathsf{DfnblC}^\star_{U[\boldsymbol{Y},X]}(x,y) \overset{def}{=} \exists f{:}\forall \boldsymbol{Y}.\forall X.(\mathfrak{T}[X] \to U[\boldsymbol{Y},X])\;.\; \mathsf{Closed}_{\Gamma^{In}}(f) \;\wedge\; (f\boldsymbol{E}|_k A\,\mathfrak{a}) = x \;\wedge\; (f\boldsymbol{F}|_k B\,\mathfrak{b}) = y$$

in place of $\mathsf{Dfnbl}^\star_{U[\boldsymbol{Y},X]}$*, for* $\Gamma^{In} = x_1{:}U_1,\ldots,x_m{:}U_m$*,* $U_i \in \mathit{In}$*,* $1 \le i \le m$*.*

Lemma 12. *For* $\mathfrak{T}[X]$ *satisfying* ***adt****, we have the derivability of*

$$\mathfrak{a}(\mathfrak{T}[R]^\star_{\mathsf{C}})\mathfrak{b} \;\Leftrightarrow\; \wedge_{1\le i\le k}\; \mathfrak{a}.f_i\; (T_i[R]^\star_{\mathsf{C}})\; \mathfrak{b}.f_i$$

Lemma 13. *With respect to the parametric PER-model of [3] it is sound to assert the following axiom schema for* $C \in \mathit{Obs}$*.*

$$\textsc{IdentC}{:}\;\; \forall x,y{:}C\;.\; x =_C y \;\Leftrightarrow\; x(C[\rho]^\star_{\mathsf{C}})y$$

Lemma 14. *For* $\mathfrak{T}[X]$ *adhering to* ***adt****, for* $f : \forall X.(\mathfrak{T}[X] \to U[X])$*, for any* $U[X]$*, and where free term variables of* f *are of types in* In*, we can derive*

$$f\; (\forall X.\mathfrak{T}[X]^\star_{\mathsf{C}} \to U[X]^\star_{\mathsf{C}})\; f$$

By Lemma 14 it is sound w.r.t. the parametric PER-model to postulate the following axiom schema. For $\mathfrak{T}[X]$ adhering to ***adt***, for $\Gamma^{In} = x_1{:}U_1,\ldots,x_m{:}U_m$, $U_i \in \mathit{In}$, $1 \le i \le m$, for any $U[X]$,

$$\textsc{CspParam}{:}\;\; \forall f{:}\forall X.(\mathfrak{T}[X]\to U[X])\;.\; \mathsf{Closed}_{\Gamma^{In}}(f) \;\Rightarrow\; f\; (\forall X.\mathfrak{T}[X]^\star_{\mathsf{C}}\to U[X]^\star_{\mathsf{C}})\; f$$

We can now show the higher-order polymorphic generalisation of Theorem 4 now validated w.r.t. the parametric PER-model:

Theorem 15. *Extending the language with the predicates* Closed *of Def. 6, given* $\textsc{CspParam}$*, for* $\mathfrak{T}[X]$ *adhering to* ***adt****, for* $\Gamma^{In} = x_1{:}U_1,\ldots,x_m{:}U_m$*,* $U_i \in \mathit{In}$*,* $1 \le i \le m$*, the following is derivable.*

$$\begin{aligned} &\forall A,B.\forall \mathfrak{a}{:}\mathfrak{T}[A], \mathfrak{b}{:}\mathfrak{T}[B]\;.\\ &\quad \exists R \subset A\times B\;.\; \mathfrak{a}(\mathfrak{T}[R]^\star_{\mathsf{C}})\mathfrak{b} \;\Leftrightarrow\\ &\qquad \textstyle\bigwedge_{C\in \mathit{Obs}} \forall f{:}\forall X.(\mathfrak{T}[X] \to C)\;.\; \mathsf{Closed}_{\Gamma^{In}}(f) \;\Rightarrow\; (f A\,\mathfrak{a}) = (f B\,\mathfrak{b}) \end{aligned}$$

Proof: $\Rightarrow$: This follows from CspParam and IdentC.

$\Leftarrow$: Along the lines of the proof of Theorem 9, and using Lemma 11 to obtain $\mathsf{Closed}_{\Gamma^{In}}(f)$ from $\mathsf{Closed}_{\Gamma^{In}}(f_U)$, and using Lemma 12 and IdentC in place of Lemma 6 and Ident. □

We now get composability validated w.r.t. the parametric PER-model:

Theorem 16 (Composability of Simulation Relations). *Given* CspParam, *for* $\mathfrak{T}[X]$ *adhering to* **adt**, *we can derive*

$$\forall A, B, G, R \subset A \times B, S \subset B \times G, \mathfrak{a}\colon \mathfrak{T}[A], \mathfrak{b}\colon \mathfrak{T}[B], \mathfrak{g}\colon \mathfrak{T}[G]. \quad \mathfrak{a}(\mathfrak{T}[R]^{\star}_{\mathsf{C}})\mathfrak{b} \ \wedge \ \mathfrak{b}(\mathfrak{T}[S]^{\star}_{\mathsf{C}})\mathfrak{g} \ \Rightarrow \ \mathfrak{a}(\mathfrak{T}[S \circ R]^{\star}_{\mathsf{C}})\mathfrak{g}$$

Proof: As for Theorem 10, but using CspParam instead of spParam. □

Finally we retrieve the notions of specification refinement. We have established the coincidence of observational equivalence and the existence of a simulation relation at higher order, but in this paper we do not tie the link to equality at existential type. This is of minor importance because we can simply redefine our notions in terms of ObsEqC (or ObsEq) instead of equality: The realisation predicate of Def. 1 then reads $\Theta_{SP}(u) = \exists X.\exists \mathfrak{x}\colon \mathfrak{T}_{SP}[X]\ .\ u\ \mathsf{ObsEqC}\ (\mathsf{pack} X \mathfrak{x}) \wedge \Phi_{SP}[X, \mathfrak{x}]$. Note that we now have to show the stability of constructors explicitly.

5 Final Remarks and Discussion

This paper has addressed specification refinement up to observational equivalence with System F using Plotkin and Abadi's logic for parametric polymorphism. At first order, specification refinement up to observational equivalence can be defined in the logic using Luo's formalism, because equality at existential type coincides (Theorem 3) with observational equivalence ObsEq (Def 2).

At higher order, *i.e.* when the data type signature has higher-order function types, we ostensibly loose the correspondence in the logic between observational equivalence and the existence of a simulation relation. We argued that at higher-order the usual notion of simulation relation is too strict, since it for function types requires that one consider arbitrary arguments, which might be other than those actually accessible in computations.

Thus an alternative simulation relation $\mathfrak{T}[R]^{\star}$ was proposed based on the $\mathsf{Dfnbl}^{\star}$ clause and data type relation (Def. 4). Then a correspondence in the logic between observational equivalence and the existence of this alternative simulation relation is re-established in any model in which the axiom schema spParam is valid (Theorem 9). For the parametric PER-model, we also achieve the correspondence (Theorem 15) by extending the logical language with basic predicates $\mathsf{Closed}_{\hat{\Gamma}}$, defining a second alternative simulation relation $\mathfrak{T}[R]^{\star}_{\mathsf{C}}$, and validating the axiom schema CspParam w.r.t the parametric PER-model. Finally, we achieve a simulation relation in the logic that composes at higher-order (theorems 10 and 16). This relates to on-going work on the semantic level.

The approach taken in this paper is conservative in that we in the outset do not want to alter either the type theory nor the parametricity axiom schema. This is motivated by the view that it is the relational proof criteria specifically for abstract data types that need amending, not the type theory itself. The parametricity axiom is left alone in order to relate to established models for relational parametricity. However, there seem to be other interesting approaches worth looking into. One alternative would be to alter the type system so as to isolate separate types for use in abstract data types, and then extend the parametricity axiom schema to deal with these types. A very promising approach to finding a non-syntactic model satisfying spParam seems to be to work along the lines of Jung and Tiuryn [19], and define a non-standard Kripke-like model to validate the logic.

Acknowledgements Thanks to Martin Hofmann, Don Sannella, Furio Honsell, Gordon Plotkin and Martin Wehr for helpful discussions. Thanks to the referees for very helpful comments. This research has been supported by EPSRC grant GR/K63795, and NFR (Norwegian Research Council) grant 110904/41.

References

1. M. Abadi, L. Cardelli, and P.-L. Curien. Formal parametric polymorphism. *Theoretical Computer Science*, 121:9–58, 1993.
2. D. Aspinall. *Type Systems for Modular Programs and Specifications.* PhD thesis, University of Edinburgh, 1998.
3. E.S. Bainbridge, P.J. Freyd, A. Scedrov, and P.J. Scott. Functorial polymorphism. *Theoretical Computer Science*, 70:35–64, 1990.
4. M. Bidoit and R. Hennicker. Behavioural theories and the proof of behavioural properties. *Theoretical Computer Science*, 165:3–55, 1996.
5. M. Bidoit, R. Hennicker, and M. Wirsing. Behavioural and abstractor specifications. *Science of Computer Programming*, 25:149–186, 1995.
6. M. Bidoit, R. Hennicker, and M. Wirsing. Proof systems for structured specifications with observability operators. *Theoretical Computer Sci.*, 173:393–443, 1997.
7. C. Böhm and A. Beraducci. Automatic synthesis of typed λ-programs on term algebras. *Theoretical Computer Science*, 39:135–154, 1985.
8. V. Breazu-Tannen and T. Coquand. Extensional models for polymorphism. *Theoretical Computer Science*, 59:85–114, 1988.
9. M. Cerioli, M. Gogolla, H. Kirchner, B. Krieg-Brückner, Z. Qian, and M. Wolf. *Algebraic System Specification and Development. Survey and Annotated Bibliography, 2nd Ed.*, volume 3 of *Monographs of the Bremen Institute of Safe Systems.* Shaker, 1997. 1st edition available in *LNCS* 501, Springer, 1991.
10. J.A. Goguen. Parameterized programming. *IEEE Transactions on Software Engineering*, SE-10(5):528–543, 1984.
11. J.A. Goguen and R. Burstall. CAT, a system for the structured elaboration of correct programs from structured specifications. Tech. Rep. CSL-118, SRI International, 1980.
12. J.E. Hannay. Specification refinement with System F. In *Proc. CSL'99*, volume 1683 of *LNCS*, pages 530–545, 1999.

13. J.E. Hannay. Specification refinement with System F, the higher-order case. Submitted for publication, 2000.
14. R. Hasegawa. Parametricity of extensionally collapsed term models of polymorphism and their categorical properties. In *Proc. TACS'91*, volume 526 of *LNCS*, pages 495–512, 1991.
15. R. Hennicker. Structured specifications with behavioural operators: Semantics, proof methods and applications. Habilitationsschrift, LMU, München, 1997.
16. C.A.R. Hoare. Proofs of correctness of data representations. *Acta Inform.*, 1:271–281, 1972.
17. F. Honsell, J. Longley, D. Sannella, and A. Tarlecki. Constructive data refinement in typed lambda calculus. In *Proc. FOSSACS 2000, LNCS*, 2000.
18. F. Honsell and D. Sannella. Pre-logical relations. In *Proc. CSL'99*, volume 1683 of *LNCS*, pages 546–561, 1999.
19. A. Jung and J. Tiuryn. A new characterization of lambda definability. In *Proc. of TLCA 93*, volume 664 of *LNCS*, pages 245–257, 1993.
20. Y. Kinoshita, P.W. O'Hearn, A.J. Power, M. Takeyama, and R.D. Tennent. An axiomatic approach to binary logical relations with applications to data refinement. In *Proc. of TACS'97*, volume 1281 of *LNCS*, pages 191–212, 1997.
21. Y. Kinoshita and A.J. Power. Data refinement for call-by-value programming languages. In *Proc. CSL'99*, volume 1683 of *LNCS*, pages 562–576, 1999.
22. Z. Luo. Program specification and data type refinement in type theory. *Math. Struct. in Comp. Sci.*, 3:333–363, 1993.
23. Q. Ma and J.C. Reynolds. Types, abstraction and parametric polymorphism, part 2. In *Proc. 7th MFPS*, volume 598 of *LNCS*, pages 1–40, 1991.
24. H. Mairson. Outline of a proof theory of parametricity. In *ACM Symposium on Functional Programming and Computer Architecture*, volume 523 of *LNCS*, pages 313–327, 1991.
25. J.C. Mitchell. On the equivalence of data representations. In V. Lifschitz, editor, *Artificial Intelligence and Mathematical Theory of Computation: Papers in Honor of John McCarthy*, pages 305–330. Academic Press, 1991.
26. J.C. Mitchell. *Foundations for Programming Languages.* MIT Press, 1996.
27. J.C. Mitchell and G.D. Plotkin. Abstract types have existential type. *ACM Trans. on Programming Languages and Systems*, 10(3):470–502, 1988.
28. N. Mylonakis. Behavioural specifications in type theory. In *Recent Trends in Data Type Spec., 11th WADT*, volume 1130 of *LNCS*, pages 394–408, 1995.
29. A.M. Pitts. Parametric polymorphism and operational equivalence. In *Proc. 2nd Workshop on Higher Order Operational Techniques in Semantics*, volume 10 of *ENTCS*. Elsevier, 1997.
30. A.M. Pitts. Existential types: Logical relations and operational equivalence. In *Proc. ICALP'98*, volume 1443 of *LNCS*, pages 309–326, 1998.
31. G. Plotkin and M. Abadi. A logic for parametric polymorphism. In *Proc. of TLCA 93*, volume 664 of *LNCS*, pages 361–375, 1993.
32. G.D. Plotkin, A.J. Power, and D. Sannella. A compositional generalisation of logical relations. Submitted for publication, 2000.
33. E. Poll and J. Zwanenburg. A logic for abstract data types as existential types. In *Proc. TLCA'99*, volume 1581 of *LNCS*, pages 310–324, 1999.
34. B. Reus and T. Streicher. Verifying properties of module construction in type theory. In *Proc. MFCS'93*, volume 711 of *LNCS*, pages 660–670, 1993.
35. J.C. Reynolds. Types, abstraction and parametric polymorphism. *Information Processing*, 83:513–523, 1983.

36. D. Sannella and A. Tarlecki. On observational equivalence and algebraic specification. *Journal of Computer and System Sciences*, 34:150–178, 1987.
37. D. Sannella and A. Tarlecki. Toward formal development of programs from algebraic specifications: Implementations revisited. *Acta Inform.*, 25(3):233–281, 1988.
38. D. Sannella and A. Tarlecki. Essential concepts of algebraic specification and program development. *Formal Aspects of Computing*, 9:229–269, 1997.
39. O. Schoett. *Data Abstraction and the Correctness of Modular Programming.* PhD thesis, University of Edinburgh, 1986.
40. T. Streicher and M. Wirsing. Dependent types considered necessary for specification languages. In *Recent Trends in Data Type Spec.*, volume 534 of *LNCS*, pages 323–339, 1990.
41. J. Underwood. Typing abstract data types. In *Recent Trends in Data Type Spec., Proc. 10th WADT*, volume 906 of *LNCS*, pages 437–452, 1994.
42. J. Zwanenburg. *Object-Oriented Concepts and Proof Rules: Formalization in Type Theory and Implementation in Yarrow.* PhD thesis, Technische Universiteit Eindhoven, 1999.

Probabilistic Asynchronous π-Calculus

Oltea Mihaela Herescu and Catuscia Palamidessi

Dept. of Comp. Sci. and Eng., The Pennsylvania State University
University Park, PA 16802-6106 USA
{herescu,catuscia}@cse.psu.edu

Abstract. We propose an extension of the asynchronous π-calculus with a notion of random choice. We define an operational semantics which distinguishes between probabilistic choice, made internally by the process, and nondeterministic choice, made externally by an adversary scheduler. This distinction will allow us to reason about the probabilistic correctness of algorithms under certain schedulers. We show that in this language we can solve the electoral problem, which was proved not possible in the asynchronous π-calculus. Finally, we show an implementation of the probabilistic asynchronous π-calculus in a Java-like language.

1 Introduction

The π-calculus ([6]) is a very expressive specification language for concurrent programming, but the difficulties in its distributed implementation challenge its candidature to be a canonical model of distributed computation. Certain mechanisms of the π-calculus, in fact, require solving a problem of distributed consensus.

The asynchronous π-calculus ([4,2]), on the other hand, is more suitable for a distributed implementation, but it is rather weak for solving distributed problems ([9]).

In order to increase the expressive power of the asynchronous π-calculus we propose a probabilistic extension, π_{pa}, based on the probabilistic automata of Segala and Lynch ([12]). The characteristic of this model is that it distinguishes between probabilistic and nondeterministic behavior. The first is associated with the random choices of the process, while the second is related to the arbitrary decisions of an external scheduler. This separation allows us to reason about adverse conditions, i.e. schedulers that "try to prevent" the process from achieving its goal. Similar models were presented in [13] and [14].

Next we show an example of distributed problem that can be solved with π_{pa}, namely the election of a leader in a symmetric network. It was proved in [9] that such problem cannot be solved with the asynchronous π-calculus. We propose an algorithm for the solution of this problem, and we show that it is correct, i.e. that the leader will eventually be elected, with probability 1, under every possible scheduler. Our algorithm is reminiscent of the algorithm used in [10] for solving the dining philosophers problem, but in our case we do not need the fairness assumption. Also, the fact that we give the solution in a language

J. Tiuryn (Ed.): FOSSACS 2000, LNCS 1784, pp. 146–160, 2000.

provided with a rigorous operational semantics allows us to give a more formal proof of correctness (the proof is omitted here due to space limitations, but the interested reader can find it in [3]).

Finally, we define a "toy" distributed implementation of the π_{pa}-calculus into a Java-like language. The purpose of this exercise is to prove that π_{pa} is a reasonable paradigm for the specification of distributed algorithms, since it can be implemented without loss of expressivity.

The novelty of our proposal, with respect to other probabilistic process algebras which have been defined in literature (see, for instance, [14]), is the definition of the parallel operator in a CCS style, as opposed to the SCCS style. Namely, parallel processes are not forced to proceed simultaneously. Note also that for general probabilistic automata it is not possible to define the parallel operator ([11]), or at least, there is no natural definition. In π_{pa} the parallel operator can be defined as a natural extension of the non probabilistic case, and this can be considered, to our opinion, another argument in favor of the suitability of π_{pa} for distributed implementation.

2 Preliminaries

In this section we recall the definition of the asynchronous π-calculus and the definition of probabilistic automata. We consider the *late* semantics of the π-calculus, because the probabilistic extension of the late semantics is simpler than the eager version.

2.1 The Asynchronous π-Calculus

We follow the definition of the asynchronous π-calculus given in [1], except that we will use recursion instead of the replication operator, since we find it to be more convenient for writing programs. It is well known that recursion and replication are equivalent, see for instance [5].

Consider a countable set of *channel names*, $x, y, \ldots$, and a countable set of *process names* $X, Y, \ldots$. The prefixes $\alpha, \beta, \ldots$ and the processes $P, Q, \ldots$ of the asynchronous π-calculus are defined by the following grammar:

$$\textit{Prefixes}\ \alpha ::= x(y) \mid \tau$$

$$\textit{Processes}\ P ::= \bar{x}y \mid \textstyle\sum_i \alpha_i.P_i \mid \nu x P \mid P \,|\, P \mid X \mid \textit{rec}_X P$$

The basic actions are $x(y)$, which represents the *input* of the (formal) name y from channel x, $\bar{x}y$, which represents the *output* of the name y on channel x, and τ, which stands for any silent (non-communication) action.

The process $\sum_i \alpha_i.P_i$ represents guarded choice on input or silent prefixes, and it is usually assumed to be finite. We will use the abbreviations $\mathbf{0}$ (*inaction*) to represent the empty sum, $\alpha.P$ (*prefix*) to represent sum on one element only, and $P + Q$ for the binary sum. The symbols νx and $|$ are the *restriction* and the *parallel* operator, respectively. We adopt the convention that the prefix operator has priority wrt $+$ and $|$. The process $rec_X P$ represents a process X defined as $X \stackrel{\text{def}}{=} P$, where P may contain occurrences of X (recursive definition). We assume that all the occurrences of X in P are prefixed.

The operators νx and $y(x)$ are *x-binders*, i.e. in the processes $\nu x P$ and $y(x).P$ the occurrences of x in P are considered *bound*, with the usual rules of scoping. The *free names* of P, i.e. those names which do not occur in the scope of any binder, are denoted by $fn(P)$. The *alpha-conversion* of bound names is defined as usual, and the renaming (or substitution) $P[y/x]$ is defined as the result of replacing all free occurrences of x in P by y, possibly applying alpha-conversion in order to avoid capture.

The operational semantics is specified via a transition system labeled by *actions* $\mu, \mu' \ldots$. These are given by the following grammar:

$$Actions\ \mu ::= x(y) \mid \bar{x}y \mid \bar{x}(y) \mid \tau$$

Essentially, we have all the actions from the syntax, plus the *bound output* $\bar{x}(y)$. This is introduced to model *scope extrusion*, i.e. the result of sending to another process a private (ν-bound) name. The bound names of an action μ, $bn(\mu)$, are defined as follows: $bn(x(y)) = bn(\bar{x}(y)) = \{y\}$; $bn(\bar{x}y) = bn(\tau) = \emptyset$. Furthermore, we will indicate by $n(\mu)$ all the *names* which occur in μ.

The rules for the late semantics are given in Table 1. The symbol $\equiv$ used in CONG stands for *structural congruence*, a form of equivalence which identifies "statically" two processes and which is used to simplify the presentation. We assume this congruence to satisfy the following:

(i) $P \equiv Q$ if Q can be obtained from P by alpha-renaming, notation $P \equiv_\alpha Q$,
(ii) $P \mid Q \equiv Q \mid P$,
(iii) $rec_X P \equiv P[rec_X P/X]$,

Note that communication is modeled by handshaking (Rules COM and CLOSE). The reason why this calculus is considered a paradigm for *asynchronous* communication is that there is no primitive *output prefix*, hence no primitive notion of continuation after the execution of an output action. In other words, the process executing an output action will not be able to detect (in principle) when the corresponding input action is actually executed.

2.2 Probabilistic Automata, Adversaries, and Executions

Asynchronous automata have been proposed in [12]. We simplify here the original definition, and tailor it to what we need for defining the probabilistic extension of the asynchronous π-calculus. The main difference is that we consider only discrete probabilistic spaces, and that the concept of deadlock is simply a node with no out-transitions.

A discrete probabilistic space is a pair (X, pb) where X is a set and pb is a function $pb : X \to (0,1]$ such that $\sum_{x \in X} pb(x) = 1$. Given a set Y, we define

$$Prob(Y) = \{(X, pb) \mid X \subseteq Y \text{ and } (X, pb) \text{ is a discrete probabilistic space}\}.$$

$$\textsc{Sum}\quad \sum_i \alpha_i.P_i \xrightarrow{\alpha_j} P_j \qquad\qquad \textsc{Out}\quad \bar{x}y \xrightarrow{\bar{x}y} \mathbf{0}$$

$$\textsc{Open}\quad \frac{P \xrightarrow{\bar{x}y} P'}{\nu y P \xrightarrow{\bar{x}(y)} P'}\ x \neq y \qquad\qquad \textsc{Res}\quad \frac{P \xrightarrow{\mu} P'}{\nu y P \xrightarrow{\mu} \nu y P'}\ y \notin n(\mu)$$

$$\textsc{Com}\quad \frac{P \xrightarrow{\bar{x}y} P' \quad Q \xrightarrow{x(z)} Q'}{P \mid Q \xrightarrow{\tau} P' \mid Q'[y/z]} \qquad\qquad \textsc{Par}\quad \frac{P \xrightarrow{\mu} P'}{P \mid Q \xrightarrow{\mu} P' \mid Q}\ bn(\mu) \cap fn(Q) = \emptyset$$

$$\textsc{Close}\quad \frac{P \xrightarrow{\bar{x}(y)} P' \quad Q \xrightarrow{x(y)} Q'}{P \mid Q \xrightarrow{\tau} \nu y(P' \mid Q')} \qquad\qquad \textsc{Cong}\quad \frac{P \equiv P' \quad P' \xrightarrow{\mu} Q' \quad Q' \equiv Q}{P \xrightarrow{\mu} Q}$$

Table 1. The late-instantiation transition system of the asynchronous π-calculus.

Given a set of states S and a set of actions A, a *probabilistic automaton* on S and A is a triple $(S, \mathcal{T}, s_0)$ where $s_0 \in S$ (initial state) and $\mathcal{T} \subseteq S \times \mathit{Prob}(A \times S)$. We call the elements of $\mathcal{T}$ *transition groups* (in [12] they are called *steps*). The idea behind this model is that the choice between two different groups is made nondeterministically and possibly controlled by an external agent, e.g. a scheduler, while the transition within the same group is chosen probabilistically and it is controlled internally (e.g. by a probabilistic choice operator). An automaton in which at most one transition group is allowed for each state is called *fully probabilistic*.

We define now the notion of execution of an automaton under a *scheduler*, by adapting and simplifying the corresponding notion given in [12]. A scheduler can be seen as a function which solves the nondeterminism of the automaton by selecting, at each moment of the computation, a transition group among all the ones allowed in the present state. Schedulers are sometimes called *adversaries*, thus conveying the idea of an external entity playing "against" the process. A process is *robust* wrt a certain class of adversaries if it gives the intended result for each possible scheduling imposed by an adversary in the class. Clearly, the reliability of an algorithm depends on how "smart" the adversaries of this class can be. We will assume that an adversary can decide the next transition group depending not only on the current state, but also on the whole history of the computation till that moment, including the random choices made by the automaton.

Given a probabilistic automaton $M = (S, \mathcal{T}, s_0)$, define $\mathit{tree}(M)$ as the tree obtained by unfolding the transition system, i.e. the tree with a root n_0 labeled by s_0, and such that, for each node n, if $s \in S$ is the label of n, then for each $(s, (X, pb)) \in \mathcal{T}$, and for each $(\mu, s') \in X$, there is a node n' child of n labeled by s', and the arc from n to n' is labeled by μ and $pb(\mu, s')$. We will denote by $nodes(M)$ the set of nodes in $tree(M)$, and by $state(n)$ the state labeling a node n.

An *adversary* for M is a function ζ that associates to each node n of $tree(M)$ a transition group among those which are allowed in $state(n)$. More formally, $\zeta : nodes(M) \rightarrow Prob(A \times S)$ such that $\zeta(n) = (X, pb)$ implies $(state(n), (X, pb)) \in \mathcal{T}$.

The *execution tree* of an automaton $M = (S, \mathcal{T}, s_0)$ under an adversary ζ, denoted by $etree(M, \zeta)$, is the tree obtained from $tree(M)$ by pruning all the arcs corresponding to transitions which are not in the group selected by ζ. More formally, $etree(M, \zeta)$ is a fully probabilistic automaton $(S', \mathcal{T}', n_0)$, where $S' \subseteq nodes(M)$, n_0 is the root of $tree(M)$, and $(n, (X', pb')) \in \mathcal{T}'$ iff $X' = \{(\mu, n') \mid (\mu, state(n')) \in X\}$ and $pb'(\mu, n') = pb(\mu, state(n'))$, where $(X, pb) = \zeta(n)$.

An *execution fragment* ξ is any path (finite or infinite) from the root of $etree(M, \zeta)$. The notation $\xi \leq \xi'$ means that ξ is a prefix of ξ'. If ξ is $n_0 \xrightarrow[p_0]{\mu_0} n_1 \xrightarrow[p_1]{\mu_1} n_2 \xrightarrow[p_2]{\mu_2} \ldots$, the *probability* of ξ is defined as $pb(\xi) = \prod_i p_i$. If ξ is maximal, then it is called *execution*. We denote by $exec(M, \zeta)$ the set of all executions in $etree(M, \zeta)$.

We define now a probability on certain sets of executions, following a standard construction of Measure Theory. Given an execution fragment ξ, let $C_\xi = \{\xi' \in exec(M, \zeta) \mid \xi \leq \xi'\}$ (*cone* with prefix ξ). Define $pb(C_\xi) = pb(\xi)$. Let $\{C_i\}_{i \in I}$ be a countable set of disjoint cones (i.e. I is countable, and $\forall i, j.\ i \neq j \Rightarrow C_i \cap C_j = \emptyset$). Then define $pb(\bigcup_{i \in I} C_i) = \sum_{i \in I} pb(C_i)$. It is possible to show that pb is well defined, i.e. two countable sets of disjoint cones with the same union produce the same result for pb. We can also define the probability of an empty set of executions as 0, and the probability of the complement of a certain set of executions as the complement wrt 1 of the probability of the set. The closure of the cones wrt the empty set, the countable union, and the complementation generates what in Measure Theory is known as a σ-field.

3 The Probabilistic Asynchronous π-Calculus

In this section we introduce the probabilistic asynchronous π-calculus (π_{pa}-calculus for short) and we give its operational semantics in terms of probabilistic automata.

The π_{pa}-calculus is obtained from the asynchronous π-calculus by replacing $\sum_i \alpha_i.P_i$ with the following *probabilistic choice operator*

$$\sum_i p_i \alpha_i.P_i$$

where the p_i's represent positive probabilities, i.e. they satisfy $p_i \in (0, 1]$ and $\sum_i p_i = 1$, and the α_i's are input or silent prefixes.

In order to give the formal definition of the probabilistic model for π_{pa}, we find it convenient to introduce the following notation for representing transition groups: given a probabilistic automaton $(S, \mathcal{T}, s_0)$ and $s \in S$, we write

$$s \{ \xrightarrow[p_i]{\mu_i} s_i \mid i \in I \}$$

iff $(s, (\{(\mu_i, s_i) \mid i \in I\}, pb)) \in \mathcal{T}$ and $\forall i \in I\; p_i = pb(\mu_i, s_i)$, where I is an index set. When I is not relevant, we will use the simpler notation $s \{ \xrightarrow[p_i]{\mu_i} s_i \}_i$. We will also use the notation $s \{ \xrightarrow[p_i]{\mu_i} s_i \}_{i:\phi(i)}$, where $\phi(i)$ is a logical formula depending on i, for the set $s \{ \xrightarrow[p_i]{\mu_i} s_i \mid i \in I \text{ and } \phi(i) \}$.

The operational semantics of a π_{pa} process P is defined as a probabilistic automaton whose states are the processes reachable from P and the $\mathcal{T}$ relation is defined by the rules in Table 2. In order to keep the presentation simple, we impose the following restrictions: In SUM we assume that all branches are different, namely, if $i \neq j$, then either $\alpha_i \neq \alpha_j$, or $P_i \not\equiv P_j$. Furthermore, in RES and PAR we assume that all bound variables are distinct from each other, and from the free variables.

The SUM rule models the behavior of a choice process. Note that all possible transitions belong to the same group, meaning that the transition is chosen probabilistically by the process itself. RES models restriction on channel y: only the actions on channels different from y can be performed and possibly synchronize with an external process. The probability is redistributed among these actions. PAR represents the interleaving of parallel processes. All the transitions of the processes involved are made possible, and they are kept separated in the original groups. In this way we model the fact that the selection of the process for the next computation step is determined by a scheduler. In fact, choosing a group corresponds to choosing a process. COM models communication by handshaking. The output action synchronizes with all matching input actions of a partner, with the same probability of the input action. The other possible transitions of the partner are kept with the original probability as well. CLOSE is analogous to COM, the only difference is that the name being transmitted is private to the sender. OPEN works in combination with CLOSE like in the standard (asynchronous) π-calculus. The other rules, OUT and CONG, should be self-explanatory.

Next example shows that the expansion law does not hold in π_{pa}. This should be no surprise, since the choices associated to the parallel operator and to the sum, in π_{pa}, have a different nature: the parallel operator gives rise to nondeterministic choices of the scheduler, while the sum gives rise to probabilistic choices of the process.

Example 1. Let $R_1 = x(z).P \mid y(z).Q$ and $R_2 = p\; x(z).(P \mid y(z).Q) + (1 - p)\; y(z).(x(z).P \mid Q)$. The transition groups starting from R_1 are:

$$R_1 \{ \xrightarrow[1]{x(z)} P \mid y(z).Q \} \qquad R_1 \{ \xrightarrow[1]{y(z)} x(z).P \mid Q \}$$

SUM	$\sum_i p_i\alpha_i.P_i \; \{\xrightarrow[p_i]{\alpha_i} P_i\}_i$	OUT	$\bar{x}y \; \{\xrightarrow[1]{\bar{x}y} \mathbf{0}\}$
OPEN	$\dfrac{P \; \{\xrightarrow[1]{\bar{x}y} P'\}}{\nu y P \; \{\xrightarrow[1]{\bar{x}(y)} P'\}} \quad x \neq y$	PAR	$\dfrac{P \; \{\xrightarrow[p_i]{\mu_i} P_i\}_i}{P \mid Q \; \{\xrightarrow[p_i]{\mu_i} P_i \mid Q\}_i}$
RES	$\dfrac{P \; \{\xrightarrow[p_i]{\mu_i} P_i\}_i}{\nu y P \; \{\xrightarrow[p'_i]{\mu_i} \nu y P_i\}_{i:y\notin fn(\mu_i)}}$ $\quad \begin{array}{l} \exists i.\; y \notin fn(\mu_i) \text{ and} \\ \forall i.\; p'_i = p_i / \sum_{j:y\notin fn(\mu_j)} p_j \end{array}$		
COM	$\dfrac{P \; \{\xrightarrow[1]{\bar{x}y} P'\} \qquad Q \; \{\xrightarrow[p_i]{\mu_i} Q_i\}_i}{P \mid Q \; \{\xrightarrow[p_i]{\tau} P' \mid Q_i[y/z_i]\}_{i:\mu_i = x(z_i)} \cup \{\xrightarrow[p_i]{\mu_i} P \mid Q_i\}_{i:\mu_i \neq x(z_i)}}$		
CLOSE	$\dfrac{P \; \{\xrightarrow[1]{\bar{x}(y)} P'\} \qquad Q \; \{\xrightarrow[p_i]{\mu_i} Q_i\}_i}{P \mid Q \; \{\xrightarrow[p_i]{\tau} \nu y(P' \mid Q_i[y/z_i])\}_{i:\mu_i = x(z_i)} \cup \{\xrightarrow[p_i]{\mu_i} P \mid Q_i\}_{i:\mu_i \neq x(z_i)}}$		
CONG	$\dfrac{P \equiv P' \qquad P' \; \{\xrightarrow[p_i]{\mu_i} Q'_i\}_i \qquad \forall i.\; Q'_i \equiv Q_i}{P \; \{\xrightarrow[p_i]{\mu_i} Q_i\}_i}$		

Table 2. The late-instantiation probabilistic transition system of the π_{pa}-calculus.

On the other hand, there is only one transition group starting from R_2, namely:

$$R_2 \; \{\xrightarrow[p]{x(z)} P \mid y(z).Q \;\; , \;\; \xrightarrow[1-p]{y(z)} x(z).P \mid Q\}$$

Figure 1 illustrates the probabilistic automata corresponding to R_1 and R_2.

As announced in the introduction, the parallel operator is associative. This property can be easily shown by case analysis.

Proposition 1. *For every process P, Q and R, the probabilistic automata of $P \mid (Q \mid R)$ and of $(P \mid Q) \mid R$ are isomorphic, in the sense that they differ only for the name of the states (i.e. the syntactic structure of the processes).*

We conclude this section with a discussion about the design choices of π_{pa}.

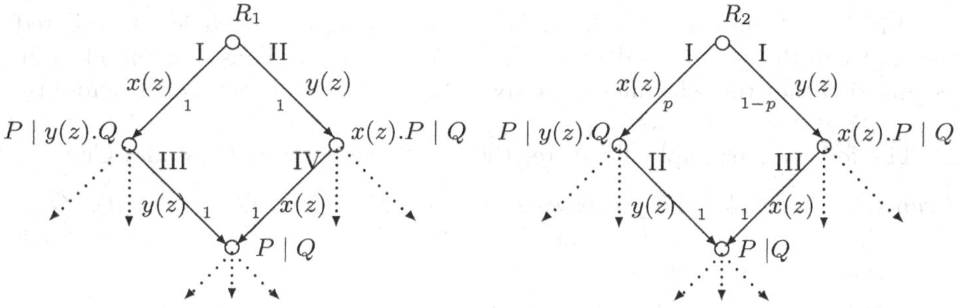

Fig. 1. The probabilistic automata R_1 and R_2 of Example 1. The transition groups from R_1 are labeled by I and II respectively. The transition group from R_2 is labeled by I.

3.1 The Rationale behind the Design of π_{pa}

In defining the rules of the operational semantics of π_{pa} we felt there was only one natural choice, with the exception of the rules COM and CLOSE. For them we could have given a different definition, with respect to which the parallel operator would still be associative.

The alternative definition we had considered for COM was:

$$\text{COM}' \quad \frac{P\{\xrightarrow[1]{\bar{x}y} P'\} \qquad Q\{\xrightarrow[p_i]{\mu_i} Q_i\}_i}{P \mid Q\{\xrightarrow[p'_i]{\tau} P' \mid Q_i\}_{i:\mu_i = x(y)}} \quad \begin{array}{l} \exists i.\ \mu_i = x(y) \text{ and} \\ \forall i.\ p'_i = p_i / \sum_{j:\mu_j = x(y)} p_j \end{array}$$

and similarly for CLOSE.

The difference between COM and COM′ is that the latter forces the process performing the input action (Q) to perform only those actions that are compatible with the output action of the partner (P).

At first COM′ seemed to be a reasonable rule. At a deeper analysis, however, we discovered that COM′ imposes certain restrictions on the schedulers that, in a distributed setting, would be rather unnatural. In fact, the natural way of implementing the π_a communication in a distributed setting is by representing the input and the output partners as processes sharing a common channel. When the sender wishes to communicate, it puts a message in the channel. When the receiver wishes to communicate, it tests the channel to see if there is a message, and, in the positive case, it retrieves it. In case the receiver has a choice guarded by input actions on different channels, the scheduler can influence this choice by activating certain senders instead of others. However, if more than one sender has been activated, i.e. more than one channel contains data at the moment in which the receiver is activated, then it will be the receiver which decides internally which channel to select. COM models exactly this situation. Note that the scheduler can influence the choices of the receiver by selecting certain outputs to be premises in COM, and delaying the others by using PAR.

With COM′, on the other hand, when an input-guarded choice is executed, the choice of the channel is determined by the scheduler. Thus COM′ models the assumption that the scheduler can only activate (at most) one sender before the next activation of a receiver.

The following example illustrates the difference between COM and COM′.

Example 2. Consider the processes $P_1 = \bar{x}_1 y$, $P_2 = \bar{x}_2 z$, $Q = 1/3\ x_1(y).Q_1 + 2/3\ x_2(y).Q_2$, and define $R = (\nu x_1)(\nu x_2)(P_1 \mid P_2 \mid Q)$. Under COM, the transition groups starting from R are

$$R\,\{\xrightarrow[1/3]{\tau} R_1, \xrightarrow[2/3]{\tau} R_2\} \qquad R\,\{\xrightarrow[1]{\tau} R_1\} \qquad R\,\{\xrightarrow[1]{\tau} R_2\}$$

where $R_1 = (\nu x_1)(\nu x_2)(P_2 \mid Q_1)$ and $R_2 = (\nu x_1)(\nu x_2)(P_1 \mid Q_2)$. The first group corresponds to the possibility that both $\bar{x}_1$ and $\bar{x}_2$ are available for input when Q is scheduled for execution. The other groups correspond to the availability of only $\bar{x}_1$ and only $\bar{x}_2$ respectively.

Under COM′, on the other hand, the only possible transition groups are

$$R\,\{\xrightarrow[1]{\tau} R_1\} \qquad R\,\{\xrightarrow[1]{\tau} R_2\}$$

Note that, in both cases, the only possible transitions are those labeled with τ, because $\bar{x}_1$ and $\bar{x}_2$ are restricted at the top level.

4 Solving the Electoral Problem in π_{pa}

In [9] it has been proved that, in certain networks, it is not possible to solve the leader election problem by using the asynchronous π-calculus. The problem consists in ensuring that all processes will reach an agreement (elect a leader) in finite time. One example of such network is the system consisting of two symmetric nodes P_0 and P_1 connected by two internal channels x_0 and x_1 (see Figure 2).

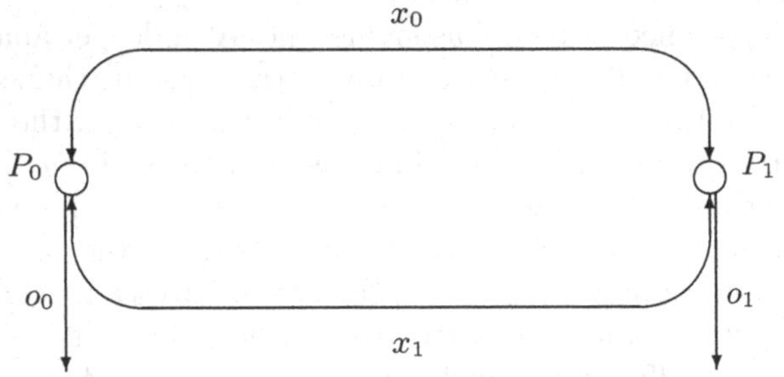

Fig. 2. A symmetric network P $= \nu x_0\ \nu x_1(P_0 \mid P_1)$. The restriction on x_0, x_1 is made in order to enforce synchronization.

In this section we will show that it is possible to solve the leader election problem for the above network by using the π_{pa}-calculus. Following [9], we will assume that the processes communicate their decision to the "external word" by using channels o_0 and o_1.

The reason why this problem cannot be solved with the asynchronous π-calculus is that a network with a leader is not symmetric, and the asynchronous π-calculus is not able to force the initial symmetry to break. Suppose for example that P_0 would elect itself as the leader after performing a certain sequence of actions. By symmetry, and because of lack of synchronous communication, the same actions may be performed by P_1. Therefore P_1 would elect itself as leader, which means that no agreement has been reached.

We propose a solution based on the idea of breaking the symmetry by repeating again and again certain random choices, until this goal has been achieved. The difficult point is to ensure that it will be achieved with probability 1 *under every possible scheduler.*

Our algorithm works as follows. Each process performs an output on its channel and, in parallel, tries to perform an input on both channels. If it succeeds, then it declares itself to be the leader. If none of the processes succeeds, it is because both of them perform exactly one input (thus reciprocally preventing the other from performing the second input). This might occur because the inputs can be performed only sequentially[1]. In this case, the processes have to try again. The algorithm is illustrated in Table 3.

$$
\begin{array}{lll}
P_i = \bar{x}_i\langle t\rangle & & \\
\quad \mid rec_X(\,1/2\;\tau.x_i(b).\,\mathit{if}\;b & & \\
\qquad\qquad \mathit{then}\;(\,(1-\varepsilon)\;x_{i\oplus 1}(b).(\bar{o}_i\langle i\rangle \mid \bar{x}_i\langle f\rangle) & & \\
\qquad\qquad\qquad + & & \\
\qquad\qquad\qquad \varepsilon\;\tau.(\bar{x}_i\langle t\rangle \mid X)) & & \\
\qquad\qquad \mathit{else}\;\bar{o}_i\langle i\oplus 1\rangle\;) & & \\
\qquad + & & \\
\qquad 1/2\;\tau.x_{i\oplus 1}(b).\,\mathit{if}\;b & & \\
\qquad\qquad \mathit{then}\;(\,(1-\varepsilon)\;x_i(b).(\bar{o}_i\langle i\rangle \mid \bar{x}_{i\oplus 1}\langle f\rangle) & & \\
\qquad\qquad\qquad + & & \\
\qquad\qquad\qquad \varepsilon\;\tau.(\bar{x}_{i\oplus 1}\langle t\rangle \mid X)) & & \\
\qquad\qquad \mathit{else}\;\bar{o}_i\langle i\oplus 1\rangle\;) & &
\end{array}
$$

Table 3. A π_{pa} solution for the electoral problem in the symmetric network of Figure 2. Here $i \in \{0,1\}$ and $\oplus$ is the sum modulo 2.

[1] In the π_{pa}-calculi and in most process algebra there is no primitive for simultaneous input action. Nestmann has proposed in [7] the addition of such construct as a way of enhancing the expressive power of the asynchronous π-calculus. Clearly, with this addition, the solution to the electoral problem would be immediate.

In the algorithm, the selection of the first input is controlled by each process with a probabilistic blind choice, i.e. a choice whose branches are prefixed by a silent (τ) action. This means that the process commits to the choice of the channel *before* knowing whether it is available. It can be proved that this commitment is essential for ensuring that the leader will be elected with probability 1 under every possible adversary scheduler. The distribution of the probabilities, on the contrary, is not essential. This distribution however affects the efficiency (i.e. how soon the synchronization protocol converges). It can be shown that it is better to split the probability as evenly as possible (hence 1/2 and 1/2).

After the first input is performed, a process tries to perform the second input. What we would need at this point is a *priority choice*, i.e. a construct that selects the first branch if the prefix is enabled, and selects the second branch otherwise. With this construct the process would perform the input on the other channel when it is available, and backtrack to the initial situation otherwise. Since such construct does not exists in the π-calculi, we use probabilities as a way of approximating it. Thus we do not guarantee that the first branch will be selected for sure when the prefix is enabled, but we guarantee that it will be selected with probability close to 1: the symbol ε represents a very small positive number. Of course, the smallest ϵ is, the more efficient the algorithm is.

When a process, say P_0, succeeds to perform both inputs, then it declares itself to be the leader. It also notifies this decision to the other process. For the notification we could use a different channel, or we may use the same channel, provided that we have a way to communicate that the output on such channel has now a different meaning. We follow this second approach, and we use boolean values **t** and **f** for messages. We stipulate that **t** means that the leader has not been decided yet, while **f** means that it has been decided. Notice that the symmetry is broken exactly when one process succeeds in performing both inputs.

In the algorithm we make use of the if-then-else construct, which is defined by the structural rules

$$\textit{if } \mathbf{t} \textit{ then } P \textit{ else } Q \equiv P \qquad \textit{if } \mathbf{f} \textit{ then } P \textit{ else } Q \equiv Q$$

As discussed in [8], these features (booleans and if-then-else) can be translated into the asynchronous π-calculus, and therefore in π_{pa}.

Next theorem states that the algorithm is correct, namely that the probability that a leader is eventually elected is 1 under every scheduler. Due to space limitations we omit the proof; the interested reader can find it in [3].

Theorem 1. *Consider the process $\nu x_0\ \nu x_1(P_0 \mid P_1)$ and the algorithm of table 3. The probability that the leader is eventually elected is* 1 *under every adversary.*

We conclude this section with the observation that, if we modify the blind choice to be a choice prefixed with the input actions which come immediately afterward, then the above theorem would not hold anymore. In fact, we can define a scheduler which selects the processes in alternation, and which suspends a process, and activates the other, immediately after the first has made a random choice and performed an input. The latter will be forced (because of the guarded choice) to perform the input on the other channel. Then the scheduler will proceed with the first process, which at this point can only backtrack. Then it will schedule the second process again, which will also be forced to backtrack, and so on. Since all the choices of the processes are obligate in this scheme, the scheduler will produce an infinite (unsuccessful) execution with probability 1.

5 Implementation of π_{pa} in a Java-like Language

In this section we propose an implementation of the *synchronization-closed* π_{pa}-calculus, namely the subset of π_{pa} consisting of processes in which all occurrences of communication actions $x(y)$ and $\bar{x}y$ are under the scope of a restriction operator νx. This means that all communication actions are forced to synchronize.

The implementation is written in a Java-like language following the idea outlined in Section 3.1. It is compositional wrt all the operators, and distributed, i.e. homomorphic wrt the parallel operator.

Channels are implemented as one-position buffers, namely as objects of the following class:

```
class Channel {
        Channel message;
        boolean isEmpty;

        public void Channel() {
                isEmpty = true;
        }

        public synchronized void send(Channel y) {
                while (!isEmpty)  wait();
                isEmpty = false;
                message = y;
                notifyAll();
        }

        public synchronized GuardState test_and_receive() {
                GuardState s = new GuardState();
                if (! isEmpty) { s.test = true;
                                 s.value = message;
                                 isEmpty = true;
                                 return s; }
                else { s.test = false;
                       s.value = null;
                       return s; }
         }
}

class GuardState {
        public boolean test;
        public Channel value;
}
```

The methods `send` and `test_and_receive` are used for implementing the output and the input actions respectively. They are both *synchronized*, because the test for the emptyness (resp. non-emptyness) of the channel, and the subsequent placement (resp. removal) of a datum, must be done atomically.

Note that, in principle, the receive method could have been defined dually to the send method, i.e. read and remove a datum if present, and suspend (wait) otherwise. This definition would work for input prefixes which are not in the context of a choice. However, it does not work for input guarded choice. In order to simulate correctly the behavior of the input guarded choice, in fact, we should check continuously for input events, until we find one which is enabled. Suspending when one of the input guards is not enabled would be incorrect. Our definition of `test_and_receive` circumvent this problem by reporting a failure to the caller, instead of suspending it.

Given the above representation of channels, the π_{pa}-calculus can be implemented by using the following encoding $[\![\cdot]\!]$:

Probabilistic Choice

$$[\![\sum_{i=1}^{m} p_i x_i(y).P_i + \sum_{i=m+1}^{n} p_i \tau.P_i]\!] =$$

```
{ boolean choice = false;
  GuardState s = new GuardState();
  float x;
  Random gen = new Random();
  while (!choice) {
     x = 1 - gen.nextFloat();  % nextFloat() returns a real in [0,1)

     if (0 < x <= p1 )
          { s = x1.test_and_receive();
            if (s.test) { y = s.value; [[ P1 ]]
                          choice = true; }
          }
     ...
     if (p1 + p2 + ... + pm-1  < x <=  p1 + p2 + ... + pm)
          { s = xm.test_and_receive();
            if (s.test) { y = s.value; [[ Pm ]]
                          choice = true; }
          }
     if (p1 + p2 + ... + pm  < x <= p1 + p2 + ... + pm+1)
          { [[ Pm+1 ]]
            choice = true; }
     ...
     if (p1 + p2 + ... + pn-1  < x <= p1 + p2 + ... + pn)
          { [[ Pn ]]
            choice = true; }
}
```

Note that with this implementation, when no input guards are enabled, the process keeps performing internal (silent) actions instead of suspending.

Output Action

$[\![\bar{x}y]\!] = \{$ `x.send(y);` $\}$

Restriction

$[\![\nu x P]\!] = \{$ `Channel x = new Channel();` $[\![P]\!] \}$

Parallel If our language is provided with a parallel operator, then we can just have a homomorphic mapping:

$$[\![P_1 \mid P_2]\!] = [\![P_1]\!] \mid [\![P_2]\!]$$

In Java, however, there is no parallel operator. In order to mimic it, a possibility is to define a new class for each process we wish to compose in parallel, and then create and start an object of that class:

```
class processP1 extends Thread {
        public void run() {
                [( P1 )]
        }
}
```

$[\![P_1 \mid P_2]\!] = \{$ `new processP1.start();` $[\![P_2]\!] \}$

Recursion Remember that the process $rec_X P$ represents a process X defined as $X \stackrel{\text{def}}{=} P$, where P may contain occurrences of X. For each such process, define the following class:

```
class X {
     static public void exec() {
            [( P )]
     }
}
```

Then define:

$[\![rec_X P]\!] = \{$ `X.exec();` $\}$

$[\![X]\!] = \{$ `X.exec();` $\}$

6 Conclusion and Future Work

We have defined a probabilistic extension π_{pa} of the asynchronous π-calculus based on the model of probabilistic automata. The main novelty is the introduction of a probabilistic choice operator. The parallel operator is still modeled nondeterministically, the idea being that it is controlled by an external scheduler. We have argued that our calculus is more powerful than the asynchronous π-calculus by showing that it is able to express the solution to the electoral problem in a symmetric network.

Future work include the embedding of the π-calculus into π_{pa} and the development of a proof system for properties of π_{pa} programs.

Acknowledgments We would like to thank Dale Miller and the anonymous FOSSACS referees for their helpful comments on a preliminary version of this paper.

References

1. R. Amadio, I. Castellani, and D. Sangiorgi. On bisimulations for the asynchronous π-calculus. *TCS*, 195(2):291–324, 1998.
2. G. Boudol. Asynchrony and the π-calculus (note). Rapport de Recherche 1702, INRIA, Sophia-Antipolis, 1992.
3. O. M. Herescu and C. Palamidessi. Probabilistic asynchronous π calculus. Tech. Rep., Dept. of Comp. Sci. and Eng., Penn State Univ., 2000. Postscript available at `http://cse.psu.edu/~catuscia/papers/prob_impl/report2.ps`.
4. K. Honda and M. Tokoro. An object calculus for asynchronous communication. In *Proc. of ECOOP*, volume 512 of *LNCS*, pages 133–147. Springer-Verlag, 1991.
5. R. Milner. *Communicating and mobile systems: the π-calculus.* Cambridge University Press, 1999.
6. R. Milner, J. Parrow, and D. Walker. A calculus of mobile processes, I and II. *Inf. and Comp.*, 100(1):1–40 & 41–77, 1992.
7. U. Nestmann. On the expressive power of joint input. In *EXPRESS '98*, volume 16.2 of *Electronic Notes in TCS*. Elsevier Science B.V., 1998.
8. U. Nestmann and B. Pierce. Decoding choice encodings. In *Proc. of CONCUR '96*, volume 1119 of *LNCS*, pages 179–194. Springer-Verlag, 1996.
9. C. Palamidessi. Comparing the expressive power of the synchronous and the asynchronous π-calculus. In *Conference Record of POPL '97*, pages 256–265, 1997.
10. M. O. Rabin and D. Lehmann. On the adantages of free choice: A symmetric and fully distributed solution to the dining philosophers problem. In *A Classical Mind: Essays in Honour of C.A.R. Hoare*, chapter 20, pages 333–352. Prentice Hall, 1994.
11. R. Segala. *Modeling and Verification of Randomized Distributed Real-Time Systems.* PhD thesis, MIT, June 1995. Tech. Rep. MIT/LCS/TR-676.
12. R. Segala and N. Lynch. Probabilistic simulations for probabilistic processes. *Nordic Journal of Computing*, 2(2):250–273, 1995.
13. M. Y. Vardi. Automatic verification of probabilistic concurrent finite-state programs. In *Proc. of FOCS*, pages 327–338. IEEE, 1985.
14. W. Yi and K. G. Larsen. Testing probabilistic and nondeterministic processes. In *Proc. of the 12th IFIP Int.l Symp. on Protocol Specification, Testing and Verification.* North Holland, 1992.

Constructive Data Refinement in Typed Lambda Calculus

Furio Honsell[1,2], John Longley[1], Donald Sannella[1], and Andrzej Tarlecki[3,4]

[1] Laboratory for Foundations of Computer Science, University of Edinburgh
[2] Dipartimento di Matematica e Informatica, Università di Udine
[3] Institute of Informatics, Warsaw University
[4] Institute of Computer Science, Polish Academy of Sciences

Abstract. A new treatment of data refinement in typed lambda calculus is proposed, phrased in terms of *pre-logical relations* [HS99] rather than logical relations, and incorporating a constructive element. Constructive data refinement is shown to have desirable properties, and a substantial example of refinement is presented.

1 Introduction

One of the activities involved in developing programs from specifications is the transformation of "abstract programs" involving types of data that are not normally available as primitive in programming languages (graphs, sets, etc.) into "concrete programs" in which a representation of these in terms of simpler types of data is provided. Apart from the change to data representation, such *data refinement* should have no effect on the results computed by the program: the concrete program should be equivalent to the abstract program in the sense that all computational observations should return the same results in both cases.

The standard treatment of data refinement in the context of typed lambda calculus, originating with Reynolds in [Rey81, Rey83] but described most clearly in [Ten94], cf. Sect. 8.5 of [Mit96], uses *logical relations* to prove the correctness of refinements. This work has its roots in [Hoa72], which proposes that the correctness of the concrete program be verified using an invariant on the domain of concrete values together with a function mapping concrete values (that satisfy the invariant) to abstract values. In algebraic terms, what is required is a homomorphism from a subalgebra of the concrete algebra to the abstract algebra. A strictly more general method is to take a homomorphic relation (a so-called *correspondence* [Sch90], cf. [Mil71]) in place of a homomorphism from a subalgebra. Logical relations extend these ideas to deal with higher-order functions.

Proof method ([Ten94]). *Let $\mathcal{A}$ and $\mathcal{B}$ be Σ-Henkin models and let OBS, the* observable types, *be a subset of Types(Σ). To show that $\mathcal{B}$ is a refinement of $\mathcal{A}$, find a logical relation $\mathcal{R}$ over $\mathcal{A}$ and $\mathcal{B}$ such that R^σ is the identity relation for each $\sigma \in OBS$. We then say that $\mathcal{B}$ is a* logical refinement *of $\mathcal{A}$ and write $\mathcal{A} \rightsquigarrow \mathcal{B}$, or $\mathcal{A} \overset{\mathcal{R}}{\rightsquigarrow} \mathcal{B}$ when we want to make $\mathcal{R}$ explicit.*

J. Tiuryn (Ed.): FOSSACS 2000, LNCS 1784, pp. 161–176, 2000.

It is well-known that the composition of two logical relations is not in general a logical relation. It follows that, given logical refinements $\mathcal{A} \overset{\mathcal{R}}{\rightsquigarrow} \mathcal{B}$ and $\mathcal{B} \overset{\mathcal{S}}{\rightsquigarrow} \mathcal{C}$, the composition $\mathcal{S} \circ \mathcal{R}$ cannot in general be used as a witness for the composed refinement $\mathcal{A} \rightsquigarrow \mathcal{C}$. (In fact, the problem is more serious than it appears at first: sometimes there is no witness for $\mathcal{A} \rightsquigarrow \mathcal{C}$ at all, see Sect. 3.) This is at odds with the *stepwise* nature of refinement, and the transitivity of the underlying concept of refinement expressed in terms of observational equivalence. It is one source of examples demonstrating the incompleteness of the above proof method; there are other examples that do not involve composition of refinement steps, see e.g. Sect. 5. The proof method is complete in the absence of higher-order term constants [Mit96].

In [HS99], a weakening of the notion of logical relations called *pre-logical relations* was studied; cf. [PPST00]. Pre-logical relations are closed under composition; in fact, they are the minimal weakening of logical relations with this property. They completely characterize observational equivalence of Henkin models, without restriction to first-order signatures. Replacing logical relations with pre-logical relations in the above gives a notion of *pre-logical refinement* which is in pleasing harmony with stepwise refinement. Indeed, it is equivalent to the underlying concept of refinement, i.e. sound and complete as a proof method.

This is an improvement but pre-logical refinement still does not entirely accord with our intuition concerning data refinement and stepwise development of programs. For one thing, like logical refinement it is a symmetric relation. We will consider a more elaborate notion of data refinement, called *constructive pre-logical refinement* (Sect. 4). This is a relation between specifications, written $SP \underset{\delta}{\overset{OBS}{\rightsquigarrow\!\!\!>}} SP'$, which incorporates a *construction* in the form of a *derived signature morphism* δ taking models of SP' to Henkin models over the signature of SP. Derived signature morphisms define the types and constants in one signature by giving terms over another signature, and this corresponds directly to the code in an ML functor body. It follows that the result of a complete chain of constructive refinements is a Henkin model, corresponding to a modular ML program, which is a solution to the original programming task. We give an extended example of constructive data refinement in the context of exact real number computation, and show that it is not a (constructive) logical refinement (Sect. 5).

Some recent accounts of data refinement in typed lambda calculus have employed variants of logical relations that are related to pre-logical relations, for instance [KOPTT97]. Our inclusion of a constructive element in the relation is new, and our example appears to be the first non-trivial concrete example of data refinement in the lambda calculus literature.

The idea of constructive pre-logical refinement comes from the world of algebraic specifications, where it is called *abstractor implementation* [ST88] or *behavioural implementation* [ST97]. This paper is an attempt to explain this idea in lambda calculus terms, since it is a substantial improvement on current accounts of data refinement in that context. One novelty with respect to existing work on abstractor implementations concerns the connection with pre-logical relations, which generalizes Schoett's characterization of observational equivalence via correspondences and makes a bridge with work on data refinement in lambda calculus based on logical relations. Another novelty concerns the use of derived signature morphisms in the typed lambda calculus for defining constructions. In order for abstractor implementations to compose, constructions are required to preserve observational equivalence, a property known as *stability* [Sch87]. This requirement is normally imposed as an assumption on the language used for defining constructions, which is left unspecified. Here, stability follows easily from the Basic Lemma of pre-logical relations. Finally, the example in Sect. 5 goes considerably beyond the simple examples of refinement of data representation that have been considered previously.

2 Preliminaries: Syntax and Semantics

For the sake of simplicity of the exposition we restrict attention to $\lambda^{\rightarrow}$, the simply-typed lambda calculus having $\rightarrow$ as its only type constructor.

Definition 2.1. *The set of* types *over a set B of* base types *(or* type constants*) is given by the grammar $\sigma ::= b \mid \sigma \rightarrow \sigma$ where b ranges over B. A* signature Σ *consists of a set B of type constants and a collection C of typed* term constants *$c : \sigma$. $Types(\Sigma)$ denotes the set of types over B.*

In a *Σ-context* $\Gamma = x_1{:}\sigma_1, \ldots, x_n{:}\sigma_n$, we require that $x_i \neq x_j$ for all $1 \leq i < j \leq n$ and $\sigma_i \in Types(\Sigma)$ for all $1 \leq i \leq n$. *Σ-terms* are given by the grammar $M ::= x \mid c \mid \lambda x{:}\sigma.M \mid M\ M$ where x ranges over variables and c over term constants. The usual typing rules associate each well-formed term M in context Γ with a type $\sigma \in Types(\Sigma)$, written $\Gamma \rhd M : \sigma$ (or $\Gamma \rhd_{\Sigma} M : \sigma$ when we need to make Σ explicit). If Γ is empty then we write simply $M : \sigma$ or $\rhd_{\Sigma} M : \sigma$.

Definition 2.2. *A Σ-*Henkin model *$\mathcal{A}$ consists of:*

- *a* carrier *set $[\![\sigma]\!]^{\mathcal{A}}$ for each $\sigma \in Types(\Sigma)$;*
- *a function $App_{\mathcal{A}}^{\sigma,\tau} : [\![\sigma \rightarrow \tau]\!]^{\mathcal{A}} \rightarrow [\![\sigma]\!]^{\mathcal{A}} \rightarrow [\![\tau]\!]^{\mathcal{A}}$ for each $\sigma, \tau \in Types(\Sigma)$;*
- *an element $[\![c]\!]^{\mathcal{A}} \in [\![\sigma]\!]^{\mathcal{A}}$ for each term constant $c : \sigma$ in Σ; and*
- *elements $K_{\mathcal{A}}^{\sigma,\tau} \in [\![\sigma \rightarrow (\tau \rightarrow \sigma)]\!]^{\mathcal{A}}$ and $S_{\mathcal{A}}^{\rho,\sigma,\tau} \in [\![(\rho \rightarrow \sigma \rightarrow \tau) \rightarrow (\rho \rightarrow \sigma) \rightarrow \rho \rightarrow \tau]\!]^{\mathcal{A}}$ for each $\rho, \sigma, \tau \in Types(\Sigma)$*

such that

- *$K_{\mathcal{A}}^{\sigma,\tau}\ x\ y = x$ and $S_{\mathcal{A}}^{\rho,\sigma,\tau}\ x\ y\ z = (x\ z)(y\ z)$; and*
- *(extensionality) if $App_{\mathcal{A}}^{\sigma,\tau}\ f\ x = App_{\mathcal{A}}^{\sigma,\tau}\ g\ x$ for every $x \in [\![\sigma]\!]^{\mathcal{A}}$, then $f = g$.*

The class of all Σ-Henkin models is denoted $Mod(\Sigma)$.

Term constants of functional type are interpreted as *total* functions. Allowing partial functions does not seem to introduce problems, but we have not checked the details. Moreover, the use of Henkin models in this paper is not essential; the definitions and results in [HS99] that we will need later also apply to non-extensional models, for instance combinatory algebras.

A Γ-*environment* η on a Henkin model $\mathcal{A}$ assigns elements of $\mathcal{A}$ to variables, with $\eta(x) \in [\![\sigma]\!]^{\mathcal{A}}$ for $x : \sigma$ in Γ. A Σ-term $\Gamma \rhd M : \sigma$ is interpreted in $\mathcal{A}$ under a Γ-environment η in the usual way with λ-abstraction interpreted via translation to combinators, written $[\![\Gamma \rhd M : \sigma]\!]^{\mathcal{A}}_{\eta}$, and this is an element of $[\![\sigma]\!]^{\mathcal{A}}$. If M is closed then we write simply $[\![M : \sigma]\!]^{\mathcal{A}}$.

We can allow terms to contain the fixed-point combinator Y (viewed as a term constant). To interpret such terms in a Henkin model $\mathcal{A}$, we need to additionally require elements $Y^{\sigma}_{\mathcal{A}} \in [\![(\sigma \to \sigma) \to \sigma]\!]^{\mathcal{A}}$ for each $\sigma \in \mathit{Types}(\Sigma)$ such that $f\ (Y^{\sigma}_{\mathcal{A}}\ f) = Y^{\sigma}_{\mathcal{A}}\ f$. We will assume that this additional structure is present whenever we consider such terms.

Definition 2.3. *A* logical relation $\mathcal{R}$ *over* Σ*-Henkin models* $\mathcal{A}$ *and* $\mathcal{B}$ *is a family of relations* $\{R^{\sigma} \subseteq [\![\sigma]\!]^{\mathcal{A}} \times [\![\sigma]\!]^{\mathcal{B}}\}_{\sigma \in \mathit{Types}(\Sigma)}$ *such that:*

– $R^{\sigma\to\tau}(f,g)$ *iff* $\forall a \in [\![\sigma]\!]^{\mathcal{A}}.\forall b \in [\![\sigma]\!]^{\mathcal{B}}.R^{\sigma}(a,b) \Rightarrow R^{\tau}(\mathit{App}_{\mathcal{A}}\ f\ a, \mathit{App}_{\mathcal{B}}\ g\ b)$.
– $R^{\sigma}([\![c]\!]^{\mathcal{A}}, [\![c]\!]^{\mathcal{B}})$ *for every term constant* $c : \sigma$ *in* Σ.

Definition 2.4. *If* $\Gamma \rhd_{\Sigma} M : \sigma$ *and* $\Gamma \rhd_{\Sigma} M' : \sigma$ *then* $\forall \Gamma.M =_{\sigma} M'$ *is a* Σ-equation. *The subscript* σ *is omitted when it is obvious. A* Σ*-Henkin model* $\mathcal{A}$ satisfies *a* Σ*-equation* $\forall \Gamma.M =_{\sigma} M'$ *if* $[\![\Gamma \rhd M : \sigma]\!]^{\mathcal{A}}_{\eta} = [\![\Gamma \rhd M' : \sigma]\!]^{\mathcal{A}}_{\eta}$ *for all* Γ*-environments* η*. It is easy to add connectives and quantifiers, giving sentences of predicate logic with equality. A* specification SP *consists of a signature* Σ *and a set* Φ *of* Σ*-sentences. Then* $\mathit{Sig}(SP) = \Sigma$*, and* $\mathit{Mod}(SP)$ *(the* models *of* SP*) is the class of all* Σ*-Henkin models satisfying all the sentences in* Φ*.*

3 Data Refinement

We begin with an analysis of the failure of composition of logical relations and its impact on composition of logical refinements.

Example 3.1. Let Σ contain two type constants, b and b', and no term constants. Consider Σ-Henkin models $\mathcal{A}, \mathcal{B}, \mathcal{C}$ which interpret b and b' as follows, and interpret function types using full set-theoretic function spaces: $[\![b]\!]^{\mathcal{A}} = \{*\} = [\![b']\!]^{\mathcal{A}}$; $[\![b]\!]^{\mathcal{B}} = \{*\}$ and $[\![b']\!]^{\mathcal{B}} = \{\circ, \bullet\}$; $[\![b]\!]^{\mathcal{C}} = \{\circ, \bullet\} = [\![b']\!]^{\mathcal{C}}$. Let $\mathcal{R}$ be the logical relation over $\mathcal{A}$ and $\mathcal{B}$ induced by $R^{b} = \{\langle *, * \rangle\}$ and $R^{b'} = \{\langle *, \circ \rangle, \langle *, \bullet \rangle\}$ and let $\mathcal{S}$ be the logical relation over $\mathcal{B}$ and $\mathcal{C}$ induced by $S^{b} = \{\langle *, \circ \rangle, \langle *, \bullet \rangle\}$ and $S^{b'} = \{\langle \circ, \circ \rangle, \langle \bullet, \bullet \rangle\}$. $\mathcal{S} \circ \mathcal{R}$ is not a logical relation because it does not relate the identity function in $[\![b]\!]^{\mathcal{A}} \to [\![b']\!]^{\mathcal{A}}$ to the identity function in $[\![b]\!]^{\mathcal{C}} \to [\![b']\!]^{\mathcal{C}}$. The problem is that the only two functions in $[\![b]\!]^{\mathcal{B}} \to [\![b']\!]^{\mathcal{B}}$ are $\{* \mapsto \circ\}$ and $\{* \mapsto \bullet\}$, and $\mathcal{S}$ does not relate these to the identity in $\mathcal{C}$. □

This simple example shows that we may have logical refinements $\mathcal{A} \overset{\mathcal{R}}{\rightsquigarrow} \mathcal{B}$ and $\mathcal{B} \overset{\mathcal{S}}{\rightsquigarrow} \mathcal{C}$ (where we take $OBS = \emptyset$ in both cases), where $\mathcal{S} \circ \mathcal{R}$ is not a logical relation and so cannot act as witness to $\mathcal{A} \rightsquigarrow \mathcal{C}$.

One possible solution might be to construct the relations at higher types from the composite relations at base types. This works if Σ contains only first-order term constants (guaranteeing that the restriction to base types lifts to a logical relation) and if OBS contains only base types (guaranteeing that the resulting logical relation is the identity relation for each $\sigma \in OBS$). The following example shows how this idea fails in the presence of second-order term constants.

Example 3.2. In the previous example, add a type constant *bool* and a term constant $c : (b \to b') \to bool$ to Σ. Let $[\![bool]\!]^{\mathcal{A}} = [\![bool]\!]^{\mathcal{B}} = [\![bool]\!]^{\mathcal{C}} = \{true, false\}$ and take $\mathcal{R}^{bool}$ and $\mathcal{S}^{bool}$ to be the identity. In each model, let the interpretation of c take constant functions to *true* and all other functions to *false*. The resulting $\mathcal{R}$ and $\mathcal{S}$ are logical relations. As before, $\mathcal{S} \circ \mathcal{R}$ is not a logical relation but now the restriction of $\mathcal{S} \circ \mathcal{R}$ to base types cannot be lifted to a logical relation either: this would relate the identity function in $[\![b]\!]^{\mathcal{A}} \to [\![b']\!]^{\mathcal{A}}$ (which is a constant function) to every function in $[\![b]\!]^{\mathcal{C}} \to [\![b']\!]^{\mathcal{C}}$, but then the constant function in $\mathcal{A}$ would be related to non-constant functions in $\mathcal{C}$, and so $[\![c]\!]^{\mathcal{A}}$ could not be related to $[\![c]\!]^{\mathcal{C}}$, otherwise *true* would be related to *false*. □

These two examples show that certain ways of composing the logical relations witnessing $\mathcal{A} \rightsquigarrow \mathcal{B}$ and $\mathcal{B} \rightsquigarrow \mathcal{C}$ do not yield a logical relation witnessing $\mathcal{A} \rightsquigarrow \mathcal{C}$. Such a witness may exist, however, and in the above example it does. For $OBS = \emptyset$, the full relation suffices; for $OBS = \{bool\}$, the full relation on b together with the empty relation on b' and the identity on *bool* lifts to a logical relation. But if we add constants $b1, b2 : b$ and $b1', b2' : b'$ with $[\![b1]\!]^{\mathcal{A}} = [\![b2]\!]^{\mathcal{A}} = [\![b1']\!]^{\mathcal{A}} = [\![b2']\!]^{\mathcal{A}} = *$, $[\![b1]\!]^{\mathcal{C}} = [\![b1']\!]^{\mathcal{C}} = \circ$ and $[\![b2]\!]^{\mathcal{C}} = [\![b2']\!]^{\mathcal{C}} = \bullet$ then there is no logical relation over $\mathcal{A}$ and $\mathcal{C}$ which is the identity on *bool* so $\mathcal{A} \not\rightsquigarrow \mathcal{C}$ for $OBS = \{bool\}$. The following proposition summarizes the situation.

Proposition 3.3. *$\mathcal{A} \rightsquigarrow \mathcal{B}$ and $\mathcal{B} \rightsquigarrow \mathcal{C}$ does not in general imply $\mathcal{A} \rightsquigarrow \mathcal{C}$.* □

Ultimately, the justification for the definition of logical refinement lies in the notion of observational equivalence, in terms of which the underlying concept of data refinement is formulated.

Definition 3.4. *Let $\mathcal{A}$ and $\mathcal{B}$ be Σ-Henkin models and let $OBS \subseteq Types(\Sigma)$. Then $\mathcal{A}$ is* observationally equivalent *to $\mathcal{B}$ with respect to OBS, written $\mathcal{A} \equiv_{OBS} \mathcal{B}$, if for any two closed Σ-terms $M, N : \sigma$ for $\sigma \in OBS$, $[\![M : \sigma]\!]^{\mathcal{A}} = [\![N : \sigma]\!]^{\mathcal{A}}$ iff $[\![M : \sigma]\!]^{\mathcal{B}} = [\![N : \sigma]\!]^{\mathcal{B}}$.*

It is usual to take OBS to be the "built-in" types for which equality is decidable, for instance *bool* and/or *nat*. Then $\mathcal{A}$ and $\mathcal{B}$ are observationally equivalent iff it is not possible to distinguish between them by performing computational experiments. Note that $OBS \subseteq OBS'$ implies $\equiv_{OBS} \supseteq \equiv'_{OBS}$.

For $OBS = \{nat\}$, the connection between logical refinement and observational equivalence is given by Mitchell's representation independence theorem.

Theorem 3.5 ([Mit96]). *Let Σ be a signature that includes a type constant nat, and let $\mathcal{A}$ and $\mathcal{B}$ be Σ-Henkin models, with $[\![nat]\!]^{\mathcal{A}} = [\![nat]\!]^{\mathcal{B}} = \mathbb{N}$. If there is a logical relation $\mathcal{R}$ over $\mathcal{A}$ and $\mathcal{B}$ with R^{nat} the identity relation on natural numbers, then $\mathcal{A} \equiv_{\{nat\}} \mathcal{B}$. Conversely, if $\mathcal{A} \equiv_{\{nat\}} \mathcal{B}$, Σ provides a closed term* *for each element of* $\mathbb{N}$, *and* Σ *contains only first-order term constants, then there is a logical relation* $\mathcal{R}$ *over* $\mathcal{A}$ *and* $\mathcal{B}$ *with* R^{nat} *the identity relation.* □

The restriction to signatures with first-order term constants in the second part of the theorem is necessary, and this is the key to the incompleteness of logical refinements as a proof method and the problem with composability of logical refinements. If $\mathcal{A} \rightsquigarrow \mathcal{B} \rightsquigarrow \mathcal{C}$ then $\mathcal{A} \equiv_{OBS} \mathcal{B} \equiv_{OBS} \mathcal{C}$, and so $\mathcal{A} \equiv_{OBS} \mathcal{C}$ since $\equiv_{OBS}$ is an equivalence relation. But then it follows that $\mathcal{A} \rightsquigarrow \mathcal{C}$ only for signatures without higher-order term constants.

An improved version of the above theorem, without the restriction to first-order signatures, holds if logical relations are replaced by *pre-logical relations.*

Definition 3.6 ([HS99]). *A* pre-logical relation $\mathcal{R}$ *over* Σ*-Henkin models* $\mathcal{A}$ *and* $\mathcal{B}$ *is a family of relations* $\{R^\sigma \subseteq [\![\sigma]\!]^{\mathcal{A}} \times [\![\sigma]\!]^{\mathcal{B}}\}_{\sigma \in Types(\Sigma)}$ *such that:*

- *If* $R^{\sigma\to\tau}(f,g)$ *then* $\forall a \in [\![\sigma]\!]^{\mathcal{A}}.\forall b \in [\![\sigma]\!]^{\mathcal{B}}.R^\sigma(a,b) \Rightarrow R^\tau(App_{\mathcal{A}}\, f\, a, App_{\mathcal{B}}\, g\, b)$.
- $R^\sigma([\![c]\!]^{\mathcal{A}}, [\![c]\!]^{\mathcal{B}})$ *for every term constant* $c : \sigma$ *in* Σ.
- $R(S_{\mathcal{A}}^{\rho,\sigma,\tau}, S_{\mathcal{B}}^{\rho,\sigma,\tau})$ *and* $R(K_{\mathcal{A}}^{\sigma,\tau}, K_{\mathcal{B}}^{\sigma,\tau})$ *for all* $\rho,\sigma,\tau \in Types(\Sigma)$.

Theorem 3.7 ([HS99]). *Let* $\mathcal{A}$ *and* $\mathcal{B}$ *be* Σ*-Henkin models and let* $OBS \subseteq Types(\Sigma)$*. Then* $\mathcal{A} \equiv_{OBS} \mathcal{B}$ *iff there exists a pre-logical relation over* $\mathcal{A}$ *and* $\mathcal{B}$ *which is a partial injection on* OBS. □

This suggests the following. (We switch to a notation that makes the set of observable types explicit.)

Definition 3.8. *Let* $\mathcal{A}$ *and* $\mathcal{B}$ *be* Σ*-Henkin models and* $OBS \subseteq Types(\Sigma)$*. Then* $\mathcal{B}$ *is a* pre-logical refinement *of* $\mathcal{A}$*, written* $\mathcal{A} \overset{OBS}{\rightsquigarrow} \mathcal{B}$*, if there is a pre-logical relation* $\mathcal{R}$ *over* $\mathcal{A}$ *and* $\mathcal{B}$ *such that* R^σ *is a partial injection for each* $\sigma \in OBS$.

We phrase this as a definition, rather than as a proof method for the underlying notion of data refinement, in contrast to logical refinements. As a proof method it is sound and complete, and therefore equivalent to this underlying notion.

Pre-logical relations compose [HS99], so pre-logical refinements compose, and this explains why stepwise refinement is sound. Another explanation goes via Theorem 3.7: $\mathcal{A} \overset{OBS}{\rightsquigarrow} \mathcal{B} \overset{OBS}{\rightsquigarrow} \mathcal{C} \Rightarrow \mathcal{A} \equiv_{OBS} \mathcal{B} \equiv_{OBS} \mathcal{C} \Rightarrow \mathcal{A} \equiv_{OBS} \mathcal{C} \Rightarrow \mathcal{A} \overset{OBS}{\rightsquigarrow} \mathcal{C}$. The set of observable types need not be the same in both steps, as the following result spells out.

Proposition 3.9. *If* $\mathcal{A} \overset{OBS}{\rightsquigarrow} \mathcal{B}$ *and* $\mathcal{B} \overset{OBS'}{\rightsquigarrow} \mathcal{C}$ *then* $\mathcal{A} \overset{OBS}{\rightsquigarrow} \mathcal{C}$ *provided* $OBS \subseteq OBS'$. □

The definition of observational equivalence may be extended to allow experiments to include the fixed-point combinator by requiring Henkin models to include elements $Y_{\mathcal{A}}^\sigma \in [\![(\sigma \to \sigma) \to \sigma]\!]^{\mathcal{A}}$ for each $\sigma \in Types(\Sigma)$ as indicated above. Theorem 3.7 still holds provided pre-logical relations are required to relate $Y_{\mathcal{A}}^\sigma$ with $Y_{\mathcal{B}}^\sigma$ for all σ.

4 Constructive Data Refinement

Pre-logical refinement, like logical refinement, is a symmetric relation. This does not fit the intuition that refinement is about going from an abstract, high-level description of a program to a concrete, more detailed description. There are at least two basic defects of the notion of pre-logical refinement of which the symmetry of the relation is merely a symptom.

First, it is a relation between Henkin models. The intuition behind stepwise refinement suggests that it should be rather a relation between *descriptions* of Henkin models, i.e. between *specifications*. The original specification of a problem rarely determines a single permissible behaviour: some of the details of the behaviour are normally left open to the implementor. So at this stage one starts with an assortment of models, corresponding to all the possible choices of behaviours. (Some of these will be isomorphic to one another, given a suitable notion of isomorphism, but if the specification permits more than one externally-visible behaviour then there will be non-isomorphic models.) The final program, on the other hand, corresponds to a single Henkin model. So the refinement process involves not just replacement of abstract data representations by more concrete ones, but also selection between permitted behaviours.

Definition 4.1. *Let SP and SP′ be specifications with* $\Sigma = Sig(SP) = Sig(SP')$ *and* $OBS \subseteq Types(\Sigma)$*. Then SP′ is a* pre-logical refinement *of SP, written* $SP \overset{OBS}{\rightsquigarrow} SP'$*, if for any* $\mathcal{B} \in Mod(SP')$ *there is some* $\mathcal{A} \in Mod(SP)$ *with a pre-logical relation* $\mathcal{R}$ *over* $\mathcal{A}$ *and* $\mathcal{B}$ *such that* R^σ *is a partial injection for each* $\sigma \in OBS$*.*

Second, the idea that refinement is a *reduction* of one as-yet-unsolved problem to another is not explicit. Intuitively, each refinement step reduces the current problem to a smaller problem, such that any solution to the smaller problem gives rise to a solution to the original problem. In pre-logical refinement of specifications, one models this by having the successive specifications accumulate more and more details arising from successive design decisions. Some parts become fully determined, and remain unchanged as a part of the specification until the final program is obtained. The parts that are not yet fully determined correspond to the unsolved parts of the original problem. (To avoid clutter, we omit the *OBS* decorations in the following diagrams.)

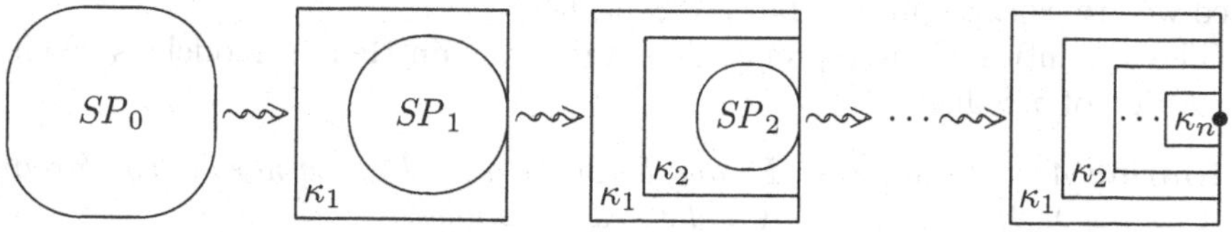

It is much cleaner to separate the finished parts from the specification, proceeding with the development of the unresolved parts only, giving

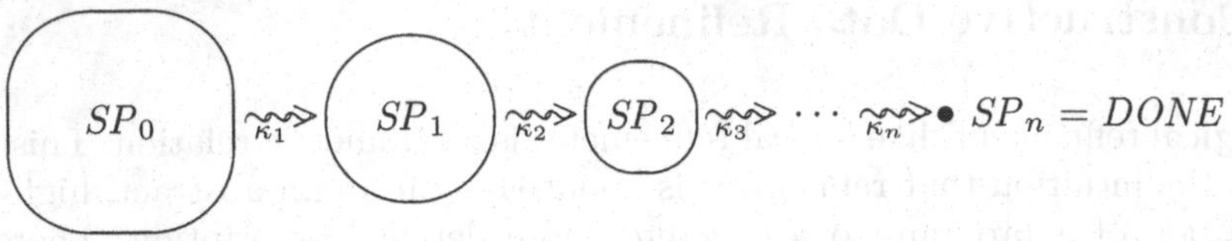

where *DONE* is a specification having a ready realisation (e.g. a specification of the built-ins of the programming language in use). The finished parts $\kappa_1, \ldots, \kappa_n$ are *constructions* extending any solution (model) of a reduced problem (specification) to a solution of the previous problem, and so we will refer to this relation as *constructive data refinement*. The signatures of successive specifications may be different, in contrast to the earlier refinement relations.

Constructive data refinement will be defined below. As constructions we will take "δ-reducts" of Σ'-Henkin models induced by "derived signature morphisms" $\delta : \Sigma \to \Sigma'$, where Σ and Σ' are the signatures before and after refinement, respectively. This amounts to giving an interpretation of the type constants and term constants in Σ as types and terms over Σ'.

Definition 4.2. *Let Σ and Σ' be signatures. A* derived signature morphism *$\delta : \Sigma \to \Sigma'$ consists of:*

- *a mapping from base types in Σ to types over Σ': for every base type b in Σ, $\delta(b) \in Types(\Sigma')$. This induces a mapping (also called δ) from $Types(\Sigma)$ to $Types(\Sigma')$, using $\delta(\sigma \to \tau) = \delta(\sigma) \to \delta(\tau)$.*
- *a type-preserving mapping from term constants in Σ to closed terms over Σ': for every $c : \sigma$ in Σ, $\rhd_{\Sigma'} \delta(c) : \delta(\sigma)$.*

This induces a mapping (also called δ) from terms over Σ to terms over Σ', using $\delta(x) = x$, $\delta(\lambda x{:}\sigma.M) = \lambda x{:}\delta(\sigma).\delta(M)$, $\delta(M\, M') = \delta(M)\, \delta(M')$, and (if we are using the Y combinator) $\delta(Y) = Y$. Composition is obvious.

Proposition 4.3. *If $\delta : \Sigma \to \Sigma'$ and $\Gamma \rhd_\Sigma M : \sigma$ then $\delta(\Gamma) \rhd_{\Sigma'} \delta(M) : \delta(\sigma)$ where $\delta(x_1{:}\sigma_1, \ldots, x_n{:}\sigma_n) = x_1{:}\delta(\sigma_1), \ldots, x_n{:}\delta(\sigma_n)$.* □

A derived signature morphism corresponds exactly to a *functor* in ML terminology, or a *parameterised program* [Gog84]: the functor parameter is a Σ'-Henkin model, and the functor body contains code which defines the components of Σ using the components of Σ'. If the fixed-point combinator is available then this code may involve recursive functions. (Recursively-defined *types* are not allowed since we are working in $\lambda^{\to}$, but see Sect. 6.)

The semantics of these programs as functions on Henkin models is given by the notion of δ-reduct.

Definition 4.4. *Let $\delta : \Sigma \to \Sigma'$ and let $\mathcal{A}'$ be a Σ'-Henkin model. The* δ-reduct *of $\mathcal{A}'$ is the Σ-Henkin model $\mathcal{A}'|_\delta$ defined as follows:*

- *$[\![\sigma]\!]^{\mathcal{A}'|_\delta} = [\![\delta(\sigma)]\!]^{\mathcal{A}'}$ for each $\sigma \in Types(\Sigma)$;*
- *$App^{\sigma,\tau}_{\mathcal{A}'|_\delta} = App^{\delta(\sigma),\delta(\tau)}_{\mathcal{A}'}$ for each $\sigma, \tau \in Types(\Sigma)$;*

– $[\![c]\!]^{\mathcal{A}'|_\delta} = [\![\delta(c)]\!]^{\mathcal{A}'}$ *for each term constant* $c : \sigma$ *in* Σ; *and*
– $K^{\sigma,\tau}_{\mathcal{A}'|_\delta} = K^{\delta(\sigma),\delta(\tau)}_{\mathcal{A}'}$, $S^{\rho,\sigma,\tau}_{\mathcal{A}'|_\delta} = S^{\delta(\rho),\delta(\sigma),\delta(\tau)}_{\mathcal{A}'}$ *and (if we are using the* Y *combinator)* $Y^{\sigma}_{\mathcal{A}'|_\delta} = Y^{\delta(\sigma)}_{\mathcal{A}'}$, *for each* $\rho, \sigma, \tau \in \mathit{Types}(\Sigma)$.

Proposition 4.5. $[\![\Gamma \rhd_\Sigma M : \sigma]\!]^{\mathcal{A}'|_\delta}_\eta = [\![\delta(\Gamma) \rhd_{\Sigma'} \delta(M) : \delta(\sigma)]\!]^{\mathcal{A}'}_\eta$. □

Σ-Henkin models and pre-logical relations between such models form a category $\mathbf{Mod}(\Sigma)$. The following property is intimately related to the concept of *stability* in [Sch87].

Proposition 4.6 (Stability). *For any* $\delta : \Sigma \to \Sigma'$, *the mapping* $\cdot|_\delta$ *extends to a functor* $\cdot|_\delta : \mathbf{Mod}(\Sigma') \to \mathbf{Mod}(\Sigma)$. *If a pre-logical relation* $\mathcal{R}'$ *in* $\mathbf{Mod}(\Sigma')$ *is a partial injection on* $OBS' \subseteq \mathit{Types}(\Sigma')$, *then* $\mathcal{R}'|_\delta$ *is a partial injection on* $\delta^{-1}(OBS')$. *Thus* $\mathcal{A}' \equiv_{OBS'} \mathcal{B}'$ *implies* $\mathcal{A}'|_\delta \equiv_{OBS} \mathcal{B}'|_\delta$ *for any* $OBS \subseteq \mathit{Types}(\Sigma)$ *such that* $\delta(OBS) \subseteq OBS'$.

Proof. *Take* $(R|_\delta)^\sigma = R^{\delta(\sigma)}$. *It follows from the Basic Lemma for pre-logical relations (see [HS99]) that this yields a pre-logical relation.* □

Now we are ready to give a formal definition of constructive data refinement.

Definition 4.7. *Let* SP *and* SP' *be specifications,* $\delta : \mathit{Sig}(SP) \to \mathit{Sig}(SP')$ *be a derived signature morphism, and let* $OBS \subseteq \mathit{Types}(\mathit{Sig}(SP))$. *Then* SP' *is a* constructive pre-logical refinement *of* SP via δ, *written* $SP \overset{OBS}{\underset{\delta}{\leadsto}} SP'$, *if for any* $\mathcal{B} \in \mathit{Mod}(SP')$ *there is some* $\mathcal{A} \in \mathit{Mod}(SP)$ *with a pre-logical relation* $\mathcal{R}$ *over* $\mathcal{A}$ *and* $\mathcal{B}|_\delta$ *such that* R^σ *is a partial injection for each* $\sigma \in OBS$.

It is easy to modify this definition to give a notion of constructive logical refinement, written $\underset{\delta}{\leadsto}$. The correspondence between derived signature morphisms as defined above and ML functors justifies the use of the word "constructive". In Sect. 5 below we give an example of constructive pre-logical refinement and show that it is not a constructive logical refinement.

Constructive pre-logical refinements compose via the composition of their underlying derived signature morphisms:

Proposition 4.8. *If* $SP \overset{OBS}{\underset{\delta}{\leadsto}} SP'$ *and* $SP' \overset{OBS'}{\underset{\delta'}{\leadsto}} SP''$ *then* $SP \overset{OBS}{\underset{\delta' \circ \delta}{\leadsto}} SP''$ *provided* $\delta(OBS) \subseteq OBS'$. □

The required relationship between OBS and OBS' is just what one would expect: as refinement progresses, the successive specifications become increasingly less abstract and so the number of non-observable types tends to decrease, while the overall task of implementing SP with observable types OBS remains the same.

As suggested above, a chain of constructive refinements is complete when the original problem has been reduced to a specification $DONE$ with a given (implemented) model $\mathcal{D}$:

$$SP_0 \overset{OBS_1}{\underset{\delta_1}{\leadsto}} SP_1 \overset{OBS_2}{\underset{\delta_2}{\leadsto}} \cdots \overset{OBS_n}{\underset{\delta_n}{\leadsto}} SP_n = DONE$$

Then, by Prop. 4.8, if the condition on $OBS_1, \ldots, OBS_n$ is satisfied, $DONE$ is a constructive pre-logical refinement of SP_0 via $\delta_n \circ \cdots \circ \delta_2 \circ \delta_1$ with respect to OBS_1: the Henkin model $\mathcal{D}|_{\delta_n \circ \cdots \circ \delta_2 \circ \delta_1}$ is observationally equivalent to some model of SP_0 with respect to OBS_1. In other words, $\delta_n \circ \cdots \circ \delta_2 \circ \delta_1$ is a program that is a solution to the original programming task.

5 An Example from Real Number Computation

We now present an extended example of constructive data refinement in the context of exact real number computation. The point of this example is that the desired refinement can be expressed in terms of pre-logical relations, but not in terms of logical relations.

We will describe a specification SP involving real numbers and some operations on them, and a specification SP' which provides a means of implementing SP using higher-type functions. We will then present a constructive pre-logical refinement $SP \underset{\delta}{\overset{OBS}{\rightsquigarrow}} SP'$ that captures this implementation; however, we will show that there is no constructive *logical* refinement $SP \underset{\delta}{\rightsquigarrow} SP'$.

5.1 A Specification for Real Number Operations

The specification SP has an underlying signature Σ consisting of the type constants *real* and *bool* and the following term constants:

$$\begin{array}{rr} 0,1 : real & sup_{[0,1]} : (real \to real) \to real \\ - : real \to real & true, false, \bot : bool \\ +, *, max : real \to real \to real & < : real \to real \to bool \end{array}$$

We declare *bool* (only) to be an observable type. As usual, we treat $+, *$ and $<$ as infixes. One could of course consider richer signatures (e.g. with division), but the signature above has the technical advantage that all the above operations are *total* functions in the intended models (see below regarding the interpretation of $sup_{[0,1]}$).

A class of intended models for SP may be given via some logical axioms, as follows. For $0, 1, -, +, *$, we take the usual axioms for a field; we also add axioms saying that the type *real* is totally ordered by $\leq$, where $t \leq u$ abbreviates the logical formula $\exists z{:}real. u = t + (z * z)$. For max and $sup_{[0,1]}$, we add the axioms

$$\forall x, y{:}real. (x \leq y \Rightarrow max\ x\ y = y) \wedge (y \leq x \Rightarrow max\ x\ y = x)$$

$$\begin{aligned} \forall f : real \to real.\ & (\exists z{:}real.\ \forall x{:}real.\ 0 \leq x \wedge x \leq 1 \Rightarrow f(x) \leq z) \Rightarrow \\ & (\forall z{:}real.\ sup_{[0,1]} f \leq z \Leftrightarrow \forall x{:}real.\ 0 \leq x \wedge x \leq 1 \Rightarrow f(x) \leq z) \end{aligned}$$

An important logical consequence of these axioms (which we shall use later) is the formula $sup_{[0,1]}(\lambda x{:}real.\, 0) = 0$.

The language we have defined is surprisingly expressive. For instance, every algebraic real number is definable by a closed term, and so any model for SP must contain a copy of at least the algebraic reals. In fact, the models we have in mind contain all the computable or *recursive* reals (though not every computable real is definable by a closed term).

The only purpose of including the type *bool* in *SP* is to allow us to make observations on real numbers. In general we do not expect to be able to tell when two real numbers are the same, but we can tell when they are different. It suffices for our purposes to include the order relation $<$ in our signature. The axioms for $<$ are:

$$\forall x, y{:}real.\, (\neg y \leq x) \Rightarrow x < y = true$$
$$\forall x, y{:}real.\, (\neg x \leq y) \Rightarrow x < y = false$$
$$\forall x, y{:}real.\, x = y \Rightarrow x < y = \bot$$

This completes the definition of *SP*.

Some brief remarks on models for *SP* may be helpful. The full set-theoretic type structure over $\mathbb{R}$ gives a model of *SP*, though we need to assign arbitrary values to the interpretation of $sup_{[0,1]}$ on functions $f : \mathbb{R} \to \mathbb{R}$ which are unbounded on $[0, 1]$. There are also natural models in which the interpretation of $real \to real$ is constrained to include only *continuous* functions (see e.g. [Nor98]).

5.2 A Specification for PCF Computations

We now present a specification SP' corresponding to the familiar functional language PCF [Plo77]. A constructive refinement $SP \underset{\delta}{\overset{OBS}{\leadsto}} SP'$ for $OBS = \{bool\}$ then amounts to a way of implementing *SP* in PCF via a "program" δ.

The signature Σ' for SP' will consist of the single type constant *nat* and:

$$0 : nat \qquad ifzero : nat \to nat \to nat \to nat$$
$$succ, pred : nat \to nat \qquad Y^\sigma : (\sigma \to \sigma) \to \sigma \qquad (\sigma \in Types(\Sigma'))$$

This is exactly the language for (a version of) PCF. The intention is that *nat* stands for the *lifted* natural numbers, with the term $\bot \equiv Y^{nat}(\lambda z{:}nat.z)$ denoting the bottom element. We freely employ syntactic sugar in PCF terms where the meaning is evident.

We now wish to add axioms to ensure that any model for SP' is a model of PCF in some reasonable sense. We do not know whether all the axioms below are strictly necessary for our purposes, but they correspond to a well-understood class of models of PCF. Let us write $t \downarrow$ as an abbreviation for the formula $ifzero\ t\ 0\ 0 = 0$ (we may read this as "t terminates"). First we have an axiom saying there is only one non-terminating element of type *nat*:

$$\forall x{:}nat.\, \neg(x\downarrow) \Leftrightarrow x = \bot$$

For 0 and *succ*, we take the usual first-order Peano axioms for the *terminating* elements. For the remaining constants, we take the axioms

$$pred\ 0 = 0 \qquad \forall x{:}nat.\ pred(succ\ x) = x$$
$$\forall y, z{:}nat.\ ifzero\ 0\ y\ z = y \qquad \forall x, y, z{:}nat.\ ifzero(succ\ x)\ y\ z = z$$
$$\forall y, z{:}nat.\ ifzero\ \bot\ y\ z = \bot$$
$$\forall f : \sigma \to \sigma.\, Y^\sigma f = f(Y^\sigma f) \qquad \forall f : \sigma \to \sigma,\ z{:}\sigma.\ z = f\ z \Rightarrow Y^\sigma f \sqsubseteq_\sigma z$$

where $t \sqsubseteq_\sigma u$ abbreviates $\forall P : \sigma \to nat.\ (P\ t\downarrow) \Rightarrow (P\ u\downarrow)$.

Note that the full set-theoretic type structure over $\mathbb{N}_\bot$ is *not* a model, because not every set-theoretic function $\mathbb{N}_\bot \to \mathbb{N}_\bot$ has a fixed point. However, the usual Scott model based on CPOs (see [Plo77]) and the game models of e.g. [AJM96] do provide models of SP', as do their recursive analogues. The extensional closed term model of PCF also provides a model (which in fact is isomorphic to the recursive game models).

5.3 A Constructive Pre-logical Refinement

We now describe a constructive refinement from SP to SP'. The basic idea is that we will represent a real number r by an infinite sequence $\boldsymbol{d} = d_0 d_1 d_2 \ldots$ of natural numbers, which in turn is represented by the function $f : \mathbb{N}_\bot \to \mathbb{N}_\bot$ given by $f(i) = d_i$. (More generally: in any model $\mathcal{B}$ of SP', including non-standard ones, there will be an inclusion from $\mathbb{N}_\bot$ to $[\![nat]\!]^{\mathcal{B}}$; for simplicity of notation we take $\mathbb{N}_\bot \subseteq [\![nat]\!]^{\mathcal{B}}$. Then we represent $\boldsymbol{d}$ by any function $f \in [\![nat \to nat]\!]^{\mathcal{B}}$ such that $f(i) = d_i$ for all $i \in \mathbb{N}$.) Operations on reals are then represented by higher-type operations on such functions. There are many ways to choose a suitable representation, and the differences between them do not matter much. For definiteness, we will work with sequences $\boldsymbol{d}$ such that $d_i \leq 2$ for all $i \geq 2$; such a sequence will represent the real number $d_0 - d_1 + \sum_{i=2}^{\infty} 2^{1-i}(d_i - 1)$. We will use the meta-notation IsReal(f) to mean that $f \in [\![nat \to nat]\!]^{\mathcal{B}}$ represents a real number in this way, and write Val(f) to denote the real number it represents. Note that there will be many sequences representing any given real number — this is in fact an essential feature of any representation of reals for which even the most basic arithmetical operations are computable. The above choice is essentially a *signed binary* representation involving infinite sequences of digits $-1, 0, 1$ (coded in PCF by $0, 1, 2$ respectively).

We can make precise the idea of implementing SP in terms of SP' by means of a derived signature morphism $\delta : \Sigma \to \Sigma'$. For the basic types, we take

$$\delta(real) = nat \to nat, \qquad \delta(bool) = nat.$$

Next, for each term constant $c : \sigma$ of Σ we need to give a term $\delta(c) : \delta(\sigma)$ in Σ'. For the constants 0 and 1, this can be done just by choosing one particular representing sequence for these real numbers, e.g.

$$\delta(0) = \lambda i{:}nat.\ 1, \qquad \delta(1) = \lambda i{:}nat.\ ifzero\ i\ 2\ 1.$$

For the booleans, we take $\delta(true) = 0$, $\delta(false) = 1$ and $\delta(\bot) = \bot$. It is also straightforward to write PCF programs *Minus*, *Plus*, *Times*, *Max*, *Less* for $\delta(-)$, $\delta(+)$, $\delta(*)$, $\delta(max)$ and $\delta(<)$ respectively. For example, we may take

$$\begin{aligned} Minus \ &= \lambda f : nat \to nat,\ i{:}nat. \\ &\quad \text{if } i = 0 \text{ then } f(1) \text{ else if } i = 1 \text{ then } f(0) \text{ else } 2 \frown f(i) \end{aligned}$$

where $\frown$ implements truncated subtraction. In any model $\mathcal{B}$, this satisfies the following condition (which should be understood as a meta-level assertion):

$$\begin{aligned} &\forall f \in [\![nat \to nat]\!]^{\mathcal{B}}.\ \text{IsReal}(f) \Rightarrow \\ &\qquad\qquad \text{IsReal}([\![Minus]\!]^{\mathcal{B}} f) \wedge \text{Val}([\![Minus]\!]^{\mathcal{B}} f) = -\text{Val}(f). \end{aligned}$$

Coding details for the other operations are given e.g. in [Plu98]. What is more surprising is that the operation $sup_{[0,1]}$ can be represented in PCF by a third-order function *Sup*, by means of a clever use of higher-type recursion (a detailed account of the algorithm with code is given in [Sim98]).

Proposition 5.1. *SP' is a constructive pre-logical refinement of SP via δ.*

Proof sketch. Starting from any $\mathcal{B} \in Mod(SP')$, we will obtain a model $\mathcal{A} \in Mod(SP)$ and a pre-logical relation $\mathcal{R}$.

The correct definition of $\mathcal{A}$ is slightly subtle — the whole point is that the obvious definition via a logical relation on $\mathcal{B}$ does not work (see below). First, we embed $\mathcal{B}$ in its chain completion *$\bar{\mathcal{B}}$ via an inclusion ι (we omit the definition). The main purpose of this step is to throw into the model all monotone functions of type nat $\to$ nat — this ensures that in $\bar{\mathcal{B}}$ we can represent all the classical reals and not just the computable ones (cf. Section 5.4 below). One can check that if $\mathcal{B}$ is a model of SP' then so is $\bar{\mathcal{B}}$. Next we define partial equivalence relations $\bar{E}^\sigma$ on $[\![\delta(\sigma)]\!]^{\bar{\mathcal{B}}}$ for each $\sigma \in Types(\Sigma)$. For the base cases, we take*

$$\bar{E}^{real}(f,g) \text{ iff } IsReal(f) \wedge IsReal(g) \wedge Val(f) = Val(g),$$
$$\bar{E}^{bool}(x,y) \text{ iff } x = y \wedge x \in \{[\![0]\!]^{\mathcal{B}}, [\![1]\!]^{\mathcal{B}}, [\![\bot]\!]^{\mathcal{B}}\}.$$

(The latter clause means that $\bar{E}$ behaves as a partial injection for observable types.) We lift this to higher types as a binary logical relation on $\bar{\mathcal{B}}$. One can show that for each constant c of Σ we have $\bar{E}(\iota[\![\delta(c)]\!]^{\mathcal{B}}, \iota[\![\delta(c)]\!]^{\mathcal{B}})$.

We now construct the required model $\mathcal{A}$ by taking $[\![\sigma]\!]^{\mathcal{A}}$ to be the set of equivalence classes of $\bar{E}^\sigma$; one can check that $\mathcal{A}$ yields a Henkin model for SP. Finally, we define relations R^σ from $[\![\sigma]\!]^{\mathcal{A}}$ to $[\![\delta(\sigma)]\!]^{\mathcal{B}}$ by $R^\sigma(a,b)$ iff $\iota(b) \in a$; clearly this defines a pre-logical relation $\mathcal{R}$ as required. □

5.4 Lack of a Constructive Logical Refinement

We now explain why SP' is not a constructive *logical* refinement of SP via δ. Intuitively, the idea is that a logical relation $\mathcal{R}$ is completely determined once we have fixed the relation at basic types — we have no freedom of choice for higher types. For certain models $\mathcal{B}$ of SP', this means that we are forced to include in the relation $R^{real \to real}$ some highly pathological elements of $[\![\delta(real \to real)]\!]^{\mathcal{B}}$, and our PCF implementation of $sup_{[0,1]}$ will fail to work for these pathological elements. This leads to a contradiction since we require $R([\![sup_{[0,1]}]\!]^{\mathcal{A}}, [\![Sup]\!]^{\mathcal{B}})$ for some model $\mathcal{A}$ of SP.

More precisely, let us take $\mathcal{B}$ to be some *effective* model of SP', such as the effective Scott domain model [Plo77] or the term model for PCF. All that we really require is that the elements of $[\![nat \to nat]\!]^{\mathcal{B}}$ correspond to just the partial recursive functions $\mathbb{N}_\bot \to \mathbb{N}_\bot$. We will show the following:

Theorem 5.2. *There is no model $\mathcal{A} \in Mod(SP)$ admitting a* logical *relation $\mathcal{R}$ over $\mathcal{A}$ and $\mathcal{B}|_\delta$ which is a partial injection on bool.*

Proof sketch. The proof of the theorem hinges on the existence of a pathological PCF implementation of the constant zero function: that is, a term Funny : $(nat \to nat) \to (nat \to nat)$ *such that* $R^{real\to real}([\![\lambda x{:}real.\,0]\!]^{\mathcal{A}}, [\![Funny]\!]^{\mathcal{B}})$, *but such that* $[\![Sup\ Funny]\!]^{\mathcal{B}} = [\![Bad]\!]^{\mathcal{B}}$, *where* $Bad = \lambda y{:}nat.\, if\ y < 2\ then\ 1\ else\ \bot$. *Since SP entails that* $sup_{[0,1]}(\lambda x{:}real.\,0) = 0$, *we have* $R^{real}([\![0]\!]^{\mathcal{A}}, [\![Bad]\!]^{\mathcal{B}})$, *which can be shown to be impossible.*

The idea behind Funny is based on the Kleene tree, *a well-known counterexample from recursion theory (see e.g. [Bee85]). Intuitively, Funny(f) gives 0 whenever f represents a* recursive *real number but diverges for certain non-recursive reals.* □

Notice how the pre-logical relation $\mathbb{R}$ in the proof of Proposition 5.1 avoids this problem: the interpretation of *Funny* in $\bar{\mathcal{B}}$ is not included in the partial equivalence relation $E^{real\to real}$, since the model contains representations of non-recursive reals on which *Funny* diverges.

The above example is robust in the sense that it is not just a feature of the particular implementation *Sup* we have chosen — it can be shown that there is *no* PCF program *Sup* that computes suprema for all relevant functions including *Funny*. Indeed, we believe that the above theorem should hold for all possible representations of the reals and all choices of the terms $\delta(c)$: the only condition on δ we require is that $\delta(real) = nat \to nat$.

6 Conclusion

The main purpose of this paper was to introduce the notion of constructive pre-logical refinement and explain how it relates to the usual account of data refinement for typed lambda calculus in terms of logical relations. In a nutshell, the relationship is that for data refinement logical relations work only because they are a special case of pre-logical relations, where the additional requirement imposed by logical relations is more of a hindrance than a help.

There are many directions in which this approach could be developed.

In Sect. 4 we considered linear chains of refinement steps. Decomposition of implementation tasks into separate subtasks can be modelled using constructions that take n-tuples of Henkin models as arguments, giving tree-shaped refinement diagrams. In particular, consider $\delta : \Sigma \to (\Sigma'_1 + \ldots + \Sigma'_n)$, where $\Sigma'_1 + \ldots + \Sigma'_n$ is a coproduct of the signatures $\Sigma'_1, \ldots, \Sigma'_n$. This induces the reduct $\cdot|_\delta : Mod(\Sigma'_1 + \ldots + \Sigma'_n) \to Mod(\Sigma)$. However, this does not give an n-ary construction, since $Mod(\Sigma'_1 + \ldots + \Sigma'_n)$ and $Mod(\Sigma'_1) \times \cdots \times Mod(\Sigma'_n)$ *do not coincide* even up to isomorphism; in other words, higher-order models do not amalgamate unambiguously. However, they *weakly amalgamate*: there is a standard (injective) construction that maps $Mod(\Sigma'_1) \times \cdots \times Mod(\Sigma'_n)$ into $Mod(\Sigma'_1 + \ldots + \Sigma'_n)$ (e.g. by taking full function spaces for extra "mixed" function types). Composing this with $\cdot|_\delta$, we obtain a function from $Mod(\Sigma'_1) \times \cdots \times Mod(\Sigma'_n)$ to $Mod(\Sigma)$ as required. This still ignores one important aspect of development, namely the possibility of mutual dependencies between subtasks. One solution, discussed thoroughly in [SST92], is to use specifications of parametric models in the development process; the same ideas should apply here, but the technical implications of using higher-order models are yet to be worked out.

This paper presents a *global* view of specifications and their refinement: constructions are required to work on the "whole system" (represented as a model of the implementing specification) and produce a whole system (represented as a model of the implemented specification). Good practice suggests that there should be a way to make the refinement steps "local" — that is, to use only *part* of the system built so far to implement some remaining parts of the requirements specification, and then add the result to the whole system built so far. Details will be provided in a longer version of the paper.

In this paper we have focused on $\lambda^{\rightarrow}$ only. But of course, less elementary type structures are also of great importance in software development using data refinement. One can consider inductive/coinductive datatypes, or more generally recursive types as in ML, or impredicative types as in Girard/Reynold's System F. For instance exact real numbers as in Sect. 5 are often implemented as streams for efficiency reasons, also in purely functional contexts, and abstract data types can be understood in the context of existential types. Notions of logical relations, appropriate for each of these type disciplines, have been proposed in the literature: see e.g. [Alt98] for inductive/coinductive types and [MM85] for System F. In order to accomodate data refinement involving such datatypes we need to introduce corresponding notions of pre-logical relation. As pointed out in [HS99], there is a standard methodology here: simply require the interpretations of the "relevant" constants in the two structures to be related. Despite its simplicity, this methodology is extremely rewarding, and it allows to harvest seredipitous results also in related areas. A case in point is offered by PER models of System F, where the extra latitude and flexibility given by defining the exponential PER pre-logically allows for a number of possibly novel natural model constructions. Finally, a notion of pre-logical relation for System F would raise the intriguing question of the relationship between this framework and the one in [Han99], where data refinements in the style of [ST88] are translated into System F using existential types.

Acknowledgements: Thanks to Samson Abramsky, Jo Hannay, Peter O'Hearn, Gordon Plotkin, John Power, John Reynolds and Bob Tennent for helpful discussion. This work has been partially supported by EPSRC grants GR/K63795 and GR/L89532, the ESPRIT-funded CoFI working group, the ESPRIT- and INCO-funded CRIT-2 project and MURST'97 and MURST'99 grants.

References

[AJM96] S. Abramsky, R. Jagadeesan, and P. Malacaria. Full abstraction for PCF. To appear in *Information and Computation* (1996).

[Alt98] T. Altenkirch. Logical relations and inductive/coinductive types. *Proc. Computer Science Logic, CSL'98.* Springer LNCS 1584, 343–354 (1998).

[Bee85] M. Beeson. *Foundations of Constructive Mathematics.* Springer (1985).

[Gog84] J. Goguen. Parameterized programming. *IEEE Trans. on Software Engineering* SE-10(5):528–543 (1984).

[Han99] J. Hannay. Specification refinement with System F. *Proc. Computer Science Logic, CSL'99*, Madrid. Springer LNCS 1683, 530–545 (1999).

[Hoa72] C.A.R. Hoare. Correctness of data representations. *Acta Informatica* 1:271–281 (1972).

[HS99] F. Honsell and D. Sannella. Pre-logical relations. *Proc. Computer Science Logic, CSL'99*, Madrid. Springer LNCS 1683, 546–561 (1999).

[KOPTT97] Y. Kinoshita, P. O'Hearn, J. Power, M. Takeyama and R. Tennent. An axiomatic approach to binary logical relations with applications to data refinement. *Proc. TACS'97*. Springer LNCS 1281, 191–212 (1997).

[Mil71] R. Milner. An algebraic definition of simulation between programs. *Proc. 2nd Intl. Joint Conf. on Artificial Intelligence*. British Computer Society, 481–489 (1971).

[Mit96] J. Mitchell. *Foundations for Programming Languages*. MIT Press (1996).

[MM85] J. Mitchell and A. Meyer. Second-order logical relations. *Proc. Logics of Programs*, Brooklyn. Springer LNCS 193, 225-236 (1997).

[Nor98] D. Normann. The continuous functionals of finite types over the reals. Technical Report 19, Dept. of Mathematics, University of Oslo (1998).

[Plo77] G. Plotkin. LCF considered as a programming language. *Theoretical Computer Science* 5:223–255 (1977).

[PPST00] G. Plotkin, J. Power, D. Sannella and R. Tennent. Lax logical relations. Submitted for publication (2000).

[Plu98] D. Plume. A calculator for exact real number computation. B.Sc. project report, Univ. of Edinburgh; available from `ftp://ftp.tardis.ed.ac.uk/users/dbp/report.ps.gz` (1998).

[Rey81] J. Reynolds. *The Craft of Programming*. Prentice Hall (1981).

[Rey83] J. Reynolds. Types, abstraction and parametric polymorphism. *Proc. 9th IFIP World Computer Congress*, Paris. North Holland, 513–523 (1983).

[SST92] D. Sannella, S. Sokołowski and A. Tarlecki. Toward formal development of programs from algebraic specifications: parameterisation revisited. *Acta Informatica* 29:689–736 (1992).

[ST88] D. Sannella and A. Tarlecki. Toward formal development of programs from algebraic specifications: implementations revisited. *Acta Informatica* 25:233–281 (1988).

[ST97] D. Sannella and A. Tarlecki. Essential concepts of algebraic specification and program development. *Formal Aspects of Computing* 9:229–269 (1997).

[Sch87] O. Schoett. Data Abstraction and the Correctness of Modular Programming. Ph.D. thesis, report CST-42-87, Dept. of Computer Science, Univ. of Edinburgh (1987).

[Sch90] O. Schoett. Behavioural correctness of data representations. *Science of Computer Programming* 14:43–57 (1990).

[Sim98] A.K. Simpson. Lazy functional algorithms for exact real functionals. *Proc. 23rd Intl. Symp. on Mathematical Foundations of Computer Science*, Brno. Springer LNCS 1450, 456–464 (1998).

[Ten94] R. Tennent. Correctness of data representations in Algol-like languages. In: *A Classical Mind: Essays in Honour of C.A.R. Hoare*. Prentice Hall (1994).

On Recognizable Stable Trace Languages

Jean-François Husson[1] and Rémi Morin[2]*

[1] IRIT, Université Paul Sabatier, 118 route de Narbonne, 31062 Toulouse, France
[2] Institut für Algebra, Technische Universität Dresden, D-01062 Dresden, Germany

Abstract. We relate several models of concurrency introduced in the literature in order to extend classical Mazurkiewicz traces. These are mainly Droste's concurrent automata and Arnold's CCI sets of P-traces, studied in the framework of local trace languages. Also, a connection between these models and classical traces is presented in details through a natural notion of projection. These relationships enable us to use efficiently Arnold's result in two other frameworks. First, we give a finite distributed implementation for regular CCI sets of P-traces (or, equivalently, finite stably concurrent automata) by means of bounded labelled Petri nets. Second, we present a new, simple and constructive method to relate Stark's trace automata with Bednarczyk's asynchronous transition systems. This improves a recent result in Scott domain theory.

Introduction. Mazurkiewicz trace languages are a well-known and widely studied model of concurrency [4]. They were introduced in [13] to provide a partial order semantics for elementary Petri nets. In the past decade several different generalizations of classical traces have been studied in the literature. First, Droste introduced concurrent automata [5] for which the independence between actions is no longer a global independence relation, but depends on the current state of the system. These automata were shown to extend Bednarczyk's asynchronous transition systems [2] and Stark's trace automata [18]. Independently, Arnold introduced an extension of classical traces by means of labelled partial orders called P-traces [1]. In particular, a strong connection between *recognizable* classical trace languages and *regular* CCI sets of P-traces was established. More recently, local trace languages were introduced to give a trace semantics for Place/Transition nets [8,14]. There a local independence relation specifies in each configuration which subsets of actions can be executed concurrently.

At some point, it seems necessary to classify and relate the different models of concurrency arisen in the literature. For instance, the synthesis problem of Petri nets consists in characterizing which automata (or languages) correspond to the behavior of a Petri net [7,15,8]. More generally, semantical studies bring relationships between models of different levels of abstraction [20,2,16,11].

In this paper, we relate three models of concurrency which are roughly at the same level of abstraction. These are CCI sets of P-traces, stably concurrent automata and a restricted subclass of local trace languages called stable trace languages. The latter are also precisely compared to classical trace languages by

* Supported by the German Research Foundation (DFG/Graduiertenkolleg)

J. Tiuryn (Ed.): FOSSACS 2000, LNCS 1784, pp. 177–191, 2000.

means of projections. We show that these relationships lead to some improvements for the theories of Petri nets, concurrent automata and dI-domains.

After some basic definitions relating recognizable local trace languages and Mukund's step transition systems [15], we introduce the subclass of stable trace languages with the help of some cube properties. The latter are actually meant to mimic the particular behaviors of stably concurrent automata. In that way, recognizable stable trace languages are easily shown to correspond to the behavior of finite stably concurrent automata. Next we focus on CCI sets of P-traces which are shown to be equivalent to some stable trace languages. Therefore they represent the behavior of stably concurrent automata. Also regular CCI sets of P-traces are associated to recognizable stable trace languages. Thus we obtain precise relationships between these three models.

These connections lead us to give a new formulation of a strong result due to Arnold [1, Th. 6.16] showing that these extensions of classical traces are closely related to the original model: *any recognizable stable trace language is the projection of a recognizable classical trace language.* This relationship holds also for non-recognizable languages over infinite alphabets. However, answering an open problem raised by Arnold, *we prove that this relationship fails in the case of non-recognizable stable trace languages over finite alphabets.* This relies on a counter-example provided by a Producer-Consumer system.

In a seminal paper [21], Zielonka proved that any recognizable classical trace language is described by an asynchronous automaton which provides a finite implementation in the form of distributed processes. In [1], Arnold introduced an extension of Zielonka's asynchronous automata, called P-asynchronous automata. However *these systems failed to describe all regular CCI sets of P-traces.* Besides, it is still an open problem to know which regular CCI sets of P-traces are described by P-asynchronous automata (obviously these are not the whole class of regular CCI sets of P-traces, see [10] for a counter-example). In order to avoid this restriction, *we present a construction of a finite distributed implementation for any recognizable stable trace language* (or any regular CCI set of P-traces) *in the form of a labelled Petri net.* This construction turns out to complete nicely a somewhat dual approach followed by Droste and Shortt [6]. There the Petri nets whose behavior corresponds to a stably concurrent automaton (or a stable trace language) are characterized by some simple conditions on the weight function.

In [17], Schmitt tackles the difficult problem to define a recognizability notion for coherent dI-domains. The basic idea is that a coherent dI-domain should be considered recognizable if it corresponds to the behavior of a finite distributed automaton. However several families of distributed automata might be considered and might give rise to different recognizability notions. The main result of [17] asserts that the coherent dI-domains obtained from either finite trace automata [18] or finite asynchronous transition systems [2] are the same. *We present here a new, simple and constructive proof of this result* — whereas Schmitt's approach is not constructive.

The proofs of our main results partly rely on technical results borrowed from [1] and [3]. A detailled study is available in [10].

1 Basic Notions

Preliminaries. We will use the following notations: for any (possibly infinite) alphabet Σ, and any words $u \in \Sigma^\star$, $v \in \Sigma^\star$, we write $u \leq v$ if u is a prefix of v, i.e. there is $z \in \Sigma^\star$ such that $u.z = v$; the empty word is denoted by ε. We write $|u|_a$ for the number of occurrences of $a \in \Sigma$ in $u \in \Sigma^\star$ and $\wp_f(\Sigma)$ denotes the set of finite subsets of Σ; for any $p \in \wp_f(\Sigma)$, $\mathrm{Lin}(p) = \{u \in p^\star \mid \forall a \in p, |u|_a = 1\}$ is the set of linearisations of p. Finally, if $\lambda : \Sigma \to \Sigma'$ is a map from Σ to Σ', we also write $\lambda : \Sigma^\star \to \Sigma'^\star$ and $\lambda : \wp_f(\Sigma) \to \wp_f(\Sigma')$ to denote the naturally associated monoid morphisms. For short, a right semi-congruence will be called right-congruence.

Local Independence Relations and Local Trace Languages. As established in [8,14], the behaviors of Petri nets are faithfully represented by local trace languages. These are a generalization of the classical Mazurkiewicz' traces [13] since they specify sets of independent actions rather than pairs.

Definition 1.1. *A* local independence relation *over Σ is a non-empty subset I of $\Sigma^\star \times \wp_f(\Sigma)$. The* (local) trace equivalence $\sim$ *induced by I is the least equivalence on $\Sigma^\star$ such that*
TE_1: $\forall u, u' \in \Sigma^\star, \forall a \in \Sigma, u \sim u' \Rightarrow u.a \sim u'.a$;
TE_2: $\forall (u,p) \in I, \forall p' \subseteq p, \forall v_1, v_2 \in \mathrm{Lin}(p'), u.v_1 \sim u.v_2$.
A (local) trace *is an $\sim$-equivalence class $[u]$ of a word $u \in \Sigma^\star$.*

By TE_1 local trace equivalences are right-congruences. TE_2 asserts that for every subset of actions which are independent after a sequence u, all sequences obtained by executing first u and then in an arbitrary order the actions from this subset, are equivalent. Note also that local trace equivalences are Parikh equivalences: $u \sim u' \Rightarrow \forall a \in \Sigma, |u|_a = |u'|_a$.

These assumptions on the trace equivalence can be translated into explicit additional conditions on the local independence relation without affecting the resulting traces. A local independence relation satisfying these additional conditions is called *complete* and can be shown to be a maximal representative among local independence relations defining the same behaviors.

Definition 1.2. *A local independence relation I over Σ is* complete *if*
Cpl_1: $(u,p) \in I \wedge\ p' \subseteq p \Rightarrow (u,p') \in I$;
Cpl_2: $(u,p) \in I \wedge\ p' \subseteq p \wedge\ v \in \mathrm{Lin}(p') \Rightarrow (u.v, p \setminus p') \in I$;
Cpl_3: $(u,\{a,b\}) \in I \wedge\ (u.ab.v, p) \in I \Rightarrow (u.ba.v, p) \in I$;
Cpl_4: $(u.a, \emptyset) \in I \Rightarrow (u,\{a\}) \in I$.

Cpl_1 makes explicit what TE_2 from Def. 1.1 guarantees for the trace equivalence: if a set of actions p can be executed concurrently after u, then so can any subset of p; moreover, following Cpl_2, the step p can be split into a sequential execution v and a concurrent step of the remaining actions. We remark now that Cpl_3 is equivalent to the requirement that $u \sim u' \wedge\ (u,p) \in I \Rightarrow (u',p) \in I$. Thus Cpl_3 states that after two equivalent sequences the independency of actions is the same; it corresponds to the right-congruence property TE_1 from Def. 1.1. Local independence relations satisfying Cpl_3 were called *consistent* in [16] and *durable* in [9]. Finally Cpl_4 guarantees that whenever $u.a$ is a sequential execution, then action a is allowed as a step after u.

In this paper, we study the local trace languages introduced in [11] as combinations of a complete local independence relation and a language of sequences.

DEFINITION 1.3. *A* local trace language *over Σ is a structure $\mathcal{L} = (\Sigma, I, L)$ where I is a complete local independence relation on Σ and $L \subseteq \Sigma^\star$ is such that $u \in L \Leftrightarrow (u, \emptyset) \in I$.*

Note here that the set of sequences L is closed for the prefix relation and the trace equivalence. Moreover any local trace language is entirely determined by its associated local independence relation.

Global Independence Relations and Mazurkiewicz Traces. Local trace languages are actually a direct generalization classical traces [13,4]. There, the independence between actions does not depend on the context of previously occurred events. Thus we consider a *global independence relation* over Σ to be a binary symmetric and irreflexive relation $\| \subseteq \Sigma \times \Sigma$. Then a *classical trace language* over $(\Sigma, \|)$ consists of a language $L \subseteq \Sigma^\star$ which is closed for the commutation of independent actions: $\forall u, v \in \Sigma^\star$, $\forall a, b \in \Sigma$, $u.ab.v \in L \wedge a \| b \Rightarrow u.ba.v \in L$.

In order to connect this approach with local trace languages, *we will only consider here prefix-closed languages.* In that way any classical trace language can be formally identified with a local trace language $\mathcal{L} = (\Sigma, I, L)$ for which $(u, p) \in I$ if the actions in p are pairwise independent w.r.t. the global independence relation. This leads us to introduce formally Mazurkiewicz trace languages within the general framework of local trace languages as follows.

DEFINITION 1.4. *Let $\|$ be a global independence relation over Σ. A* Mazurkiewicz trace language *over $(\Sigma, \|)$ is a local trace language $\mathcal{L} = (\Sigma, I, L)$ such that $\forall u \in \Sigma^\star$, $\forall n \in \mathbb{N}$, $\forall a_1, ..., a_n \in \Sigma$:*

$$(u, \{a_1, ..., a_n\}) \in I \Leftrightarrow u.a_1...a_n \in L \wedge \ \forall i, j \in [1, n] \text{ distinct}, a_i \| a_j.$$

Now associating any prefix-closed classical trace language L over a fixed independent alphabet $(\Sigma, \|)$ to the Mazurkiewicz trace language $\mathcal{L} = (\Sigma, I, L)$, where I is defined as in Def. 1.4, we build clearly a *one-to-one correspondence between prefix-closed classical trace languages and Mazurkiewicz trace languages.*

Despite of this nice formal connection, we should stress here that the local independence relation associated to a Mazurkiewicz trace language may have some unusual (but technically necessary) properties. In particular, if the language L is not *forward-closed* w.r.t. the global independence relation $\|$ then there are a word u and two actions a and b such that $u.a \in L$, $u.b \in L$, $a \| b$ but $u.ab \notin L$; in that case, a and b are not independent after u: $(u, \{a, b\}) \notin I$.

Recognizable Languages and Finite Step Transition Systems. The model of step transition systems was introduced by Mukund [15] in order to extend the so-called synthesis problem of elementary Petri nets [7] to the more general model of Place/Transition nets.

DEFINITION 1.5. *A* step transition system *over the alphabet* Σ *is a structure* $\mathcal{A} = (Q, s, \Sigma, \longrightarrow)$ *where* Q *is a set of states,* $s \in Q$ *is an initial state and* $\longrightarrow \subseteq Q \times \wp_f(\Sigma) \times Q$ *is a set of labelled transitions such that*

- $\forall q_1, q_2 \in Q$: $q_1 \xrightarrow{\emptyset} q_2 \Leftrightarrow q_1 = q_2$;
- $\forall q_1, q_2 \in Q$, $\forall p' \subseteq p \in \wp_f(\Sigma)$: $q_1 \xrightarrow{p} q_2 \Rightarrow \exists q_3 \in Q$, $q_1 \xrightarrow{p'} q_3 \xrightarrow{p \setminus p'} q_2$;
- $\forall q_1, q_2, q_3 \in Q$, $\forall p \in \wp_f(\Sigma)$: $q_1 \xrightarrow{p} q_2 \wedge q_1 \xrightarrow{p} q_3 \Rightarrow q_2 = q_3$.

The step transition system $\mathcal{A}$ *is* finite *if* Σ *and* Q *are finite.*

As usual, for any word $u = a_1...a_n \in \Sigma^\star$, we write $q \xrightarrow{u} q'$ if there are states $q_0,..., q_n$ such that $q_0 = q$, $q_n = q'$ and for each $i \in [1, n]$, $q_{i-1} \xrightarrow{\{a_i\}} q_i$. Let us also stress here that we only consider deterministic step transition systems. This is actually meant to make sure that the local independence relations intuitively associated to them are complete — in particular, they satisfy Cpl_3.

DEFINITION 1.6. *The local trace language associated to a step transition system* $\mathcal{A} = (Q, s, \wp_f(\Sigma), \longrightarrow)$ *is the structure* $\mathcal{L} = (\Sigma, I, L)$ *where*

- $\forall u \in \Sigma^\star$: $u \in L \Leftrightarrow \exists q \in Q, s \xrightarrow{u} q$;
- $\forall u \in \Sigma^\star$, $\forall p \in \wp_f(\Sigma)$: $(u, p) \in I \Leftrightarrow \exists q_1, q_2 \in Q, s \xrightarrow{u} q_1 \xrightarrow{p} q_2$.

Step transition systems define naturally a notion of recognizability which extends a similar notion well-known and widely studied in the case of classical language theory or classical trace languages.

DEFINITION 1.7. *A local trace language is* recognizable *if it is the language of a* finite *step transition system.*

Note here that if $\mathcal{L} = (\Sigma, I, L)$ is recognizable then L is a recognizable language of $\Sigma^\star$, but the converse is false — except, e.g., for Mazurkiewicz trace languages over finite independent alphabets.

2 Stable Trace Languages

We introduce in this section the subclass of stable trace languages. These later generalize Mazurkiewicz traces and Nielsen, Sassone and Winskel's generalized trace languages [16].

Cube Properties in Local Trace Languages. Stable trace languages are characterized by cube properties that can be formalized as follows.

DEFINITION 2.1. *A* stable trace language *is a local trace language* $\mathcal{L} = (\Sigma, I, L)$ *such that*

S_1: $\forall u \in \Sigma^\star$, $\forall n \geq 2$, $\forall a_1, ..., a_n \in \Sigma$ *distinct:*

$$[\forall \sigma : [1, n] \to [1, n] \text{ onto} : u.a_1...a_n \sim u.a_{\sigma(1)}...a_{\sigma(n)}] \Rightarrow (u, \{a_1, ..., a_n\}) \in I$$

S_2: *$\forall u \in \Sigma^\star$, $\forall a, b, c \in \Sigma$ distinct:*
$$[(u, \{a, c\}) \in I \wedge (u.a, \{b, c\}) \in I] \Rightarrow [(u, \{a, b\}) \in I \Leftrightarrow (u.c, \{a, b\}) \in I]$$

Condition S_1 asserts that whenever a set of actions may be executed in any order after a given sequence without affecting the resulting trace then these actions are mutually independent. Note here that the converse always holds. Therefore S_1 means simply that the independence relation I is somehow determined by its trace equivalence $\sim$. Now, the second condition S_2 requires that the concurrency between actions satisfies some local properties. As explained by the following proposition, this insures that the set of traces of a stable trace language satisfies some *cube properties* (CP) similar to those used to characterize stably concurrent automata.

PROPOSITION 2.2. *Let $\mathcal{L} = (\Sigma, I, L)$ be a local trace language satisfying S_1. In the following diagrams, for all $u, v \in \Sigma^\star$, we note $[u] \longrightarrow [v]$ if there is $a \in \Sigma$ such that $u.a \sim v$. The language $\mathcal{L}$ is stable iff $\forall u \in \Sigma^\star$, $\forall a, b, c \in \Sigma$ distinct:*

(CP)
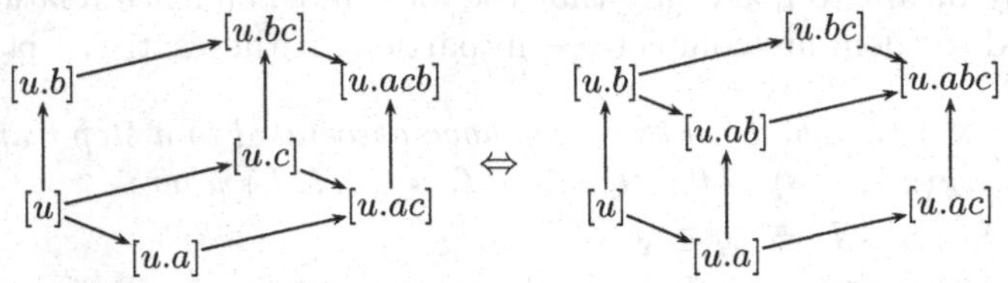

It is clear that any Mazurkiewicz trace language is a stable trace language. Let us also mention here that Nielsen, Sassone and Winskel's *generalized trace languages* [16] can be identified to the stable trace languages which satisfy the following additional *coherence property*: if $(u, \{a, b\}) \in I$, $(u, \{a, c\}) \in I$ and $(u, \{b, c\}) \in I$ then $(u, \{a, b, c\}) \in I$.

Stably Concurrent Automata. We present now the very natural connection between stable trace languages and stably concurrent automata.

DEFINITION 2.3. *[3] An* automaton with concurrency relations *over the alphabet Σ is a structure $\mathcal{A} = (Q, s, \Sigma, \longrightarrow, (\|_q)_{q \in Q})$ such that*

1. *Q is a non-empty set of states, with an initial state s;*
2. *$\longrightarrow \subseteq Q \times \Sigma \times Q$ is a set of transitions assumed deterministic, i.e. whenever $p \xrightarrow{a} q$ and $p \xrightarrow{a} r$ then $q = r$;*
3. *$(\|_q)_{q \in Q}$ is a family of irreflexive, symmetric binary relations on Σ; it is required that whenever $a \|_p b$ then there exist transitions $p \xrightarrow{a} q$, $p \xrightarrow{b} q'$, $q \xrightarrow{b} r$ and $q' \xrightarrow{a} r$.*

Note that we only consider automata with concurrency relations provided with a *single initial state*. On the other hand, the set of states and the alphabet may be infinite. The language L associated to an automaton with concurrency relations is the set of finite sequences $u = a_1 ... a_n \in \Sigma^\star$ such that there are states $q_0, ..., q_n$ for which $s = q_0$ and for each $i \in [1, n]$, $q_{i-1} \xrightarrow{a_i} q_i$. For short, these conditions will be denoted by $s \xrightarrow{u} q_n$. Now the independence relations $\|_q$

provide naturally an equivalence relation over L as follows. The trace equivalence $\sim$ associated to $\mathcal{A}$ is the least equivalence over L such that $\forall u, v \in \Sigma^\star$, $\forall a, b \in \Sigma$: $s \xrightarrow{u} p \xrightarrow{ab} q \xrightarrow{v} r \wedge\ a\|_q b \Rightarrow u.ab.v \sim u.ba.v$.

For many different reasons, it appears that one may expect the independence relations $\|_q$ to depend locally of each other. In that way, a particular attention has been devoted to stably concurrent automata. In the following definition, for all actions a, b and c, and for all state q, we note $a\|_{q.c}b$ if there exists a state $q' \in Q$ such that $q \xrightarrow{c} q'$ and $a\|_{q'}b$.

DEFINITION 2.4. *[3] A automaton with concurrency relations $\mathcal{A}$ is called* stably concurrent automaton *if for all $q \in Q$ and all actions a, b, $c \in \Sigma$, the following equivalence holds: $a\|_q c \wedge\ b\|_q c \wedge\ a\|_{q.c}b \Leftrightarrow a\|_q b \wedge\ b\|_{q.a}c \wedge\ a\|_{q.b}c$. We say that $\mathcal{A}$ is finite if Q and Σ are finite.*

A fundamental property of stably concurrent automata is the following correspondence between the trace equivalence $\sim$ and the family of independence relations $(\|_q)_{q\in Q}$: $\forall u \in \Sigma^\star$, $\forall a, b \in \Sigma$ distinct, $u.ab \sim u.ba \Leftrightarrow s \xrightarrow{u} q \wedge\ a\|_q b$. Therefore the assumption on $(\|_q)_{q\in Q}$ in Def. 2.4 corresponds precisely to the cube properties (CP) of Prop. 2.2. Also, the independency of actions is entirely determined by the trace equivalence. This remark lead us to represent the behavior of stably concurrent automata by stable trace languages as follows.

DEFINITION 2.5. *Let $\mathcal{A}$ be a stably concurrent automaton over Σ, L be its language and $\sim$ be its trace equivalence. The stable trace language associated to $\mathcal{A}$ is $\mathcal{L}(\mathcal{A}) = (\Sigma, I, L)$ where $\forall u \in \Sigma^\star$, $\forall n \in \mathbb{N}$, $\forall a_1, ..., a_n \in \Sigma$ distinct:*

$$(u, \{a_1, ..., a_n\}) \in I \Leftrightarrow \begin{cases} u.a_1...a_n \in L \\ \forall \sigma : [1, n] \to [1, n] \text{ onto} : u.a_1...a_n \sim u.a_{\sigma(1)}...a_{\sigma(n)} \end{cases}.$$

We easily check that $\mathcal{L}(\mathcal{A})$ is indeed a stable trace language. Moreover the restriction of the trace equivalence of $\mathcal{L}(\mathcal{A})$ to L is precisely the trace equivalence of $\mathcal{A}$. We stress that $\mathcal{L}(\mathcal{A})$ is a representation of the behavior of $\mathcal{A}$ equivalent to the *labelled dI-domain* usually considered (see e.g. [3]). Furthermore any stable trace language is the language of a stably concurrent automaton. Besides a stable trace language is recognizable if and only if it is the trace language of a *finite* stably concurrent automaton.

Full Stable Trace Languages Are Stable Right-Congruences. Although stable trace languages play a central role to relate stably concurrent automata with CCI sets of P-traces, we need to introduce first an equivalent representation in the form of particular right-congruences.

DEFINITION 2.6. *Let $\sim$ be a right-congruence over $\Sigma^\star$. The associated* diamond relation *$\sim^\diamond$ is the least right-congruence over $\Sigma^\star$ such that*

$$\forall u \in \Sigma^\star, \forall a, b \in \Sigma, u.ab \sim u.ba \Rightarrow u.ab \sim^\diamond u.ba.$$

We say that the right-congruence $\sim$ is homotopic *if $\sim^\diamond = \sim$.*

It is clear that for all right-congruence $\sim$, $\sim^\diamond \subseteq \sim$. The converse inclusion holds in particular for the trace equivalence of any local trace language which is thus a homotopic right-congruence.

DEFINITION 2.7. *A right-congruence over $\Sigma^\star$ is* stable *if it is homotopic and satisfies axiom* (CP) *of Prop. 2.2, whenever $a, b, c \in \Sigma$ are distinct and $u \in \Sigma^\star$.*

Clearly, the trace equivalence of a stable trace language is a stable right-congruence. However, different stable trace languages may determine the same trace equivalence. That is why we focus now on *full local trace languages.* The latter are defined as the local trace languages $\mathcal{L} = (\Sigma, I, L)$ such that $L = \Sigma^\star$.

PROPOSITION 2.8. *An equivalence relation over $\Sigma^\star$ is the trace equivalence of a stable trace language if and only if it is a stable right-congruence. Moreover, in that case, it is the trace equivalence of a unique* full *stable trace language.*

3 CCI Sets of P-Traces

We show here a one-to-one correspondence between Arnold's CCI sets of P-traces [1] and full stable trace languages. Moreover, regular CCI sets of P-traces correspond to recognizable full stable trace languages.

P-Traces. In this section we consider a fixed alphabet Σ. Note here that we shall consider a slight extension of Arnold's approach since Σ may be infinite.

DEFINITION 3.1. *[1] A* P-trace *t over Σ is a triple $(E_t, \prec_t, \xi_t)$ where $(E_t, \prec_t)$ is a finite partial order and ξ_t is a mapping from E_t to Σ such that for all $x, y \in E_t$, $\xi_t(x) = \xi_t(y) \Rightarrow (x \prec_t y$ or $y \prec_t x)$.*

DEFINITION 3.2. *A* linear extension *of a P-trace $t = (E_t, \prec_t, \xi_t)$ is a total order $\prec$ over E_t such that $\prec_t \subseteq \prec$.*

Now, linear extensions of a P-trace t can easily be identified to words over Σ. Formally, let n be the cardinal of E_t. For any linear extension $\prec$ of t, there is only one way to write $E_t = \{e_1, ..., e_n\}$ with $e_i \prec e_j \Leftrightarrow i \leq j$. Then the word associated to $\prec$ is $\xi_t(e_1)...\xi_t(e_n)$. Clearly, this mapping from linear extensions of t to words is one-to-one. In the following, we shall identify any linear extension of t with its associated word.

DEFINITION 3.3. *Let t be a P-trace over Σ. We note $LE(t)$ the set of all the words associated to a linear extension of t.*

P-traces are naturally structured with a notion of isomorphism: two P-traces $t = (E_t, \prec_t, \xi_t)$ and $t' = (E_{t'}, \prec_{t'}, \xi_{t'})$ are isomorphic if there is a bijection σ from E_t to $E_{t'}$ such that
- $\forall x, y \in E_t : x \prec_t y \Leftrightarrow \sigma(x) \prec_{t'} \sigma(y)$;
- $\forall x \in E_t : \xi_t(x) = \xi_{t'}(\sigma(x))$.

Clearly, two isomorphic P-traces admit the same linear extensions. Noteworthy is the converse property due to Szpilrajn [19].

PROPOSITION 3.4. *Two P-traces t and t' are isomorphic iff $LE(t) = LE(t')$.*

CCI Sets of P-Traces Are Stable Right-Congruences Too. As in the classical case, a P-trace is meant to represent one concurrent execution of a distributed system. In order to describe all the possible behaviors of a system, one has to consider sets of P-traces.

DEFINITION 3.5. *[1] Let $\mathcal{P}$ be a set of P-traces over Σ. We say that $\mathcal{P}$ is consistent and complete if*
- $\bigcup_{t \in \mathcal{P}} LE(t) = \Sigma^\star$ *[Complete]*
- $\forall t, t' \in \mathcal{P},\ t \neq t' \Rightarrow LE(t) \cap LE(t') = \emptyset$ *[Consistent]*

Each consistent and complete set of P-traces determines an equivalence relation $\sim$ over $\Sigma^\star$ whose equivalence classes are the linear extensions of its elements. This equivalence will be called the *trace equivalence* of $\mathcal{P}$.

However, this equivalence relation is sometimes not a right-congruence, which is admittedly still a natural assumption for traces. That is why, following Arnold, we focus on ideal sets of P-traces. These are defined according to the following partial order of P-traces.

DEFINITION 3.6. *We say that a P-trace $t = (E_t, \prec_t, \xi_t)$ is a prefix of a P-trace $t' = (E_{t'}, \prec_{t'}, \xi_{t'})$ if the following conditions are satisfied:*
- $E_t \subseteq E_{t'}$;
- $\forall x \in E_t, \xi_t(x) = \xi_{t'}(x)$;
- $\prec_t = \prec_{t'} \cap (E_t \times E_t)$;
- $\forall x \in E_t, \forall y \in E_{t'} : y \prec_{t'} x \Rightarrow y \in E_t$.

DEFINITION 3.7. *A set of P-traces over Σ is* ideal *if for all $t \in \mathcal{P}$, if t' is a prefix of t then $t' \in \mathcal{P}$. A complete, consistent and ideal set of P-traces will be called CCI for short.*

Useful consequence of [1, Prop. 3.1 and 3.3], our first result relates CCI sets of P-traces and stable right-congruences as follows.

THEOREM 3.8. *An equivalence relation over $\Sigma^\star$ is the trace equivalence of a CCI set of P-traces if and only if it is a stable right-congruence (Def. 2.7).*

Thus any CCI set of P-traces describes a stable right-congruence and consequently it is associated to a uniquely determined full stable trace language (Prop. 2.8). Conversely, any (full) stable trace language can be associated to a CCI set of P-traces which is essentially unique up to the natural isomorphism notion defined as follows. We say that two sets of P-traces $\mathcal{P}_1$ and $\mathcal{P}_2$ are isomorphic if there is a bijection σ from $\mathcal{P}_1$ to $\mathcal{P}_2$ such that for all P-trace $t \in \mathcal{P}_1$, $\sigma(t)$ and t are isomorphic P-traces. Clearly, two CCI sets of P-traces are isomorphic iff their associated trace equivalences are equal. Thus, up to an isomorphism, Prop. 2.8 and Th. 3.8 show that *each stable trace language can be associated to the unique CCI set of P-traces which determines the same trace equivalence.*

Now the behaviors of stably concurrent automata are not full stable trace languages — except if one provide them with an additional sink state. Thus the traces of a stably concurrent automaton are described by a consistent and ideal set of P-traces (it is complete only if its language is $\Sigma^\star$). This result completes actually some similar connections established independently in [3].

Regular CCI Sets of P-Traces vs Recognizable Languages. Theorem 3.8 and Proposition 2.8 establish a one-to-one correspondence between CCI sets of P-traces and full stable trace languages. We explain here that this relationship also holds between *recognizable* stable trace languages and *regular* CCI sets of P-traces. The latter were introduced by Arnold as follows.

DEFINITION 3.9. *Let $\mathcal{P}$ be a CCI set of P-traces over a* finite alphabet Σ *and let $\sim$ be its associated trace equivalence. We consider the equivalence relation $\equiv$ over $\Sigma^\star$ such that $u \equiv v$ if $\forall w, w' \in \Sigma^\star, u.w \sim u.w' \Leftrightarrow v.w \sim v.w'$.*
The set $\mathcal{P}$ is called regular *if the equivalence $\equiv$ is of finite index.*

Using [3, Prop. 2.7], we can now complete Prop. 2.8 and Th. 3.8 as follows.

PROPOSITION 3.10. *A CCI set of P-traces is regular if and only if its associated full stable trace language is recognizable.*

4 Stable Trace Languages vs Mazurkiewicz Ones

We now show how stable trace languages relate to Mazurkiewicz ones. We explain that stable trace languages form a true generalization of Mazurkiewicz trace languages through the particularly useful example of a Producer-Consumer system. However, any stable trace language may be regarded simply as a *labelled* Mazurkiewicz trace language. This will be formalized here by a notion of projections.

Projections of Local Trace Languages. We first recall the natural structure of local trace languages by morphisms introduced in [11].

DEFINITION 4.1. *Let $\mathcal{L} = (\Sigma, I, L)$ and $\mathcal{L}' = (\Sigma', I', L')$ be two local trace languages. A* morphism *λ from $\mathcal{L}$ to $\mathcal{L}'$ is a map $\lambda : \Sigma \to \Sigma'$ such that*
– *$\forall (u,p) \in I$, $(\lambda(u), \lambda(p)) \in I'$;*
– *$\forall (u, \{a,b\}) \in I$: $a \neq b \Rightarrow \lambda(a) \neq \lambda(b)$.*

Note that if two distinct actions a and b are independent after u then their images should be independent after $\lambda(u)$ in order to respect concurrency: that is why we require that $\lambda(a) \neq \lambda(b)$. Clearly if u_1 and u_2 are trace equivalent according to I then $\lambda(u_1)$ and $\lambda(u_2)$ are trace equivalent according to I'.

In this paper, we introduce particular morphisms which insure several nice correspondences between the related local trace languages.

DEFINITION 4.2. *A* projection *from $\mathcal{L} = (\Sigma, I, L)$ to $\mathcal{L}' = (\Sigma', I', L')$ is a morphism $\lambda : \mathcal{L} \to \mathcal{L}'$ whose underlying map $\lambda : \Sigma \to \Sigma'$ is onto and such that $\forall (u', p') \in I'$, $\exists! (u,p) \in I$, $\lambda(u) = u' \wedge \lambda(p) = p'$.*

We remark first that the trace equivalence is faithfully preserved and reflected by projections. Moreover there is a one-to-one correspondence between the traces of $\mathcal{L}$ and those of $\mathcal{L}'$.

LEMMA 4.3. *Let λ be a projection from $\mathcal{L} = (\Sigma, I, L)$ to $\mathcal{L}' = (\Sigma', I', L')$. Then $\lambda : \Sigma^\star \to \Sigma'^\star$ induces a bijection between L and L'. Moreover, for all u_1, u_2 in L, $u_1 \sim u_2 \Leftrightarrow \lambda(u_1) \sim \lambda(u_2)$.*

Therefore, projections of local trace languages should be regarded as simple and faithful labellings. If $\lambda : \mathcal{L} \to \mathcal{L}'$ is a projection then *we will say that $\mathcal{L}'$ is the image of $\mathcal{L}$ through the projection λ.* It is clear that the image of a recognizable local trace language through a projection is recognizable.

Projections of Mazurkiewicz Trace Languages. The connection between Mazurkiewicz trace languages and stable trace languages is first established by Theorem 4.4 below. It asserts that any stable trace language is the projection of a Mazurkiewicz trace language. This result can be established by means of known relationships between stably concurrent automata, prime event structures, and dI-domains [12,20] — at least if we assume that all alphabet is countable. However, a direct proof can be achieved without this assumption. It follows in fact the same basic idea since it relies on equivalences of prime intervals [16,17,11].

THEOREM 4.4. *A local trace language (over a possibly infinite alphabet) is stable if and only if it is the image of a Mazurkiewicz trace language through a projection.*

The connection between projections of Mazurkiewicz languages and stable languages expressed in the preceding theorem also applies to the subclasses of recognizable languages (over finite alphabets). *This very interesting result will be used in the two last sections of this paper.* It is a direct reformulation of Arnold's work [1, Th. 6.16] with the help of Prop. 3.10.

THEOREM 4.5. *A stable trace language is recognizable if and only if it is the image of a recognizable Mazurkiewicz trace language through a projection.*

The Producer-Consumer System. We are now interested by languages over *finite* alphabets. An open problem raised by Arnold [1] is to know whether each stable trace language over a finite alphabet is the image of a Mazurkiewicz trace language over a finite alphabet through a projection[1]. *We give a negative answer to this question through the example of a Producer-Consumer system.*

We consider the alphabet $\Sigma = \{p, c\}$ where p represents a production of one item and c a consumption. The language of the system describes all the possible sequences for which at each stage there may not be more consumptions than productions. Formally, $L = \{u \in \Sigma^\star \mid \forall v \leq u, |v|_p \geq |v|_c\}$. Thus p, pc, ppc and pcp are sequential executions of the system. We now want to model a possible independency between the producer and the consumer. Provided that there has been already enough items produced, the producer and the consumer can act simultaneously. For instance, $ppc \sim pcp$. This can be represented by the local independence relation I defined as follows:

[1] The question raised by Arnold dealt with CCI sets of P-traces, i.e. *full* stable trace languages. We leave it to the reader to adapt our counter-example accordingly.

– $(u, \emptyset) \in I \Leftrightarrow u \in L$;
– $(u, \{c\}) \in I \Leftrightarrow u \in L \wedge |u|_p \geq |u|_c + 1$;
– $(u, \{p\}) \in I \Leftrightarrow u \in L$;
– $(u, \{p, c\}) \in I \Leftrightarrow u \in L \wedge |u|_p \geq |u|_c + 1$.

Clearly, $\mathcal{L} = (\Sigma, I, L)$ is a stable trace language. We now prove by contradiction that $\mathcal{L}$ is *not* the image of a Mazurkiewicz trace language over a *finite* alphabet through a projection. Let us assume that $\mathcal{L}$ is the image of a Mazurkiewicz trace language $\mathcal{L}' = (\Sigma', I', L')$ over a finite independent alphabet $(\Sigma', \|')$ through a projection λ. Let n denote the size of Σ'. We consider the sequence $u = (p.c)^{n+1}$ consisting of $n + 1$ productions and $n + 1$ consumptions. There is a unique sequence $v \in L'$ such that $\lambda(v) = u$. Let us write $v = a_1.b_1.a_2.b_2...a_{n+1}.b_{n+1}$. Clearly, $\lambda(a_i) = p$ and $\lambda(b_i) = c$ for all $i \in [1, n + 1]$. We easily check that for any $i \in [1, n]$, we have $b_i \not\| a_i$ and for all $j \in [i + 1, n]$, $b_i \| a_j$. Now there are $i_1, i_2 \in [1, n]$ such that $i_1 < i_2$ and $b_{i_1} = b_{i_2}$ because $\mathrm{Card}(\Sigma') = n$. Hence $b_{i_1} \| a_{i_2} \not\| b_{i_2}$. Contradiction.

5 Distributed Implementation of Stable Trace Languages

In this section, we establish that each recognizable stable trace language admits a distributed implementation in the form of a finite bounded Petri net. According to Prop. 3.10, this result also holds for regular CCI sets of P-traces. Furthermore, this means that the labelled dI-domain of any finite stably concurrent automaton is also described by a finite bounded Petri net.

We consider here the classical model of Place/Transition nets.

DEFINITION 5.1. *A* Petri net *is a quadruple* $\mathcal{N} = (S, T, W, M_{in})$ *where*
– S *is a set of places and* T *is a set of transitions such that* $S \cap T = \emptyset$;
– W *is a map from* $(S \times T) \cup (T \times S)$ *to* $\mathbb{N}$, *called* weight function;
– M_{in} *is a map from* S *to* $\mathbb{N}$, *called* initial marking.

Given a Petri net $\mathcal{N} = (S, T, W, \mathrm{M}_{in})$, $\mathrm{Mar}_{\mathcal{N}}$ denotes the set of all markings of $\mathcal{N}$ that is to say functions $\mathrm{M} : S \to \mathbb{N}$; a step $p \in \wp_f(T)$ is *enabled* at $\mathrm{M} \in \mathrm{Mar}_{\mathcal{N}}$ if $\forall s \in S$, $\mathrm{M}(s) \geq \sum_{t \in p} W(s, t)$; in this case, we note $\mathrm{M}\,[p\rangle\,\mathrm{M}'$ where $\mathrm{M}'(s) = \mathrm{M}(s) + \sum_{t \in p}(W(t, s) - W(s, t))$ and say that the transitions of p may be *fired* concurrently and lead to the marking M'. A *step firing sequence* consists of a sequence of markings $\mathrm{M}_0,..., \mathrm{M}_n$ and a sequence of steps $p_1,..., p_n \in \wp_f(T)$ such that $\mathrm{M}_0 = \mathrm{M}_{in}$ and $\forall k \in [1, n]$, $\mathrm{M}_{k-1}\,[p_k\rangle\,\mathrm{M}_k$. In that case, M_n is said *reachable*.

DEFINITION 5.2. *A* labelled Petri net *is a structure* (S, T, W, M_{in}, ξ) *where* (S, T, W, M_{in}) *is a Petri net and* ξ *is a map from* T *to an alphabet* Σ *such that for all firing sequence* $M_{in} = M_0\,[p_1\rangle\,...M_{n-1}\,[p_n\rangle\,M_n$ *and all transitions* $t, t' \in T$:

$$M_n\,[\{t\}\rangle \wedge M_n\,[\{t'\}\rangle \wedge \xi(t) = \xi(t') \Rightarrow t = t'.$$

The restriction adopted for the labelling $\xi : T \to \Sigma$ insures that two transitions enabled by a common reachable marking correspond to two distinct actions. In other words, the labelling is deterministic.

DEFINITION 5.3. *The local trace language associated to a labelled Petri net* $\mathcal{N} = (S, T, W, M_{in}, \xi)$ *is* $\mathsf{t}(\mathcal{N}) = (\Sigma, I, L)$ *where* $I = \{(\xi(t_1 ... t_n), \xi(p)) \mid (t_1 ... t_n, p) \in T^\star \times \wp_f(T) \wedge \ M_{in}\,[\{t_1\}\rangle\, M_1 ... [\{t_n\}\rangle\, M_n\,[p\rangle\,\}$ *and the set of sequential executions is* $L = \{u \in \Sigma^\star \mid (u, \emptyset) \in I\}$.

Let us now focus on *finite* Petri nets — that is to say with a finite number of places and transitions — which are also *bounded*, which means that there are only a finite number of reachable markings. It is clear that local trace languages of such Petri nets are recognizable. Using Th. 4.5 and Zielonka's theorem [21] we can establish the converse property for stable trace languages. *Roughly*, the proof proceeds as follows. Given a recognizable stable trace $\mathcal{L}$, we consider a recognizable Mazurkiewicz trace language $\mathcal{L}_M = (\Sigma_M, I_M, L_M)$ over $(\Sigma_M, \|_M)$ and a projection $\lambda : \mathcal{L}_M \to \mathcal{L}$ by using Th. 4.5. Then Zielonka's theorem [21] yields an asynchronous automaton $\mathcal{A}$ over $(\Sigma_M, \|_M)$ recognizing L_M. We regard $\mathcal{A}$ as if all its states were final and describe its behavior by a (1-safe) Petri net labelled by ξ. Then the trace language of this Petri net *includes* $\mathcal{L}_M$. The technical point is then to add some places and to adapt the weight function in order to restrict the behavior of the net to L_M, *without affecting the independency of the transitions.* Finally, the labelling of the final net is changed into $\lambda \circ \xi$.

THEOREM 5.4. *Any recognizable stable trace language is the local trace language of a finite bounded labelled Petri net.*

6 Asynchronous Transition Systems vs Trace Automata

Motivated by domain theoretic considerations, Schmitt established in [17] that any finite stable trace automaton is covered by a finite asynchronous transition system — which thus describes the same coherent dI-domain. We explain here how Theorem 4.5 provides a new approach to prove easily this result and yields an algorithm for the construction of such an asynchronous transition system.

DEFINITION 6.1. *Let* $(\Sigma, \|)$ *be an independent alphabet. An* independent automaton *over* $(\Sigma, \|)$ *is a structure* $\mathcal{A} = (Q, s, \Sigma, \longrightarrow, \|)$ *where* Q *is a set of states, with initial state* $s \in Q$ *and* $\longrightarrow \subseteq Q \times \Sigma \times Q$ *is a transition relation such that* $q \xrightarrow{a} q_1 \wedge q \xrightarrow{a} q_2 \Rightarrow q_1 = q_2$.

A trace automaton *is an independent automaton which satisfies the* Forward Diamond *property* FD*:*

FD*:* $q \xrightarrow{a} q_1 \wedge q \xrightarrow{b} q_2 \wedge a \| b \Rightarrow \exists q_3 \in Q,\ q_2 \xrightarrow{a} q_3 \wedge q_1 \xrightarrow{b} q_3$.

An asynchronous transition system *over* $(\Sigma, \|)$ *is an independent automaton which satisfies* FD *and the* Independent Diamond *property* ID*:*

ID*:* $q \xrightarrow{a} q_1 \wedge q_1 \xrightarrow{b} q_2 \wedge a \| b \Rightarrow \exists q_3 \in Q,\ q_1 \xrightarrow{b} q_3 \wedge q_3 \xrightarrow{a} q_2$.

We shall assume in this paper that *all states of an independent automaton are reachable*[2]. We note that each trace automaton may be regarded as an automaton

[2] This means that $\forall q \in Q, \exists u \in \Sigma^\star, s \xrightarrow{u} q$.

with concurrency relation (Def. 2.3) for which $a\|_q b \Leftrightarrow a\|b \wedge q \xrightarrow{a} q' \wedge q \xrightarrow{b} q''$. It is clear that each asynchronous transition system, regarded as an automaton with concurrency relations, is in fact a stably concurrent automaton. That is not true for trace automata in general (only one implication is fulfilled). That is why Schmitt introduced *stable* trace automata as follows.

DEFINITION 6.2. *A trace automaton* $\mathcal{A} = (Q, s, \Sigma, \longrightarrow, \|)$ *is* stable *if for all states* $q, r \in Q$ *and for all actions* a, b *and* c *pairwise independent w.r.t.* $\|$:

$$\left[q \xrightarrow{abc} r \wedge q \xrightarrow{acb} r \wedge q \xrightarrow{bca} r\right] \Rightarrow \left[q \xrightarrow{cab} r \wedge q \xrightarrow{cba} r\right].$$

We remark here that a trace automaton is a stably concurrent automaton iff it is stable. Therefore any asynchronous transition system is a stable trace automaton. In order to strengthen this trivial relationship between stable trace automata and asynchronous transition systems, Schmitt used folding morphisms, which correspond somehow to projections.

DEFINITION 6.3. *Let* $\mathcal{A} = (Q, s, \Sigma, \longrightarrow)$ *and* $\mathcal{A}' = (Q', s', \Sigma', \longrightarrow')$ *be two trace automata. A* folding morphism *from* $\mathcal{A}$ *to* $\mathcal{A}'$ *is a pair of maps* $\sigma : Q \to Q'$ *and* $\lambda : \Sigma \to \Sigma'$ *such that*
- $\sigma(s) = s'$;
- $q_1 \xrightarrow{a} q_2 \Rightarrow \sigma(q_1) \xrightarrow{\lambda(a)} \sigma(q_2)$;
- $q_1 \xrightarrow{a} q_2 \wedge q_1 \xrightarrow{b} q_3 \wedge a \neq b \Rightarrow \lambda(a) \neq \lambda(b)$;
- $\sigma(q_1) \xrightarrow{a'} q_2' \Rightarrow \exists q_2 \in Q, \exists a \in \Sigma, q_1 \xrightarrow{a} q_2 \wedge \lambda(a) = a'$;
- $\forall q \in Q,\ q \xrightarrow{a} q' \wedge q \xrightarrow{b} q'' \Rightarrow [a\|b \Leftrightarrow \lambda(a)\|'\lambda(b)]$.

In that case, we say that $\mathcal{A}$ *covers* $\mathcal{A}'$.

We can now state the main result of [17].

THEOREM 6.4. *Any finite stable trace automaton is covered by some finite asynchronous transition system.*

Let us now present a new, simple and constructive proof of this result. Let $\mathcal{A} = (Q, s, \Sigma, \longrightarrow, \|)$ be a finite stable trace automaton. Viewed as a stably concurrent automaton, it describes a recognizable stable trace language $\mathcal{L} = (\Sigma, I, L)$. Applying Theorem 4.5, yields a recognizable Mazurkiewicz trace language $\mathcal{L} = (\Sigma_M, I_M, L_M)$ over an independent alphabet $(\Sigma_M, \|_M)$ and a projection $\lambda_M : \mathcal{L}_M \to \mathcal{L}$. We consider $\mathcal{A}_M = (Q_M, s_M, \Sigma_M, \longrightarrow_M, F_M)$ to be the minimal automaton of L_M, where F_M denotes the set of final states. Since L_M is recognizable and prefix-closed, $\mathcal{A}_M$ is finite and $F_M = Q_M$. We also remark that $\mathcal{A}_M$ *satisfies the Independent Diamond property* ID *w.r.t.* $\|_M$, because L_M is closed for the commutation of independent actions. We consider the synchronized product $\mathcal{A} \times \mathcal{A}_M = (Q \times Q_M, (s, s_M), \Sigma \times \Sigma_M, \longrightarrow_\times, \|_\times)$ where

$$(q, q_M) \xrightarrow{a, a_M}_\times (q', q_M') \text{ iff } q \xrightarrow{a} q' \wedge q_M \xrightarrow{a_M} q_M' \wedge \lambda(a_M) = a$$

and $(a, a_M)\|_\times(b, b_M)$ iff $a\|b \wedge a_M\|_M b_M$. We easily check that $\mathcal{A} \times \mathcal{A}_M$ is a finite asynchronous transition system — once restricted to its reachable states. Moreover the pair $\sigma_1 : (q, q_M) \mapsto q$ and $\lambda_1 : (a, a_M) \mapsto a$ is a folding morphism from $\mathcal{A} \times \mathcal{A}_M$ to $\mathcal{A}$.

Let us stress finally that the construction of $\mathcal{A}_M$ from $\mathcal{A}$ is essentially provided by Arnold's proof of [1, Th. 6.16]. One can actually deduce from this proof some upper bounds for the sizes of Σ_M and Q_M (w.r.t. the sizes of Q and Σ). This is definitively impossible when following Schmitt's approach.

Acknowledgments The authors are grateful to A. Arnold and B. Rozoy for their help and their useful advices. The second author thanks M. Droste and D. Kuske for motivating discussions while preparing the last improvements of this paper.

References

1. Arnold A.: *An extension of the notion of traces and asynchronous automata.* Theoretical Informatics and Applications **25** (1991) 355–393
2. Bednarczyk M.: *Categories of asynchronous systems.* PhD thesis (University of Sussex, 1987)
3. Bracho F., Droste M., Kuske D.: *Representations of computations in concurrent automata by dependence orders.* TCS **174** (1997) 67–96
4. Diekert V., Rozenberg G.: *The Book of Traces.* (World Scientific, 1995)
5. Droste M.: *Concurrency, automata and domains.* LNCS **443** (1990) 195–208
6. Droste M., Shortt R.M.: *From Petri nets to automata with concurrency.* – Unpublished manuscript (1999) –
7. Ehrenfeucht A., Rozenberg G.: *Partial (Set) 2-structures.* Part II: State spaces of concurrent systems, Acta Informatica **27** (1990) 343–368
8. Hoogers P.W., Kleijn H.C.M., Thiagarajan P.S.: *A Trace Semantics for Petri Nets.* Information and Computation **117** (1995) 98–114
9. Husson J.-Fr.: *Modélisation de la causalité par des relations d'indépendances.* Thesis (Université Paul Sabatier de Toulouse, 1996)
10. Husson J.-Fr., Morin R.: *Relationships between Arnold's CCI sets of P-traces and Droste's stably concurrent automata.* Technical report MATH-AL-1-00 (Technische Universität Dresden, 2000)
11. Kleijn H.C.M., Morin R., Rozoy B.: *A General Categorical Connection between Local Event Structures and Local Traces.* FCT'99, LNCS **1684** (1999) 338–349
12. Kuske D.: *Nondeterministic automata with concurrency relations and domains.* CAAP'94, LNCS **787** (1994) 202–217
13. Mazurkiewicz A.: *Concurrent program schemes and their interpretations.* Aarhus University Publication (DAIMI PB-78, 1977)
14. Morin R., Rozoy B.: *On the Semantics of Place/Transition Nets.* Concur'99, LNCS **1664** (1999) 447–462
15. Mukund M.: *Petri Nets and Step Transition Systems.* International Journal of Foundations of Computer Science **3** (1992) 443–478
16. Nielsen M., Sassone V., Winskel G.: *Relationships between Models of Concurrency.* LNCS **803** (1994) 425–475
17. Schmitt V.: *Stable trace automata vs. full trace automata.* TCS **200** (1998) 45–100
18. Stark E.W.: *Connections between concrete and abstract model of concurrent systems.* LNCS **442** (1990) 53–79
19. Szpilrajn E.: *Sur l'extension de l'ordre partiel.* Fund. Math. **16** (1930) 386–389
20. Winskel G.: *Event structures.* LNCS **255** (1987) 325–392
21. Zielonka W.: *Notes on finite asynchronous automata.* Theoretical Informatics and Applications **21** (1987) 99–135

The State Explosion Problem from Trace to Bisimulation Equivalence

François Laroussinie and Philippe Schnoebelen

Lab. Spécification & Vérification, ENS de Cachan & CNRS UMR 8643,
61, av. Pdt. Wilson, 94235 Cachan Cedex France
{fl,phs}@lsv.ens-cachan.fr

Abstract. We show that any relation between the simulation preorder and bisimilarity is EXPTIME-hard when systems are given as networks of finite state systems (or equivalently as automata with boolean variables, etc.). We also show that any relation between trace inclusion and ready trace equivalence or possible-futures equivalence is EXPSPACE-hard for these systems.
These results match the already known upper bounds and partially answer a conjecture by Rabinovich. They strongly suggest that there is no way to escape the state explosion problem when checking behavioural relations.
For the branching-time relations, our proof uses a new construction that immediately applies to timed automata, a family of systems for which these complexity results are new.

1 Introduction

The *model-checking approach* to automated or computer-aided verification is now widely recognized as a promising development for system design, especially in the area of critical systems [CGL96]. The main practical limitation of model-checking is the well-known *state explosion problem*: the systems we check are built by composing several subsystems, they use variables and/or clocks, and a flat equivalent transition system would have an exponential number of states. Therefore, even if model-checking flat systems is tractable, verifying non-flat systems has been a major challenge since the beginning.

The state explosion problem can be considered from a pragmatic or from a theoretical angle. The pragmatical approach aims, e.g., at designing symbolic methods that may bypass the state explosion in many practical cases [BCM+92]. The theoretical approach studies the structural complexity of model-checking *non-flat systems*, i.e. systems described as combinations of finite-state components. The goal here is to understand better which verification problems have to face state explosion in an intrinsic way, which special way of combining subsystems could avoid state explosion, and what are the theoretical limits of all approaches, even the best pragmatical ones.

But what exactly are these non-flat systems ? Different models exist: synchronized products of finite-state automata are a natural possibility, automata

J. Tiuryn (Ed.): FOSSACS 2000, LNCS 1784, pp. 192–207, 2000.

acting on boolean variables are another one, as well as 1-safe Petri nets. From a structural complexity perspective, these brands of non-flat systems can all be succinctly encoded into each other and the complexity results hold robustly across many variant presentations. In this paper we consider synchronized products of automata (see section 2) but we keep the more general terminology of "non-flat systems" in this introduction.

An overview of existing results. The literature is limited but the main questions have been answered:

Classical verification problems: The complexity classes of the main questions for non-flat systems, like reachability, termination, deadlock-freedom, etc., are known (e.g., these three examples are PSPACE-complete). Most of these problems have been investigated in the framework of 1-safe Petri nets, where they were natural questions since the beginning. An excellent survey is [Esp98].

Temporal logic: Model-checking PLTL, CTL, or CTL* formulas on non-flat systems is PSPACE-complete [KVW98]. Model-checking the branching-time mu-calculus is EXPTIME-complete, even when restricted to the alternation-free fragment [Rab97b, KVW98].

Behavioural equivalences and preorders: Trace equivalence of non-flat systems is EXPSPACE-complete [Rab97a] while bisimilarity is EXPTIME-complete [JM96], as is simulation equivalence [HKV97].

Behavioural equivalences. This third set of problems is where the existing results are the most incomplete when assessing the state explosion problem. One of the difficulties here is that the linear time – branching time spectrum contains dozens of different semantical equivalences [Gla90] (cf. Fig. 1).

However, some general methods apply to several equivalences at once:
(1) [JM96] shows EXPTIME-completeness of seven truly concurrent variants of bisimulation. One single construction suffices for the lower bounds since all seven equivalences coincide in the absence of concurrency.
(2) [Rab97a] shows that *all equivalences lying between trace equivalence and bisimilarity* are PSPACE-hard. Note that this apply to all classical equivalences from [Gla90] and also to any new equivalence, however fancy, one would care to define [1].

Rabinovich's result is impressive, even more since it has been convincingly argued [Gla90, Pnu85, Mil89] that any interesting equivalence lies between these two extremes. However, the result is not optimal since not one relation between trace equivalence and bisimilarity is known to be in PSPACE for non-flat systems. Indeed, [Rab97a] conjectures that all these equivalences are EXPTIME-hard.

[1] A similar approach appears in [Jan95] where a single construction shows undecidability, over P/T nets, of all equivalences between trace equivalence and bisimilarity.

Our contribution. We partially answer Rabinovich's conjecture. We prove EXPTIME-hardness of all equivalences (actually any relation) lying between the simulation preorder and strong bisimilarity, and EXPSPACE-hardness of all equivalences (actually any relation) lying between trace inclusion and ready trace equivalence or possible-futures equivalence.

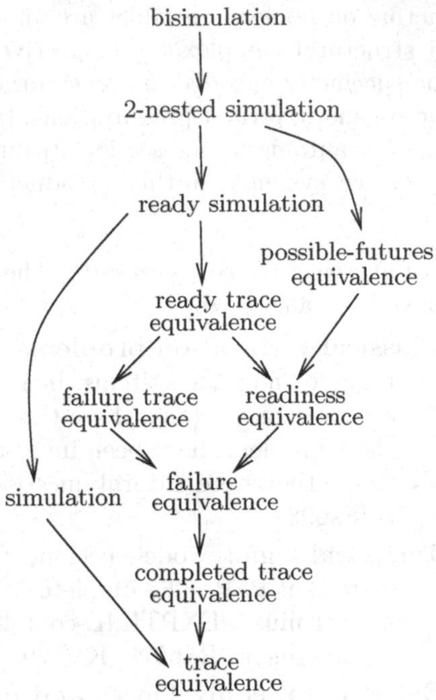

Fig. 1. The linear time – branching time spectrum [Gla90]

These results have several important corollaries. First, they close (on non-flat systems) the gap between lower-bound and upper-bound for the 11 relations van Glabbeek singles out as most fundamental in his linear time – branching time spectrum.

Secondly, they entail EXPTIME-hardness (over non-flat systems) of all model-checking problems for temporal or modal logics able to specify bisimilarity or simulation. For example, since the branching-time modal mu-calculus can state bisimilarity through a simple (modal depth 2) formula [And93], EXPTIME-hardness of bisimilarity entails EXPTIME-hardness of model-checking mu-calculus formula over non-flat systems (a result already known from [KVW98, Rab97b]).

Finally, our technique is interesting in itself: our construction for the branching-time relations differs from the approach in [JM96] [2]. It originates from our investigations of complexity questions for Timed Automata [AL99] and readily gives EXPTIME-hardness of all relations between (strong timed–) bisimilarity and simulation. To our knowledge this is the first complexity characterization of behavioural equivalences over these models.

Plan of the paper. We first give basic definitions on (flat and non-flat) systems, the behavioural equivalences we need (§ 2) and alternating Turing machines (§ 3). We then prove our generic EXPTIME lower bound (§ 4) and our generic EXPSPACE lower bound (§ 5). Upper bounds are given when they match the lower bounds.

Acknowledgments. This work owes much to the comments and suggestions we got from L. Jategaonkar and the anonymous referees who saw an earlier version.

[2] Additionally, an incorrect labeling of the nets and the omission of some crucial part of the construction make the proof of Theo. 5.7. in [JM96] hard to repair [Jat99].

2 Equivalences and Preorders between Non-flat Systems

Transition systems. A flat (transition) system is a tuple $C = \langle \Sigma, Q, \longrightarrow \rangle$ where Σ is a finite alphabet, Q is a finite set of states, and $\longrightarrow \subseteq Q \times \Sigma \times Q$ is the transition relation. The size $|C|$ of C is $|\Sigma| + |Q| + |\longrightarrow|$. As usual, we write $q \xrightarrow{a} q'$ when $(q, a, q') \in \longrightarrow$, and let $ready(q)$ denote the *set of actions ready in* q, i.e. $\{a \in \Sigma \mid q \xrightarrow{a} q' \text{ for some } q'\}$.

Traces. A *trace* from $q \in Q$ is any $w = a_1 \dots a_n \in \Sigma^*$ such that there exists $q_0, q_1, \dots, q_n \in Q$ with $q = q_0$ and $q_{i-1} \xrightarrow{a_i} q_i$ for $i = 1, \dots, n$ (written $q_0 \xrightarrow{w} q_n$). If $X_i = ready(q_i)$ for $i = 0, \dots, n$, then $(X_0, a_1, X_1, a_2, X_2, \dots, a_n, X_n)$ is a *ready trace* from q. We write $Tr(q)$ (resp. $RT(q)$, $PF(q)$) for the set of traces (resp. ready traces, possible futures) from q (where $(w, S) \in \Sigma^* \times \mathcal{P}(\Sigma^*)$ is a *possible future* of p if there exists q s.t. $p \xrightarrow{w} q$ and $S = Tr(q)$). Trace inclusion, trace equality, ready trace equivalence and possible-futures equivalence, denoted $\subseteq_{Tr}$, $=_{Tr}$, $=_{RT}$ and $=_{PF}$, have the obvious definition.

Bisimulations. A *simulation* over C is any $R \subseteq Q \times Q$ satisfying the following transfer property: for all qRq' and $q \xrightarrow{a} r$, there is a $q' \xrightarrow{a} r'$ s.t. $q'Rr'$. A *bisimulation* is any symmetric simulation. The largest simulation over C exists, is denoted $\sqsubseteq$, and is called the simulation preorder. The largest bisimulation is denoted $\leftrightarrow$ and is called bisimilarity.

The hierarchy of equivalences. [Gla90, Gla93] survey the main behavioural equivalences (and preorders) used in the semantics of concurrent systems. Van Glabbeek list dozens of different possibilities between the weakest (trace equivalence) and the strongest (bisimilarity). The most important stepping stones in this hierarchy are given in Fig. 1.

As usual, for any such behavioural relation $\mathcal{R}$, we write $(C, q) \mathcal{R} (C', q')$ when $q \mathcal{R} q'$ inside a disjoint sum system $C + C'$. We write $C \mathcal{R} C'$ when C and C' come with (often implicit) initial states, and $(C, q_0) \mathcal{R} (C', q_0')$.

Non-flat systems. A non-flat system is a product of flat systems. Formally, it is a vector $\mathcal{S} = (C_1, \dots, C_k)$ where $C_i = \langle \Sigma_i, Q_i, \longrightarrow_i \rangle$ for $i = 1, \dots, k$. The *flattening* $C_\mathcal{S}$ of $\mathcal{S}$ is the transition system $\langle \Sigma, Q, \longrightarrow \rangle$ given by $\Sigma \stackrel{\text{def}}{=} \Sigma_1 \cup \dots \cup \Sigma_k$, $Q \stackrel{\text{def}}{=} Q_1 \times \dots \times Q_k$ and where $\longrightarrow$ is the set of all triples $((q_1, \dots, q_k), a, (r_1, \dots, r_k))$ from $Q \times \Sigma \times Q$ s.t. for $i = 1, \dots, k$ either $q_i \xrightarrow{a}_i r_i$ or ($a \notin \Sigma_i$ and $q_i = r_i$). In this paper we only need *binary* synchronization, i.e. where a given a belongs to at most two different Σ_i.

For a behavioural relation $\mathcal{R}$, deciding whether $\mathcal{S} \mathcal{R} \mathcal{S}'$ means deciding whether $C_\mathcal{S} \mathcal{R} C_{\mathcal{S}'}$. A *naive algorithm* for this problem is any algorithm that computes $C_\mathcal{S}$ and $C_{\mathcal{S}'}$. Let $|\mathcal{S}| \stackrel{\text{def}}{=} |C_1| + \dots + |C_k|$. Then $|C_\mathcal{S}|$ is $O(|C_1| \times \dots \times |C_k|)$, hence $O(2^{|\mathcal{S}|})$. This is known as *state explosion.*

Non-flat systems in the literature. [Rab97b] uses automata acting on boolean variables (or more generally on variables with a finite domain), [Esp98, JM96] use 1-safe labeled Petri nets. Product of finite automata are sometimes called *concurrent systems* [KVW98, Rab97a]. When relabeling of actions is allowed, any of these models can be directly translated into any other [3]. For maximal generality, we prove our hardness results for products without relabeling (and our upper bounds through naive algorithms that easily handle relabelings) which is one more way we strengthen the results from [Rab97a].

3 Alternating Machines

An *Alternating Turing Machine* [CKS81] (an ATM for short) is a tuple $A = \langle Q, \Sigma, \delta, l, q_0, q_F \rangle$ where $Q = \{q, \dots\}$ is the *set of states*, $\Sigma = \{a, ..\}$ is the tape *alphabet* containing a special *blank symbol* (denoted by $\diamondsuit$), $\delta \subseteq Q \times \Sigma \times Q \times \Sigma \times \{L, R\}$ is the set of *transitions*, $q_0 \in Q$ is the *initial state*, $q_F \in Q$ is the final (accepting) state and $l : Q \to \{\vee, \wedge\}$ labels each state as either disjunctive or conjunctive.

Q is thus partitioned by l into $Q_\vee$ and $Q_\wedge$. We use letters $r, r', \dots$ to denote conjunctive states, $s, s', \dots$ for disjunctive states and $q, q', \dots$ for both. W.l.o.g. we require that $q_0, q_F \in Q_\vee$, that $\Sigma = \{a, b\}$, that each $q \neq q_F$ is the source of a transition, and that an ATM has clean alternation, i.e. it moves from disjunctive to conjunctive states and *vice versa.* We assign to each transition in δ a number $k \in \{1, \dots, |\delta|\}$ and we will denote by t_k the k-th transition.

A *configuration* of A (also called an *instantaneous description*, or an *i.d.*) is a triple $\alpha = (q, i, w)$ where $q \in Q$ is the *current state*, $w \in \Sigma^*$ is a word describing the *tape content*, and $0 < i \leq |w|$ is the *position of the head* on the tape (i.e. A is currently seeing $w(i)$). We use letters $\beta, \dots$ to denote disjunctive i.d.'s (that is, i.d.'s with a disjunctive control state) and $\gamma, \dots$ for the conjunctive i.d.'s. An i.d. (q, i, w) is *final* iff $q = q_F$.

An ATM moves like an usual non-deterministic TM: if $\alpha = (q, i, w)$, $w(i) = a$ and $(q, a, q', b, D) \in \delta$, then A may move from α to $\alpha' = (q', i', w')$, written $\alpha \longrightarrow \alpha'$, where w' is w updated by writing a b in position i and i' is $i + 1$ if $D = R$ or $i - 1$ if $D = L$. (As usual, if i' falls outside of w', we pad w' with an extra $\diamondsuit$ and perhaps readjust i'.) We say α' is a *successor* of α : there can only be a finite number of such successors.

The moves of an ATM starting from some i.d. α_0 can be arranged into a tree: the root node is labeled with α_0, and any node labeled by some α has one child for every α' s.t. $\alpha \longrightarrow \alpha'$. The order of the branches is not relevant so that there is only one tree starting from a given α_0. We call it the *run* of A from α_0.

[3] There exist other varieties of non-flat systems. Quite often they rely on a direct synchronization mechanism and can be accounted for in our formalism. The few exceptions (e.g., the Message Sequence Charts of [MPS98] or the Communicating Hierarchical State Machine of [AKY99]) have only recently been considered from a complexity-theoretic point of view, and they are obvious candidates for continuations of our work.

The run of A on some input word x is its run from $\alpha(x) \stackrel{\text{def}}{=} (q_0, 1, x)$. Note that a run may be infinite, and that a node is a leaf if and only if it is labeled by a configuration without any successor.

For ATM's, *accepting runs* are defined by seeing the run as an AND-OR tree. Formally, for $n \in \mathbb{N}$, we say a run rooted at some disjunctive β is accepting in n steps iff it is a final configuration or $n \geq 1$ and *one* of its children is accepting in $n-1$ steps, while a run rooted at some conjunctive [4] γ is accepting in n steps iff $n \geq 1$ and *all* its children are accepting in $n-1$ steps (and there is at least one child). We say A accepts x in n steps iff the run from $\alpha(x)$ is accepting in n steps. A word x is accepted by A iff there exists $n \geq 0$ s.t. A accepts x in n steps.

We say A is *linearly-bounded* on x if any configuration (q, w, i) in the run of A on some x has $|w| \leq |x|$ (that is, the machine never uses more tape than what is needed by the input). A classical result says that the problem LB-ATM-ACCEPT :

input: an ATM A and a word $x \in \Sigma^*$ s.t. A is linearly-bounded on x,
output: yes iff A accepts x, no otherwise.

is EXPTIME-complete.

4 EXPTIME-Hard Relations

Theorem 4.1. *Any relation lying between the simulation preorder and bisimilarity is EXPTIME-hard on non-flat systems.*

This is our main technical result and the rest of this section is devoted to the proof, a logspace reduction from LB-ATM ACCEPT. The proof of EXPTIME-hardness of bisimilarity in [JM96] is also based on a reduction from LB-ATM ACCEPT but, as mentioned in the introduction, the encoding is quite different.

The proofs of the next two lemmas assume familiarity in handling simulations and bisimulations.

4.1 Modeling an ATM by a Non-flat System

Let A, w_0 be an ATM with a word of length n such that $A = \langle Q, \Sigma, \delta, l, q_0, q_F \rangle$ is linearly-bounded on w_0. We build a concurrent system $\mathcal{S}_{A,w_0} = (\mathcal{B}, C_1, \ldots, C_n)$ which models the run of A over w_0. Each C_i models the i-th tape cell: it can be in state a or b, and its initial state is $w_0(i)$. The tape cell synchronizes with the head of the ATM, hence for each transition $t_k = (q, e, q', e', d) \in \delta$, C_i has a transition $e \xrightarrow{t_k, i} e'$. See Fig. 2 for an example of C_i component for a set of transitions.

$\mathcal{B}$ is the control part of A. Write $Q^- = \{q^- \mid q \in Q\}$ (resp. $Q^+ = \{q^+ \ldots\}$) for a set of copies of states from Q tagged by a "$-$" (resp. by a "$+$"). The states of $\mathcal{B}$ is $Q_\mathcal{B} \stackrel{\text{def}}{=} Q^- \times \{1, \ldots, n\} \cup Q^+_\vee \times \{1, \ldots, n\} \cup Q^+_\wedge \times \{1, \ldots, n\} \times \{t_1, \ldots, t_{|\delta|}\}$.

[4] Remember $q_F \notin Q_\wedge$.

$t_1 = (s_1, a, r_1, b, R)$
$t_2 = (s_1, b, r_2, b, R)$
$t_3 = (r_1, a, s_2, a, L)$
$t_4 = (r_1, a, s_3, b, R)$
$t_5 = (r_2, b, s_3, a, R)$
$t_6 = (r_2, a, s_4, a, L)$
...

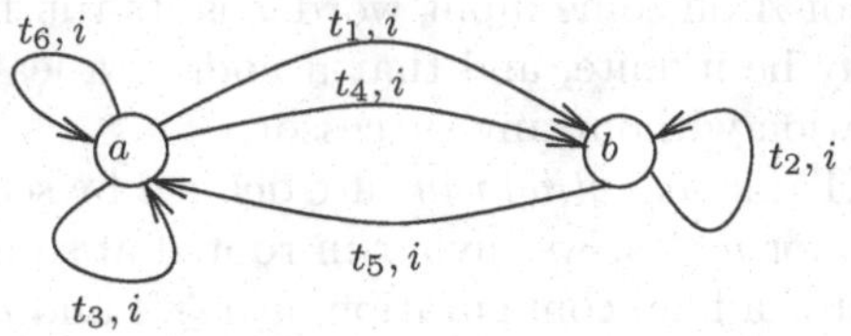

Fig. 2. System C_i

A state (q^-, i) of $\mathcal{B}$ encodes a control state of A and a position of A's head over the tape. For each $t_k = (q, e, q', e', d) \in \delta$ and for any i, $\mathcal{B}$ has a transition $(q^-, i) \xrightarrow{t_k, i} (q'^-, i + d)$ where $i + d$ denotes $i + 1$ (resp. $i - 1$) if $d = R$ and $i < n$ (resp. $d = L$ and $i > 1$).

These transitions are called "type 1" and they synchronize with the corresponding transitions from the C_i's: a transition labeled "t_k, i" is enabled in $\mathcal{S}_{A,w_0}$ iff the current control state is q, the position of the head is i, and if C_i contains the right value. Firing this transition modifies the value of C_i, the control state and the head position so that the behaviour of A and its tape is faithfully emulated by the type 1 transitions.

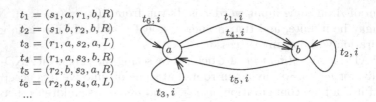

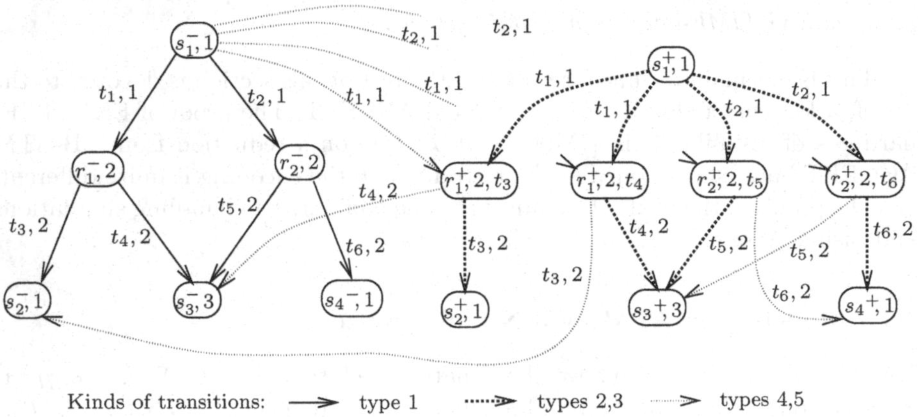

Fig. 3. (Part of) system $\mathcal{B}$

An example of such type 1 transitions is displayed in the left part of Fig. 3, assuming δ as in the previous example.

The q^+ states behave slightly differently. To begin with, disjunctive and conjunctive states are not dealt in the same way. Assume $s \in Q_\vee$ is disjunctive. For each $t_k = (s, e, r, e', d)$ and $t_{k'} = (r, f, s', f', d')$ in δ, for any i, $\mathcal{B}$ has a (type 2) transition $(s^+, i) \xrightarrow{t_k, i} (r^+, i + d, t_{k'})$. These transitions correspond to "firing t_k and picking $t_{k'}$ as next transition".

The transitions for conjunctive states are defined accordingly: if t_k is some (r, e, s, e', d), then $\mathcal{B}$ has (type 3) transitions $(r^+, i, t_k) \xrightarrow{t_k, i} (s^+, i + d)$.

Here is the idea behind these transitions: assume an i.d. s, i, w is not accepting. A strategy for establishing this had an opponent firing any transition t_k from s, and the defender may picking a $t_{k'}$ (one must exist) leading to a rejecting i.d., etc. In $\mathcal{S}_{A,w_0}$, this strategy is implemented by having s^- (the opponent) firing a type 1 transition t_k, forcing s^+ to fire the type 2 t_k transition that selects $t_{k'}$ for the next move.

The (type 4) transitions move from s^- states to the Q^+ part: formally $\mathcal{B}$ has all $(s^-, i) \xrightarrow{t_k, i} (r^+, i', t_{k'})$ s.t. $(s^+, i) \xrightarrow{t_k, i} (r^+, i', t_{k'})$. The purpose is to allow in s^- everything allowed in s^+.

The (type 5) transitions allow firing any $t_{k'}$ from a (r^+, i, t_k) where $\mathcal{B}$ has already commited to t_k. Assume $t_k = (r, e, s, e', d)$, then for all $t_{k'} \neq t_k$ starting from r, i.e. $t_{k'}$ is some (r, f, s', f', d'), $\mathcal{B}$ has one of the following transitions depending on the values of e and f:

- $(r^+, i, t_k) \xrightarrow{t_{k'}, i} (s'^-, i + d')$ if $e = f$. For example, see transition "$t_4, 2$" from $(r_1^+, 2, t_3)$ or transition "$t_3, 2$" from $(r_1^+, 2, t_4)$ in Fig. 3.
- $(r^+, i, t_k) \xrightarrow{t_{k'}, i} (s'^+, i + d')$ if $e \neq f$. For example, see transition "$t_6, 2$" from $(r_2^+, 2, t_5)$ or transition "$t_5, 2$" from $(r_2^+, 2, t_6)$ in Fig. 3.

Intuitively if t_k and $t_{k'}$ are both enabled (according to the value of C_i), then the transition leads to the corresponding s^- state, otherwise it leads to the corresponding s^+ state.

Finally, $\mathcal{B}$ has special (type 6) transitions in (q_F^-, i) states: $(q_F^-, i) \xrightarrow{\text{acc}} (q_F^-, i)$. These are the only transitions without synchronization, they do not exist from the q_F^+ states and they distinguish between the Q^- and the Q^+ parts of $\mathcal{B}$.

With this we have completed the description of $\mathcal{B}$. The size of $\mathcal{S}_{A,w_0}$ is $O(n \times |Q| \times |\delta|^2)$ and $\mathcal{S}_{A,w_0}$ can be built using only four counters, that is in space $\ln(n) + \ln(|Q|) + 2\ln(|\delta|)$.

4.2 Relating A on w_0 and $\mathcal{S}_{A,w_0}$

A configuration of $\mathcal{S}_{A,w_0}$ has the form $\langle \rho, e_1, \dots, e_n \rangle$ where ρ is a $\mathcal{B}$ state and $e_i \in \{a, b\}$ is a C_i state. We write such a configuration as $\langle \rho, w \rangle$ where $w \in \Sigma^n$ is given by $w(i) = e_i$ for $i = 1, \dots, n$.

$\langle \rho, w \rangle$ is said to be disjunctive (resp. conjunctive) depending on whether ρ contains a disjunctive or conjunctive state of A.

We now link i.d.'s of A and configurations of $\mathcal{S}_{A,w_0}$: Given an i.d. $\alpha = (q, i, w)$, α^- denotes the $\mathcal{S}_{A,w_0}$ configuration $\langle (q^-, i), w \rangle$. Given a disjunctive i.d. $\beta = (s, i, w)$, β^+ represents $\langle (s^+, i), w \rangle$. Given a conjunctive i.d. $\gamma = (r, i, w)$ and a transition t_k whose source node is r, γ_k^+ denotes $\langle (r^+, i, t_k), w \rangle$.

Lemma 4.2. *If A does not accept w_0, then $\langle(q_0^-, 1), w_0\rangle \leftrightarrow \langle(q_0^+, 1), w_0\rangle$.*

Proof. Remember that $\beta, \ldots$ (resp. $\gamma, \ldots$) denote disjunctive (resp. conjunctive) i.d.'s. Consider the following relation R between the configurations of $\mathcal{S}_{A,w_0}$:

$$R \stackrel{\text{def}}{=} \{(\beta^-, \beta^+) \mid \beta \text{ is rejecting}\} \cup \mathtt{Id} \cup$$
$$\{(\gamma^-, \gamma_k^+) \mid \gamma \longrightarrow_k \beta \text{ and } \gamma \text{ and } \beta \text{ are rejecting}\}$$

We can show that R is bisimulation: since A rejects w_0, then $(\langle(q_0^-, 1), w_0\rangle, \langle(q_0^+, 1), w_0\rangle) \in R$, and it remains to check that R has the transfer property in both directions (see Appendix A for details).

Lemma 4.3. *If A accepts w_0, then $\langle(q_0^-, 1), w_0\rangle \not\sqsubseteq \langle(q_0^+, 1), w_0\rangle$.*

Proof. By induction on the number of steps for accepting. See Appendix B.

Corollary 4.4. *For any relation $\mathcal{R}$ s.t. $\leftrightarrow \subseteq \mathcal{R} \subseteq \sqsubseteq$, A does not accept w_0 iff $\langle(q_0^-, 1), w_0\rangle \mathcal{R} \langle(q_0^+, 1), w_0\rangle$.*

which concludes the proof of Theorem 4.1.

4.3 Upper Bounds

Theorem 4.1 is in a sense optimal since the lower bounds it exhibits are optimal for the relations singled out in Fig. 1:

Theorem 4.5. *Bisimulation, 2-nested simulation, ready simulation, and simulation on non-flat systems are EXPTIME-complete.*

Proof (sketch). There only remain to show membership in EXPTIME. In all four cases this can be done by a reduction to model checking of a simple branching-time mu-calculus formula. Such a reduction expresses a relation $\mathcal{R}$ via a mu-calculus formula $\varphi_{\mathcal{R}}$ in a way s.t. $C\mathcal{R}C'$ iff $(\tilde{C}, \tilde{C'}) \models \varphi_{\mathcal{R}}$ where $\tilde{C}$ is a variant of C where the actions have been relabeled to avoid conflicts with C'. For bisimulation this is done in [And93], and the same technique apply to the other equivalences. We then rely on EXPTIME-completeness of mu-calculus model-checking for non-flat systems [KVW98, Rab97b]. □

4.4 Extension to Timed Automata

Timed Automata [AD94] can be seen as a special kind of non-flat systems. We denote by $\mathbb{N}$ the set of natural numbers and by $\mathbb{R}$ the set of non–negative real numbers. If $Cl = \{x, y, \ldots\}$ is a set of clocks, $\mathcal{L}(Cl)$ denotes *clocks constraints* over Cl, that is the set of formulas built using boolean connectives over atomic formulas of the form $x \bowtie m$ or $x - y \bowtie m$ with $x, y \in Cl$, $m \in \mathbb{N}$ and $\bowtie \in \{=, <, >, \leq, \geq\}$. A time assignment v for Cl is a function from Cl to $\mathcal{R}$. We denote by $\mathcal{R}^{Cl}$ the set of time assignments for Cl. For $v \in \mathcal{R}^{Cl}$ and $d \in \mathcal{R}$, $v + d$ denotes the time assignment which maps each clock x in Cl to the value $v(x) + d$. For $Cl' \subseteq Cl$, $[Cl' \leftarrow 0]v$ denotes the assignment for Cl which maps each clock in Cl' to the value 0 and agrees with v over $Cl \backslash Cl'$. Given a condition $g \in \mathcal{L}(Cl)$ and a time assignment $v \in \mathcal{R}^{Cl}$, we note $v \models g$ when g holds for v. We define the timed automata (TA):

Definition 4.6. *A timed automaton TA over Σ is a tuple $\langle N, \eta_0, Cl, E\rangle$ where N is a finite set of nodes, $\eta_0 \in N$ is the initial node, Cl is a finite set of clocks, $E \subseteq N \times \mathcal{L}(Cl) \times \Sigma \times 2^{Cl} \times N$ corresponds to the set of edges: $e = \langle \eta, g, a, r, \eta' \rangle \in E$ represents an edge from the node η to the node η' with action a, r denotes the set of clocks to be reset and g is the enabling condition (the guard) over the clocks of TA. We use the notation $\eta \xrightarrow{g,a,r} \eta'$.*

A *configuration* of TA is a pair (η, v) where η is a node of TA and v a time assignment for Cl. Informally, the system starts at node η_0 with the assignment v_0 which maps all clocks to 0. The values of the clocks may increase synchronously with time. At any time, the automaton whose current node is η can change node by following an edge $\langle \eta, g, a, r, \eta' \rangle \in E$ provided the current values of the clocks satisfy g. With this transition the clocks in r get reset to 0. Let Θ denote the set of delay actions $\{\varepsilon(d) \mid d \in \mathbb{R}\}$. Formally the semantics of TA is defined as a *labeled timed transition system*:

Definition 4.7. *A labeled timed transition system over Σ is a tuple $\mathcal{S} = \langle S, s_0, \longrightarrow \rangle$, where S is a set of states, s_0 is the initial state, $\longrightarrow \subseteq S \times (\Sigma \cup \Theta) \times S$ is a transition relation. We require that for any $s \in S$ and $d \in \mathcal{R}$, there exists a unique state s^d such that $s \xrightarrow{\varepsilon(d)} s^d$ and that $(s^d)^e = s^{d+e}$.*

The labeled timed transition system associated with TA is $\langle S_{TA}, s_0, \longrightarrow_{TA} \rangle$, where S_{TA} is the set of configuration of TA, s_0 is the initial configuration (η_0, v_0), and $\longrightarrow_{TA}$ is the transition relation defined as follows:

$$(\eta, v) \xrightarrow{a} (\eta', v') \text{ iff } \exists \langle \eta, g, a, r, \eta' \rangle \in E \text{ s.t. } v \models g \text{ and } v' = [r \leftarrow 0]v$$
$$(\eta, v) \xrightarrow{\varepsilon(d)} (\eta', v') \text{ iff } \eta = \eta' \text{ and } v' = v + d$$

The standard notion of bisimulation (and simulation) can be naturally extended to timed systems [Čer93]: A strong timed (bi)simulation between TA and TB is a (bi)simulation between the associated labeled timed transition systems.

Theorem 4.8. *Any relation lying between the simulation preorder and bisimilarity is EXPTIME-hard on timed automata.*

Proof (sketch). Let A, w_0 be an ATM with a word of length n. We transform the automaton $\mathcal{B}$ defined in section 4.1 into a timed automaton TB in such a way that the clocks Cl of TB encode the tape content. This encoding is used in [AL99]. The transitions of TB use guards over the clocks to ensure a correct behavior, and reset operations are used to modify the tape content according to the performed transition. Therefore we obtain a single timed automaton instead of a parallel composition of finite automata.

TB uses $2n+1$ clocks: $\{x_1,\dots,x_n,y_1,\dots,y_n,t\}$. The clock t is used to ensure a delay of length 1 between two transitions of TB. The clocks x_i and y_i encode the value of the i-th tape cell by the following convention: $C_i = a$ (resp. $C_i = b$) iff $x_i = y_i$ (resp. $x_i < y_i$). Let t_i be the ATM transition (q,e,q',e',d) : the transition $(q,k) \xrightarrow{t_i,k} (q',k+d)$ we used in $\mathcal{B}$ is replaced by a transition $(q,k) \xrightarrow{t=1\wedge g,t_i,r} (q',k+d)$ where g is $x_i = y_i$ (resp. $x_i < y_i$) if $e = a$ (resp. $e = b$), the reset set r is $\{t, x_i\}$ (resp. $\{t, x_i, y_i\}$) if $e' = b$ (resp. $e' = a$). The initialization of the tape with the input word w_0 can be encoded by adding the transitions $init^- \xrightarrow{t=1,s_0,r_w} (q_0^-,1)$ and $init^+ \xrightarrow{t=1,s_0,r_{w_0}} (q_0^+,1)$, where $r_{w_0} = \{t\} \cup \{x_i \mid w_0(i) = b\}$. The acc transition of $\mathcal{B}$ are kept in TB. Lemmas 4.2 and 4.3 still hold for the initial configurations $(init^-, u_0)$ and $(init^+, v_0)$ where u_0 and v_0 map any clock in Cl to 0.

Remark 4.9. Note that bisimulation and simulation for timed automata are EXPTIME-complete since the model-checking problem for the timed μ-calculus (which allows to express bisimilarity and similarity) is EXPTIME-complete [AL99].

5 EXPSPACE-Hard Relations

Theorem 5.1. *Any relation lying between trace inclusion and the intersection of ready trace equivalence and possible-futures equivalence is EXPSPACE-hard on non-flat systems.*

Proof (sketch). We adapt the proof, from [JM96], that trace inclusion is EXPSPACE-hard on non-flat systems.

Their proof is a reduction from the problem of deciding whether the language defined by a regular expression with interleaving is Σ^*, which is known to be EXPSPACE-complete [MS94]. Given any regular expression e built from $\{\cup, *, ., \|\}$ with $|e| = n$, Jategaonkar and Meyer build a non-flat system $Net(e)$ over the alphabet $\Sigma \cup \{\mathbf{1}, \surd\}$ s.t. $Tr(Net(e))$ is (the prefix-closure of) $\{\mathbf{1}^{4n} a_1 \mathbf{1}^{4n} \dots \mathbf{1}^{4n} a_k \mathbf{1}^{4n} \surd \mid a_1 \dots a_k \in L(e)\}$.

Let $=_{RT.PF}$ be the equivalence defined as the intersection of $=_{RT}$ and $=_{PF}$. We can modify the previous model in a simple way to obtain $Net(e,n)$ with $n \geq |e|$ so that, for $L(e) = \Sigma^*$ iff $Net(e,n) =_{RT.PF} Net(\Sigma^*,n)$ iff $Net(\Sigma^*,n) \subseteq_{Tr} Net(e,n)$. This will entail the result.

The main idea is to add a state *end* from which the enabled transitions are labeled by $\Sigma \cup \{\mathbf{1}\}$ and lead to *end*. From any state q, we add transitions $q \xrightarrow{\Sigma} end$. By this way we have that $RT(Net(e,n))$ is (the prefix-closure of)

$$\{(\overbrace{\{\mathbf{1}\},\mathbf{1},\dots,\{\mathbf{1}\},\mathbf{1}}^{4n},\Sigma,a_1,\{\mathbf{1}\},\mathbf{1},\dots,\Sigma,a_k,\{\mathbf{1}\},\mathbf{1},\dots,\{\surd\},\surd,\emptyset) \mid a_1\dots a_k \in L(e)\}$$

$$\cup \{(\overbrace{\{\mathbf{1}\},\mathbf{1},\dots,\{\mathbf{1}\},\mathbf{1}}^{4n},\Sigma,b_1,\{\mathbf{1}\},\mathbf{1},\dots,\Sigma,b_k,\{\mathbf{1}\}) \mid b_1,\dots,b_k \in \Sigma\}$$

and $PF(Net(e,n))$ is the set of pairs (w, S) s.t. $w = \mathbf{1}^{4n}a_1\mathbf{1}^{4n}\ldots\mathbf{1}^k \in Tr(Net(e,n))$ and S is the prefix-closure of $S_1 \cup S_2$ or S_2 with:

$$S_1 = \{w' \mid w.w'\surd \in Tr(Net(e,n))\}$$
$$S_2 = \{w' = \mathbf{1}^{4n-k}b_1\mathbf{1}^{4n}\ldots b_l\mathbf{1}^{4n} \mid b_1\ldots b_l \in \Sigma^*\}$$

Note that for $(w, S) \in PF(Net(\Sigma^*, n))$, S is the prefix-closure of:

$$\{w' = \mathbf{1}^{4n-k}b_1\mathbf{1}^{4n}\ldots b_l\mathbf{1}^{4n}\surd \mid b_1\ldots b_l \in \Sigma^*\}$$

Clearly, $Net(\Sigma^*, n) \subseteq_{Tr} Net(e,n)$ iff $Net(e,n) =_{RT} Net(\Sigma^*, n)$ iff $Net(e,n) =_{PF} Net(\Sigma^*, n)$ iff $L(e) = \Sigma^*$. This gives the result. □

5.1 Upper Bounds

Theorem 5.1 is in a sense optimal since the lower bounds it exhibits are optimal for the relations singled out in Fig. 1:

Theorem 5.2. *Possible-futures equivalence, ready trace equivalence, failure trace equivalence, readiness equivalence, failures equivalence, completed trace equivalence and trace equivalence on non-flat systems are EXPSPACE-complete.*

Proof (sketch). We only need to prove membership in EXPSPACE. In all cases, this can be done by the naive algorithm, noting that the problems are in PSPACE for flat systems (by simple reductions to language equivalence of non-deterministic automata).

6 Conclusion

We have shown that for non-flat systems, any relation between the simulation preorder and bisimilarity is EXPTIME-hard, and that any relation between trace inclusion and ready trace equivalence is EXPSPACE-hard.

This is a partial answer to the questions raised by Rabinovich [Rab97a] [5]. Indeed, these results cover a large array of relations, and they give lower bounds matching the (obvious) upper bounds in the 11 relations van Glabbeek singles out as most prominent in his branching time – linear time spectrum.

For the EXPTIME-hard relations, our construction also applies to timed automata, where the lower bounds were not known.

This theoretical study has practical implications. It strongly suggests that there is no way to escape state explosion when checking non-flat systems for some behavioural relation, at least not by some smart choice of which behavioural equivalence is chosen [6]. Attempts at general solutions should rather aim at finding a smart limitation of how non-flat systems may be described. In such a

[5] Additionally, our hardness results do not need his *hide* operator to further relabel the products of systems.

[6] Since our results are not a complete answer, we cannot rule out the dim possibility that some PSPACE-easy relation exist in the branching time–linear time spectrum.

quest, one should aim at forbidding the construction of our $\mathcal{S}_{A,w_0}$ system (or any reasonably succinct equivalent encoding).

A related idea is to focus on the complexity of deciding whether $\mathcal{S} \sim C$ *where* C *is a fixed system* and where $\mathcal{S}$ is then the only input. For this measure, called *implementation complexity*, the results are no longer uniform. For example, for simulation we have that deciding whether $\mathcal{S} \sqsubseteq C$ is still EXPTIME-complete [HKV97] while for bisimulation, we have the following:

Proposition 6.1. *When* C *is fixed, deciding whether* $\mathcal{S} \underline{\leftrightarrow} C$ *is PSPACE-complete.*

Proof (Sketch). PSPACE membership combines the ability to build a CTL formula Φ_C such that $\mathcal{S} \underline{\leftrightarrow} C$ iff $\mathcal{S} \models \Phi_C$ [BCG88] and the fact that CTL model checking of non-flat systems is PSPACE-complete [KVW98]. PSPACE-hardness is by reduction of the reachability problem in $\mathcal{S}$.

References

[AD94] R. Alur and D. L. Dill. A theory of timed automata. *Theoretical Computer Science*, 126(2):183–235, 1994.

[AKY99] R. Alur, S. Kannan, and M. Yannakakis. Communicating hierarchical state machines. In *Proc. 26th Int. Coll. Automata, Languages, and Programming (ICALP'99), Prague, Czech Republic, July 1999*, volume 1644 of *Lecture Notes in Computer Science*, pages 169–178. Springer, 1999.

[AL99] L. Aceto and F. Laroussinie. Is your model checker on time ? In *Proc. 24th Int. Symp. Math. Found. Comp. Sci. (MFCS'99), Szklarska Poreba, Poland, Sep. 1999*, volume 1672 of *Lecture Notes in Computer Science*, pages 125–136. Springer, 1999.

[And93] H. R. Andersen. *Verification of Temporal Properties of Concurrent Systems.* PhD thesis, Aarhus University, Denmark, June 1993. Available as DAIMI PB–445.

[BCG88] M. C. Browne, E. M. Clarke, and O. Grumberg. Characterizing finite Kripke structures in propositional temporal logic. *Theoretical Computer Science*, 59(1–2):115–131, 1988.

[BCM+92] J. R. Burch, E. M. Clarke, K. L. McMillan, D. L. Dill, and L. J. Hwang. Symbolic model checking: 10^{20} states and beyond. *Information and Computation*, 98(2):142–170, 1992.

[Čer93] K. Čerāns. Decidability of bisimulation equivalence for parallel timer processes. In *Proc. 4th Int. Workshop Computer Aided Verification (CAV'92), Montreal, Canada, June–July 1992*, volume 663 of *Lecture Notes in Computer Science*, pages 302–315. Springer, 1993.

[CGL96] E. M. Clarke, O. Grumberg, and D. Long. Model-checking. In M. Broy, editor, *Deductive Program Design, Proc. NATO-ASI Summer School, Marktoberdorf, Germany, 26 July - 7 Aug 1994*, volume F-152 of *NATO ASI Series.* Springer, 1996.

[CKS81] A. K. Chandra, D. C. Kozen, and L. J. Stockmeyer. Alternation. *Journal of the ACM*, 28(1):114–133, 1981.

[Esp98] J. Esparza. Decidability and complexity of Petri net problems — an introduction. In *Advances in Petri Nets 1998*, volume 1491 of *Lecture Notes in Computer Science*, pages 374–428. Springer, 1998.

[Gla90] R. J. van Glabbeek. The linear time – branching time spectrum. In *Proc. Theories of Concurrency (CONCUR'90), Amsterdam, NL, Aug. 1990*, volume 458 of *Lecture Notes in Computer Science*, pages 278–297. Springer, 1990.

[Gla93] R. J. van Glabbeek. The linear time – branching time spectrum II: The semantics of sequential systems with silent moves. In *Proc. 4th Int. Conf. Concurrency Theory (CONCUR'93), Hildesheim, Germany, Aug. 1993*, volume 715 of *Lecture Notes in Computer Science*, pages 66–81. Springer, 1993.

[HKV97] D. Harel, O. Kupferman, and M. Y. Vardi. On the complexity of verifying concurrent transition systems. In *Proc. 8th Int. Conf. Concurrency Theory (CONCUR'97), Warsaw, Poland, Jul. 1997*, volume 1243 of *Lecture Notes in Computer Science*, pages 258–272. Springer, 1997.

[Jan95] P. Jančar. Undecidability of bisimilarity for Petri nets and some related problems. *Theoretical Computer Science*, 148(2):281–301, 1995.

[Jat99] L. Jategaonkar. Personal communication, August 1999.

[JM96] L. Jategaonkar and A. R. Meyer. Deciding true concurrency equivalences on safe, finite nets. *Theoretical Computer Science*, 154(1):107–143, 1996.

[KVW98] O. Kupferman, M. Y. Vardi, and P. Wolper. An automata-theoretic approach to branching-time model checking, 1998. Full version of the CAV'94 paper, accepted for publication in J. ACM.

[Mil89] R. Milner. *Communication and Concurrency*. Prentice Hall Int., 1989.

[MPS98] A. Muscholl, D. Peled, and Z. Su. Deciding properties for message sequence charts. In *Proc. Int. Conf. Foundations of Software Science and Computation Structures (FOSSACS'98), Lisbon, Portugal, Mar.-Apr. 1999*, volume 1378 of *Lecture Notes in Computer Science*, pages 226–242. Springer, 1998.

[MS94] A. J. Mayer and L. J. Stockmeyer. Word problems—this time with interleaving. *Information and Computation*, 115(2):293–311, 1994.

[Pnu85] A. Pnueli. Linear and branching structures in the semantics and logics of reactive systems. In *Proc. 12th Coll. Automata, Languages and Programming (ICALP'85), Nafplion, Greece, Jul. 1985*, volume 194 of *Lecture Notes in Computer Science*, pages 15–32. Springer, 1985.

[Rab97a] A. Rabinovich. Complexity of equivalence problems for concurrent systems of finite agents. *Information and Computation*, 139(2):111–129, 1997.

[Rab97b] A. Rabinovich. Symbolic model checking for μ-calculus requires exponential time. Tech. report, Dept. Comp. Sci., Tel Aviv University, Israel, August 1997.

A Proof of Lemma 4.2

We have to show that R has the transfer property in both directions:
1. Consider a pair $(\beta^-, \beta^+) \in R$, with $\beta = (s, i, w)$ a rejecting (disjunctive) i.d. β is not a final configuration, no `acc` transition is enabled from β^-: and we just have to check the transfer property for transitions labeled by t_k, i:

– Assume a type 1 move $\beta^- \xrightarrow{t_k,i} \langle (r^-,i'),w' \rangle$. In A, this corresponds to $(s,i,w) \longrightarrow_k (r,i',w')$. Let γ be (r,i',w'). Since β is disjunctive and rejecting, γ is rejecting. Thus there exists a move $\gamma \longrightarrow_{k'} \beta'$ s.t. β' is rejecting. Moreover the (type 2) transition $\beta^+ \xrightarrow{t_k,i} \gamma^+_{k'}$ is allowed in $\mathcal{S}_{A,w_0}$. Therefore, for any transition $\beta^- \xrightarrow{t_k,i} \gamma^-$, there exists $\beta^+ \xrightarrow{t_k,i} \gamma^+_{k'}$ s.t. $(\gamma^-,\gamma^+_{k'}) \in R$.
– The other possible moves for this pair are type 4 transitions $\beta^- \longrightarrow \gamma^+_{k'}$ and type 2 transitions $\beta^+ \longrightarrow \gamma^+_{k'}$: they can be imitated by the other side, relying on $(\gamma^+_{k'},\gamma^+_{k'}) \in \mathtt{Id} \subseteq R$.

2. Consider a pair $(\gamma^-,\gamma^+_k) \in R$ with $\gamma = (r,i,w)$. γ is a rejecting i.d. and there exists a move $\gamma \longrightarrow_k \beta$ leading to a rejecting $\beta = (s,i',w')$. We check the transfer property:

– Assume a type 1 move $\gamma^-_k \xrightarrow{t_{k'},i} \beta^-$. Then $\gamma \longrightarrow_{k'} \beta$ and either $k = k'$ or $k \neq k'$. If $k = k'$, then $\gamma^+ \xrightarrow{t_{k'},i} \beta^+$ and since β is not accepting, $(\beta^-,\beta^+) \in \mathcal{R}$. When $k \neq k'$, both t_k and $t_{k'}$ are enabled from γ, so that t_k and $t_{k'}$ require the same letter on the tape cell, and there exists a type 5 move $\gamma^+ \xrightarrow{t_{k'},i} \beta^-$. We use the fact that $(\beta^-,\beta^-) \in \mathtt{Id} \subseteq \mathcal{R}$.
– Assume a type 3 move $\gamma^+_k \xrightarrow{t_k,i} \beta^+$ with $\beta = (s^+,i',w')$, it can be simulated by $\gamma^- \xrightarrow{t_k,i} \beta^-$ because β is not accepting, so that $(\beta^-,\beta^+) \in R$.
– Other moves from γ^+_k reach a β^- (because t_k is enabled from γ) and can be easily imitated.

3. Finally, the pairs from $\mathtt{Id}$ obviously enjoy the transfer property.

B Proof of Lemma 4.3

We show by induction on l that

1. If β is accepting in l steps, then $\beta^- \not\sqsubseteq \beta^+$.
2. If $\gamma = (r,i,w)$ is accepting in l steps, then $\gamma^- \not\sqsubseteq \gamma^+_k$ for any k s.t. the source node of t_k is r.

– $l = 0$: if β accepts in 0 steps, then it is final and $\beta^- \xrightarrow{\mathsf{acc}}$ cannot be matched from β^+. A conjunctive configuration γ cannot be accepting in 0 steps.
– Assume the property holds for any $l' \leq l$. We have two cases:
  - A disjunctive β accepts in $l+1$ steps. Then there exists t_k s.t. $\beta \longrightarrow_k \gamma$ where $\gamma = (r,i,w)$ is accepting in l steps. In $\mathcal{S}_{A,w_0}$, the transition $\beta^- \xrightarrow{t_k,i} \gamma^-$ has to be matched by a transition labeled with "t_k,i" which leads to a configuration $\gamma^-_{k'}$ and, by i.h., $\gamma^- \not\sqsubseteq \gamma^+_{k'}$.
  - A conjunctive $\gamma = (r,i,w)$ accepts in $l+1$ steps. We must show that $\gamma^- \not\sqsubseteq \gamma^+_k$ for any k s.t. t_k starts from r. There are two cases:
    * t_k is enabled from γ: since γ accepts, any move from γ leads to an i.d. accepting in l steps. In $\mathcal{S}_{A,w_0}$, the transition $\gamma^- \xrightarrow{k,i} \beta^-$ can only be matched from γ^+_k by $\gamma^+_k \xrightarrow{k,i} \beta^+$ and, by i.h., $\beta^- \not\sqsubseteq \beta^+$.

* t_k is not enabled from γ: any transition $t_{k'}$ enabled from γ leads to an i.d. accepting in l steps and one such a transition exists. In $\mathcal{S}_{A,w_0}$, the move $\gamma^- \xrightarrow{k',i} \beta^-$ can only be matched from γ_k^+ by $\gamma_k^+ \xrightarrow{k',i} \beta^+$ and, by i.h., $\beta^- \not\sqsubseteq \beta^+$.

In both cases, we found a transition from γ^- which cannot be simulated from γ^+ and then $\gamma^- \not\sqsubseteq \gamma_k^+$.

Now, since we assume that $(q_0, 1, w_0)$ is accepting, the proof is complete.

A Proof System for Timed Automata

Huimin Lin[1]* and Wang Yi[2]

[1] Laboratory for Computer Science
Institute of Software, Chinese Academy of Sciences
lhm@ox.ios.ac.cn
[2] Department of Computer Systems
Uppsala University
yi@docs.uu.se

Abstract. A proof system for timed automata is presented, based on a CCS-style language for describing timed automata. It consists of the standard monoid laws for bisimulation and a set of inference rules. The judgments of the proof system are *conditional equations* of the form $\phi \triangleright t = u$ where ϕ is a clock constraint and t, u are terms denoting timed automata. It is proved that the proof system is complete for timed bisimulation over the recursion-free subset of the language. The completeness proof relies on the notion of *symbolic timed bisimulation*. The axiomatisation is also extended to handle an important variation of timed automata where each node is associated with an invariant constraint.

1 Introduction

Timed automata [AD94] has been recognised as a fundamental model for real time systems. By now the theory of timed automata has been well developed, but there is still one aspect missing: axiomatisation.

Timed automata extend traditional finite automata with a finite set of real-valued *clock variables* (or *clocks* for short) by annotating each transition with, in addition to an action label, a clock constraint (enabling condition) and a subset of clocks (reset set). Intuitively a timed automaton may stay at a node with clocks increasing uniformly (to model time passage), or choose a transition whose clock constraint is satisfied, make the move, reset the subset of clocks associated with the transition to zero, and arrive at the target node of the transition (to model control state switch). The explicit presence of clock variables and resetting, features that mainly associated with the so-called "imperative languages", distinguishes timed automata from process calculi such as CCS, CSP and their timed extensions which are "applicative" in nature and therefore more amenable to axiomatisation.

The aim of this paper is to propose a proof system for timed automata. We adapt the *symbolic bisimulation* technique originally developed for value-passing processes [HL95, HL96] to the timed setting. We first present a simple CCS-style

* Supported by research grants from National Science Foundation of China and Chinese Academy of Sciences

J. Tiuryn (Ed.): FOSSACS 2000, LNCS 1784, pp. 208–222, 2000.

language in which each term represents a timed automaton. The language has a conditional construct $\phi \rightarrow t$ (read "if ϕ then t") where ϕ is a clock constraint. Action prefixing is of the form $a(\mathbf{x}).t$, meaning to perform action a and reset the clocks in $\mathbf{x}$ to zero, then behave like t. An inference system is then formulated with judgments being *conditional equations* of the form

$$\phi \rhd t = u$$

Intuitively it means that "t and u are timed bisimilar for each clock valuation satisfying ϕ". A typical inference rule takes the form:

$$\text{GUARD} \quad \frac{\phi \wedge \psi \rhd t = u \qquad \phi \wedge \neg\psi \rhd \mathbf{0} = u}{\phi \rhd (\psi \rightarrow t) = u}$$

It performs a case analysis on the constraint ψ: $\psi \rightarrow t$ behaves like t when ψ is true, and like the inactive process $\mathbf{0}$ otherwise. Note that the guarding constraint ψ of $\psi \rightarrow t$ in the conclusion is *part of the object language* describing timed automata, while in the premise it is shifted to the condition part of the judgment in our *meta language* for reasoning about timed automata.

The crucial rule, as might be expected, is the one for action prefixing:

$$\text{ACTION} \quad \frac{\phi{\downarrow_{\mathbf{xy}}}{\Uparrow} \rhd t = u}{\phi \rhd a(\mathbf{x}).t = a(\mathbf{y}).u} \quad \mathbf{y} \cap \mathcal{C}(t) = \mathbf{x} \cap \mathcal{C}(u) = \emptyset$$

Here $\downarrow_{\mathbf{xy}}$ and $\Uparrow$ are postfixing operations on clock constraints. $\phi{\downarrow_{\mathbf{xy}}}{\Uparrow}$ is a clock constraint obtained from ϕ by first setting the clocks in $\mathbf{xy}$ to zero (operator $\downarrow_{\mathbf{xy}}$), then removing up-bounds on all clocks of ϕ (operator $\Uparrow$). Readers familiar with Hoare Logic may notice some similarity between this rule and the rule dealing with assignment there:

$$\{P[e/x]\}\ x := e\ \{P\}$$

But here the operator $\downarrow_{\mathbf{xy}}$ is slightly more complicated than substitution with zero, because clocks are required to increase uniformly. We also need $\Uparrow$ to allow time to pass indefinitely.

Traditionally axiomatisation for so-called "pure" process algebras are based on equational reasoning, i.e. "replacing equal for equal". Since timed automata involve clock constrains and clock resetting, it is not surprising that pure equational reasoning along is no longer adequate. The inference system proposed in this paper can be viewed as extending pure equational reasoning by formulating suitable rules for the specific constructs present in timed automata. It turns out that with this extension the standard monoid laws for bisimulation are sufficient for timed bisimulation, i.e. the proof system consisting of the set of inference rules and the four monoid laws are sound and complete for timed bisimulation. The proof of the completeness result relies on developing a theory of timed symbolic bisimulation which is a binary relation indexed by clock constraints. It captures the standard definition of timed bisimulation in the sense that t and

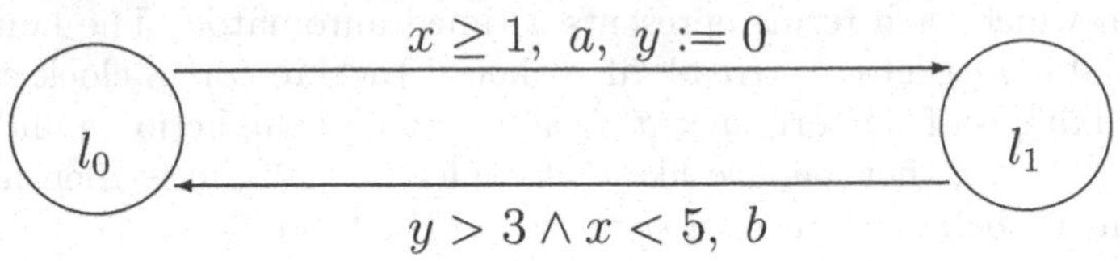

Fig. 1. A Timed Automaton.

u are symbolically bisimilar over indexing constraint ϕ if and only if they are timed bisimilar for any time valuation satisfying ϕ.

In the remaining of this section we briefly discuss related work. The language for timed automata is presented in the next section, with a symbolic operational semantics which associates each term in the language to a timed automaton. Section 3 develops a theory of symbolic bisimulation for timed automata. The proof system is presented in Section 4, together with its completeness proof. Section 5 discusses how to extend the language to include *invariants*. The paper is concluded with Section 6 where further research direction is also outlined.

Related work The first process algebra for timed automata is proposed in [WPD94] as the very first input language for the UPPAAL tool. The only previous attempt to axiomatizing timed automata we are aware is [DAB96], which develops a large set of sound axioms for timed bisimulation. However, no completeness result is reported.

On the other hand, most timed extensions of process algebras came with axiomatisation on various equivalence relations including bisimulation. Of particular interest is [Bor96] which also adapts the symbolic bisimulation technique of [HL95, HL96] to a timed process language and proposed a symbolic style proof system. As noted by the author, the language considered in that paper is quite different from timed automata as it does not involve clock variables.

2 A Language for Timed Automata

The theory of timed automata was introduced in [AD94] and has since then established as a standard model for real time systems. We first give a brief review for the readers unfamiliar with timed automata and then present an algebraic language in which each term denotes a timed automaton.

2.1 Timed Automata

A timed automaton is a standard finite-state automaton extended with a finite collection of real-valued clocks. In a timed automaton each transition is labelled with a *guard* (a constraint over clocks), a *synchronisation action*, and a *reset set* (a subset of clocks to be reset). Intuitively, a timed automaton starts an execution with all clocks initialised to zero. Clocks increase at the same rate while the automaton stays within a node. A transition can be taken if the clocks fulfill the guard. By taking the transition, all clocks in the clock reset are set to zero, while the others are unchanged. Thus transitions occur instantaneously. Semantically, a state of an automaton is a pair of a control node and a *clock valuation*, i.e. the current setting of the clocks. Transitions in the semantic interpretation are either labelled with a synchronisation action (if it is an instantaneous switch from the current node to another) or a positive real number i.e. a time delay (if the automaton stays within a node letting time pass).

Consider the timed automaton of Figure 1. It has two control nodes l_0 and l_1 and two real–valued clocks x and y. A *state* of the automaton is of the form $(l, \langle s, t\rangle)$, where l is a control node, and s and t are non–negative reals giving the value of the two clocks x and y. Assuming that the automaton starts to operate in the state $(l_0, \langle 0, 0\rangle)$, it may stay in node l_0 for any amount of time, while the values of the clocks increase uniformly, at the same rate. Thus from the initial state, all states of the form $(l_0, \langle t, t\rangle)$ with $t \geq 0$ are reachable. However, only at the states $(l_0, \langle t, t\rangle)$, where $t \geq 1$, the edge from l_0 to l_1 is enabled. Additionally, edges are labelled with synchronization actions and simple assignments reseting clocks. For instance, when following the edge from l_0 to l_1 the action a is performed to synchronize with the environment and the clock y is reset to 0, leading to states of the form $(l_1, \langle t, 0\rangle)$, where $t \geq 1$.

For the formal definition, we assume a finite set of alphabets $\mathcal{A}$ for synchronization actions and a finite set of real-valued variables $\mathcal{C}$ for clocks. We use a, b etc. to range over $\mathcal{A}$ and x, y etc. to range over $\mathcal{C}$. Subsets of $\mathcal{C}$ will be denoted by $\mathbf{x}, \mathbf{y}$ with elements x_i, x_j, ..., y_i, y_j, ... We use $\mathcal{B}(C)$, ranged over by ϕ, ψ etc., to denote the set of conjunctive formulas of atomic constraints of the form: $x_i \bowtie m$ or $x_i - x_j \bowtie n$ where $x_i, x_j \in \mathcal{C}$, $\bowtie \in \{\leq, <, \geq, >\}$, and m, n are natural numbers. The elements of $\mathcal{B}(C)$ are called *clock constraints.*

Definition 2.1. *A timed automaton over actions $\mathcal{A}$ and clocks $\mathcal{C}$ is a tuple $\langle N, l_0, E\rangle$ where*

- *N is a finite set of nodes,*
- *$l_0 \in N$ is the initial node,*
- *$E \subseteq N \times \mathcal{B}(C) \times \mathcal{A} \times 2^{C} \times N$ is the set of edges.*

When $\langle l, g, a, r, l'\rangle \in E$, we write $l \stackrel{g,a,r}{\longrightarrow} l'$.

We shall present the operational semantics for timed automata in terms of a process algebraic language in which each term denotes an automaton.

Sometimes to describe progress properties, nodes of timed automata are associated with *invariants* that control the amount of time an automaton can stay at a node. Such an extension will be discussed in Section 5.

$$\text{DELAY}\quad \frac{}{t\rho \xrightarrow{d} t(\rho + d)}$$

$$\text{ACTION}\quad \frac{}{(a(\mathbf{x}).t)\rho \xrightarrow{a} t\rho\{\mathbf{x} := 0\}} \qquad \text{CHOICE}\quad \frac{t\rho \xrightarrow{a} t'\rho'}{(t+u)\rho \xrightarrow{a} t'\rho'}$$

$$\text{GUARD}\quad \frac{t\rho \xrightarrow{a} t'\rho'}{(\phi \rightarrow t)\rho \xrightarrow{a} t'\rho'}\ \rho \models \phi \qquad \text{REC}\quad \frac{(t[\mathbf{fix}Xt/X])\rho \xrightarrow{a} t'\rho'}{(\mathbf{fix}Xt)\rho \xrightarrow{a} t'\rho'}$$

Fig. 2. Standard Transitional Semantics

2.2 The Language

We preassume a set of process variables, ranged over by $X,\ Y,\ Z,\ \ldots$. The language for timed automata over $\mathcal{C}$ can be given by the following BNF grammar:

$$t ::= \mathbf{0} \mid \phi \rightarrow t \mid a(\mathbf{x}).t \mid t + t \mid X \mid \mathbf{fix}Xt$$

$\mathbf{0}$ is the inactive process which can do nothing, except for allowing time to pass. $\phi \rightarrow t$, read "if ϕ then t", is the usual (one-armed) conditional construct. $a(\mathbf{x}).r$ is action prefixing. $+$ is nondeterministic choice.

A recursion $\mathbf{fix}Xt$ binds X in t. This is the only binding operator in this language. It induces the notions of bound and free process variables as usual. Terms not containing free variables are *closed.* A recursion $\mathbf{fix}Xt$ is *guarded* if every occurrence of X in t is within the scope of an action prefixing.

The set of clock variables used in a term t is denoted $\mathcal{C}(t)$.

A *clock valuation* is a function from $\mathcal{C}$ to $\mathbf{R}^{\geq 0}$, and we use ρ to range over clock valuations. The notations $\rho\{\mathbf{x} := 0\}$ and $\rho + d$ are defined thus

$$\rho\{\mathbf{x} := 0\}(y) = \begin{cases} 0 & \text{if } y \in \mathbf{x} \\ \rho(y) & \text{otherwise} \end{cases}$$
$$(\rho + d)(x) = \rho(x) + d \quad \text{for all } x$$

Given a clock valuation $\rho : \mathcal{C} \rightarrow \mathbf{R}^{\geq 0}$, a term can be interpreted according to rules in Figure 2, where the symmetric rule for $+$ has been omitted. The transitional semantics uses two types of transition relations: action transition $\xrightarrow{a}$ and delay transition $\xrightarrow{d}$. We call $t\rho$ a *process*, where t is a term and ρ a valuation; we use $p,\ q, \ldots$ to range over the set of processes. We also write μ for either an action or a delay (a real number).

Definition 2.2. *A symmetric relation R over processes is a timed bisimulation if $(p, q) \in R$ implies*

whenever $p \xrightarrow{\mu} p'$ then $q \xrightarrow{\mu} q'$ for some q' with $(p', q') \in R$.

We write $p \sim q$ if $(p, q) \in R$ for some timed bisimulation R.

$$\text{ACTION}\ \frac{}{a(\mathbf{x}).t \xrightarrow{\mathrm{tt},a,\mathbf{x}} t} \qquad \text{CHOICE}\ \frac{t \xrightarrow{b,a,r} t'}{t+u \xrightarrow{b,a,r} t'}$$

$$\text{GUARD}\ \frac{t \xrightarrow{\psi,a,r} t'}{\phi{\rightarrow}t \xrightarrow{\phi\wedge\psi,a,r} t'} \qquad \text{REC}\ \frac{t[\mathbf{fix}Xt/X] \xrightarrow{b,a,r} t'}{\mathbf{fix}Xt \xrightarrow{b,a,r} t'}$$

Fig. 3. Symbolic Transitional Semantics

The symbolic transitional semantics of this language is reported in Figure 3. Again the symmetric rule for + has been omitted. According to the symbolic semantics, each guarded closed term of the language gives rise to a timed automaton; On the other hand, it is not difficult to see that every timed automaton can be generated from a guarded closed term in the language. In the sequel we will use the phrases "timed automata" and "terms" interchangeably.

The two versions of transitional semantics can be related as follows:

Lemma 2.3. *1. If $t \xrightarrow{\phi,a,\mathbf{x}} t'$ then $t\rho \xrightarrow{a} t'\rho\{\mathbf{x} := 0\}$ for any $\rho \models \phi$.*
2. If $t\rho \xrightarrow{a} t'\rho'$ then there exist ϕ, $\mathbf{x}$ such that $\rho \models \phi$, $\rho' = \rho\{\mathbf{x} := 0\}$ and $t \xrightarrow{\phi,a,\mathbf{x}} t'$.

3 Constraints and Symbolic Bisimulation

This section is devoted to defining a symbolic version of timed bisimulation. To easy the presentation we shall fix two timed automata and symbolically, i.e. without evaluating clock constraints, compare them for bisimulation. To avoid clock variables of one automaton being reset by the other, we always assume the sets of clocks of the two timed automata under consideration are disjoint and write C for the union of the two clock sets. Let N be the largest natural number occurring in the constraints of the two automata. An atomic constraint over C with ceiling N has one of the two forms: $x \bowtie m$ or $x - y \bowtie n$ where $x, y \in C, \bowtie \in \{\leq, <, \geq, >\}$ and $m, n \leq N$ are natural numbers.

In the following, "atomic constraint" always means "atomic constraint over C with ceiling N". Note that given two timed automata there are only finite number of such atomic constraints. We shall use c to range over atomic constraints.

A constraint, or *zone*, is a boolean combination of atomic constraints. A constraint ϕ is consistent if there is some ρ such that $\rho \models \phi$. Let ϕ and ψ be two constraints. We write $\phi \Rightarrow \psi$ to mean $\rho \models \phi$ implies $\rho \models \psi$ for any ρ. Note that the relation $\Rightarrow$ is decidable.

A *region constraint*, or *region* for short, ϕ is a consistent constraint containing only the following atomic conjuncts:

- For each $i \in \{1, \ldots, n\}$ either $x_i = m_i$ or $m_i < x_i < m_i + 1$ or $x_i > N$;
- For each pair of $i, j \in \{1, \ldots, n\}$, $i \neq j$, either $x_i - m_i = x_j - m_j$ or $x_i - m_i < x_j - m_j$ or $x_i - m_i > x_j - m_j$.

where the m_i in $x_i - m_i$ of the second clause refers to the m_i related to x_i in the first clause. In words, m_i is the integral part of x_i and $x_i - m_i$ its fractional part.

Given a set of clock variables C and a ceiling N, the set of region constraints over C is finite. and is denoted $\mathcal{RC}_N^C$. In the sequel, we will omit the sub- and super-scripts when they can be supplied by the context.

Fact 1 *Let ϕ be a region constraint. If $\rho \models \phi$ and $\rho' \models \phi$ then*

- *For all $i \in \{1, \ldots, n\}$, if $\rho(x_i) \leq N$ then $\lfloor \rho(x_i) \rfloor = \lfloor \rho'(x_i) \rfloor$.*
- *For any $i, j \in \{1, \ldots, n\}$, $i \neq j$,*
  - *$\{\rho(x_i)\} = \{\rho(x_j)\}$ iff $\{\rho'(x_i)\} = \{\rho'(x_j)\}$ and*
  - *$\{\rho(x_i)\} < \{\rho(x_j)\}$ iff $\{\rho'(x_i)\} < \{\rho'(x_j)\}$.*

where $\lfloor x \rfloor$ and $\{x\}$ are the integral and fractional parts of x, respectively.

That is, two valuations satisfying the same region constraint must agree on their integral parts as well as on the ordering of their fractional parts. Note that this is precisely the definition of region equivalence due to Alur and Dill [AD94].

The notion of a region constraint enjoy an important property: processes in the same region behave uniformly with respect to timed bisimulation ([Cer92]):

Fact 2 *Let t, u be two timed automata with disjoint sets of clock variables and ϕ a region constraint over the union of the two clock sets. Suppose that both ρ and ρ' satisfy ϕ. Then $t\rho \sim u\rho$ iff $t\rho' \sim u\rho'$.*

Fact 3 *Suppose that ϕ is a region constraint and ψ a zone. Then either $\phi \Rightarrow \psi$ or $\phi \Rightarrow \neg\psi$.*

So a region is either entirely contained in a zone, or is completely outside a zone. In other words, regions are the finest polyhedra that can be described by our constraint language.

A *canonical* constraint is a disjunction of regions. Given a constraint we can first transform it into disjunctive normal form, then decompose each disjunct into a disjoint set of regions. Both steps can be effectively implemented. As a corollary to Fact 3, if we write $\mathcal{RC}(\phi)$ for the set of regions contained in the zone ϕ, then $\bigvee \mathcal{RC}(\phi) = \phi$, i.e. $\bigvee \mathcal{RC}(\phi)$ is the canonical form of ϕ.

We will need two operators to deal with resetting. The first one is $\downarrow_{\mathbf{x}}$ where $\mathbf{x} \subseteq C \subseteq \mathcal{C}$. We first define it on regions, then generalise it to zones. By the abuse of notation, we will write $c \in \phi$ to mean c is a conjunct of ϕ.

For a region ϕ,

$$\begin{aligned}\phi{\downarrow_{\mathbf{x}}} = \phi \downarrow'_{\mathbf{x}} &\wedge \bigwedge\{ x_i = 0 \mid x_i \in \mathbf{x} \} \wedge \bigwedge\{ x_i = x_j \mid x_i, x_j \in \mathbf{x} \} \\ &\wedge \bigwedge\{ x_i = x_j - m \mid x_i \in \mathbf{x}, x_j \notin \mathbf{x}, x_j = m \in \phi \} \\ &\wedge \bigwedge\{ x_i < x_j - m \mid x_i \in \mathbf{x}, x_j \notin \mathbf{x}, x_j > m \in \phi \}\end{aligned}$$

and $\downarrow'_{\mathbf{x}}$ is defined by

$$\begin{array}{ll} tt \downarrow'_{\mathbf{x}} = tt & \\ (c \wedge \phi) \downarrow'_{\mathbf{x}} = \phi \downarrow'_{\mathbf{x}} & \text{if } \mathbf{x} \cap fv(c) \neq \emptyset \\ (c \wedge \phi) \downarrow'_{\mathbf{x}} = c \wedge \phi \downarrow'_{\mathbf{x}} & \text{if } \mathbf{x} \cap fv(c) = \emptyset \end{array}$$

where $fv(c)$ is the set of clock variables appearing in (atomic constraint) c.

Lemma 3.1. *1. $\rho \models \phi$ implies $\rho\{\mathbf{x} := 0\} \models \phi\downarrow_{\mathbf{x}}$.*
2. If ϕ is a region constraint then so is $\phi\downarrow_{\mathbf{x}}$.

For a canonical constraint $\bigvee_i \phi_i$ with each ϕ_i a region, $(\bigvee_i \phi_i)\downarrow_{\mathbf{x}} = \bigvee_i(\phi_i\downarrow_{\mathbf{x}})$. For an arbitrary constraint ϕ, $\phi\downarrow_{\mathbf{x}}$ is understood as the result of applying $\downarrow_{\mathbf{x}}$ to the canonical form of ϕ.

The second operator $\_\Uparrow$ is defined similarly. We first define it on regions:

$$\phi\Uparrow = \phi\Uparrow' \wedge \bigwedge_{i \neq j} e_{ij}(\phi)$$

where $\_\Uparrow'$ is defined by

$$\begin{array}{l} tt\Uparrow' = tt \\ (x < m \wedge \phi)\Uparrow' = x \leq N \wedge \phi\Uparrow' \\ (x = m \wedge \phi)\Uparrow' = m \leq x \wedge \phi\Uparrow' \\ (c \wedge \phi)\Uparrow' = c \wedge \phi\Uparrow' \quad \text{for other atomic constraint c} \end{array}$$

and

$$e_{ij}(\phi) = \begin{cases} x_i - m_i = x_j - m_j & x_i = m_i, x_j = m_j \in \phi \\ m_i - m_j - 1 < x_i - x_j < m_i - m_j & \text{otherwise} \end{cases}$$

For an arbitrary constraint ϕ, $\phi\Uparrow$ is understood as the result of applying $\Uparrow$ to each disjunct of the canonical form of ϕ.

Definition 3.2. *ϕ is $\Uparrow$-closed if and only if $\phi\Uparrow = \phi$.*

Lemma 3.3. *1. $\phi\Uparrow$ is $\Uparrow$-closed.*
2. $\rho \models \phi$ implies $\rho \models \phi\Uparrow$.
3. If ϕ is $\Uparrow$-closed then $\rho \models \phi$ implies $\rho + d \models \phi$ for all $d \in \mathbf{R}^{\geq 0}$.

Symbolic bisimulation will be defined as a family of binary relations indexed by clock constraints. Following [Cer92] we use constraints over the union of the (disjoint) clock sets of two timed automata as indices. Given a constraint ϕ, a finite set of constraints Φ is called a *ϕ-partition* if $\bigvee \Phi = \phi$. A ϕ-partition Φ is called *finer* than another such partition Ψ if Φ can be obtained from Ψ by decomposing some of its elements. By the corollary to Fact 3, $\mathcal{RC}(\phi)$ is a ϕ-partition, and is the finest such partition. In particular, if ϕ is a region constraint then $\{\phi\}$ is the only partition of ϕ.

Definition 3.4. *A constraint indexed family of symmetric relations over terms* $\mathbf{S} = \{ S^{\phi} \mid \phi \Uparrow\text{-closed} \}$ *is a timed symbolic bisimulation if* $(t, u) \in S^{\phi}$ *implies*

> *whenever* $t \xrightarrow{\psi, a, \mathbf{x}} t'$ *then there is a* $\phi \wedge \psi$*-partition* Φ *such that for each* $\phi' \in \Phi$ *there is* $u \xrightarrow{\psi', a, \mathbf{y}} u'$ *for some* ψ', $\mathbf{y}$ *and* u' *such that* $\phi' \Rightarrow \psi'$ *and* $(t', u') \in S^{\phi' \downarrow_{\mathbf{xy}} \Uparrow}$.

We write $t \sim^{\phi} u$ *if* $(t, u) \in S^{\phi} \in \mathbf{S}$ *for some symbolic bisimulation* $\mathbf{S}$.

It is easy to see that the $\phi \wedge \psi$-partition Φ used in the above definition can be replaced by any partition finer than Φ.

Timed symbolic bisimulation captures $\sim$ in the following sense:

Theorem 3.5. $t \sim^{\phi} u$ *iff* $t\rho \sim u\rho$ *for any* $\rho \models \phi$.

Proof. ($\Longrightarrow$) Assume $(t, u) \in S^{\phi} \in \mathbf{S}$ for some symbolic bisimulation $\mathbf{S}$. Define

$$R = \{ (t\rho, u\rho) \mid \text{there exists some } \phi \text{ such that } \rho \models \phi \text{ and } (t, u) \in S^{\phi} \in \mathbf{S} \}$$

We show R is a timed bisimulation. Suppose $(t\rho, u\rho) \in R$, i.e. there is some ϕ such that $\rho \models \phi$ and $(t, u) \in S^{\phi}$.

- $t\rho \xrightarrow{a} t'\rho'$. By Lemma 2.3 there are ψ, $\mathbf{x}$ such that $\rho \models \psi$, $\rho' = \rho\{\mathbf{x} := 0\}$ and $t \xrightarrow{\psi, a, \mathbf{x}} t'$. So there is a $\phi \wedge \psi$-partition Φ with the properties specified in Definition 3.4. Since $\rho \models \phi \wedge \psi$, $\rho \models \phi'$ for some $\phi' \in \Phi$. Let $u \xrightarrow{\psi', a, \mathbf{y}} u'$ be the symbolic transition associated with this ϕ', as guaranteed by Definition 3.4. Then $\phi' \Rightarrow \psi'$ and $(t', u') \in S^{\phi' \downarrow_{\mathbf{xy}} \Uparrow}$. Since $\rho \models \psi'$, $u\rho \xrightarrow{a} u'\rho\{\mathbf{y} := 0\}$. By Lemma 3.1, $\rho\{\mathbf{xy} := 0\} \models \phi' \downarrow_{\mathbf{xy}}$. By Lemma 3.3, $\rho\{\mathbf{xy} := 0\} \models \phi' \downarrow_{\mathbf{xy}} \Uparrow$. Therefore $(t'\rho\{\mathbf{xy} := 0\}, u'\rho\{\mathbf{xy} := 0\}) \in R$. Since $t'\rho\{\mathbf{xy} := 0\} \equiv t'\rho\{\mathbf{x} := 0\}$ and $u'\rho\{\mathbf{xy} := 0\} \equiv u'\rho\{\mathbf{y} := 0\}$, this is the same as $(t'\rho\{\mathbf{x} := 0\}, u'\rho\{\mathbf{y} := 0\}) \in R$.
- $t\rho \xrightarrow{d} t(\rho + d)$. Then also $u\rho \xrightarrow{d} u(\rho + d)$. Since ϕ is $\Uparrow$-closed, $\rho + d \models \phi$. Therefore $(t(\rho + d), u(\rho + d)) \in R$.

($\Longleftarrow$) Assume $t\rho \sim u\rho$ for any $\rho \models \phi_0$, we show $t \sim^{\phi_0} u$ as follows. For each $\Uparrow$-closed ϕ define

$$S^{\phi} = \{ (t, u) \mid \forall \phi' \in \mathcal{RC}(\phi)\ \exists \rho \models \phi' \ \textit{s.t.}\ (t\rho, u\rho) \in R \}$$

and let $\mathbf{S} = \{ S^{\phi} \mid \phi \text{ is } \Uparrow - \text{closed} \}$ Then by Fact 2 $(t, u) \in S^{\phi_0}$. $\mathbf{S}$ is well-defined because R is a timed bisimulation. We show $\mathbf{S}$ is a symbolic bisimulation. Suppose $(t, u) \in S^{\phi}$ and let $t \xrightarrow{\psi, a, \mathbf{x}} t'$. Define $\Phi' = \{ \phi' \mid \phi' \in \mathcal{RC}(\phi) \text{ and } \phi' \Rightarrow \psi \}$. Then Φ' is a $\phi \wedge \psi$-partition. For each $\phi' \in \Phi'$, there exists ρ s.t. $\rho \models \phi'$ with $(t\rho, u\rho) \in R$. By the definition of Φ', $\rho \models \psi$. By Lemma 2.3, $t\rho \xrightarrow{a} t'\rho\{\mathbf{x} := 0\}$. Since $(t\rho, u\rho) \in R$, $u\rho \xrightarrow{a} u'\rho'$ for some u' and ρ' with $(t'\rho\{\mathbf{x} := 0\}, u'\rho') \in R$. By Lemma 2.3 again, $u \xrightarrow{\psi', a', \mathbf{y}} u'$ for some ψ' and $\mathbf{y}$ with $\rho \models \psi'$ and $\rho' = \rho\{\mathbf{y} := 0\}$. Hence $(t\rho\{\mathbf{x} := 0\}, u\rho\{\mathbf{y} := 0\}) \in R$, which is the same as $(t\rho\{\mathbf{xy} := 0\}, u\rho\{\mathbf{xy} := 0\}) \in R$. ¿From $\rho \models \phi'$, by Lemma 3.1 we have $\rho\{\mathbf{xy} := 0\} \models \phi' \downarrow_{\mathbf{xy}}$. Since ϕ' is a region constraint, so is $\phi' \downarrow_{\mathbf{xy}}$ which is the only element of $\mathcal{RC}(\phi' \downarrow_{\mathbf{xy}})$. Therefore $(t', u') \in S^{\phi' \downarrow_{\mathbf{xy}} \Uparrow}$.

S1 $X + \mathbf{0} = X$
S2 $X + X = X$
S3 $X + Y = Y + X$
S4 $(X + Y) + Z = X + (Y + Z)$

Fig. 4. The Equational Axioms

4 The Proof System

The proof system consists of a set of equational axioms in Figure 4 and a set of inference rules in Figure 5. The judgments of the inference system are *conditional equations* of the form

$$\phi \rhd t = u$$

with ϕ a constraint and t, u terms. Its intended meaning is "$t\rho \sim u\rho$ for any $\rho \models \phi$". $t = u$ abbreviates $\mathbf{tt} \rhd t = u$.

The equational axioms are the standard monoid laws for bisimulation [Mil89]. The set of inference rules extends equational reasoning by introducing a rule for each construct in the process language. CONGR-+ expresses the fact that bisimulation is preserved by +. The rule GUARD permits a case analysis on conditional. It is all we need to reason with this construct. ACTION is the introduction rule for action prefixing. This rule is complicated by the fact that an action has associated with it a clock resetting, hence necessitates the two operators $\downarrow_{\mathbf{xy}}$ and $\Uparrow$. It requires a side condition to make sure clock resetting in one process does not interfere with the other. Finally, the two rules PARTITION and ABSURD have nothing to do with any specific constructs in the language. They are so-called "structural rules" used to "glue" pieces of derivations together.

Let us write $\vdash \phi \rhd t = u$ to mean $\phi \rhd t = u$ can be derived from this proof system.

Some useful properties of the proof system are summarised in the following proposition:

Proposition 4.1. *1.* $\vdash \phi{\rightarrow}(\psi{\rightarrow}t) = \phi \wedge \psi{\rightarrow}t$
2. $\vdash t = t + \phi{\rightarrow}t$
3. If $\phi \Rightarrow \psi$ *then* $\vdash \phi \rhd t = \psi{\rightarrow}t$
4. $\vdash \phi \wedge \psi \rhd t = u$ *implies* $\vdash \phi \rhd \psi{\rightarrow}t = \psi{\rightarrow}u$
5. $\vdash \phi{\rightarrow}(t + u) = \phi{\rightarrow}t + \phi{\rightarrow}u$

The rule PARTITION has a more general form:

Proposition 4.2. *Suppose Φ is a finite set of constraints and $\bigvee \Phi = \phi$. If $\vdash \psi \rhd t = u$ for each $\psi \in \Phi$, then $\vdash \phi \rhd t = u$.*

Soundness of the proof system is stated below:

Theorem 4.3. *If $\vdash \phi \rhd t = u$ and ϕ is $\Uparrow$-closed then $t \sim^{\phi} u$.*

Now we discuss the completeness of the proof system, and we shall confine to the recursion-free subset of the language. As usual the completeness proof uses the notion of a normal form.

$$\text{EQUIV} \quad \frac{}{t = t} \quad \frac{t = u}{u = t} \quad \frac{t = u \quad u = v}{t = v}$$

$$\text{AXIOM} \quad \frac{}{t = u} \quad t = u \text{ is an axiom instance}$$

$$\text{CONGR-+} \quad \frac{t = t'}{t + u = t' + u}$$

$$\text{GUARD} \quad \frac{\phi \wedge \psi \rhd t = u \qquad \phi \wedge \neg\psi \rhd \mathbf{0} = u}{\phi \rhd \psi \rightarrow t = u}$$

$$\text{ACTION} \quad \frac{\phi{\downarrow_{\mathbf{xy}}}\Uparrow \rhd t = u}{\phi \rhd a(\mathbf{x}).t = a(\mathbf{y}).u} \quad \mathbf{y} \cap \mathcal{C}(t) = \mathbf{x} \cap \mathcal{C}(u) = \emptyset$$

$$\text{PARTITION} \quad \frac{\phi_1 \rhd t = u \qquad \phi_2 \rhd t = u}{\phi \rhd t = u} \quad \phi \Rightarrow \phi_1 \vee \phi_2$$

$$\text{ABSURD} \quad \frac{}{\mathsf{ff} \rhd t = u}$$

Fig. 5. The Inference Rules

Definition 4.4. *A term t is a normal form if $t \equiv \sum_i \phi_i \rightarrow a_i(\mathbf{x}_i).t_i$ and each t_i is a normal form.*

Definition 4.5. *The height of a term t, denoted $\mid t \mid$, is defined thus:*

- $\mid \mathbf{0} \mid = 0$
- $\mid t + u \mid = \ max\{\mid t \mid, \mid u \mid\}$
- $\mid \phi \rightarrow t \mid = \mid t \mid$
- $\mid a(\mathbf{x}).t \mid = 1 + \mid t \mid$

Lemma 4.6. *For every term t there exists a normal form t' such that $\mid t \mid = \mid t' \mid$ and $\vdash t = t'$.*

Theorem 4.7. *For recursion-free terms t and u, $t \sim^{\phi} u$ implies $\vdash \phi \rhd t = u$.*

Proof. By Lemma 4.6 we assume t, u are in normal form:

$$t \equiv \sum_{i \in I} \phi_i \rightarrow a_i(\mathbf{x}_i).t_i$$

$$u \equiv \sum_{j \in J} \psi_j \rightarrow b_j(\mathbf{y}_j).u_j$$

Without loss of generality, we may assume $a_i = b_j = a$ for all i and j.

Apply induction on the joint height of t and u. The base case is trivial. For the induction step, let $\phi' \in \mathcal{RC}(\phi)$. For each $i \in I$, $t \stackrel{\phi_i,a,\mathbf{x}_i}{\longrightarrow} t_i$. Since $t \sim^{\phi} u$, there exists a $\phi \wedge \phi_i$-partition Φ with the properties specified in Definition 3.4. Without lose of generality, we assume each element of Φ is a region constraint, i.e. $\Phi = \mathcal{RC}(\phi \wedge \phi_i)$. Since ϕ' is a region, by Fact 3 there are two cases:
(case 1) $\phi' \wedge \phi_i = \mathsf{ff}$, i.e. $\phi' \notin \Phi$. By GUARD and ABSURD we can derive $\vdash \phi' \rhd \phi_i \rightarrow a(\mathbf{x}_i).t_i = \mathbf{0}$.
(case 2) $\phi' \Rightarrow \phi_i$, i.e. $\phi' \in \Phi$. By the definition of symbolic bisimulation, there is some $j \in J$ such that $\phi' \Rightarrow \psi_j$, $u \stackrel{\psi_j,a,\mathbf{y}_j}{\longrightarrow} u_j$ and $t_i \sim^{\phi'\downarrow_{\mathbf{x}_i\mathbf{y}_j}\Uparrow} u_j$. By induction we have

$$\vdash \phi'\downarrow_{\mathbf{x}_i\mathbf{y}_j}\Uparrow \rhd t_i = u_j$$

By ACTION,

$$\vdash \phi' \rhd a(\mathbf{x}_i).t_i = a(\mathbf{y}_j).u_j$$

Since $\phi' \Rightarrow \phi_i$ and $\phi' \Rightarrow \psi_j$, by Proposition 4.1,

$$\vdash \phi' \rhd \phi_i \rightarrow a(\mathbf{x}_i).t_i = \psi_j \rightarrow a(\mathbf{y}_j).u_j$$

Symmetrically, for each $j \in J$, either $\vdash \phi' \rhd \psi_j \rightarrow a(\mathbf{y}_j).u_j = \mathbf{0}$ or there is some $i \in I$ such that

$$\vdash \phi' \rhd \psi_j \rightarrow a(\mathbf{y}_j).u_j = \phi_i \rightarrow a(\mathbf{x}_i).t_i$$

Therefore, using S1 – S4 and CONGR-+, we can conclude

$$\vdash \phi' \rhd t = \sum_{i \in I} \phi_i \rightarrow a_i(\mathbf{x}_i).t_i + \sum_{j \in J} \psi_j \rightarrow b_j(\mathbf{y}_j).u_j$$

and

$$\vdash \phi' \rhd u = \sum_{i \in I} \phi_i \rightarrow a_i(\mathbf{x}_i).t_i + \sum_{j \in J} \psi_j \rightarrow b_j(\mathbf{y}_j).u_j$$

Hence

$$\vdash \phi' \rhd t = u$$

Finally an application of Proposition 4.2 gives the required

$$\vdash \phi \rhd t = u$$

5 Invariants

One important variation on the notion of timed automata is to associate an invariant condition to each node of the automaton to model progress behaviours. According to the transitional semantics of Figure 2 a process can delay forever at any location (node). To disallow such arbitrary delays each location in a timed automata is assigned an *invariant constraint*, with the interpretation that delay transitions at a node will not be possible when the invariant at the node is violated.

To describe timed automata with invariants we extend our language as follows

$$s ::= \{\phi\}t$$
$$t ::= \mathbf{0} \mid \phi \rightarrow t \mid a(\mathbf{x}).s \mid t + t \mid X \mid \mathbf{fix} X t$$

In this language, invariants can not occur at places which do not correspond to locations in timed automata. For instance, strings having the forms $\phi \rightarrow \{\psi\}t$, $\{\phi\}t + \{\psi\}u$ or $\mathbf{fix}X\{\phi\}t$ are *not* terms of the language, while $\{\phi\}(t+u)$ and $\phi \rightarrow a(\mathbf{x}).\{\psi\}t$ are allowed.

We assign each term t an invariant constraint $Inv(t)$ by letting

$$Inv(t) = \begin{cases} \phi & \text{if } t \text{ has the form } \{\phi\}t' \\ \mathrm{tt} & \text{otherwise} \end{cases}$$

Furthermore, we add a side condition to the rule DELAY in Figure 2, plus a new rule INV to deal with invariants:

$$\text{DELAY} \quad \frac{}{t\rho \xrightarrow{d} t(\rho + d)} \quad \rho + d' \models Inv(t) \text{ for any } 0 \leq d' \leq d$$

$$\text{INV} \quad \frac{t\rho \xrightarrow{a} t'\rho'}{(\{\phi\}t)\rho \xrightarrow{a} t'\rho'} \quad \rho \models \phi$$

For the symbolic transitional semantics, we simply forget the invariants (recall that symbolic transitions correspond to edges of automata, while invariants reside in nodes):

$$\text{INV} \quad \frac{t \xrightarrow{\psi,a,r} t'}{\{\phi\}t \xrightarrow{\psi,a,r} t'}$$

A slightly modified version of Lemma 2.3 holds:

Lemma 5.1. *1. If $t \xrightarrow{\phi,a,\mathbf{x}} t'$ then $t\rho \xrightarrow{a} t'\rho\{\mathbf{x} := 0\}$ for any $\rho \models \phi \wedge Inv(t)$.*
2. If $t\rho \xrightarrow{a} t'\rho'$ then there exist ϕ, $\mathbf{x}$ such that $\rho \models \phi \wedge Inv(t)$, $\rho' = \rho\{\mathbf{x} := 0\}$ and $t \xrightarrow{\phi,a,\mathbf{x}} t'$.

Definition 2.2 of timed bisimulation remains the same, since the intended effects of invariants have already been manifested in the the transition rules for the standard transitional semantics. On the other hand, the definition of symbolic timed bisimulation, Definition 3.4, should be modified slightly to accommodate invariants:

Definition 5.2. *A constraint indexed family of symmetric relations over terms $\mathbf{S} = \{ S^\phi \mid \phi \Uparrow\!-closed\}$ is a timed symbolic bisimulation if $(t,u) \in S^\phi$ implies*

1. *$\phi \Rightarrow (Inv(t) \Rightarrow Inv(u))$ and*
2. *whenever $t \xrightarrow{\psi,a,\mathbf{x}} t'$ then there is a $Inv(t) \wedge \phi \wedge \psi$-partition Φ such that for each $\phi' \in \Phi$ there is $u \xrightarrow{\psi',a,\mathbf{y}} u'$ for some ψ', $\mathbf{y}$ and u' such that $\phi' \Rightarrow \psi'$ and $(t',u') \in S^{\phi'\downarrow_{\mathbf{xy}}\Uparrow}$.*

We write $t \sim^\phi u$ if $(t,u) \in S^\phi \in \mathbf{S}$ for some symbolic bisimulation $\mathbf{S}$.

We have the counterpart of Theorem 3.5:

Theorem 5.3. *$t \sim^{\phi} u$ iff $t\rho \sim u\rho$ for any $\rho \models \phi$.*

The proof of this theorem is very similar to that of Theorem 3.5, with the uses of Lemma 2.3 replaced by Lemma 5.1.

Concerning the proof system, we add a rule to deal with the construct $\{\phi\}t$:

$$\text{INV} \quad \frac{\phi \wedge \psi \rhd t = u \qquad \phi \wedge \neg\psi \rhd \{\mathsf{ff}\}\mathbf{0} = u}{\phi \rhd \{\psi\}t = u}$$

This rule appears similar to the GUARD rule. However, there is a crucial difference: When the guard ψ is false $\psi \rightarrow t$ behaves like $\mathbf{0}$, the process which is inactive but can allow time to pass; On the other hand, when the invariant ψ is false $\{\psi\}t$ behaves like $\{\mathsf{ff}\}\mathbf{0}$, the process usually referred to as *time-stop*, which is not only inactive but also "still", can not even let time elapse.

With these modifications the completeness result carries over to the new setting:

Theorem 5.4. *For recursion-free terms t and u in the extended language, $t \sim^{\phi} u$ implies $\vdash \phi \rhd t = u$.*

The proof uses the following normal form taking invariants into account:

$$\{\psi\}\sum_{i \in I} \phi_i \rightarrow a_i(\mathbf{x}_i).t_i$$

The technical details of the proof are almost the same as that of Theorem 4.7.

6 Conclusion

We have proposed a theory of symbolic bisimulation and presented a proof system for timed automata. Using conditional equations as judgments the proof system separates manipulation of time from reasoning about process equivalence. As a result the proof system is much simpler than purely equational formulation. It is shown that by generalising pure equational reasoning to a set of inference rules dealing with specific language constructs needed for timed automata, the standard monoid laws for bisimulation are sufficient for characterizing bisimulation in the timed world. This result agrees with the previous works on proof systems for value-passing processes [HL96] and for π-calculus [Lin94], providing a further evidence that the four monoid laws capture the essence of bisimulation.

The proof system presented in the current paper is complete only over finite timed automata, i.e. the subset of timed automata which do not involve loops. We conjecture that by adding a suitable version of *unique fixpoint induction* [Mil84], together with the standard laws for folding/unfolding recursions, a complete proof system for the whole set of timed automata can be achieved. A similar result has been reported in [AJ94] for regular timed CCS [Wan91]. We leave this as a topic for future research.

References

[AD94] R. Alur and D.L. Dill. A theory of timed automata. *Theoretical Computer Science*, 126:183–235, 1994.

[AJ94] L. Aceto and A. Jeffrey. A complete axiomatization of timed bisimulation for a class of timed regular behaviours. Report 4/94, Sussex University, 1994.

[Bor96] M. Boreale. Symbolic Bisimulation for Timed Processes. In *AMAST'96*, LNCS 1101 pp.321-335. Springer–Verlag. 1996.

[Cer92] K. Čeräns. Decidability of Bisimulation Equivalences for Parallel Timer Processes. In *CAV'92*, LNCS 663, pp.302-315. Springer–Verlag. 1992.

[DAB96] P.R. D'Argenio and Ed Brinksma. A Calculus for Timed Automata (Extended Abstract). In *FTRTFTS'96*, LNCS 1135, pp.110-129. Springer–Verlag. 1996.

[HL95] M. Hennessy and H. Lin. Symbolic bisimulations. *Theoretical Computer Science*, 138:353–389, 1995.

[HL96] M. Hennessy and H. Lin. Proof systems for message-passing process algebras. *Formal Aspects of Computing*, 8:408–427, 1996.

[Lin94] H. Lin. Symbolic bisimulations and proof systems for the π-calculus. Report 7/94, Computer Science, University of Sussex, 1994.

[Mil84] R. Milner. A complete inference system for a class of regular behaviours. *J. Computer and System Science*, 28:439–466, 1984.

[Mil89] R. Milner. *Communication and Concurrency.* Prentice-Hall, 1989.

[Wan91] Wang Yi. *A Calculus of Real Time Systems.* Ph.D. thesis, Chalmers University, 1991.

[WPD94] Wang Yi, Paul Pettersson, and Mats Daniels. Automatic Verification of Real-Time Communicating Systems By Constraint-Solving. In *Proc. of the 7th International Conference on Formal Description Techniques*, 1994.

Categorical Models for Intuitionistic and Linear Type Theory

Maria Emilia Maietti, Valeria de Paiva, and Eike Ritter*

School of Computer Science, University of Birmingham
Edgbaston, Birmingham B15 2TT, United Kingdom
{mem,vdp,exr}@cs.bham.ac.uk

Abstract. This paper describes the categorical semantics of a system of mixed intuitionistic and linear type theory (ILT). ILT was proposed by G. Plotkin and also independently by P. Wadler. The logic associated with ILT is obtained as a combination of intuitionistic logic with intuitionistic linear logic, and can be embedded in Barber and Plotkin's Dual Intuitionistic Linear Logic (DILL). However, unlike DILL, the logic for ILT lacks an explicit modality ! that translates intuitionistic proofs into linear ones. So while the semantics of DILL can be given in terms of monoidal adjunctions between symmetric monoidal closed categories and cartesian closed categories, the semantics of ILT is better presented via fibrations. These interpret double contexts, which cannot be reduced to linear ones. In order to interpret the intuitionistic and linear identity axioms acting on the same type we need fibrations satisfying the comprehension axiom.

1 Introduction

This paper arises from the need to fill a gap in the conceptual development of the xSLAM project. The xSLAM project is concerned with the design and implementation of abstract machines based on linear logic. For xSLAM we initially developed a linear λ-calculus by adding explicit substitutions to Barber and Plotkin's DILL [GdPR00]. We then considered the categorical models one obtains for both intuitionistic and linear logic with explicit substitutions on the style of Abadi et al. [GdPR99].

The DILL system [BP97] distinguishes between intuitionistic and linear variables: linear variables are used once during evaluation, intuitionistic ones arbitrarily often. This is a key feature for the optimisation which linear logic provides for the implementation of functional programming languages. But in DILL the intuitionistic implication is defined in terms of linear implication and the modality ! via the standard Girard translation, namely $A \to B = (!A) \multimap B$. This is not appropriate for implementations of functional languages. The reason is that in the translation of the simply-typed λ-calculus into DILL !'s occur only in types

* Research supported by EPSRC-grant GR/L28296 under the title "The eXplicit Substitution Linear Abstract Machine".

J. Tiuryn (Ed.): FOSSACS 2000, LNCS 1784, pp. 223–237, 2000.

$!A \multimap B$, and the linearity is in effect not used. Indeed, a function of this type is applied only to arguments with no free linear variables, and during the execution of the program these arguments will be substituted only for intuitionistic variables. Finally we want to detect immediately when a function is intuitionistic. Hence it is more appropriate to have both $\rightarrow$ and $\multimap$ as primitive operations and disregard !. This leads to consideration of the mixed intuitionistic and linear type theory (henceforth named ILT) described by Plotkin [Plo93] and Wadler [Wad90] obtained from DILL by (i) adding intuitionistic implication, and (ii) removing the modality ! from the type operators.

The syntactic behaviour of ILT is very similar to that of DILL. But when it comes to semantics, the situation is a little more complicated. It is not obvious how to restrict the idea of a symmetric monoidal adjunction, so that we capture all the behaviour of intuitionistic implication, without at the same time, importing all the machinery for modelling the modality !. But if we step back and look at our models for calculi of explicit substitution, we can see that modelling intuitionistic logic using fibrations can be combined with modelling (intuitionistic) linear logic using symmetric monoidal closed categories, and in a way that does not bring in all the machinery for !.

The expert reader will note that the fibration modelling of intuitionistic logic is only necessary for dealing with predicates and/or dependent types; and this paper is only concerned with propositional intuitionistic logic. However, fibration modelling does provide a means of adding linear type theory to intuitionistic type theory in the required way. This is the main result we establish in this paper.

The paper is organised as follows. In the first section we describe the calculus ILT. In the next section we define IL-indexed categories and prove soundness and completeness of ILT with respect to them. In the third section we show that ILT is the internal language of (a suitable restriction of) IL-indexed categories. Finally in the fourth section we add exponentials to these IL-indexed categories and we prove the equivalence between them and the models given by a symmetric monoidal adjunction between a symmetric monoidal closed category with finite products and a cartesian closed category that is the co-Kleisli category with respect to the comonad induced by the adjunction.

2 Intuitionistic and Linear Type Theory

The system of mixed intuitionistic and linear logic that we model in this paper, to be called Intuitionistic and Linear Type Theory or ILT for short, borrows from Girard's Logic of Unity the elegant idea of separating assumptions into two classes: intuitionistic, which can be freely duplicated (shared) or discarded (ignored); and linear, which are constrained to be used exactly once. Syntactically, this strict separation is achieved by maintaining judgements with double-sided ("dual") contexts $\Gamma \mid \Delta \vdash A$, where, as a convention, Γ and Δ contain non-linear (intuitionistic) and linear assumptions, respectively. Another distinguishing feature of ILT is that it has both intuitionistic ($A \rightarrow B$) and linear implications ($A \multimap B$), as well as additive ($A \& B$) and multiplicative ($A \otimes B$) conjunctions with their units (1 and I), but no modality (or exponential) types $!A$. This system should not be confused with BI the logic of bunched implications proposed by O'Hearn and Pym [OP99], whose propositional fragment has the same operators, but with very different behaviour.

The system ILT closest relative is Barber and Plotkin's DILL [BP97] and most of its syntactic properties can be easily derived from DILL's properties. But semantics is a different story: DILL's rather elegant semantics in terms of a monoidal adjunction between a symmetric monoidal closed category L and a cartesian closed category C is not suitable for ILT, as ILT has no terms (or morphisms) corresponding to the modality *per se*. For instance, ILT has no term corresponding to $\mathsf{id}\colon !A \to !A$. This section describes briefly the system ILT.

The set of types we shall work with is

$$A ::= G \mid A \multimap B \mid A \to B \mid A \otimes B \mid I \mid A \& B \mid T$$

The syntax of preterms is defined inductively by

$$\begin{aligned} M, N ::= {} & a \mid x \mid \lambda a^A.M \mid \lambda x^A.M \mid M\,{}_iN \mid M_l N \\ & \mid M \otimes N \mid \texttt{let}\ M\ \texttt{be}\ a \otimes b\ \texttt{in}\ N \mid (M, N) \mid \mathsf{Fst}(M) \mid \mathsf{Snd}(M) \\ & \mid \circ \mid \bullet \mid \texttt{let}\ M\ \texttt{be}\ \bullet\ \texttt{in}\ N \end{aligned}$$

where a and x range over countable sets of linear and intuitionistic variables, respectively. This distinction of variables is not strictly necessary, but we adopt it here to aid legibility. Because the two let-expressions behave so similarly we sometimes write $\texttt{let}\ M\ \texttt{be}\ p\ \texttt{in}\ N$ to cover both, where p is either $a \otimes b$ or $\bullet$. The typing rules for ILT are standard, see Table 1.

We have three kinds of equations, β and η-equations and commuting conversions. The last kind of equations, familiar in the setting of linear lambda-calculi, arise due to the form of η-rules for the tensor product and its unit. For the presentation of these equations we use contexts-with-holes, written $C[\_]$. They are given by the grammar

$$\begin{aligned} C[\_] ::= {} & \_ \mid \lambda a^A.C[\_] \mid \lambda x^A.C[\_] \mid C[\_]_i M \mid M_i C[\_] \mid C[\_]_l M \mid M_l C[\_] \\ & \mid C[\_] \otimes M \mid M \otimes C[\_] \mid \texttt{let}\ C[\_]\ \texttt{be}\ p\ \texttt{in}\ N \mid \texttt{let}\ M\ \texttt{be}\ p\ \texttt{in}\ C[\_] \end{aligned}$$

Note that this definition implies that there is exactly one occurrence of the symbol $\_$ in a context-with-hole $C[\_]$. The term $C[M]$ denotes the replacement of $\_$ in $C[\_]$ by M with the possible capture of free variables. This capture is the difference between the replacement of $\_$ and substitution for a free variable: If $C[\_]$ is the context-with-hole $(\lambda a^A.\_)$, then $C[a] = \lambda a^A.a$, whereas $(\lambda a^A.b)[a/b] = \lambda c^A.a$. The equations for ILT are given in Table 2.

Note that in ILT linear variables can move across the divisor of the context as expressed in the following lemma.

Lemma 1 *For every ILT derivable judgement* $\Gamma \mid a_1 : A_1, \ldots, a_n : A_n, \Sigma \vdash M : B$ *we can derive* $\Gamma, x_1 : A_1, \ldots, x_n : A_n \mid \Sigma \vdash M[x_1/a_1, \ldots x_n/a_n] : B$.

$$\Gamma \mid a : A \vdash a : A \qquad \Gamma, x : A \mid \_ \vdash x : A$$

$$\frac{\Gamma \mid \Delta, a : A \vdash M : B}{\Gamma \mid \Delta \vdash \lambda a^A.M : A \multimap B} \qquad \frac{\Gamma \mid \Delta_1 \vdash M : A \multimap B \quad \Gamma \mid \Delta_2 \vdash N : A}{\Gamma \mid \Delta \vdash M\,{}_l N : B}$$

$$\frac{\Gamma, x : A \mid \Delta \vdash M : B}{\Gamma \mid \Delta \vdash \lambda x^A.M : A \to B} \qquad \frac{\Gamma \mid \Delta \vdash M : A \to B \quad \Gamma \mid \_ \vdash N : A}{\Gamma \mid \Delta \vdash M\,{}_i N : B}$$

$$\frac{\Gamma \mid \Delta_1 \vdash M : A \quad \Gamma \mid \Delta_2 \vdash N : B}{\Gamma \mid \Delta \vdash M \otimes N : A \otimes B}$$

$$\frac{\Gamma \mid \Delta_1 \vdash M : A \otimes B \quad \Gamma \mid a : A, b : B, \Delta_2 \vdash N : C}{\Gamma \mid \Delta \vdash \texttt{let } M \texttt{ be } a \otimes b \texttt{ in } N : B}$$

$$\frac{\Gamma \mid \Delta \vdash M : A \quad \Gamma \mid \Delta \vdash N : B}{\Gamma \mid \Delta \vdash (M, N) : A \& B} \qquad \frac{\Gamma \mid \Delta \vdash M : A \& B}{\Gamma \mid \Delta \vdash \mathsf{Fst}(M) : A} \qquad \frac{\Gamma \mid \Delta \vdash M : A \& B}{\Gamma \mid \Delta \vdash \mathsf{Snd}(M) : B}$$

$$\frac{}{\Gamma \mid \emptyset \vdash \bullet : I} \qquad \frac{\Gamma \mid \Delta_1 \vdash M : I \quad \Gamma \mid \Delta_2 \vdash N : C}{\Gamma \mid \Delta \vdash \texttt{let } M \texttt{ be } \bullet \texttt{ in } N : C}$$

$$\frac{}{\Gamma \mid \Delta \vdash \circ : 1}$$

Where applicable Δ_1, Δ_2 are disjoint and Δ is a permutation of Δ_1, Δ_2.

Table 1. The typing rules of ILT

β-equations:

$$\begin{array}{rclrcl} (\lambda x{:}\,A.M)_i N &=& M[N/x] & (\lambda a{:}\,A.M)_l N &=& M[N/a] \\ \texttt{let } M \otimes N \texttt{ be } a \otimes b \texttt{ in } R &=& R[M/a, N/b] & \texttt{let } \bullet \texttt{ be } \bullet \texttt{ in } M &=& M \\ \mathsf{Fst}(M, N) &=& M & \mathsf{Snd}(M, N) &=& N \end{array}$$

η-equations:

$$\begin{array}{rclrcll} \lambda a : A.M_l a &=& M & \lambda x : A.M_i x &=& M & \text{if } x \notin FV(M) \\ \texttt{let } a \otimes b \texttt{ be } M \texttt{ in } a \otimes b &=& M & \texttt{let } \bullet \texttt{ be } M \texttt{ in } \bullet &=& M & \text{if } \Gamma \mid \Delta \vdash M : 1 \\ (\mathsf{Fst}(M), \mathsf{Snd}(M)) &=& M & \circ &=& M & \end{array}$$

Commuting conversions:

$$\begin{array}{rcl} \texttt{let } M \texttt{ be } * \texttt{ in } C[N] &=& C[\texttt{let } M \texttt{ be } * \texttt{ in } N] \\ \texttt{let } M \texttt{ be } a \otimes b \texttt{ in } C[N] &=& C[\texttt{let } M \texttt{ be } a \otimes b \texttt{ in } N] \end{array}$$

Table 2. The equations of ILT

3 Categorical Semantics of ILT

The basis for our categorical model of ILT is Ehrhard's notion of a D-category for modelling dependent types [Ehr88], which goes back to Lawvere's idea of hyperdoctrines satisfying the comprehension axiom [Law70]. Hyperdoctrines model many-sorted predicative logic, where predicates are indexed over sorts or sets. A suitable adjunction allows the interpretation of the comprehension axiom, that is the creation of a subset defined by a predicate indexed over a set. Ehrhard generalized this idea in terms of fibrations introducing D-categories to interpret the Calculus of Constructions [Ehr88]. Here we adopt D-categories to model ILT. The fact of no having type dependencies will be clearly expressed by some restrictions that we will put on the particular D-categories we use to prove that ILT is their internal language.

In order to make more explicit the structure we need to interpret our calculus we recall the definition of D-categories in terms of indexed categories, which are categorically equivalent to fibrations. A D-category is a split indexed category $E\colon \mathcal{B}^{op}\to\mathbf{Cat}$[1] where the base category $\mathcal{B}$ models contexts and the fibre over an object Γ models terms whose free variables are contained in the context modelled in Γ. We require both $\mathcal{B}$ and each fibre $E(\Gamma)$, for Γ in $\mathcal{B}$, to have *a terminal object* $\top$. We also require that for every f morphism in the base category $E(f)$ *preserves the terminal object.* The fibration associated to this indexed category is the projecting functor $p : Gr(E)\to\mathcal{B}$, where $Gr(E)$ is the Grothendieck completion (see also page 107 of [Jac99]). We recall that the objects of the Grothendieck completion of E are the couples (Γ, A) where Γ is an object of $\mathcal{B}$ and A is an object of $E(\Gamma)$. The morphisms of $Gr(E)$ between (Γ, A) and (Δ, C) are couples (f, h) where $f : \Gamma \to \Delta$ is a morphism in $\mathcal{B}$ and $h : A \to E(f)(C)$ is a morphism in $E(\Gamma)$. For every object Γ in $\mathcal{B}$ the category $E(\Gamma)$ is said the fibre of p under the object Γ.

The key construction of a D-category to interpret contexts and substitutions is the requirement called the "comprehension property" i.e. the requirement that the terminal object functor $\mathcal{T}\colon\mathcal{B}\to Gr(E)$ has got a *right adjoint* $G\colon Gr(E)\to\mathcal{B}$. Recall that the functor $\mathcal{T}$ is defined as follows: for every object Γ in the base category $\mathcal{B}$, $\mathcal{T}(\Gamma) \equiv (\Gamma, \top)$ and for every morphism f, $\mathcal{T}(f) \equiv (f, \mathsf{Id})$. Actually $\mathcal{T}$ is an embedding functor of the base category $\mathcal{B}$ into the fibres of E. The right adjoint to $\mathcal{T}$ assures that every object, which for example interprets a sequent $\Gamma \vdash A$ in the fibre over the object interpreting the context Γ, can be put in correspondence to a context, in the example Γ, A, in the base category. Moreover by $\mathcal{T}$ a morphism in the fibre corresponds to a morphism in the base category and this allows to model substitution by the re-indexing functor.

The idea for the model of ILT is to modify this setting to capture the separation between intuitionistic and linear variables in ILT (with their corresponding substitutions) and simultaneously to model the two identity axioms, i.e. the assumptions of intuitionistic and linear variables, acting on the same types. The

[1] Note that from now on when we refer to indexed categories we mean split indexed categories, i.e. the pseudofunctor towards **Cat** is actually a functor.

base category $\mathcal{B}$ models only the intuitionistic contexts of ILT, *i.e.*, objects in $\mathcal{B}$ model contexts $(\Gamma \mid \_)$. Each fibre over an object in $\mathcal{B}$ modelling a context $\Gamma \mid \_$ models terms $\Gamma \mid \Delta \vdash M{:}A$ for any context Δ. We require a terminal object in $\mathcal{B}$. The fibres are now symmetric monoidal closed categories with finite products (SMCP categories) and model the linear constructions of ILT. The functors between the fibres have to preserve the SMCP structure.

Since we no longer require each fibre to have a terminal object, we replace the right adjoint to the terminal object functor $\mathcal{T}$ by a right adjoint G to the unit functor $U{:}\mathcal{B}{\to}Gr(E)$, assigning to each object Γ in $\mathcal{B}$ the object (Γ, I). This right-adjoint G is the comprehension functor. In this way we obtain that morphisms in the base correspond to morphisms with domain I in the fibre, *i.e.*, terms with no free linear variables.

Now we can model substitution for intuitionistic variables by reindexing along morphisms in the base as usual: this adjunction $U \dashv G$ enforces the restriction that only terms with no free linear variables can be substituted for intuitionistic variables. Intuitionistic function spaces are modelled in the standard way by the right adjoint to weakening.

Definition 2 *Let $\mathcal{B}$ be a category with a terminal object $\top$. An* IL-indexed category *is a functor $E{:}\mathcal{B}^{op}{\to}$***Cat** *such that the following conditions are satisfied. (Note that we write $f * (-)$ for the application of the functor E to f, for any morphism f in $\mathcal{B}$.)*

(i) *$E(\Gamma)$ is a symmetric monoidal category with finite products, i.e. a SMCP category, for each object Γ of $\mathcal{B}$. Moreover for each morphism f in $\mathcal{B}$, the functor f^* preserves this SMCP structure on the nose, i.e. it is a SMCP functor.*
For every object Γ in $\mathcal{B}$, we denote the terminal object of $E(\Gamma)$ by $\top$, the unique map towards $\top$ from every object C of $E(\Gamma)$ by ter_C, the product of two objects A and B by $A \times B$, the projections by π_1 and π_2 and the unique map from A to $B \times C$ given two maps t and s from A to B and A to C respectively by $< t, s >$.

(ii) *For each object Γ of $\mathcal{B}$ the functor $U{:}\mathcal{B}{\to}Gr(E)$, given by $U(\Gamma) \equiv (\Gamma, I)$ and $U(f) \equiv (f, \mathsf{Id})$ has a right adjoint $G{:}Gr(E){\to}\mathcal{B}$. The object $G(\Gamma, A)$ is abbreviated $\Gamma.A$ in the sequel and the morphism $G(f, h)$ is written $f.h$. Furthermore $(\mathsf{Fst}, \mathsf{Snd}){:}(\Gamma.A, I){\to}(\Gamma, A)$ denotes the counit of this adjunction. The natural isomorphism between $\mathsf{Hom}_{Gr(E)}((-, I), (-, A))$ and $\mathsf{Hom}_{\mathcal{B}}(-, -.A)$ is denoted by $[-, -]$.*

(iii) *For every object Γ of $\mathcal{B}$ and A of $E(\Gamma)$, the functor $\mathsf{Fst}^*_A{:}E(\Gamma){\to}E(\Gamma.A)$ has a right adjoint $\Pi_A{:}E(\Gamma.A){\to}E(\Gamma)$. We will write in the sequel Cur^I for the natural isomorphism between $\mathrm{Hom}_{E(\Gamma.A)}(\mathsf{Fst}^*_A(B), C)$ and $\mathrm{Hom}_{E(\Gamma)}(B, \Pi_A(C))$ and App_I for its counit.*

(iv) *The Beck-Chevalley-condition for the adjunctions $\mathsf{Fst}^*_A \vdash \Pi_A$ is satisfied in the strict sense, i.e. the equation $f^*(\mathsf{Cur}^I_A(t)) = \mathsf{Cur}^I_A((f.\mathsf{Id})^*(t))$ holds for every $f{:}\Delta{\to}\Gamma$, $A \in E(\Gamma)$, $B \in E(\Gamma.A)$.*

Next, we define the interpretation of the ILT-calculus, which is the minimal ILT-theory corresponding to the notion of IL-indexed category.

Definition 3 *Given any IL-indexed category $E\colon \mathcal{B}^{op} \to \mathbf{Cat}$ we define a map $[\![-]\!]$ from types to objects in $E(\top)$, from intuitionistic contexts Γ to objects in $\mathcal{B}$, from linear contexts Δ to objects in $E(\top)$, from double contexts to objects of suitable fibres and from terms $\Gamma \mid \Delta \vdash M\colon A$ to morphisms $[\![M]\!]\colon [\![\Delta]\!] \to [\![A]\!]$ in $E([\![\Gamma]\!])$ by induction over the structure:*

(i) On intuitionistic and linear contexts respectively:

$$[\![-]\!] = \top \qquad [\![\Gamma, x\colon A]\!] = [\![\Gamma]\!].[\![A]\!] \qquad\qquad [\![-]\!] = I \qquad [\![\Delta, a\colon A]\!] = [\![\Delta]\!] \otimes [\![A]\!]$$

where I is the tensor-unit in the category $E(\top)$ and also $[\![\Delta]\!]$ and $[\![A]\!]$ are objects of $E(\top)$.
On double contexts: $[\![\Gamma \mid \Delta]\!] = \mathsf{Fst}^*_{[\![\Gamma]\!]}([\![\Delta]\!])$ because $[\![\Delta]\!]$ being a linear context is an object of $E(\top)$.

(ii) On types:

$$[\![A \to B]\!] = \Pi_{[\![A]\!]}.[\![B]\!] \qquad [\![A \multimap B]\!] = [\![A]\!] \multimap [\![B]\!] \qquad [\![A \otimes B]\!] = [\![A]\!] \otimes [\![B]\!]$$
$$[\![I]\!] = I \qquad [\![A \& B]\!] = [\![A]\!] \times [\![B]\!] \qquad [\![1]\!] = \top$$

(iii) On terms (assuming that $\Gamma = x_1\colon A_1, \ldots, x_n\colon A_n$):

$$[\![\Gamma, x\colon A \mid - \vdash x\colon A]\!] = \mathsf{Snd} \qquad\qquad [\![\Gamma | a\colon A \vdash a\colon A]\!] = \mathsf{Id}$$

$$\frac{[\![\Gamma \vdash M\colon A]\!] = t}{[\![\Gamma, x\colon B \vdash M\colon A]\!] = \mathsf{Fst} * t} \qquad\qquad [\![\Gamma \mid \Delta \vdash \circ : 1]\!] = ter_{[\![\Delta]\!]}$$

$$\frac{[\![\Gamma, x\colon A \mid \Delta \vdash M\colon B]\!] = t}{[\![\Gamma \mid \Delta \vdash \lambda x^A.M\colon A \to B]\!] = \mathsf{Cur}^I(t)} \qquad \frac{[\![\Gamma \mid \Delta \vdash M\colon A \to B]\!] = t \quad [\![\Gamma \mid - \vdash N\colon A]\!] = s}{[\![\Gamma \mid \Delta \vdash M_I N\colon B]\!] = \langle \mathsf{Id}, s\rangle * (\mathsf{App}_I \cdot t)}$$

$$\frac{[\![\Gamma \mid \Delta \vdash M\colon A]\!] = t \qquad [\![\Gamma \mid \Delta \vdash N\colon B]\!] = s}{[\![\Gamma \mid \Delta \vdash (M, N)\colon A \times B]\!] = < t, s >}$$

$$\frac{[\![\Gamma \mid \Delta \vdash M\colon A \times B]\!] = t}{[\![\Gamma \mid \Delta \vdash \mathsf{Fst}(M)\colon A]\!] = \pi_1(t)} \qquad \frac{[\![\Gamma \mid \Delta \vdash M\colon A \times B]\!] = t}{[\![\Gamma \mid \Delta \vdash \mathsf{Snd}(M)\colon B]\!] = \pi_2(t)}$$

$$\frac{[\![\Gamma \mid \Delta_1 \vdash M\colon A]\!] = t \qquad [\![\Gamma \mid \Delta_2 \vdash N\colon B]\!] = s}{[\![\Gamma \mid \Delta \vdash M \otimes N\colon A \otimes B]\!] = (t \otimes s) \cdot \pi}$$

$$\frac{[\![\Gamma \mid \Delta_1 \vdash M\colon A \times B]\!] = m \qquad [\![\Gamma \mid \Delta_2, a\colon A, b\colon B \vdash N\colon C]\!] = n}{[\![\Gamma \mid \Delta \vdash \texttt{let } M \texttt{ be } a \otimes b \texttt{ in } N\colon C]\!] = n \cdot (\mathsf{Id} \otimes m) \cdot \pi}$$

$$[\![\Gamma \mid \emptyset \vdash \bullet : I]\!] = \mathsf{Id} \qquad \frac{[\![\Gamma \mid \Delta_1 \vdash M\colon I]\!] = m \qquad [\![\Gamma \mid \Delta_2 \vdash N\colon C]\!] = n}{[\![\Gamma \mid \Delta \vdash \texttt{let } M \texttt{ be } \bullet \texttt{ in } N\colon C]\!] = n \cdot \psi \cdot (\mathsf{Id} \otimes m) \cdot \pi}$$

where ψ is one part of the isomorphism between $[\![\Delta_2]\!]$ and $[\![\Delta_2]\!] \otimes I$

$$\frac{[\![\Gamma \mid \Delta, a\colon A \vdash M\colon B]\!] = t}{[\![\Gamma \mid \Delta \vdash \lambda a^A.M\colon A \multimap B]\!] = \mathsf{Cur}^L(t)}$$

where Cur^L is the corresponding natural transformation for the adjunction between $(-) \otimes [\![A]\!]$ and $[\![A]\!] \multimap (-)$ in $E([\![\Gamma]\!])$

$$\frac{[\![\Gamma \mid \Delta_1 \vdash M: A \multimap B]\!] = t \qquad [\![\Gamma \mid \Delta_2 \vdash N: A]\!] = s}{[\![\Gamma \mid \Delta \vdash M_L N: B]\!] = \mathsf{App}_L \cdot (t \otimes s) \cdot \pi}$$

where App_L *is the counit of the right adjoint to tensor and* π *is the canonical morphism from* $[\![\Delta]\!]$ *to* $[\![\Delta_1]\!] \otimes [\![\Delta_2]\!]$.

Next, we turn to the soundness of this categorical semantics. As always, the key lemmata concern substitution. In particular they are needed to prove the validity of introduction and elimination rules regarding intuitionistic implication and of all the conversion rules involving substitution. As we have two kinds of substitution, we have to show two substitution lemmata, namely for substitution of intuitionistic and linear variables.

Lemma 4 *(i) Assume* $[\![\Gamma, x: A \mid \Delta \vdash M: B]\!] = t$ *and* $[\![\Gamma \mid \_ \vdash N: A]\!] = s$. *Then* $[\![\Gamma \mid \Delta \vdash M[N/x]: B]\!] = \langle \mathsf{Id}, s \rangle * t$.
(ii) Assume $[\![\Gamma \mid \Delta_1, a: A \vdash M: B]\!] = t$ *and* $[\![\Gamma \mid \Delta_2 \vdash N: A]\!] = s$. *Then* $[\![\Gamma \mid \Delta \vdash M[N/a]: B]\!] = t \cdot (\mathsf{Id} \otimes s) \cdot \pi$, *where* π *is the canonical morphism from* $[\![\Delta]\!]$ *to* $[\![\Delta_1 \otimes \Delta_2]\!]$.

Proof. Induction over the structure of M.

The soundness proof is now routine.

Theorem 5 *Given an IL- indexed category* $E: \mathcal{B}^{op} \to \mathbf{Cat}$ *under the above interpretation* $[\![]\!]$ *the following facts hold.*

(i) Assume $\Gamma \mid \Delta \vdash M: A$. *Then* $[\![\Gamma \mid \Delta \vdash M: A]\!]$ *is a morphism from* $[\![\Delta]\!]$ *to* $[\![A]\!]$ *in* $E([\![\Gamma]\!])$;
(ii) Assume $\Gamma \mid \Delta \vdash M = N: A$. *Then* $[\![\Gamma \mid \Delta \vdash M: A]\!] = [\![\Gamma \mid \Delta \vdash N: A]\!]$.

Now we turn to the completeness theorem.

Theorem 6 *If* $[\![\Gamma \mid \Delta \vdash M: A]\!] = [\![\Gamma \mid \Delta \vdash N: A]\!]$ *where* $[\![]\!]$ *is the above defined interpretation, for every IL- indexed category* $E: \mathcal{B}^{op} \to \mathbf{Cat}$ *and for every derived sequents* $\Gamma \mid \Delta \vdash M: A$ *and* $\Gamma \mid \Delta \vdash N: A$ *then we can derive in ILT* $\Gamma \mid \Delta \vdash M = N: A$.

Proof. As usual the proof is based on the construction of a term model out of ILT. Since the interpretation of ILT in the syntactic model turns out to be the identity then the completeness immediately follows.
First recall that in order to prove that two functors $U : \mathcal{B} \to Gr(E)$ and $G : Gr(E) \to \mathcal{B}$ define a right adjunction $U \dashv G$, we give two data: firstly, a natural transformation $\alpha_D : \mathsf{Hom}(U(-), D) \to \mathsf{Hom}(-, G(D))$ for each object D in $Gr(E)$, and secondly the co-unit, that is a natural transformation $\epsilon : U \cdot G \to 1$ such that for every object C in $\mathcal{B}$ and every f in $\mathsf{Hom}(U(C), D)$ we have $\epsilon_D \cdot U(\alpha_D(f)) = f$.

Now we proceed by defining the syntactic IL-indexed category starting from an ILT-theory, based on the ILT-calculus and possibly some ground types with the corresponding terms.

Definition 7 *Given an ILT-theory $\mathcal{T}$ with any set of ground types $\mathcal{G}$ we define the* syntactic IL- indexed category $F(\mathcal{T})$ *in the following way.*
The base category:

- *Objects of the base category $\mathcal{B}(\mathcal{T})$ are lists of types $(A_1, \ldots, A_n)$. The terminal object is the empty context $[\,]$.*
- *Morphisms from $(A_1, \ldots, A_n)$ to $(B_1, \ldots, B_m)$ are lists of terms $(M_1, \ldots, M_m)$ such that $x_1\colon A_1, \ldots, x_n\colon A_n \mid \_ \vdash M_i\colon B_i$ for some intuitionistic variables $x_1, \ldots, x_n$. We will write $\boldsymbol{A}$ for $(A_1, \ldots, A_n)$ whenever convenient.*
- *Two morphisms $(M_1, \ldots, M_m)$ and $(N_1, \ldots, N_m)$ from $(A_1, \ldots, A_n)$ to $(B_1, \ldots, B_m)$ supposing that $x_1\colon A_1, \ldots, x_n\colon A_n \mid \_ \vdash M_i\colon B_i$ and $y_1\colon A_1, \ldots, y_n\colon A_n \mid \_ \vdash N_i\colon B_i$ are equal if we derive $x_1\colon A_1, \ldots, x_n\colon A_n \vdash M_i = N_i[\boldsymbol{x}/\boldsymbol{y}]\colon B_i$. We will write $(\boldsymbol{M})$ for $(M_1, \ldots, M_m)$ whenever convenient.*
- *The identity morphism on $(\boldsymbol{A})$ is the list $(\boldsymbol{x})$;*
- *Composition is given by intuitionistic substitution: given morphisms $(M_1, \ldots,$*
$M_m)$ from $(A_1, \ldots, A_n)$ to $(B_1, \ldots, B_m)$ with $x_1\colon A_1, \ldots, x_n\colon A_n \mid \_ \vdash M_i\colon B_i$ and $(N_1, \ldots, N_n)$ from $(C_1, \ldots, C_k)$ to $\boldsymbol{A}$ such that $y_1\colon C_1, \ldots, y_k\colon C_k \mid \_ \vdash N_j\colon A_j$, we define $\boldsymbol{M} \cdot \boldsymbol{N}$ to be $(M_1[\boldsymbol{N}/\boldsymbol{x}], \ldots, M_m[\boldsymbol{N}/\boldsymbol{x}])$.

The fibres:

- *The objects of the fibres of $E(\boldsymbol{A})$ are types A.*
- *A morphism from A to B in $E(\boldsymbol{A})$ is a term M such that $x_1\colon A_1, \ldots, x_n\colon A_n \mid a\colon A \vdash M\colon B$. Two morphisms M and N from A to B in $E(\boldsymbol{A})$ such that $x_1\colon A_1, \ldots, x_n\colon A_n \mid a\colon A \vdash M\colon B$ and $y_1\colon A_1, \ldots, y_n\colon A_n \mid b\colon A \vdash N\colon B$ are equal if we derive $\boldsymbol{x}\colon \boldsymbol{A} \mid a\colon A \vdash M = N[\boldsymbol{x}/\boldsymbol{y}, a/b]\colon B$.*
- *For any morphism $\boldsymbol{M}$ from $\boldsymbol{A}$ to $\boldsymbol{B}$, the functor $E(\boldsymbol{M})$ is the identity on the objects and transforms any morphism M with $\boldsymbol{y}\colon \boldsymbol{B} \mid a\colon A \vdash M\colon B$ to $M[\boldsymbol{M}/\boldsymbol{y}]$.*

The structure in a fibre is given in the following.

- *The tensor product of two objects A and B in the fibre $E(\boldsymbol{A})$ is the type $A \otimes B$. The tensor product of two morphisms M and N in $E(\boldsymbol{A})$ is the term* `let` $a \otimes b$ `be` z `in` $M \otimes N$ *if $x_1\colon A_1, \ldots, x_n\colon A_n \mid a\colon A \vdash M\colon B$ and $y_1\colon A_1, \ldots, y_n\colon A_n \mid b\colon A \vdash N\colon B$.*
- *The unit of the category $E(\boldsymbol{A})$ is given by the type I.*
- *The product and terminal object in $E(\boldsymbol{A})$ are given by the products and the type 1 in the syntax in the standard way.*
- *The right adjoint to the tensor product in $E(\boldsymbol{A})$ is given by the natural transformation mapping the morphism M from $C \otimes A$ to B to $\lambda a\colon A.M[c \otimes a/b]$ where $\boldsymbol{x}\colon \boldsymbol{A} \mid b\colon C \otimes A \vdash M\colon B$; the co-unit is the natural transformation whose component at the object B is given by the morphism* `let` $a \otimes b$ `be` c `in` ab *with $\boldsymbol{x}\colon \boldsymbol{A} \mid c\colon A \multimap B \otimes A \vdash$* `let` $a \otimes b$ `be` c `in` $ab\colon B$.

The comprehension property:

- *The right adjoint G to the functor U is given by*

$$G(((A_1,\dots A_n),A)) = (A_1,\dots,A_n,A)$$
$$G(((M_1,\dots M_n),M)) = (M_1,\dots,M_n,M[x/a])$$

if $\boldsymbol{x}{:}\,\boldsymbol{A} \mid a{:}\,A \vdash M{:}\,B$, since by lemma 1 we can derive $\boldsymbol{x}{:}\,\boldsymbol{A}, x{:}\,A \mid \vdash M[x/a]{:}\,B$. For any morphism $((M_1,\dots M_n),M)$ with $\boldsymbol{x}{:}\,\boldsymbol{A} \mid a{:}\,I \vdash M{:}\,B$ the natural isomorphism $[\boldsymbol{M},M]$ is $(M_1,\dots,M_n,M[\bullet/a])$. The co-unit for the object $((A_1,\dots,A_n),A)$ is the morphism $((x_1,\dots,x_n),\texttt{let} * \texttt{be}\ a\ \texttt{in}\ x)$.

The intuitionistic function space:

- *The right adjoint to $\mathsf{Fst}^*{:}\,E(\boldsymbol{A}){\rightarrow}E((\boldsymbol{A},A))$ is the functor $\Pi_A(-){:}\,E((\boldsymbol{A},A)){\rightarrow}E(\boldsymbol{A})$ which maps every object C of $E((\boldsymbol{A},A))$ to $A \rightarrow C$ and every morphism M in $E((\boldsymbol{A},A))$ to $\lambda x^A.M$. The natural transformation Cur^I maps the morphism M from C to B in $E(\boldsymbol{A},A)$ to $\lambda x{:}\,A.M$ if $\boldsymbol{x}{:}\,\boldsymbol{A}, x{:}\,A \mid \_ \vdash M{:}\,B$; the co-unit is the natural transformation whose component at the object B is given by the term ax where $\boldsymbol{x}{:}\,\boldsymbol{A}, x{:}\,A \mid a{:}\,A \rightarrow B \vdash ax{:}\,B$.*

Note the subtle difference in the definition of the base category and the fibre: we define objects in the base category to be lists of types, whereas objects in the fibre are singleton types. Having products in the calculus, we could have chosen a uniform definition and defined the objects of $\mathcal{B}$ to be types rather than lists of types. However, this means we would need to use projections in the syntax to access the components of the product, which is rather cumbersome. In contrast we have no choice for the definition of the fibres but to use types as objects. The reason is that with the other choice there is no way of turning the fibre into a symmetric monoidal closed category, as there is no way of defining $C{\multimap}A{\otimes}B$ in terms of $C{\multimap}A$ and $C{\multimap}B$. This is not problem for a cartesian closed category, as in this case we have $C \rightarrow A \times B \equiv (C \rightarrow A) \times (C \rightarrow B)$.

The key part of the completeness theorem is the following proposition, whose proof is a routine verification:

Proposition 8 *For any ILT-theory $\mathcal{T}$ the syntactic IL-indexed category $F(\mathcal{T})$ is an IL-indexed category.*

The syntactic IL-indexed category allow us to prove completeness for ILT with respect to IL-indexed categories.

4 ILT as an Internal Language

Starting from the above soundness and completeness theorems we want to see if ILT is actually an internal language of IL-indexed categories. To this purpose we define the following categories $\mathsf{TH}(ILT)$ and **IL-ind**.

Definition 9 *The objects of* $\mathsf{TH}(ILT)$ *are the ILT-theories, i.e. type theories whose inference rules include the ILT ones. The morphisms are translations that send types to types so as to preserve* $I, \top, \otimes, \&, \multimap, \rightarrow$. *They send terms to terms so as to preserve the introduction and elimination constructors corresponding to the above types and they send intuitionistic (linear) variables to intuitionistic (linear) variables respecting their typability such that the typability judgement and equality between terms are preserved.*

Definition 10 *The objects of the category* **IL-ind** *are IL-indexed categories and the morphisms between* $E: \mathcal{B}^{op} \rightarrow \mathbf{Cat}$ *and* $E': \mathcal{B}'^{op} \rightarrow \mathbf{Cat}$ *are given by a functor* $H : \mathcal{B} \rightarrow \mathcal{B}'$ *preserving the terminal object and a natural transformation* $\alpha : E \Rightarrow E' \cdot H$ *such that for every object* Δ *in* $\mathcal{B}$ $\alpha_\Delta : E(\Delta) \rightarrow E'(H(\Delta))$ *is a SMCP-functor. Finally the comprehension adjunction is preserved and the intuitionistic function spaces too as expressed by the conditions described in the following (where we differentiate the structure of* E *from that one of* E' *with the prime).*

1. *For every object* Δ *in* $\mathcal{B}$ *and* A *in* $E(\Delta)$, *and for every morphism* $(f, t) : (\Delta, A) \rightarrow (\Gamma, C)$ *in* $Gr(E)$ *we have* $H(G(\Delta, A)) = G'(H(\Delta), \alpha_\Delta(A))$ *and* $H(G(f, t)) = G'(H(f), \alpha_\Delta(t))$.
2. *For every* $(f, t) : (\Delta, I) \rightarrow (\Gamma, C)$ $H([f, t]) = [(H(f), \alpha_\Delta(t))]'$
3. *For every object* Δ *in* $\mathcal{B}$, A *in* $E(\Delta)$ *and* C *in* $E(\Delta.A)$ *and every morphism* f *in* $E(\Delta.A)$ *we have that* $\alpha_\Delta(\Pi_A(C)) = \Pi_{\alpha_\Delta(A)}(\alpha_{\Delta.A}(C))$ *and* $\alpha_\Delta(\mathsf{Cur}^I(f)) = \mathsf{Cur}^{I'}(\alpha_{\Delta.A}(f))$.

Formally the fact that ILT is the internal language of our IL-indexed categories is proved by providing an equivalence between the category of ILT-theories $\mathsf{TH}(ILT)$ and that one of IL-indexed categories **IL-ind**. But we can prove the above equivalence only if we put some restrictions on the IL-indexed categories.

Definition 11 *An IL-indexed category* $E: \mathcal{B}^{op} \rightarrow \mathbf{Cat}$, *is a restricted IL-indexed category if the following conditions hold:*

1. *for every object* $\Delta \in Ob(\mathcal{B})$, *meaning with* $\iota_\Delta : \Delta \rightarrow \top$ *the unique map towards the terminal object* $\top$ *in* $\mathcal{B}$, *the functor* $E(\iota_\Delta) : E(\top) \rightarrow E(\Delta)$ *is bijective on the objects;*
2. *the right adjoint* G *restricted to the fibres of* $\top$ *corresponding to* $E(\top)$ *is bijective on the objects;*

Finally we call **rIL-ind** the full subcategory of **IL-ind** whose object are restricted IL-indexed categories.
Now we are ready to prove the following:

Proposition 12 *There exist two functors* $L : \mathsf{TH}(ILT) \rightarrow$ **rIL-ind** *and* $F :$ **rIL-ind** $\rightarrow \mathsf{TH}(ILT)$ *that give rise to an equivalence between* $\mathsf{TH}(ILT)$ *and* **rIL-ind**.

Proof. Given an ILT-theory $\mathcal{T}$ we define $F(\mathcal{T})$ in an analogous way to the definition of the syntactic ILT-category in Definition 7, but we take $\mathcal{B}(\mathcal{T})$ to be the category whose objects are the ILT-types and whose morphisms between the types A and C are $x : A \mid \vdash c : C$. Hence we define $G((A, B)) \equiv A\&B$. We can easily see that $F(\mathcal{T})$ is a restricted IL-indexed category.
We can obviously lift any translation to become a morphism between IL-indexed categories. Given an IL-indexed category $E: \mathcal{B}^{op} \to \mathbf{Cat}$ we now define an ILT-theory $L(E)$ out of it in the following way:

Definition 13 *The language of $L(E)$ is defined as follows:*

1. *the types of $L(E)$ are the objects of the fibre $E(\top)$;*
2. *the preterms of $L(E)$ are the morphisms of $E(\Delta)$ for every object Δ of $\mathcal{B}$;*
3. *The inference rules are defined as the interpretation function in the Definition 3. Note that two typed terms represented by two morphisms in the same fibre are equal if they are equal as morphisms.*

The functor L can be easily extended on the morphisms of IL-indexed categories to define translations. What remains to be checked is that the two compositions $L \cdot F$ and $F \cdot L$ are naturally isomorphic to the corresponding identity functors. For every ILT-theory $\mathcal{T}$ it is easy to check that $L(F(\mathcal{T}))$ can be translated into $\mathcal{T}$ via a natural isomorphism.

For every restricted IL-indexed category $E: \mathcal{B}^{op} \to \mathbf{Cat}$ we prove that $F(L(E))$ is equivalent to E by the added requirements on IL-indexed categories. The base category $\mathcal{B}$ is equivalent to the $\mathcal{B}(F(L(E)))$ since by the comprehension adjunction with respect to E together with the first requirement we can build a faithful, full and surjective functor from $\mathcal{B}(F(L(E)))$ towards $\mathcal{B}$. The natural transformation on each fibre is given by the projecting functors on the objects and by the identity on morphisms. The components of this natural transformations are really isomorphisms by the second requirement on the restricted indexed category.

Note that the internal language could be naturally enriched with explicit substitutions on terms to represent the composition in the fibre by explicit substitutions of linear variables and the morphism assignment of E by explicit substitutions of intuitionistic variables. But if we want to interpret explicit substitution operations on contexts in a different way from those on terms, then we need to add another fibration to each SMCP fibre in the style of [GdPR99], passing to a complicated doubly indexed category.

Moreover, observe that every categorical model defined by Benton [Ben95] given by a symmetric monoidal adjunction $F \vdash K$ with $F : \mathcal{C} \to \mathcal{S}$, $\mathcal{C}$ a cartesian closed category, $\mathcal{S}$ a symmetric monoidal closed category with finite products, provides an IL-indexed category, by taking as a base the cartesian closed category $\mathcal{C}$ and as the fibre over an object C of the base the symmetric monoidal closed category with finite products whose objects are those of $\mathcal{S}$ but whose morphism from A to B are the $\mathcal{S}$-morphism $F(C)\otimes A \multimap B$. The intuitionistic space between A and B is given by the usual $F(A) \multimap B$.

Then, if the adjunction $F \vdash K$ satisfies the requirement that $\mathcal{C}$ is the co-Kleisli category with respect to the comonad induced by the adjunction and K the embedding functor via the counit, the above IL-indexed category is also restricted.

5 The Connection to the Exponentials

In this section we show how to regain exponentials. We characterise exponentials by a universal construction, namely as the left adjunction to the functor which replaces all linear variables in a term by the intuitionistic ones.
Note that since ILT is the internal language of a restricted IL-indexed category, its base category is actually cartesian closed so we can give the following definition to get exponentials:

Definition 14 *An* **rIL-indexed category with exponentials** *is a restricted IL-indexed category* $E\colon \mathcal{B}^{\mathrm{op}} \to \mathbf{Cat}$ *such that the functor* $\mathcal{I}\colon E(\top) \to \mathcal{B}$ *given by* $\mathcal{I}(A) = \top.A$, $\mathcal{I}(t) = id.t$ *has a symmetric monoidal left adjoint to form a symmetric monoidal adjunction. We write* ! *for the left adjoint.*

Note that $\mathcal{I}$ is a monoidal functor by using the internal language. It is also possible to define the exponentials by the condition $\mathsf{Hom}_{E(\Gamma)}(!^*A, B) \cong \mathsf{Hom}_{E(\Gamma\cdot A)}(I, B)$ plus a Beck-Chevalley-condition [HS99]. It is easy to see that these two definitions are equivalent: if you specialise the second condition to the case $\Gamma = \top$ and use the adjunction between $\mathcal{B}$ and $Gr(E)$ putting $!(\top.A) \equiv !^*(A)$, you obtain the first condition by the first requirement of restricted indexed categories. The converse argument goes as follows:

$$\begin{aligned}
&\mathsf{Hom}_{E(\Gamma)}(!^*A, B) \cong \mathsf{Hom}_{E(\Gamma)}(I, !^*A \multimap B) \cong \mathsf{Hom}_{\mathcal{B}}(\Gamma, \top.(!^*A \multimap B))\\
&\cong \mathsf{Hom}_{E(\top)}(!\Gamma, !^*A \multimap B) \cong \mathsf{Hom}_{E(\top)}(!\Gamma \otimes !^*A, B) \cong \mathsf{Hom}_{E(\top)}(!(\Gamma \times (\top.A)), B)\\
&\cong \mathsf{Hom}_{\mathcal{B}}(\Gamma.A, \top.B) \cong \mathsf{Hom}_{E(\Gamma\cdot A)}(I, B)
\end{aligned}$$

where the second-but-last equivalence uses the fact that the adjunction between $E(\top)$ and $\mathcal{B}$ is monoidal.

It is instructive to examine the relation between a rIL-indexed category and certain Benton's linear-nonlinear categories as expressed in the following.

Definition 15 *The category* $\mathbf{Ben}_r$ *has as objects Benton's models* $F \vdash K$ *[Ben95], i.e. a symmetric monoidal adjunction between a cartesian closed category* $\mathcal{C}$ *and a symmetric monoidal closed category with finite products* $\mathcal{S}$ *where* $F : \mathcal{C} \to \mathcal{S}$*, such that* $\mathcal{C}$ *is the co-Kleisli category with respect to the comonad induced by the adjunction and* K *is the embedding functor via the counit. The morphisms between* $F \dashv K$ *and* $F' \vdash K'$*, with* $F : \mathcal{C} \to \mathcal{S}$ *and* $F' : \mathcal{C}' \to \mathcal{S}'$*, are functors* $M : \mathcal{S} \to \mathcal{S}'$ *preserving the SMCP structure and the symmetric monoidal comonad.*

We recall that the category **Ben** of Benton's models and couples of functors (H_1, H_2) with $H_1 : \mathcal{S} \to \mathcal{S}'$, $H_2 : \mathcal{C} \to \mathcal{C}'$ commuting with the adjoints and preserving the monoidal adjunction has $\mathbf{Ben}_r$ as a co-reflective subcategory:

$$\mathbf{Ben}_r \; \underset{R}{\overset{I}{\rightleftarrows}} \; \mathbf{Ben}$$

assigning to each Benton's model the corresponding one given by the monoidal adjunction with the co-Kleisli category. Morever note that the category $\mathbf{Ben}_r$ is equivalent to the category $\mathbf{Bier}$ of Bierman's models (see [Bie94]) with functors preserving the relevant structure.

Definition 16 *The category* **rIL-indE** *has restricted IL-indexed categories as objects and as morphisms IL-morphisms preserving the adjunction that define exponentials, i.e. a morphism between* $E : \mathcal{B}^{op} \to \mathbf{Cat}$ *and* $E' : \mathcal{B}'^{op} \to \mathbf{Cat}$ *is a rIL-ind morphism given by* $H : B \to \mathcal{B}'$ *and* $\alpha : E \Rightarrow E' \cdot H$ *such that it also satisfies the following conditions:*

- *for every object Δ in $\mathcal{B}$, $!H(\Delta) = \alpha_\top(!\Delta)$;*
- *for every object Δ in $\mathcal{B}$ and A in $E(\top)$ and for every morphism $t : \Delta \to I(A)$ in $\mathcal{B}$, $\phi'(H(t)) = \alpha_\top(\phi(t))$, where ϕ' and ϕ are the bijections of the corresponding adjunctions.*

Proposition 17 *The category* $\mathbf{Ben}_r$ *of suitable Benton's models is equivalent to the category* **rIL − indE**.

Proof. We already saw how every linear-nonlinear category in $\mathbf{Ben}_r$ gives rise to an rIL-indexed category in section 4. The exponentials in Benton's setting satisfy the universal property for exponentials in a rIL-indexed category with exponentials. Conversely, any rIL-indexed category with exponentials $E : \mathcal{B} \to \mathbf{Cat}$ gives rise to a linear-nonlinear category: the symmetric monoidal closed category is $E(\top)$, and the cartesian closed category is the base category $\mathcal{B}$, which we prove to be cartesian closed by means of its internal language ILT. Now we can observe by the internal language that the adjunction $! \vdash I$ gives rise to a symmetric monoidal adjunction between $E(\top)$ and $\mathcal{B}$. Using the equivalence between the two definitions of exponentials given above one shows that these functors define an equivalence.

By the above proposition we conclude that we can embed the category $\mathbf{Ben}$ into the category **IL-ind** through the reflection into $\mathbf{Ben}_r$, as an alternative to the embedding into **IL-ind** obtained by taking the cartesian closed category of a Benton's model as the base category of the indexed category.

$$
\begin{array}{ccccc}
\mathbf{Bier} & \overset{\simeq}{\longrightarrow} & \mathbf{Ben}_r & \underset{R}{\overset{I}{\rightleftarrows}} & \mathbf{Ben} \\
& & \downarrow{\scriptstyle\simeq} & & \downarrow \\
& & \mathbf{rIL-indE} & \hookrightarrow \; \mathbf{rIL-ind} \; \hookrightarrow & \mathbf{IL-ind}
\end{array}
$$

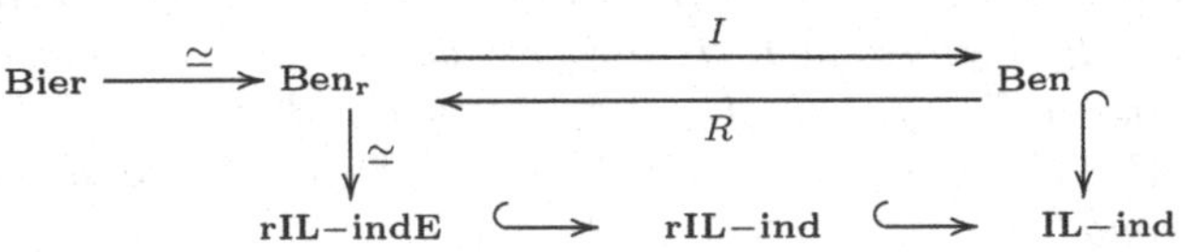

Here we could also prove that **rIL-indE** is a reflective subcategory of **rIL-ind**, whose reflection is given by freely adding the ! modality to the internal language of a rIL-indexed category and then considering the syntactic category associated.

In the context of Benton's model, once the SMCP category $\mathcal{S}$ is fixed one is free to choose a functor $F : \mathcal{C} \to \mathcal{S}$ to represent exponentials. In the context of rIL-indexed categories with exponentials the choice of F is determined by the choice of the indexed category E, that is the substitution along intuitionistic variables.

6 Conclusion

We have produced a sound and complete model for the type theory ILT. Moreover we showed that, with a suitable restriction, IL-categories are the internal language for this type theory. The reasons for developing ILT are of a pragmatic nature: in applications within linear functional programming, it seems a good idea to have both intuitionistic and linear implication co-existing, instead of having intuitionistic implication a derived operation, obtained from Girard's translation.

We hope to find a good representation in terms of one-dimensional categories for IL-indexed categories. Maybe in order to achieve this we need to extend ILT with a connective reflecting the logical role of the operation "|" acting on ILT-contexts.

References

[Ben95] Nick Benton. A mixed linear and non-linear logic: Proofs, terms and models. In *Proceedings of Computer Science Logic '94, Kazimierz, Poland.* LNCS No. 933, Berlin, Heidelberg, New York, 1995.

[Bie94] G. Bierman. What is a categorical model of intuitionistic linear logic? In *Proc. of the Second International Conference on Typed Lambda Calculus and Applications.*, volume 902 of *Lecture Notes in Computer Science.* Springer Verlag, 1994.

[BP97] A. Barber and G. Plotkin. Dual intuitionistic linear logic. Technical report, LFCS, University of Edinburgh, 1997.

[Ehr88] Th. Ehrhard. A categorical semantics of constructions. In Computer Science Press, editor, *Logic in Computer Science*, IEEE, pages 264–273, 1988.

[GdPR99] Neil Ghani, Valeria de Paiva, and Eike Ritter. Categorical models of explicit subsitutions. In *Proc. of FoSSaCS'99*, volume 1578 of LNCS, 1999.

[GdPR00] N. Ghani, V. de Paiva, and E. Ritter. Linear explicit substitutions. *Journal of the IGPL*, to appear 2000.

[HS99] Martin Hofmann and Thomas Streicher. Personal communication, 1999.

[Jac99] B. Jacobs. *Categorical Logic and Type Theory.*, volume 141 of *Studies in Logic.* Elsevier, 1999.

[Law70] F.W. Lawvere. Equality in hyperdoctrines and comprehension schema as an adjoint functor. *Proc. Sympos. Pure Math.*, XVII:1–14, 1970.

[OP99] P. O'Hearn and D.J. Pym. The logic of bunched implications. *Bulletin of Symbolic Logic*, 5(2):215–244, 1999.

[Plo93] G.D. Plotkin. Type theory and recursion. In *Proc. of Logic in Computer Science*, 1993.

[Wad90] P. Wadler. Linear types can change the world! In M. Broy and C. Jones, editors, *Programming Concepts and Methods*, 1990.

Locality and Polyadicity in Asynchronous Name-Passing Calculi

Massimo Merro*

INRIA Sophia-Antipolis, France

Abstract. We give a *divergence-free* encoding of polyadic *Local* π into its monadic variant. Local π is a sub-calculus of asynchronous π-calculus where the recipients of a channel are local to the process that has created the channel. We prove the encoding *fully-abstract* with respect to barbed congruence. This implies that in Local π (i) polyadicity does not add extra expressive power, and (ii) when studying the theory of polyadic Local π we can focus on the simpler monadic variant. Then, we show how the idea of our encoding can be adapted to name-passing calculi with *non-binding input prefix*, such as *Chi*, *Fusion* and πF *calculi*.

1 Introduction

Local π, in short Lπ, is a variant of the asynchronous π-calculus [11, 5] where the recipients of a channel are local to the process that has created the channel. More precisely, in a process $(\boldsymbol{\nu} a)\, P$ all possible inputs at a appear – and are syntactically visible – in P; no further inputs may be created, inside or outside P. The locality property of channels is achieved by imposing that only the output capability of names may be transmitted, i.e., the recipient of a name may only use it in output actions. Lπ is a very expressive fragment of asynchronous π-calculus, and its theory has been studied in [15]; similar calculi are discussed, or at least mentioned, in [12, 4, 1, 30]. Lπ borrows ideas from some experimental programming languages (or proposals of programming languages), most notably Pict [20], Join [8], and Blue [6], and can be regarded as a basis for them (the restriction on output capabilities is not explicit in Pict, but, as we understand from the Pict users, most Pict programs obey it). The locality property makes Lπ particularly suitable for giving the semantics to, and reasoning about, concurrent or distributed object-oriented languages [14]. For instance, the locality property can guarantee unique identity of objects – a fundamental feature of objects.

As for most name-passing calculi, the theoretical developments on Lπ have been conducted on a monadic calculus, that is, a calculus in which only single names can be transmitted. On the other hand, most applications in name-passing calculi use polyadic communications, i.e., communications involving tuples of names. So, an interesting issue is to investigate whether monadic and polyadic name-passing calculi have the same expressive power. In this paper we show that,

* Funded by the European Union, under the Marie Curie TMR programme.

J. Tiuryn (Ed.): FOSSACS 2000, LNCS 1784, pp. 238–251, 2000.

under the locality hypothesis on channels, monadic and polyadic π-calculi have the same expressive power. More precisely, we give an encoding $\langle\!\langle \cdot \rangle\!\rangle$ of polyadic Lπ into monadic Lπ, and we prove it *fully-abstract* with respect to *barbed congruence* [18]. Our encoding is *divergence-free*, that is, it does not introduce infinite internal computations. Furthermore, we show how the idea of our encoding can be easily adapted to name-passing calculi with *non-binding input prefix*, such as *Chi calculus* [9], *Fusion calculus* [19] and πF-*calculus* [10], and we propose a simple encoding of polyadicity for these calculi.

The first attempt of encoding polyadicity in name-passing calculi is by Robin Milner [16]. Milner gives a simple encoding of polyadic into monadic synchronous π-calculus. Milner's encoding is not fully-abstract. In order to recover the full abstraction Yoshida [29], and Quaglia and Walker [21], have introduced two different *type systems* for monadic processes which model the communication protocol underlying Milner's encoding. A different approach has been followed by Gonthier and Fournet in the *Join-calculus* [8], an "extended subset" of the asynchronous π-calculus. In [8], among other results, a direct, although complex, fully-abstract encoding of polyadic processes into monadic ones is proposed. All these approaches will be discussed at the end of the paper.

In this extended abstract proofs are just sketched; complete proofs can be found in [13].

Outline The paper is structured as follows. In Section 2 we describe the polyadic Lπ calculus giving some properties of it; in Section 3 we recall a few correctness criteria for encodings; in Section 4 we present the encoding of polyadic Lπ into monadic Lπ; in Section 5 we prove the full abstraction of the encoding; in Section 6 we investigate other possible encodings of polyadicity in Lπ; in Section 7 we show how the idea of our encoding can be adapted in name-passing calculi with non-binding input prefix; in Section 8 we conclude and discuss related works.

2 The Polyadic Lπ

Polyadic Lπ, in short L$\widetilde{\pi}$, is an asynchronous fragment of Milner's polyadic π-calculus [16]. We use small letters $a, b, c, \ldots, x, y$ for *names*; capital letters P, Q, R for *processes*; and $\widetilde{a}$ to denote a tuple of names $a_1, \ldots, a_n$. L$\widetilde{\pi}$ has operators of inaction, input prefix, asynchronous output, parallel composition, restriction and replicated input:

$$P ::= \mathbf{0} \;\Big|\; a(\widetilde{x}).\,P \;\Big|\; \overline{a}\langle\widetilde{b}\rangle \;\Big|\; P \mid P \;\Big|\; (\nu a)\,P \;\Big|\; !a(\widetilde{x}).\,P$$

where in input processes $a(\widetilde{x}).\,P$ names in $\widetilde{x}$ are all distinct and may not occur free in P in input position. This syntactic constraint ensures that only the output capability of names may be transmitted.

We use σ for *substitutions*; $P\sigma$ is the result of applying σ to P, with the usual renaming convention to avoid captures; $\{\widetilde{b}/\widetilde{a}\}$ is the simultaneous substitution of names $\widetilde{a}$ with names $\widetilde{b}$. Parallel composition has the lowest precedence among the operators, and $\prod_n P_n$ is an abbreviation for the process $P_1 \mid \ldots \mid P_n$. We write $(\nu\tilde{a})\, P$ for $(\nu a_1) \ldots (\nu a_n)\, P$ and $\overline{a}b$ for $\overline{a}\langle b\rangle$. The *labeled transition system* is the usual one (in the late style [17]). *Structural congruence*, written $\equiv$ and defined as usual (see [16]), allows us to ignore certain structural differences between processes. Transitions are of the form $P \xrightarrow{\mu} P'$, where *action* μ can be: τ (interaction); $a(\tilde{b})$ (input); $(\nu\tilde{c})\, \overline{a}\langle\tilde{b}\rangle$ (output) where $\tilde{c} \subseteq \tilde{b}$ and $\overline{a}(\tilde{b})$ is an abbreviation for $(\nu\tilde{b})\, \overline{a}\langle\tilde{b}\rangle$. In these actions, a is the *subject* and $\tilde{b}$ the *object*. We write $\xrightarrow{\hat{\mu}}$ to mean $P \xrightarrow{\mu} Q$, if $\mu \neq \tau$, and either $P = Q$ or $P \xrightarrow{\tau} Q$, if $\mu = \tau$. Relation $\Longrightarrow$ is the reflexive and transitive closure of $\xrightarrow{\tau}$; moreover, $\stackrel{\mu}{\Longrightarrow}$ stands for $\Longrightarrow\xrightarrow{\mu}\Longrightarrow$, and $\stackrel{\hat{\mu}}{\Longrightarrow}$ for $\stackrel{\mu}{\Longrightarrow}$ if $\mu \neq \tau$, and for $\Longrightarrow$ if $\mu = \tau$. Free and bound names (fn, bn) of actions and processes are defined as usual.

We assume Milner's *sorting system*, under which all processes are well-sorted [16]. Names are partitioned into a collection of *sorts*. A *sorting function* is defined which maps sorts onto sequences of sorts. If a sort $\mathtt{S}$ is mapped onto a sequence of sorts $\tilde{\mathtt{T}}$ this means that channels in $\mathtt{S}$ can only carry tuples in $\tilde{\mathtt{T}}$. A sorting system is necessary to prevent arity mismatching in communications, like in $\overline{a}\langle b, c\rangle \mid a(x).\, P$. Substitutions must map names onto names of the same sort.

The *behavioral equivalence* we are interested in is *barbed congruence* [18]. It is well-known that barbed congruence represents a uniform mechanism for defining a behavioral equivalence in any process calculus possessing (i) an *interaction relation* (the τ-steps in π-calculus), modeling the evolution of the system, and (ii) an *observability predicate* $\downarrow_a$ for each name a which indicates the possibility for a process of accepting a communication at a with the environment. $P \downarrow_a$ holds if there is a derivative P', and an action μ, with subject a, such that $P \xrightarrow{\mu} P'$. We also write $P \Downarrow_a$ if there is a derivative P' such that $P \Longrightarrow P' \downarrow_a$. We recall that a *context* $C[\cdot]$ is a process with exactly one hole, written $[\cdot]$, where a process may be plugged in.

Definition 1 (barbed bisimilarity, congruence). Barbed bisimilarity, *written $\dot{\approx}$, is the largest symmetric relation on π-calculus processes such that $P \dot{\approx} Q$ implies:*

1. *If $P \xrightarrow{\tau} P'$ then there exists Q' such that $Q \Longrightarrow Q'$ and $P' \dot{\approx} Q'$.*
2. *If $P \downarrow_a$ then $Q \Downarrow_a$.*

Let $\mathcal{L}$ be a set of processes in π_a, and $P, Q \in \mathcal{L}$. Two processes P and Q are barbed congruent *in $\mathcal{L}$, written $P \cong_{\mathcal{L}} Q$, if for each context $C[\cdot]$ in $\mathcal{L}$ it holds that $C[P] \dot{\approx} C[Q]$.*

The main inconvenience of barbed congruence is that it uses quantification over contexts in the definition, and this can make proofs of process equalities heavy. Simpler proof techniques are based on *labeled characterizations* without context quantification.

Definition 2 (ground bisimilarity). Ground bisimilarity, *written $\approx$, is the largest symmetric relation on processes such that if $P \approx Q$, $P \xrightarrow{\mu} P'$, $\mathrm{bn}(\mu) \cap \mathrm{fn}(Q) = \emptyset$, then there exists Q' such that $Q \stackrel{\hat{\mu}}{\Longrightarrow} Q'$ and $P' \approx Q'$.*

We recall that in the asynchronous calculi without matching, like $\mathrm{L}\widetilde{\pi}$, ground bisimilarity coincides with early, late, and open bisimilarities [23]. All these relations are congruences and imply barbed congruence.

In the technical part of this paper we shall need a means to count the number of silent moves performed by a process in order to use *up-to techniques* [27, 24]. The *expansion* relation [3], written $\lesssim$, is an asymmetric variant of $\approx$ such that $P \lesssim Q$ holds if $P \approx Q$, and Q has at least as many τ-moves as P.

Definition 3 (expansion). *$\lesssim$ is the largest relation on processes such that $P \lesssim Q$ implies:*

1. *whenever $P \xrightarrow{\mu} P'$, and $\mathrm{bn}(\mu) \cap \mathrm{fn}(Q) = \emptyset$, there exists Q' such that $Q \stackrel{\mu}{\Longrightarrow} Q'$ and $P' \lesssim Q'$;*
2. *whenever $Q \xrightarrow{\mu} Q'$, and $\mathrm{bn}(\mu) \cap \mathrm{fn}(P) = \emptyset$, there exists P' such that $P \xrightarrow{\hat{\mu}} P'$ and $P' \lesssim Q'$.*

In both monadic and polyadic $\mathrm{L}\pi$, barbed congruence is a relation strictly larger than ground bisimilarity. For instance, in $\mathrm{L}\pi$, if $P = \overline{a}b$ and $Q = (\boldsymbol{\nu} c)\,(\overline{a}c \mid\, !c(x).\,\overline{b}x)$ then $P \cong_{\mathrm{L}\pi} Q$ (see [15]) but $P \not\approx Q$. In [15], Merro and Sangiorgi give two labeled characterizations of barbed congruence for monadic $\mathrm{L}\pi$. One of them is based on an encoding of $\mathrm{L}\pi$ into $\pi\mathrm{I}$, a calculus where all names emitted are private [25]. The (polyadic version of the) encoding (essentially Boreale's [4]) is an homomorphism on all operators except output, for which we have:

$$[\![\overline{a}\langle\widetilde{b}\rangle]\!] \stackrel{\mathrm{def}}{=} (\boldsymbol{\nu}\widetilde{c})\,(\overline{a}\langle\widetilde{c}\rangle \mid \widetilde{c} \rightarrow \widetilde{b})$$

where $\widetilde{b} = (b_1, \ldots, b_n)$, $\widetilde{c} = (c_1, \ldots, c_n)$; names b_i and c_i have the same sort for all i; $\widetilde{c} \cap (\{a\} \cup \widetilde{b}) = \emptyset$; $\widetilde{c} \rightarrow \widetilde{b} \stackrel{\mathrm{def}}{=} \prod_{j=1}^{n} !c_j(\widetilde{x}).\,[\![\overline{b_j}\langle\widetilde{x}\rangle]\!]$ with $\widetilde{x} = (x_1, \ldots, x_{m_j})$.

Remark 1. Being recursively defined, the process $\widetilde{c} \rightarrow \widetilde{b}$ is not in $\mathrm{L}\widetilde{\pi}$, but it is ground bisimilar to a process of $\mathrm{L}\widetilde{\pi}$ (using replication instead of recursion).

Given two tuples of names $\widetilde{b} = (b_1, \ldots, b_n)$ and $\widetilde{c} = (c_1, \ldots, c_n)$ where names b_i and c_i have the same sort for all i, we denote with $\widetilde{c} \rhd \widetilde{b}$ the process $\prod_{j=1}^{n} !c_j(\widetilde{x}).\,\overline{b_j}\langle\widetilde{x}\rangle$. Note that $[\![\widetilde{c} \rhd \widetilde{b}]\!] = \widetilde{c} \rightarrow \widetilde{b}$.

Below, we report a simple adaption to the polyadic case of a few results on $[\![\cdot]\!]$ that have already appeared in the literature: Theorem 1 provides an adequacy result w.r.t. barbed bisimilarity; Theorem 2 gives a characterization of barbed congruence in $\mathrm{L}\widetilde{\pi}$ for image-finite processes. We recall that the class of *image-finite processes* (to which most of the processes one would like to write belong) is the largest subset $\mathcal{I}$ of π-calculus process which is derivation closed and such that $P \in \mathcal{I}$ implies that, for all μ, the set $\{P' \;:\; P \stackrel{\mu}{\Longrightarrow} P'\}$, quotiented by alpha conversion, is finite.

Theorem 1 (Boreale [4]). *Let P and Q be two $\mathrm{L}\widetilde{\pi}$-processes then*

$$P \stackrel{\bullet}{\approx} Q \text{ iff } [\![P]\!] \stackrel{\bullet}{\approx} [\![Q]\!].$$

Theorem 2 (Merro and Sangiorgi [15]). *Let P and Q be two L$\overline{\pi}$-processes. Then*

1. $P \cong_{\mathrm{L}\overline{\pi}} Q$ implies $[\![P]\!] \approx [\![Q]\!]$, *for P and Q image-finite processes;*
2. $[\![P]\!] \approx [\![Q]\!]$ implies $P \cong_{\mathrm{L}\overline{\pi}} Q$.

Remark 2. Theorem 2 has been proved in [15] with respect to asynchronous barbed congruence (where only output barbs are taken into account) and an asynchronous variant of $\approx$. The adaptation to the synchronous case is straightforward.

3 Correctness Criteria for Encodings

When studying an encoding between two languages it is necessary to have some *correctness criteria* in order to assess the encoding. The most common correctness criteria for an encoding between two process calculi are based on the notions of *operational correspondence* and *full abstraction.* The former relates the execution steps as defined by an operational semantics of the source and target calculi. The latter relates the source and the target calculi at the level of behavioral equivalences. More formally, let us denote with $(\mathcal{S}, \asymp_{\mathrm{s}}, \longrightarrow_{\mathrm{s}})$ and $(\mathcal{T}, \asymp_{\mathrm{t}}, \longrightarrow_{\mathrm{t}})$ two process calculi equipped with behavioral equivalences $\asymp_{\mathrm{s}}$ and $\asymp_{\mathrm{t}}$, and transition relations $\longrightarrow_{\mathrm{s}}$ and $\longrightarrow_{\mathrm{t}}$, respectively. Let $[\![\cdot]\!] : \mathcal{S} \longmapsto \mathcal{T}$ be an encoding from $\mathcal{S}$ to $\mathcal{T}$. A formal definition of operational correspondence is the following:

Definition 4 (operational correspondence). *Given two process calculi $(\mathcal{S}, \asymp_{\mathrm{s}}, \longrightarrow_{\mathrm{s}})$ and $(\mathcal{T}, \asymp_{\mathrm{t}}, \longrightarrow_{\mathrm{t}})$, an encoding $[\![\cdot]\!] : \mathcal{S} \mapsto \mathcal{T}$ enjoys a (strong)* operational correspondence *if for each $S \in \mathcal{S}$ the following two properties holds:*

1. *If $S \longrightarrow_{\mathrm{s}} S'$ then $[\![S]\!] \longrightarrow_{\mathrm{t}} \asymp_{\mathrm{t}} [\![S']\!]$.*
2. *If $[\![S]\!] \longrightarrow_{\mathrm{t}} T$ then there is S' such that $S \longrightarrow_{\mathrm{s}} S'$ and $T \asymp_{\mathrm{t}} [\![S']\!]$.*

Requirements 1 and 2 assert that all possible executions of S may be simulated, up to behavioral equivalence, by its translation, and vice-versa. A notion of *weak operational correspondence* can be easily derived from Definition 4 by simply replacing $\longrightarrow_{\mathrm{s}}$ and $\longrightarrow_{\mathrm{t}}$ with their reflexive transitive closure, in requirements 1 and 2.

Full abstraction has two parts: *soundness*, which says that the equivalence between the translations of two source terms implies that of the source terms themselves; and *completeness*, which says the converse. While soundness is a necessary property and can be usually derived from the operational correspondence, completeness is in general hard to achieve because it implies a strong relationship between source and target calculi.

Definition 5 (soundness, completeness, and full abstraction). *Let $(\mathcal{S}, \asymp_{\mathrm{s}}, \longrightarrow_{\mathrm{s}})$ and $(\mathcal{T}, \asymp_{\mathrm{t}} \longrightarrow_{\mathrm{t}})$ be two process calculi. An encoding $[\![\cdot]\!] : \mathcal{S} \longmapsto \mathcal{T}$ is* sound *if $[\![S_1]\!] \asymp_{\mathrm{t}} [\![S_2]\!]$ implies $S_1 \asymp_{\mathrm{s}} S_2$ for each $S_1, S_2 \in \mathcal{S}$; it is* complete *if $S_1 \asymp_{\mathrm{s}} S_2$ implies $[\![S_1]\!] \asymp_{\mathrm{t}} [\![S_2]\!]$ for each $S_1, S_2 \in \mathcal{S}$; it is* fully-abstract *if it is sound and complete.*

Full abstraction will represent our correctness criterion for the encoding of polyadicity that we are going to present in the next section.

4 Encoding Polyadicity

In this section we give an encoding of polyadic Lπ into monadic Lπ. We present our encoding by comparison with Milner's encoding of polyadic synchronous π-calculus into monadic synchronous π-calculus [16]. Milner's idea is quite simple: One can emulate sending a tuple $\widetilde{b}$ by sending a fresh channel w along which all names b_i are transmitted sequentially. More precisely, Milner gives an encoding $\{\!|\cdot|\!\}$ from polyadic processes to monadic ones which is an homomorphism on all operators except input and output for which we have:

- $\{\!| a(x_1,\dots,x_n).\,P |\!\} \stackrel{\text{def}}{=} a(w).\,\mathrm{INP}\langle w,x_1,\dots,x_n\rangle.\,\{\!| P |\!\}$
- $\{\!| \overline{a}\langle b_1,\dots,b_n\rangle.\,Q |\!\} \stackrel{\text{def}}{=} (\boldsymbol{\nu} w)\ (\overline{a}w.\,\mathrm{OUT}\langle w,b_1,\dots,b_n\rangle.\,\{\!| Q |\!\})$

where

- $\mathrm{INP}\langle w,x_1,\dots,x_n\rangle \stackrel{\text{def}}{=} w(x_1).\,w(x_2)\dots w(x_n)$
- $\mathrm{OUT}\langle w,b_1,\dots,b_n\rangle \stackrel{\text{def}}{=} \overline{w}b_1.\,\overline{w}b_2\dots\overline{w}b_n$

and w is a fresh name, i.e., it is not free in the translated processes. Intuitively, $\mathrm{INP}\langle w,\widetilde{x}\rangle$ and $\mathrm{OUT}\langle w,\widetilde{b}\rangle$ model a protocol which takes care of instantiating each variable x_i with the correspondent name b_i by using a fresh channel w. Since w is private to $\mathrm{INP}\langle w,\widetilde{x}\rangle$ and $\mathrm{OUT}\langle w,\widetilde{b}\rangle$ no interferences are possible. It is easy to show that there is an *operational correspondence* between a polyadic process P and its translation $\{\!| P |\!\}$: (i) if $P \stackrel{\tau}{\longrightarrow} P'$ then $\{\!| P |\!\} \stackrel{\tau}{\longrightarrow} \gtrsim \{\!| P' |\!\}$ and (ii) if $\{\!| P |\!\} \stackrel{\tau}{\longrightarrow} P_1$ then there exists P' such that $P \stackrel{\tau}{\longrightarrow} P'$ and $P_1 \gtrsim \{\!| P' |\!\}$ where $\lesssim$ is the *expansion relation* (see Definition 3). From the operational correspondence one can derive the *soundness* of the encoding when considering *barbed congruence* as the behavioral equivalence in both source and target languages. Unfortunately, as it is well-known, Milner's encoding is not complete and therefore it is not *fully-abstract.* As a counterexample take $R = a(\widetilde{x}).\,a(\widetilde{y}).\,\mathbf{0}$ and $S = a(\widetilde{x}).\,\mathbf{0} \mid a(\widetilde{y}).\,\mathbf{0}$; then R and S are barbed congruent but their encodings are not: $\{\!| S |\!\}$ may perform two consecutive inputs along a while in $\{\!| R |\!\}$ the input protocol $\mathrm{INP}\langle w,\widetilde{x}\rangle$ blocks the second input along a. In synchronous π-calculus, a similar counterexample can be given by using outputs instead of inputs. These counterexamples essentially say that Milner's encoding is not fully-abstract because the protocols $\mathrm{INP}\langle w,\widetilde{x}\rangle$ and $\mathrm{OUT}\langle w,\widetilde{b}\rangle$ prevent the continuations $\{\!| P |\!\}$ and $\{\!| Q |\!\}$ from evolving. Thus, one might think of adapting, somehow, Milner's encoding so that the protocols $\mathrm{INP}\langle w,\widetilde{x}\rangle$ and $\mathrm{OUT}\langle w,\widetilde{b}\rangle$ (or a variant of them) are in parallel with the continuations and not in sequence. In (full) π-calculus, such an adaptation is not possible because of the binding nature of the input prefix. This problem can be avoided in Lπ by relying on Lemma 1 which gives, under certain hypotheses, an interesting encoding for the substitution operator. Recall the definition of $\widetilde{a} \rhd \widetilde{b}$ from Section 2.

Lemma 1 (Merro and Sangiorgi [15]). *Let $\widetilde{a}$ and $\widetilde{b}$ be two tuples with the same arity and such that $\widetilde{a} \cap \widetilde{b} = \emptyset$, and let P be an L$\widetilde{\pi}$-process such that all names $a_i \in \widetilde{a}$ do not appear free in input position in P. It holds that $(\boldsymbol{\nu}\widetilde{a})\,(\widetilde{a} \triangleright \widetilde{b} \mid P) \cong_{\mathrm{L}\widetilde{\pi}} P\{\widetilde{b}/\widetilde{a}\}$.*

In the following we show how Lemma 1 can be used to define an encoding $\langle\!|\cdot|\!\rangle$ of polyadic Lπ-processes into monadic ones. For simplicity, we restrict ourselves to processes transmitting pairs of names. The general case, when tuples of arbitrary size are transmitted, can be derived straightforwardly. The encoding $\langle\!|\cdot|\!\rangle$ is an homomorphism on all operators except input and output, for which we have:

- $\langle\!| a(\widetilde{x}).\,P |\!\rangle \stackrel{\mathrm{def}}{=} a(w).\,(\boldsymbol{\nu}\widetilde{x})\,(\mathrm{INP}\langle w, \widetilde{x}\rangle \mid \langle\!| P |\!\rangle)$
- $\langle\!| \overline{a}\langle\widetilde{b}\rangle |\!\rangle \stackrel{\mathrm{def}}{=} (\boldsymbol{\nu}w)\,(\overline{a}w \mid \mathrm{OUT}\langle w, \widetilde{b}\rangle)$

where $w \notin \mathrm{fn}(\langle\!| P |\!\rangle)$, and supposing $\widetilde{x} = (x_1, x_2)$, $\widetilde{y} = (y_1, y_2)$, $\widetilde{b} = (b_1, b_2)$, and $\widetilde{x} \triangleright \widetilde{y} = !x_1(z).\,\overline{y_1}z \mid !x_2(z).\,\overline{y_2}z$ we define

- $\mathrm{INP}\langle w, \widetilde{x}\rangle \stackrel{\mathrm{def}}{=} (\boldsymbol{\nu}c_1c_3)\,(\overline{w}c_1 \mid c_1(c_2).\,(\overline{c_2}c_3 \mid c_3(y_1).\,c_1(y_2).\,\widetilde{x} \triangleright \widetilde{y}))$
- $\mathrm{OUT}\langle w, \widetilde{b}\rangle \stackrel{\mathrm{def}}{=} w(c_1).\,(\boldsymbol{\nu}c_2)\,(\overline{c_1}c_2 \mid c_2(c_3).\,(\overline{c_3}b_1 \mid \overline{c_1}b_2))$.

Like Milner's encoding, $\langle\!|\cdot|\!\rangle$ is based on the send of a private channel w used by $\mathrm{INP}\langle w, \widetilde{x}\rangle$ and $\mathrm{OUT}\langle w, \widetilde{b}\rangle$ for transmitting names b_i. Unlike Milner's encoding, in $\langle\!|\cdot|\!\rangle$ the send of names b_i produces n forwarders $x_i \triangleright b_i$ in parallel. More precisely, by Lemma 1, it holds that:

$$\langle\!| \overline{a}\langle\widetilde{b}\rangle \mid a(\widetilde{x}).\,P |\!\rangle \xrightarrow{\;\tau\;} \gtrsim (\boldsymbol{\nu}\widetilde{x})\,(\widetilde{x} \triangleright \widetilde{b} \mid \langle\!| P |\!\rangle) \cong_{\mathrm{L}\pi} \langle\!| P |\!\rangle\{\widetilde{b}/\widetilde{x}\} \equiv \langle\!| P\{\widetilde{b}/\widetilde{x}\} |\!\rangle.$$

The encoding $\langle\!|\cdot|\!\rangle$ is sound with respect to barbed congruence. Unfortunately, in this form, the encoding is not yet fully-abstract because it is not complete. As a counterexample take the processes $R = \overline{a}\langle\widetilde{b}\rangle$ and $S = (\boldsymbol{\nu}\widetilde{d})\,(\overline{a}\langle\widetilde{d}\rangle \mid \widetilde{d} \triangleright \widetilde{b})$, with $\widetilde{b} = (b_1, b_2)$ and $\widetilde{d} = (d_1, d_2)$; then $R \cong_{\mathrm{L}\widetilde{\pi}} S$ (see [15]) but $\langle\!| R |\!\rangle \not\cong_{\mathrm{L}\pi} \langle\!| S |\!\rangle$, indeed let $C[\cdot] = [\cdot] \mid T$ in which $T = a(w).\,(\boldsymbol{\nu}c_1c_3h)\,(\overline{w}c_1 \mid c_1(c_2).\,(\overline{c_2}c_3 \mid c_3(y_1).\,c_1(y_2).\,(\overline{y_1}h \mid h(x).\,\overline{m})))$, then $C[\langle\!| R |\!\rangle] \not\Downarrow_m$ while $C[\langle\!| S |\!\rangle] \Downarrow_m$. Notice that we may not find a similar counterexample by using two ground bisimilar processes R and S. This information allows us to give an amended variant of $\langle\!|\cdot|\!\rangle$. By Theorem 2 we know that the encoding $[\![\cdot]\!]$ of Section 2 maps barbed congruent processes into ground bisimilar processes; that is, it holds that $P \cong_{\mathrm{L}\widetilde{\pi}} Q$ iff $[\![P]\!] \approx [\![Q]\!]$ (on image-finite processes). So, we can refine the encoding $\langle\!|\cdot|\!\rangle$ by simply combining $\langle\!|\cdot|\!\rangle$ with $[\![\cdot]\!]$. More precisely, we define an encoding $\{\!|\cdot|\!\}$ of L$\widetilde{\pi}$ into Lπ as the composition of $[\![\cdot]\!]$ and $\langle\!|\cdot|\!\rangle$, thus if P is an L$\widetilde{\pi}$-process

$$\{\!| P |\!\} \stackrel{\mathrm{def}}{=} \langle\!| [\![P]\!] |\!\rangle.$$

Notice that both encodings $[\![\cdot]\!]$ and $\langle\!|\cdot|\!\rangle$ are *divergence-free*, that is, they do not introduce infinite internal computations, so also the encoding $\{\!|\cdot|\!\}$ does not introduce divergence.

5 Proving the Full Abstraction of $\langle\!\langle\!\![\cdot]\!\!\rangle\!\rangle$

In this section we shall prove that, on image-finite and well-sorted processes, $\langle\!\langle\!\![\cdot]\!\!\rangle\!\rangle$ is fully abstract with respect to barbed congruence. To this end we study the encoding $[\![\langle\!| \cdot |\!\rangle]\!]$ obtained by inverting the order of the application of the encodings $[\![\cdot]\!]$ and $\langle\!| \cdot |\!\rangle$. We first prove an operational correspondence, up to expansion, between processes P and $[\![\langle\!| P |\!\rangle]\!]$. This will allows us to prove the soundness of $\langle\!\langle\!\![\cdot]\!\!\rangle\!\rangle$. Then we derive the completeness of $\langle\!\langle\!\![\cdot]\!\!\rangle\!\rangle$ from a completeness result for $[\![\langle\!| \cdot |\!\rangle]\!]$.

Lemma 2 will allow us to prove the operational correspondence between processes P and $[\![\langle\!| P |\!\rangle]\!]$.

Lemma 2 (Boreale [4]).

1. *Let $\widetilde{a}$, $\widetilde{b}$, $\widetilde{c}$ be tuples of names of the same size such that $(\widetilde{a} \cup \widetilde{c}) \cap \widetilde{b} = \emptyset$. Then $(\boldsymbol{\nu}\widetilde{b})\,(\widetilde{a} \to \widetilde{b} \mid \widetilde{b} \to \widetilde{c}) \gtrsim \widetilde{a} \to \widetilde{c}$.*
2. *Let P be an $\mathrm{L}\widetilde{\pi}$ process and $\widetilde{a}$ and $\widetilde{b}$ two tuples of names such that the names in $\widetilde{a}$ do not occur free in P in input-subject position and $\widetilde{a} \cap \widetilde{b} = \emptyset$. Then $(\boldsymbol{\nu}\widetilde{a})\,(\widetilde{a} \to \widetilde{b} \mid [\![P]\!]) \gtrsim [\![P]\!]\{\widetilde{b}/\widetilde{a}\}$.*

Remark 3. Lemma 2(2) can be seen as a variant of Lemma 1 up to $[\![\cdot]\!]$. Actually, Lemma 1 follows directly from Lemma 2(2) and Theorem 2(2).

Lemma 3. *Let P be a well-sorted process in $\mathrm{L}\widetilde{\pi}$ then:*

1. *Suppose that $P \xrightarrow{\alpha} P'$. Then we have:*
   (a) *if $\alpha = a(\widetilde{x})$ then $[\![\langle\!| P |\!\rangle]\!] \xrightarrow{a(w)} \gtrsim (\boldsymbol{\nu}\widetilde{x})\,([\![\mathrm{INP}\langle w, \widetilde{x}\rangle]\!] \mid [\![\langle\!| P' |\!\rangle]\!])$;*
   (b) *if $\alpha = (\boldsymbol{\nu}\widetilde{c})\,\overline{a}\langle\widetilde{b}\rangle$, with $\widetilde{c}$ eventually empty, then*
   $[\![\langle\!| P |\!\rangle]\!] \xrightarrow{\overline{a}(p)} \gtrsim (\boldsymbol{\nu}\widetilde{c})\,((\boldsymbol{\nu}w)\,(p \to w \mid [\![\mathrm{OUT}\langle w, \widetilde{b}\rangle]\!]) \mid [\![\langle\!| P' |\!\rangle]\!])$,
   with $p \notin fn(P')$;
   (c) *if $\alpha = \tau$ then $[\![\langle\!| P |\!\rangle]\!] \xrightarrow{\tau} \gtrsim [\![\langle\!| P' |\!\rangle]\!]$.*
2. *Suppose that $[\![\langle\!| P |\!\rangle]\!] \xrightarrow{\alpha} P_1$. Then there exists $P' \in \mathrm{L}\widetilde{\pi}$ such that:*
   (a) *if $\alpha = a(w)$ then $P \xrightarrow{a(\widetilde{x})} P'$, for some $\widetilde{x}$, with*
   $P_1 \gtrsim (\boldsymbol{\nu}\widetilde{x})\,([\![\mathrm{INP}\langle w, \widetilde{x}\rangle]\!] \mid [\![\langle\!| P' |\!\rangle]\!])$;
   (b) *if $\alpha = \overline{a}(p)$ then $P \xrightarrow{(\boldsymbol{\nu}\widetilde{c})\,\overline{a}\langle\widetilde{b}\rangle} P'$, with $\widetilde{c}$ eventually empty, $p \notin fn(P')$ and*
   $P_1 \gtrsim (\boldsymbol{\nu}\widetilde{c})\,((\boldsymbol{\nu}w)\,(p \to w \mid [\![\mathrm{OUT}\langle w, \widetilde{b}\rangle]\!]) \mid [\![\langle\!| P' |\!\rangle]\!])$;
   (c) *if $\alpha = \tau$ then $P \xrightarrow{\tau} P'$ with $P_1 \gtrsim [\![\langle\!| P' |\!\rangle]\!]$.*

Proof. By transition induction. The only subtle points arise in parts 1(c) and 2(c) where also Lemma 2 is used. Details can be found in [13].

Remark 4. Note that the lemma above is not true when considering ill-sorted processes. For instance, if $P = \overline{a}\langle b, c\rangle \mid a(x).\,Q$ then $[\![\langle\!| P |\!\rangle]\!] \xrightarrow{\tau}$ while $P \not\xrightarrow{\tau}$.

From Lemma 3 we can derive a weak operational correspondence.

Lemma 4.

1. *If* $P \Longrightarrow P'$ *then* $[\![\langle\!| P |\!\rangle]\!] \Longrightarrow\gtrsim [\![\langle\!| P' |\!\rangle]\!]$;
2. *If* $[\![\langle\!| P |\!\rangle]\!] \Longrightarrow P_1$ *then there is* P' *s.t.* $P \Longrightarrow P'$ *and* $P_1 \gtrsim [\![\langle\!| P' |\!\rangle]\!]$;
3. $P \Downarrow_a$ *iff* $[\![\langle\!| P |\!\rangle]\!] \Downarrow_a$.

Proof. Parts 1 and 2 are proven by induction on the number of τ-moves by exploiting Lemma 3. Part 3 follows from parts 1 and 2, and Lemma 3.

Lemmas 3 and 4 allow us to prove the following two lemmas which will be useful for proving the soundness of $\langle\!\![\![\cdot]\!]\!\!\rangle$.

Lemma 5. *Let* P *and* Q *be two* $\mathrm{L}\widetilde{\pi}$*-processes. Then*

$$[\![\langle\!| P |\!\rangle]\!] \stackrel{\centerdot}{\approx} [\![\langle\!| Q |\!\rangle]\!] \text{ implies } P \stackrel{\centerdot}{\approx} Q.$$

Proof. We use Lemmas 3 and 4 and the fact that $\lesssim \stackrel{\centerdot}{\approx} \gtrsim \, \subset \, \stackrel{\centerdot}{\approx}$ to prove that the relation $\mathcal{R} = \{(P, Q) : [\![\langle\!| P |\!\rangle]\!] \stackrel{\centerdot}{\approx} [\![\langle\!| Q |\!\rangle]\!]\}$ is a barbed bisimulation.

Lemma 6. *Let* P *and* Q *be two* $\mathrm{L}\widetilde{\pi}$*-processes. Then*

$$\langle\!\![\![P]\!]\!\!\rangle \stackrel{\centerdot}{\approx} \langle\!\![\![Q]\!]\!\!\rangle \text{ implies } P \stackrel{\centerdot}{\approx} Q.$$

Proof. Since $\langle\!\![\![\cdot]\!]\!\!\rangle \stackrel{\text{def}}{=} \langle\!| [\![\cdot]\!] |\!\rangle$, by Theorem 1, we have $[\![\langle\!| [\![P]\!] |\!\rangle]\!] \stackrel{\centerdot}{\approx} [\![\langle\!| [\![Q]\!] |\!\rangle]\!]$. By Lemma 5 we have $[\![P]\!] \stackrel{\centerdot}{\approx} [\![Q]\!]$. By Theorem 1 we have $P \stackrel{\centerdot}{\approx} Q$.

The following lemma will allow us to prove the completeness of $\langle\!\![\![\cdot]\!]\!\!\rangle$.

Lemma 7. *Let* P *and* Q *be two* $\mathrm{L}\widetilde{\pi}$*-processes. Then*

$$P \approx Q \text{ implies } [\![\langle\!| P |\!\rangle]\!] \approx [\![\langle\!| Q |\!\rangle]\!].$$

Proof. We prove that $\mathcal{S} = \{([\![\langle\!| P |\!\rangle]\!], [\![\langle\!| Q |\!\rangle]\!]) : P \approx Q\}$ is a ground bisimulation up to context and up to $\gtrsim$ [24]. Details can be found in [13].

Finally we prove that, on image-finite and well-sorted processes, the encoding $\langle\!\![\![\cdot]\!]\!\!\rangle$ is fully-abstract with respect to barbed congruence.

Theorem 3 (full abstraction of $\langle\!\![\![\cdot]\!]\!\!\rangle$). *Let* P *and* Q *be two image-finite and well-sorted processes in* $\mathrm{L}\widetilde{\pi}$*, then*

$$P \cong_{\mathrm{L}\widetilde{\pi}} Q \text{ iff } \langle\!\![\![P]\!]\!\!\rangle \cong_{\mathrm{L}\pi} \langle\!\![\![Q]\!]\!\!\rangle.$$

Proof. The soundness follows from the compositionality of $[\![\cdot]\!]$ and $\langle\!| \cdot |\!\rangle$, and Lemma 6. As for completeness, by Theorem 2(1) we have $[\![P]\!] \approx [\![Q]\!]$. By Lemma 7 we have $[\![\langle\!| [\![P]\!] |\!\rangle]\!] \approx [\![\langle\!| [\![Q]\!] |\!\rangle]\!]$. By the monadic variant of Theorem 2(2) we have $\langle\!| [\![P]\!] |\!\rangle \cong_{\mathrm{L}\pi} \langle\!| [\![Q]\!] |\!\rangle$, i.e., $\langle\!\![\![P]\!]\!\!\rangle \cong_{\mathrm{L}\pi} \langle\!\![\![Q]\!]\!\!\rangle$.

6 What about $\llparenthesis \cdot \rrparenthesis$ and $[\![\llparenthesis \cdot \rrparenthesis]\!]$?

We have proved that the encoding $\{\![\cdot]\!\}$ is fully-abstract w.r.t. barbed congruence. Other possible candidates for a fully-abstract encoding of polyadic Lπ into monadic Lπ are: $\llparenthesis \cdot \rrparenthesis$ and $[\![\llparenthesis \cdot \rrparenthesis]\!]$. Unfortunately, none of them is fully-abstract w.r.t. barbed congruence or ground bisimilarity.

In Section 4 we already showed that $\llparenthesis \cdot \rrparenthesis$ is not fully-abstract w.r.t. barbed congruence. The encoding $\llparenthesis \cdot \rrparenthesis$ is not fully-abstract w.r.t. ground bisimilarity either. As a counterexample take $P = (\boldsymbol{\nu} a)\, (\overline{a}\langle\widetilde{b}\rangle \mid a(\widetilde{x}).\, \overline{c}\langle\widetilde{x}\rangle)$ and $Q = \overline{c}\langle\widetilde{b}\rangle$; then $P \approx Q$, but $\llparenthesis P \rrparenthesis \approx (\boldsymbol{\nu}\widetilde{x})\, (\widetilde{x} \triangleright \widetilde{b} \mid \llparenthesis \overline{c}\langle\widetilde{x}\rangle \rrparenthesis)$, and $\llparenthesis Q \rrparenthesis = \llparenthesis \overline{c}\langle\widetilde{b}\rangle \rrparenthesis$, and therefore $\llparenthesis P \rrparenthesis \not\approx \llparenthesis Q \rrparenthesis$.

By Lemma 7 the encoding $[\![\llparenthesis \cdot \rrparenthesis]\!]$ is complete w.r.t. ground bisimilarity. Since the encoding $[\![\llparenthesis \cdot \rrparenthesis]\!]$ enjoys an operational correspondence up to expansion (Lemma 3), one may hope that $[\![\llparenthesis \cdot \rrparenthesis]\!]$ is sound w.r.t. ground bisimilarity and therefore fully-abstract. Unfortunately, $[\![\llparenthesis \cdot \rrparenthesis]\!]$ is not sound w.r.t. ground bisimilarity. As a counterexample take $P = (\boldsymbol{\nu}\widetilde{c})\, \overline{a}\langle\widetilde{c}\rangle$ and $Q = (\boldsymbol{\nu}\widetilde{c})\, (\overline{a}\langle\widetilde{c}\rangle \mid \overline{c_1}\langle b\rangle)$, with $\widetilde{c} = (c_1, c_2)$; then $P \cong_{\mathrm{L}\widetilde{\pi}} Q$ (see [15]) and also $\llparenthesis P \rrparenthesis \cong_{\mathrm{L}\pi} \llparenthesis Q \rrparenthesis$, by Theorem 2 $[\![\llparenthesis P \rrparenthesis]\!] \approx [\![\llparenthesis Q \rrparenthesis]\!]$, but $P \not\approx Q$. The encoding $[\![\llparenthesis \cdot \rrparenthesis]\!]$ is not fully-abstract w.r.t. barbed congruence either. As a counterexample take the processes $P = \overline{a}\langle\widetilde{b}\rangle$ and $Q = (\boldsymbol{\nu}\widetilde{d})\, (\overline{a}\langle\widetilde{d}\rangle \mid \widetilde{d} \triangleright \widetilde{b})$, with $\widetilde{b} = (b_1, b_2)$ and $\widetilde{d} = (d_1, d_2)$; then, as already shown in Section 4, $P \cong_{\mathrm{L}\widetilde{\pi}} Q$ and $\llparenthesis P \rrparenthesis \not\cong_{\mathrm{L}\pi} \llparenthesis Q \rrparenthesis$; since the encoding $[\![\cdot]\!]$ is sound w.r.t. barbed congruence (which follows by Theorem 1 and the compositionality of $[\![\cdot]\!]$) we have that $[\![\llparenthesis P \rrparenthesis]\!] \not\cong_{\mathrm{L}\pi} [\![\llparenthesis Q \rrparenthesis]\!]$.

7 An Encoding of Polyadicity in Calculi with Non-binding Input Prefix

In Section 4, we said that Milner's encoding is not fully-abstract because the protocols $\mathrm{INP}\langle w, \widetilde{x}\rangle$ and $\mathrm{OUT}\langle w, \widetilde{b}\rangle$ prevent the continuations $\{\!|P|\!\}$ and $\{\!|Q|\!\}$ to evolve. Actually, the real problem is the binding nature of the input prefix. Indeed, we can easily change the encoding of $\overline{a}\langle\widetilde{b}\rangle.\, P$ by putting the protocol $\mathrm{OUT}\langle w, \widetilde{b}\rangle$ in parallel with the continuation but we cannot do the same with the encoding of input prefixes.

On the contrary, in calculi where the input prefix is non-binding, such as *Chi calculus* [9], *Fusion calculus* [19] and πF-*calculus* [10], we can adapt Milner's encoding by simply putting the protocol $\mathrm{INP}\langle w, \widetilde{x}\rangle$ in parallel with the continuation. We conjecture that, in these calculi, such a variant of Milner's encoding is fully-abstract.

Let us consider, for instance, the Fusion calculus. [1] For our purposes it suffices to consider a finite fragment. The extension of our encoding when infinite processes are allowed is straightforward. The grammar of finite Fusion calculus has operators of inaction, *non-binding input prefix*, output prefixing, parallel composition, and restriction:

[1] Actually, it might be easier to work with the πF-*calculus*. We consider the Fusion calculus and not πF only because the theory of Fusion is more stable.

$$P ::= \mathbf{0} \;\Big|\; a\langle\widetilde{x}\rangle.\,P \;\Big|\; \overline{a}\langle\widetilde{b}\rangle.\,P \;\Big|\; P\,|\,P \;\Big|\; (a)P$$

Conventions about names are as in π-calculus, except for the non-binding input prefix for which we have:

$$\mathrm{fn}(a\langle\widetilde{x}\rangle.\,P) \stackrel{\mathrm{def}}{=} \{a\} \cup \{x_1, \ldots, x_n\} \cup \mathrm{fn}(P) \text{ and } \mathrm{bn}(a\langle\widetilde{x}\rangle.\,P) \stackrel{\mathrm{def}}{=} \mathrm{bn}(P).$$

We write $(\widetilde{x})P$ for $(x_1)\ldots(x_n)P$. Conventions about processes and substitutions are as in π-calculus. The *reduction semantics* is defined by means of a notion of structural congruence (essentially the same as in π-calculus) and a reduction relation. For simplicity, we give the basic reduction rules for the monadic calculus, the generalization to the polyadic case is slightly more complex:

$$\texttt{(comm1)} : (x)(P\,|\,a\langle x\rangle.\,Q\,|\,\overline{a}\langle y\rangle.\,R) \longrightarrow (x)((P\,|\,Q\,|\,R)\{y/x\})$$

$$\texttt{(comm2)} : (y)(P\,|\,a\langle x\rangle.\,Q\,|\,\overline{a}\langle y\rangle.\,R) \longrightarrow (y)((P\,|\,Q\,|\,R)\{x/y\})$$

Notice that the restrictions (x) and (y) in the derivatives make sense only when $x = y$, otherwise, up to structural congruence, they disappear. The definitions of observability, barbed bisimilarity, and barbed congruence are essentially the same as in π-calculus. Finally, an important derived process, called fusion, can be defined as follows: $\{\widetilde{x} = \widetilde{y}\} \stackrel{\mathrm{def}}{=} (u)(\overline{u}\langle\widetilde{x}\rangle.\,\mathbf{0} \mid u\langle\widetilde{y}\rangle.\,\mathbf{0})$.

In Fusion calculus, communications can arise only in the presence of a scoping construct delimiting their effects (see reduction rules `(comm1)` and `(comm2)`). So, to observe all potential communications (and their effects) it makes sense to consider a notion of barbed congruence obtained by closing barbed bisimulation under contexts that bind all free names of the tested processes. Similar *closing contexts* have been used in typed calculi [26]. As in the definition of *testing equivalences* [7], these contexts signal success by emitting along names that do not appear in the tested processes.

Definition 6 (closed barbed congruence). *Two processes P and Q are* closed barbed congruent, *written $\cong_c$, if for each context $C[\cdot]$ such that $\mathrm{fn}(P) \cap \mathrm{fn}(C[P]) = \mathrm{fn}(Q) \cap \mathrm{fn}(C[Q]) = \emptyset$, it holds that $C[P] \stackrel{\bullet}{\approx} C[Q]$.*

It is immediate to adapt this definition to other calculi, such as π-calculus. Actually, in π-calculus and CCS, closed barbed congruence coincides with barbed congruence: One can prove that closed barbed congruence coincides with the closure under substitutions of early bisimulation, by adapting the proofs in [22, 2]; since the closure under substitutions of early bisimulation is known to coincide with barbed congruence, the two definitions of barbed congruence coincide. Unfortunately, standard and closed barbed congruence do not coincide in Fusion.

Milner's encoding can be rewritten in Fusion calculus so that the instantiation of names does not block the continuations:

$$(\!| a\langle x_1, \dots, x_n\rangle. P |\!) \stackrel{\text{def}}{=} (w)aw.(wx_1.wx_2.\dots.wx_n \mid (\!| P |\!))$$

$$(\!| \overline{a}\langle b_1, \dots, b_n\rangle. Q |\!) \stackrel{\text{def}}{=} (w)\overline{a}w.(\overline{w}b_1.\overline{w}b_2.\dots.\overline{w}b_n \mid (\!| Q |\!))$$

Note that the continuations $(\!| P |\!)$ and $(\!| Q |\!)$ may evolve without waiting for the n communications along the private channel w. This encoding is not sound w.r.t. standard barbed congruence and not even w.r.t. *hyperequivalence* [19], because, in some sense, the encoding breaks the preemptive power of fusions. More precisely, if we take $R = \{a = b\} \mid \{c = d\}$ and $S = \{a = b\}.\{c = d\}^2$, then R and S are not equivalent while their translations are. Nevertheless, we believe that the encoding $(\!| \cdot |\!)$ is fully abstract with respect to closed barbed congruence. Our conjecture is due to the fact that closed barbed congruence is insensitive to fusion prefixing, that is, it handles fusion actions as silent moves. As a consequence, the counterexample above is not valid anymore because processes $\{a = b\} \mid \{c = d\}$ and $\{a = b\}.\{c = d\}$ are closed barbed congruent. Unfortunately, we cannot prove the full abstraction of $(\!| \cdot |\!)$ by using the same proof techniques of Section 5 because we do not know yet a labeled characterization of closed barbed congruence in Fusion.

8 Conclusions and Related Works

We have presented a *divergence-free* encoding $\langle\!\langle \cdot \rangle\!\rangle$ of polyadic Lπ into monadic Lπ inspired by Milner's encoding. The encoding exploits a property of Lπ saying that, under certain hypotheses, substitution can be encoded in terms of links, restriction, and parallel composition. This property allows us to define an encoding of polyadicity where the machinery emulating the transmission of tuples does not block continuations.

We have proved that, on image-finite and well-sorted processes, $\langle\!\langle \cdot \rangle\!\rangle$ is fully-abstract with respect to barbed congruence. This shows that in Lπ (i) polyadicity does not add extra expressive power, and (ii) when studying the theory of polyadic Lπ we can focus on the simpler monadic variant. Finally, we have proposed an encoding of polyadicity in name-passing calculi with non-binding input prefix, such as *Chi*, *Fusion* and *πF calculi* [9, 19, 10], which is based on the same idea of $\langle\!\langle \cdot \rangle\!\rangle$.

Of course, our encodings (as the Milner's one) do not preserve well-sortedness. This is a minor point because in monadic calculi there cannot be arity mismatching.

Note that we have used synchronous barbed congruence where both input and output actions are observed. Sometimes, in asynchronous calculi, only output barbs are taken into account validating the law $a(\widetilde{x}).\overline{a}\langle\widetilde{x}\rangle = \mathbf{0}$. This law may be questioned because it introduces divergences. For instance, from $a(\widetilde{x}).\overline{a}\langle\widetilde{x}\rangle = \mathbf{0}$ we can derive the equality $!a(\widetilde{x}).\overline{a}\langle\widetilde{x}\rangle \mid \overline{a}b = \overline{a}b$ between a divergent and a non-divergent process. Our encoding is not complete w.r.t. asynchronous barbed

[2] A formal definition for S is $(uz)(ua.zc \mid \overline{u}b.\overline{z}d)$

congruence precisely because $\langle\!\langle a(\widetilde{x}).\,\overline{a}\langle\widetilde{x}\rangle \rangle\!\rangle$ and $\langle\!\langle \mathbf{0} \rangle\!\rangle$ are not asynchronous barbed congruent. However, we believe that $\langle\!\langle \cdot \rangle\!\rangle$ is fully-abstract w.r.t. a variant of asynchronous barbed congruence which is sensitive to divergence, along the lines of [28].

The works which are most closely related to ours are [29, 21] where type systems for monadic π-processes are introduced in order to capture the communication protocol underlying Milner's encoding. More precisely, in [29] a notion of graph type is introduced and studied. Nodes of a graph type represent atomic actions, and edges an activation ordering between them. The approach in [21] is similar but the type system is simpler. Both papers show a full abstraction result with respect to typed contextual equivalences that reject all contexts which do not respect the protocol imposed by the encoding. While [29, 21] work on the full π-calculus our result only applies in Lπ. This is because Lemmas 1 and 2 only work on Lπ-processes. On the other hand, we prove a sharper result because we get the completeness of the encoding with respect to all monadic contexts without rejecting "hostile" contexts.
In [8], Fournet and Gonthier provide, among other results, a fully-abstract encoding of polyadic into monadic Join Calculus. Apart from the differences among the two process calculi, the encoding in [8] is technically quite different from ours; for instance, as the authors themselves say, their translation encodes and then subsequently decodes tuples twice.

Acknowledgments A series of discussions with Davide Sangiorgi has inspired the work reported in the paper. I thank Paola Quaglia, David Walker and Björn Victor for insightful discussions on the encoding of polyadicity in π and Fusion calculi. I thank Ilaria Castellani, Silvano Dal-Zilio, Christine Röckl, and the anonymous referees for useful comments on the paper.

References

[1] R. Amadio. An asynchronous model of locality, failure, and process mobility. In *Proc. Coordination'97*, LNCS 1282, Springer Verlag, 1997.
[2] R. Amadio, I. Castellani, and D. Sangiorgi. On bisimulations for the asynchronous π-calculus. *Theoretical Computer Science*, 195:291–324, 1998.
[3] S. Arun-Kumar and M. Hennessy. An efficiency preorder for processes. *Acta Informatica*, 29:737–760, 1992.
[4] M. Boreale. On the expressiveness of internal mobility in name-passing calculi. *Theoretical Computer Science*, 195:205–226, 1998.
[5] G. Boudol. Asynchrony and the π-calculus. Technical Report RR-1702, INRIA-Sophia Antipolis, 1992.
[6] G. Boudol. The pi-calculus in direct style. In *Proc. 24th POPL*. ACM Press, 1997.
[7] R. De Nicola and R. Hennessy. Testing equivalences for processes. *Theoretical Computer Science*, 34:83–133, 1984.
[8] C. Fournet and G. Gonthier. The Reflexive Chemical Abstract Machine and the Join calculus. In *Proc. 23th POPL*. ACM Press, 1996.
[9] Y. Fu. A proof theoretical approach to communication. In *24th ICALP*, volume 1256 of *Lecture Notes in Computer Science*. Springer Verlag, 1997.

[10] P. Gardner and L. Wischik. The πF-calculus: a π-calculus with fusions. Personal Communication, 1999.
[11] K. Honda and M. Tokoro. An Object Calculus for Asynchronous Communication. In Proc. *ECOOP'91,* LNCS 512, Springer Verlag, 1991.
[12] K. Honda and M. Tokoro. A Small Calculus for Concurrent Objects. In *OOPS Messanger*, Association for Computing Machinery. 2(2):50-54, 1991.
[13] M. Merro. Locality and polyadicity in asynchronous name-passing calculi. Available at *http://www-sop.inria.fr/meije/personnel/Massimo.Merro.html.*, 1999.
[14] M. Merro, H. Hüttel, J. Kleist, and U. Nestmann. Migrating Objects as Mobile Processes. To appear as a INRIA/BRICS Technical Report, 1999.
[15] M. Merro and D. Sangiorgi. On asynchrony in name-passing calculi. In *25th ICALP*, volume 1443 of *Lecture Notes in Computer Science.* Springer Verlag, 1998. The full-paper will appear as an INRIA Technical report.
[16] R. Milner. The polyadic π-calculus: a tutorial. Technical Report ECS–LFCS–91–180, LFCS, Dept. of Comp. Sci., Edinburgh Univ., October 1991.
[17] R. Milner, J. Parrow, and D. Walker. A calculus of mobile processes, (Parts I and II). *Information and Computation*, 100:1–77, 1992.
[18] R. Milner and D. Sangiorgi. Barbed bisimulation. In W. Kuich, editor, *19th ICALP*, LNCS 623, Springer Verlag, 1992.
[19] J. Parrow and B. Victor. The fusion calculus: Expressiveness and symmetry in mobile processes. In *Proc. LICS'98*, IEEE Computer Society Press., 1998.
[20] B. C. Pierce and D. N. Turner. Pict: A programming language based on the pi-calculus. To appear in *Proof, Language and Interaction: Essays in Honour of Robin Milner*, MIT Press.
[21] P. Quaglia and Walker D.. On encoding pπ in mπ. In *Proc. FST & TCS*, volume 1530 of *Lecture Notes in Computer Science*, pages 42–53. Springer Verlag, 1998.
[22] D. Sangiorgi. *Expressing Mobility in Process Algebras: First-Order and Higher-Order Paradigms.* PhD thesis CST–99–93, University of Edinburgh, 1992.
[23] D. Sangiorgi. Lazy functions and mobile processes. Technical Report RR-2515, INRIA-Sophia Antipolis, 1995.
[24] D. Sangiorgi. Locality and non-interleaving semantics in calculi for mobile processes. *Theoretical Computer Science*, 155:39–83, 1996.
[25] D. Sangiorgi. π-calculus, internal mobility and agent-passing calculi. *Theoretical Computer Science*, 167(2):235–274, 1996.
[26] D. Sangiorgi. The name discipline of receptiveness. In *24th ICALP*, volume 1256 of *Lecture Notes in Computer Science.* Springer Verlag, 1997. To appear in TCS.
[27] D. Sangiorgi and R. Milner. The problem of "Weak Bisimulation up to". In *Proc. CONCUR '92*, LNS 630, Springer Verlag, 1992.
[28] D. Walker. Bisimulation and divergence. *Information and Computation*, 85(2):202–241, 1990.
[29] N. Yoshida. Graph types for monadic mobile processes. In *Proc. FST & TCS*, LCNS 1180, Springer Verlag, 1996.
[30] N. Yoshida. Minimality and Separation Results on Asynchronous Mobile Processes: representability theorem by concurrent combinators. In *9th CONCUR*, LNCS 1466, Springer Verlag, 1998.

On Rational Graphs

Christophe Morvan

IRISA, Campus de Beaulieu,
35042 Rennes, France
christophe.morvan@irisa.fr

Abstract. Using rationality, like in language theory, we define a family of infinite graphs. This family is a strict extension of the context-free graphs of Muller and Schupp, the equational graphs of Courcelle and the prefix recognizable graphs of Caucal. We give basic properties, as well as an internal and an external characterization of these graphs. We also show that their traces form an AFL of recursive languages, containing the context-free languages.

1 Introduction

When dealing with computers, infinite graphs are natural objects. They emerge naturally in recursive program schemes or communicating automata, for example. Studying them as families of objects is comparatively recent: Muller and Schupp (in [MS 85]) first captured the structure of the graphs of pushdown automata, then Courcelle (in [Co 90]) defined the set of regular (equational) graphs. More recently Caucal introduced (in [Ca 96]) a characterization of graphs in terms of inverse (rational) substitution from the complete binary tree. Step by step, like Chomsky's languages family, a hierarchy of graph families is built: the *graphs of pushdown automata*, *regular graphs* and *prefix-recognizable graphs*.

To define infinite objects conveniently, we have to use finite systems. For infinite graphs, two kinds of finite systems are employed: internal systems or external systems. Roughly speaking an internal characterization is a *machine* producing the arcs of the graph. An external characterization yields the structure of the graph (usually "up to isomorphism"). There is, of course a relationship between internal and external characterization: for example the pushdown automata are an internal characterization of the connected regular graphs of finite degree whereas the *deterministic graph grammars* are an external system for the family of regular graphs.

The purpose of this article is to give both internal and external characterization of a wider family of graphs. Using words for vertices, *rationality* (like in language theory) will provide an internal characterization; it will also give basic results for this family: for example rational graphs will be recognized by transducers; a rational graph is a recursive set; determinism for rational graphs will be decidable. Then *inverse substitution* from the complete binary tree (like in [Ca 96]) will be an external characterization of this family. Strangely this extension will prove to be a slight extension of the *prefix-recognizable graphs*: instead

J. Tiuryn (Ed.): FOSSACS 2000, LNCS 1784, pp. 252–266, 2000.

of taking the inverse image of the complete binary tree by a rational substitution we will consider the inverse image of the complete binary tree by a linear substitution (*i.e.*, a substitution where the image of each letter is a linear language). Finally properties of the traces of these graphs will be investigated: we will show that the traces of these graphs form an *abstract family of (recursive) languages* containing the context-free languages.

2 Rational Graphs

In this section we will define a new family of infinite graphs, namely the set of *rational graphs*. We will state some results for this family and give examples of rational graphs.

2.1 Partial Semigroups

This paragraph introduces rationality for partial semigroups and uses this notion to give a natural introduction for rational graphs.
We start by recalling some standards notations: for any set E, its cardinal is denoted by $|E|$; its powerset is denoted by 2^E. Let the set of nonnegative integers be denoted by $\mathbb{N}$. A semigroup S is a set equipped with an operation $\cdot : S \times S \to S$ such that: for all u, v in S there exists w in S such that $\cdot(u, v) = w$ denoted by $u \cdot v = w$ and this operation is associative (*i.e.*, $\forall u, v, w \in S, (u \cdot v) \cdot w = u \cdot (v \cdot w)$. Finally, a monoid M is a semigroup with a (unique) neutral element (denoted ε along these lines) *i.e.*, an element $\varepsilon \in M$ such that for all element u in M $u \cdot \varepsilon = \varepsilon \cdot u = u$.
Now, a *partial semigroup* is a set S equipped with $\cdot : S \times S \to S$, a partial operation, with $\mathcal{D} \subseteq S \times S$ the domain of $\cdot$; set $\mathcal{D}$ need not be $S \times S$. Moreover we impose this operation to be *associative* as follows: $[(u, v) \in \mathcal{D} \wedge ((u \cdot v), w) \in \mathcal{D}] \Leftrightarrow [(v, w) \in \mathcal{D} \wedge (u, (v \cdot w)) \in \mathcal{D}]$ and in that case, $u \cdot (v \cdot w) = (u \cdot v) \cdot w$. Meaning that if multiplication is defined on the one side, then it is defined on the other side and both agree.
Notice that a partial semigroup S such that $\mathcal{D}$ is $S \times S$ is a semigroup.

Example 2.1. Given two semigroups $(S_1, \cdot_1)$ and $(S_2, \cdot_2)$ such that $S_1 \cap S_2$ is empty. The union $S = S_1 \cup S_2$, with the partial operation $\cdot$ defined as $\cdot_1$ over the elements of S_1 and $\cdot_2$ over the element of S_2, is a partial semigroup.

Taking a new element $\perp$ we complete any partial semigroup S into a semigroup $S \cup \{\perp\}$ by extending its operation $\cdot$ as follows:
$a \cdot b = \perp$ for all $a, b \in S \cup \{\perp\}$ such that $(a, b) \notin \mathcal{D}$.
Also the product $S \times S'$ of two partial semigroups S and S' is a partial semigroup for operation $\cdot$ defined componentwise:
$(a, a') \cdot (b, b') = (a \cdot b, a' \cdot b')$ for all $(a, b) \in \mathcal{D}$ and $(a', b') \in \mathcal{D}'$.
In order to define the rational subsets of a partial semigroup, we have to extend its operation to its subsets:

$$A \cdot B := \{a \cdot b \mid a \in A \wedge b \in B \} \text{ for every } A, B \subseteq S$$

The powerset 2^S of S, is a semigroup for $\cdot$ so defined.
Now, a subset P of a partial semigroup S is a *partial subsemigroup* of S, if P is a partial semigroup for $\cdot$ of S *i.e.*, $P \cdot P$ is a subset of P.
For any subset P of a partial semigroup S, following subset $P^+ = \bigcup_{n \geqslant 1} P^n$ (with $P^1 = P$ and $P^{n+1} = P^n \cdot P$ for every $n \geqslant 1$) is the smallest (for inclusion) partial subsemigroup of S containing P. Set P^+ is called the *partial semigroup generated* by P. In particular $(P^+)^+ = P^+$. Also, S is *finitely generated* if $S = P^+$ for some finite P.
A set $P \subseteq S$ is a *code* if there is no two factorization in P^+ of the same element:
$u_1 \cdots u_m = v_1 \cdots v_n \wedge u_1, \ldots, u_m, v_1, \ldots, v_n \in P \Rightarrow m = n \wedge \forall\, i \in [1 \cdots n], u_i = v_i$
A partial semigroup S is *free* if there is code P such that $P^+ = S$.
For every $W \subseteq 2^S$, we denote by $\bigcup W = \{a \mid \exists P \in W, a \in P\}$. Operator $+$ commutes with operator $\bigcup$, *i.e.*, $\bigcup(W^+) = (\bigcup W)^+$ for every $W \subseteq 2^S$.
The (left) *residual* $u^{-1}P$ of $P \subseteq S$ by $u \in S$ is following subset:
$u^{-1}P := \{v \in S \mid u \cdot v \in P\}$
and satisfies following basic equality:
$(u \cdot v)^{-1}P = v^{-1}(u^{-1}P)$ for all $u, v \in S$ and $P \subseteq S$.

Definition 2.2. Let $(S, \cdot)$ be a partial semigroup. The family $Rat(S)$ of rational subsets of S is the least family $\mathcal{R}$ of subsets of S satisfying the following conditions:

(i) $\emptyset \in \mathcal{R}$; $\{m\} \in \mathcal{R}$ for all m in S;
(ii) if $A, B \in \mathcal{R}$ then $A \cup B, A \cdot B$ and $A^+ \in \mathcal{R}$.

In order to generalize well known results for monoids in the case of partial semigroups, and as our purpose is to deal with graphs, we will set some notations and definitions for graphs and automata.
Let P be a subset of S. A (simple oriented labelled) P-*graph* G over V with arcs labelled in P is a subset of $V \times P \times V$. An element (s, a, t) in G is an *arc* of *source* s, *goal* t and *label* a (s and t are *vertices* of G). We denote by $Dom(G)$, $Im(G)$ and V_G the sets respectively of sources, goals and vertices of G. Each (s, a, t) of G is identified with labelled transition $s \xrightarrow[G]{a} t$ or simply $s \xrightarrow{a} t$ if G is understood.
A graph G is *deterministic* if distinct arcs with same source have distinct label: $r \xrightarrow{a} s \wedge r \xrightarrow{a} t \Rightarrow s = t$. A graph is (source) *complete* if, for every label a, every vertex is source of an arc labelled a: $\forall a \in P$, $\forall s \in V_G$, $\exists t\ s \xrightarrow{a} t$.
Set $2^{V \times P^+ \times V}$ of P^+-graphs with vertices in V is a semigroup for *composition relation*: $G \cdot H := \{r \xrightarrow{a \cdot b} t \mid \exists s, r \xrightarrow[G]{a} s \wedge s \xrightarrow[H]{b} t\}$ for any $G, H \subseteq V \times P^+ \times V$.
Relation $\xrightarrow[G^+]{u}$ denoted by $\xRightarrow[G]{u}$ or simply $\xRightarrow{u}$ if G is understood, is the existence of a *path* in G labelled u in P^+. For any L in S, we denote by $s \xRightarrow{L} t$ that there exists u in L such that $s \xRightarrow{u} t$.

The *trace* (or set of path labels) $L(G,E,F)$ of G from a set E to a set F is the following subset of P^+:

$$L(G,E,F) \ := \ \{u \in S \mid \exists\, s \in E,\ \exists\, t \in F,\ s \overset{u}{\underset{G}{\Longrightarrow}} t\ \}$$

Given $P \subseteq S$, a *P-automaton* A is a P-graph G whose vertices are called *states*, with an *initial state* i and a subset F of *final states*; the automaton *recognizes* subset $L(A)$ of P^+: $L(A) := L(G,\{i\},F)$. An automaton is finite (resp. deterministic, complete) if its graph is finite (resp. deterministic, complete). This allows to state a standard result for rational subsets.

Proposition 2.3. *Given a subset P of a partial semigroup S, $Rat(P^+)$ is*

(i) the smallest subset of 2^S containing $\emptyset$ and $\{a\}$ for each $a \in P$, and closed for $\cup, \cdot, +$
(ii) the set of subsets recognized by finite P-automata,
(iii) the set of subsets recognized by finite and deterministic P-automata.

We simply translated the standards definitions of rational subsets of monoids given for example in [Be 79]. An interesting example of a partial semigroup is the subject of these lines: the set of arcs (labelled with an element of a finite set) between elements of a free monoid is a partial semigroup; its rational subsets are the rational graphs.

2.2 Partial Semigroups and Graphs

In this section, we will consider an important example of partial semigroup: the set of rational graphs. So consider an arbitrary finite set X and denote X^* its associated free monoid. We will consider graphs as subsets of $X^*\times\mathcal{A}\times X^*$ (the set of graphs over X^* with arcs labelled in $\mathcal{A}$). For convenience, set $2^{X^*\times\mathcal{A}\times X^*}$ is denoted $G_{\mathcal{A}}(X^*)$.
Now, with $(u,a_i,v)\cdot_i(u',a_i,v') = (u\cdot u',a_i,v\cdot v')$, set $X^*\times\{a_i\}\times X^*$ (a_i in $\mathcal{A}$) is a monoid. As stated in Example 2.1 the union of these monoids (namely $X^*\times\mathcal{A}\times X^*$) is a partial semigroup. We denote by $\cdot$ the operation in $X^*\times\mathcal{A}\times X^*$ (which is $\cdot_i$ for each $X^*\times\{a_i\}\times X^*$).
Remark: this $\cdot$ operation for graphs is indeed, similar to the synchronization product for transition systems defined by Nivat and Arnold in [AN 88].
We are now able to define the set of rational graphs.

Definition 2.4. The set of rational graphs, denoted $Rat(X^*\times\mathcal{A}\times X^*)$ is the family of rational subsets of $X^*\times\mathcal{A}\times X^*$.

Let us now recall that a *transducer* is a finite automaton over pairs (see for example [Au 88] [Be 79]). A rational relation (*i.e.*, a rational subset of $X^*\times X^*$) is recognized by a rational transducer.
There is a strong relationship between rational graphs and rational relations and to characterize the family of rational graphs in a more practical way we will use *labelled transducers*.

Definition 2.5. A *labelled transducer* $T = \langle Q, I, F, E, L\rangle$ over X, is composed of a finite set of states Q, a set of initial states $I \subseteq Q$, a set of final states $F \subseteq Q$, a finite set of transitions (or edges) $E \subseteq Q \times X^* \times X^* \times Q$ and an application L from F into $2^{\mathcal{A}}$.

Like for P-graphs, transition (p, u, v, q) of transducer T will be denoted by $p \xrightarrow[T]{u/v} q$ or simply $p \xrightarrow{u/v} q$ if T is understood. Now similarly an element $(u, d, v) \in X^* \times \mathcal{A} \times X^*$ is *recognized* by transducer T if there is a path $p_0 \xrightarrow[T]{u_1/v_1} p_1 \cdots p_{n-1} \xrightarrow[T]{u_n/v_n} p_n$ and $p_0 \in I$, $p_n \in F$, $u = u_1 \cdots u_n$, $v = v_1 \cdots v_n$ and $d \in L(p_n)$.
Remark: an illustration of transducer execution will be given in Example 2.7.

Proposition 2.6. *A graph G in $G_{\mathcal{A}}(X^*)$ is rational if and only if it satisfies one of the following equivalent properties:*

(i) G belongs to the smallest subset of $G_{\mathcal{A}}(X^*)$ containing:
$\emptyset$,$\{\varepsilon \xrightarrow{d} \varepsilon\}$,$\{x \xrightarrow{d} \varepsilon\}$ and $\{\varepsilon \xrightarrow{d} x\}$, for all $x \in X$, all $d \in \mathcal{A}$, and closed under $\cup$, $\cdot$ and $+$;
(ii) G is a finite union of rational relations over each letter:
$G = \bigcup_{d \in \mathcal{A}} R_d$, for $R_d \in Rat(X^* \times \{d\} \times X^*)$;
(iii) G is recognized by labelled rational transducer.

This Proposition states that for any graph G in $Rat(X^* \times \mathcal{A} \times X^*)$, the relation: $\xrightarrow[G]{d} := \{(u, v) \mid u \xrightarrow[G]{d} v\}$ is rational for each d in $\mathcal{A}$. Therefore we also introduce $\xrightarrow[G]{} := \bigcup_{d \in \mathcal{A}} \xrightarrow[G]{d}$, which is also a rational relation. Naturally we denote by $\xrightarrow[G]{d}(u)$ (resp. $\xrightarrow[G]{}(u)$) the image of word u by relation $\xrightarrow[G]{d}$ (resp. $\xrightarrow[G]{}$) (and similarly for subsets of X). Also for a rational graph G there are possibly many transducers generating it, thus we will denote by $\Theta(G)$ the set of transducers generating G.

We will now give some examples of rational graphs.

Example 2.7. This graph :

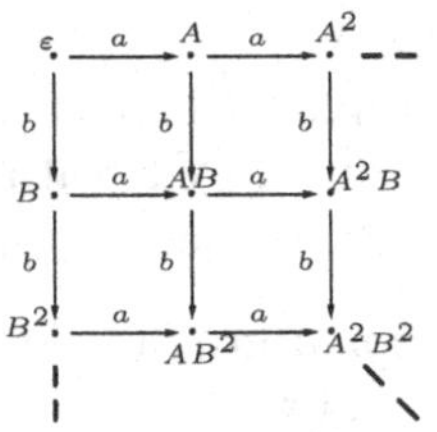

is a rational graph generated by this transducer :

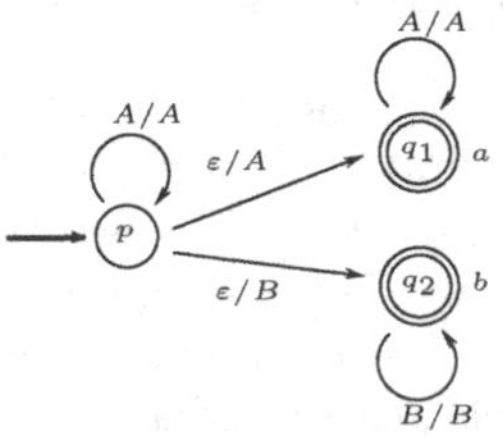

Notice that its second order monadic theory is undecidable and therefore rational graphs have an undecidable second order monadic theory.
Why does the arc (AB, b, AB^2) belong to the graph? Simply because the following path is in the transducer:

$$p \xrightarrow{A/A} p \xrightarrow{\varepsilon/B} q_2 \xrightarrow{B/B} q_2$$

and that b is associated to the final state q_2.

Example 2.8. This graph :

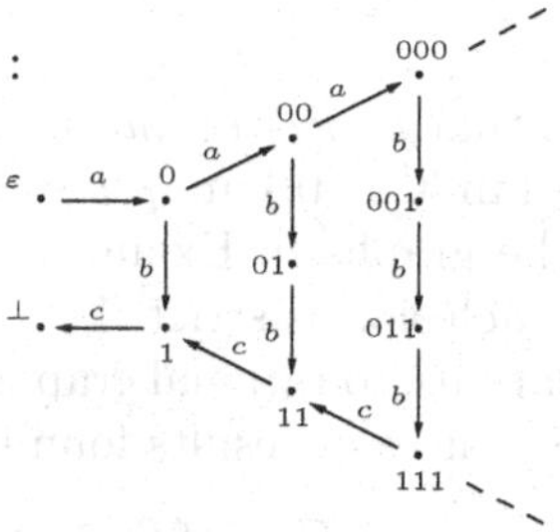

is rational, generated by this transducer :

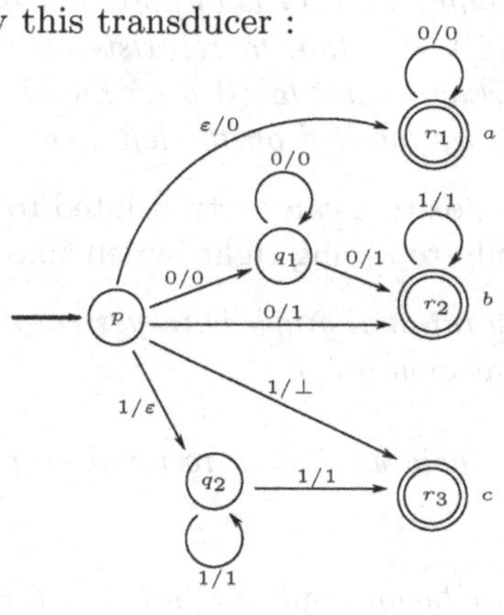

We finish with a last example showing that the transition graphs of *Petri nets* are rational graphs.

Example 2.9. For more detail on Petri nets the reader may refer to [Re 85]. A Petri net can be seen as a finite set of transitions of this form:
$A_1^{n_1} A_2^{n_2} \cdots A_m^{n_m} \xrightarrow{d} A_1^{l_1} A_2^{l_2} \cdots A_m^{l_m}$, with A_i^x representing there are x coins in place A_i (d represents the label (if any) of the transition). Following transducer generates the transition graph associated to the above transition:

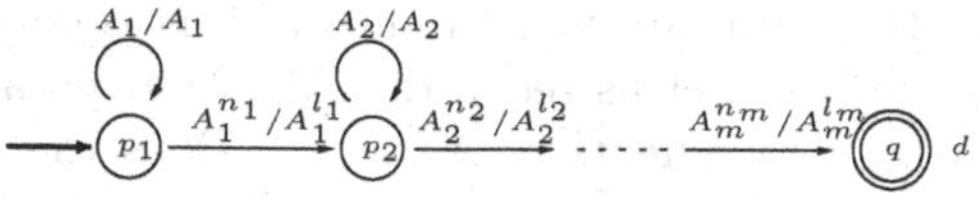

Each vertex of the generated graph correspond to a marking of the Petri net. Each arc of the graph represents that a transition has been fired.

2.3 Some Results for Rational Graphs

This section will introduce results for this family of graphs. Some of these results are just a reformulation of known results over rational relations. Others are simple facts on these graphs and their boundary.
The first fact is that this family is an extension of previous families. Simply recall that every *prefix-recognizable graph* (defined in [Ca 96]) is a finite union of graphs of the following form :

$$(U \xrightarrow{a} V) \cdot W := \{ uw \xrightarrow{a} vw \mid u \in U \wedge v \in V \wedge w \in W \}$$

with U, V, W rational sets.
This characterization ensures that *prefix-recognizable graphs* are rational graphs. As the regular graphs (defined in [Co 90]) are *prefix-recognizable graphs*, they are rational too. Furthermore, the graphs in Examples 2.7 and 2.8 are not *prefix-recognizable graphs* thus the inclusion is strict. Let us now translate some well-known results for rational relations, to rational graphs (the proofs will be omitted they are mostly direct consequences of results found in [Au 88] and [Be 79]).

Proposition 2.10. *A rational graph G is of finite out-degree if and only if there exists a transducer $T \in \Theta(G)$ such that there exists no cycle in T labelled on the left with the empty word which is not labelled on the right with the empty word. In other words the only cycles labelled on the left ε, are labelled on the right ε.*

Remark: naturally this proposition can be translated to characterize the graphs of finite in-degree, by simply replacing right by left and vice-versa.

Proposition 2.11. *Every rational graph is recursive: it is decidable whether an arc (u, d, v) belongs to a rational graph.*

Theorem 2.12. *It is decidable whether a rational graph is deterministic (from its transducer).*

Proposition 2.13. *The inclusion and equality of deterministic rational graphs is decidable.*

Remark: unfortunately this result ceases to be true for general rational graphs ([Be 79] Theorem 8.4, page 90).
We have already seen that the second order monadic theory of these graphs is undecidable in general. We will now see that it is also the case for the first order theory.

Proposition 2.14. *The first order theory of rational graphs is undecidable.*

Proof. We will prove this proposition by reducing Post's correspondence problem (P.C.P.) to this problem. Let us recall the P.C.P.: given an alphabet X and (u_0, v_0), (u_1, v_1),..., (u_n, v_n) elements of $X^* \times X^*$. Does there exist a sequence $0 \leqslant i_1, i_2, \ldots, i_m \leqslant n$, such that $u_0 u_{i_1} \cdots u_{i_m} = v_0 v_{i_1} \cdots v_{i_m}$? To an instance of P.C.P. (i.e. a family (u_i, v_i)) we associate following transducer:

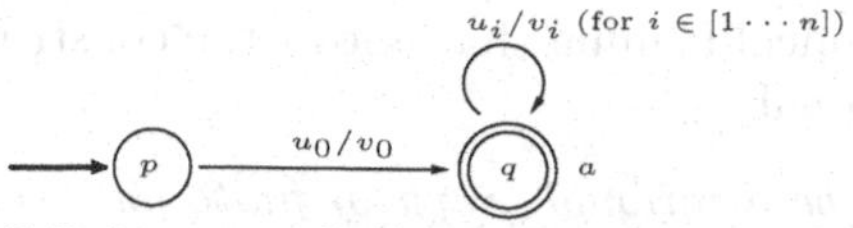

The resolution of P.C.P. becomes finding a vertex s such that $s \xrightarrow{a} s$ is an arc of the graph generated by the transducer. It is a first order instance, therefore,as P.C.P. is undecidable, the first order theory of rational graphs is not decidable in general. □

Before giving another negative decision result, let us denote by $\tilde{u}$ the mirror of word u (defined by induction on the length of u: $\tilde{\varepsilon} = \varepsilon$ and $\widetilde{au} = \tilde{u}a$ (for any u with $|u| \geqslant 0$).

Proposition 2.15. *Accessibility is not decidable for rational graphs in general.*

Proof. Once again, we use P.C.P. Using the same notations as earlier define a (word) rewriting system G, using two new symbols # and \$, in the following way:

$$G \begin{cases} \$ \longrightarrow u_i\$\widetilde{v_i}\ \forall i \in \{0, \cdots, n\} \\ \$ \longrightarrow \# \\ A\#A \longrightarrow \#\quad \forall A \in X \end{cases}$$

Now "P.C.P. has a solution" is equivalent to the existence of a derivation from $u_0\$\widetilde{v_0}$ to #. But, considering the following transducer:

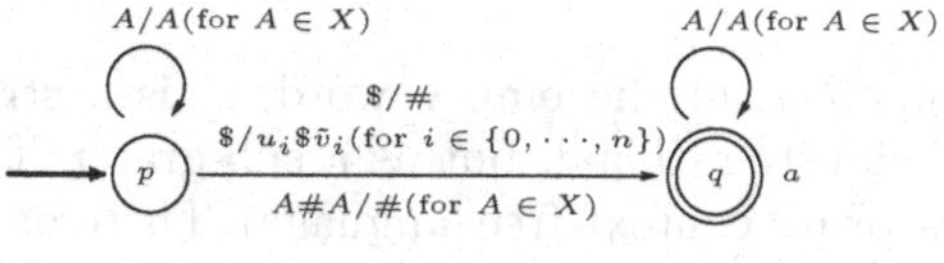

the question becomes: is there a path leading from $u_0\$\widetilde{v_0}$ to the vertex # ? Answering the last question would allow P.C.P. to be solved in the general case which is a contradiction. Therefore accessibility is undecidable for the rational graphs in general. □

Remark: the transitive closure of a rational graph is, at least, uneffective. If this construction were effective and rational, then accessibility for rational graph would be decidable.
Now we will see a case where accessibility is decidable for rational graphs. A transducer T is *increasing* if every pair (u, v) recognized by T is such that the length of v (denoted by $|v|$) is greater or equal to the length of u : $|v| \geqslant |u|$.

Proposition 2.16. *The accessibility is decidable for any rational graph with an increasing transducer.*

Proof. Let us denote by $T^{\leqslant n}(u)$ following set: $T^{\leqslant n}(u) := \bigcup_{i=0}^{n} T^i(u)$. For all $n \in \mathbb{N}$ this set is rational.
Now, let G be a rational graph generated by an increasing transducer T and let u and v be two vertices of G. Let us put $n_0 = |\{w \in X^* \mid |u| \leqslant |w| \leqslant |v|\}| = |X|^{|u|} + \cdots + |X|^{|v|}$. Vertex v is accessible from u if and only if v belongs to $T^{\leqslant n_0}(u)$. Thus accessibility is decidable for rational graphs with an increasing transducer. □

We now give a technical Lemma that allows the construction of a graph that is not *structurally* rational.

Lemma 2.17. *Let G be a rational graph of finite out-degree. There exists two integers p and q such that for every $(s, a, t) \in G$ we have $|t| \leqslant p.|s| + q$*

Example 2.18. Consider an infinite tree in $X^* \times \mathcal{A} \times X^*$ such that every vertex of depth n has $2^{2^{2^n}}$ sons. This tree is not *strucurally* rational, in other words whatever name are given to its vertices this graph is never a rational graph. This is a direct consequence of previous lemma: say n is the length of the root, there are at most $|X|^{(np^l + p^{l-1}q + \cdots + q)}$ vertices of depth l.

Despite these results the transducers are not able to capture the structure of rational graphs.
For example, this transducer:

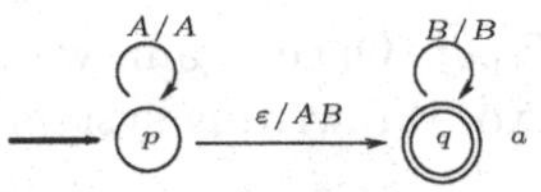

generates this graph:

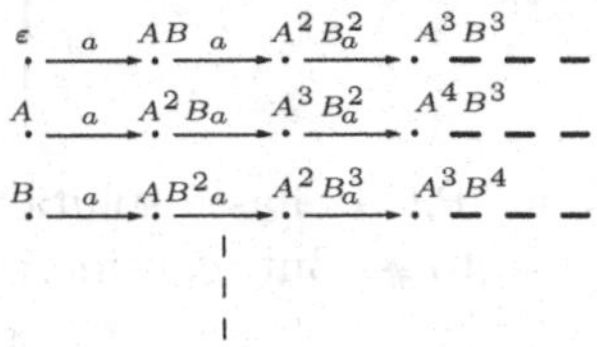

The connected component of the empty word, ε, is a straight-line. It is "up to isomorphism" obviously rational, but as a sub-graph of this graph, it is not rational (its vertices form a context-free language). Therefore we need an external ("up to isomorphism") characterization of these graphs. This is the subject of the next section.

3 An External Characterization

In this section, we will characterize rational graphs using inverse linear substitutions. Labelled transducers are an internal representation of rational graphs, it clearly depends on the name of the vertices. But often in graph theory, the name of the vertices is not relevant, it carries no information. An external characterization, like the graph grammars for equational graphs, produces graphs without giving names for vertices. It only gives the *structure* of the graph. Inverse linear substitution is an external characterization of rational graphs.

3.1 Graph Isomorphism

An external characterization of rational graphs is given "up to isomorphism". Two graphs G_1 and G_2 in $G_{\mathcal{A}}(X^*)$ are *isomorphic*, if there is a bijection ψ : $V(G_1) \to V(G_2)$ such that: $s_1 \xrightarrow[G_1]{d} s_2$(*i.e.*, $(s_1, d, s_2) \in G_1$) if and only if $\psi(s_1) \xrightarrow[G_2]{d} \psi(s_2)$.

Two isomorphic graphs have the same structure: they are the same up to a renaming of the vertices.
Now let us consider the equivalence ($\equiv$) generated by graph isomorphism: we say that G_1 is equivalent to G_2 (denoted $G_1 \equiv G_2$) if G_1 and G_2 are isomorphic. This equivalence relation provides us with a partition of $G_{\mathcal{A}}(X^*)$ denoted $Graph_{\mathcal{A}} := G_{\mathcal{A}}(X^*)/\equiv$. This allows the introduction of the set of *structural rational graphs*:

$$GRat_{\mathcal{A}} := \{[G]_{\equiv} \in Graph_{\mathcal{A}} \mid G \in Rat(X^* \times \mathcal{A} \times X^*)\}$$

This set is the set of graphs that are isomorphic to some rational graph.
Set $Graph_{\mathcal{A}}$ (and $GRat_{\mathcal{A}}$) does not depend on the choice of set X, therefore we can choose X to be any two letters alphabet with no loss of generality.

Lemma 3.1. *For all subset X' (with at least two elements) of X and all class $[G]_{\equiv}$ of $Graph_{\mathcal{A}}$ ($= G_{\mathcal{A}}(X^*)/\equiv$) there exists G_0 in $G_{\mathcal{A}}(X'^*)$ such that $G_0 \in [G]_{\equiv}$.*

We now have to characterize the structure of $GRat_{\mathcal{A}}$. This is the goal of the next section.

3.2 Substitution

Recall the definition of the *prefix-recognizable graphs* (family REC_{Rat}). This family has been defined as the set of graphs obtained from the complete binary tree by inverse rational substitution, followed by rational restriction. We will use the same process (actually a linear context-free substitution) to obtain the family of rational graphs.
A *substitution* over a free monoid X^* is a morphism $\varphi : \mathcal{A}^* \to 2^{X^*}$, which associates to each letter in $\mathcal{A}$ a language in X^*. Our purpose is to study graphs, starting from the complete binary tree (Λ) labelled $X = \{A, B\}$. To move by inverse arcs, we use a new alphabet : $\overline{X} = \{\overline{A}, \overline{B}\}$ and we say that $x \xrightarrow{\overline{A}} y$ if $y \xrightarrow{A} x$. Given a language L and two vertices x and y, recall that $x \underset{\Lambda}{\overset{L}{\Longrightarrow}} y \Leftrightarrow \exists u \in L, x \underset{\Lambda}{\overset{u}{\Longrightarrow}} y$. Now, given a substitution $\varphi : \mathcal{A}^* \to 2^{(X \cup \overline{X})^*}$, we can define the graph $\varphi^{-1}(\Lambda)$ in the following way:

$$\varphi^{-1}(\Lambda) = \{x \xrightarrow{d} y \mid d \in \mathcal{A} \wedge x \underset{\Lambda}{\overset{\varphi(d)}{\Longrightarrow}} y\}$$

Given a language L, we define now $L_{\Lambda} = \{s \mid r \underset{\Lambda}{\overset{L}{\Longrightarrow}} s\}$. It allows us to consider the graph $\varphi^{-1}(\Lambda)_{|L_{\Lambda}}$: it is the image of the complete binary tree by an inverse substitution followed by a restriction; if L is rational, we say a rational restriction.

Example 3.2. Example 2.7 states that the grid is a rational graph. Following substitution: $h(a) = \{\overline{B}^m A B^m \mid m \geqslant 0\}$, $h(b) = \{B\}$ over the complete binary tree on $\{A, B\}$, followed with the restriction to $L = A^* B^*$ produces a graph isomorphic to the grid:

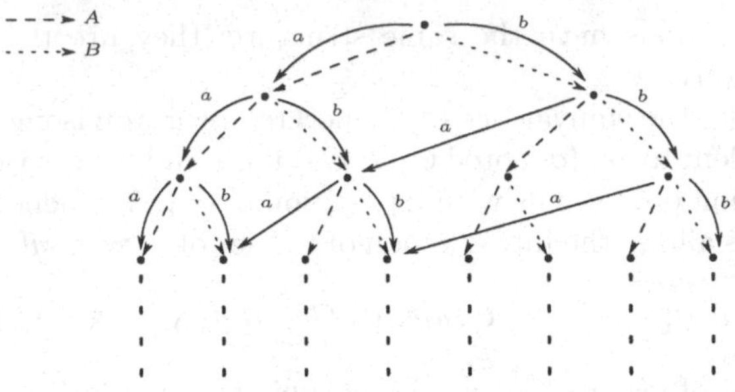

Now, it is well know that there is a close relationship between *linear languages* and rational relations (a linear language is a context-free language generated by a grammar with only, at most, one non-terminal on the right hand side of each rule). And indeed, if we denote the set of linear languages over the alphabet $X \cup \overline{X}$ by $Lin(X \cup \overline{X})$, we have the following proposition.

Proposition 3.3. *The set $GRat_{\mathcal{A}}$ is a subset of the family of the graphs obtained from the complete binary tree (Λ) by an inverse* linear *substitution, followed by a rational restriction:*

$$GRat_{\mathcal{A}} \subseteq \{[\varphi^{-1}(\Lambda)_{|L_\Lambda}]_{\equiv} \mid \forall d \in \mathcal{A}, \varphi(d) \in Lin(X \cup \overline{X}) \wedge L \in Rat(X)\}$$

Proof (Sketch). We first transform the transducer generating the graph (G) so that each vertex begins with the same prefix. Then we produce linear languages (L_d) such that $(u, d, v) \in X^* \times \mathcal{A} \times X^*$ is an arc of G if and only if $\widetilde{\overline{u}}v \in L_d$. We then define $\varphi(d)$ to be L_d. It only remains to define L (the rational restriction) to be $L := Dom(G) \cup Im(G)$ □

The converse of this result would help us to grab the structure of rational graphs. Unfortunately it is not obvious. Actually the following example illustrate the difficulty of the naive converse of Proposition 3.3.

Example 3.4. Consider $\varphi(a) = \{\overline{B}BA^nB^n | n \in \mathbb{N}\}$, it is a linear substitution. Consider $L = BA^*B^*$ and the graph $G = \varphi^{-1}(\Lambda)_{|L_\Lambda}$. Structurally, graph G is rational (it is the star). But the graph naturally associated to G (according to $\varphi(a)$ and L) is $G' = \{(B, a, BA^nB^n) | n \in \mathbb{N}\}$, which is not rational.

So there is a deep isomorphism problem to get the converse. Actually, we will try to inject rationality in the "linear language" to achieve a complete characterization of rational graphs.

A natural way to introduce rationality into $Lin(X \cup \overline{X})$ would be to impose the projections over barred and non-barred letters to be rational. The next example shows that again, things are not so nice.

Example 3.5. Consider $\varphi(a) = \{\overline{A}\overline{B}BA^nB^m | n \geqslant m\} \cup \{\overline{B}BA^nB^m | m > n\}$ φ is a linear substitution. Moreover it has rational projections over barred and non-barred letters. Consider $L = BA^*B^*$ and the graph $G = \varphi^{-1}(\Lambda)_{|L_\Lambda}$.

Structurally, graph G is rational (it is two stars). But the graph naturally associated to G (according to $\varphi(a)$ and L) is $G' = \{(BA, a, BA^nB^m) | \ n \geqslant m\} \cup \{(B, a, BA^nB^m) | \ m > n\}$, which is not rational (its intersection with the recognizable set $\{BA\} \times \{a\} \times BA^*B^*$ is $\{(BA, a, BA^nB^m) | \ n \geqslant m\}$ which is not rational).

Now consider the set $Ratlin(X \cup \overline{X})$ of linear languages (called rational-linear) over $(X \cup \overline{X})^*$ such that the production of their grammars are of following form: $p \rightarrow \overline{u}qv$ (with $\overline{u} \in \overline{X}^*$ and $v \in X^*$) or $p \rightarrow \varepsilon$.

Theorem 3.6. *Set $GRat_{\mathcal{A}}$ is precisely the set of graphs obtained from the complete binary tree (Λ) by a* rational-linear *substitution, followed by a rational restriction :*

$$GRat_{\mathcal{A}} = \{[\varphi^{-1}(\Lambda)_{|L_\Lambda}]_{\equiv} \mid \forall d \in \mathcal{A}, \varphi(d) \in Ratlin(X \cup \overline{X}) \land L \in Rat(X)\}$$

Proof (Sketch). The first inclusion is treated in Proposition 3.3. For the reverse inclusion we first take a graph G image of a *rational-linear* substitution, followed by a rational restriction then we need to check that it is possible to produce a transducer from the grammars of $\varphi(d)$ for each d. Then we show that this graph contains G, finally, using rational intersection we obtain precisely G. □

Now that an external characterization of the rational graphs has been given, the next section will consider the properties of the *traces* of rational graphs.

4 The Traces of Rational Graphs

We have already seen that there is a strong connection between language theory and rational graphs. In this section we will see another connection between graphs and languages, in terms of *traces*.
We first recall that the *trace* of a graph G leading from a vertex set I (of initial states) to a vertex set F (of final states) is the set of all the path labels in the graph, leading from a vertex in the set of initial states to a vertex in the set of final states:

$$L(G, I, F) := \{u \mid \exists s \in I \ \exists t \in F, s \underset{G}{\overset{u}{\Longrightarrow}} t\}$$

In other words the trace of a graph is "the language of its labels". For example the traces of the finite graphs are all rational languages and the traces of *prefix-recognizable graphs* are all context-free languages. Notice by the way that the traces of rational graphs contain therefore every context free language.

Proposition 4.1. *The traces of rational graph leading from a rational vertex set to a context free vertex set (or vice-versa) is recursive*

Proof. In order to check whether a word u is in the trace of graph G (from a set I to a set F), it is just to check if the set $S = \underset{G}{\overset{u(|u|)}{\longrightarrow}}(\underset{G}{\overset{u(|u|-1)}{\longrightarrow}}(\cdots \underset{G}{\overset{u(1)}{\longrightarrow}}(I)\cdots))$ intersects set F. If set I is rational (*resp.* context-free) its image by a rational transduction is rational (*resp.* context-free), hence by a simple induction, set S is rational (*resp.* context-free). Therefore it is decidable whether $S \cap F$ is empty. □

Let us denote by *TR* the family of the traces of rational graphs leading from a rational vertex set to a rational vertex set: $TR = \{L(G, I, F) | \, G \in Rat(X^* \times \mathcal{A} \times X^*) \wedge I, F \in Rat(X^*)\}$ (notice that we could as well restrict ourselves to a unique initial state and a unique final state). Now we will show that set *TR* form an *Abstract Family of Languages* (AFL), that is, it satisfies following properties:

- closure for intersection with a rational (regular) language,
- closure under non-erasing (monoid)morphism, and inverse morphism,
- for each $L, L' \in TR$ we have $L \cdot L', L \cap L', L^+, L^* \in TR$.

Proposition 4.2. *The intersection of two elements of TR is an element of TR.*

Proof. Consider two elements L and L' of *TR*. Say $L = L(G, I, F)$ and $L' = L(G', I, F)$. The language $L \cap L'$ is actually the trace of $G \cdot (\{\$\} \times \mathcal{A} \times \{\$\}) \cdot G'$ (with $\$$ a new symbol) between $I_G \cdot \{\$\} \cdot I_{G'}$ and $F_G \cdot \{\$\} \cdot F_{G'}$. Hence $L \cap L'$ in an element of *TR*. □

As rational languages are traces of rational graphs (finite graphs are rational graphs), family *TR* is closed under intersection with rational languages.
Now let us recall that a finite (*resp.* rational) substitution $\sigma : \mathcal{A}^* \to 2^{\mathcal{A}^*}$ is a morphism such that for each letter d in $\mathcal{A}$ $\sigma(d)$ is a finite (*resp.* rational) subset of $\mathcal{A}^*$. A substitution is *non-erasing* if $\varepsilon \notin \sigma(d)$ for all $d \in \mathcal{A}$.

Proposition 4.3. *Family TR is closed under non-erasing finite substitution.*

Proof (Sketch). Consider σ a non-erasing finite substitution, and L a language in *TR*. We take a graph G such that $L = L(G, I, F)$, and T a transducer generating G. We, then, construct a new transducer such that each production d in T is replaced by a path u (in the corresponding graph), for each $u \in \sigma(d)$. The trace of the graph generated by this transducer is $\sigma(L)$ □

Following corollary is a direct consequence of this proposition.

Corollary 4.4. *Family TR is closed under non-erasing morphism.*

Notice that the condition "non-erasing" is essential for our proof. A interesting question is whether this condition is necessary.

Proposition 4.5. *Assume that L is an element of TR and that σ is a finite substitution over $\mathcal{A}^*$ then $\sigma^{-1}(L)$ is a language of TR.*

Proof (Sketch). This proposition is a consequence of Elgot and Mezei's theorem, which states that the composition of two rational relations is a rational relation (see for example [Be 79], Theorem 4.4 p 68). Using this we can produce a rational graph in which a finite number of finite path are replaced by arcs. Which proves the Proposition. □

Remark: Note that it is not as straightforward for inverse rational substitution. Actually it seems that it is not true for inverse rational substitution: consider any rational graph with one label (a) and the inverse rational substitution $\sigma(a) = a^*$. The graph image with the same approach would be the transitive closure of the original graph, which is not effectively rational (and might not even be structurally rational) as stated in the remark after Proposition 2.15.
Following corollary is an obvious consequence of proposition 4.5.

Corollary 4.6. *Family TR is closed under inverse morphism.*

Proposition 4.7. *Family TR is closed under concatenation, Kleene plus and star.*

Proof (Sketch). The argument is more or less the same as for finite automata. We use operation over rational relations to get the results. □

As stated earlier, we only have now to summary these results.

Theorem 4.8. *The traces of rational graphs, leading from a rational vertex set to a rational vertex set, form an AFL (Abstract Family of Languages).*

Proof. This result is simply a brief summary of corollaries 4.4, 4.6 and propositions 4.2 and 4.7. □

Now we have an abstract family of languages that contains the context free languages. This AFL is a subset of the recursive languages. It seems that this family is composed of the context sensitive languages.

Conjecture 4.9. *The traces of the rational graphs are precisely the context sensitives languages.*

Notice also that recently graphs of linear bounded machines (which characterize context sensitive languages) have been studied in [KP 99].

5 Conclusion

In this paper, a general family of graphs has been introduced. Rational graphs are a strict extension of previously studied families. It is a well grounded family, related to well known structures of language theory. We have given both an internal and an external characterization, as well as some basic properties.

Unfortunately, or fortunately depending on the point of view, it is a very expressive family. Therefore many decision results are lost. An interesting question is to study restrictions of this family that will retain decision results from former families.

Traces of rational graphs are another aspect of this family. We have shown that it forms an abstract family of recursive languages. An interesting question is to know if these traces are precisely the context sensitive languages.

Rational trees also seem to be an interesting field of research, but this has not been done yet.

Acknowledgements

The author would like to express his gratitude to Didier Caucal for his help along the preparation of this paper.

References

[AN 88] A. Arnold and M. Nivat, *Comportements de processus*, Colloque AFCET "les mathématiques de l'informatique", pp. 35–68, 1982.

[Au 88] J.-M. Autebert and L. Boasson, *Transductions rationelles*, Ed. Masson, pp. 1–133, 1988.

[Be 79] J. Berstel *Transductions and context-free languages*, Ed. Teubner, pp. 1–278, 1979.

[Ca 96] D. Caucal *On transition graphs having a decidable monadic theory*, LNCS 1099, pp. 194–205, 1996,

[Co 90] B. Courcelle *Graph rewriting: an algebraic and logic approach*, Handbook of TCS, Vol. B, Elsevier, pp. 193–242, 1990.

[GG 66] S. Ginsburg and S. A. Greibach *Mappings which preserve context sensitive languages*, Information and Control 9, pp. 563–582, 1966.

[HU 79] J. E. Hopcroft and J. D. Ullman *Introduction to automata theory, langages and computation*, Ed. Addison-Wesley pp. 1–284, 1979.

[KP 99] T. Knapik and E. Payet *Synchronization product of Linear Bounded Machines*, LNCS 1684, pp. 362–373, 1999.

[MS 85] D. Muller and P. Schupp *The theory of ends, pushdown automata, and second-order logic*, TCS 37, pp. 51–75, 1985.

[Ni 68] M. Nivat *Transduction des langages de Chomsky*, Ann. de l'Inst. Fourier 18, pp. 339-456, 1968.

[Re 85] W. Reisig *Petri nets.* EATCS Monographs on Theoretical Computer Science, Vol. 4, Springer Verlag, 1985.

[Sc 76] M.P. Schützenberger *Sur les relations rationnelles entre monoïdes libres*, TCS 3, pp. 243–259, 1976.

Sequential and Concurrent Abstract Machines for Interaction Nets

Jorge Sousa Pinto*

Laboratoire d'Informatique (LIX - CNRS UMR 7650)
École Polytechnique
91128 Palaiseau Cedex, France
pinto@lix.polytechnique.fr

Abstract. This paper is a formal study of how to implement interaction nets, filling an important gap in the work on this graphical rewriting formalism, very promising for the implementation of languages based on the λ-calculus. We propose the first abstract machine for interaction net reduction, based on a decomposition of interaction rules into more atomic steps, which tackles all the implementation details hidden in the graphical presentation. As a natural extension of this, we then give a concurrent shared-memory abstract machine, and show how to implement it, resulting in the first parallel implementation of interaction nets.

1 Introduction

Interaction Nets (INs) are an extension of Proof-Nets for the multiplicative fragment of Linear Logic [5], proposed by Yves Lafont [8, 9] as a simple and inherently parallel graphical formalism for programming. By way of a number of translations of the λ-calculus, interaction nets have proved to be a useful new paradigm for implementing functional languages, specifically when controlling the sharing of terms is a priority. The research effort has however been directed more at these translations than at the implementation of interaction net reduction – in particular, no parallel implementations exist. In this paper we study the sequential and concurrent implementation of interaction nets, by means of abstract machines in which interaction steps are decomposed into simple machine operations.

The interest of interaction nets for functional programming is twofold: on one hand they allow to control the amount of shared reductions performed. In particular, they have been used for the implementation of Optimal Reduction (as formalized in [12], and brought to practice in successive studies [10, 6, 1]), but also other efficient strategies for the λ-calculus have been proposed [13].

On the other hand, we have their potential (which has not yet been fully explored) to be implemented *in parallel*: unlike general graph-rewriting systems,

* On leave from Universidade do Minho. Research partially supported by PRAXIS XXI grant BD/11261/97.

J. Tiuryn (Ed.): FOSSACS 2000, LNCS 1784, pp. 267–282, 2000.

interaction nets possess locality and confluence properties which allow for all the active pairs in a given net to be reduced simultaneously, without interference.

Implementations of INs have to this point been quite ad-hoc, since the formalism, being a graphical representation, has always been assumed to be trivial, and no formal studies of its implementation have been undertaken. However, there is a considerable gap between this presentation and a running implementation, in the sense that each basic interaction rewriting step may require many 'rewiring' steps, implemented by non-trivial sequences of machine operations.

Additionally, a decomposition of interaction steps into sequences of basic, close-to-machine operations is essential if parallel implementations are to be studied. We may then investigate whether the benefits are limited to the potential parallelism contained in the nets (simultaneous redexes) or if there are other opportunities for parallelizing, at the level of small-grain machine operations.

Abstract machines for the λ-calculus such as the SECD machine [11] or Krivine's machine [3] have been proposed as implementation devices encompassing (and decomposing) both the β-reduction relation and the variable substitution mechanism. A mechanism along these lines does not however exist for interaction nets. In this paper we introduce such an abstract machine, providing a suitable decomposition of interaction rewriting steps into fine grain operations.

From this machine we then obtain a concurrent (multi-threaded, shared memory) version as a simple generalization, where basic machine tasks are distributed among threads. This may be implemented on any platform offering support for multi-threaded computation, although some care is required to guarantee correctness. The result is the first parallel reducer for interaction nets.

Structure of the Paper. We start by briefly reviewing interaction nets and some details of their implementation. In Sect.3 we introduce notation and then define machine configurations as appropriate tuples of data-structures, and show how to obtain a configuration from a net, before giving the definition of the sequential abstract machine. Section 4 is devoted to the study of correctness of this machine. We then present the concurrent machine in Sect.5. In Sect.6 we mention some implementation aspects, notably with respect to the parallel implementation of the concurrent abstract machine, and finally conclude in Sect.7.

2 Background and Motivation

An interaction net is an undirected graph built from a set of cells or agents, each of which contains a *principal port*, and a number (possibly zero) of *auxiliary ports*. Edges in this graph connect any two ports, but no more than one edge may be connected to the same port. A *free port* in the net has a hanging edge connected to it, i.e, an edge which is not connected to anything at the other extremity. The *observable interface* of a net is the set of its free ports arranged in a sequence. Computation (in the form of graph-rewriting) takes place only at special edges of the net, those connecting two cells by their principal ports. Such a pair of cells is called an *active pair*, and it may be rewritten using an

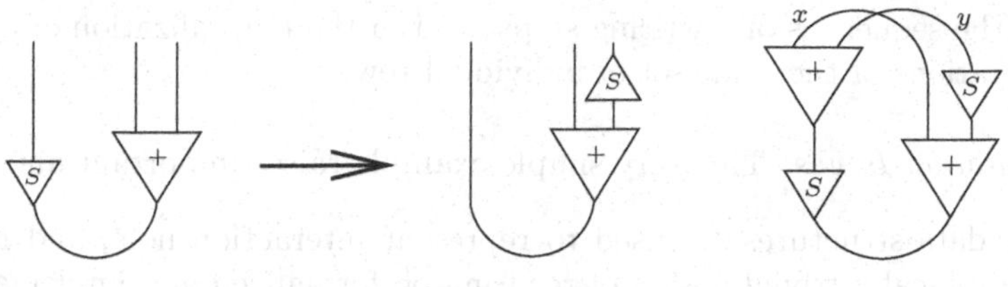

Fig. 1. Example interaction rule and its representation using Lafont's notation

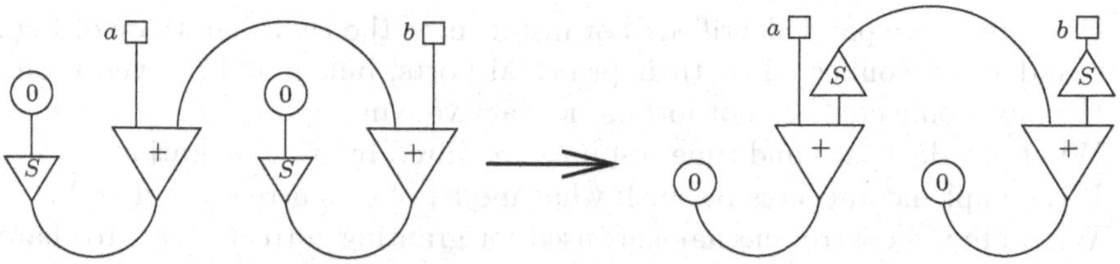

Fig. 2. Example interaction net

appropriate *interaction rule*. An interaction system specifies a set of agents (from which to build nets) and rules (with which to rewrite them).

An Example. The left-hand side of Fig.1 represents an interaction rule in a system containing agents (0, S, and +) and rules for natural numbers arithmetic. The cells are the following: 0 is a single-port agent, representing the constant 0. S is a constructor with two ports, the principal port representing the successor of the number in the auxiliary port. Finally, the + agent has two auxiliary ports, one of which is for the sum of the numbers in the principal port and in the other auxiliary port. We define addition inductively on its first argument, so this must be associated to a principal port, where interaction is possible.

The rule is to be applied as a graph-rewriting rule: in a net in which a sub-net matching the left side of the rule occurs, this sub-net may be substituted by the net on the right. The *interface preservation* property ensures that there is a wire in the right-hand side net to connect to every wire left hanging when the sub-net is removed from the initial net. Figure 2 is an example of how this rule can be applied. We distinguish observable values (a and b) graphically using small squares. In the figure, the two active pairs are reduced in parallel, using the rule in Fig.1. The reader will have no difficulty in writing the interaction rule (between the 0 and + agents) that would be needed for reduction to proceed.

The motivations for parallelism can be easily understood. Interaction always happens *locally*, when two cells are connected via their principal ports. The rewritable elements are always pairs of cells, so any cell can be involved in at most one such element; no critical pairs exist. Any two active pairs in a net can be rewritten in arbitrary order; strong local confluence holds, resulting in the fact that the sequences of rewriting steps used in the normalization of a net are all permutations of the same set of individual rewrites.

Implementation Issues. This very simple example raises important questions:

1. What data-structures are used to represent interaction nets, and how can the graphically trivial notion of rewiring be formalized and implemented?
2. How is the observable interface updated (this is a particular case of rewiring)?
3. Each application of an interaction rule involves producing a copy of its right-hand side. How is this accounted for?
4. How are active pairs identified? For instance, in the right-hand side of Fig.2, 0 and + are connected by their principal ports, but + and S, even though they are connected, do not form a new active pair.
5. What are the space and time resources required by each operation?
6. If the implementation is parallel, what model of concurrency is used?
7. What are the control mechanisms used for granting correct access to shared resources by the different parallel processing elements?

An abstract machine, by decomposing interaction into atomic operations, should provide answers to these questions, and should be directly implementable.

A Language for Interaction Nets. The language we use to describe nets was originally given by Lafont [8] and developed in [4]. Agents are written as algebraic constructors with arity equal to the number of auxiliary ports. Active pairs are then equations, equalities between terms with variables. A wire linking two leaves (two auxiliary ports) in two such terms (trees) is represented by two occurrences of the same variable. Variables are allowed as members in equations, to allow for modular descriptions. Each variable occurs *exactly twice* in the net.

A net may then be described as a pair $\langle \mathbf{t} \mid \Delta \rangle$, with $\mathbf{t}$ a sequence of terms (its observable interface) and Δ a multiset of equations. With respect to rules, each one may be represented succinctly as a net with one active pair (and empty observable interface), by wiring together each free port occurring in the left-hand side of the rule and the corresponding port in its right-hand side (see Fig. 1).

Semantics. We briefly review a calculus for interaction nets [4], inspired by the Chemical Abstract Machine [2]. Let $\rightleftharpoons$ be the smallest equivalence satisfying the structural rules $\Delta, t = u, \Theta \rightleftharpoons \Delta, u = t, \Theta$ and $\Delta, t = u, v = w, \Theta \rightleftharpoons \Delta, v = w, t = u, \Theta$. $\mathcal{N}$ is the function giving the set of variables occurring in a term. We give a set of conditional reduction rules for interaction nets. We assume no variable occurs simultaneously in a rule and in the net.

Interaction: $(\alpha(t'_1, \ldots, t'_n), \beta(u'_1, \ldots, u'_m))$ is an interaction rule $\Rightarrow$
$\langle \mathbf{t} \mid \alpha(t_1 \ldots t_n) = \beta(u_1 \ldots u_m), \Gamma \rangle \longrightarrow$
$\langle \mathbf{t} \mid t_1 = t'_1, \ldots, t_n = t'_n, u_1 = u'_1, \ldots, u_m = u'_m, \Gamma \rangle$.

Indirection: $x \in \mathcal{N}(u) \;\Rightarrow\; \langle \mathbf{t} \mid x = t, u = v, \Gamma \rangle \longrightarrow \langle \mathbf{t} \mid u[t/x] = v, \Gamma \rangle$.

Collect: $x \in \mathcal{N}(\mathbf{t}) \;\Rightarrow\; \langle \mathbf{t} \mid x = u, \Delta \rangle \longrightarrow \langle \mathbf{t}[u/x] \mid \Delta \rangle$.

Multiset: $\Theta \rightleftharpoons^* \Theta', \langle \mathbf{t_1} \mid \Theta' \rangle \longrightarrow \langle \mathbf{t_2} \mid \Delta' \rangle, \Delta' \rightleftharpoons^* \Delta \;\Rightarrow\; \langle \mathbf{t_1} \mid \Theta \rangle \longrightarrow \langle \mathbf{t_2} \mid \Delta \rangle$.

Properties. Some properties of this system, proved in [4], are *strong local confluence* (diamond property) and *uniqueness of normal forms.* A standard result of (abstract) rewrite systems also yields, as a consequence of strong confluence:

Lemma 1. *Any normalizing interaction net is* strongly *normalizing.*

Remarks. Each variable occurs exactly once in the term (or list) where it is substituted, and no two rules may perform substitution of the same variable.

The above semantics defines a notion of canonical forms for interaction nets: $P \Downarrow Q$ iff $P \longrightarrow^* Q$ and $Q \not\longrightarrow$. These canonical forms correspond to irreducible nets $\langle \mathbf{t} \mid \varepsilon \rangle$ or $\langle \mathbf{t} \mid \mathcal{LC} \rangle$, with $\mathcal{LC}$ a list of cycles of the form $x = t$, with $x \in \mathcal{N}(t)$.

Structural Equivalence of Interaction Nets. Two interaction nets are *α-convertible*, written $\mathcal{A} \approx_\alpha \mathcal{B}$, if they are the same up to renaming of variables. We define *structural equivalence* ($\equiv$) as satisfying $\mathcal{A} \equiv \langle \mathbf{t} \mid \Delta \rangle$ whenever $\mathcal{A} \approx_\alpha \langle \mathbf{t} \mid \Theta \rangle$ and $\Theta \rightleftharpoons \Delta$. This is clearly an equivalence relation that is preserved by reduction.

3 A Sequential Abstract Machine for Interaction Nets

Interaction Systems. An interaction system is a tuple $\langle \Sigma, \mathcal{R}, \mathcal{V} \rangle$, where Σ is a set of *agents* and $\mathcal{R}$ is a set of *interaction rules.* Greek letters $\alpha, \beta, \ldots$ range over agents. n^α is the *arity* of agent α. $\mathcal{V}$ is the set of variables in the system, ranged over by $x, y \ldots$, and which allows one to define the set *Terms* for this system, which are either variables or *agent terms* of the form $\alpha(t_1, \ldots, t_{n^\alpha})$, with $t_1, \ldots, t_{n^\alpha} \in$ *Terms*. We will sometimes write this as $\alpha(\boldsymbol{t})$.

The function $\mathcal{N}$: *Terms* $\rightarrow \mathcal{P}(\mathcal{V})$ returns the set of variables in a term (it can be trivially extended to pairs, sequences, and sequences of pairs of terms). The $\widehat{\ }$ operator is applied to a rule to produce a copy of it in which all variable names are fresh (w.r.t. a certain context – a machine configuration) and unique.

We then define $\mathcal{T}$ as the subset of *Terms* in which each variable occurs at most once. This linearity condition may be generalized to lists of terms and lists of pairs of terms, allowing substitution to be defined trivially as assignment, since no erasing or copying of the substituted term will happen: $t[u/x] = t[x := u]$.

Each rule $r \in \mathcal{R}$ in the system is a tuple $r = (t_1, t_2, \phi_r)$ where $t_1, t_2 \in \mathcal{T}$ but $t_1, t_2 \notin \mathcal{V}$, $\mathcal{N}(t_1) \cap \mathcal{N}(t_2) = \emptyset$, and $\phi_r : \mathcal{N}(t_1) \cup \mathcal{N}(t_2) \rightarrow \mathcal{N}(t_1) \cup \mathcal{N}(t_2)$ is a fixpoint-free involutive permutation (or involution) on variables, i.e, $y = \phi_r(x)$ implies $x = \phi_r(y)$, and $\phi_r(x) \neq x$. We shall denote by $\phi_r[x \leftrightarrow y]$ the permutation which maps x to y, y to x, and any other variable z to $\phi_r(z)$. We require that no two interaction rules exist in $\mathcal{R}$ for the same pair of agents, and also that $\mathcal{R}$ is closed under symmetry so that the order of t_1 and t_2 is irrelevant. To write rules as given before in this framework, it suffices to give different names to the two occurrences of each variable, and store the linking information in ϕ_r.

We finally define a set $\mathcal{T}_a$ of *annotated terms.* These are either variables, or terms of the form $\{X\}.t$ with $t \in \mathcal{T}$, and X a list of variables, possibly containing the symbol $\square$. We shall see in Sect.3 how these annotations will be used.

Configurations. A machine configuration is a tuple $\langle \Gamma \mid S \mid \phi_N \mid V \mid C \rangle$, where no variable occurs repeatedly in two different components of the tuple:

- $\Gamma : \mathcal{V} \to \mathcal{T}_a$ is a *Heap*, a mapping such that $x \in dom(\Gamma)$ implies $x \notin \{\mathcal{N}(\Gamma(y)) \mid y \in dom(\Gamma)\}$, and $x, y \in dom(\Gamma)$ implies $\mathcal{N}(\Gamma(x)) \cap \mathcal{N}(\Gamma(y)) = \emptyset$. We use the notation $\Gamma[x \mapsto \{N\}.t]$ to refer to the heap which maps x to $\{N\}.t$ and any other variable y to $\Gamma(y)$;
- $S \in (\mathcal{T}_a \times \mathcal{T}_a)^*$ is a sequence of *Pairs* of terms, representing equations;
- $\phi_N : N \to N$ is a fixpoint-free *Involution* on variables, with $N = \mathcal{N}(S) \cup \mathcal{N}(V) \cup \mathcal{N}(C) \cup dom(\Gamma) \cup \{\mathcal{N}(\Gamma(x)) \mid x \in dom(\Gamma)\}$;
- $V \in (\mathcal{T}_a \cup \{\square\})^*$ is the *Observable Interface* of the net (a sequence of terms);
- $C \in ((\mathcal{V} \times \mathcal{T}_a) \cup \{\square\})^*$ is a sequence of *Cycles*.

Interaction Functions. We will use the usual $[\ldots]$ notation for lists, ε for the empty list, : for *cons*, @ for *append*. For an interaction system $\mathcal{S}$, we define:

$$\begin{aligned}\mathcal{I}_\mathcal{S}(\alpha(\boldsymbol{t}), \beta(\boldsymbol{u})) &= [(\nu(t_1), \nu(tt_1)), \ldots (\nu(t_{n^\alpha}), \nu(tt_{n^\alpha})),\\ &\quad (\nu(u_1), \nu(uu_1)), \ldots (\nu(u_{n^\beta}), \nu(uu_{n^\beta}))];\\ \Phi_\mathcal{S}(\alpha(\boldsymbol{t}), \beta(\boldsymbol{u})) &= \phi\phi_r;\end{aligned}$$

where $r = (\alpha(\boldsymbol{t'}), \beta(\boldsymbol{u'}), \phi_r) \in \mathcal{R}$, $\widehat{r} = (\alpha(tt_1, \ldots tt_{n^\alpha}), \beta(uu_1, \ldots uu_{n^\beta}), \phi\phi_r)$ is a fresh copy of r, and ν annotates (agent) terms with a sequence of the variables occurring in them: $\nu(x) = x$, $\nu(\alpha(\boldsymbol{t})) = \{an(\alpha(\boldsymbol{t})) : \square : \varepsilon\}.\alpha(\boldsymbol{t})$, with an defined by $an(x) = [x] \mid an(\alpha(t_1, \ldots t_{n^\alpha})) = an(t_1) \,@ \cdots @\, an(t_{n^\alpha})$. We will denote by $\circ$ an auxiliary function on lists for removing the first occurrence of the $\square$ mark.

Loading the Abstract Machine. In order to obtain initial configurations $\Sigma[\mathbf{t} \mid \Delta]$ corresponding to an interaction net $\langle \mathbf{t} \mid \Delta \rangle$ we first need to obtain a net $\langle \mathbf{t}' \mid \Delta' \rangle$ by splitting variables and linking split pairs in an involution ϕ_N. Then $\Sigma[\mathbf{t} \mid \Delta]$ is any configuration $\langle\, \emptyset \mid \nu_{lp}(seq(\Delta')) \mid \phi_N \mid \nu_l(\mathbf{t}') : \square : \varepsilon \mid \square : \varepsilon \,\rangle$, where $seq(\Delta')$ is a list obtained by arbitrarily ordering the set Δ', and ν_l, ν_{lp} generalize the previously defined ν for lists of terms and lists of pairs of terms, respectively.

The basic idea. We describe the machine succinctly: equation pairs are stored in the list S. Each execution step pops a pair, and an appropriate rule is selected (by pattern-matching) to handle that pair.

If it is an active pair $(\alpha(\boldsymbol{t}), \beta(\boldsymbol{u}))$, an interaction will be performed, invoking the interaction functions and pushing the newly generated pairs $\mathcal{I}_\mathcal{S}(\alpha(\boldsymbol{t}), \beta(\boldsymbol{u}))$ onto the stack, and including in the involution the pairs given by $\Phi_\mathcal{S}(\alpha(\boldsymbol{t}), \beta(\boldsymbol{u}))$.

If it is a pair of variables (x, y) such that $\phi_N(x) = z$ and $\phi_N(y) = w$, we remove from ϕ_N the pairs $x \leftrightarrow z$ and $y \leftrightarrow w$, and add to it the pair $z \leftrightarrow w$.

For a pair $(x, \alpha(\boldsymbol{t}))$, we simply create a new entry $x \mapsto \alpha(\boldsymbol{t})$ in the heap.

The machine stops when S is empty. For now we consider that the sequence of pairs is accessed using a LIFO strategy, thus as a stack. However it is not important how we implement the multiset of equations as a linear data-structure; by opting for a stack we simply increase the locality of the machine.

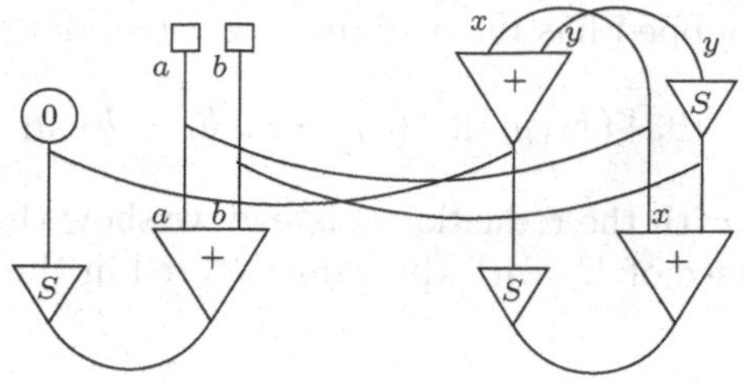

Fig. 3. Example of the rewiring involved in the application of an interaction rule

Rewiring is handled by the two last cases. Using proof-net terminology, a cut between two axioms gives origin to a single axiom, whereas a cut between an axiom and any other net results in this last net being stored in the heap. For this reason, final configurations are totally contained in the heap, since the information progressively stored in it has not been used anywhere. We thus need a set of *post-processing* rules that will traverse the observable interface and update every variable x_i in it with the value stored in the heap for $\phi_N(x_i)$. We shall not worry about post-processing here.

An Example. Let us see how this machine deals with a simplified version of the example in Sect.2. First observe, on the right in Fig.1, the interaction rule for the pair $(+, S)$ redrawn to reflect our notation for rules, giving $r_1 = (S(+(x_1, y_1)), +(x_2, S(y_2)), \{x_1 \leftrightarrow x_2, y_1 \leftrightarrow y_2\})$.

We show in Fig.3 a net consisting of a single active pair, together with a copy of the rule mentioned. The rewiring that needs to be done is shown in the picture, and consists in wiring together all the corresponding arguments of each agent in the active pair in the net and in the rule (and removing the active pair from both). Formally, we start with an initial configuration

$$\Sigma_0 = \langle \emptyset \mid [(S(0), +(a_2, b_2))] \mid \{a_1 \leftrightarrow a_2, b_1 \leftrightarrow b_2\} \mid [a_1, b_1, \square] \mid [\square] \rangle,$$

The first step of the abstract machine produces a new configuration by popping the pair from the stack and invoking the interaction functions:

$$\mathcal{I}_S(S(0), +(a_2, b_2)) = [(b_2, S(y_2)), (a_2, x_2), (0, +(x_1, y_1))],$$
$$\Phi_S(S(0), +(a_2, b_2)) = \{x_1 \leftrightarrow x_2, y_1 \leftrightarrow y_2\},$$

resulting in the configuration

$$\Sigma_1 = \langle \emptyset \mid [(b_2, S(y_2)), (a_2, x_2), (0, +(x_1, y_1))] \mid \{a_1 \leftrightarrow a_2, b_1 \leftrightarrow b_2, x_1 \leftrightarrow x_2, y_1 \leftrightarrow y_2\} \mid [a_1, b_1, \square] \rangle.$$

The pair at the top is now made of a variable and an agent term, which will now be associated to the variable, in the heap.

$$\Sigma_2 = \langle \{b_2 \mapsto S(y_2)\} \mid [(a_2, x_2), (0, +(x_1, y_1))] \mid \{a_1 \leftrightarrow a_2, b_1 \leftrightarrow b_2, x_1 \leftrightarrow x_2, y_1 \leftrightarrow y_2\} \mid [a_1, b_1, \square] \rangle.$$

The next pair to be popped has two variables, so we update the involution:

$$\Sigma_3 = \langle \{b_2 \mapsto S(y_2)\} \mid [(0, +(x_1, y_1))] \mid \{a_1 \leftrightarrow x_1, b_1 \leftrightarrow b_2, y_1 \leftrightarrow y_2\} \mid [a_1, b_1, \Box] \rangle.$$

We shall not proceed with the reduction. Instead we show the result of updating the Observable Interface of Σ_3 with the values stored in the heap:

$$\Sigma_3' = \langle \emptyset \mid [(0, +(x_1, y_1))] \mid \{a_1 \leftrightarrow x_1, y_1 \leftrightarrow y_2\} \mid [\Box, a_1, S(y_2)] \rangle.$$

A Machine with Substitutions. The above machine has some drawbacks that we will eliminate by refining its definition. The first problem has to do with cycles: in fact, not every pair $(x, \alpha(\boldsymbol{t}))$ should be moved to the heap, since it may happen that $\phi_N(x) \in \mathcal{N}(\boldsymbol{t})$. This is an example of a vicious circle, which may be generated during reduction. Our machine would store $x \mapsto \alpha(\ldots, \phi_N(x), \ldots)$ in the heap. Now since $\phi_N(x)$ occurs only in the term associated with x, its value may never be substituted in the interface, thus this part of the net will be forever lost in the heap. Configurations where this happens are called *degenerate*.

We must then include a special structure (C) in configurations, to store these pairs, and the machine must specify how the test $\phi_N(x) \in \mathcal{N}(\boldsymbol{t})$ is performed.

A different kind of degenerate configuration exists, in which active pairs, rather than cycles, are irrecoverably contained in the heap. Suppose for instance the stack looks again like $(x, \alpha(\boldsymbol{t})) : (y, \beta(\boldsymbol{u})) : \cdots$, but we now have $\phi_N(x) = y$. After a first step of operation we get a heap $\Gamma[x \mapsto \alpha(\boldsymbol{t})]$ and stack $(y, \beta(\boldsymbol{u})) : \cdots$. A second machine step produces a heap $\Gamma[x \mapsto \alpha(\boldsymbol{t}), y \mapsto \beta(\boldsymbol{u})]$, and the active pair is lost forever in it, since no substitution of x or y can be made.

It is easy to show other examples where degenerate configurations are created, either with lost cycles or lost active pairs. We will solve this problem by performing substitution of variables stored in the heap *during* the operation of the machine. For every non-active pair at the top of the stack, we will exhaustively substitute variables before actually popping it.

Looking again at the previous example, instead of performing the second step given above, we would substitute the variable y with the term $\Gamma[\phi_N(y)]$, to get the stack $(\alpha(\boldsymbol{t}), \beta(\boldsymbol{u})) : \cdots$, where the active pair has been recovered.

Implementing Substitutions on the Top of the Stack. In order to allow for the exhaustive substitution of variables on the top of the stack to be handled efficiently, we add to each term an *annotation list* containing all the variables in it. These are included in the configurations when the machine is loaded, and kept up-to-date (at a low cost) by every machine rule. Instead of traversing a whole term (a tree) looking for variables with values in the heap, we simply traverse *circularly* this annotation structure. The $\Box$ mark is initially placed at the end of every such annotation list so it can be detected when it has been fully traversed.

The Abstract Machine. We will now reformulate our configurations by including explicitly a *processing element* or *thread*. Configurations will be of the form $\langle \Gamma \mid S \mid \phi_N \mid V \mid C \mid t \rangle$, with t a *Thread*, built from the following signature:

$$\mathsf{process} : \mathcal{T}_a \times \mathcal{T}_a \to Thread \qquad \mathsf{enlist} : (\mathcal{T}_a \times \mathcal{T}_a)^* \to Thread$$
$$\mathsf{delist} : Thread \qquad \mathsf{cycle} : \mathcal{V} \times \mathcal{T}_a \to Thread$$

Each operator corresponds to a state of the machine, in which it performs one specific action. When it is $\mathsf{process}(t, u)$, it processes the pair (t, u) using the rules previously outlined; when it is delist it will take a pair from the Pairs stack to be processed; when it is $\mathsf{enlist}(l)$ it will add to the stack all the pairs in l; finally, when it is $\mathsf{cycle}(x, t)$ it will add the cycle (x, t) to the Cycles structure. The abstract machine is loaded with $t = \mathsf{delist}$, and stops with $S = \varepsilon$ and $t = \mathsf{delist}$.

We give in Table 1 the abstract machine rules, where the families of rules I to III correspond to pair-processing as sketched before (including variable substitution), and Family IV manages the life-cycle of the thread.

As an example of the flexibility of this presentation of the machine, consider what needs to be changed if we want to access the Pairs structure as a Queue: rule T.2 simply has to give instead $S@[(t, u)]$ in its right-hand side.

A final remark: observe that all the machine rules perform simple tasks such as assignments and rotating lists one position, except for rule I, which depends of course on the size of the right-hand side of the interaction rule applied.

Properties. It is immediate to verify the determinism of this set of rules. Most of the proofs of properties stated here are left for the long version of this paper.

Definition 1 (Correct and Complete Annotations). *We say a configuration has* correct annotations *if for every annotated term* $\{A\}.\alpha(\mathbf{t})$ *occurring in it we have* $\mathbf{set}(\mathring{A}) \subseteq \mathcal{N}(\mathbf{t})$. *It has* complete annotations *if* $\mathbf{set}(\mathring{A}) \supseteq \mathcal{N}(\mathbf{t})$.

Proposition 1. *Let* $\langle \mathbf{t} \mid \Delta \rangle$ *be an interaction net. If* $\Sigma[\mathbf{t} \mid \Delta] \longrightarrow^* \Sigma'$, *then* Σ' *has correct and complete annotations.*

Proof. Straightforward induction on the reductions. $\Sigma[\mathbf{t} \mid \Delta]$ has correct and complete annotations, and every machine rule preserves the property. □

Definition 2 (Degeneracy). *A configuration is* degenerate *if the heap contains an active pair* $\{x \mapsto \alpha(\mathbf{t}), y \mapsto \beta(\mathbf{u})\}$ *with* $\phi_N(x) = y$, *or a cycle* $\{x_i \mapsto t_i\}, i = 1 \ldots N$, *with* $\phi_N(x_i) \in \mathcal{N}(t_{i+1})$ *for* $i = 1 \ldots N-1$, *and* $\phi_N(x_N) \in \mathcal{N}(t_1)$.

Proposition 2. *If* $\Sigma[\mathbf{t} \mid \Delta] \longrightarrow^* \Sigma'$, $\langle \mathbf{t} \mid \Delta \rangle$ *is an IN, then* Σ' *is not degenerate.*

We remark that if $\Sigma \longrightarrow \Sigma'$, Σ' may be degenerate even if Σ is not.

4 Correctness of the Sequential Abstract Machine

Our first goal will now be to define the interpretation of a machine configuration as an interaction net. We will then introduce some notation and give several lemmas needed for the correctness proof.

Table 1. Abstract machine rules

I	Permut Thread	ϕ_N process $(\{l_1\}.\alpha(\boldsymbol{t}),\{l_2\}.\beta(\boldsymbol{u}))$	$\phi_N \cup \Phi_S\,(\alpha(\boldsymbol{t}),\beta(\boldsymbol{u}))$ enlist $(\mathcal{I}_S\,(\alpha(\boldsymbol{t}),\beta(\boldsymbol{u})))$

II.1	Permut Thread	$\phi_N[x \leftrightarrow y]$ process(x,y)	$\phi_N[x \leftrightarrow y]$ cycle(x,y)
II.2	Heap Permut Thread	$\Gamma\,[z \mapsto \{X\}.\sigma(\boldsymbol{v})]$ $\phi_N[x \leftrightarrow z]$ process(x,y)	Γ ϕ_N process $(\{X\}.\sigma(\boldsymbol{v}),y)$
II.3	Heap Permut Thread	$\Gamma\,[z \mapsto \bot, w \mapsto \{Y\}.\tau(\boldsymbol{u})]$ $\phi_N[x \leftrightarrow z, y \leftrightarrow w]$ process(x,y)	Γ $\phi_N[x \leftrightarrow z]$ process $(x,\{Y\}.\tau(\boldsymbol{u}))$
II.4 $y \neq z, x \neq w$	Heap Permut Thread	$\Gamma\,[z \mapsto \bot, w \mapsto \bot]$ $\phi_N[x \leftrightarrow z, y \leftrightarrow w]$ process(x,y)	Γ $\phi_N[z \leftrightarrow w]$ delist

III.0	Thread	process $(\{Y\}.\alpha(\boldsymbol{t}),x)$	process $(x,\{Y\}.\alpha(\boldsymbol{t}))$
III.1	Heap Permut Thread	$\Gamma\,[x \mapsto \{X\}.\beta(\boldsymbol{u})]$ $\phi_N[x \leftrightarrow y]$ process $(z,\{y:T\}.\alpha(\boldsymbol{t}))$	Γ ϕ_N process$(z,\{(\mathring{X})\,@T\}.\alpha(\boldsymbol{t})[y:=\beta(\boldsymbol{u})])$
III.2 $x \neq z$	Heap Permut Thread	$\Gamma\,[x \mapsto \bot]$ $\phi_N[x \leftrightarrow y]$ process $(z,\{y:T\}.\alpha(\boldsymbol{t}))$	Γ $\phi_N[x \leftrightarrow y]$ process $(z,\{T@[y]\}.\alpha(\boldsymbol{t}))$
III.3	Permut Thread	$\phi_N[x \leftrightarrow y]$ process $(x,\{y:T\}.\alpha(\boldsymbol{t}))$	$\phi_N[x \leftrightarrow y]$ cycle $(x,\{y:T\}.\alpha(\boldsymbol{t}))$
III.4	Heap Permut Thread	$\Gamma\,[x \mapsto \{X\}.\beta(\boldsymbol{u})]$ $\phi_N[x \leftrightarrow z]$ process $(z,\{\Box:T\}.\alpha(\boldsymbol{t}))$	Γ ϕ_N process $(\{X\}.\beta(\boldsymbol{u}),\{\Box:T\}.\alpha(\boldsymbol{t}))$
III.5	Heap Permut Thread	$\Gamma[x \mapsto \bot]$ $\phi_N[x \leftrightarrow z]$ process $(z,\{\Box:T\}.\alpha(\boldsymbol{t}))$	$\Gamma\,[z \mapsto \{T@[\Box]\}.\alpha(\boldsymbol{t})]$ $\phi_N[x \leftrightarrow z]$ delist

T.1	Pairs Thread	$(t,u):S$ delist	S process(t,u)
T.2	Pairs Thread	S enlist$((t,u):T)$	$(t,u):S$ enlist(T)
T.3	Thread	enlist(ε)	delist
T.4	Cycles Thread	C cycle(t,u)	$(t,u):C$ delist

Definition 3 (Updating). *Let $\Sigma = \langle \Gamma \mid S \mid \phi_N \mid V \mid C \mid t\rangle$. The* update *of Σ is the configuration $\mathbf{U}[\Sigma]$ that results from recursively substituting (updating annotations) every variable x occurring in any component S, V, C, t of Σ with the value stored for the variable $\phi_N(x)$ in the heap Γ, removing this entry from the heap and the pair $x \leftrightarrow \phi_N(x)$ from the permutation.*

It is straightforward to expand the post-processing rules with others for updating the stack and the thread. Together they implement the above notion of updating.

Proposition 3. *If Σ is non-degenerate then $\mathbf{U}[\Sigma]$ has an empty heap.*

Definition 4 (Collapsing). *From an interaction net $N = \langle \mathbf{t} \mid \Delta\rangle$ and an involution ϕ we obtain the* collapse *of N by ϕ, a net denoted by $\mathbf{Clp}[N, \phi]$, by substituting in $\mathbf{t}$ and Δ every pair of variables x, y such that $\phi(x) = y$ with a fresh variable, which we will by convention call k_{xy}.*

Auxiliary Functions. We need a family of auxiliary functions defined as follows: $\lfloor\rfloor_0$ takes a term and removes its annotation, $\lfloor x\rfloor_0 = x \mid \lfloor\{N\}.\alpha(\mathbf{t})\rfloor_0 = \alpha(\mathbf{t})$; $\lfloor\rfloor_1$ takes a list of terms and removes the $\Box$ mark as well as all the annotations, $\lfloor\varepsilon\rfloor_1 = \varepsilon \mid \lfloor\Box : t\rfloor_1 = \lfloor t\rfloor_1 \mid \lfloor h : t\rfloor_1 = \lfloor h\rfloor_0 : \lfloor t\rfloor_1$; $\lfloor\rfloor_2$ takes a list of pairs of terms and returns the corresponding multiset of equations, $\lfloor\varepsilon\rfloor_2 = \emptyset \mid \lfloor\Box : t\rfloor_2 = \lfloor t\rfloor_2 \mid \lfloor(h_1, h_2) : t\rfloor_2 = \{\lfloor h_1\rfloor_0 = \lfloor h_2\rfloor_0\} \cup \lfloor t\rfloor_2$. Finally, $\lfloor\rfloor_t$ takes a thread and returns a set containing the pair being processed by the thread, or the empty set if the thread does not contain any pair, $\lfloor\mathsf{process}(t_1, t_2)\rfloor_t = \{\lfloor t_1\rfloor_0 = \lfloor t_2\rfloor_0\} \mid \lfloor\mathsf{delist}\rfloor_t = \emptyset \mid \lfloor\mathsf{enlist}(l)\rfloor_t = \lfloor l\rfloor_2 \mid \lfloor\mathsf{cycle}(x, t)\rfloor_t = \{x = \lfloor t_2\rfloor_0\}$. We shall use the notation $\lfloor\rfloor$ for any of $\lfloor\rfloor_0$, $\lfloor\rfloor_1$, $\lfloor\rfloor_2$, $\lfloor\rfloor_t$, whenever the distinction is clear from context. We also need an auxiliary function $r_\Box$ to rotate a list until $\Box$ is at the end, easily defined as: $r_\Box(\Box : t) = t@(\Box : \varepsilon) \mid r_\Box(h : t) = r_\Box(t@(h : \varepsilon))$.

Definition 5 (Interpretation). *The* interpretation *of a machine configuration Σ is an interaction net $[\![\Sigma]\!]$ obtained as follows:*

1. *We compute $\mathbf{U}[\Sigma] = \langle \Gamma^{U[\Sigma]} \mid S^{U[\Sigma]} \mid \phi_N^{U[\Sigma]} \mid V^{U[\Sigma]} \mid C^{U[\Sigma]} \mid t^{U[\Sigma]}\rangle$.*
2. *We then build the net $N^\Sigma = \langle \lfloor r_\Box(V^{U[\Sigma]})\rfloor \mid \lfloor S^{U[\Sigma]}\rfloor \cup \lfloor C^{U[\Sigma]}\rfloor \cup \lfloor t^{U[\Sigma]}\rfloor\rangle$.*
3. *$[\![\Sigma]\!] = \mathbf{Clp}[N^\Sigma, \phi_N^{U[\Sigma]}]$ concludes our construction.*

Notice that the interpretation of a configuration is *unique*. It is immediate to see that all the configurations $\Sigma[\mathbf{t} \mid \Delta]$ have the same interpretation $\langle \mathbf{t} \mid \Delta\rangle$.

The interpretation of a degenerate configuration disregards all the active pairs and cycles contained in the heap of a degenerate configuration. This is appropriate in the sense that this is information that cannot be read back.

Lemma 2. *If Σ is an irreducible configuration, then $[\![\Sigma]\!]$ is in normal form.*

Proof. Immediate. Δ^Σ may be empty (if C^Σ is), or contain cycles. $\Box$

Notation. In what follows we do not distinguish notationally between the reduction $\longrightarrow$ (or its transitive $\longrightarrow^*$ or refexive $\longrightarrow^{\equiv}$ closures) of machine configurations and of interaction nets, since the distinction can be made from context. The same is true for structural equivalence ($\equiv$).

Lemma 3. *Let Σ be a configuration with correct annotations, $\Sigma \longrightarrow \Sigma'$ using any rule except I, II.4, and III.5, and Σ, Σ' non-degenerate. Then $[\![\Sigma]\!] \equiv [\![\Sigma']\!]$.*

Lemma 4. *Let $\Sigma \longrightarrow \Sigma'$, with Σ, Σ' non-degenerate and correctly-annotated. Then $[\![\Sigma]\!] \longrightarrow^{\equiv} [\![\Sigma']\!]$.*

Lemma 5. *The set of rules II.1 to II.3, III.0 to III.4, and T.1 to T.4 is normalizing, with the same normal forms as the complete set of rules (i.e, they have an empty S component and* delist *thread), together with all the configurations to which one of the rules I, II.4, or III.5 can be applied.*

Proposition 4 (Correctness). *Let $N = \langle \mathsf{t} \mid \Delta \rangle$ be an interaction net. Then*

$$N \Downarrow \overline{N} \;\; \textit{iff} \;\; \Sigma[\mathsf{t} \mid \Delta] \longrightarrow^* \overline{\Sigma},$$

with $\overline{\Sigma}$ an irreducible machine configuration, and $[\![\overline{\Sigma}]\!] \equiv \overline{N}$.

Observe that a result such as $[\![\Sigma]\!] \longrightarrow [\![\Sigma']\!] \Rightarrow \Sigma \longrightarrow^* \Sigma'$ does *not* hold, since the semantics is non-deterministic and besides, it allows for variables in the observable interface to be updated at any time.

5 A Concurrent Abstract Machine

The machine we have been considering is inherently sequential: it is always deterministically decided which rule is applied at each stage. However, the way the machine has been formulated makes it trivial to obtain a concurrent machine from it, simply by including more processing threads within a configuration.

Definition 6 (Multi-thread Configuration). *An n*-thread configuration *is:*

$$\langle \Gamma \mid S \mid \phi_N \mid V \mid C \mid [t_1, \ldots t_n] \rangle$$

where $[t_1, \ldots t_n]$ is a list of threads and all other components are as before.

Definition 7 (Concurrent reduction). $\stackrel{ct}{\longrightarrow}$ *is the smallest relation verifying*

$$\frac{\langle \Gamma \mid S \mid \phi_N \mid V \mid C \mid t_i \rangle \longrightarrow \langle \widehat{\Gamma} \mid \widehat{S} \mid \widehat{\phi_N} \mid \widehat{V} \mid \widehat{C} \mid \widehat{t_i} \rangle}{\langle \Gamma \mid S \mid \phi_N \mid V \mid C \mid [t_1 \ldots t_i \ldots t_n] \,\rangle \stackrel{ct}{\longrightarrow} \langle\, \widehat{\Gamma} \mid \widehat{S} \mid \widehat{\phi_N} \mid \widehat{V} \mid \widehat{C} \mid [t_1 \ldots \widehat{t_i} \ldots t_n] \,\rangle}$$

This definition is intuitive: a pool of threads work on the shared data-structures, each thread proceeding individually and deterministically, according to the sequential machine rules. Each $\xrightarrow{ct}$ *step* is a step of one of the individual threads.

Non-determinism is introduced because it may be the case that several threads are willing to operate. For instance, when several threads are in the delist state and the list is not empty, one of them will fetch the top pair and change state to process, while the others will keep trying to access the list.

The resulting machine almost falls into the standard producers-consumers synchronization model of shared-memory computation, with the synchronization problem solved by implementing a shared queue of tasks (pairs to be processed). The diference is that every thread is a consumer and *may be a producer*, of tasks.

Properties. The definition of the reduction of a multi-thread configuration as individual reductions of any of its threads makes all the inductively proved properties of the sequential machine also valid for the concurrent one. Lemmas 2, 3, 4, and 5, and Propositions 1 and 3, all hold, with the interpretation of a multi-thread configuration modified to include all the pairs being processed by threads, and irreducible configurations having an empty Pairs list and all threads delist.

Unfortunately, Prop.2 is no longer true, which destroys our correctness result. This is due to a race condition when traversing an annotation list to perform substitutions, which allows the generation of irrecoverable cycles in the heap.

As an example of such a situation, consider the following 2-thread configuration (we omit the V and C components), for a net containing a 2-cell cycle which we show may get lost in the heap. Consider that $w \in \mathcal{N}(t)$ and $z \in \mathcal{N}(u)$.

$$
\begin{aligned}
& \langle \emptyset \mid (x, [w : \Box].t) : (y, [z : \Box].u) : S \mid \phi_N[x \leftrightarrow z, y \leftrightarrow w] \mid [\mathsf{delist}, \mathsf{delist}] \rangle. \\
\xrightarrow{ct}{}^{*}_{T.1}\ & \langle \emptyset \mid S \mid \phi_N[x \leftrightarrow z, y \leftrightarrow w] \mid [\mathsf{process}(x, [w : \Box].t), \mathsf{process}(y, [z : \Box].u)] \rangle. \\
\xrightarrow{ct}_{III.2}\ & \langle \emptyset \mid S \mid \phi_N[x \leftrightarrow z, y \leftrightarrow w] \mid [\mathsf{process}(x, [w : \Box].t), \mathsf{process}(y, [\Box : z].u)] \rangle. \\
\xrightarrow{ct}_{III.2}\ & \langle \emptyset \mid S \mid \phi_N[x \leftrightarrow z, y \leftrightarrow w] \mid [\mathsf{process}(x, [\Box : w].t), \mathsf{process}(y, [\Box : z].u)] \rangle. \\
\xrightarrow{ct}_{III.5}\ & \langle \{x \mapsto [w : \Box].t\} \mid S \mid \phi_N[x \leftrightarrow z, y \leftrightarrow w] \mid [\mathsf{delist}, \mathsf{process}(y, [\Box : z].u)] \rangle. \\
\xrightarrow{ct}_{III.5}\ & \langle \{x \mapsto [w : \Box].t, y \mapsto [z : \Box].u\} \mid S \mid \phi_N[x \leftrightarrow z, y \leftrightarrow w] \mid [\mathsf{delist}, \mathsf{delist}] \rangle.
\end{aligned}
$$

Recovering Correctness. First, we remark that this form of degenerate configurations is not very harmful, since one could simply forbid nets containing cycles. However, a simple way exists to recover lost cycles, by keeping in the configurations an additional component: a list of variables stored in the heap, kept up-to-date by the rules. After post-processing, and according to Prop.3 (remember post-processing rules implement updating of configurations with empty lists of Pairs), this list will be empty if the configuration is not degenerate. If it is not empty, then the machine may be restarted with any pair (variable, term) still stored in the heap. Once a pair in a cycle is recovered in this way, regular machine operation will proceed to store the cycle in the appropriate structure.

6 Implementing the Abstract Machine

Sequential Implementation. The abstract machine may be programmed sequentially in a straightforward way. It suffices to choose appropriate data-structures for configurations, and to map machine operations into these structures. The 'motor' that runs the machine is simply a loop that pops a pair of terms from the stack and decides which machine operation to apply. We remark this decision is not complex, as the number of operations might lead one to think: the form of the pair being processed restricts the pattern-matching to a family of rules.

Optimizations. During operation of the machine the size of Pairs tends to grow considerably. One possible optimization with respect to keeping the list reasonably small is to give priority to the execution of rules that remove pairs from it. This is a straightforward modification: it suffices to add a second list of pairs to the configurations (for active pairs), and to substitute rules T.1 to T3. by a new set of rules that manages the two lists according to the desired priority scheme.

Concurrent Implementation. A well-suited technology exists for implementing our concurrent abstract machine: POSIX Threads, which are lightweight processes running in the address space of the same UNIX process, individually scheduled. This technology has the advantage of producing implementations that may be run (without modifications in the code) in machines with any number of processors. If conveniently supported by the kernel of the operating system, threads will run in true parallelism, assigned to different processors.

The way to implement our abstract machine using this technology is to launch as many threads (running the same code, as specified by the machine rules) as there are processors in the machine (this can be done automatically at run-time).

Now it is time to ask whether the correspondence between the resulting implementation and the abstract machine is perfect. In a uniprocessor machine this is indeed the case: a single thread is executed at any time, and this is what the machine captures, even though in practice each machine operation is decomposed into a sequence of program instructions, which means that time-slicing between threads may occur in the middle of the execution of an operation.

In the case of multiprocessors, however, in order to obtain a correct implementation, one has to stipulate that *a parallel reduction step is any sequence of concurrent reduction steps in which every thread is involved at most once.*

To illustrate this point, consider the situation of two threads in the delist state. The outcome if both execute rule T.1 simultaneously is not predictable. The correct behaviour is that two different configurations may result, corresponding to the two orders in which the threads may take pairs from the list.

Now the parallel reducer must keep to this behaviour, protecting the access to the Pairs and Cycles data-structures by means of some synchronization mechanism: the first thread to gain access to a shared structure will make the other thread(s) *block* until the first one liberates the structure. *Locks* [7] are used to implement a linearizable queue, and this is thus not a wait-free implementation.

We leave a detailed treatment of this matter for the long version of this paper; there is another situation requiring locking, which concerns the case of two adjacent pairs of variables (two axiom cuts) being processed simultaneously.

Other situations are critical with respect to race conditions in true parallelism. Take for example the two threads $\mathsf{process}(x, \{\Box : T\}.t)$ and $\mathsf{process}(y, \{\Box : T'\}.u)$, with $\phi_N(x) = y$. Our abstract machine prevents this from generating a lost active pair in the heap: once one of the threads executes rule III.5, the other will be unable to execute it (executing III.4 instead). But in true parallelism the threads may execute III.5 simultaneously, giving a degenerate configuration. We remark that the problem now is not in the access to the data structures.

One solution to this problem not requiring additional synchronization is the mechanism explained in Sect.5 to recover entries in the heap back to Pairs. This optimistic solution relies on the low probability of the race situations to occur.

7 Conclusions

We have presented an abstract machine which provides answers to the questions raised in Sect.2. Specifically, the machine proposes concrete data-structures, together with an algorithm for implementing interaction net reduction. We have also specified how rules are represented and applied. Identification of active pairs is automatic, and question 2 is answered by the post-processing operations. With respect to 5, all the machine rules perform simple operations in constant time.

We have implemented this machine following Sect.6, and obtained a robust reducer that performs well. The *granularity* of the machine operations is quite small, while still keeping the operations sufficiently atomic: our tests show that each interaction is decomposed in between 7 and 12 machine operations.

The concurrent machine additionally provides answers to questions 6 and 7, resulting in the first parallel implementation of interaction nets, with the significant advantage of running on commonly available workstations. We remark that this parallel implementation is not limited by the number of active pairs in particular nets, since all rewiring operations are performed in parallel. Our current research involves studying the performance of this implementation.

References

[1] Andrea Asperti, Cecilia Giovannetti, and Andrea Naletto. The bologna optimal higher-order machine. *Journal of Functional Programming*, 6(6):763–810, November 1996.

[2] Gérard Berry and Gérard Boudol. The Chemical Abstract Machine. In *Conference Record of the Seventeenth Annual ACM Symposium on Principles of Programming Languages*, pages 81–94, 1990.

[3] P.-L. Curien. An abstract framework for environment machines. *Theoretical Computer Science*, 82(2):389–402, May 1991.

[4] Maribel Fernndez and Ian Mackie. A calculus for interaction nets. In Gopalan Nadathur, editor, *Principles and Practice of Declarative Programming'99 Conference*

Proceedings, number 1702 in Lecture Notes in Computer Science. Springer-Verlag, September/October 1999.

[5] Jean-Yves Girard. Linear logic. *Theoretical Computer Science*, 50:1–102, 1987.

[6] Georges Gonthier, Martn Abadi, and Jean-Jacques Lvy. The geometry of optimal lambda reduction. In *Proceedings of ACM Symposium Principles of Programming Languages*, pages 15–26, January 1992.

[7] P. Jayanti. Wait-free computing. In *Distributed Algorithms, 9th International Workshop, WDAG '95*, volume 972 of *Lecture Notes in Computer Science*, pages 19–50, 1995.

[8] Yves Lafont. Interaction nets. In *Seventeenth Annual Symposium on Principles of Programming Languages*, pages 95–108, San Francisco, California, 1990. ACM Press.

[9] Yves Lafont. From proof nets to interaction nets. In J.-Y. Girard, Y. Lafont, and L. Regnier, editors, *Advances in Linear Logic*, pages 225–247. Cambridge University Press, 1995. Proceedings of the Workshop on Linear Logic, Ithaca, New York, June 1993.

[10] John Lamping. An algorithm for optimal lambda-calculus reductions. In *Proceedings of the Seventeenth ACM Symposium on Principles of Programming Languages*, pages 16–30. ACM, ACM Press, January 1990.

[11] Peter Landin. The mechanical evaluation of expressions. *Computer Journal*, 6(4), 1963.

[12] Jean-Jacques Lévy. *Réductions Correctes et Optimales dans le Lambda Calcul.* Thèse de Doctorat d'Etat, University of Paris VII, 1978.

[13] Ian Mackie. YALE: Yet another lambda evaluator based on interaction nets. In *Proceedings of the 3rd ACM SIGPLAN International Conference on Functional Programming (ICFP'98)*, pages 117–128. ACM Press, September 1998.

On Synchronous and Asynchronous Mobile Processes

Paola Quaglia[1*] and David Walker[2]

[1] Aethra Telecomunicazioni, Italy
[2] Oxford University Computing Laboratory, U.K.

Abstract. This paper studies the relationship between synchronous and asynchronous mobile processes, in the setting of the π-calculus. A type system for processes of the asynchronous monadic subcalculus is introduced and used to obtain a full-abstraction result: two processes of the polyadic π-calculus are typed barbed congruent iff their translations into the subcalculus are asynchronous-monadic-typed barbed congruent.

1 Introduction

This paper studies the relationship between synchronous and asynchronous mobile processes, in the setting of the π-calculus [MPW92, Mil99]. A primitive of the π-calculus, inherited from its ancestor CCS [Mil89], is a form of handshake communication. The (polyadic) π-term $\overline{x}\langle a_1 a_2\rangle . P$ expresses a process that may send the pair of names a_1, a_2 via the link named x and continue as P, and the term $x(y_1 y_2).Q$ a process that may receive a pair of names via x (a reader unfamiliar with π-calculus may care to refer to section 2). Interaction between these processes is expressed by

$$\overline{x}\langle a_1 a_2\rangle . P \mid x(y_1 y_2).Q \longrightarrow P \mid Q\{a_1 a_2/y_1 y_2\}\,,$$

where $\{a_1 a_2/y_1 y_2\}$ indicates substitution of the as for the ys in Q. The fact that interaction is expressed by handshake communication is important for the tractability of the π-calculus, and that of many other theories of concurrent systems that are based on communication primitives of a similar nature.

On the other hand, many concurrent systems, especially distributed systems, use forms of asynchronous communication, in which the act of sending a datum and the act of receiving it are separate. Relatedly, many languages for programming concurrent or distributed systems have asynchronous primitives, an important reason for this being that they are amenable to efficient implementation. Language features for synchronized communication are often implemented using asynchronous primitives.

The π-calculus has a subcalculus in which communication may be understood as asynchronous [HT91, Bou92]. The key step in achieving this is the decree that in the subcalculus, the only output-prefixed terms are those of the form $\overline{x}\langle a\rangle . \mathbf{0}$,

* This work was done while the author was at BRICS, Aarhus University, Denmark.

J. Tiuryn (Ed.): FOSSACS 2000, LNCS 1784, pp. 283–296, 2000.

where $\mathbf{0}$ expresses a process that has no capabilities. In a term of the subcalculus, a subterm $\overline{x}\langle \boldsymbol{a} \rangle. \mathbf{0}$ at top level may be thought of as a datum $\boldsymbol{a}$ that has been sent but not received and that is available to any subterm at top level of the form $x(\boldsymbol{y}). Q$.

The theory of the asynchronous subcalculus is much less tractable than that of the π-calculus. It is the subcalculus, however, that is the basis for the concurrent programming language Pict [PT97]. Further, the join-calculus [FG96], which is itself closely related to the asynchronous π-calculus, is the basis for a language for programming distributed systems [FM97]. Language features for synchronized communication are implemented in many languages, among them Pict and the join-language, by means of compilations based on well-known asynchronous communication protocols. The first study of such a compilation carried out using a mathematical model of mobile processes was in [Bou92], where a specific translation was shown to be computationally adequate with respect to Morris's extensional operational preorder. The present paper studies the translation of [Bou92], but extended in a straightforward way to polyadic π-terms. Thus the translation considered is from $p\pi$, the set of polyadic π-terms, to $am\pi$, the set of asynchronous monadic π-terms.

The paper is concerned with the effect of the translation on behavioural equivalence. The standard equivalence on π-terms is barbed congruence. Roughly, two terms are barbed congruent if no difference in behaviour can be observed between the systems obtained by placing them into an arbitrary π-context. The notion of observation is natural, and the basis for observation of difference in behaviour is a kind of bisimulation game. The definition of barbed congruence, involving as it does quantification over a class of contexts, is also appropriately sensitive to the (sub)calculus under consideration. For instance on polyadic terms a typing discipline is used to separate out ill-formed terms such as $\overline{x}\langle a_1 a_2 a_3 \rangle. P \mid x(y_1 y_2). Q$, in which sender and receiver disagree on the length of tuple to be communicated. Given a sorting λ of the kind introduced in [Mil91] that achieves this separating out, polyadic terms that respect λ are barbed λ-congruent if no difference in behaviour can be observed between the systems obtained by placing them into an arbitrary context that itself respects λ.

The translation from $p\pi$ to $am\pi$ is not fully abstract. The reason, briefly, is that there are $am\pi$-contexts that do not conform to the protocol underlying the translation, and some such contexts are able to expose differences between the translations of $p\pi$-terms that are barbed λ-congruent. The aim of this paper is to obtain a full-abstraction theorem for the translation by giving a characterization of a suitable class of $am\pi$-contexts. The basis for the characterization is a type system for $am\pi$-terms. This type system is based on a graph, derived in a simple manner from the sorting, that describes aspects of the protocol that is at the core of the translation. The full-abstraction theorem asserts that for any sorting λ, two $p\pi$-terms are barbed λ-congruent if and only if their translations are barbed λ^{am}-congruent. Barbed λ^{am}-congruence is the natural variant of barbed congruence on well-typed $am\pi$-terms.

The study of type systems for mobile processes is an important topic, both to aid rigorous analysis of systems and to assist in programming. The present paper develops techniques introduced in [QW98], and builds on earlier work on types for mobile processes, for instance in [Hon93, KPT96, PS96, PS97, San97, Tur96]. The paper [QW98] proves a full-abstraction theorem for a translation from $p\pi$ to the monadic π-calculus. The present paper studies a translation from $p\pi$ to the *asynchronous* monadic subcalculus. Because of the separation of sending and receiving in the asynchronous subcalculus, the technical details in the present paper differ greatly from – and are considerably more difficult than – those in [QW98]. We wish to mention in particular the paper [Yos96], where a notion of graph type for monadic processes is introduced and studied. Nodes of a graph type represent atomic actions, and edges an activation ordering between them. Although [Yos96] and the present paper both use graphs for similar purposes, the technical developments in the two papers are entirely different.

We believe that the present paper is the first to prove a full-abstraction theorem for the translation studied in [Bou92]. The present paper studies the translation extended to polyadic terms in order to show the generality of the techniques used. The type system introduced is of a kind that is well understood, and its rules are, in our view, informative. One or two of the rules are quite complicated, however. We believe that this complication may be intrinsic; we tried many alternatives before reaching the system described here. In the space available it is not possible to explain why simpler-looking systems are inadequate. Instead, we explain the main features of the system, using examples where appropriate, and give enough of the technical development to outline the structure of the argument. An important point is that the class of typeable $am\pi$-contexts contains much more than just the translations of well-sorted polyadic contexts.

Several papers study translations between subcalculi of the π-calculus. For instance, in addition to [Bou92] mentioned earlier, [Bor98] studies a translation from the *asynchronous* $p\pi$ to the subcalculus of the π-calculus, πI, in which only private names may be communicated. Also, [MS98] studies in depth a subcalculus, $L\pi$, of the asynchronous monadic calculus in which only the output capability of names may be communicated. In particular a full-abstraction result is shown for the translation from $L\pi$ to the subcalculus $L\pi I$ of πI. The subcalculus $L\pi$ is closely related to the join-calculus, about which many results, including results on translations, are shown in [Fou98].

In the papers just mentioned, a summation operator on terms is lacking. Encodings of asynchronous processes involving forms of summation in the summation-free subcalculus, another topic that is important in programming-language implementation, are studied in [NP96, Nes97]. Summation is also absent from the calculus considered in the present paper. In [Pal97], a result is shown that is paraphrased (Remark 6.1, p. 264) as follows: "There exists no uniform encoding of the π-calculus [with guarded summation] into the asynchronous π-calculus preserving a reasonable semantics", where *uniform* and *reasonable* are given specific meanings. The translation of [Bou92] is uniform and the semantics studied in the present paper is reasonable, in the senses of [Pal97].

In our view, the main theorem of the present paper is of intrinsic interest: it shows precisely how the class of $am\pi$-contexts needs to be cut down to obtain full abstraction. Moreover, the characterization uses standard machinery of type systems, albeit with some inevitable complication. Further, the characterization is closely tied, via the type system, to the protocol that is at the core of the translation: it shows clearly how that protocol affects process equivalence. Finally, because of the importance of type systems for mobile processes in general, we believe that several ideas needed for the proof of completeness may be useful for tackling other problems.

In section 2 we recall necessary background material, in section 3 we introduce the type system for asynchronous monadic processes, and in section 4 we briefly outline the proof of the main result.

2 Background

In this section we recall necessary definitions and notations. We refer to the papers cited in the Introduction for further explanation.

We presuppose a countably-infinite set, N, of names, ranged over by lower-case letters. We write $\boldsymbol{x}$ for a tuple $x_1 \ldots x_n$ of names.

The *prefixes* are given by

$$\pi \ ::= \ \overline{x}\langle \boldsymbol{y} \rangle \ \mid \ x(\boldsymbol{z})$$

where $\boldsymbol{z}$ is a tuple of distinct names. In each case, x is the *subject*.

The *(polyadic) processes* are given by

$$P ::= \mathbf{0} \ \mid \ \pi.P \ \mid \ P \mid P' \ \mid \ \nu z\, P \ \mid \ !P\,.$$

We write $p\pi$ for the set of processes, and use P, Q, R to range over $p\pi$. A process is *monadic* if for each subterm $\overline{x}\langle \boldsymbol{y} \rangle.P$ or $x(\boldsymbol{y}).P$ of it, $\boldsymbol{y}$ is of length 1. A process is *asynchronous* if for each subterm $\overline{x}\langle \boldsymbol{y} \rangle.P$ of it, P is $\mathbf{0}$. We abbreviate $\overline{x}\langle \boldsymbol{y} \rangle.\mathbf{0}$ to $\overline{x}\langle \boldsymbol{y} \rangle$. We write $am\pi$ for the set of processes that are asynchronous and monadic.

In $x(\boldsymbol{z}).P$ and in $\nu z\, P$ the displayed occurrences of $\boldsymbol{z}$ and z are *binding* with *scope* P. An occurrence of a name in a term is *free* if it is not within the scope of a binding occurrence of the name. We write $\mathrm{fn}(P)$ for the set of names that have a free occurrence in P, and $\mathrm{fn}(P, Q, \ldots)$ for $\mathrm{fn}(P) \cup \mathrm{fn}(Q) \cup \ldots$.

We write $\{y_1 \cdots y_n/x_1 \ldots x_n\}$ for the substitution that maps x_i to y_i for each i and is otherwise the identity, and $P\{y_1 \cdots y_n/x_1 \ldots x_n\}$ for the process obtained by applying it to P, with change of bound names if necessary to avoid captures.

We adopt the following conventions on bound names: processes that are α-convertible are identified; and when a collection of processes and other entities such as substitutions or sets of names is considered, it is assumed that the bound names of the processes are chosen to be different from their free names and from the names of the other entities.

A *context* is obtained when the *hole* $[\cdot]$ replaces an occurrence of $\mathbf{0}$ in a process. We write $C[P]$ for the process obtained by replacing the occurrence of the hole in the context C by P.

Structural congruence is the smallest congruence, $\equiv$, on processes such that

1. $P_1 \mid (P_2 \mid P_3) \equiv (P_1 \mid P_2) \mid P_3$, $P_1 \mid P_2 \equiv P_2 \mid P_1$, $P \mid \mathbf{0} \equiv P$
2. $\nu z\, \nu w\, P \equiv \nu w\, \nu z\, P$, $\nu z\, \mathbf{0} \equiv \mathbf{0}$
3. $\nu z\, (P_1 \mid P_2) \equiv P_1 \mid \nu z\, P_2$ provided $z \notin \mathrm{fn}(P_1)$
4. $!P \equiv P \mid !P$.

Reduction is the smallest relation, $\longrightarrow$, on processes such that

1. $\overline{x}\langle \boldsymbol{y} \rangle. P \mid x(\boldsymbol{z}). Q \longrightarrow P \mid Q\{\boldsymbol{y}/\boldsymbol{z}\}$ provided $|\boldsymbol{y}| = |\boldsymbol{z}|$
2. $P \longrightarrow P'$ implies $P \mid Q \longrightarrow P' \mid Q$
3. $P \longrightarrow P'$ implies $\nu z\, P \longrightarrow \nu z\, P'$
4. $P \equiv Q \longrightarrow Q' \equiv P'$ implies $P \longrightarrow P'$.

If x is a name then $\overline{x}$ is a *co-name*. The *observability predicates*, $\downarrow_{\overline{x}}$, are defined by: $P \downarrow_{\overline{x}}$ if P has an unguarded subterm $\overline{x}\langle \boldsymbol{y} \rangle. Q$ with the displayed occurrence of x free in P. (An occurrence of a term is *unguarded* if it is not underneath a prefix.)

Barbed bisimilarity is the largest symmetric relation, $\dot{\approx}$, such that if $P \mathrel{\dot{\approx}} Q$ then $P \downarrow_{\overline{x}}$ implies $Q \longrightarrow^* \downarrow_{\overline{x}}$, and $P \longrightarrow P'$ implies $Q \longrightarrow^* \dot{\approx} P'$. The normal definition of barbed bisimilarity on π-calculus requires also that: $P \downarrow_x$ implies $Q \longrightarrow^* \downarrow_x$. On the asynchronous subcalculus, however, it is normal to take the observables to be the co-names only. On the full calculus, closing under contexts one obtains the same relation (barbed congruence) whether or not names are deemed observable. We therefore work with the definition as stated.

Now fix a set $\mathcal{S}$ of *sorts*, ranged over by s, t, and a *sorting* $\lambda : \mathcal{S} \rightharpoonup \mathcal{S}^+$, where $\mathcal{S}^+$ is the set of nonempty tuples of sorts. We use Ψ to range over finite partial functions from names to sorts. We write $\mathrm{n}(\Psi)$ for the domain of Ψ, and $x : s$ for (x, s). In particular, if $\mathrm{n}(\Psi) = \{x_1, \ldots, x_n\}$ and $\Psi(x_i) = s_i$ for each i, we write $\{x_1 : s_1, \ldots, x_n : s_n\}$ for Ψ. We write Ψ, Ψ' for $\Psi \cup \Psi'$, provided $x \in \mathrm{n}(\Psi) \cap \mathrm{n}(\Psi')$ implies $\Psi(x) = \Psi'(x)$; and we write $\Psi, x : s$ for $\Psi, \{x : s\}$. Note: we will later consider functions from names to other sets, and will then use similar notations.

P is a λ*-process* if a judgment $\Psi \vdash P$ can be inferred using the rules in table 1, where the prefix rules share the side condition that $\lambda(s) = (t_1 \ldots t_n)$, and the output-prefix rule has in addition the side condition: $x = y_i$ implies $s = t_i$, and $y_i = y_j$ implies $t_i = t_j$. In accordance with the convention on bound names, in writing $\Psi \vdash P$ it is assumed that the bound names of P are chosen to be different from the names in Ψ. So in particular $z \notin \mathrm{n}(\Psi)$ in the restriction rule, and $z_1, \ldots, z_n \notin \mathrm{n}(\Psi)$ in the input-prefix rule.

Basic properties of the type system are: preservation of typing under $\equiv$, subject reduction, and freedom from arity-disagreements:

Lemma 1. 1. If $\Psi \vdash P$ and $Q \equiv P$, then $\Psi \vdash Q$.
2. If $\Psi \vdash P$ and $P \longrightarrow P'$, then $\Psi \vdash P'$.
3. If P is a λ-process and $P \longrightarrow^* \nu \boldsymbol{w}\, (\overline{x}\langle \boldsymbol{y} \rangle. P_1 \mid x(\boldsymbol{z}). P_2 \mid P_3)$, then $|\boldsymbol{y}| = |\boldsymbol{z}|$.

$$\frac{}{\Psi \vdash \mathbf{0}} \qquad \frac{\Psi \vdash P}{\Psi \vdash !P} \qquad \frac{\Psi \vdash P_1 \quad \Psi \vdash P_2}{\Psi \vdash P_1 \mid P_2} \qquad \frac{\Psi, z : s \vdash P}{\Psi \vdash \nu z\, P}$$

$$\frac{\Psi \vdash P}{\Psi, x : s, y_1 : t_1, \ldots, y_n : t_n \vdash \overline{x}\langle y_1 \ldots y_n \rangle . P}$$

$$\frac{\Psi, z_1 : t_1, \ldots, z_n : t_n \vdash P}{\Psi, x : s \vdash x(z_1 \ldots z_n). P}$$

Table 1. The typing rules for $p\pi$

The appropriate barbed congruence for λ-processes is defined as follows:

Definition 2. 1. A context C is a $\lambda(\Psi)$-*context* if for some Ψ' there is an inference of $\Psi' \vdash C$ in which the hole is typed by $\Psi \vdash [\cdot]$.
2. P and Q are *barbed λ-congruent*, $P \approx_\lambda Q$, if there is Ψ such that $\Psi \vdash P, Q$ and $C[P] \approx C[Q]$ for every $\lambda(\Psi)$-context C.

3 The Asynchronous Monadic Type System

Definition 3. The translation $[\![\cdot]\!]$ from $p\pi$ to $am\pi$ is defined by the following clauses (where for clarity we give the clauses for triples; the general case is then as expected), together with the stipulation that $[\![\cdot]\!]$ is a homomorphism for the other operators:

$$[\![\overline{x}\langle a_1 a_2 a_3\rangle . P]\!] = \nu w\, (\overline{x}w \mid w(v_1). (\overline{v_1}a_1 \mid w(v_2). (\overline{v_2}a_2 \mid w(v_3). (\overline{v_3}a_3 \mid [\![P]\!]))))$$
$$[\![x(y_1 y_2 y_3). P]\!] = x(w). \nu v_1\, (\overline{w}v_1 \mid v_1(y_1). \nu v_2\, (\overline{w}v_2 \mid v_2(y_2). \nu v_3\, (\overline{w}v_3 \mid v_3(y_3). [\![P]\!])))$$

where $w, v_1, v_2, v_3 \notin \mathrm{fn}([\![P]\!])$.

Communication of an n-tuple in $p\pi$ is mimicked by a sequence of $2n+1$ reductions in $am\pi$. In the case $n = 2$ we have:

$$\begin{aligned}
& [\![\overline{x}\langle a_1 a_2\rangle . P \mid x(y_1 y_2). Q]\!] \\
\longrightarrow\ & \nu w\, (w(v_1). (\overline{v_1}a_1 \mid w(v_2). (\overline{v_2}a_2 \mid [\![P]\!])) \mid \nu v_1\, (\overline{w}v_1 \mid v_1(y_1). \nu v_2\, (\overline{w}v_2 \mid v_2(y_2). [\![Q]\!]))) \\
\longrightarrow\ & \nu w\, \nu v_1\, (\overline{v_1}a_1 \mid w(v_2). (\overline{v_2}a_2 \mid [\![P]\!]) \mid v_1(y_1). \nu v_2\, (\overline{w}v_2 \mid v_2(y_2). [\![Q]\!])) \\
\longrightarrow\ & \nu w\, (w(v_2). (\overline{v_2}a_2 \mid [\![P]\!]) \mid \nu v_2\, (\overline{w}v_2 \mid v_2(y_2). [\![Q]\!]\{a_1/y_1\})) \\
\longrightarrow\ & \nu v_2\, (\overline{v_2}a_2 \mid [\![P]\!] \mid v_2(y_2). [\![Q]\!]\{a_1/y_1\}) \\
\longrightarrow\ & [\![P]\!] \mid [\![Q]\!]\{a_1 a_2/y_1 y_2\} .
\end{aligned}$$

The first reduction, via x, establishes a private link w between sender and receiver. In the second reduction the receiver uses w to transmit a private link v_1, and in the third the sender transfers a_1 along v_1. The receiver then transmits another private link v_2 via w, and in the last reduction the sender transfers a_2 along v_2. This completes the protocol for communicating the pair a_1, a_2 via x. In a slight variant of the protocol, the private name v_1 is used to send both a_1 and a_2. Although we have not studied this variant, we imagine that a similar analysis may be carried through.

We refer to names, such as w in the example above, that are passed in the first step of the protocol as *primary* names; and we refer to names, such as v_1 and v_2 in the example, that are used to pass names that occur in the process being translated as *secondary* names. We introduce *m-sorts* for classifying these names, and a graph, both derived from the sorting λ.

Definition 4. The set of *m-sorts* is $\mathcal{S}^m = \mathcal{S}_1^m \cup \mathcal{S}_2^m$ where the set of *primary m-sorts* is

$$\mathcal{S}_1^m = \{\circ^s \mid s \in \mathcal{S}\} \cup \{s^i \mid 1 \leq i \leq |\lambda(s)|, s \in \mathcal{S}\} \cup \{\bullet\}$$

and the set of *secondary m-sorts* is

$$\mathcal{S}_2^m = \{\circ^{s^i} \mid 1 \leq i \leq |\lambda(s)|, s \in \mathcal{S}\} \cup \{\delta^{s^i} \mid 1 \leq i \leq |\lambda(s)|, s \in \mathcal{S}\}.$$

We use σ to range over primary m-sorts, δ to range over secondary m-sorts, α to range over m-sorts, and $\circ$ to range over the $\circ^s$ and the $\circ^{s^i}$.

Definition 5. The labelled directed graph $\mathcal{G}_\lambda$ has set of nodes $\mathcal{S}_1^m$ and arrows as follows, where $\lambda(s) = (t_1 \dots t_n)$:

$$\circ^s \rightarrow s^1 \xrightarrow{\delta_1 t_1} s^2 \xrightarrow{\delta_2 t_2} \dots s^n \xrightarrow{\delta_n t_n} \bullet \qquad \text{where } \delta_i \text{ is } \delta^{s^i}.$$

We use the following notations: $\xrightarrow{\delta t}$ for $\exists \sigma, \sigma'. \sigma \xrightarrow{\delta t} \sigma'$; $\xrightarrow{\delta t} \sigma$ for $\exists \sigma'. \sigma' \xrightarrow{\delta t} \sigma$; $\sigma \rightarrow \sigma'$ for $\exists \delta, t. \sigma \xrightarrow{\delta t} \sigma'$; σ^+ for the σ' such that $\sigma \rightarrow \sigma'$, provided $\sigma \neq \bullet$; and σ^{++} for the σ'' such that $\sigma \rightarrow \sigma' \rightarrow \sigma''$, provided $\sigma, \sigma' \neq \bullet$.

Referring to the example above, suppose $\lambda(s) = (t_1 t_2)$ and x is of sort s and a_i is of sort t_i for each i. The type system will assign different primary m-sorts to various occurrences of the primary name w to capture their different roles in the translated process. The occurrence in $\overline{x}w$ will be assigned primary m-sort $\circ^s$, those in $\overline{w}v_1$ and $w(y_1)$ primary m-sort s^1, and those in $\overline{w}v_2$ and $w(y_2)$ primary m-sort s^2. The name w is first carried by x, then carries v_1, then carries v_2, and finally disappears (represented in $\mathcal{G}_\lambda$ by $\bullet$), having completed its contribution to the protocol. A secondary name is sent and then used once for communication: for each i the occurrence of the secondary name v_i in $\overline{w}v_i$ will be assigned secondary m-sort $\circ^{s^i}$, and the occurrences in $\overline{v_i}a_i$ and $v_i(y_i)$ secondary m-sort δ^{s^i}. Note that v_1 carries a_1 of sort t_1 and v_2 carries a_2 of (possibly different) sort t_2. This information is recorded in the labels of $\mathcal{G}_\lambda$.

In general the m-sorts assigned to names in a type judgment will give information about how the names occur in the process in question. The judgments are of the form $\Psi; \Delta; \Gamma; \Omega; \Pi \vdash M$ with M an $am\pi$-process. The function Ψ associates sorts with names, as in the type system for $p\pi$. The functions Δ and Γ associate m-sorts with names that occur free at the top level in M. More precisely, Δ gives information about input prefixes of the form $x(y)$, and Γ information about output particles of the form $\overline{x}y$. Further, Ω gives information about free names in prefixes *not* at the top level in M, and Π certain associations between names. We explain this further after introducing the type system.

Notation 6. We use Δ, Γ to range over finite partial functions from N to $\mathcal{S}^m$.
We use Ω to range over finite partial functions from N to $\mathcal{S}^m_1 \cup (\mathcal{S}^m_1 \times \mathsf{N})$. We write Ω^z for the function with domain $\mathrm{n}(\Omega) - \{z\}$ such that for $x \in \mathrm{n}(\Omega^z)$,

$$\Omega^z(x) = \begin{cases} \sigma & \text{if } \Omega(x) = (\sigma, z) \\ \Omega(x) & \text{otherwise.} \end{cases}$$

We use Π to range over finite partial functions from N to N. We write Π^z for the function obtained from Π by deleting any pair in which z occurs.

Definition 7. M is a λ^{am}*-process* if a judgment $\Psi; \Delta; \Gamma; \Omega; \Pi \vdash M$ can be inferred using the rules in table 2, where:

1. In accordance with the convention on bound names, in writing $\Psi; \Delta; \Gamma; \Omega; \Pi \vdash M$ it is assumed that the bound names of M are chosen to be different from the names in $\mathrm{n}(\Psi, \Delta, \Gamma, \Omega, \Pi)$. So in particular $z \notin \mathrm{n}(\Psi, \Delta, \Gamma, \Omega, \Pi)$ in the restriction rules, and $w \notin \mathrm{n}(\Psi)$ in i_x, and $v \notin \mathrm{n}(\Psi)$ in i_w, and $a \notin \mathrm{n}(\Psi, w)$ in i_v.
2. i_x is two rules written as one: if $(\circ^s)^{++} = \bullet$ then $\{w : (\circ^s)^{++}\}$ is read as $\emptyset$.
3. i_w is two rules written as one: if $\sigma^+ = \bullet$ then $\{w : \sigma^+\}$ is read as $\emptyset$.
4. i_v is three rules written as one: if $\sigma = \bullet$ then $\{w : \sigma\}$ and $\{w : \sigma^+\}$ and $\{w : (\sigma, v)\}$ are all read as $\emptyset$; if $\sigma \neq \bullet$ but $\sigma^+ = \bullet$ then $\{w : \sigma^+\}$ is read as $\emptyset$.
5. The side condition (comp) of *par* is: $\Delta_1, \Gamma_1, \Omega_1, \Pi_1$ and $\Delta_2, \Gamma_2, \Omega_2, \Pi_2$ are complementary, as defined below.

Definition 8. $\Delta_1, \Gamma_1, \Omega_1, \Pi_1$ and $\Delta_2, \Gamma_2, \Omega_2, \Pi_2$ are *complementary* if

1. $\mathrm{n}(\Delta_1) \cap \mathrm{n}(\Delta_2) = \mathrm{n}(\Gamma_1) \cap \mathrm{n}(\Gamma_2) = \mathrm{n}(\Omega_1) \cap \mathrm{n}(\Omega_2) = \emptyset$
2. $\Delta_1, \Delta_2; \Gamma_1, \Gamma_2; \Omega_1, \Omega_2; \Pi_1, \Pi_2$ are compatible, where

Definition 9. $\Delta, \Gamma, \Omega, \Pi$ are *compatible* if

1. if $x \in \mathrm{n}(\Delta) \cap \mathrm{n}(\Gamma)$ then $\Delta\lceil x$ and $\Gamma\lceil x$ are x-partners (see below)
2. if $x \in \mathrm{n}(\Omega) \cap \mathrm{n}(\Gamma)$ then $x \in \mathrm{n}(\Pi)$ and $\Omega(x) = (\Gamma(x)^+, \Pi(x))$, or $x \notin \mathrm{n}(\Pi)$ and $\Omega(x) = \Gamma(x)^+$

$$nil \quad \frac{}{\Psi;\ \ \emptyset;\ \ \emptyset;\ \ \emptyset;\ \ \emptyset \vdash \mathbf{0}}$$

$$o_x \quad \frac{}{\Psi, x : s;\ \ \emptyset;\ \ \{w : \mathrm{o}^s\};\ \ \emptyset;\ \ \emptyset \vdash \overline{x}w} \qquad w \notin \mathrm{n}(\Psi, x)$$

$$o_w \quad \frac{}{\Psi;\ \ \emptyset;\ \ \{w : \sigma, v : \mathrm{o}^\sigma\};\ \ \emptyset;\ \ \{(w, v)\} \vdash \overline{w}v} \qquad w, v \notin \mathrm{n}(\Psi) \text{ and } w \neq v$$

$$o_v \quad \frac{}{\Psi, a : t;\ \ \emptyset;\ \ \{v : \delta\};\ \ \emptyset;\ \ \emptyset \vdash \overline{v}a} \qquad \xrightarrow{\delta t} \text{ and } v \notin \mathrm{n}(\Psi, a)$$

$$i_x \quad \frac{\Psi;\ \ \emptyset;\ \ \{w : (\mathrm{o}^s)^+\};\ \ \{w : (\mathrm{o}^s)^{++}\};\ \ \emptyset \vdash M}{\Psi, x : s;\ \ \emptyset;\ \ \emptyset;\ \ \emptyset;\ \ \emptyset \vdash x(w).\, M}$$

$$i_w \quad \frac{\Psi;\ \ \{w : \sigma^+\};\ \ \{v : \delta^\sigma\};\ \ \emptyset;\ \ \emptyset \vdash M}{\Psi;\ \ \{w : \sigma\};\ \ \emptyset;\ \ \emptyset;\ \ \emptyset \vdash w(v).\, M} \qquad w \notin \mathrm{n}(\Psi)$$

$$i_v \quad \frac{\Psi, a : t;\ \ \emptyset;\ \ \{w : \sigma\};\ \ \{w : \sigma^+\};\ \ \emptyset \vdash M}{\Psi;\ \ \{v : \delta\};\ \ \emptyset;\ \ \{w : (\sigma, v)\};\ \ \emptyset \vdash v(a).\, M} \qquad \xrightarrow{\delta t} \sigma \text{ and } v \notin \mathrm{n}(\Psi, w)$$

$$par \quad \frac{\Psi;\ \ \Delta_1;\ \ \Gamma_1;\ \ \Omega_1;\ \ \Pi_1 \vdash M_1 \qquad \Psi;\ \ \Delta_2;\ \ \Gamma_2;\ \ \Omega_2;\ \ \Pi_2 \vdash M_2}{\Psi;\ \ \Delta_1, \Delta_2;\ \ \Gamma_1, \Gamma_2;\ \ \Omega_1, \Omega_2;\ \ \Pi_1, \Pi_2 \vdash M_1 \mid M_2} \qquad \text{comp}$$

$$res_1 \quad \frac{\Psi, z : s;\ \ \Delta;\ \ \Gamma;\ \ \Omega;\ \ \Pi \vdash M}{\Psi;\ \ \Delta;\ \ \Gamma;\ \ \Omega;\ \ \Pi \vdash \nu z\, M}$$

$$res_2 \quad \frac{\Psi;\ \ \Delta, \Delta';\ \ \Gamma, \Gamma';\ \ \Omega;\ \ \Pi \vdash M}{\Psi;\ \ \Delta;\ \ \Gamma;\ \ \Omega^z;\ \ \Pi^z \vdash \nu z\, M} \qquad \Delta', \Gamma' \text{ are } z\text{-partners}$$

$$rep \quad \frac{\Psi;\ \ \emptyset;\ \ \emptyset;\ \ \emptyset;\ \ \emptyset \vdash M}{\Psi;\ \ \emptyset;\ \ \emptyset;\ \ \emptyset;\ \ \emptyset \vdash !M}$$

Table 2. The typing rules for *amπ*

3. if $x \in \mathrm{n}(\Omega) \cap \mathrm{n}(\Delta) - \mathrm{n}(\Gamma)$ then $\Omega(x) = (\sigma, y)$ where $\sigma = \Delta(x)$ or $\sigma = \Delta(x)^+$, and if $y \in \mathrm{n}(\Gamma)$ then $\sigma = \Delta(x)$
4. if $\Pi(x) \in \mathrm{n}(\Delta)$ and $\Gamma(x)^+ \neq \bullet$, then $x \in \mathrm{n}(\Omega)$.

Definition 10. Δ and Γ are *x-partners* if $\Gamma = \{x : \circ^s\}$ and $\Delta = \{x : (\circ^s)^+\}$, or $\Gamma = \{x : \circ^\sigma\}$ and $\Delta = \{x : \delta^\sigma\}$, or $\Gamma = \{x : \alpha\}$ and $\Delta = \{x : \alpha\}$.

The origin of the subtlety of the type system is, as one might expect, the separation between sending and receiving. The crux is to find an appropriate rule for typing compositions. The most delicate point is how to capture compatibility of an output particle and an input-prefixed process when the subject of the particle is a primary name and the subject of the top-level input prefix is a secondary name. To make this clearer we first examine in detail how the translations of $\overline{x}\langle a_1 a_2\rangle.\,\mathbf{0}$ and $x(y_1 y_2).\,\mathbf{0}$ are typed. Suppose $\lambda(s) = (t_1 t_2)$ so that in $\mathcal{G}_\lambda$ we have

$$\circ^s \rightarrow \sigma_1 \xrightarrow{\delta^{\sigma_1} t_1} \sigma_2 \xrightarrow{\delta^{\sigma_2} t_2} \bullet \quad \text{where } \sigma_i \text{ is } s^i.$$

Let $\Psi = \{x : s, a_1 : t_1, a_2 : t_2\}$ and $\Psi_1 = \Psi, \{y_1 : t_1\}$ and $\Psi_2 = \Psi, \{y_1 : t_1, y_2 : t_2\}$. Then the type inferences are:

$$\dfrac{\dfrac{}{\Psi;\emptyset;\{w:\circ^s\};\emptyset;\emptyset \vdash \overline{x}w}\,o_x \qquad \dfrac{\dfrac{\dfrac{}{\Psi;\emptyset;\{v_1:\delta^{\sigma_1}\};\emptyset;\emptyset \vdash \overline{v_1}a_1}\,o_v \qquad \dfrac{\dfrac{\dfrac{}{\Psi;\emptyset;\{v_2:\delta^{\sigma_2}\};\emptyset;\emptyset \vdash \overline{v_2}a_2}\,o_v \qquad \dfrac{}{\Psi;\emptyset;\emptyset;\emptyset;\emptyset \vdash \mathbf{0}}\,nil}{\Psi;\emptyset;\{v_2:\delta^{\sigma_2}\};\emptyset;\emptyset \vdash \overline{v_2}a_2 \mid \mathbf{0}}\,par}{\Psi;\{w:\sigma_2\};\emptyset;\emptyset;\emptyset \vdash w(v_2).\,(\overline{v_2}a_2 \mid \mathbf{0})}\,i_w}{\Psi;\{w:\sigma_2\};\{v_1:\delta^{\sigma_1}\};\emptyset;\emptyset \vdash \overline{v_1}a_1 \mid w(v_2).\,(\overline{v_2}a_2 \mid \mathbf{0})}\,par}{\Psi;\{w:\sigma_1\};\emptyset;\emptyset;\emptyset \vdash w(v_1).\,(\overline{v_1}a_1 \mid w(v_2).\,(\overline{v_2}a_2 \mid \mathbf{0}))}\,i_w}{\dfrac{\Psi;\{w:\sigma_1\};\{w:\circ^s\};\emptyset;\emptyset \vdash \overline{x}w \mid w(v_1).\,(\overline{v_1}a_1 \mid w(v_2).\,(\overline{v_2}a_2 \mid \mathbf{0}))}{\Psi;\emptyset;\emptyset;\emptyset;\emptyset \vdash [\![\overline{x}\langle a_1a_2\rangle.\,\mathbf{0}]\!] = \nu w\,(\overline{x}w \mid w(v_1).\,(\overline{v_1}a_1 \mid w(v_2).\,(\overline{v_2}a_2 \mid \mathbf{0})))}\,res_2}\,par$$

$$\dfrac{\dfrac{\dfrac{}{\Psi;\emptyset;\{w:\sigma_1, v_1:\circ^{\sigma_1}\};\emptyset;\{(w,v_1)\} \vdash \overline{w}v_1}\,o_w \qquad \dfrac{\dfrac{\dfrac{\dfrac{}{\Psi_1;\emptyset;\{w:\sigma_2, v_2:\circ^{\sigma_2}\};\emptyset;\{(w,v_2)\} \vdash \overline{w}v_2}\,o_w \qquad \dfrac{\dfrac{}{\Psi_2;\emptyset;\emptyset;\emptyset;\emptyset \vdash \mathbf{0}}\,nil}{\Psi_1;\{v_2:\delta^{\sigma_2}\};\emptyset;\emptyset;\emptyset \vdash v_2(y_2).\,\mathbf{0}}\,i_v}{\Psi_1;\{v_2:\delta^{\sigma_2}\};\{w:\sigma_2, v_2:\circ^{\sigma_2}\};\emptyset;\{(w,v_2)\} \vdash \overline{w}v_2 \mid v_2(y_2).\,\mathbf{0}}\,par}{\Psi_1;\emptyset;\{w:\sigma_2\};\emptyset;\emptyset \vdash N = \nu v_2\,(\overline{w}v_2 \mid v_2(y_2).\,\mathbf{0})}\,res_2}{\Psi;\{v_1:\delta^{\sigma_1}\};\emptyset;\{w:(\sigma_2,v_1)\};\emptyset \vdash v_1(y_1).\,N}\,i_v}{\Psi;\{v_1:\delta^{\sigma_1}\};\{w:\sigma_1, v_1:\circ^{\sigma_1}\};\{w:(\sigma_2,v_1)\};\{(w,v_1)\} \vdash \overline{w}v_1 \mid v_1(y_1).\,N}\,par\ (\star)}{\dfrac{\Psi;\emptyset;\{w:\sigma_1\};\{w:\sigma_2\};\emptyset \vdash \nu v_1\,(\overline{w}v_1 \mid v_1(y_1).\,N)}{\Psi;\emptyset;\emptyset;\emptyset;\emptyset \vdash [\![x(y_1y_2).\,\mathbf{0}]\!] = x(w).\,\nu v_1\,(\overline{w}v_1 \mid v_1(y_1).\,N)}\,i_x}\,res_2$$

Note that when rule i_v is applied to type $v_1(y_1).\,N$ in the typing of $[\![x(y_1y_2).\,\mathbf{0}]\!]$, the Ω-component in the conclusion keeps track of the fact that the primary name w is used for sending in the continuation of the input-prefixed process. This information is vital for checking the admissibility of possible parallel compositions. The judgment

$$J = \langle\ \Psi;\{v_1:\delta^{\sigma_1}\};\emptyset;\{w:(\sigma_2,v_1)\};\emptyset \vdash v_1(y_1).\,\nu v_2\,(\overline{w}v_2 \mid v_2(y_2).\,\mathbf{0}) = v_1(y_1).\,N\ \rangle$$

illustrates this point well. First, to type the composition of $v_1(y_1).\,N$ and an output particle of the form $\overline{w}u$, the datum u must be v_1. (The reader may care to check that *par* is applicable at $(\star)$ in the inference above, using clause 2 of definition 9.) But secondly, things are quite different when $v_1(y_1).N$ is composed with an input-prefixed process of the form $w(u).M$ (see clause 3 of definition 9). For consider the first two reduction steps in

$$[\![\overline{x}\langle a_1a_2\rangle.P \mid x(y_1y_2).Q]\!] \longrightarrow^* [\![P]\!] \mid [\![Q]\!]\{a_1a_2/y_1y_2\},$$

when P and Q are both $\mathbf{0}$. Then since typeability should be invariant under structural congruence, it should be possible to 'compose' the judgment J both with

$$\Psi; \{w : \sigma_1\}; \emptyset; \emptyset; \emptyset \vdash w(v_1).(\overline{v_1}a_1 \mid w(v_2).(\overline{v_2}a_2 \mid \mathbf{0}))$$

(consider the process reached after one reduction step), and with

$$\Psi; \{w : \sigma_2\}; \emptyset; \emptyset; \emptyset \vdash w(v_2).(\overline{v_2}a_2 \mid \mathbf{0})$$

(consider the process reached after the second reduction step).

Notation 11. We write Σ for $\Psi; \Delta; \Gamma; \Omega; \Pi$, and similarly Σ_0 for $\Psi_0; \Delta_0; \Gamma_0; \Omega_0; \Pi_0$, and Σ' for $\Psi'; \Delta'; \Gamma'; \Omega'; \Pi'$ etc.

Due to lack of space we omit some basic lemmas about the type system. We state, however, that typing is preserved by the translation, and that the translation of a $p\pi$-term has no other typings:

Lemma 12. 1. If $\Psi \vdash P$ then $\Psi; \emptyset; \emptyset; \emptyset; \emptyset \vdash [\![P]\!]$.
2. If $\Sigma \vdash [\![P]\!]$ then $\Delta = \Gamma = \Omega = \Pi = \emptyset$ and $\Psi \vdash P$.

Other important facts about the type system, the latter being a special case of a more general result, are:

Lemma 13. 1. If $\Sigma \vdash M$ and $N \equiv M$, then $\Sigma \vdash N$.
2. If $\Psi; \emptyset; \emptyset; \emptyset; \emptyset \vdash M$ and $M \longrightarrow M'$, then $\Psi; \emptyset; \emptyset; \emptyset; \emptyset \vdash M'$.

These essential properties of a viable type system are not easy to achieve in conjunction with lemma 18 below, which is crucial for the proof of the completeness of the type system.

We now define the appropriate form of barbed congruence for $am\pi$-processes, based on the type system. First we have:

Definition 14. Σ is *balanced* if

1. $\mathrm{n}(\Psi) \cap \mathrm{n}(\Delta, \Gamma, \Omega) = \emptyset$
2. $\Delta, \Gamma, \Omega, \Pi$ are compatible
3. $\mathrm{n}(\Delta) = \mathrm{n}(\Gamma, \Omega)$.

The class of $am\pi$-processes that are typed by balanced Σs contains the translations of λ-processes and enjoys good closure properties. We then have:

Definition 15. 1. K is a $\lambda^{am}(\Sigma)$-*context* if for some balanced Σ' there is an inference of $\Sigma' \vdash K$ in which the hole is typed by $\Sigma \vdash [\cdot]$; and K is *m-closed* if in addition $\Delta' = \Gamma' = \Omega' = \Pi' = \emptyset$.
2. M and N are *barbed* λ^{am}-*congruent*, $M \approx_\lambda^{am} N$, if there is a balanced Σ such that $\Sigma \vdash M, N$ and $K[M] \approx K[N]$ for every m-closed $\lambda^{am}(\Sigma)$-context K.

4 Summary of Main Results

The principal result is that two λ-processes are barbed λ-congruent if and only if their translations are barbed λ^{am}-congruent:

Theorem 16 (Full Abstraction). $[\![P]\!] \approx_{\lambda}^{am} [\![Q]\!]$ if and only if $P \approx_{\lambda} Q$.

The 'only if' is the easier assertion to prove. The main lemma needed for it is:

Lemma 17. If R is a λ-process then $[\![R]\!] \approx R$.

Using this lemma, the proof of soundness is completed as follows. Suppose $[\![P]\!] \approx_{\lambda}^{am} [\![Q]\!]$ and $\Sigma \vdash [\![P]\!], [\![Q]\!]$ where $\Sigma = \Psi; \emptyset; \emptyset; \emptyset; \emptyset$, so $K[[\![P]\!]] \stackrel{\cdot}{\approx} K[[\![Q]\!]]$ for every m-closed $\lambda^{am}(\Sigma)$-context K. Then $\Psi \vdash P, Q$, and if C is a $\lambda(\Psi)$-context then $[\![C]\!]$ is an m-closed $\lambda^{am}(\Sigma)$-context and hence

$$C[P] \stackrel{\cdot}{\approx} [\![C[P]]\!] = [\![C]\!][[\![P]\!]] \stackrel{\cdot}{\approx} [\![C]\!][[\![Q]\!]] = [\![C[Q]]\!] \stackrel{\cdot}{\approx} C[Q],$$

so $P \approx_{\lambda} Q$.

As just noted, the translation of a $\lambda(\Psi)$-context is a $\lambda^{am}(\Psi; \emptyset; \emptyset; \emptyset; \emptyset)$-context. The class of $\lambda^{am}(\Sigma)$-contexts contains much more than just parts of translations of $\lambda(\Psi)$-contexts, however. To prove completeness we have to understand precisely what it does contain. The main lemma needed is:

Lemma 18. If K is a $\lambda^{am}(\Sigma_0)$-context with Σ_0 balanced, then there is a $\lambda(\Psi_0)$-context C such that if $\Psi_0 \vdash M$ then $\nu \boldsymbol{u}\, K[M] \approx_{\lambda}^{am} [\![C]\!][\nu \boldsymbol{u_0}\, M]$ where $\boldsymbol{u} = \mathrm{n}(\Delta)$ and $\boldsymbol{u_0} = \mathrm{n}(\Delta_0)$.

Proof. The proof is a fairly complicated induction on the inference of $\Sigma \vdash K$. Let $M^* = \nu \boldsymbol{u_0}\, M$. We sketch just the argument for composition.

Suppose that $K = K' \mid K''$ and $\Sigma \vdash K$ is inferred from $\Sigma' \vdash K'$ and $\Sigma'' \vdash K''$. There are several cases. We outline the argument for just one of them: when Σ' and Σ'' are not balanced and there is w such that $\Gamma'(w) = \Delta''(w) = \sigma$.

First it can be shown that there is $K^* \equiv K$ such that

$$K^* = [\nu v\,]\nu \boldsymbol{x}\, (\overline{w}v \mid w(u).\, [\nu a\,](\overline{u}a \mid K_1) \mid v(y).\, K_2\, \big[\mid K_3 \big])$$

where $u \notin \mathrm{fn}(K_1)$ and K_3, if present, is balanced. Note: [ ] around an expression indicates that it may be absent. Further, $|\, K^* \,| \leq |\, K \,|$, where $|\, T \,|$ is the size of a term T.

Then let $K_1^* = \overline{w}v \mid w(u).\, [\nu a](\overline{u}a \mid K_1) \mid v(y).\, K_2$ and suppose that $\Sigma_1 \vdash K_1^*$ where $\mathrm{n}(\Delta_1) = \boldsymbol{u}_1$. Then $\nu \boldsymbol{u}_1\, K_1^* \approx_{\lambda}^{am} \nu \boldsymbol{u}_1\, K_1^{**}$ where

$$K_1^{**} = [\nu a\,](\overline{v}a \mid K_1) \mid v(y).\, K_2$$

and K_1^{**} is balanced and $|\, K_1^{**} \,| < |\, K_1^* \,|$.

By induction hypothesis there is C_1 such that $\nu \boldsymbol{u}_1\, K_1^{**}[M] \approx_{\lambda}^{am} [\![C_1]\!][M^*]$. Moreover, if K_3 is present in K^* then by induction hypothesis there is C_2 such that $\nu \boldsymbol{u}_2\, K_3[M] \approx_{\lambda}^{am} [\![C_2]\!][M^*]$ where $\Sigma_2 \vdash K_3$ and $\boldsymbol{u}_2 = \mathrm{n}(\Delta_2)$.

Set $C = \nu \boldsymbol{x}\, (C_1 \,\big[\,|\, C_2\big]\,)$. Then:

$$\begin{aligned}
\nu \boldsymbol{u}\, K[M] \equiv{}& \nu \boldsymbol{u}\, K^*[M] \\
\equiv{}& [\nu v\,]\nu \boldsymbol{x}\, (\nu \boldsymbol{u}_1\, K_1^*[M] \,\big[\,|\, \nu \boldsymbol{u}_2\, K_3[M]\big]\,) \\
\approx_\lambda^{am}{}& [\nu v\,]\nu \boldsymbol{x}\, (\nu \boldsymbol{u}_1\, K_1^{**}[M] \,\big[\,|\, \nu \boldsymbol{u}_2\, K_3[M]\big]\,) \\
\approx_\lambda^{am}{}& \nu \boldsymbol{x}\, ([\![C_1]\!][M^*] \,\big[\,|\, [\![C_2]\!][M^*]\big]\,) \\
={}& [\![C]\!][M^*]\,.
\end{aligned}$$

□

Using this lemma we may show completeness, that is, if $P \approx_\lambda Q$ then $[\![P]\!] \approx_\lambda^{am} [\![Q]\!]$. For suppose that $\Psi \vdash P, Q$ and let Σ be $\Psi; \emptyset; \emptyset; \emptyset; \emptyset$. Then Σ is balanced and $\Sigma \vdash [\![P]\!], [\![Q]\!]$. Moreover if K is an m-closed $\lambda^{am}(\Sigma)$-context then using lemma 17 and lemma 18 there is C such that

$$K[[\![P]\!]] \approx_\lambda^{am} [\![C]\!][[\![P]\!]] = [\![C[P]]\!] \dot{\approx} C[P] \approx C[Q] \dot{\approx} [\![C[Q]]\!] = [\![C]\!][[\![Q]\!]] \approx_\lambda^{am} K[[\![Q]\!]]\,.$$

Hence $[\![P]\!] \approx_\lambda^{am} [\![Q]\!]$.

This completes the outline of the proof of the full-abstraction theorem. □

References

[Bor98] M. Boreale. On the Expressiveness of Internal Mobility in Name-Passing Calculi. *Theoretical Computer Science*, 195(2):205–226, 1998.

[Bou92] G. Boudol. Asynchrony and the π-calculus (note). Rapports de Recherche 1702, INRIA Sophia Antipolis, 1992.

[Fou98] C. Fournet. The Join-Calculus: a Calculus for Distributed Mobile Programming. Thesis École Polytechnique 1998.

[FG96] C. Fournet and G. Gonthier. The reflexive chemical machine and the join-calculus. In *Proc. 23rd Annual ACM SIGPLAN–SIGACT Symp. on Principles of Programming Languages*, 372–385, 1996.

[FM97] C. Fournet and L. Maranget. The join-calculus language. `http://join.inria.fr`.

[Hon93] K. Honda. Types for Dyadic Interaction. In *Proc. CONCUR'93*, 509–523. Springer 1993.

[HT91] K. Honda and M. Tokoro. An Object Calculus for Asynchronous Communication. In P. America, editor, *Proc. European Conference on Object-Oriented Programming, ECOOP '91*. Springer 1991.

[KPT96] N. Kobayashi and B. Pierce and D. Turner. Linearity and the Pi-Calculus. In *Proc. 23rd Annual ACM SIGPLAN–SIGACT Symp. on Principles of Programming Languages*, 358–371, 1996.

[MS98] M. Merro and D. Sangiorgi. On asynchrony in name-passing calculi. In *Proc. 25th International Colloquium ICALP'98*. Springer 1998.

[Mil89] R. Milner. **Communication and Concurrency**. Prentice Hall 1989.

[Mil91] R. Milner. The Polyadic π-Calculus: a Tutorial. In **Logic and Algebra of Specification**, Springer 1992, 203–246.

[Mil99] R. Milner. **Communicating and mobile systems: the π-calculus**. CUP 1999.

[MPW92] R. Milner, J. Parrow, and D. Walker. A Calculus of Mobile Processes, Part I and II. *Information and Computation*, 100(1):1–77, 1992.

[Nes97] U. Nestmann. What is a 'Good' Encoding of Guarded Choice? In *Proc. EXPRESS'97*, Electronic Lecture Notes in Computer Science, vol. 7, 1997.

[NP96] U. Nestmann and B. Pierce. Decoding Choice Encodings. In *Proc. International Conference on Concurrency Theory CONCUR'96*, 179–194. Springer 1996.

[Pal97] C. Palamidessi. Comparing the Expressive Power of the Synchronous and the Asynchronous π-calculus. In *Proc. 24th Annual ACM SIGPLAN–SIGACT Symp. on Principles of Programming Languages*, 256–265, 1997.

[PS96] B. Pierce and D. Sangiorgi. Typing and Subtyping for Mobile Processes. Mathematical Structures in Computer Science 6(5), 409–454, 1996.

[PS97] B. Pierce and D. Sangiorgi. Behavioral Equivalence in the Polymorphic Pi-Calculus. In *Proc. 24th Annual ACM SIGPLAN-SIGACT Symp. on Principles of Programming Languages*, 1997.

[PT97] B. Pierce and D. Turner. Pict: A Programming Language Based on the Pi-Calculus. Indiana University technical report 1997.

[QW98] P. Quaglia and D. Walker. On Encoding $p\pi$ in $m\pi$. In *Proc. 18th Conference on Foundations of Software Technology and Theoretical Computer Science, FST&TCS '98*, 42–53. Springer, 1998.

[San97] D. Sangiorgi. The name discipline of uniform receptiveness. In *Proc. 24th International Colloquium ICALP'97*, 303–313. Springer 1997.

[Tur96] D. Turner. The Polymorphic Pi-Calculus: Theory and Implementation. PhD thesis, University of Edinburgh 1996.

[Yos96] N. Yoshida. Graph Types for Monadic Mobile Processes. In *Proc. 17th Conference on Foundations of Software Technology and Theoretical Computer Science, FST&TCS '97*, 371–386. Springer, 1996.

Type Inference for First-Order Logic

Aleksy Schubert*

Institute of Informatics
Warsaw University
ul. Banacha 2
02–097 Warsaw
Poland
alx@mimuw.edu.pl

Abstract. Although type inference for dependent types is in general undecidable, people experience that the algorithms for type inference in Elf programming language stop in common cases. The present paper is a partial explanation of this behaviour. It shows that for a wide range of terms — terms that correspond to first-order logic proofs — the formalism of dependent types gives decidable type inference. We remark also that imposing that the context and the type of a judgement are first-order is not sufficient for obtaining decidability.

1 Introduction

Lambda calculus with dependent types is a formalism defined in [HHP87] in order to provide a means for defining logics. For example, one can define first-order logic within the formalism. This definition leads to a restriction on dependent types which constitutes by itself an interesting type system for λ-terms.

Dependent types formalism has also been used as a base for the programming language Elf [Pfe91]. The clauses of Elf are expressions of dependent types. This allows to reason about properties of programs inside the language. Although the problem of inferring types in the language is undecidable, as shown in [Dow93], it comes out that for many practical programs the algorithm used in the framework halts. This paper is a partial explanation for the phenomenon. The type inference for a wide range of terms: terms that correspond to proofs in first-order logic, is decidable.

Interestingly enough, the border-line between decidability and undecidability is very slight here. The problem of type inference for the first-order logic inside dependent types is defined as follows: given a first-order context Γ and a Curry-term M, check if there exists a first-order type such that $\Gamma \vdash M : \tau$ is the end of some first-order derivation (i.e. a derivation that can be translated into first-order logic). If the condition that $\Gamma \vdash M : \tau$ is the end of some first-order derivation is relaxed so that $\Gamma \vdash M : \tau$ may be the end of any derivation in

* This work was supported by Polish national research funding agency KBN grant no. 8 T11C 035 14.

J. Tiuryn (Ed.): FOSSACS 2000, LNCS 1784, pp. 297–313, 2000.

dependent types, then the problem becomes undecidable. This holds even for a class of terms M that fall within an extension of the first-order logic where quantification over first-order function symbols is allowed.

The techniques used in this paper are based on the old idea that typing problems correspond to problems of solving appropriate equations. We reduce type inference for first-order logic to special kind of equations with explicit substitutions. These equations are subject to a further reduction that is very similar to usual Robinson's unification. So obtained equations are translated in turn to second-order unification equations. As it is proved in [Gol81], second-order unification is undecidable, so in general it cannot serve as a method for providing decidability. In the present study, we get a particular form of equations which allows us to design a procedure to solve them. We deal only with equations of the three forms

$$F_1(t_1,\ldots,t_n) = F_2(s_1,\ldots,s_m); \qquad F_1(t_1,\ldots,t_n) = f(s_1,\ldots,s_m);$$
$$f_1(t_1,\ldots,t_n) = f_2(s_1,\ldots,s_m)$$

where none of second-order variables may occur in terms $t_1,\ldots,t_n,s_1,\ldots s_n$. The latter condition is very important here as when we drop it the problem becomes undecidable. In [Sch98], it is shown that already solving equations f the form $F_1(t_1,\ldots,t_n) = f(s_1,\ldots,s_m)$, where second-order variables may occur in $s_1,\ldots,s_n$, is undecidable.

The paper is organised as follows: Section 2 contains basic definitions and formulation of problems we deal with; Section 3 presents a sketch of the undecidability result for type inference with relaxed first-order constraints, and Section 4 contains a sketch of the decidability result for the first-order type inference.

2 Basic Definitions

We introduce the definition of the system λP. The basic insight behind this system is that types of terms may depend on terms. ¿From the perspective of programming language this corresponds to providing devices for defining types such as `list(n)` that represent lists of length n. From the point of view off logic, this allows to implement rules of substitution. We follow hereafter the presentation in [SU98].

2.1 Language of λP

The set of *pure* λ*-terms* is defined according to the following grammar:

$$M ::= x \mid (\lambda x.M) \mid (MM)$$

Contexts are used in the typing system as well. These are sequences of pairs: $(\alpha : \boldsymbol{\kappa})$ or $(x : \tau)$, where α is a kind variable, $\boldsymbol{\kappa}$ a kind, x is an object variable and τ a type.

Pure λ-terms and contexts form a base for Curry style λ-calculus, λP, the expressions of which are inferred according to the following rules:

2.2 Rules of λP

Kind formation rules:

$$(type) \vdash * : \Box \qquad (\text{kind-abs})\frac{\Gamma, x:\tau \vdash \boldsymbol{\kappa} : \Box}{\Gamma \vdash (\Pi x:\tau)\boldsymbol{\kappa} : \Box}$$

Kinding rules:

$$(\text{kind-var})\frac{\Gamma \vdash \boldsymbol{\kappa} : \Box}{\Gamma, \alpha : \boldsymbol{\kappa} \vdash \alpha : \boldsymbol{\kappa}}(\alpha \notin \text{Dom}(\Gamma))$$

$$(\text{kind-app})\frac{\Gamma \vdash \phi : (\Pi x:\tau)\boldsymbol{\kappa} \quad \Gamma \vdash M : \tau}{\Gamma \vdash \phi M : \boldsymbol{\kappa}[x := M]} \quad (\text{kind-abs})\frac{\Gamma, x:\tau \vdash \sigma : *}{\Gamma \vdash (\forall x:\tau)\sigma : *}$$

Typing rules:

$$(\text{var})\frac{\Gamma \vdash \tau : *}{\Gamma, x:\tau \vdash x : \tau}(\alpha \notin \text{Dom}(\Gamma))$$

$$(\text{app})\frac{\Gamma \vdash N : (\forall x:\tau)\sigma \quad \Gamma \vdash M : \tau}{\Gamma \vdash NM : \sigma[x := M]} \quad (\text{abs})\frac{\Gamma, x:\tau \vdash M : \sigma}{\Gamma \vdash \lambda x.M : (\forall x:\tau)\sigma}$$

Weakening rules:

$$(\text{trm} - \text{kd})\frac{\Gamma \vdash \tau : * \quad \Gamma \vdash \boldsymbol{\kappa} : \Box}{\Gamma, x:\tau \vdash \boldsymbol{\kappa} : \Box}(x \notin \text{Dom}(\Gamma))$$

$$(\text{typ} - \text{kd})\frac{\Gamma \vdash \boldsymbol{\kappa} : \Box \quad \Gamma \vdash \boldsymbol{\kappa}' : \Box}{\Gamma, \alpha : \boldsymbol{\kappa} \vdash \boldsymbol{\kappa}' : \Box}(\alpha \notin \text{Dom}(\Gamma))$$

$$(\text{trm} - \text{typ})\frac{\Gamma \vdash \tau : * \quad \Gamma \vdash \phi : \boldsymbol{\kappa}}{\Gamma, x:\tau \vdash \phi : \boldsymbol{\kappa}}(x \notin \text{Dom}(\Gamma))$$

$$(\text{typ} - \text{typ})\frac{\Gamma \vdash \boldsymbol{\kappa} : \Box \quad \Gamma \vdash \phi : \boldsymbol{\kappa}'}{\Gamma, \alpha : \boldsymbol{\kappa} \vdash \phi : \boldsymbol{\kappa}'}(\alpha \notin \text{Dom}(\Gamma))$$

$$(\text{trm} - \text{trm})\frac{\Gamma \vdash \tau : * \quad \Gamma \vdash M : \sigma}{\Gamma, x:\tau \vdash M : \sigma}(x \notin \text{Dom}(\Gamma))$$

$$(\text{typ} - \text{trm})\frac{\Gamma \vdash \boldsymbol{\kappa} : \Box \quad \Gamma \vdash M : \sigma}{\Gamma, \alpha : \boldsymbol{\kappa} \vdash M : \sigma}(\alpha \notin \text{Dom}(\Gamma))$$

Conversion rules:

$$(\text{kd} - \text{conv})\frac{\Gamma \vdash \phi : \boldsymbol{\kappa} \quad \boldsymbol{\kappa} =_\beta \boldsymbol{\kappa}'}{\Gamma \vdash \phi : \boldsymbol{\kappa}'} \quad (\text{typ} - \text{conv})\frac{\Gamma \vdash M : \sigma \quad \sigma =_\beta \sigma'}{\Gamma \vdash M : \sigma'}$$

The definitions in Subsection 2.2 and 2.1 allow to infer types for Curry-style terms. The system λP is usually defined in the Church version as follows. First, raw expressions are described according to the following grammar:

$$\begin{aligned}
&\Gamma ::= \{\} \mid \Gamma, (x : \phi) \mid \Gamma, (\alpha : \kappa); \\
&\kappa ::= * \mid (\Pi x : \phi)\kappa; \\
&\phi ::= \alpha \mid (\forall x : \phi)\phi \mid (\phi(M); \\
&M ::= x \mid (MM) \mid (\lambda x : \phi.M)
\end{aligned}$$

Some of these expressions, designated by inference rules, are called Church terms. The inference rules have exactly the same form in most cases as the rules for inferring Curry types. The exception is the rule (abs) which looks as follows

$$(\text{abs})\frac{\Gamma, x : \tau \vdash M : \sigma}{\Gamma \vdash \lambda x : \tau.M : (\forall x : \tau)\sigma}$$

Note that the definition of types for the Church version also changes — the definition depends on the definition of terms which is different in Curry and Church styles. These versions are essentially equivalent as shown in [vBLRU97].

In this document, we use the word 'subtype' to mean subexpression. We do not employ any other kind of 'subtyping' relation here.

Definition 1 (type assignment)
A *derivation* is a tree labelled with rules of λP so that for each node its label premises are in bijection with conclusions in labels of its sons. Derivations are usually denoted by letters like $\mathcal{P}, \mathcal{Q}\ldots$

We say that *a derivation $\mathcal{P}$ assigns a type τ to a term M* iff the derivation ends with the assertion $\Gamma \vdash M : \tau$ for some Γ.

Except where stated explicitly otherwise, we write $(\forall x : \sigma)\tau$ as $\sigma \to \tau$ provided that x does not occur free in τ.

We shall be using extensively the notation $l((\forall x : \sigma_1)\sigma_2)$ and $l(\sigma_1 \to \sigma_2)$ to denote σ_1 together with $r((\forall x : \sigma_1)\sigma_2)$ and $r(\sigma_1 \to \sigma_2)$ to denote σ_2.

We denote the α-conversion relation, applied for both types or λ-terms by $\equiv_\alpha$.

We have to formulate the exact problem we should solve. The notion of signature is central in the syntactic part in any presentation of the first-order logic. Thus, we have to determine what part of λP syntax corresponds to the notion.

Definition 2 (signature first-order context)
The *signature first-order context* is a λP context such that:

1. There is only one type variable 0 (which should be regarded as a type constant), representing the type individuals;
2. All kinds are of the form $0 \Rightarrow \cdots \Rightarrow 0 \Rightarrow *$;
3. There is a finite number of distinguished constructor variables, representing relation symbols in the signature (they must be of appropriate kinds, depending on arity);

4. Function symbols in the signature are represented by distinguished object variables of types $0 \to \cdots \to 0 \to 0$, depending on arity;
5. Constant symbols are represented by distinguished object variables of type 0.

A λP context obtained from a signature Σ is denoted by Γ_Σ.

The proof theory for first-order logic introduces a notion of a context (environment) in which a formula is interpreted. This context is reflected by the following notion (this notion is in the spirit of [SU98]):

Definition 3 (first-order context)
A *first-order context* over a signature context Γ_Σ is a context in dependent types of the form $\Gamma_\Sigma \cup \{x_1 : \phi_1, \ldots, x_n : \phi_n\}$ where each ϕ_i is either first-order type or 0.

The notion of an algebraic term is crucial in the presentation of the first-order logic. These terms have their counterparts in λP. The most straightforward definition of such terms looks as follows:

Definition 4 (homogeneous first-order term)
We say that t is a *homogeneous first-order term* in a first-order context Γ iff

- $t = x$ where $\Gamma(x) = 0$ (i.e. x is a constant symbol or a first-order variable),
- $t = ft_1 \ldots t_n$ where $\Gamma(f) = \underbrace{0 \to \cdots \to 0}_{n-times} \to 0$ and each t_i is a homogeneous first-order term in Γ.

The next step in our presentation is to define what is the equivalent of the first-order formula.

Definition 5 (first-order type)
We say that a type ϕ is a *first-order type* in the context Γ iff it is of the form

- $P(t_1, \ldots, t_n)$ where $\Gamma(P) = \underbrace{0 \Rightarrow \cdots \Rightarrow 0}_{n-times} \Rightarrow *$, $P \neq 0$ and each t_i is homogeneous first-order term in Γ, or
- $(\forall x_1 : 0) \cdots (\forall x_n : 0).\phi_1 \to \cdots \to \phi_m$ where each ϕ_i is a first-order type in $\Gamma \cup \{x_1 : 0, \ldots, x_n : 0\}$.

At last, we have to define which derivations of λP may be regarded as first-order derivations.

Definition 6 (first-order derivations)
We say that a derivation $\mathcal{P}$ in dependent types is a *first-order derivation* iff each judgement $\Gamma \vdash M : \tau$ in the derivation is such that Γ is a first-order context over a fixed signature first-order context Γ_Σ and τ is either a first-order type or a type of the form $\underbrace{0 \to \cdots \to 0}_{n-times} \to 0$ where $n \geq 0$.

This definition of derivation allows to introduce one-to-one correspondence between derivations in λP and some first-order logic proofs. We do not present details due to limited space.

We can now describe precisely the set of problems we deal with.

Problem 1. The problem of *type inference with a first-order context* is defined as follows:
Given: A Curry-style term M and a first-order context Γ.
Question: Does there exist a derivation in λP that ends with $\Gamma \vdash M : \tau$ for a first-order type τ?

Problem 2. The problem of *first-order type inference* is defined as follows:
Given: A Curry-style term M and a first-order context Γ.
Question: Does there exist a first-order derivation that ends with $\Gamma \vdash M : \tau$ for a first-order type τ?

Note that in all the above-mentioned questions we assume that a context Γ is a first-order context. This is not standard for type inference problems as usually these are formulated with arbitrary contexts. We may assume that contexts from the *Given* parts in definitions of problems are first-order contexts as procedure checking if the context has the property is easy.

3 Undecidability of Type Inference with a First-Order Context

Our undecidability proof is almost identical to the proof presented in [Dow93].

Theorem 1. *undecidability of Problem 1 The problem of type inference with a first-order context is undecidable.*

Proof. We present a description of changes that should be made in Dowek's proof in order to get our claim. The context Γ

$$[0 : \text{Type}; a : 0 \to 0; b : 0 \to 0; c : 0; d : 0; P : 0 \to \text{Type}; F : (\forall x : 0)(Px) \to 0]$$

used in [Dow93] should be replaced by

$$[0 : \text{Type}; a : 0 \to 0; b : 0 \to 0; c : 0; d : 0; P : 0 \to \text{Type}; F : (\forall x : 0)(Px) \to (Pc)].$$

The replacement enforces only a little change in types used in the proof (some occurrences should be replaced by $P(c)$), but this does not harm reasonings in Dowek's proof.

The undecidability is essentially obtained because we can quantify over first-order function symbols here. The type $\forall x_1 : 0 \to 0 \cdots \forall x_n : 0 \to 0.(\beta x_1 \cdots x_n)$ used in the proof is the only element that goes beyond first-order logic.

4 First-Order Type Inference

This material presents a proof for decidability of first-order type inference where signatures have at least one constant symbol. Such signatures give rise to a very wide class of instances and the restriction does not seem to be significant. In fact, the construction mentioned here requires only some minor modifications in order to provide a solution for the full problem. We lay aside the most general presentation for the sake of simplicity.

4.1 Generation of Equations

In our algorithm, we use some equations. Thus, we have to define the entities to be equated.

Definition 7 (e-terms)
The set of *e-terms over the signature* Σ *and variables* X, denoted by $T^{e}_{\Sigma}(X)$, is defined as follows

- $x \in T^{e}_{\Sigma}(X)$ if $x \in X$;
- $f(t_1, \dots, t_n) \in T^{e}_{\Sigma}(X)$ if $f \in \Sigma$, has arity n ($n \geq 0$) and $t_i \in T^{e}_{\Sigma}(X)$ for $i = 1, \dots, n$;
- $t\langle x := s\rangle \in T^{e}_{\Sigma}(X)$ where $t \in T^{e}_{\Sigma}(X)$, $x \in X$, and s is an e-term over Σ with variables from X.

We extend this notion to types using a set $\mathcal{X}$ of type variables.

Definition 8 (e-types)
The set of *e-types over the signature* Σ*, variables* X *and type variables* $\mathcal{X}$, denoted by $\mathcal{T}^{e}_{\Sigma}(X, \mathcal{X})$, is defined as follows

- $P(t_1, \dots, t_n) \in \mathcal{T}^{e}_{\Sigma}(X, \mathcal{X})$, if $t_i \in T^{e}_{\Sigma}(X)$ for $i = 1, \dots, n$;
- $\alpha \in \mathcal{T}^{e}_{\Sigma}(X, \mathcal{X})$, if $\alpha \in \mathcal{X}$;
- $\tau_1 \to \tau_2 \in \mathcal{T}^{e}_{\Sigma}(X, \mathcal{X})$, if $\tau_1, \tau_2 \in \mathcal{T}^{e}_{\Sigma}(X, \mathcal{X})$ and $x \in X$;
- $(\forall x : 0)\tau \in \mathcal{T}^{e}_{\Sigma}(X, \mathcal{X})$, if $\tau \in \mathcal{T}^{e}_{\Sigma}(X, \mathcal{X})$ and $x \in X$;
- $\tau\langle x := s\rangle \in \mathcal{T}^{e}_{\Sigma}(X, \mathcal{X})$, if $\tau \in \mathcal{T}^{e}_{\Sigma}(X, \mathcal{X})$ and s is a homogeneous first-order term over Σ with variables from X.

We use the notation $\tau\langle \boldsymbol{x} := \boldsymbol{t}\rangle$ in order to shorten $\tau\langle x_1 := t_1\rangle \cdots \langle x_n := t_n\rangle$. The set of *free first-order variables* in an e-type (e-term) τ, denoted by $\mathrm{Vars}(\tau)$, is defined so that x is bounded in $(\forall x)\tau'$ and $\tau\langle x := t\rangle$.

We introduce the notation $\mathrm{TV}(\tau)$ to denote the set of all type variables in τ. Notations $\mathrm{Vars}(\cdots)$ and $\mathrm{TV}(\cdots)$ are extended so that they can be applied to sets of e-types.

The notion of (semantical) substitution is not straightforward here so we present its definition. This notion describes a different operation than the one defined later in Definition 13.

Definition 9 (first-order substitution)
A *first-order* substitution is a partial function from first-order variables to e-terms with finite domain. We usually denote such a substitution by $[x_1 := t_1, \dots, x_n := t_n]$. This function acts on e-terms so that no free variable gets bounded, which may be expressed as follows:

- $x_i[x_1 := t_1, \dots, x_i := t_i, \dots, x_n := t_n] = t_i$;
- $y[x_1 := t_1, \dots, x_n := t_n] = y$ where for each $i = 1, \dots, n$ we have $x_i \neq y$;
- $f(s_1, \dots, s_n)[x_1 := t_1, \dots, x_n := t_n] = f(s'_1, \dots, s'_n)$ where $s'_i = s_i[x_1 := t_1, \dots, x_n := t_n]$;
- $t\langle x := u\rangle[x_1 := t_1, \dots, x_n := t_n] = t'\langle x' := u'\rangle$ where $u' = u[x_1 := t_1, \dots, x_n := t_n]$, the variable x' does not occur in any of terms $x_1, \dots, x_n$, $t_1, \dots, t_n$ and $t' = t[x := x'][x_1 := t_1, \dots, x_n := t_n]$;

- $\alpha[x_1 := t_1, \ldots, x_n := t_n] = \alpha$;
- $P(s_1, \ldots, s_n)[x_1 := t_1, \ldots, x_n := t_n] = P(s'_1, \ldots, s'_n)$ where $s'_i = s_i[x_1 := t_1, \ldots, x_n := t_n]$;
- $\tau_1 \to \tau_2[x_1 := t_1, \ldots, x_n := t_n] = \tau'_1 \to \tau'_2$ where $\tau'_i = \tau_i[x_1 := t_1, \ldots, x_n := t_n]$;
- $((\forall x : 0)\tau)[x_1 := t_1, \ldots, x_n := t_n] = ((\forall x' : 0)\tau')$ where x' does not occur in $x_1, \ldots, x_n, t_1, \ldots, t_n$ and $\tau' = \tau[x := x'][x_1 := t_1, \ldots, x_n := t_n]$;
- $\tau\langle x := u\rangle[x_1 := t_1, \ldots, x_n := t_n] = \tau'\langle x' := u'\rangle$ where $u' = u[x_1 := t_1, \ldots, x_n := t_n]$, the variable x' does not occur in any of terms $x_1, \ldots, x_n$, $t_1, \ldots, t_n$ and $\tau' = \tau[x := x'][x_1 := t_1, \ldots, x_n := t_n]$.

The set Paths(τ) of *paths* in an e-type τ (an e-term) is a set of sequences of natural numbers defined so that subsequent numbers represent which part of an e-type or an e-term is taken. For instance, the path 12 points to τ_2 in $(\forall x)(\tau_1 \to \tau_2)$, and the path 3 points to t in $\tau'\langle x := t\rangle$.

We have already introduced types with explicit substitutions (e-types). These substitutions allow to delay some substitution until a type variable is substituted, but then substitutions must be applied. The whole just described work is done by $\leadsto$-reduction.

Definition 10 (reduction for e-terms and e-types)
The *reduction for e-terms* is defined as:

1. $t_1 = f(s_1, \ldots, s_n) \leadsto f(s'_1, \ldots, s'_n)$ where for some $i \in \{1, \ldots n\}$ we have $s_i \leadsto s'_i$ and for $j \neq i$ we have $s_j = s'_j$;
2. $t\langle x := s\rangle \leadsto t'\langle x := s\rangle$ when $t \leadsto t'$;
3. $t_1 = t\langle x := s\rangle \leadsto t[x := s]$ when t is irreducible ($[x := s]$ is the usual substitution);
4. $\tau_1 = P(s_1, \ldots, s_n)$ and $\tau_2 = P(s'_1, \ldots, s'_n)$ for some predicate $P \in \Sigma$ and for some $i \in \{1, \ldots n\}$ we have $s_i \leadsto s'_i$ and for $j \neq i$ we have $s_j = s'_j$;
5. $\tau_1 = \sigma_1 \to \sigma_2$ and $\tau_2 = \sigma'_1 \to \sigma_2$ where $\sigma_1 \leadsto \sigma'_1$;
6. $\tau_1 = \sigma_1 \to \sigma_2$ and $\tau_2 = \sigma_1 \to \sigma'_2$ where $\sigma_2 \leadsto \sigma'_2$;
7. $\tau_1 = (\forall y : 0)\sigma_1$ and $\tau_2 = (\forall y : 0)\sigma'_1$ where $\sigma_1 \leadsto \sigma'_1$;
8. $\tau_1 = \sigma\langle x := s\rangle$ and $\tau_2 = \sigma'\langle x := s\rangle$, where $s \in T^{\mathrm{e}}_{\Sigma}(X)$, $x \in X$, and $\sigma \leadsto \sigma'$;
9. $\tau_1 = (\sigma_1 \to \sigma_2)\langle x := s\rangle$ and $\tau_2 = \sigma_1\langle x := s\rangle \to \sigma_2\langle x := s\rangle$, where $s \in T^{\mathrm{e}}_{\Sigma}(X)$, $x \in X$;
10. $\tau_1 = ((\forall y : 0)\sigma)\langle x := s\rangle$ and $\tau_2 = ((\forall y : 0)\sigma\langle x := s\rangle)$, where $s \in T^{\mathrm{e}}_{\Sigma}(X)$, $x \neq y$ (if $x = y$ perform α-conversion first and then reduce according to the present rule).
11. $\tau_1 = P(t_1, \ldots, t_m)\langle x := s\rangle$ and $\tau_2 = P(t'_1, \ldots, t'_m)$, where $s \in T^{\mathrm{e}}_{\Sigma}(X)$, $x \in X$, $P \in \Sigma$ and has the arity m, and $t'_i = t_i\langle x := s\rangle$ for $i = 1, \ldots, m$.

As usual, we extend $\leadsto$ to its reflexive-transitive closure $\leadsto^*$.

We point out that according to the definition above an e-type of the form $\alpha\langle x := t\rangle$, where α is a variable, is irreducible.

The reduction $\leadsto^*$ has several good properties the proofs of which are omitted here: it has Church-Rosser property, it is strongly normalising, and decidable.

Thus, we can define that $NF^{\rightsquigarrow}(\tau)$ and $NF^{\rightsquigarrow}(t)$ which are normal forms of respectively the e-type τ and the e-term t.

The following interesting fact gives a nice insight about what is going on in e-types.

Property 1. If τ is an e-type in the normal form such that $\mathrm{TV}(\tau) = \emptyset$ then it has no subtype (subterm) of the form $\sigma\langle x := t\rangle$ $(s\langle x := t\rangle)$.

Definition 11 (equality for e-terms and e-types)
The *equality for e-terms and e-types* is defined as the least congruence containing $\rightsquigarrow^* \cup \equiv_\alpha$ and is denoted by $\simeq$.

Definition 12 (e-equation)
We write $\tau_1 \doteq \tau_2$ to denote that the pair of e-types τ_1, τ_2 is an *e-equation*. Sets of e-equations are denoted by $\mathcal{E}, \mathcal{F}, \ldots$. The set $\mathcal{E}^{\mathrm{e}}_{\Sigma}(X, \mathcal{X})$ is the set of e-equations among e-types from $\mathcal{T}^{\mathrm{e}}_{\Sigma}(X, \mathcal{X})$.

Now, we define a notion of substitution we deal with.

Definition 13 (substitutions)
Each partial function from type variables to some $\mathcal{T}^{\mathrm{e}}_{\Sigma}(X, \mathcal{Y})$ is called a *substitution*.

We extend a substitution $S : \mathcal{X} \rightharpoonup \mathcal{T}^{\mathrm{e}}_{\Sigma}(X, \mathcal{Y})$ to e-types inductively as follows:

- $S(0) = 0$;
- $S(P(t_1, \ldots, t_m)) = P(t_1, \ldots, t_m)$;
- $S(\alpha) = \alpha$ if $\alpha \notin \mathrm{Dom}(S)$;
- $S(\alpha) = S(\alpha)$ if $\alpha \in \mathrm{Dom}(S)$;
- $S((\forall x : 0)\sigma_2) = (\forall x : 0)S(\sigma_2)$;
- $S(\sigma_1 \to \sigma_2) = S(\sigma_1) \to S(\sigma_2)$;
- $S(\sigma\langle x := s\rangle) = S(\sigma)\langle x := s\rangle$.

Note that in the definition above we do not have any kind of renaming of individual variables while substituting under quantifier. This approach is intentional here. We agree with the fact that some symbols may get bounded during such a substitution.

Definition 14 (solution of a set of equations)
We say that a substitution $S : \mathcal{X} \rightharpoonup \mathcal{T}^{\mathrm{e}}_{\Sigma}(X, \emptyset)$ is a *solution of a set of e-equations* $\mathcal{E}$ iff for each e-equation $[\tau_1 \doteq \tau_2] \in \mathcal{E}$ we have $S(\tau_1) \simeq S(\tau_2)$.

We define $S(\Gamma)^{\rightsquigarrow}$ for a context Γ as the sequence Γ with each $x : \tau$ replaced by $x : NF^{\rightsquigarrow}(S(\tau))$.

We cannot hope for a most-general solution property here.

Example 1. Consider a signature context $\Gamma_\Sigma = \{P : 0 \Rightarrow *, c : 0\}$. The set of equations $\mathcal{E} = \{\alpha\langle x := c\rangle\langle y := c\rangle \doteq P(c)\}$ has two solutions $S_1(\alpha) = P(x)$ and $S_2(\alpha) = P(y)$, but there is no S_3 such that $S_3 \circ S_2 = S_1$ or $S_3 \circ S_1 = S_2$. Thus, neither S_1 nor S_2 can be the most general solution.

Definition 15 (generation of equations)
Here is a nondeterministic procedure **gener** that takes as an input a Curry-style term M, an enriched first-order context Γ, and a path ρ (intentionally leading to M in a bigger term) and generates a set of e-equations included in $\mathcal{E}^{\mathrm{e}}_{\Sigma\cup\{c_0,c_1\}}(\Gamma^0, \mathcal{X})$ where c_0, c_1 are fresh first-order constants. The procedure follows

1. $\mathbf{gener}(x, \Gamma, \rho) = \{\alpha_{x,\rho} \doteq \Gamma(x)\}$ when $x \in \mathrm{Dom}(\Gamma)$ and $\Gamma(x) \neq 0$;
2. $\mathbf{gener}(x, \Gamma, \rho) = \{c_0 \doteq c_1\}$ when $x \notin \mathrm{Dom}(\Gamma)$ or $x \in \mathrm{Dom}(\Gamma)$ and $\Gamma(x) = 0$;
3. $\mathbf{gener}(MN, \Gamma, \rho) = \{\alpha_{M,\rho\cdot l} \doteq (\forall x : 0)\alpha^0_{MN,\rho}, \alpha^0_{MN,\rho}\langle x := N\rangle \doteq \alpha_{MN,\rho}\} \cup \mathcal{E}_M \cup \mathcal{E}_N$ provided that N is a homogeneous first-order term, x is a fresh first-order variable, $\mathcal{E}_M = \mathbf{gener}(M, \Gamma, \rho \cdot l)$ and $\mathcal{E}_N = \mathbf{gener}(N, \Gamma, \rho \cdot r)$;
4. $\mathbf{gener}(MN, \Gamma, \rho) = \{\alpha_{M,\rho\cdot l} \doteq \alpha_{N,\rho\cdot r} \to \alpha_{MN,\rho}\} \cup \mathcal{E}_M \cup \mathcal{E}_N$ provided that N is not a homogeneous first-order term, $\mathcal{E}_M = \mathbf{gener}(M, \Gamma, \rho \cdot l)$ and $\mathcal{E}_N = \mathbf{gener}(N, \Gamma, \rho \cdot r)$;
5. nondeterministically choose one of either (5a) or (5b):
   (a) $\mathbf{gener}(\lambda x.M, \Gamma, \rho) = \{\alpha_{\lambda x.M,\rho} \doteq \alpha_{x,\rho} \to \alpha_{M,\rho\cdot l}\} \cup \mathcal{E}_M$ where the set of equations $\mathcal{E}_M = \mathbf{gener}(M, \Gamma \cup \{x : \alpha_{x,\rho}\}, \rho \cdot l)$,
   (b) $\mathbf{gener}(\lambda x.M, \Gamma, \rho) = \{\alpha_{\lambda x.M,\rho} \doteq (\forall x : 0)\alpha_{M,\rho\cdot l}\} \cup \mathcal{E}_M$ where the set of equations $\mathcal{E}_M = \mathbf{gener}(M, \Gamma \cup \{x : 0\}, \rho \cdot l)$.

We divide the set of variables $\mathcal{X}$ so that $\mathcal{X} = \mathcal{X}_0 \cup \mathcal{X}_1$ where $\mathcal{X}_0 \cap \mathcal{X}_1 = \emptyset$ and $\mathcal{X}_1 = \{\alpha_{M,\rho} \mid M \in \lambda P, \text{ and } \rho \text{ is a path }\}$.

Theorem 2. *There exists a nondeterministic algorithm which for each first-order context Γ and a Curry style term M has a run that gives a set of e-equations $\mathcal{E}$ such that the following sentences are equivalent:*

1. *There exists a type τ such that $\Gamma \vdash M : \tau$ has a first-order derivation.*
2. *$\mathcal{E}$ has a solution.*

Proof. The algorithm is described by the procedure **gener**. The procedure gives nondeterministically a set of equations $\mathcal{E}$. By straightforward induction on the term M, we prove both implications of the theorem. Details are omitted due to lack of space.

4.2 Simplification of Equations

Generally, types in equations from the previous subsection contain first-order quantifiers of type 0 and arrows. We get rid of arrows using a procedure similar to the one in Robinson's unification.

In order to shorten the notation, we should denote by $\forall^n\tau$ an e-type of the form $(\forall x_1 : 0) \cdots (\forall x_n : 0)\tau$ where $n \geq 0$. In order to distinguish different $\forall^n$'s, we sometimes supplement them with a subscript.

We present a procedure to simplify equations. The general idea behind the procedure is to unify equations in the fashion of Robinson's unification with additional work connected with pushing explicit substitutions and first-order quantifiers to leaves.

Definition 16 (simplification procedure)
The procedure processes step by step pairs $(\mathcal{Q}, S)$ where $\mathcal{Q}$ is a sequence of equations to be solved and S is a substitution. The input of the procedure is a pair $(\mathcal{Q}_0, \emptyset)$, where $\mathcal{Q}_0$ is the set of equations we are interested in.

The intended property of the abovementioned substitution S is that if equations in $\mathcal{Q}$ are solvable by a substitution S' then $S' \circ S$ solves $\mathcal{Q}_0$.

The procedure terminates either when it explicitly fails or when the sequence $\mathcal{Q}$ consists only of pairs of one the following three shapes:

$$\forall_1^n \alpha\langle \boldsymbol{x} := \boldsymbol{t}\rangle \doteq \forall_2^n \alpha'\langle \boldsymbol{y} := \boldsymbol{s}\rangle \tag{1}$$
$$\forall_1^n \alpha\langle \boldsymbol{x} := \boldsymbol{t}\rangle \doteq \forall_2^n P(s_1, \ldots, s_m) \tag{2}$$
$$\forall_1^n P(t_1, \ldots, t_n) \doteq \forall_2^n P(s_1, \ldots, s_n) \tag{3}$$

where $\boldsymbol{x}$, $\boldsymbol{y}$, $\boldsymbol{t}$, $\boldsymbol{s}$ stand for appropriate vectors of variables and terms, and $n \geq 0$.

In the procedure, we use two kinds of type variables: normal variables and travelling variables. Travelling variables are used only in the proof of termination. They may be omitted in a working version of the algorithm. All variables in the input are marked as normal.

At each step, the following cases are checked (we omit cases symmetric wrt. $\doteq$):

1. Let $\mathcal{Q} = \parallel \forall^n(\sigma_1 \to \sigma_2)\langle \boldsymbol{y} := \boldsymbol{t}\rangle \doteq \tau \parallel \cdot \mathcal{Q}'$. The present pair is transformed to
$$(\parallel \forall^n(\sigma_1\langle \boldsymbol{y} := \boldsymbol{t}\rangle \to \sigma_2\langle \boldsymbol{y} := \boldsymbol{t}\rangle) \doteq \tau \parallel \cdot \mathcal{Q}', S).$$
2. Let $\mathcal{Q} = \parallel \forall^n((\forall x : 0)\sigma_2)\langle \boldsymbol{y} := \boldsymbol{t}\rangle \doteq \tau \parallel \cdot \mathcal{Q}'$. The present pair is transformed to
$$(\parallel \forall^n((\forall x' : 0)\sigma_2\langle x := x'\rangle\langle \boldsymbol{y}' := \boldsymbol{t}'\rangle) \doteq \tau \parallel \cdot \mathcal{Q}', S)$$
where x' does not occur in any of terms in $\boldsymbol{t}$, and $\langle \boldsymbol{y}' := \boldsymbol{t}'\rangle$ are those explicit substitutions for which y's do not occur in $\forall^n$.
3. Let $\mathcal{Q} = \parallel \forall^n P(s_1, \cdots, s_m)\langle \boldsymbol{y} := \boldsymbol{t}\rangle \doteq \tau \parallel \cdot \mathcal{Q}'$. The present pair is transformed to
$$(\parallel \forall^n P(s_1\langle \boldsymbol{y} := \boldsymbol{t}\rangle, \ldots, s_m\langle \boldsymbol{y} := \boldsymbol{t}\rangle) \doteq \tau \parallel \cdot \mathcal{Q}', S).$$
4. Let $\mathcal{Q} = \parallel \forall_1^n(\sigma_1 \to \sigma_2) \doteq \forall_2^n(\tau_1 \to \tau_2) \parallel \cdot \mathcal{Q}'$. The present pair is transformed to
$$(\parallel \forall_1^n \sigma_1 \doteq \forall_1^n \tau_1 \parallel \cdot \parallel \forall_2^n \sigma_2 \doteq \forall_2^n \tau_2 \parallel \cdot \mathcal{Q}', S)$$
5. Let $\mathcal{Q} = \parallel \forall_1^n \alpha\langle \boldsymbol{x} := \boldsymbol{t}\rangle \doteq \forall_2^n \tau_1 \to \tau_2 \parallel \cdot \mathcal{Q}'$ where $\boldsymbol{x}$ is the set of variables $x_1, \ldots, x_m$, the vector $\boldsymbol{t}$ is the set of terms $t_1, \ldots, t_m$, and α is a type variable such that no cycle containing α in the graph $G_{\mathcal{Q}}$ has an edge from E_s. The present pair is transformed to
$$\begin{aligned}(\parallel \forall_1^n(\alpha_1 \to \alpha_2)\langle \boldsymbol{x} := \boldsymbol{t}\rangle \doteq \forall_2^n \tau_1 \to \tau_2 \parallel \cdot \mathcal{Q}'[\alpha := \alpha_1 \to \alpha_2)],\\ [\alpha := \alpha_1 \to \alpha_2] \circ S)\end{aligned}$$
where α_1, α_2 are fresh variables. Additionally, we mark variables α_1, α_2 as travelling.
6. Let $\mathcal{Q} = \parallel \forall_1^n \alpha\langle \boldsymbol{x} := \boldsymbol{t}\rangle \doteq \forall_2^n((\forall y : 0)\tau) \parallel \cdot \mathcal{Q}'$ where $\boldsymbol{x}$ is the set of variables $x_1, \ldots, x_m$, the vector $\boldsymbol{t}$ is the set of terms $t_1, \ldots, t_m$, and α is a type variable

such that no cycle in the graph $G_{\mathcal{Q}}$ contains a vertice with α and an edge from E_s simultaneously. The present pair is transformed to

$$(\| \forall_1^n((\forall y' : 0)\alpha_1)\langle \boldsymbol{x} := \boldsymbol{t}\rangle \doteq \forall_2^n((\forall y : 0)\tau) \| \cdot \mathcal{Q}'[\alpha := ((\forall y' : 0)\alpha_1)], \\ [\alpha := ((\forall y' : 0)\alpha_1)] \circ S)$$

where α_1 is a fresh type variable, and y' is a fresh first-order variable. Additionally, we mark variable α_1 as travelling.

7. Let $\mathcal{Q} = \| \sigma \doteq \tau \| \cdot \mathcal{Q}'$ and let $\sigma \doteq \tau$ be of one of the shapes (1–3). The present pair is transformed to

$$(\mathcal{Q}' \cdot \| \sigma \doteq \tau \|, S).$$

8. In all other cases fail.

Theorem 3. *1. The procedure terminates for all inputs of the form* $(\mathcal{Q}, \emptyset)$.
2. A system $\mathcal{Q}$ *has a solution iff the result of the* simplification procedure *applied to* $(\mathcal{Q}, \emptyset)$ *is* $(\mathcal{Q}', S)$ *where* $\mathcal{Q}'$ *has a solution and each equation in the sequence is in one of the forms (1–3) described in Definition 16.*

Proof. The termination is obtained due to similar reasoning to the one in Robinson's unification. For the proof of the second claim, one should show that each rule of the *simplification procedure* is sound and complete and then the claim follows by induction. Details are omitted due to lack of space.

4.3 Removal of First-Order Quantifiers

We obtain a set of e-equations by means of the *simplification procedure.* These equations have a special form. They still contain first-order quantifiers which do not allow for a direct translation into second-order unification. We introduce a procedure to remove them. The procedure uses as a intermediate data structure a special kind of graph which is defined as follows

Definition 17 (graph of fixing)
A *graph of fixing* for a set of equations $\mathcal{E}$ is defined as each graph with vertices

$$V_{\mathcal{E}} = X_{\mathcal{E}} \times \mathrm{TV}(\mathcal{E})$$

where $X_{\mathcal{E}}$ is the set of first-order variables quantified in $\mathcal{E}$, and $\mathrm{TV}(\mathcal{E})$ is defined as the set of type variables in $\mathcal{E}$. The edges of such graphs are meant to be unordered pairs.

We will start the procedure of removal of first-order quantifiers with a fixing graph in which an edge between (x, α) and (x', α') informs that there exists an equation with α and α' where x and x' are quantified in the same place in both sides of equation. We will be processing fixing graphs then in order to approach the situation that each edge between (x, α) and (x', α') informs that either x and x' should occur at exactly the same places in terms that result in applying a solution to α and α' respectively.

The procedure that removes quantifiers gives as a result a new set of equations with some negative constraints. These constraints say that some symbol may not occur in a type variable. We remove quantifiers as follows:

Definition 18 (removal of first-order quantifiers)
The input for the procedure is a triple $(\Sigma, X, \mathcal{E})$ where Σ is a signature, X is a set of first-order variables, and $\mathcal{E}$ is a set of e-equations included in $\mathcal{E}^{e}_{\Sigma}(X, \mathcal{X})$. The output is a triple $(\Sigma', \mathcal{E}', \phi)$, where Σ' is a signature, $\mathcal{E}'$ is a set of e-equations included in $\mathcal{E}^{e}_{\Sigma'}(\emptyset, \mathcal{X})$, and $\phi : \mathrm{TV}(\mathcal{E}') \to P(X_{\mathcal{E}})$. Equations are modified according to the following schema:

1. We build a graph of fixing $G_{\mathcal{E}}$ and $\phi_{\mathcal{E}}\mathrm{TV}(\mathcal{E}') \to P(X_{\mathcal{E}})$. They are the result of the hereafter mentioned iteration:
   (a) We begin with $G^0_{\mathcal{E}} = \langle V_{\mathcal{E}}, E_0 \rangle$ and $\phi_0 : \mathrm{TV}(\mathcal{E}) \to P(X_{\mathcal{E}})$ where

$$E_0 = \{((x_i, \alpha), (x'_i, \alpha')) \mid [\forall x_1 \ldots \forall x_i \ldots \forall x_n \alpha\langle \cdots \rangle \doteq \forall x'_1 \ldots \forall x'_i \ldots \forall x'_n \alpha'\langle \cdots \rangle] \in \mathcal{E}\}$$
$$\phi_0(\alpha) = \emptyset \text{ for each } \alpha.$$

   (b) We transform $G^n_{\mathcal{E}}$ into $G^{n+1}_{\mathcal{E}}$ only if there exists a path ρ in $G^n_{\mathcal{E}}$ from (x_i, α) to (x_j, α) where $x_i \neq x_j$. We define E_{n+1} and ϕ_{n+1} as follows
      i. take an edge in ρ — $((y, \beta), (y', \beta'))$,
      ii. remove the edge — the resulting set is E_{n+1},
      iii. $\phi_{n+1}(\gamma) = \phi_n(\gamma)$ for $\gamma \neq \beta$,
      $\phi_{n+1}(\gamma) = \phi_n(\gamma) \cup \{y\}$ when there is an equation in $\mathcal{E}$

$$\forall z_1 \ldots \forall z_i \ldots \forall z_m \beta\langle \boldsymbol{z}^1 := \boldsymbol{t} \rangle \doteq \forall z'_1 \ldots \forall z'_i \ldots \forall z'_m \beta'\langle \cdots \rangle$$

      where $z_i = y$ and $z'_i = y'$ and $\boldsymbol{z}^1$ does not contain y,
      $\phi_{n+1}(\gamma) = \phi_n(\gamma)$ when the former condition does not hold.
2. We produce a new set of equations $\mathcal{E}'$ by means of two steps:
   (a) we generate a function $\psi : V_{\mathcal{E}} \to \mathrm{Const}$ such that $\psi^{-1}(c)$ is either $\emptyset$ or a connected component in $G_{\mathcal{E}}$;
   (b) we remove quantifiers in each equation:

$$\forall z_1 \ldots \forall z_i \ldots \forall z_n \alpha\langle \boldsymbol{z}^1 := \boldsymbol{t}^1 \rangle \doteq \forall z'_1 \ldots \forall z'_i \ldots \forall z'_n \beta\langle \boldsymbol{z}^2 := \boldsymbol{t}^2 \rangle$$

   using the following rules
   - if (z_i, α) and (z'_i, β) are in the same connected component then we replace both the variables by $\psi((z_i, \alpha))$;
   - if (z_i, α) and (z'_i, β) are in different connected components then
     • if $z_i \in \phi(\alpha)$ we replace x_i and x_j by $\psi((z_i, \beta))$,
     • if $z'_i \in \phi(\beta)$ we replace x_i and x_j by $\psi((z_i, \alpha))$,

     (if both cases hold we take the first option).

The signature we return contains: all the symbols from Σ, all the symbols from X, and all the first-order constants introduced in the abovementioned procedure.

The following fact is necessary to establish the correctnes of the abovementioned definition.

Property 2. Let $\forall z_1 \ldots \forall z_i \ldots \forall z_n \alpha\langle \boldsymbol{z}^1 := \boldsymbol{t}^1 \rangle \doteq \forall z'_1 \ldots \forall z'_i \ldots \forall z'_n \beta \langle \boldsymbol{z}^2 := \boldsymbol{t}^2 \rangle$ be an equation. If G_k does not contain the edge $((z_i, \alpha), (z'_i, \beta))$ then either $z_i \in \phi_k(\alpha)$ or $z'_i \in \phi_k(\beta)$.

Proof. Induction on k.

The following fact explains why we should break paths from (x_i, α) to (x_j, α). Existence of such path means that x_i and x_j are equal.

Property 3. Let ρ be a path in G_k for some k and let S be a solution of $\mathcal{E}$. If for each edge $((z_i, \alpha), (z'_i, \beta))$ on ρ and for each equation of the form

$$\forall z_1 \ldots \forall z_i \ldots \forall z_n \alpha\langle \boldsymbol{z}^1 := \boldsymbol{t}^1 \rangle \doteq \forall z'_1 \ldots \forall z'_i \ldots \forall z'_n \beta \langle \cdots \rangle$$

we have that $z_i \notin \boldsymbol{z}^1$, then there exists a position w such that for each vertice (y, γ) in we have that y is on w in $S(\gamma)$.

Proof. Induction on the length of ρ.

Property 4. The procedure of *removal of first-order quantifiers*

1. terminates,
2. $\mathcal{E}$ has a solution $T : \mathcal{X} \rightharpoonup \mathcal{T}^{e}_{\Sigma}(X, \emptyset)$ iff the result $\mathcal{E}'$ of *removal of first-order quantifiers* has a solution $T' : \mathcal{X} \rightharpoonup \mathcal{T}^{e}_{\Sigma'}(X \backslash (\Sigma \cup \mathrm{Dom}(\Gamma)), \emptyset)$

Proof. The property (1) is obvious.

The proof of (2) has two parts. We present a scetch of them here.

($\Rightarrow$) If $\mathcal{E}$ has a solution T then we can construct a solution T' of $\mathcal{E}'$. This is done by replacing each constant x in $T(\alpha)$ by $\psi((x, \alpha))$. As there are no paths from (x_i, α) to (x_j, α) in $G_{\mathcal{E}}$, each first-order variable in α obtains a different constant. Bullets in the point (2b) of Definition 18 guarantee that this operation results in a solution.

($\Leftarrow$) If $\mathcal{E}'$ has a solution T' then we can reconstruct T that solves E by simply replacing fresh constants by first-order variables they replaced. The existence of ρ in the point (1b) of Definition 18 guarantees that only one first-order variable may correspond to a constant in a type variable.

4.4 From Equations to Second-Order

We finally obtained a set of e-equations that can easily be transformed to a special form of second-order unification equations. We have to deal with constraints, though. The translation is defined as

Definition 19 (translation to second-order)

For each type variable α, let A_α be the set of all the variables x such that there exists a type $\alpha\langle \boldsymbol{y} := \boldsymbol{t} \rangle \langle x := s \rangle \langle \boldsymbol{z} := \boldsymbol{u} \rangle$ in the set being translated. Assuming $A_\alpha = \{x_1, \ldots, x_n\}$, we replace each $\alpha\langle \boldsymbol{y} := \boldsymbol{t} \rangle$ by $F_\alpha(t'_1, \ldots, t'_n\}$ where $t'_i = t_j[x_{j+1} := t_{j+1}] \cdots [x_n := t_n]$ if $x_i = y_j$ and $t'_i = x_i$ if there is no $y_j = x_i$.

Constraints are translated to second-order constraints by replacing α's by corresponding F's.

Immediately, we obtain the following property:

Property 5. For a given set $\mathcal{E}$ of equations of the form (1–3) in Definition 16, there exists a set $\mathcal{E}'$ of second-order unification equations such that $\mathcal{E}$ is solvable if and only if $\mathcal{E}'$ is solvable.

Moreover, the translation from $\mathcal{E}$ to $\mathcal{E}'$ is effective.

The transformation that allows to get rid of constraints looks as follows

Definition 20 (removing constraints)
Let $\mathcal{E}$ be a set of second-order equations with constraints ϕ. For each constant $c \in \Sigma$ we introduce two constants c_1 and c_2. For each second-order variable F of arity n we introduce two variables F_1 and F_2 both of arities $n+k$ where k is the number of constants in Σ. We define two operations $|\cdot|_1$ and $|\cdot|_2$ as follows:

- $|c|_i = c_i$,
- $|f(t_1,\dots,t_n)|_i = f(|t_1|_i,\dots,|t_n|_i)$,
- $|F(t_1,\dots,t_n)|_i = F_i(|t_1|_i,\dots,|t_n|_i,c_i^1,\dots,c_i^k)$ where $\{c^1,\dots,c^k\}$ is the set of all constants in Σ.

Each equation $t_1 = t_2$ in $\mathcal{E}$ is replaced by a pair of equations $|t_1|_1 = |t_2|_1$ and $|t_1|_2 = |t_2|_2$. For each variable F in $\mathcal{E}$ we supply additional equations $F_1(a,\dots,a,c_1^1,\dots,c_1^k) = F_2(a,\dots,a,c_1^1,\dots,c_1^k)$ and $F_1(a,\dots,a,c_2^1,\dots,c_2^k) = F_2(a,\dots,a,c_2^1,\dots,c_2^k)$ where a is a fresh constant. At last for each constraint $\phi(F)$ we supply the equation

$$F_1(a,\dots,a,c_1^1,\dots,c_1^k) = F_2(a,\dots,a,d^1,\dots,d^k)$$

where $d^i = c_1^i$ if $c^i \notin \phi(F)$ and $d^i = c_2^i$ if $c^i \in \phi(F)$.

Immediately we obtain the following property:

Property 6. For a given set $\mathcal{E}$ of equations with constraints ϕ, there exists a set $\mathcal{E}'$ of second-order unification equations such that $\mathcal{E}$ is solvable if and only if $\mathcal{E}'$ is solvable.

The translation from $\mathcal{E}$ to $\mathcal{E}'$ is effective and involves only equations of the form (1–3) in Definition 21.

4.5 Solving of Final Equations

In Subsection 4.2, we obtained sets of equations. Each equation is in one of three forms.

Definition 21 (head equations)
The sets of equations in one of the following forms

1. $F_1(t_1,\dots,t_n) = F_2(s_1,\dots,s_m)$;
2. $F_1(t_1,\dots,t_n) = P(s_1,\dots,s_m)$;
3. $P_1(t_1,\dots,t_n) = P_2(s_1,\dots,s_m)$;

where F_1, F_2 are second-order variables, and P_1, P_2 symbols of first-order constants, is called the set of *head equations.*

Now, we describe a procedure to solve such sets of equations.

We need the following facts:

Theorem 4. *complete set of solutions for second-order matching For each set E of second-order matching equations, if the set is solvable then it has a finite number of solutions with domains equal to* TV(E) *and all of them can be effectively generated.*

Property 7. If the set E of second-order unification has only equations of the form $F_1(t_1, \ldots, t_n) = F_2(s_1, \ldots, t_m)$, then it has a ground solution provided that the signature has at least one constant symbol.

The first one is proved in [HL78]. The second is obvious — the solution assigns the same term with no arguments on all the second-order variables. This construction is applicable, though, only if we have at least one constant symbol in the signature.

Definition 22 (solving procedure)

The nondeterministic procedure to solve our second-order equations is defined as follows:

1. Check if there are equations of the form $P_1(t_1, \ldots, t_n) = P_2(s_1, \ldots, s_m)$, where the sides of the equation are different. If so fail else remove all equations of the form $P(t_1, \ldots, t_n) = P(t_1, \ldots, t_n)$
2. Find the complete set A of solutions for all the equations of the form $F(t_1, \ldots, t_n) = P(s_1, \ldots, t_m)$ (the set exists by Theorem 4). If there are no such equations then go to step 5.
3. Choose one of the solutions and apply to all equations.
4. Go to step 1.
5. There are only equations of the form $F_1(t_1, \ldots, t_n) = F_2(s_1, \ldots, t_m)$. These equations have always a solution (provided that there is at least one constant in the signature) so we accept in this case.

We have the following theorem:

Theorem 5. *The problem, if a given set of head equations is solvable, is decidable.*

At last, we obtain:

Theorem 6. *The first-order type inference problem is decidable.*

Proof. A consequence of Theorem 2, Theorem 3, Fact 5 and Theorem 5.

5 Acknowledgements

I would like to thank Paweł Urzyczyn for encouraging me to work on the problem. He is also a person to thank for his digging in early versions of the paper. His remarks were very helpful during the preparation of the document. Also, I would like to thank Gilles Dowek for a discussion we had about the problems. In fact, much of the ideas in the proof presented in Subsection 4.5 is due to him. The present proof, due to his remarks, is much simpler than my primary version. Anonymous referees contributed to better presentation of the paper so my thanks go for them too.

References

[Dow93] Gilles Dowek, *The undecidability of typability in the lambda-pi-calculus*, Typed Lambda Calculi and Applications (M. Bezem and J.F. de Groote, eds.), LNCS, no. 664, 1993, pp. 139–145.

[Gol81] W. D. Goldfarb, *The undecidability of the second-order unification problem*, TCS (1981), no. 13, 225–230.

[HHP87] R. Harper, F. Honsell, and G. Plotkin, *A Framework for Defining Logics*, Proceedings of Logic in Computer Science, 1987, pp. 194–204.

[HL78] G. Huet and B. Lang, *Proving and applying program transformations expressed with second order patterns*, Acta Informatica (1978), no. 11, 31–55.

[Pfe91] Frank Pfenning, *Logic Programming in the LF Logical Framework*, Logical Frameworks (Gherard Huet and Gordon Plotkin, eds.), Cambridge University Press, 1991.

[Sch98] A. Schubert, *Second-order unification and type inference for church-style polymorphism*, Proc. of POPL, 1998.

[SU98] M.H. Sørensen and P. Urzyczyn, *Lectures on Curry-Howard Isomorphism*, Tech. Report 14, DIKU, 1998.

[TvD88] A.S. Troelstra and D. van Dalen, *Constructivism in Mathematics, An Introduction, Volume II*, Studies in Logic and the Foundations of Mathematics, vol. 123, North-Holland, 1988.

[vBLRU97] Stefan van Bakel, Luigi Liquori, Simona Ronchi Della Rocca, and PawełUrzyczyn, *Comparing cubes of typed and type assignment systems*, Annals of Pure and Applied Logic (1997), no. 86, 267–303.

[Vor96] Andrei Voronkov, *Proof search in intuitionistic logic based on constraint satisfaction*, Theorem Proving with Analytic Tableaux and Related Methods (Terrasini, Palermo) (P. Miglioli, U. Moscato, D. Mundici, and M. Ornaghi, eds.), LNAI, no. 1071, Springer Verlag, 1996, pp. 312–329.

An Algebraic Foundation for Adaptive Programming

Peter Thiemann

Institut für Informatik
Universität Freiburg, Germany
thiemann@informatik.uni-freiburg.de

Abstract. An adaptive program is an object-oriented program which is abstracted over the particular class structure. This abstraction fosters software reuse, because programmers can concentrate on specifying how to process the objects which are essential to their application. The compiler of an adaptive program takes care of actually locating the objects. The adaptive programmer merely writes a traversal specification decorated with actions. The compiler instantiates the specification with the actual class structure and generates code that traverses a collection of objects, performing visits and actions according to the specification. Previous approaches to compiling adaptive programs rely on standard methods from automata theory and graph theory to achieve their goal. We introduce a new foundation for the compilation of adaptive programs, based on the algebraic properties of traversal specifications. Exploiting these properties, we develop the underlying theory for an efficient compilation algorithm. A key result is the derivation of a normal form for traversal specifications. This normal form is the basis for directly generating a traversal automaton with a uniformly minimal number of states.

Key words: object-oriented programming, semantics, finite automata, compilation

1 Introduction

An adaptive program [12, 14, 11, 15] is an object-oriented program which is abstracted over the particular class structure. Adaptive programming moves the burden of navigating through a linked structure of objects of many different classes from the programmer to the compiler. The key idea is to only specify the landmarks for navigation and the actions to be taken at the landmarks, and leave to the compiler the task of generating traversal code to locate the "landmark" classes and to perform the actions.

This abstraction fosters software reuse in two dimensions. First, the same adaptive program applies unchanged to many similar problems. For example, consider the adaptive program *Average* that visits objects of class *Item* and computes the average of the field *amount* therein. This program can be compiled with respect to a class structure for a company, instantiating *Item* to *Employee*

J. Tiuryn (Ed.): FOSSACS 2000, LNCS 1784, pp. 314–328, 2000.

and *amount* to *salary*, to compute the average salary of the employees. But the same program can also be compiled by instantiating *Item* to *InventoryItem* and *amount* to *price*. This instance computes the average price of all items in stock.

Second, adaptive programming is attractive for programming in an evolving environment. Here, "evolving" means that classes, instance variables, and methods are added, deleted, and renamed, as customary in refactoring [13, 5, 8]. In this situation, many adaptive programs need merely be recompiled without change, thus alleviating the tedious work of refactoring considerably.

An adaptive program consists of two parts: a traversal specification and wrapper (action) specifications. The traversal specification mentions classes whose objects must (or must not) be visited in a certain order and the instance variables that must (or must not) be traversed. A wrapper specification links a class to an action that has to be performed when the traversal encounters an object of that class. Following Palsberg et al [15, 14], our semantics only considers actions to be performed on the first encounter with an object.

Although a traversal specification only mentions names of classes and instance variables that are relevant for the programming task at hand, the actual class structure, for which the adaptive program is compiled, may contain intermediate classes and additional instance variables. The compiler automatically generates all the code to traverse or ignore these objects. Likewise, wrapper specifications need only be present for classes whose objects require special treatment. Hence, the programmer writes the important parts of the program and the compiler fills in the boring rest.

1.1 Related Work

Due to the high-level programming style of adaptive programs, their compilation is an interesting problem. Palsberg et al [15] define a formal semantics for adaptive programs, formalizing Lieberherr's original approach to compilation [11], and identify a number of restrictions. A subsequent paper [14] removes the restrictions and simplifies the semantics, but leads to a compilation algorithm which runs in exponential time in the worst case. Both papers rely on the theory of finite automata and employ standard constructions, like minimization and the powerset construction (which leads to the exponential worst case behavior). In addition, these works employ a more restrictive notion of traversal specification than the present paper.

Finally, Lieberherr and Patt-Shamir [12] introduce further generalizations and simplifications which lead to a polynomial-time compilation algorithm. However, whereas the earlier algorithms perform "static compilation", which processes all compile-time information at compile time, their polynomial-time algorithm performs "dynamic compilation", which means that a certain amount of compile-time information is kept until run time and hence compile-time work is spread over the code implementing the traversal. They employ yet another notion of traversal specification. While this is more general than their earlier work, the relation to our specifications is not clear.

The algebraic approach is based on a notion of derivatives which is closely related to quotients of formal languages [9] and to derivatives of regular expressions [6, 7, 4]. However, traversal specifications differ from standard regular expressions, so our derivatives are novel to this work.

There is a companion paper dealing with the practical aspects of compiling adaptive programs by partial evaluation [17].

1.2 Contribution of This Work

The algebraic foundations of adaptive programming are based on the algebraic properties of traversal specifications. Exploiting the algebraic laws, we define a normal form for traversal specifications. If the specification contains alternative paths (like + in a regular expression) then the size of the normal form can be exponential in the size of the original specification, so that its computation takes exponential time, too. We show that the exponential bound is tight by exhibiting a suitable specification. For a specification without alternatives (coined "multiplicative specification" [14]) this step takes linear time.

Starting from a traversal specification in normal form our algorithm computes the state skeleton of the uniformly minimal traversal automaton, using a notion of derivatives for traversal specifications. Uniform minimality means that the number of states is minimal over all automatons that implement the traversal for all possible class structures. This step takes linear time for multiplicative specifications and exponential time in the worst case for general specifications. We show that the exponential bound is tight.

Only the final compilation step requires the actual class structure. It constructs the actual traversal automaton from the state skeleton and the class structure. It takes time proportional to the product of the sizes of both. We prove that the resulting automaton implements the semantics of a traversal specification. Hence the automaton is equivalent to the one constructed with "static compilation" by Palsberg et al [14].

The main technical contribution of this work is the exploration of the algebra of traversal specifications, in particular Theorems 1 and 2, which demonstrate that the formally constructed automaton is indeed uniformly minimal. These theorems can also be viewed as normal form results for a certain class of regular expressions.

Overview Section 2 establishes some formal preliminaries and defines a semantics of adaptive programs. Section 3 explores traversal specifications and their algebraic properties; culminating in the first compilation step. Section 4 deals with the second compilation step, the construction of the uniformly minimal traversal automaton. Section 5 considers extensions and further work, and Section 6 concludes. A companion technical report [16] contains an appendix with all proofs.

2 Semantics of Adaptive Programs

This section first recalls the basic concepts of class graphs and object graphs used to define the semantics of adaptive programs. Then, we define a generalized (with respect to previous work [14, 15]) notion of traversal specifications and use it to define a semantics of adaptive programs.

2.1 Graphs

A *labeled directed graph* is a triple (V, E, L) where V is a set of nodes, L is a set of labels, and $E \subseteq V \times L \times V$ is the set of edges. Write $u \xrightarrow{l} v$ for the edge $(u, l, v) \in E$; then u is the source, l the label, and v the target of the edge.

Let $G = (V, E, L)$ be a labeled directed graph. A *path from* v_0 *to* v_n is a sequence $(v_0, l_1, v_1, l_2, \ldots, l_n, v_n)$ where $n \geq 0$, $v_0, \ldots, v_n \in V$, $l_1, \ldots, l_n \in L$, and, for all $1 \leq i \leq n$, there is an edge $v_{i-1} \xrightarrow{l_i} v_i \in E$. The set of all paths in G is $\mathsf{Paths}(G)$.

If $p = (v_0, l_1, \ldots, v_n)$ and $p' = (v'_0, l'_1, \ldots, v'_m)$ are paths with $v_n = v'_0$ then define the concatenation $p \cdot p' = (v_0, l_1, \ldots, v_n, l'_1, \ldots, v'_m)$. For sets of paths P and P' let $P \cdot P' = \{p \cdot p' \mid p \in P, p' \in P', p \cdot p' \text{ is defined}\}$.

2.2 Class Graphs and Object Graphs

Let $\mathcal{C}$ be a set of class names and $\mathcal{N}$ be a set of instance names, totally ordered by $\leq$. A *class graph* is a finite labeled directed graph $\mathcal{G}_C = (\mathcal{C}, \mathcal{E}_C, \mathcal{N} \cup \{\diamond\})$.

There are two kinds of edges in the class graph. A *construction edge* has the form $u \xrightarrow{l} v$ where $l \in \mathcal{N}$ $(l \neq \diamond)$. It indicates that objects of class u have an instance variable l containing objects of class v. There is at most one construction edge with source u and label l. Each cycle in $\mathcal{G}_C$ involves at least one construction edge.

An edge $u \xrightarrow{\diamond} v$ is a *subclass edge*, indicating that v is a subclass of u. Without lack of generality [3, 15, 12] we assume that class graphs are *simple*, i.e., every class is either *abstract* (all outgoing edges are subclass edges) or *concrete* (all outgoing edges are construction edges). In addition, if $u \xrightarrow{\diamond} v \in \mathcal{E}_C$ then v is concrete.

Figure 1 shows an example class graph with an abstract class A and three concrete classes B, C, and D. Dashed arrows indicate subclass edges, solid arrow indicate construction edges. Class A has subclasses B and C. Class B has one instance variable a of class D. Class C has an instance variable b of class D and another c of class A.

Let Ω be a set of objects. An *object graph* is a finite labeled graph $(\Omega, \mathcal{E}_O, \mathcal{N})$ such that there is at most one edge with source u and label l. The edge $u \xrightarrow{l} v$ means that the instance variable l in object u holds the object v.

Figure 2 shows an example object graph corresponding to the class structure in Fig. 1. The objects $C1$ and $C2$ have class C, $B1$ class B, and $D1$, $D2$, and $D3$ are object identities of class D.

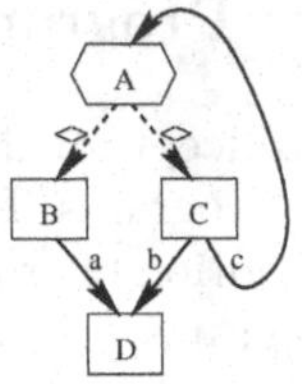

Fig. 1. Example class graph

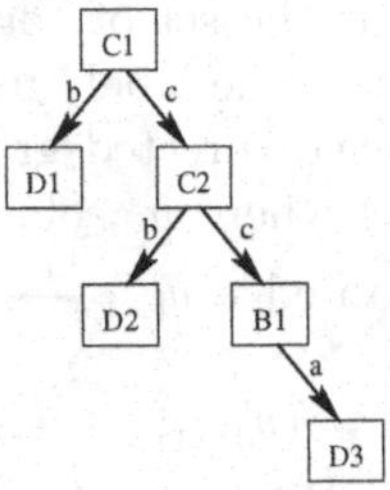

Fig. 2. Example object graph

A *class map* is a mapping $\mathsf{Class} : \Omega \to \mathcal{C}$ from objects to class names of concrete classes. The *subclass map* $\mathsf{Subclasses} : \mathcal{C} \to \mathcal{P}(\mathcal{C})$ maps a class name to the set of class names of all its subclasses, including itself. $\mathsf{Subclasses}(A)$ is the set of all $B \in \mathcal{C}$ such that there is a path $(A, \diamond, \ldots, \diamond, B)$ in the class graph.

2.3 Traversal Specifications

A traversal specification answers the question "where do we go from here?" at some point of a traversal of an object or class graph. Hence, a traversal specification is either B (denoting a path to an object of class B), a concatenation of specifications, or an alternative of specifications. Figure 3 shows the formal syntax.

The semantics of a traversal specification is specified relative to a starting node A. It is a set of paths in a class graph.

$$\begin{array}{ll}
\mathsf{RPathSet}(A, B) & = \{(A, l_1, A_1, \ldots, l_n, A_n) \in \mathsf{Paths}(\mathcal{G}_C) \mid A_n \in \mathsf{Subclasses}(B)\} \\
\mathsf{RPathSet}(A, \rho_1 \cdot \rho_2) & = \bigcup_{B \in \mathsf{Target}(\rho_1)} \mathsf{RPathSet}(A, \rho_1) \cdot \mathsf{RPathSet}(B, \rho_2) \\
\mathsf{RPathSet}(A, \rho_1 + \rho_2) & = \mathsf{RPathSet}(A, \rho_1) \cup \mathsf{RPathSet}(A, \rho_2)
\end{array}$$

The function Target yields the set of possible target classes of a traversal.

$$\begin{array}{ll}
\mathsf{Target}(B) & = \{B\} \\
\mathsf{Target}(\rho_1 \cdot \rho_2) & = \mathsf{Target}(\rho_2) \\
\mathsf{Target}(\rho_1 + \rho_2) & = \mathsf{Target}(\rho_1) \cup \mathsf{Target}(\rho_2)
\end{array}$$

$$\begin{aligned} \rho ::= {} & B && \text{simple path to } B \\ \mid {} & \rho \cdot \rho && \text{concatenation} \\ \mid {} & \rho + \rho && \text{alternative} \end{aligned}$$

Fig. 3. Traversal specifications

The definition of the semantics naturally adapts to object graphs, by replacing occurrences of class names with objects of the respective classes:

$$\begin{aligned} \mathsf{RPathSet}_{\mathcal{G}_O}(A, B) = \{\, & (o_0, l_1, o_1, \ldots, l_n, o_n) \in \mathsf{Paths}(\mathcal{G}_O) \mid \\ & \mathsf{Class}(o_0) \in \mathsf{Subclasses}(A), \\ & \mathsf{Class}(o_n) \in \mathsf{Subclasses}(B)\} \end{aligned}$$

2.4 Semantics

An adaptive program is a pair (ρ, W) of a traversal specification ρ and a *wrapper map* W. The map W maps a class name $A \in \mathcal{C}$ to an action to be executed when visiting an object of class A. Given an object graph $\mathcal{G}_O$, the semantics of (ρ, W) with respect to some initial object o is completely determined by listing the objects in the order in which they are traversed. Formally,

$$\mathsf{Trav}(\rho, o) = \mathsf{Seq}(\mathsf{RPathSet}_{\mathcal{G}_O}(o, \rho))$$

where

$$\begin{aligned} & \mathsf{Seq}(\Pi) && = o_0 \mathsf{Seq}(\Pi_1) \ldots \mathsf{Seq}(\Pi_n) \\ & \text{where} \\ & \{o_0\} && = \{o \in \Omega \mid o \ldots \in \Pi\} \\ & \{l_1, \ldots, l_n\} && = \{l \in \mathcal{N} \mid o_0 l \ldots \in \Pi\} \quad l_i < l_{i+1} \\ & \Pi_i && = \{w \in \Omega(\mathcal{N}\Omega)^* \mid o_0 l_i w \in \Pi\} \end{aligned}$$

To see that $\mathsf{Trav}(\rho, o)$ is well-defined, observe that

1. o_0 is uniquely determined in the first expansion of $\mathsf{Seq}()$ because each path in $\mathsf{RPathSet}_{\mathcal{G}_O}(o, \rho)$ starts with the inital object o;
2. o_0 is uniquely determined in every recursive expansion of $\mathsf{Seq}()$ because the initial segment $o_0 l_i$ of a path in an *object graph* completely determines the next object (there are no inheritance edges in an object graph).

To run the adaptive program on o means to execute the wrappers specified by W in the sequence prescribed by $\mathsf{Trav}(\rho, o)$.

3 Traversal Algebra

In this section, we investigate some algebraic laws that hold for traversal specifications and define a normal form for them. Working towards a compilation

$$
\begin{aligned}
(\rho_1 \cdot \rho_2) \cdot \rho_3 &= \rho_1 \cdot (\rho_2 \cdot \rho_3) \\
(\rho_1 + \rho_2) + \rho_3 &= \rho_1 + (\rho_2 + \rho_3) \\
\rho_1 + \rho_2 &= \rho_2 + \rho_1 \\
\rho + \rho &= \rho \\
\rho_1 \cdot (\rho_2 + \rho_3) &= (\rho_1 \cdot \rho_2) + (\rho_1 \cdot \rho_3) \\
(\rho_1 + \rho_2) \cdot \rho_3 &= (\rho_1 \cdot \rho_3) + (\rho_2 \cdot \rho_3)
\end{aligned}
$$

Fig. 4. Laws for traversal specifications

algorithm, we define a notion of derivative for traversal specifications, where taking the derivative of a specification corresponds to visiting a certain node during a traversal. Finally, we consider the complexity of the resulting compilation algorithm.

3.1 Algebraic Laws

Traversal specifications obey some algebraic laws. The concatenation of specifications $\cdot$ is associative. The alternative of specifications $+$ is associative, commutative, and idempotent. Furthermore, concatenation $\cdot$ distributes over $+$. Figure 4 shows the resulting laws.

Lemma 1. *The algebraic laws given in Fig. 4 are correct, in the sense that if* $\rho_1 = \rho_2$ *is a law then, for all* A, $\mathsf{RPathSet}(A, \rho_1) = \mathsf{RPathSet}(A, \rho_2)$.

A further law compresses a concatenation of simple paths even further.

Lemma 2. $A \cdot A = A$

Given an arbitrary total ordering on the set of class names, a traversal specification is in *normal form* if it has the form $w_1 + w_2 + \ldots + w_n$ where each w_i is a *traversal word* (that is, it is generated by the grammar $w ::= B \mid B \cdot w$) and $w_i < w_{i+1}$ in the induced lexicographic ordering. The function norm maps a traversal specification to its normal form. In the algorithm, $\square$ denotes the empty traversal specification.

$$
\begin{aligned}
\text{norm}(\rho) &= \text{sort}(\text{norm'}(\rho, \square)) \\
\text{norm'}(B, w_1 + \ldots + w_n) &= \text{prefix}(B, w_1) + \ldots + \text{prefix}(B, w_n) \\
\text{norm'}(\rho_1 \cdot \rho_2, L) &= \text{norm'}(\rho_1, \text{norm'}(\rho_2, L)) \\
\text{norm'}(\rho_1 + \rho_2, L) &= \text{norm'}(\rho_1, L) + \text{norm'}(\rho_2, L)
\end{aligned}
$$

$$
\text{prefix}(B, w) = \begin{cases} B & \text{if } w = \square \\ w & \text{if } w = B \cdot w' \\ B \cdot w & \text{otherwise} \end{cases}
$$

The function sort merges traversal specifications by sorting an alternative of words and removing duplicates. The function norm has exponential complexity in the worst case. To see that, consider the family of specifications $\rho_n = (A_1 + B_1) \cdots (A_n + B_n)$ for distinct A_i and B_i. Each ρ_n has size linear in n, but $\mathrm{norm}(\rho_n) = A_1 \cdot A_2 \cdots A_n + \ldots + B_1 \cdot B_2 \cdots B_n$ has size proportional to 2^n.

Lemma 3. *For all A and ρ: $\mathsf{RPathSet}(A, \rho) = \mathsf{RPathSet}(A, \mathrm{norm}(\rho))$.*

3.2 Second Normal Form

Further simplifications are possible for specifications in normal form. First, define another ordering on words. A word v is less than or equal to a word $w \cdot A_{n+1}$ if v is a subsequence of w followed by a non-empty ascending sequence of superclasses of A_{n+1}.

Definition 1. *Let $m \geq 0$. Define $v \preceq_m w$ iff there is some $n \geq 0$ such that $v = A_1 A_2 \cdots A_n B_1 B_2 \cdots B_{m+1}$ and there exist $\alpha_1, \ldots, \alpha_{n+1}$ such that $w = \alpha_1 A_1 \alpha_2 A_2 \cdots A_n \alpha_{n+1} A_{n+1}$ where $A_{n+1} \in \mathsf{Subclasses}(B_1)$ and, for all $1 \leq i \leq m$, $B_i \in \mathsf{Subclasses}(B_{i+1})$.*

Write $v \preceq w$ if there exists some m such that $v \preceq_m w$.

We will be most interested in the special case where $m = 0$. It turns out that $\preceq_0$ is related to the reverse inclusion of the corresponding path sets.

Proposition 1. *The relation $\preceq$ is a partial ordering on the set of normalized traversal words.*

Corollary 1. *The relation $\preceq_0$ is a partial ordering on traversal words.*

Lemma 4. *For all words v and w, if $w \preceq_0 v$ then, for all A, $\mathsf{RPathSet}(A, v) \subseteq \mathsf{RPathSet}(A, w)$.*

The proof is by induction on v.

The lemma does not extend to $\preceq_m$ for $m > 0$, hence it does not hold for $\preceq$. To see this, consider three distinct class names A, B, and D so that $A \cdot B \preceq D$ if $D \in \mathsf{Subclasses}(A)$ and $A \in \mathsf{Subclasses}(B)$. Now, $\mathsf{RPathSet}(D, D)$ contains (D), but $(D) \notin \mathsf{RPathSet}(A \cdot B,)$, since every element of the latter contains A.

As a corollary, we have the following additional law.

Lemma 5. *Suppose $w \preceq_0 v$ then $v + w = w$.*

Proof. We need to show that, for each A, $\mathsf{RPathSet}(A, v + w) = \mathsf{RPathSet}(A, w)$. The inclusion $\mathsf{RPathSet}(A, w) \subseteq \mathsf{RPathSet}(A, v + w)$ is obvious by definition. The reverse inclusion is Lemma 4.

Definition 2. *A traversal specification ρ is in* second normal form *(2NF) if it is in normal form $\rho \equiv w_1 + \ldots + w_n$ and, for all $i, j \in \{1, \ldots, n\}$, if $i \neq j$ then $w_i \not\preceq_0 w_j$.*

To get norm to produce traversal specifications in 2NF, it suffices to have sort not just remove duplicates but also remove each word w if there is another word v such that $v \preceq_0 w$. Call this modified function sort$'$.

$$\partial_X(A) \equiv A$$
$$\partial_X(A \cdot w) \equiv \begin{cases} w & \text{if } X = A \\ A \cdot w & \text{otherwise} \end{cases}$$
$$\partial_X(w_1 + \ldots + w_n) \equiv \partial_X(w_1) + \ldots + \partial_X(w_n)$$

Fig. 5. Derivative of a traversal specification

3.3 Formal Derivatives

Another view of a traversal specification is to consider it as a state in a traversal. For example, the specification A means "continue until you find some object of class A", and the specification $B \cdot A$ means "search for some B-object and then continue looking for some A-object". Clearly, whenever a traversal visits a node of class X in the object graph, the traversal specification might change to reflect the new state of the traversal. For example, if the traversal hits upon a B-object in state $B \cdot A$, the traversal continues through B's instance variables in state A. In principle, the new state should be $B \cdot A + A$ because, by definition, the traversal should still look for As following some B. However, Lemma 5 shows that A is equivalent to $B \cdot A + A$.

Formally, when a traversal in state ρ encounters an X-object, the new traversal specification for the instance variables is the *derivative* of the old specification ρ with respect to the class X, that is $\partial_X(\rho)$. The definition in Fig. 5 assumes that ρ is already in normal form.

Lemma 6. *If ρ is in (second) normal form then so is* $\text{sort}'(\partial_X(\rho))$*, for all* X.

Computation of $\partial_X(\rho)$ takes time linear in the length of ρ. Subsequent normalization boils down to a single run of sort′ on the derivative, which takes $O(n^2 \log n)$ where n is the length of ρ (since each comparison may take time linear in n).

3.4 The State Skeleton

Let $\text{Der}(\rho)$ be the set of all iterated derivatives of a traversal specification ρ. Since it only depends on ρ, it is possible to precompute $\text{Der}(\rho)$ before a concrete class graph is given.

The complexity for computing $\text{Der}(\rho)$ is clearly its size $|\text{Der}(\rho)|$ for some ρ in normal form. First, for words the table

w	$\text{Der}(w)$	$\|\text{Der}(w)\|$
A	$\{A\}$	1
$A \cdot w$	$\{A \cdot w\} \cup \text{Der}(w)$	$1 + \|\text{Der}(w)\|$

determines the number of derivatives. That is, $|\text{Der}(w)|$ is linear in the size of w.

For a general specification $\rho = w_1 + \ldots + w_n$ which also includes alternatives $\mathrm{Der}(w_1 + \ldots + w_n) \subseteq \{v_1 + \ldots + v_n \mid v_i \in \mathrm{Der}(w_i)\}$ (some alternatives may be deleted due to Lemma 5), it holds that $|\mathrm{Der}(w_1 + \ldots + w_n)| \leq |\mathrm{Der}(w_1)| \cdot \ldots \cdot |\mathrm{Der}(w_n)| \sim |w_1| \cdots |w_n|$. Depending on the structure of ρ, $|w_1| \cdots |w_n|$ can range from linear in $|\rho|$ (for $n = 1$) to exponential in $|\rho|$. To demonstrate the latter, consider the following example. Let $w_i = A_i \cdot B_i \cdot C$ where all A_i and B_i and C are distinct. In this case, $|\mathrm{Der}(w_1 + \ldots + w_n)| = 2^n + 1$ (by straightforward induction using Lemma 5) whereas the size of $w_1 + \ldots + w_n$ is linear in n. Therefore, the exponential bound is tight.

3.5 Compiling Traversal Specifications

Compiling a traversal specification means to compute the set of its iterated derivatives. In the case of a multiplicative specification [14] (which does not use +), compilation takes linear time. Firstly, normalization of a specification boils down to removing repeated class names, which can be done in linear time. Secondly, computing the normalized derivative takes unit time. Finally, the number of normalized derivatives is linear in the size of the multiplicative specification.

For general specifications, compilation takes exponential time in the worst case, for two reasons. First, the normalization of a traversal specification may take exponential time and, second, the traversal specification may have an exponential number of derivatives.

From now on we can safely assume that the function $\partial_X(\rho)$ only deals with specifications in 2NF. Once the elements of $\mathrm{Der}(\rho)$ have been computed, the compiler assigns numbers to them and reduces the computation of $\partial_X(\rho)$ to a constant-time table lookup.

Starting from a specification ρ and a designated source class A, a compiled traversal specification is a quadruple (A, P, ρ_0, ∂) where $\rho_0 \in P$ is the initial traversal specification in 2NF, $P = \mathrm{Der}(\rho_0)$ is the set of normalized iterated derivatives of ρ_0, and $\partial : P \times \mathcal{C} \to P$ is the table of derivatives.

4 Adaption to a Class Structure

Given a specific class graph $\mathcal{G}_C = (\mathcal{C}, \mathcal{E}_C, \mathcal{N} \cup \{\diamond\})$ and a compiled traversal specification (A, P, ρ_0, ∂), the next task is to produce a target program which implements the traversal. The abstract model of the target program is a finite automaton, the traversal automaton. We describe its construction and prove its correctness with respect to the traversal specification. Then, we show that it is uniformly minimal, ie., it has the least number of states among those automata that implement the semantics of ρ_0 and work for all possible class graphs.

4.1 Traversal Automaton

The first step towards the target program is the construction of the traversal automaton. The traversal automaton is a non-deterministic finite automaton $\mathcal{A} = (Q, \Sigma, \delta, q_0, F)$ [9] where

- $Q = \mathcal{C} \times \{\text{in}, \text{out}\} \times P$ is the set of states;
- $\Sigma = \mathcal{C} \cup \mathcal{N} \cup \{\diamond\}$ is the alphabet;
- $q_0 = (A, \text{in}, \rho_0)$ is the initial state;
- $F = \{(A, \text{out}, \rho) \mid A \in \mathcal{C}, \rho \in P$ and there exists some B and ρ' such that $\rho = B + \rho' \vee \rho = B, A \in \mathsf{Subclasses}(B)\}$ is the set of final states;
- $\delta((A, \text{in}, \rho), A) = \{(A, \text{out}, \rho)\}$ and $\delta((A, \text{out}, \rho), l) = \{(B, \text{in}, \partial_A(\rho)) \mid A \xrightarrow{l} B \in \mathcal{E}_C\}$ defines the transition function.

As usual, $L(\mathcal{A}, q)$ is the language recognized from initial state $q \in Q$.

Inheritance edges in the class graph are the only sources of non-determinism in $\mathcal{A}$. All transitions on construction edges are deterministic because there is at most one construction edge with a given source u and label l.

The next Lemma shows that the automaton $\mathcal{A}$ indeed implements the semantics of the traversal specification ρ_0.

Lemma 7. *The automaton $\mathcal{A}$ recognizes $\mathsf{RPathSet}_{\mathcal{G}_O}(A, \rho_0)$.*

We actually prove a more general claim: for all $A \in \mathcal{C}$, for all $\rho \in P$, $L(\mathcal{A}, (A, \text{in}, \rho)) = \mathsf{RPathSet}(A, \rho)$. This can be shown using induction on the length n of a path $(A_0, l_1, A_1, l_2, \ldots, l_n, A_n)$.

4.2 Minimal Traversal Automaton

The step from the traversal automaton to generated code is simple. The states of the automaton correspond to a set of mutually recursive procedures/methods, each of which implements one step of the traversal and – possibly – an action. If there were equivalent states they would have to employ equivalent code to continue the traversal. In other words, the compiled code would suffer from code duplication. Hence, the traversal automaton should have as few states as possible.

Standard results from automata theory [9, Sec. 3.4] show that a minimal (deterministic) finite automaton always exists. This minimal automaton has the property that for all its states q and q', if $q \neq q'$ then $L(\mathcal{A}, q) \neq L(\mathcal{A}, q')$, that is, q and q' are *distinguishable*. Theorem 1 below demonstrates that the set $\text{Der}(\rho)$ generates distinguishable states under certain assumptions on the class graph.

Since we want to compute the uniformly minimal automaton, ie., an automaton which works regardless of the actual class graph, we make the following two assumptions.

Assumption 1 (REACHABILITY) *Let B be an arbitrary class. For all concrete classes A there is a label $l \neq \diamond$ such that $A \xrightarrow{l} B \in \mathcal{E}_C$.*

Assumption 2 (RICHNESS) *Given a specification ρ, there is always a sufficient number of classes not mentioned in ρ.*

These assumptions are technical devices to enable a proof of the following development. They are not the weakest possible assumptions, but rather they are chosen to make the proofs palatable. They are not meant to be imposed on class graphs submitted to the compiler. If a class graph violates the assumptions, then the generated automaton may not be minimal for this particular class graph.

The intuition behind the assumptions is to guarantee the existence of a suitably connected set of classes which are not mentioned in the specification which is compiled. This is usually true because any given specification only mentions a very small subset of the classes in a system.

From now on, REACHABILITY and RICHNESS are implicitly assumed for all statements.

Theorem 1. *Let $\rho_1, \rho_2 \in \mathrm{Der}(\rho)$, all in 2NF, such that $\rho_1 \not\equiv \rho_2$.*
For all $A \in \mathcal{C}$, $\mathsf{RPathSet}(A, \rho_1) \neq \mathsf{RPathSet}(A, \rho_2)$.

We need a number of auxiliary lemmas to prove this theorem. First, we establish that the inclusion of path sets for words implies that the words are related by $\preceq_0$.

Lemma 8. *Let v and w be words in normal form.*
Suppose $\forall A \,.\, \mathsf{RPathSet}(A, v) \subseteq \mathsf{RPathSet}(A, w)$. Then $w \preceq_0 v$.

The proof is by induction on the length of w.

Since Lemma 4 provides the other implication, we have proved the following theorem.

Theorem 2. *Let v and w be words in normal form.*
$\forall A \,.\, \mathsf{RPathSet}(A, v) \subseteq \mathsf{RPathSet}(A, w)$ if and only if $w \preceq_0 v$.

Exploiting that $\preceq_0$ is a partial order immediately yields the following.

Corollary 2. *Let v and w be words in normal form. $\forall A \,.\, \mathsf{RPathSet}(A, v) = \mathsf{RPathSet}(A, w)$ if and only if $w \equiv v$.*

This result for words extends to traversal specifications in strong 2NF. To obtain the strong form of 2NF, we replace $\preceq_0$ by $\preceq$ in the definition of 2NF.

Theorem 3. *Suppose ρ and ρ' are in strong 2NF. Then $\forall A \,.\, \mathsf{RPathSet}(A, \rho) = \mathsf{RPathSet}(A, \rho')$ if and only if $\rho \equiv \rho'$.*

Theorem 1 follows immediately from Theorem 3. Theorem 3 characterizes all specifiable traversals since it establishes a one-to-one correspondence between traversal specifications in strong 2NF and specifiable path sets.

From another point of view, we have proved a normal form result for a certain kind of regular expressions, namely traversal specifications. Theorem 3 completely characterizes them, by putting the languages in one-to-one correspondence with expressions in normal form.

1. $(A, \mathrm{in}, \rho_0) \in Q$.
2. If $q = (A, \mathrm{in}, \rho) \in Q$ then let $q' = (A, \mathrm{out}, \rho)$ in
   - $q' \in Q$; and
   - if $q' \in F$ then active(q'); and
   - if active(q') then active(q); and
   - if active(q') then $(q, A, q') \in \delta$.
3. If $q = (A, \mathrm{out}, \rho) \in Q$ then
   for each $A \xrightarrow{l} B \in \mathcal{E}_C$ let $q' = (B, \mathrm{in}, \partial_A(\rho))$ in
   - $q' \in Q$; and
   - if active(q') then active(q); and
   - if active(q') then $(q, l, q') \in \delta$.

Fig. 6. Constraint system specifying those states of $\mathcal{A}$ which are reachable and active

4.3 Generation of the Automaton

The naive construction of the automaton $\mathcal{A}$ is too costly because not all states of $\mathcal{A}$ are accessible from the initial state. Fortunately, it is easy to restrict the construction of the state space of $\mathcal{A}$ so that only accessible states are constructed.

Likewise, naive use of $\mathcal{A}$ to control a traversal leads to unnecessary visits because some states of $\mathcal{A}$ are *sink states.* A state q is a sink state if there is no path from q to a final state or, equivalently, $L(\mathcal{A}, q) = \emptyset$. The non-sink states are easily identified by marking all those states that have a path to a final state (analogous to the construction of an automaton for INIT(L) from an automaton for L [9]). The remaining unmarked states are sink states.

Both properties can be computed in one traversal of the reachable part of the automaton. This traversal takes $O(|\mathcal{E}_C| \cdot |\mathrm{Der}(\rho_0)|)$ time. The constraint system in Fig. 6 specifies the traversal. In the specification, the predicate active(q) is true iff q is not a sink state. It can be implemented using standard techniques in the complexity given above.

5 Extensions and Further Work

The algebraic approach using derivatives of traversal specifications is also suitable for dynamic compilation [12]. In this case, the compilation time is constant for each class (i.e., linear in the size of the class structure) and the amount of work left to run time is comparable to that in Lieberherr and Patt-Shamir's approach [12]. However, their approach employs a different notion of traversal specification.

It is easy to generalize the framework to multiple source classes since traversal specifications do not mention source classes to begin with. Also the adaption to multiple target classes requires no change in the method, due to our removal of the notion of well-formedness. Well-formedness was only a real requirement in the early work which relied on identifying the set of states of the traversal automaton with the set of classes [15]. The later works have been able to dispense with well-formedness, too [12].

Further operators like negation and intersection could be allowed for traversal specifications. While the algebraic approach seems to work with these operators in principle, its impact on normal forms and the remaining development of Sec. 4 has been left to further investigation. In the database community [1, 10, 2], more expressive path expressions have been considered, including l^{-1} (find an object o so that the current one is the value of instance variable $o.l$) and $\mu(l)$ (find the closest reachable object with instance variable l) [18]. These would also be interesting to investigate.

6 Conclusion

We have presented a new algebraic foundation for compiling adaptive programs. Our approach provides a simple and intuitive algorithm based on formal derivatives of traversal specifications, while maintaining and verifying the previously established complexity bounds. We have implemented the compilation of adaptive programs using partial evaluation, thus substantiating earlier claims in this regard. We hope that this new perspective provides further insight into the structure of adaptive programs.

References

[1] Serge Abiteboul, Dallan Quass, Jason McHugh, Jennifer Widom, and Janet Wiener. The Lorel query language for semistructured data. *Journal of Digital Libraries*, 1(1):68–88, 1997.

[2] Serge Abiteboul and Victor Vianu. Regular path queries with constraints. In *PODS '97. Proceedings of the Sixteenth ACM SIG-SIGMOD-SIGART Symposium on Principles of Database Systems*, pages 122–133, Tucson, Arizona, May 1997. ACM Press.

[3] Paul L. Bergstein. Object-preserving class transformations. In *OOPSLA'91, ACM SIGPLAN Sixth Annual Conference on Object-Oriented Programming Systems, Languages, and Applications*, pages 299–313. ACM, November 1991. SIGPLAN Notices (26)11.

[4] Gerard Berry and Ravi Sethi. From regular expressions to deterministic automata. *Theoretical Computer Science*, 48:117–126, 1986.

[5] W. Brown, R. Malveau, H. McCormick, and T. Mowbray. *AntiPatterns: Refactoring Software, Architectures, and Projects in Crisis.* John Wiley and Sons, 1998.

[6] Janusz A. Brzozowski. Derivatives of regular expressions. *Journal of the ACM*, 11(4):481–494, 1964.

[7] John H. Conway. *Regular Algebra and Finite Machines.* Chapman and Hall, 1971.

[8] Martin Fowler. *Refactoring: Improving the Design of Existing Code.* Addison-Wesley, 1999.

[9] John E. Hopcroft and Jeffrey D. Ullman. *Introduction to automata theory, languages and computation.* Addison-Wesley, 1979.

[10] Michael Kifer, Wong Kim, and Yehoshua Sagiv. Querying object oriented databases. In Michael Stonebraker, editor, *Proceedings of the SIGMOD International Conference on Management of Data*, volume 21 of *SIGMOD Record*, pages 393–402, New York, NY, USA, June 1992. ACM Press.

[11] Karl J. Lieberherr. *Adaptive Object-Oriented Software: The Demeter Method with Propagation Patterns*. PWS Publishing Company, Boston, 1996.

[12] Karl J. Lieberherr and Boaz Patt-Shamir. Traversals of object structures: Specification and efficient implementation. Technical Report NU-CCS-97-15, College of Computer Science, Northeastern University, Boston, MA, July 1997.

[13] W. Opdyke. *Refactoring Object-Oriented Frameworks*. PhD thesis, University of Illinois at Urbana-Champain, 1992.

[14] Jens Palsberg, Boaz Patt-Shamir, and Karl Lieberherr. A new approach to compiling adaptive programs. *Science of Computer Programming*, 29(3):303–326, September 1997.

[15] Jens Palsberg, Cun Xiao, and Karl Lieberherr. Efficient implementation of adaptive software. *ACM Transactions on Programming Languages and Systems*, 17(2):264–292, March 1995.

[16] Peter Thiemann. An algebraic foundation for adaptive programming. `http://www.informatik.uni-freiburg.de/~thiemann/papers/adaptive-lncs.ps%.gz`, October 1999.

[17] Peter Thiemann. Compiling adaptive programs by partial evaluation. In David Watts, editor, *Proc. of the 9th International Conference on Compiler Construction*, Lecture Notes in Computer Science, Berlin, Germany, March 2000. Springer-Verlag. Preliminary version available from `http://www.informatik.uni-freiburg.de/~thiemann/papers/compile.ps.gz`.

[18] Jan Van den Bussche and Gottfried Vossen. An extension of path expressions to simplify navigation in object-oriented queries. In *Proc. of Intl. Conf. on Deductive and Object-Oriented Databases (DOOD)*, volume 760 of *Lecture Notes in Computer Science*, pages 267–282, 1993.

Predicate Logic and Tree Automata with Tests

Ralf Treinen*

Laboratoire de Recherche en Informatique
Université Paris-Sud
F-91495 Orsay cedex, France
http://www.lri.fr/~treinen

Abstract. We investigate the question whether the well-known correspondence between tree automata and the weak second order logic of two successor functions (*WS2S*) can be extended to tree automata with tests. Our first insight is that there is no generalization of tree automata with tests that has a decidable emptiness problem and that is equivalent to the full class of formulae in some extension of *WS2S*, at least not when we are asking for an conservative extension of the classical correspondence between *WS2S* and tree automata to tree automata with tests.
As a consequence we can extend the correspondence between tree automata and *WS2S* to automata with tests only when we admit a restriction of the class of formulae. We present a logic, called *WS2Sy*, and a restriction of the class of formula, called *uniform*, that is equivalent to tree automata with tests.

1 Introduction

The equivalence of tree automata and weak second-order logic of 2 successor functions, short *WS2S*, is known for more then 30 years [10]. During the current decade, a lot of work has been done on classes of tree automata that are stronger than classical tree automata (see [4] and [8] for a survey). The general frame to obtain these stronger classes of tree automata is to augment the automaton model with tests. In the case of tree automata with tests between brothers [1], for instance, we can write a transition rule like $f(q_1, q_2) \rightarrow^{1=2} q$ that will accept a tree $f(t_1, t_2)$ in state q if t_1 is accepted in state q_1, t_2 is accepted in q_2, and if in addition $t_1 = t_2$. These tests increase in a considerable way the expressiveness of tree automata. Tree automata with equality tests between brothers as sketched above can for instance recognize the set of balanced trees (which is not possible with classical tree automata).

Defining new classes of tree automata is of course only interesting when the usual "nice" properties of automata are preserved. The most important of these is the decidability of the emptiness of the language recognized by such an automaton. Furthermore we expect a good class of recognizable languages to

* Partially supported by the Esprit Working Group 22457 - CCL II

J. Tiuryn (Ed.): FOSSACS 2000, LNCS 1784, pp. 329–343, 2000.

be closed under operations such as union, intersection, complement and (maybe restricted classes of) homomorphisms and inverse homomorphisms.

Several classes of tree automata with "nice" properties have been identified (see [4] for an excellent overview of tree automata and tree automata with tests). In light of the above mentioned equivalence between tree automata and the logic *WS2S* it is a natural question whether there are similar logical characterizations of tree automata with tests. Before attacking this question we will try to explain in an informal manner the logic *WS2S* and its correspondence with tree automata.

The second-order logic *WS2S* comes with a standard interpretation. There are two sorts: the sort of words over the alphabet $\{1, 2\}$ and the sort of *finite* sets of words. There are a constant for the empty word, unary functions to append a symbol 1, resp. 2 at the end of a word, and the elementship relation between words and sets. An example of a formula in this logic, expressing that the word x is a prefix of the word y is (the convention is that word variables are written in lower case and set variables in upper case):

$$\forall Y(y \in Y \wedge \forall z([z1 \in Y \vee z2 \in Y] \rightarrow z \in Y) \rightarrow x \in Y)$$

A tree automaton with k states can be translated into a formula of *WS2S* in the following sense: We represent a tree over an alphabet of n symbols by n sets, each of them representing the occurrences (addresses of nodes) of the tree marked with one the symbols. The formula has to state that these sets are pairwise disjoint (since an occurrence can carry only one symbol), that their union is closed under prefix (using the prefix predicate defined above) and that the arity of the function symbols is respected, that there is an assignment of states to the occurrences (this is expressed by an existential quantification over k sets similar to what we did to represent the term itself) respecting the transition rules of the automaton such that the root is marked with an accepting state.

Given a formula ϕ with n free variables (by a slight variation of the logic we can assume that only set variables are involved) we first have to say how to represent an n-tuple of sets as a tree: We take as tree signature the n-tuples over $\{0, 1\}$, a tree representing a n-tuple of sets has at occurrence π the symbol 1 in the i-th component if and only if π belongs to the i-th set. Since all sets in *WS2S* are finite a finite tree is sufficient (there is also a technically *much* more involved variant for infinite sets and infinite trees due to Rabin [7]). Now, the idea to get an automaton that corresponds to a given formula is to first construct automata for the atomic formula of the logic, and then to apply the closure of tree automata by union, complement and projection (corresponding to disjunction, negation and existential quantification).

In fact there is a problem with the translation of formulae into automata that is easily overseen when sketched as we did above: For this translation to work we need an additional closure property of tree automata (which, luckily, does hold for classical tree automata): closure by *cylindrification*. The problem is apparent when we have constructed a tree automaton for a formula $\phi(X_1, X_2)$ and another one for a formula $\psi(X_2, X_3)$ and when we now want to construct from these the automaton for $\phi(X_1, X_2) \wedge \psi(X_2, X_3)$. We cannot just take the intersection of these two automata since the two "components" of the trees recognized by the respective automata do not correspond to the same variables. In fact we have to cylindrify both automata, that is add to the first automaton a third component and to the second automaton a new first component that are in fact completely ignored by the rules of the automata (the origin of the name "cylindrification" is the intuition of a two-dimensional geometrical figure that is slided along the third dimension through space). Finally we can take the intersection of the two cylindrified automata.

Here lies the problem when we ask for a logical characterization of tree automata with tests: The closure properties of the logic, including the "implicit" closure by cylindrification that simply stems from the presence of variables in the logic, require any class of automata that corresponds to the *full* class of formulae of some logic to be closed under cylindrification.

If we need cylindrification for our class of automata to correspond to some logic then we could simply extend our automaton model accordingly and try to show that the "nice" properties of automata still hold. The automata model that we get from *Tree Automata with Tests (TAT)* when we close under cylindrification are *Tree Automata with Component-wise Tests (TACT)* that will be formally defined in Section 3. Unfortunately, emptiness of TACT-automata is undecidable as we will show in Section 4, that is, our original program simply has to fail.

Hence we propose to ask for a *subset* of the set of formulae of some suitable logic that is equivalent to our class of formulae. We define in Section 5 such a logic *WS2Sy* and its two subclasses of so-called *restricted* and *uniform* formulae. We state the exact correspondence between TACT and TAT automata and the subclasses of restricted, resp. uniform formulae of *WS2Sy* in Section 6 and prove this correspondence in Section 7 and 8. The technical part of the paper only considers automata with tests between brothers, we briefly discuss extension to other classes of automata with tests in Section 9.

2 Preliminaries

A *signature* Σ consists of a set of symbols (also denoted Σ) and an *arity function* $\alpha: \Sigma \to \mathbf{N}_0$. Often one writes Σ_n for $\{f \in \Sigma \mid \alpha(f) = n\}$. For a signature Σ the set $T(\Sigma)$ of Σ *ground terms* is the smallest set such that if $f \in \Sigma_n$ and $t_1, \ldots, t_n \in T(\Sigma)$ then $f(t_1, \ldots, t_n) \in T(\Sigma)$. The set of *occurrences* $O(t)$ of a tree $t = f(t_1, \ldots, t_n)$ is $\{\epsilon\} \cup \bigcup_{i=1}^{n} \{iw | w \in O(t_i)\}$. If $\pi \in O(t)$ then the *subtree* $t\mid_\pi$ of t at π is defined by $t\mid_\epsilon = t$ and $f(t_1, \ldots, t_n)\mid_{i\pi} = t_i\mid_\pi$.

Given signatures Σ, Γ, a *renaming* ρ is a function $\rho: \Sigma \to \Gamma$ such that $\alpha(\rho(f)) \le \alpha(f)$ for all $f \in \Sigma$. A renaming $\rho: \Sigma \to \Gamma$ extends to a tree homomorphism $\rho: T(\Sigma) \to T(\Gamma)$ by $\rho(f(t_1, \ldots, t_n)) = (\rho(f))(\rho(t_1), \ldots, \rho(t_{\alpha(\rho(f))}))$ (hence, arguments not needed in Γ are simply dropped).

An instance of the *Post Correspondence Problem (short: PCP)* is a finite sequence $P = ((p_i, q_i))_{i=1,\ldots,m}$ of pairs of words from $\{a, b\}^*$. A *solution* of such an instance of PCP is a nonempty sequence $(i_1, \ldots, i_n)$, $1 \leq i_j \leq m$, such that $p_{i_1} \cdots p_{i_n} = q_{i_1} \cdots q_{i_n}$. According to a classical result due to Post [6], it is undecidable whether an instance of the PCP has a solution or not.

3 Tree Automata with Component-wise Tests

Definition 1 (Tuple Signature). *For any finite alphabet Γ and $n \geq 0$, the signature $\Gamma^{(n)}$ consists of the set of function symbols $(\Gamma \cup \{\bot\})^n$, where $\bot$ is a new symbol. The symbol $(\bot \ldots \bot)$ is a constant, all other symbols are binary.*

Example 1. Let $\Gamma = \{0, 1\}$. The signature $\Gamma^{(2)}$ contains the binary symbols $00, 01, 0\bot, 10, 11, 1\bot, \bot 0, \bot 1$ and the constant $\bot\bot$.

Definition 2 (Projection and Component of a Tree). *Let τ be a $\Gamma^{(n)}$-tree and $1 \leq i \leq n$.*

1. *The* i-th component *of τ, denoted τ^i, is the $\Gamma^{(1)}$-tree given by the renaming $(f_1 \ldots f_i \cdots f_n) \mapsto f_i$ for all $f_j \in \Gamma \cup \{\bot\}$.*
2. *The* i-th projection *of τ, denoted $\tau^{\langle i \rangle}$, is the $\Gamma^{(n-1)}$-tree given by the renaming $(f_1 \ldots f_{i-1} f_i f_{i+1} \cdots f_n) \mapsto (f_1 \ldots f_{i-1} f_{i+1} \cdots f_n)$ for all $f_j \in \Gamma \cup \{\bot\}$.*

Note that both projection and selection of a component can change the set of occurrences of a tree since a binary symbol may become a constant, as is illustrated in the example given on Figure 1.

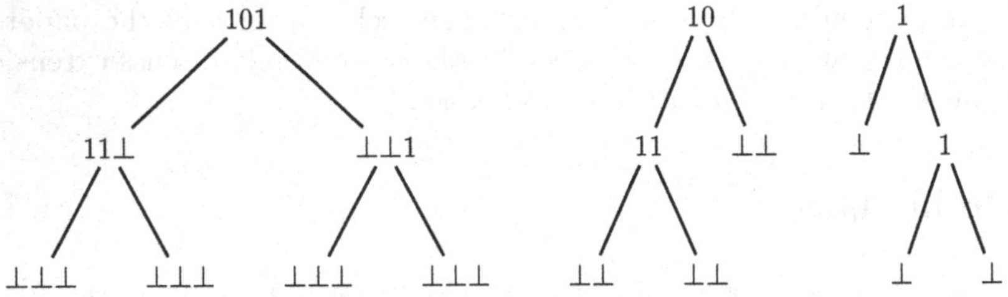

(a) Tree τ (b) $\tau^{\langle 3 \rangle}$ (c) τ^3

Fig. 1. Example of projection and component.

Definition 3 (Tree Automata). *A* tree automaton with component-wise tests between brothers (short: TACT) *is a quintuplet $(\Gamma, n, Q, Q_f, \Delta)$ where*

- *Γ is a finite alphabet and $n \geq 1$,*
- *Q is a finite set of states,*

- $Q_f \subseteq Q$ *is the set of accepting states,*
- Δ *is a set of transition rules of one of the following forms:*
  - $(\bot \dots \bot) \rightarrow q$, $q \in Q$.
  - $f(q_1, q_2) \rightarrow^c q$ *where* c *is a boolean combination of tests* $1.i = 2.i$ *with* $1 \leq i \leq n$, $f \in \Gamma^{(n)} - (\bot \dots \bot)$, $q, q_1, q_2 \in Q$.

A tree automaton with tests between brothers (short: TAT) *is a TACT automaton* $(\Gamma, n, Q, Q_f, \Delta)$ *where all tests of rules in* Δ *are either* ***True****, or* $1.1 = 2.1 \wedge \dots \wedge 1.n = 2.n$*, or* $1.1 \neq 2.1 \vee \dots \vee 1.n \neq 2.n$.

A tree automaton (short: TA) *is a TACT* $(\Gamma, n, Q, Q_f, \Delta)$ *where all tests of rules in* Δ *are* ***True****.*

Note that in a TAT all tests operate uniformly on *all* components. Hence TAT's are exactly the tree automata with tests between brothers introduced in [1], and TA are classical tree automata. In the examples we will simply drop a test True on a transition rule and write it as the rule of a classical tree automaton.

Definition 4. *The TACT A* tests only on the set of components I *if whenever A contains a transition rule with a test c and* $1.i = 2.i$*, resp.* $1.i \neq 2.i$ *is an atomic test in c, then* $i \in I$.

Definition 5 (Acceptance by a TACT). *A tree t* satisfies *the test* $1.i = 2.i$ *iff* $(t\mid_1)^i = (t\mid_2)^i$*, this extends in the canonical way to boolean combinations of tests.*

The rewriting relation of a TACT $A = (\Gamma, n, Q, Q_f, \Delta)$ *is the smallest binary relation* $\rightarrow_A \subseteq T(\Gamma^{(n)}) \times Q$ *with*

- $a \rightarrow_A q$ *if* $a \rightarrow q \in \Delta$
- $f(t_1, t_2) \rightarrow_A q$ *if* $f(q_1, q_2) \rightarrow^c q \in \Delta$*,* $f(t_1, t_2)$ *satisfies c,* $t_1 \rightarrow_A q_1$ *and* $t_2 \rightarrow_A q_2$.

The automaton A accepts *a tree t if* $t \rightarrow_A q$ *for some accepting state* $q \in Q_f$. *The set* L_A recognized *by A is the set of all trees accepted by A.*

Definition 6 (Deterministic and Complete TACT). *A TACT A is* deterministic *if for every tree t there is at most one state q such that* $t \rightarrow_A q$*, and* complete *if for every tree t there is at least one state q with* $t \rightarrow_A q$.

The following proposition is immediate from our definitions:

Proposition 1. *Every TA-recognizable set is TAT-recognizable, and every TAT-recognizable set is TACT-recognizable.*

4 The Emptiness Problem for TACT

Theorem 1. *The emptiness-problem for TACT automata (even when restricted to the class of TACT without negative constraints) is undecidable.*

Proof: We reduce the Post Correspondence Problem to the emptiness problem of TACT automata. Let $P = ((p_i, q_i))_{i=1,\dots,m}$ be an instance of PCP.

First some terminology: a tree $t \in T(\Gamma^{(n)})$ is a *comb* if every binary node of t has the constant $(\bot \dots \bot)$ as its left son. For example, the tree of Figure 2 is not a comb but its right subtree is. For a comb $t \in T(\Gamma^{(n)})$ and $1 \leq i \leq n$, the *i-th word coded by* t is the word $t \downarrow_i \in \Gamma^*$ defined by

$$t \downarrow_i = \begin{cases} \epsilon & \text{if } t^i = \bot \\ c \cdot t \,|_2 \!\downarrow_i & \text{if } t^i = c(\bot, t\,|_2) \end{cases}$$

For instance, if t is the right subtree of the tree depicted in Figure 2 then $t \downarrow_1 = aabb$ and $t \downarrow_3 = fa$.

We define the signature of our automaton as $\{f, a, b\}^{(4)}$. The automaton L_P is constructed in three steps:

The first step is to construct an automaton that accepts a comb if it encodes two pairs of words such that the second pair is obtained from the first pair by application of one step of the PCP instance P. For reasons that will be apparent in the last step this automaton comes in a positive and in a negative version that differ in the choice of the components that code the two pairs. More exactly:

For any word $v \in \Gamma^*$, let $A_v^{i,j}$ for $i \neq j$ be the automaton that accepts t iff t is a comb, $t \downarrow_i = fw$ and $t \downarrow_j = wv$ for some $w \in \Gamma^*$. If $v = v_1 \cdots v_n$ then the rules of the automaton are (here for $i = 1$ and $j = 2$), where _ stands for any symbol from $\{a, b, f, \bot\}$ and α, β for any symbol from $\{a, b\}$:

$$\begin{aligned}
(\bot\bot\bot\bot) &\to q_l \\
(\bot\bot\bot\bot) &\to q_n \\
(\bot\bot__)(q_l, q_n) &\to q_n \\
(\bot v_i__)(q_l, q_i) &\to q_{i-1} \quad i = 2, \dots, n \\
(f v_1__)(q_l, q_1) &\to q_0 \\
(\alpha v_1__)(q_l, q_1) &\to q_\alpha \\
(\alpha\beta__)(q_l, q_\beta) &\to q_\alpha \\
(f\beta__)(q_l, q_\beta) &\to q_0
\end{aligned}$$

The only accepting state is q_0.

From the boolean closure of (classical) tree automata we get an automaton A_P^+ that accepts t iff t is a comb and for some i we have that $t \downarrow_1 = fw_1$, $t \downarrow_2 = fw_2$, $t \downarrow_3 = w_1 p_i$ and $t \downarrow_4 = w_2 q_i$. Analogously, the automaton A_P^- accepts t iff t is a comb and for some i we have that $t \downarrow_1 = w_1 p_i$, $t \downarrow_2 = w_2 q_i$, $t \downarrow_3 = fw_1$ and $t \downarrow_4 = fw_2$. Let Q^+ resp. Q^- be the accepting states of these two automata. In case of the tree t of Figure 2, for example, A_P^+ accepts $t\,|_{12}$ and A_P^- accepts $t\,|_2$.

The second step is to construct automata that in addition test whether the newly constructed pair is of the form (w, w) for some non-empty word w. We can easily derive from A^+_P this automaton AE^+_P (with set of accepting states $Q^+_=$) that emulates A^+_P and verifies in addition that $t\downarrow_3 = t\downarrow_4 \neq \epsilon$, and analogously AE^-_P (with set of accepting states $Q^-_=$) that emulates A^-_P and verifies in addition that $t\downarrow_1 = t\downarrow_2 \neq \epsilon$. In case of the tree t of Figure 2, AE^-_P accepts $t|_2$.

Note that the first two steps used only classical tree automata. The third step is now to build the final automaton which uses these four automata as sub-automata (we hence assume their states-spaces to be disjoint) to accept a solution sequence of P. This is where equality tests come in.

$$\begin{array}{lll}
(\bot\bot\bot\bot) & \rightarrow & p_\bot \\
(ffff)(p_\bot, p_\bot) & \rightarrow & p^+ \\
(ffff)(p^+, q^+) & \rightarrow^{1.1=2.1\wedge 1.2=2.2} & p^- \quad q^+ \in Q^+ \\
(ffff)(p^-, q^-) & \rightarrow^{1.3=2.3\wedge 1.4=2.4} & p^+ \quad q^- \in Q^- \\
(ffff)(p^+, q^+) & \rightarrow^{1.1=2.1\wedge 1.2=2.2} & p_f \quad q^+ \in Q^+_= \\
(ffff)(p^-, q^-) & \rightarrow^{1.3=2.3\wedge 1.4=2.4} & p_f \quad q^- \in Q^-_=
\end{array}$$

where p_f is the only accepting state. An example of the representation of the solution of an instance of PCP as accepted by this automaton is given in Figure 2. In this example, the accepting run assigns the occurrence 11 the state p^+, the ocurrence 1 the state p^- and the occurrence ϵ the accepting state p_f. □

The undecidability result holds even in case of signatures with only two components. For a proof, it suffices to encode in the above proof the first and second, respectively third and forth component of the signature into one symbol.

5 The Logic *WS2Sy*

The logic *WS2Sy* is a two-sorted logic with the sorts w (for *word*) and s (for *set*). We will write variables of sort w in lower case and variables of sort s in upper case. Function symbols are a constant ϵ of sort w and two monadic function symbols 1 and 2 of profile $\mathtt{w} \rightarrow \mathtt{w}$. We write applications of these function symbols in postfix notation, that is $x1121$ for $1(2(1(1(x))))$. Relation symbols are $\in$ of profile $\mathtt{w} \times \mathtt{s}$, and for every $n \geq 1$ a $n+1$-ary predicate Sy of profile $\mathtt{w} \times \mathtt{s} \times \ldots \times \mathtt{s}$.

The standard interpretation of *WS2Sy* assigns the sort w as universe the set $\{1,2\}^*$ and the sort s as universe the set of all finite subsets of $\{1,2\}^*$. The constant ϵ is interpreted as the empty word, and the function 1 (resp. 2) as the function that appends 1 (resp. 2) to a word. The predicate symbol $\in$ denotes set membership. The synchronisation predicate $Sy(w, M_1, \ldots, M_n)$ holds if for all $1 \leq i \leq n$ and all $x \in \{1,2\}^*$ we have that $w1x \in M_i$ iff $w2x \in M_i$.

The notion of a *free occurrence* of a variable in a formula is defined as usual. A *WS2Sy*-formula ϕ is called *restricted* if whenever ϕ contains a subformula of the form $Sy(x, X_1, \ldots, X_n)$ then $X_1, \ldots, X_n$ are free variable occurrences (here,

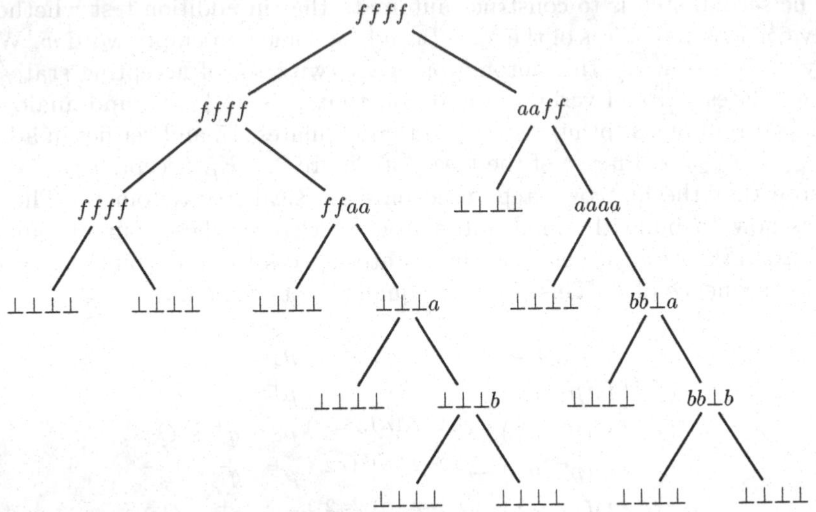

Fig. 2. Example of the representation of the solution $((\epsilon,\epsilon),(a,aab),(aabb,aabb))$ of the PCP instance $((a,aab),(abb,b))$.

there is no restriction on x being free or bound). A *WS2Sy*-formula ϕ is called *uniform* if whenever ϕ contains a subformula of the form $Sy(x, X_1, \ldots, X_n)$ then $X_1, \ldots, X_n$ are exactly the free variable occurrences of ϕ (hence, x is bound). As a consequence, every uniform formula of *WS2Sy* is restricted, and the classical logic *WS2S* is obtained from *WS2Sy* by omiting the synchronisation predicates.

The logic *WS2Sy* allows to define the usual set-theoretic notions as union, intersection, singleton sets, etc. that we will use freely in the sequel. Furthermore, the prefix relation on words (denoted $x \leq y$) is expressible in *WS2S* as has been demonstrated in Section 1, hence in *WS2Sy*.

Following the classical translation of the logic *WS2S* into tree automata, we define the one-sorted version $WS2Sy_0$ of *WS2Sy* where only set-variables and predicates on sets are used. The predicates of $WS2Sy_0$ are $X_1 = X_2 1$, $X_1 = X_2 2$, $X_1 = \epsilon$, $X_1 \subseteq X_2$, and $Sy(X_0, X_1, \ldots, X_n)$. In the standard interpretation of $WS2Sy_0$ we have that $M_1 = M_2 1$ is true iff M_2 is some singleton set $\{m_2\}$ and $M_1 = \{m_2 1\}$ and analogous for $M_1 = M_2 2$; $M_1 = \epsilon$ is true iff $M_1 = \{\epsilon\}$; $\subseteq$ is set inclusion; and $Sy(M_0, M_1, \ldots, M_n)$ is true in $WS2Sy_0$ iff M_0 is some singleton set $\{m_0\}$ and $Sy(m_0, M_1, \ldots, M_n)$ is true in *WS2Sy*. We can now translate in a straightforward way any formula $\Phi(x_1, \ldots, x_n, Y_1, \ldots, Y_m)$ of *WS2Sy* into a formula $\Phi_0(X_1, \ldots, X_n, Y_1, \ldots, Y_m)$ of $WS2Sy_0$ such that

$$w_1, \ldots, w_n, M_1, \ldots, M_m \models \Phi \text{ iff } \{w_1\}, \ldots, \{w_n\}, M_1, \ldots, M_m \models \Phi_0$$

and any formula $\Phi(X_1, \ldots, X_n, Y_1, \ldots, Y_m)$ of $WS2Sy_0$ (for an appropriate enumeration of the variables) into a formula $\Phi_1(x_1, \ldots, x_n, Y_1, \ldots, Y_m)$ of *WS2Sy* such that

$$M_1, \ldots, M_n, N_1, \ldots, N_m \models \Phi \text{ iff exists } m_i \text{ such that } M_i = \{m_i\} \text{ for all } i \text{ and } m_1, \ldots, m_n, N_1, \ldots, N_m \models \Phi_1$$

We say that a set S of n-tuples of sets of words over $\{1,2\}$ is definable in *WS2Sy* (resp. restricted *WS2Sy* or uniform *WS2Sy*) if there is *WS2Sy*-formula (resp. restricted *WS2Sy*-formula or uniform *WS2Sy*-formula) $\Phi(X_1, \ldots, X_n)$ such that

$$(M_1, \ldots, M_n) \in S \text{ iff } M_1, \ldots, M_n \models \Phi$$

According to the translation between *WS2Sy* and $WS2Sy_0$ that we have mentioned above it does not matter whether we take *WS2Sy* or $WS2Sy_0$ to define the notion of definability.

6 Recognizability and Definability

Before we can formulate the correspondence between definability in (subclasses of) *WS2Sy* and recognizability by (subclasses of) TACT we need translations of tuples of finite sets of words into trees, and vice versa.

Definition 7. *The* tree representation *of a finite set* $W \subset \{1,2\}^*$ *is the tree* $\overline{W} \in T(\{0,1\}^{(1)})$ *defined by*

$$\overline{W} = \begin{cases} \bot & \text{if } W = \emptyset \\ 0(\overline{1^{-1}W}, \overline{2^{-1}W}) & \text{if } W \neq \emptyset \text{ and } \epsilon \notin W \\ 1(\overline{1^{-1}W}, \overline{2^{-1}W}) & \text{if } W \neq \emptyset \text{ and } \epsilon \in W \end{cases}$$

where $1^{-1}W = \{w \mid 1w \in W\}$ *and* $2^{-1}W = \{w \mid 2w \in W\}$.

The tree representation $\overline{(W_1, \ldots, W_n)}$ *of an n-tuple* $(W_1, \ldots, W_n)$ *of finite subsets of* $\{1,2\}^*$ *is the tree* $t \in T(\{0,1\}^{(n)})$ *with* $t^{\langle i \rangle} = \overline{W_i}$ *for all i.*

The tree representation $\overline{S}$ *of a set of tuples of finite subsets of* $\{1,2\}^*$ *is* $\{\overline{(W_1, \ldots, W_n)} \mid (W_1, \ldots, W_n) \in S\}$.

Note that the tree representation of a tuple of sets is uniquely defined since $(\bot \ldots \bot)$ is a constant.

Example 2. The tree representation of the set $\{\epsilon, 2\}$ is the right tree of Figure 1.

The tree representation of the triple of sets $(\{\epsilon, 1\}, \{1\}, \{\epsilon, 2\})$ is the left tree of Figure 1.

Theorem 2. *Let S be a set of n-tuples of words.*

1. *If S is definable in restricted WS2Sy then $\overline{S}$ is TACT-recognizable.*
2. *If S is definable in uniform WS2Sy then $\overline{S}$ is TAT-recognizable.*
3. *If S is definable in WS2S then $\overline{S}$ is TA-recognizable ([10]).*

The proof of the first two items of this theorem is subject of Section 7, the last item is due to [10].

Definition 8. *The* tuple representation $\langle\langle t \rangle\rangle$ *of a tree* $t \in T(\Gamma^{(n)})$ *for finite* Γ, *say* $\Gamma = \{c_1, \ldots, c_m\}$, *is the* $n(m+1)$*-tuple of finite subsets of* $\{1,2\}^*$

$$(M_0^1, M_1^1, \ldots, M_m^1, \ldots, M_0^n, M_1^n, \ldots, M_m^n)$$

defined by

$$M_0^i = \{w \mid \textit{the i-th component of the root of } t\mid_w \textit{ is } \perp\}$$
$$M_j^i = \{w \mid \textit{the i-th component of the root of } t\mid_w \textit{ is } c_j\}$$

The tuple representation $\langle\langle S \rangle\rangle$ *of a set of trees in* $T(\Gamma^{(n)})$ *is* $\{\langle\langle t \rangle\rangle \mid t \in S\}$.

Example 3. The tuple representation of the middle tree of Figure 1 is

$$(\{11,12,2\}, \{\}, \{\epsilon,1\}, \{11,12,2\}, \{\epsilon\}, \{1\})$$

Theorem 3. *Let* $S \subseteq T(\Gamma^{(n)})$.

1. *If S is TACT-recognizable then $\langle\langle S \rangle\rangle$ is definable in restricted WS2Sy.*
2. *If S is TAT-recognizable then $\langle\langle S \rangle\rangle$ is definable in uniform WS2Sy.*
3. *If S is TA-recognizable then $\langle\langle S \rangle\rangle$ is definable in WS2S ([10]).*

The proof of the first two items of this theorem is subject of Section 8, the last item is due to [10].

7 Translating Formulae to Automata

In this section we prove Theorem 2 by translating a restricted *WS2Sy*$_0$-formula $\Phi(X_1, \ldots, X_n)$ into a TACT-automaton A_Φ over $\{0,1\}^{(n)}$ such that A_Φ is a TAT when Φ is uniform, and that A_Φ is a classical tree automaton when Φ is a *WS2S* formula.

The first step is to construct automata for the atomic formulae of *WS2Sy*$_0$. Automata for the atomic formulae $X_1 = X_2.0$, $X_1 = X_2.1$, $X_1 = \epsilon$ and $X_1 \subseteq X_2$ can be found in the literature (for instance [4]). It remains to give an automaton for the synchronization predicates:

The automaton A_n is defined as $(\{0,1\}, n, \{q_0, q_1\}, \{q_1\}, \Delta)$ where Δ contains the rules

$$\begin{array}{rcl}
(\bot \ldots \bot) & \rightarrow & q_0 \\
(\bot _ \ldots _)(q_0, q_0) & \rightarrow & q_0 \\
(0_ \ldots _)(q_0, q_0) & \rightarrow & q_0 \\
(1_ \ldots _)(q_0, q_0) & \rightarrow^{1.2=2.2 \wedge \ldots \wedge 1.n=2.n} & q_1 \\
(0_ \ldots _)(q_0, q_1) & \rightarrow & q_1 \\
(0_ \ldots _)(q_1, q_0) & \rightarrow & q_1
\end{array}$$

Proposition 2. *Let S^n be the set of all n-tuples of sets of words such that $S \models Sy(X_1, X_2, \ldots, X_n)$. The language recognized by A_n is $\overline{S_n}$.*

In the case of the equivalence between *WS2S* and classical tree automata the translation of an arbitrary formula is obtained once the closure of the class of recognizable sets by the boolean operation, cylindrification and projection is established. In case of *WS2Sy* and TACT we need, however, a more specific property of TACT-recognizable sets than just closure by certain operations: The closure must not affect the set of components on which the automaton performs tests. This invariant of the closure operations is needed because in the closure by projection of the i-th component we need as a hypothesis that the automaton does not test on the i-th component. An even stronger invariant will be needed to prove that uniform *WS2Sy* translates to TAT automata.

Proposition 3. *If L is recognizable by a TACT A that tests only on the set of components I then there exists a complete and deterministic TACT that tests only on I and that recognizes L.*

Proof: Completion is achieved by adding a sink state. The determinisation is the same as in [4]. Since all rules in the determined automaton have tests that are boolean combinations of tests in the original automaton the set of tested components is not touched by this operation. □

It should be remarked that the determinisation of a tree automaton with tests requires the set of constraints to be closed under negation (see [4]).

Proposition 4. *If L is recognized by a TACT A that tests only on the set of components I then there exists a TACT that tests only on I and that recognizes $T(\Gamma^{(n)}) - L$.*

If L_1, L_2 are recognized by TACTs A_1, A_2 that test only on the set of components I then there exists a TACT that tests only on I and that recognizes $L_1 \cup L_2$, resp. $L_1 \cap L_2$.

Proof: This is now straightforward (again, see [4]). We just remark that the closure of the language of constraints by conjunction is used in case of the intersection. □

Definition 9. *Let L be a set of $\Gamma^{(n)}$-trees. For $1 \leq i \leq n$ the i-th* projection *of L is*

$$\exists i : L = \{t^{\langle i \rangle} \mid t \in L\}$$

For $1 \leq i \leq n+1$, the $i+1$-th cylindrification *of L is*

$$\updownarrow i : L = \{t \in T(\Gamma^{(n+1)}) \mid t^{\langle i \rangle} \in L\}$$

Proposition 5. *If L is recognizable by a TACT A that tests only on the set of components I then there exists a TACT that recognizes $\updownarrow i : L$ and tests only on $\{j \mid j < i\} \cup \{j+1 \mid j > i\}$.*

Proof: Let L be recognized by the TACT $(\Gamma, n, Q, Q_f, \Delta)$. To ease notation we show the construction for the case $i = n+1$. It is straightforward to show that $\updownarrow n+1 : L$ is recognized by the TACT $(\Gamma, n+1, Q, Q_f, \Delta')$ where

$$\begin{aligned}\Delta' = &\{(\bot \cdots \bot\bot) \rightarrow q \mid (\bot \cdots \bot) \rightarrow q \in \Delta\}\\ \cup &\{(\bar{f}f)(q_1, q_2) \rightarrow^c q \mid \bar{f}(q_1, q_2) \rightarrow^c q \in \Delta, f \neq \bot, \bar{f} \neq \bar{\bot}\}\\ \cup &\{(\bar{\bot}f)(q_1, q_2) \rightarrow q \mid (\bot \cdots \bot) \rightarrow q \in \Delta, f \neq \bot\}\end{aligned}$$

□

Proposition 6. *Let $L \subseteq T(\Gamma^{(n)})$ be recognized by a TACT A that tests only on the set of components I and $i \notin I$. There exists a TACT that recognizes $\exists i : L$ and tests only on $\{j \mid j < i\} \cup \{j-1 \mid j > i\}$.*

Proof: Let L be recognized by the TACT $A = (\Gamma, n+1, Q, Q_f, \Delta)$. To ease notation we show the construction for the case $i = n+1$.

We can assume w.l.o.g that A is reduced, that is that there is for every $q \in Q$ a term $t \in T(\Gamma^{(n)})$ such that $t \rightarrow_A^* q$ (this can simply be obtained by dropping all states that recognize the empty set). We construct an automaton for $\exists n : L$ as $A = (\Gamma, n, Q, Q_f, \Delta')$ where

$$\begin{aligned}\Delta' = &\{(\bot \cdots \bot) \rightarrow q \mid (\bot \cdots \bot\bot) \rightarrow q \in \Delta\}\\ \cup &\{(\bot \cdots \bot) \rightarrow q \mid (\bot \cdots \bot f)(q_1, q_2) \rightarrow q \in \Delta, f \neq \bot\}\\ \cup &\{\bar{f}(q_1, q_2) \rightarrow^c q \mid \bar{f}f(q_1, q_2) \rightarrow^c q, \bar{f} \neq \bar{\bot}\}\end{aligned}$$

The proof that A' accepts $\exists n+1 : L$ is exactly as in the case of classical tree automata (see, e.g., [4]). The restriction that the automaton A does not use a test on the $n+1$-th component ensures that the constraints pose no problem here. □

Proof of Theorem 2: Let a restricted formula Φ be given. We can assume without loss of generality that every bound variable of Φ has exactly one binding quantifier and that no variable of Φ has both bound and free occurrences in Φ. We construct inductively an automaton for all subformulae of Φ.

We get an automaton for atomic formulae as in the case of classic tree automata, resp. by Proposition 2. Then we cylindrify to have components according to all free and bound variables of Φ. This yields, by Proposition 5, an automaton which does not test on components corresponding to bound variables. In case of composite formulae we conclude by Propositions 4 and 6.

If the formula Φ is uniform then the automata corresponding to the atomic formulae have (after cylindrification) only tests `True`, $1.1 = 2.1 \wedge \ldots \wedge 1.n = 2.n$ and $1.1 \neq 2.1 \vee \ldots \vee 1.n \neq 2.n$, where we assume for simplicity that the components corresponding to the global variables are $1, \ldots, n$. Since all closure operations on automata construct tests that are boolean combinations of tests of the input automata, the final automaton too has only tests of this form. Since the final automaton works on the components $1, \ldots, n$ it is indeed a TAT. □

8 Translating Automata to Formulae

In this section we prove Theorem 3 by translating a TACT-automaton $A = (\Gamma, n, Q, Q_f, \Delta)$, where Γ has cardinality m, into a formula Φ with $n(m+1)$ free variables.

Let $\Gamma = \{c_1, \ldots, c_m\}$, we will use in addition the convention $c_0 = \bot$. Let $Q = \{q_1, \ldots, q_q\}$. We can assume w.l.o.g. that all constraints of the productions of A are conjunctions of equations and inequations since a boolean combination of constraints can be brought into an equivalent disjunctive normal form and a rule $f(q_1, q_2) \rightarrow^{c_1 \vee c_2} q$ can be split into two rules $f(q_1, q_2) \rightarrow^{c_1} q$ and $f(q_1, q_2) \rightarrow^{c_2} q$.

First we define some auxiliary formulas: The formula *partition*$(Y, Y_1, \ldots, Y_k)$ states that $(Y_1, \ldots, Y_k)$ is a partition of Y:

$$\mathit{partition}(Y, Y_1, \ldots, Y_k) = Y = Y_1 \cup \ldots \cup Y_k \wedge \bigwedge_{i \neq j} Y_i \cap Y_j = \emptyset$$

The formula *term*$(X, X_1, \ldots, X_{n(m+1)})$ states that, for some tree $t \in T(\Gamma^{(n)})$, X is the set of occurrence of t and $(X_1, \ldots, X_{n(m+1)}) = \langle\langle t \rangle\rangle$:

$$\begin{aligned} \mathit{term}(X, X_1, \ldots, X_{n(m+1)}) = & \bigwedge_{i=0 \ldots n-1} \mathit{partition}(X, X_{i(m+1)+1}, \ldots, X_{i(m+1)+m+1}) \\ & \wedge \forall x, y (x \leq y \wedge y \in X \rightarrow x \in X) \\ & \wedge \forall x (x \in X_0^1 \cap \ldots \cap X_0^n \rightarrow (x0 \notin X \wedge x1 \notin X)) \\ & \wedge \forall x (x \notin X_0^1 \cap \ldots \cap X_0^n \rightarrow (x0 \in X \wedge x1 \in X)) \end{aligned}$$

The first clause of the formula *term* says that each component of every occurrence is marked with exactly one symbol and that X is the set of occurrences, the second clause says that the set of occurrences is prefix-closed, the third clause says that any occurrence marked $(\bot \ldots \bot)$ is a leaf and the forth clause that every occurrence not marked with $(\bot \ldots \bot)$ has two subtrees. Finally, the formula is

$$\begin{aligned}
\phi_A(X_0^1, X_1^1, \ldots, X_m^1, \ldots, X_0^n, X_1^n, \ldots, X_m^n) &= \exists X, Y_1, \ldots, Y_k \Big(\\
& term(X, X_0^1, \ldots, X_m^n) \\
& \wedge\ partition(X, Y_1, \ldots, Y_q) \\
& \wedge \bigvee_{q_i \in Q_f} \epsilon \in Y_i \\
& \wedge \forall x (x \in X_0^1 \cap \ldots \cap X_0^n \to \bigvee_{(\bot \cdots \bot \to q_i \in \Delta)} x \in Y_i) \\
& \wedge \bigwedge_{(i_1 \ldots i_n) \neq (0 \ldots 0)} \forall x (x \in X_{i_1} \cap \ldots \cap X_{i_n} \to \bigvee_{(i_1 \ldots i_n)(q_j, q_k) \to^c q_l \in \Delta} (\\
& \quad x \in Y_l \wedge x1 \in Y_j \wedge x2 \in Y_k \\
& \quad \wedge \bigwedge_{1.i = 2.i \in c} Sy(x, X_0^i, \ldots, X_m^i) \wedge \bigwedge_{1.i \neq 2.i \in c} \neg Sy(x, X_0^i, \ldots, X_m^i))) \Big)
\end{aligned}$$

In this formula, the first conjunct says that the free variables are the encoding of a $\Gamma^{(n)}$-tree with set of occurrences X. The second conjunct says that every occurrence of the tree is assigned a state. The third conjunct expresses that the root of the tree is assigned an accepting state, and the last two conjuncts express that the assignment is according to the transitions rules of the automaton: The forth conjunct covers the case of the constant $(\bot \ldots \bot)$ and the complex last conjunct the case of a binary function symbol.

Note that the formula ϕ_A is restricted. If the automaton is in fact a TAT automaton then the formula ϕ_A is equivalent to a uniform *WS2Sy*-formula since

$$Sy(x, X_0^i, \ldots, X_m^i) \wedge Sy(x, X_0^j, \ldots, X_m^j)$$

is equivalent to the formula

$$Sy(x, X_0^i, \ldots, X_m^i, X_0^j, \ldots, X_m^j)$$

Finally, if the automaton A is a classical tree automaton then ϕ_A contains no synchronization predicate and is hence a *WS2S*-formula.

9 Other Classes of Automata with Tests

So far we have only considered the class of automata with tests between brothers introduced in [1]. We can easily extend the results of this paper to classes of automata with "deep" tests that can perform tests like $11.i = 222.i$, where a tree t satisfies this test if $(t\ |_{11})^{\langle i \rangle} = (t\ |_{222})^{\langle i \rangle}$ [5]. This generalization is easily achieved by defining a generalization of *WS2Sy* with stronger synchronization predicates. These classes of automata are, however, of limited interest since already the class of automata with tests between cousin positions (that is $p.i = q.i$ where p and q have length 2) has an undecidable emptiness problem [9].

There is a very interesting class of tree automata with tests that has a decidable emptiness problem: the class of *reduction automata* [3] and *generalized reduction automata* [2]. These automata allow "deep" (in the above sense) tests but come with a syntactic restriction that ensures that on every branch of a tree only a bounded number of equality tests can be performed. Hence, the undecidability proof of this paper does not directly apply to a generalization of these automata to component-wise tests since we used the fact that we can perform an unbounded number of equality tests on the left spine of the tree (see Section 4). Hence, it is still possible that the results known for (generalized) reduction automata can be lifted to component-wise tests, and that a corresponding logic with a restriction on the set of admissible formulae can be found.

References

1. B. Bogaert and S. Tison. Equality and disequality constraints on brother terms in tree automata. In P. Enjalbert, A. Finkel, and K. W. Wagner, editors, *9th Annual Symposium on Theoretical Aspects of Computer Science*, volume 577 of *Lecture Notes in Computer Science*, pages 161–171, Paris, France, 1992. Springer-Verlag.
2. A.-C. Caron, H. Comon, J.-L. Coquidé, M. Dauchet, and F. Jacquemard. Pumping, cleaning and symbolic constraints solving. In *Proc. Int. Conference on Algorithms, Languages and Programming*, pages 436–449, 1994.
3. A.-C. Caron, J.-L. Coquidé, and M. Dauchet. Encompassment properties and automata with constraints. In C. Kirchner, editor, *5th International Conference on Rewriting Techniques and Applications*, volume 690 of *Lecture Notes in Computer Science*, pages 328–342, Montreal, Canada, June 1993. Springer-Verlag.
4. H. Comon, M. Dauchet, R. Gilleron, F. Jacquemard, D. Lugiez, S. Tison, and M. Tommasi. Tree automata. Techniques and Applications, Apr. 1999. Available at `http://www.grappa.univ-lille3.fr/tata/`.
5. J. Mongy. *Transformations de noyaux reconnaissables d'arbres. Forêts RATEG.* PhD thesis, Laboratoire d'Informatique Fondamentale de Lille, Université Lille 1, Villeneuve d'Asq, France, 1981. In French.
6. E. L. Post. A variant of a recursively unsolvable problem. *Bulletin of the AMS*, 52:264–268, 1946.
7. M. Rabin. Decidability of second-order theories and automata on infinite trees. *Trans. Amer. Math. Soc.*, 141:1–35, 1969.
8. F. Seynhaeve. *Automates, Réécriture et Contraintes : Résultats de Décidabilité et d'Indécidabilité.* PhD thesis, Université de Lille 1, Villeneuve d'Ascq, France, May 1999. In French.
9. F. Seynhaeve, M. Tommasi, and R. Treinen. Grid structures and undecidable constraint theories. In M. Bidoit and M. Dauchet, editors, *Theory and Practice of Software Development*, volume 1214 of *Lecture Notes in Computer Science*, pages 357–368, Lille, France, Apr. 1997. Springer-Verlag. Extended version to appear in *Theoretical Computer Science.*
10. J. Thatcher and J. Wright. Generalized finite automata with an application to a decision problem of second-order logic. *Math. Systems Theory*, 2:57–82, 1968.

Compositional Verification in Linear-Time Temporal Logic*
Extended Abstract

Yih-Kuen Tsay

Department of Information Management, National Taiwan University
tsay@im.ntu.edu.tw

Abstract. In the compositional verification of a concurrent system, one seeks to deduce properties of the system from properties of its constituent modules. This paper supplements our previous work on the same subject to provide a comprehensive compositional framework in linear-time temporal logic. It has been shown by many that specifying properties of a module in the assumption-guarantee style is effective in achieving compositionality. We consider two forms of temporal formulas that correspond to two interpretations of an assumption-guarantee specification and investigate how they can be applied in compositional verification. We argue by examples that the two forms complement each other and both are needed to facilitate the compositional approach. We also show how to handle assumption-guarantee specifications where the assumption contains a liveness property.

1 Introduction

A concurrent system typically is or can be decomposed as the parallel composition of several modules. In the compositional verification of a system, one seeks to deduce properties of the system from properties of its constituent modules. We assume that the system to be verified is closed, i.e., the system is meant to be executed in isolation (without any interferences, except perhaps part of the initialization, from the environment). Nonetheless, we provide sufficient details showing how the results of this paper can be extended straightforwardly to the compositional verification of an open system, which is essentially a module.

Properties of a system are represented by assertions on computations of the system and so are properties of a module. Computations of a system are the sequences of states produced when the system is executed in isolation. In contrast, computations of a module are the sequences of states produced when the module is executed in parallel with an arbitrary but (syntactically) compatible environment, i.e., the computations of an imaginary system obtained from composing the module with the arbitrary environment. A system or module

* This research was supported in part by grants NSC 86-2213-E-002-002 and NSC 87-2213-E-002-015 from the National Science Council, Taiwan (R.O.C.) and a research award from College of Management, National Taiwan University.

J. Tiuryn (Ed.): FOSSACS 2000, LNCS 1784, pp. 344–358, 2000.

satisfies a certain property if the corresponding assertion holds for each of its computations.

A module will behave properly only if its environment does. When specifying properties of a module, one should therefore include (1) assumed properties about its environment and (2) guaranteed properties of the module if the environment obeys the assumption. This type of specification is essentially a generalization of pre and post-conditions for sequential programs [14]. The generalization was adopted in the early 1980's by Misra and Chandy [23], Jones [15], and Lamport [19] and became the so-called *assumption-guarantee* (also known as rely-guarantee or assumption-commitment) paradigm.

Consider an assumption-guarantee specification with assumption A and guarantee G. There are at least two possible interpretations of the specification over a sequence of states. Informally, one interpretation states that G holds at least one step longer than A does. The other states that G holds as long as A does, which is a weaker interpretation than the first. A third even weaker interpretation is the ordinary implication from A to G; however, it is practically equivalent to the second interpretation, as a module should not have the ability to predict the future behavior of its environment and hence the future violation of A by its environment. We refer to properties according to the first interpretation as *strong* assumption-guarantee properties and those according to the second as *weak* assumption-guarantee properties. As has been pointed out by Abadi and Lamport [2], if A and G cannot be falsified simultaneously by any step of the module or its environment, then the two interpretations are equivalent.

In this paper, we intend to further advance the use of temporal logic in specifying and reasoning about assumption-guarantee properties and investigate how this kind of properties can be applied in compositional verification. Temporal logic is one convenient formalism for specifying the behavior of a concurrent system. The idea of representing concurrent systems and their specifications as formulas in temporal logic was first proposed by Pnueli [24].

We have proposed in [16] to formulate assumption-guarantee specifications using the linear-time temporal logic (LTL) of Manna and Pnueli [21]. We showed how to specify and reason about strong assumption-guarantee properties in the full set of LTL. Our formulation of assumption-guarantee specifications as well as the derived composition rules are syntactic and entirely within LTL. *This paper complements and differs from our previous work in three aspects: First, we consider both strong and weak (not just strong) assumption-guarantee properties in this paper. Second, we emphasize the use of assumption-guarantee specifications in compositional verification rather than hierarchical development. Last, we extend the previous work to include composition rules that permit assumptions with liveness properties.* Hiding (of local variables) is not treated here for a more focused exposition; it can be handled syntactically in the same way as in our previous work. Together this paper and the previous work provide a comprehensive compositional framework in LTL.

Related works on assumption-guarantee specifications, including [23, 15, 19, 12, 1, 3, 2, 9, 10, 27], typically reason about relevant properties at the semantic level or define a special-purpose logic. In [1], Abadi and Lamport gave a comprehensive treatment of compositionality in a general semantic setting with agents (which are used essentially for identifying a module). Their semantic composition rule used the notion of the "realizable part" of a specification which in general cannot be extracted by simpler operations on the specification. Xu, Cau, and Collette [27] provided an explanation of the difference between two well-known composition rules respectively for message-passing and shared-variable models. They show that the two rules can be derived from a more general one. In [4], Alur and Henzinger suggested the notion of local liveness in place of the weaker notion of receptiveness involved in the compositionality issue. They argue that receptiveness is unnecessarily weak and computationally hard to check, while local liveness on the other hand is satisfied by most existing models and is easier to check. A collection of survey papers on the general subject of compositional verification has recently been published as [11].

Barringer and Kuiper [6] are, to our knowledge, the first to formulate assumption-guarantee specifications in temporal logic. They used the notion of an agent and considered only strong assumption-guarantee properties. Manna and Pnueli proposed a compositional verification rule using weak assumption-guarantee properties in their recent book [22]. Using the Temporal Logic of Actions (TLA, a variant of temporal logic) [20], the work of Abadi and Lamport [2] is an improvement over earlier temporal logic-based works in handling hiding and liveness properties. They focused on assumption-guarantee specifications where the assumption and the guarantee cannot be falsified simultaneously. With a limited set of temporal operators in TLA, they had to work mostly at the semantic level. Abadi and Lamport's formulation of an assumption-guarantee specification allows liveness properties in the assumption part. However, their composition rule only works for safety assumptions. Collette [10], adapting the work of [2], proposed a UNITY-like [7] logic for assumption-guarantee specifications with restricted forms of assumption and guarantee.

Assumption-guarantee specifications have also found applications in the area of model checking [8]. They are useful for compositional (or modular) model checking, which provides one possible way to tackle the state-explosion problem. Virtually all existing works on modular model checking are for branching-time temporal logic or a combination of linear-time and branching-time logics. Grumberg and Long [13] considered a subset of CTL (Computation Tree Logic, a branching-time temporal logic) for which satisfaction is preserved under parallel composition. In their work, the assumption of the specification of a module is represented by another abstract module; the composition of the two modules is then checked against the desired property. In [5], Aziz et. al. proposed to reduce the size of each module of a system via an equivalence so that the given specification is preserved. Their method handles full CTL. The complexity of modular model checking of CTL formulas has been shown to be at least as high as that of (propositional) LTL formulas by Kupferman and Vardi [26, 17, 18].

2 Preliminaries

2.1 Temporal Logic

Linear-time temporal logic (LTL) is a logic for expressing assertions on infinite sequences of states, where each state is an assignment to a predefined universe of variables. An LTL formula is interpreted with respect to a position $i \geq 0$ in a sequence of states. *State formulas* are the basic type of LTL formula built only from variables, constants, functions, and predicates using the usual first-order logic connectives. The interpretation of a state formula in position i is performed as usual using the particular interpretation of variables in state i (plus the fixed interpretations of constants, functions, and predicates). General LTL formulas also contain temporal operators; in this paper, we will use only the following:

- $\bigcirc$ means "in the next state". The formula $\bigcirc\varphi$ is true in position i of a sequence σ (denoted $(\sigma, i) \models \bigcirc\varphi$) iff φ is true in position $i+1$ of σ (i.e., $(\sigma, i+1) \models \varphi$).
- $\Box$ means "always in the future (including the present)"; $(\sigma, i) \models \Box\varphi$ iff $\forall k \geq i : (\sigma, k) \models \varphi$.
- $\circleddash$ means "in the previous state, if there is any"; $(\sigma, i) \models \circleddash\varphi$ iff $(i > 0) \rightarrow ((\sigma, i-1) \models \varphi)$. $\circleddash$ is a weaker version of $\ominus$, which means "in the previous state"; $(\sigma, i) \models \ominus\varphi$ iff $(i > 0) \wedge ((\sigma, i-1) \models \varphi)$. It follows that $(\sigma, i) \models \circleddash\varphi$ iff $(\sigma, i) \models \neg\ominus\neg\varphi$.
- $\boxminus$ means "always in the past (including the present)"; $(\sigma, i) \models \boxminus\varphi$ iff $\forall k : 0 \leq k \leq i : (\sigma, k) \models \varphi$.
- For a variable u, the interpretation of u^- (the previous value of u) in position i is the same as the interpretation of variable u in position $i-1$; by convention, the interpretation of u^- in position 0 is the same as the interpretation of u in position 0.[1]
- *first* is an abbreviation for $\circleddash$*false*, which is true only in position 0.

We say that a sequence σ satisfies a formula φ (or φ holds for σ) if $(\sigma, 0) \models \varphi$. A formula φ is *valid*, denoted $\models \varphi$ or simply φ when it is clear that validity is intended, if φ is satisfied by every sequence.

A formula without temporal operators but possibly with "$^-$"-superscribed variables is called a *transition formula*; this definition is slightly different from that in [21], where a transition formula always contains $\neg$*first* as a conjunct. A formula without any future operator $\bigcirc$, $\Box$, or $\Diamond$ (though liveness is considered, $\Diamond$ is not explicitly used in this paper) is called a *past formula*; in particular, a transition formula is a past formula. A *safety formula* is one that specifies a safety property and a *liveness formula* is one that specifies a liveness property. Of

[1] In contrast to Lamport and others who use "$^+$"-superscribed (or primed) variables to denote their values in the next state, we use "$^-$"-superscribed variables to denote their values in the previous state. The reason is that (for conformity) we wish to use only past operators, except the outmost $\Box$, in the safety part of a specification. The introduction of "$^-$"-superscribed variables is convenient but not essential, since they can be encoded by the $\circleddash$ operator.

$$\textbf{local } a, b : \textbf{integer where } a = b = 0$$

$$P_a :: \begin{bmatrix} \textbf{loop forever do} \\ [a := b+1] \end{bmatrix} \parallel P_b :: \begin{bmatrix} \textbf{loop forever do} \\ [b := a+1] \end{bmatrix}$$

Fig. 1. Program KEEP-AHEAD.

particular importance, formulas of the form $\Box H$, where H is a past formula, are for certain safety formulas; they will be referred to as *canonical safety formulas*. Specific forms of liveness formulas are not important for our purposes. Formulas of the form $\Box H \wedge L$, where H is a past formula and L a liveness formula, will be referred to as *canonical formulas*.

2.2 Specifying Concurrent Systems

A concurrent system consists of a set of variables, an initial condition on the variables, and a set of transitions that specify how the system may change the values of its variables in an execution step. Semantically, a concurrent system is associated with a set of computations or sequences of states, each of which represents a possible execution of the system. We will mostly concentrate on safety properties of a system. For our purpose, we distinguish two kinds of specification: system specification and requirement specification.

System specifications are basically programs in the form of a temporal formula. Consider Program KEEP-AHEAD in Figure 1. The system specification of KEEP-AHEAD is given by $\Phi_{\text{KEEP-AHEAD}}$ as defined below.

$$\Phi_{\text{KEEP-AHEAD}} \triangleq (a = 0) \wedge (b = 0) \wedge \Box \begin{pmatrix} (a = b^- + 1) \wedge (b = b^-) \\ \vee\ (b = a^- + 1) \wedge (a = a^-) \\ \vee\ (a = a^-) \wedge (b = b^-) \end{pmatrix}$$

The formula $\Phi_{\text{KEEP-AHEAD}}$ states that the values of a and b are initially 0. It also states via the disjunction of three transition formulas that, in each step of an execution, either the value of a becomes $b + 1$ (while the value of b is unchanged), the value of b becomes $a + 1$, or nothing is changed. The transition formula $(a = a^-) \wedge (b = b^-)$ is called a stuttering transition and is included to make the specification invariant under stuttering.

We regard system specifications as formal definitions of concurrent systems so that we can do without a formal semantics of the programming language; programs are informal notations for readability. To take fairness into account, one may conjoin an appropriate liveness formula to the system specification. The safety formula in a system specification can be put in the canonical form of $\Box H$, specifically in the form of $\Box((\mathit{first} \wedge \mathit{Init}) \vee (\neg \mathit{first} \wedge N))$, where *Init* is a state formula and N the disjunction of several transition formulas. As N will

```
module Ma
in       b   : integer
own out a    : integer where a = 0

       loop forever do
       [a := b + 1]
```

∥

```
module Mb
in       a   : integer
own out b    : integer where b = 0

       loop forever do
       [b := a + 1]
```

Fig. 2. Program KEEP-AHEAD as the parallel composition of two modules.

always contain a stuttering transition, $\Box((\mathit{first} \wedge \mathit{Init}) \vee (\neg \mathit{first} \wedge N))$ simplifies to $\Box((\mathit{first} \wedge \mathit{Init}) \vee N)$.

Requirement specification is the usual type of temporal-logic specification. A property is represented by a temporal formula. A system (program) S is said to satisfy a formula φ if every computation of S satisfies φ. Let Φ_S denote the system specification of S. We will regard $\Phi_S \to \varphi$ as the formal definition of the fact that S satisfies φ, denoted as $S \models \varphi$. The safety formula in a requirement specification can usually be put in the canonical form.

2.3 Parallel Composition as Conjunction

Program KEEP-AHEAD can be decomposed as the parallel composition of two modules as shown in Figure 2. A module may read but not change the value of an **in** (input) variable. A *compatible* environment of a module may read but not change the value of an **own out** (owned output) variable of the module. In the system $M_a \parallel M_b$, M_b is the environment of M_a and M_a is the environment of M_b; both are clearly compatible with each other.

The system specifications Φ_{M_a} and Φ_{M_b} of modules M_a and M_b respectively are defined as follows:

$$\Phi_{M_a} \triangleq (a=0) \wedge \Box \begin{pmatrix} (a = b^- + 1) \wedge (b = b^-) \\ \vee\, (a = a^-) \end{pmatrix}$$

$$\Phi_{M_b} \triangleq (b=0) \wedge \Box \begin{pmatrix} (b = a^- + 1) \wedge (a = a^-) \\ \vee\, (b = b^-) \end{pmatrix}$$

It is perhaps more accurate to say that Φ_{M_a} is the system specification of an imaginary system composed of M_a and an arbitrary but compatible environment; analogously, for Φ_{M_b}. A little calculation shows that

$$\models \Phi_{M_a} \wedge \Phi_{M_b} \leftrightarrow \Phi_{\text{KEEP-AHEAD}}.$$

This formally confirms that $M_a \parallel M_b$ is equivalent to Program KEEP-AHEAD.

A module M is said to satisfy a formula φ if every computation of M satisfies φ. Let Φ_M denote the system specification of M. Like in the case of specifying properties of a concurrent system, we will regard $\Phi_M \rightarrow \varphi$ as the formal definition of the fact that M satisfies φ, denoted as $M \models \varphi$. Since parallel composition is conjunction, it follows that, if M is a module of system S, then $M \models \varphi$ implies $S \models \varphi$.

3 Assumption-Guarantee Specifications

We shall concentrate on assumption-guarantee specifications where both the assumption and the guarantee are safety properties; liveness will be treated in Section 6. We assume that safety properties are expressed as canonical safety formulas of the form $\Box H$, where H is a past formula.

3.1 Strong Assumption-Guarantee Formulas

Strong assumption-guarantee formulas specify strong assumption-guarantee properties. A strong assumption-guarantee property of a module with assumption A and guarantee G asserts the following:

> For every computation of the module, G holds initially and, for every $i > 1$, if A holds for the prefix of length $i - 1$ (i.e., with $i - 1$ states), then G also holds for the prefix of length i.

Notice that, if a safety property does not hold for a prefix of a computation, then the property will not hold for any longer prefix. The above assertion therefore says that G holds at least one step longer than A does.

As A and G are given respectively as $\Box H_A$ and $\Box H_G$, where H_A and H_G are past formulas, the strong assumption-guarantee property can be expressed as $\Box(\circleddash \boxminus H_A \rightarrow \boxminus H_G)$,[2] which is equivalent to $\Box(\circleddash \boxminus H_A \rightarrow H_G)$. Note that $\Box(\circleddash \boxminus H_A \rightarrow H_G)$ implies that H_G holds initially, since $\circleddash \boxminus H_A$ always holds in position 0 of a sequence. To summarize, we define strong assumption-guarantee formulas of the form $A \rhd G$ as follows:

$$A \rhd G \ (i.e., \Box H_A \rhd \Box H_G) \triangleq \Box(\circleddash \boxminus H_A \rightarrow H_G)$$

Note that $A \rhd G$ is also a canonical safety formula.

Theorem 1. *Suppose that H_{G_1} and H_{G_2} are past formulas. Then,*

$$\models (\Box H_{G_1} \rhd \Box H_{G_2}) \wedge (\Box H_{G_2} \rhd \Box H_{G_1}) \rightarrow \Box H_{G_1} \wedge \Box H_{G_2}.$$

The above theorem is essentially the composition principle formulated by Misra and Chandy [23]. This small result shows that strong assumption-guarantee formulas have a mutual induction mechanism built in and hence permit "circular

[2] Since H_A and H_G are past formulas, "$\Box H_A$ holds for the prefix of length $i - 1$ of σ" can be formally stated as "$(\sigma, i) \models \circleddash \boxminus H_A$" and "$\Box H_G$ holds for the prefix of length i of σ" as "$(\sigma, i) \models \boxminus H_G$".

reasoning" (there is of course no real cycle if one looks at the semantic models and reasons state by state from the initial one), i.e., deducing new properties from mutually dependent properties.

We now state a general rule for composing strong assumption-guarantee properties; this rule has been proven in [16].

Theorem 2. *Suppose that* $A_i \equiv \Box H_{A_i}$*,* $G_i \equiv \Box H_{G_i}$*,* $A \equiv \Box H_A$*, and* $G \equiv \Box H_G$*, all in the canonical form. Then,*

$$\frac{\begin{array}{l} 1. \models \Box\left(\boxminus H_A \wedge \boxminus \bigwedge_{i=1}^{n} H_{G_i} \rightarrow H_{A_j}\right) \textit{ for } 1 \le j \le n \\ 2. \models \Box\left(\ominus \boxminus H_A \wedge \boxminus \bigwedge_{i=1}^{n} H_{G_i} \rightarrow H_G\right) \end{array}}{\models \bigwedge_{i=1}^{n} (A_i \rhd G_i) \;\rightarrow\; (A \rhd G)}$$

Intuitively, Premise 1 of the above composition rule says that the assumption about the environment of a module should follow from the guarantees of other modules and the assumption about the environment of the entire (open) system, while Premise 2 says that the guarantee of the entire system should follow from the guarantees of individual modules and the assumption about its environment. For closed systems, we take A to be *true* and simplify the rule as follows:

Theorem 3. *Suppose that* $A_i \equiv \Box H_{A_i}$*,* $G_i \equiv \Box H_{G_i}$*, and* $G \equiv \Box H_G$*, all in the canonical form. Then,*

$$\frac{\begin{array}{l} 1. \models \Box\left(\boxminus \bigwedge_{i=1}^{n} H_{G_i} \rightarrow H_{A_j}\right) \textit{ for } 1 \le j \le n \\ 2. \models \Box\left(\boxminus \bigwedge_{i=1}^{n} H_{G_i} \rightarrow H_G\right) \end{array}}{\models \bigwedge_{i=1}^{n} (A_i \rhd G_i) \;\rightarrow\; G}$$

Theorem 1, stated earlier, follows immediately from this theorem.

3.2 Weak Assumption-Guarantee Formulas

Weak assumption-guarantee formulas specify weak assumption-guarantee properties. A weak assumption-guarantee property of a module with assumption A and guarantee G asserts the following:

> For every computation of the module, if A holds for some prefix of the computation, then G also holds for the same prefix.

Notice again that, if a safety property does not hold for a prefix of a computation, then the property will not hold for any longer prefix. The above assertion therefore says that G holds as long as A does.

With A and G given respectively as $\Box H_A$ and $\Box H_G$, the weak assumption-guarantee property can be expressed as $\Box(\boxminus H_A \rightarrow \boxminus H_G)$, which is equivalent to $\Box(\boxminus H_A \rightarrow H_G)$. Hence, we define weak assumption-guarantee formulas of the form $A \trianglerighteq G$ as follows:

$$A \trianglerighteq G \ (i.e., \Box H_A \trianglerighteq \Box H_G) \ \stackrel{\Delta}{=} \ \Box(\boxminus H_A \rightarrow H_G)$$

Weak assumption-guarantee formulas lack the kind of mutual induction mechanism built into strong assumption-guarantee formulas and cannot be readily composed.

A Quick Comparison between Strong and Weak Assumption-Guarantee Formulas: For a property $\Box H_A \triangleright \Box H_G$ to hold for the computations of a module M, no step of an environment compatible with M should be able to falsify both H_A and H_G. On the other hand, $\Box H_A \trianglerighteq \Box H_G$ does not have this constraint. This distinction is further elaborated in Section 7.

4 Compositional Verification

We present two compositional verification rules: one using strong assumption-guarantee formulas and the other using weak assumption-guarantee formulas.

Theorem 4 (Rule MOD-S). *Suppose that A_i, G_i, and G are canonical safety formulas. Then,*

$$\frac{\begin{array}{l} M_i \models A_i \triangleright G_i \ \mathit{for}\ 1 \leq i \leq n \\ \models \bigwedge_{i=1}^{n} (A_i \triangleright G_i) \rightarrow G \end{array}}{\mathop{\|}_{i=1}^{n} M_i \models G}$$

The first premise may be established by applying a verification rule for canonical safety formulas from [22, Chapter 4] (recall that $(A_i \triangleright G_i) \equiv \Box(\circleddash \boxminus H_{A_i} \rightarrow H_{G_i})$ is a canonical safety formula), while the second premise may be established by applying the composition rule from Theorem 3 or the simpler Theorem 1. If all the modules are finite, then both of the two premises may be established by a suitable model checker. Nonetheless, Theorem 3 may still be useful for reducing the complexity of checking validity.

Regarding compositional verification using weak assumption-guarantee formulas, Manna and Pnueli have proposed in [22, Page 337] a compositional verification rule where the property of a module is exactly in the form of a weak assumption-guarantee formula. Consider a system S that is equivalent to $\mathop{\|}_{i=1}^{n} M_i$. Translated into our notation, the compositional verification rule reads as follows.

Theorem 5 (Rule MOD-W). *Suppose that S is a system equivalent to $\mathop{\|}_{i=1}^{n} M_i$ and A and G are canonical safety formulas. Then,*

$$\frac{\begin{array}{l} S \models A \\ M_j \models A \trianglerighteq G \ \mathit{for\ some}\ j \end{array}}{S \models G}$$

As pointed out in [22], Rule MOD-W is normally applied in an incremental manner. One typically starts with A replaced by *true* and proves some property $\Box H_1$ of a module; one then uses $\Box H_1$ in place of A to prove another property $\Box H_2$ of another module; and so on.

The rule could have been formulated as:

$$\frac{\begin{array}{l} S \models \Box H_A \\ M_j \models \Box H_A \to \Box H_G \text{ for some } j \end{array}}{S \models \Box H_G}$$

The new rule seems to look simpler. However, to establish $M_j \models \Box H_A \to \Box H_G$, it is inevitable in practice to face the proof obligation of $M_j \models \Box(\boxminus H_A \to H_G)$; this is due to the inability of a module to predict the future of its environment. Rule MOD-W makes this clearer.

5 Examples

We consider two examples. The examples are very simple and are intended to contrast the respective strengths of strong and weak assumption-guarantee specifications, demonstrating their complementary roles in compositional verification (rather than their abilities in tackling large systems). In each example, a system is decomposed as the parallel composition of two modules and a property of the system is proven compositionally. We argue that Rule MOD-S is more effective for the first example, while Rule MOD-W is more effective for the second.

5.1 Example 1

Consider again Program KEEP-AHEAD that appeared in Section 2. It is easy to see that the values of a and b are monotonically (but not strictly) increasing in KEEP-AHEAD, i.e., KEEP-AHEAD $\models \Box((a \geq a^-) \land (b \geq b^-))$. Can the property be verified compositionally?

Theorem 1 suggests that we decompose $\Box((a \geq a^-) \land (b \geq b^-))$ as the conjunction of $\Box(b \geq b^-) \rhd \Box(a \geq a^-)$ and $\Box(a \geq a^-) \rhd \Box(b \geq b^-)$. Unfortunately, neither $M_a \models \Box(b \geq b^-) \rhd \Box(a \geq a^-)$ nor $M_b \models \Box(a \geq a^-) \rhd \Box(b \geq b^-)$. For Module M_a, the assumption $\Box(b \geq b^-)$ says nothing about the initial value of b (permitting b to be an arbitrary negative integer initially), it therefore cannot guarantee that the value of a is monotonically increasing in the very first step (a is 0 initially and may become $b+1$ in the first step). An analogy applies to Module M_b.

A simple remedy is to first strengthen the proof obligation as KEEP-AHEAD $\models \Box((\mathit{first} \to a \geq 0) \land (a \geq a^-) \land (\mathit{first} \to b \geq 0) \land (b \geq b^-))$. Again, Theorem 1 suggests that we decompose

$$\Box((\mathit{first} \to a \geq 0) \land (a \geq a^-) \land (\mathit{first} \to b \geq 0) \land (b \geq b^-))$$

as the conjunction of

$$\Box((\mathit{first} \to b \geq 0) \land b \geq b^-) \rhd \Box((\mathit{first} \to a \geq 0) \land a \geq a^-)$$

$$\textbf{local } x, y : \textbf{integer where } x = y = 0$$

$$P_x :: \left[\begin{array}{l}\textbf{loop forever do}\\ \left[\begin{array}{l} l_1 : \textbf{await } x < y+1 \\ l_2 : x := x+1 \end{array}\right]\end{array}\right] \parallel P_y :: \left[\begin{array}{l}\textbf{loop forever do}\\ \left[\begin{array}{l} m_1 : \textbf{await } y < x+1 \\ m_2 : y := y+1 \end{array}\right]\end{array}\right]$$

Fig. 3. Program KEEP-UP.

and

$$\Box((\mathit{first} \rightarrow a \geq 0) \wedge a \geq a^-) \rhd \Box((\mathit{first} \rightarrow b \geq 0) \wedge b \geq b^-).$$

It turns out that $M_a \models \Box((\mathit{first} \rightarrow b \geq 0) \wedge b \geq b^-) \rhd \Box((\mathit{first} \rightarrow a \geq 0) \wedge a \geq a^-)$ and $M_b \models \Box((\mathit{first} \rightarrow a \geq 0) \wedge a \geq a^-) \rhd \Box((\mathit{first} \rightarrow b \geq 0) \wedge b \geq b^-)$. Applying Rule MOD-S, we successfully prove KEEP-AHEAD $\models \Box((\mathit{first} \rightarrow a \geq 0) \wedge (a \geq a^-) \wedge (\mathit{first} \rightarrow b \geq 0) \wedge (b \geq b^-))$ and hence KEEP-AHEAD $\models \Box((a \geq a^-) \wedge (b \geq b^-))$ in a compositional way.

It would be inconvenient, if not impossible, to achieve compositionality for the example using Rule MOD-W. With this rule, one somehow has to first establish either KEEP-AHEAD $\models \Box(a \geq a^-)$ or KEEP-AHEAD $\models \Box(b \geq b^-)$. To establish KEEP-AHEAD $\models \Box(a \geq a^-)$ first, for example, one may attempt to prove KEEP-AHEAD $\models \Box(b \geq b^-)$ and $M_a \models \Box(b \geq b^-) \unrhd \Box(a \geq a^-)$. But, KEEP-AHEAD $\models \Box(b \geq b^-)$ then has to be established first, leading to a cycle.

5.2 Example 2

For the second example, we take Program KEEP-UP from [22, Chapter 4], which is recreated in Figure 3. The program is decomposed as the composition of modules M_x and M_y as shown in Figure 4. The system specifications of KEEP-UP, M_x, and M_y are omitted for brevity. Note that in M_x the input variable y is explicitly given an initial value 0 and similarly in M_y the input variable x is given an initial value 0.

It can be shown that KEEP-UP $\models \Box(|x-y| \leq 1)$. In [22], the property $\Box(|x-y| \leq 1)$ is proven compositionally by repeated applications of Rule MOD-W. Note that $\Box(|x-y| \leq 1)$ is equivalent to $\Box((x \leq y+1) \wedge (y \leq x+1))$, or $\Box(x \leq y+1) \wedge \Box(y \leq x+1)$. Briefly, the compositional verification proceeds as follows:

1. Prove KEEP-UP $\models \Box(x \geq x^-)$ by applying Rule MOD-W with A replaced by *true* and establishing the premise $M_x \models \mathit{true} \unrhd \Box(x \geq x^-)$; prove KEEP-UP $\models \Box(y \geq y^-)$ in an analogous way. These two proofs are independent of each other.
2. Prove KEEP-UP $\models \Box(x \leq y+1)$ by applying Rule MOD-W with A replaced by $\Box(y \geq y^-)$, which was proven in the previous step, and establishing the

module M_x
in y : **integer where** $y = 0$
own out x : **integer where** $x = 0$

loop forever do
$\begin{bmatrix} l_1 : \textbf{await } x < y + 1 \\ l_2 : x := x + 1 \end{bmatrix}$

$\|$

module M_y
in x : **integer where** $x = 0$
own out y : **integer where** $y = 0$

loop forever do
$\begin{bmatrix} m_1 : \textbf{await } y < x + 1 \\ m_2 : y := y + 1 \end{bmatrix}$

Fig. 4. Program KEEP-UP as the parallel composition of two modules.

premise $M_x \models \Box(y \geq y^-) \trianglerighteq \Box(x \leq y + 1)$; prove KEEP-UP $\models \Box(y \leq x + 1)$ in an analogous way. Again, these two proofs are independent of each other.

An attempt to use Rule MOD-S would fail. The property $\Box(x \leq y+1) \wedge \Box(y \leq x + 1)$ indeed follows from the conjunction of $\Box(x \leq y + 1) \rhd \Box(y \leq x + 1)$ and $\Box(y \leq x + 1) \rhd \Box(x \leq y + 1)$ like in the first example. However, it is not possible to establish either $M_x \models \Box(x \leq y + 1) \rhd \Box(y \leq x + 1)$ or $M_x \models \Box(y \leq x + 1) \rhd \Box(x \leq y + 1)$. This is due to the fact that both $(x \leq y + 1)$ and $(y \leq x + 1)$ are state formulas that may be falsified by a transition of some environment compatible with M_x (the environment is allowed to change y in an arbitrary way); a module cannot possibly satisfy an assumption-guarantee property if the guarantee part can be falsified by its environment. Analogous arguments applies for M_y.

6 Liveness

To allow liveness properties, we simply strengthen an assumption-guarantee specification by conjoining it with the ordinary implication between the assumption and the guarantee. We consider the extension of a strong assumption-guarantee formula; the extension of a weak one can be done analogously. We will present just one inference rule for composing such properties.

As the generalized definition of a strong assumption-guarantee formula with assumption $A \equiv \Box H_A \wedge L_A$ (in the canonical form) and guarantee $G \equiv \Box H_G \wedge L_G$, we define $A \rhd G$ as follows:

$$A \rhd G \triangleq (\Box H_A \rhd \Box H_G) \wedge (A \rightarrow G)$$

where the $\rhd$ on the right hand side is as defined in Section 3. This generalized definition is consistent with the definition of $\rhd$ for safety assumptions and guarantees, since if A and G are safety formulas, the implication $A \rightarrow G$, i.e., $\Box H_A \rightarrow \Box H_G$, will be subsumed by $\Box H_A \rhd \Box H_G$.

Now that the assumptions may contain liveness properties, we no longer have symmetric composition rules like that in Theorem 2, as mutual dependency on liveness properties leads to unsound rules. Theorem 2 was generalized in our previous work [16] to permit liveness in the guarantee parts. Below is an asymmetric composition rule for two modules; its proof can be found in the full paper [25].

Theorem 6. *Suppose that* $A_1 \equiv \Box H_{A_1}$, $G_1 \equiv \Box H_{G_1} \wedge L_{G_1}$, $A_2 \equiv \Box H_{A_2} \wedge L_{A_2}$, $G_2 \equiv \Box H_{G_2} \wedge L_{G_2}$, $A \equiv \Box H_A \wedge L_A$, *and* $G \equiv \Box H_G \wedge L_G$, *all in the canonical form. Then,*

$$\begin{array}{ll}
1.\ (a) & \models \Box\Big(\boxminus H_A \wedge \boxminus(H_{G_1} \wedge H_{G_2}) \rightarrow H_{A_1} \wedge H_{A_2}\Big) \\
\quad (b) & \models A \wedge G_1 \rightarrow A_2 \\
2.\ (a) & \models \Box\Big(\circleddash \boxminus H_A \wedge \boxminus(H_{G_1} \wedge H_{G_2}) \rightarrow H_G\Big) \\
\quad (b) & \models A \wedge G_1 \wedge G_2 \rightarrow G \\
\hline
 & \models (A_1 \rhd G_1) \wedge (A_2 \rhd G_2) \ \rightarrow\ (A \rhd G)
\end{array}$$

Again, take A to be *true* for a closed system.

This composition rule looks unsophisticated and may seem not to be very useful. As a matter of fact, many practical systems exhibit the type of dependency treated by the rule. Take network protocols as an example. An upper-layer protocol relies on the liveness properties of a lower-layer one to ensure liveness in the service that it provides, but the lower-layer protocol does not assume liveness about the upper-layer one. We believe that two modules with more complicated dependency on liveness should be verified as one single module.

7 Discussion: Guidelines of Usage

We give a few guidelines for using the proposed compositional approach.

- *What type of systems can be treated with the compositional approach?*
  Our approach works for a system where each shared variable is owned and can be modified by exactly one of its modules. This is partly due to the fact that only this type of systems allow parallel composition to be conveniently modeled as conjunction in LTL. There certainly are ways to circumvent this limitation; introducing the notion of agents is one possibility [1]. However, we do not think that compositional verification should be applied to two modules that may change a same shared variable. Sharing variables in such a manner indicates that the two modules are tightly coupled and are best treated as one single module.
- *How does one decide which form of assumption-guarantee specification should be used?*
  The desired property of a system gives much hint on what the guarantee parts should look like, as seen from the examples in Section 5. Here is the first thing to check: does the guarantee part involve a variable owned by the environment? For instance, in Example 1 the guarantee part in each of the two assumption-guarantee properties does not involve a variable owned by

the environment. A module M cannot possibly satisfy a property $A \rhd G$ if some environment compatible with M is capable of falsifying G, which is more likely to happen when G involves a variable owned by the environment. If the environment is capable of falsifying G, then one may try to find a suitable A' such that in falsifying G the environment also has to pay the price of falsifying A'. $A' \trianglerighteq G$ could turn out to be a property of M useful for proving the desired property of the system.

– *What changes are needed to the approach if one prefers using "+"-superscribed (or primed) rather than "−"-superscribed variables in expressing transitions of a system (like in TLA)?*
  We have opted for using "−"-superscribed variables, as it leads to a more succinct formulation of assumption-guarantee specifications and rules for composing such specifications. The required changes are quite straightforward. If $A \equiv Init_A \wedge \Box N_A$ and $G \equiv Init_G \wedge \Box N_G$, where N_A and N_G are transition formulas using primed variables, then $A \rhd G$ translates into

$$Init_G \wedge (Init_A \rightarrow N_G) \wedge \Box(\boxminus((first \rightarrow Init_A) \wedge N_A) \rightarrow \bigcirc N_G).$$

  Note that $\Box(\boxminus((first \rightarrow Init_A) \wedge N_A) \rightarrow \bigcirc N_G)$ is a safety formula, though not in the canonical form. The composition rules can be changed accordingly.

We have omitted the treatment of hiding, i.e., assumptions and guarantees with existentially quantified variables, to focus on showing the complementary roles of strong and weak assumption-guarantee specifications. Hiding is a powerful means of expressiveness. The formulation of strong assumption-guarantee specifications with hiding have been considered in our previous work [16]; the same technique applies to weak assumption-guarantee specifications.

References

[1] M. Abadi and L. Lamport. Composing specifications. *ACM Transactions on Programming Languages and Systems*, 15(1):73–132, January 1993.

[2] M. Abadi and L. Lamport. Conjoining specifications. *ACM Transactions on Programming Languages and Systems*, 17(3):507–534, May 1995.

[3] M. Abadi and G.D. Plotkin. A logical view of composition. *Theoretical Computer Science*, 114(1):3–30, June 1993.

[4] R. Alur and T.A. Henzinger. Local liveness for compositional modeling of fair reactive systems. In *Computer Aided Verification, Proceedings of the 7th International Conference, LNCS 939*, pages 166–179, 1995.

[5] A. Aziz, T.R. Shiple, V. Singhal, and A.L. Sangiovanni-Vincentelli. Formula-dependent equivalence for compositional CTL model checking. In *Computer Aided Verification, LNCS 818*, pages 324–337, June 1994.

[6] H. Barringer and R. Kuiper. Hierarchical development of concurrent systems in a temporal logic framework. In S.D. Brookes, A.W. Roscoe, and G. Winskel, editors, *Seminar on Concurrency, LNCS 197*, pages 35–61. Springer-Verlag, 1984.

[7] K.M. Chandy and J. Misra. *Parallel Program Design: A Foundation.* Addison-Wesley, 1988.

[8] E.M. Clarke, D.E. Long, and K.L. McMillan. Compositional model checking. In *Proceedings of the 4th IEEE Symposium on Logic in Computer Science*, pages 353–362, 1989.

[9] P. Collette. Application of the composition principle to Unity-like specifications. In *TAPSOFT '93: Theory and Practice of Software Development, LNCS 668*, pages 230–242. Springer-Verlag, 1993.

[10] P. Collette. *Design of Compositional Proof Systems Based on Assumption-Guarantee Specifications — Application to UNITY.* PhD thesis, Université Catholique de Louvain, June 1994.

[11] W.-P. de Roever, H. Langmåck, and A. Pnueli. *Compositionality: The Significant Difference.* Springer-Verlag, 1998. Lecture Notes in Computer Science 1536.

[12] P. Grønning, T.Q. Nielsen, and H.H. Løvengreen. Refinement and composition of transition-based rely-guarantee specifications with auxiliary variables. In K.V. Nori and C.E. Veni Madhavan, editors, *Foundations of Software Technology and Theoretical Computer Science, LNCS 472*, pages 332–348. Springer-Verlag, 1991.

[13] O. Grumberg and D.E. Long. Model checking and modular verification. *ACM Transactions on Programming Languages and Systems*, 16(3):843–871, May 1994.

[14] C.A.R. Hoare. An axiomatic basis for computer programs. *Communications of the ACM*, 12(8):576–580, 1969.

[15] C.B. Jones. Tentative steps towards a development method for interfering programs. *ACM Transactions on Programming Languages and Systems*, 5(4):596–619, October 1983.

[16] B. Jonsson and Y.-K. Tsay. Assumption/guarantee specifications in linear-time temporal logic. *Theoretical Computer Science*, 167:47–72, October 1996. An extended abstract appeared earlier in TAPSOFT '95, LNCS 915.

[17] O. Kupferman and M.Y. Vardi. Module checking. In O. Grumberg, editor, *Computer-Aided Verification, CAV '96, LNCS 1102*, pages 75–86. Springer-Verlag, August 1996.

[18] O. Kupferman and M.Y. Vardi. Module checking revisited. In *Computer-Aided Verification, CAV '97, LNCS 1254*. Springer-Verlag, June 1997.

[19] L. Lamport. Specifying concurrent program modules. *ACM Transactions on Programming Languages and Systems*, 5(2):190–222, 1983.

[20] L. Lamport. The temporal logic of actions. *ACM Transactions on Programming Languages and Systems*, 16(3):872–923, May 1994.

[21] Z. Manna and A. Pnueli. *The Temporal Logic of Reactive and Concurrent Systems: Specification.* Springer-Verlag, 1992.

[22] Z. Manna and A. Pnueli. *Temporal Verification of Reactive Systems: Safety.* Springer-Verlag, 1995.

[23] J. Misra and K.M. Chandy. Proofs of networks of processes. *IEEE Transactions on Software Engineering*, 7(4):417–426, July 1981.

[24] A. Pnueli. The temporal semantics of concurrent programs. *Theoretical Computer Science*, 13:45–60, 1982.

[25] Y.-K. Tsay. Compositional verification in linear-time temporal logic (the full version). Send requests to `tsay@im.ntu.edu.tw`.

[26] M.Y. Vardi. On the complexity of modular model checking. In *Proceedings of the 10th IEEE Symposium on Logic in Computer Science*, pages 101–111, June 1995.

[27] Q. Xu, A. Cau, and P. Collette. On unifying assumption-commitment style proof rules for concurrency. In B. Jonsson and J. Parrow, editors, *CONCUR '94: Concurrency Theory, LNCS 836*, pages 267–282. Springer-Verlag, 1994.

On the Semantics of Refinement Calculi

Hongseok Yang[1] and Uday S. Reddy[2]

[1] University of Illinois at Urbana-Champaign,
hyang@cs.uiuc.edu
[2] University of Birmingham,
u-reddy@cs.uiuc.edu

Abstract. Refinement calculi for imperative programs provide an integrated framework for programs and specifications and allow one to develop programs from specifications in a systematic fashion. The semantics of these calculi has traditionally been defined in terms of predicate transformers and poses several challenges in defining a state transformer semantics in the denotational style. We define a novel semantics in terms of sets of state transformers and prove it to be isomorphic to positively multiplicative predicate transformers. This semantics disagrees with the traditional semantics in some places and the consequences of the disagreement are analyzed.

1 Introduction

Two dominant semantic views of imperative programs are in terms of *state transformers*, initiated by McCarthy [17], Scott and Strachey [30], and *predicate transformers*, initiated by Dijkstra [11]. State transformers give a clear correspondence with the operational semantics, where commands do, after all, transform the state of a machine. The predicate transformer view, on the other hand, has been argued to be suitable for showing that programs achieve certain goals, i.e., to questions of correctness. A definitive relationship between the two views was established by Plotkin [28], following other work [9, 31, 4], where it is shown that Dijkstra's predicate transformers are isomorphic to nondeterministic state transformers defined using the Smyth powerdomain. The isomorphism establishes a tight connection between the predicate transformer view and operational behavior, which is not obvious otherwise. It is also of important conceptual value as it allows the two semantic views to coexist side by side. The ideas expressed using either view can be converted into the other, and there is no conflict between the two views.

In more recent work, predicate transformers have been put to new uses. Refinement calculi, developed by Hehner [16], Back [3, 5], Morris [24], Morgan [19] and Nelson [27], extend Dijkstra's programming language with "specification statements." Typically written as $[\varphi, \psi]$, a specification statement stands for some statement that is yet to be developed but which is expected to satisfy the specification $\langle\varphi, \psi\rangle$, i.e., transform states satisfying φ to states satisfying ψ.

J. Tiuryn (Ed.): FOSSACS 2000, LNCS 1784, pp. 359–374, 2000.

Such specification statements serve as space fillers in the initial stages of program development, and they are refined to actual program statements in later stages.

The semantics of such extended languages for program refinement has only been defined in terms of predicate transformers. No semantics is known in terms of state transformers. Moreover, the predicate transformers involved in the semantics go beyond Dijkstra's predicate transformers. (They do not satisfy Dijkstra's healthiness conditions such as continuity.) Since, by Plotkin's result, state transformers are isomorphic to Dijkstra's predicate transformers, we already know that there are no conventional state transformers corresponding to these new predicate transformers. This leaves the operational interpretation of the refinement calculi very much in the dark.

In this paper, we develop a semantic interpretation of refinement calculi in terms of state transformers. The basic idea is that statements in refinement calculi are to be interpreted as *sets of state transformers* that satisfy the specifications embedded in the statements. In Denney's terminology [10], this interpretation represents "under-determinism" as opposed to "nondeterminism." We also need a notion of *guarded* state transformers, similar to the idea of partial functions, which are defined only for some subset of the set of all states. We are able to show that suitable sets of guarded state transformers are isomorphic to positively multiplicative predicate transformers. This parallels Plotkin's original isomorphism result for Dijkstra's predicate transformers.

All the constructs of refinement calculi can be interpreted using sets of guarded state transformers. This gives a natural semantics of specification statements as collections of program statements that meet those specifications. However, this semantics does not match up exactly with the traditional predicate transformer semantics of refinement calculi. The predicate transformers used in the latter are not in general positively multiplicative, a property used in our isomorphism result.

We examine the consequences of this mismatch, and show that there are refinement laws that are intuitively *unreasonable* but hold in the traditional semantics though not in ours. The conclusion is that a better semantics of refinement calculus is obtained by restricting to positively multiplicative predicate transformers which have a natural equivalence with state transformer sets.

We believe these results go a long way towards demystifying refinement calculi. The absence of an operational reading for the constructs of refinement calculi has contributed to some of the mysteries surrounding the traditional treatment of the subject. The predicate transformer semantics implies that the theory of these calculi is internally consistent. However, the mysteries point to problems in *interpreting* the theory. Our contribution is in clarifying the interpretation which, we hope, might lead to a wider appreciation of the theory itself.

Related Work The early work on relating state transformers and predicate transformers is mentioned in Plotkin [28]. In later work, Apt and Plotkin [1, 2] extended [28] to countable nondeterminism, and Smyth [29] to non-flat state spaces. Bonsangue and Kok [7] found correspondences for safety and liveness predicate transformers and, in [8], for Nelson's predicate transformers [27]. We should remark that all this work is for *programming* languages, not for specification languages used in refinement. However, there are close relationships between the results needed in this paper and the earlier results, especially those of Apt and Plotkin [1, 2]. Morgan [20], Gardiner [12] and Naumann [25] also considered multiplicative predicate transformers and the correspondence with relations (which may be seen as infinitely nondeterministic state transformers). Gardiner et al. [13] and Naumann [25] used this correspondence to lift type structure to specification languages.

After the present work was completed, we were made aware of Ewen Denney's dissertation [10], which echoes very similar ideas to our work. In particular, it interprets specifications via under-determinism. On the other hand, Denney focuses on functional programming languages whereas we are looking at imperative programming and the correspondence between state transformer and predicate transformer interpretations. We also highlight the interaction between nondeterminism and under-determinism (cf. Sec. 3.2).

Overview In Sec. 2, we give a brief summary of the refinement calculus we use in this paper and define its predicate transformer semantics. Section 3 introduces the state transformer concepts that are used in our semantics and show their isomorphism with positively multiplicative predicate transformers. The state transformer semantics of the calculus is defined in Sec. 4. Finally, in Sec. 5, we discuss problems and issues that lie outside our isomorphism.

2 Refinement Calculus

Refinement calculi are obtained by extending a programming language with additional notations for expressing specifications. Program statements and specification statements are then freely intermixed. A refinement relation $\sqsubseteq$ is defined between statements in the extended language. A collection of refinement laws, axiomatizing the refinement relation, is devised, by which a specification can be refined to an executable program in a series of steps. The subject is extensively covered in the two text books [6, 21] as well as the collection [23].

Here, we use a variant of the Morgan-Gardiner refinement calculus [19, 22] as the basis of our study. For simplicity, we treat basic imperative programs over a fixed collection of program variables. However, we will allow locally bound constant identifiers in specifications.

Assume a finite set $\mathcal{V}$ of typed *variable identifiers*, and a countably infinite set $\mathcal{I}$ of *constant identifiers*, disjoint from $\mathcal{V}$. Using these we form a collection of *expressions*, *assertions* and *atomic commands*, whose structure we unspecified except to note that both variable identifiers and constant identifiers can occur in them. The collection of statements in the Dijkstra's programming language is given by the context-free syntax:

$$
\begin{array}{rcl}
C & ::= & A \mid \mathbf{skip} \mid \mathbf{abort} \mid C_1; C_2 \mid \mathbf{if}\, G\, \mathbf{fi} \mid \mathbf{do}\, G\, \mathbf{od} \\
G & ::= & \epsilon \mid E \rightarrow C \mid G_1 \,[\!]\, G_2
\end{array}
$$

where A and E range over atomic commands and boolean expressions respectively, and G stands for guarded commands.

To obtain a refinement calculus, we extend the collection of statements by two clauses:

$$C \ ::= \ \ldots \mid v_1, \ldots, v_n\colon [\varphi, \psi] \mid \mathbf{con}\ i\colon \tau = E \ \mathbf{in}\ C$$

The statement $v_1, \ldots, v_n\colon [\varphi, \psi]$ is called a *specification statement* or a *prescription*. The intended meaning is that it stands for some arbitrary program statement that satisfies the specification $\langle \varphi, \psi \rangle$, i.e., transforms states satisfying φ to those satisfying ψ, by modifying at most the variables $v_1, \ldots, v_n$. The variables $v_1, \ldots, v_n$ are said to constitute the *frame* of the statement. When the frame includes all the variables in $\mathcal{V}$, we use the abbreviation $[\varphi, \psi]$ for $\mathcal{V}\colon [\varphi, \psi]$. For example, the statement $r\colon [n \geq 0,\ r^2 - 1 < n \leq r^2]$ specifies the action of assigning to r the integer square root of n.

The construct $\mathbf{con}\ i\colon \tau = E\ \mathbf{in}\ C$ specifies an action that satisfies the specification C when i is given the value of E in the current state. For example,

$$\mathbf{con}\ k\colon \mathsf{int} = |n|\ \mathbf{in}\ n\colon [\mathsf{true},\ |n| = k + 1]$$

specifies that n must be modified so as to increase its absolute value by 1. This is a variant of the constant-introduction construct of Morgan and Gardiner [22] where we require the initial value to be explicitly declared. We consider the Morgan-Gardiner construct in Section 5 as it raises interesting semantic issues.

Predicate Transformer Semantics

A predicate transformer interpretation for the refinement calculus has been defined by Morgan and Gardiner [19, 14] (as well as other authors on the subject). Here, we use a semantic version of this interpretation by taking predicates as sets of states. Our treatment closely follows Plotkin [28]. See also [26, 8, 7] for similar presentations.

Let Σ be the set of states for the variables in $\mathcal{V}$. For technical reasons, we assume that Σ is countable. A *predicate* is a subset $a \subseteq \Sigma$. A *predicate transformer* is a monotone function $t : \mathcal{P}(\Sigma) \to \mathcal{P}(\Sigma)$. Predicate transformers are partially ordered by the pointwise ordering:[1] $t_1 \sqsubseteq t_2 \iff \forall a' \in \mathcal{P}(\Sigma).\, t_1(a') \subseteq t_2(a')$. The poset of predicate transformers is denoted PT.

A predicate transformer is said to be *completely multiplicative* if for any family $F' \subseteq \mathcal{P}(\Sigma)$, $t(\bigcap F') = \bigcap t(F')$. We call it *positively multiplicative* if this property holds for all nonempty families $F' \subseteq \mathcal{P}(\Sigma)$. Define the poset:

$$\mathsf{PTM}^{+} = \{t : \mathcal{P}(\Sigma) \to \mathcal{P}(\Sigma) \mid t \text{ is positively multiplicative }\}, \text{ ordered pointwise}$$

If t is any predicate transformer and $x \in t(\Sigma)$, define

$$L_t(x) = \bigcap \{a' \mid x \in t(a')\}.$$

[1] We often use primed variable names (such as a') as arguments for predicate transformers to denote the fact that they are sets of post-states.

Program Operations

Skip	:	$\mathcal{D}$	Do	:	$\mathsf{Bool} \times \mathcal{D} \to \mathcal{D}$
Conv	:	$\text{d-ST} \to \mathcal{D}$	Empty	:	$\mathsf{Bool} \times \mathcal{D}$
Comp	:	$\mathcal{D}^2 \to \mathcal{D}$	Guard	:	$\mathsf{Bool} \times \mathcal{D} \to \mathsf{Bool} \times \mathcal{D}$
Cond	:	$\mathsf{Bool} \times \mathcal{D} \to \mathcal{D}$	Bar	:	$(\mathsf{Bool} \times \mathcal{D})^2 \to \mathsf{Bool} \times \mathcal{D}$

Specification Operations

$$\mathsf{Pres}_R : \mathcal{P}(\Sigma)^2 \to \mathcal{D}$$
$$\mathsf{Con}_A : (\Sigma \to A) \times (A \to \mathcal{D}) \to \mathcal{D}$$

where $R \subseteq \Sigma \times \Sigma$ is an equivalence relation
A is a countable set
d-ST $= \Sigma \to \Sigma$, ordered discretely
Bool $= \Sigma \to \{\mathsf{tt}, \mathsf{ff}\}$, ordered discretely

Table 1. Signature of the Semantic Algebra

Lemma 1. *A predicate transformer t is positively multiplicative iff, for all $x \in t(\Sigma)$, $x \in t(L_t(x))$. In this case, $L_t(x)$ is the least a' such that $x \in t(a')$.*

Lemma 2. *For any predicate transformer t, there is a least positively multiplicative predicate transformer t^* above t, given by $t^*(a') = \{x \in t(\Sigma) \mid L_t(x) \subseteq a'\}$.*

Note that $L_{t^*}(x)$ and $L_t(x)$ are the same. By forcing $t^*(L_{t^*}(x))$ to include x, we obtain a positively multiplicative predicate transformer. We call t^* the *positively multiplicative closure* of t.

Lemma 3. PTM^+ *is a complete lattice with least upper bounds given by $\bigsqcup_{i \in I} t_i = (\lambda a. \bigcup_{i \in I} t_i(a))^*$. The least element $\bot_{\mathsf{PTM}^+}$ is $\lambda a'. \emptyset$.*

Note that PTM^+ is not a complete sublattice of PT because the least upper bounds in PTM^+ are different from those in PT.

We work in the category of complete lattices with monotone functions as morphisms. By Tarski's fixed point theorem, every monotone function $f : L \to L$ has a least fixed point, given by $\mathbf{fix}(f) = \bigsqcap\{t \in L \mid f(t) \sqsubseteq t\}$.

To define the semantics of the refinement calculus, we use an algebraic approach as in [28]. Table 1 shows the signature of a semantic algebra $\mathcal{D}$, where all the operations are meant to be monotone maps. For the predicate transformer semantics $\mathcal{D} = \mathsf{PTM}^+$, but the same signature will be used for the state transformer semantics to be introduced later. The program operations are as in [28] and we recall their definitions in Table 2. The only difference from [28] is that we are using *positively multiplicative* predicate transformers instead of continuous ones.

$$
\begin{array}{rcl}
\mathsf{Skip} & = & \lambda a'.a' \\
\mathsf{Conv}(m) & = & \lambda a'.m^{-1}(a') \\
\mathsf{Comp}(t_1,t_2) & = & t_1 \circ t_2 \\
\mathsf{Cond}(p,t) & = & \lambda a'.p^{+} \cap t(a') \\
\mathsf{Do}(p,t) & = & \mathbf{fix}_{\mathsf{PTM}^{+}}(\lambda t'.\,\lambda a'.\,(p^{-} \cap a') \cup (p^{+} \cap (t \circ t')(a'))) \\
\mathsf{Empty} & = & (\lambda x.\,\mathsf{ff}, \lambda a'.\,\emptyset) \\
\mathsf{Guard}(p,t) & = & (p,t) \\
\mathsf{Bar}((p_1,t_1),(p_2,t_2)) & = & (p_1 \vee p_2,\ \lambda a'.\,(p_1^{+} \cup p_2^{+}) \cap (p_1^{-} \cup t_1(a')) \cap (p_2^{-} \cup t_2(a')))
\end{array}
$$

where $p^{+} = p^{-1}(\mathsf{tt})$, $p^{-} = p^{-1}(\mathsf{ff})$ and $(p \vee q)(x) = p(x) \vee q(x)$

Table 2. Program Operations for PTM^{+}

For interpreting specification constructs, we define two new operators:

1. **Prescription:** The operation Pres_R captures the semantics of Morgan's specification statement $\boldsymbol{v}\colon [\varphi, \psi]$. The idea that only variables $\boldsymbol{v}$ can be modified can be represented by an equivalence relation $R \subseteq \Sigma \times \Sigma$, which equates states that possibly differ only in variables $\boldsymbol{v}$. We write $[x]_R$ for the equivalence class of x under R. Define a family of operations indexed by equivalence relations $R \subseteq \Sigma \times \Sigma$:

$$
\begin{array}{rcl}
\mathsf{Pres}_R & : & \mathcal{P}(\Sigma) \times \mathcal{P}(\Sigma) \to \mathsf{PTM}^{+} \\
\mathsf{Pres}_R(b,b') & = & \lambda a'.\{x \in b \mid b' \cap [x]_R \subseteq a'\}
\end{array}
$$

2. **Constant introduction:** The family of operations $\mathsf{Con}_A : (\Sigma \to A) \times (A \to \mathsf{PTM}^{+}) \to \mathsf{PTM}^{+}$ captures the introduction of constant identifiers of type A.

$$
\mathsf{Con}_A(e,f) \;=\; \lambda a'.\,\{x \in \Sigma \mid x \in f(e(x))(a')\}
$$

We note that two of Dijkstra's healthiness conditions are violated by these predicate transformers. When R relates all pairs of states,

- $\mathsf{Pres}_R(b,\emptyset)$ is not strict (unless $b = \emptyset$).
- $\mathsf{Pres}_R(b,\Sigma)$ is not continuous. Note that Σ can be expressed as a lub $\bigcup_i a'_i$ for an increasing sequence of finite sets a'_i. $\mathsf{Pres}_R(b,\Sigma)(\Sigma) = b$, but for every finite a', $\mathsf{Pres}_R(b,\Sigma)(a') = \emptyset$.

Lemma 4. *All the operators above are well-defined and monotone.*

Note that the operators are not necessarily continuous. For example, Comp is not continuous.

The semantics of the refinement language is as follows. Since commands have free identifiers (for constants), we use *environments* for giving values to the identifiers [15, 18]. *Env* denotes the set of environments. The semantic functions are defined in Table 3, parameterized by a semantic algebra $\mathcal{D}$. By instantiating the definition by $\mathcal{D} = \mathsf{PTM}^{+}$, we obtain the predicate transformer semantics.

$$\begin{array}{lcl}
\mathcal{P} & : & \text{Predicates} \to \text{Env} \to \mathcal{P}(\Sigma) \\
\mathcal{E} & : & \text{Expressions} \to \text{Env} \to (\Sigma \to \text{Value}) \\
\mathcal{A} & : & \text{Atomic commands} \to \text{Env} \to \textsf{d-ST} \\
\mathcal{C} & : & \text{Statements} \to \text{Env} \to \mathcal{D} \\
\mathcal{G} & : & \text{Guarded Commands} \to \text{Env} \to \textsf{Bool} \times \mathcal{D}
\end{array}$$

Interpretation of Commands

$$\begin{array}{rcl}
\mathcal{C}[\![A]\!]e & = & \textsf{Conv}(\mathcal{A}[\![A]\!]e) \\
\mathcal{C}[\![\textbf{skip}]\!]e & = & \textsf{Skip} \\
\mathcal{C}[\![\textbf{abort}]\!]e & = & \bot \\
\mathcal{C}[\![C_1; C_2]\!]e & = & \textsf{Comp}(\mathcal{C}[\![C_1]\!]e, \mathcal{C}[\![C_2]\!]e) \\
\mathcal{C}[\![\textbf{if}\, G\, \textbf{fi}]\!]e & = & \textsf{Cond}(\mathcal{G}[\![G]\!]e) \\
\mathcal{C}[\![\textbf{do}\, G\, \textbf{od}]\!]e & = & \textsf{Do}(\mathcal{G}[\![G]\!]e) \\
\mathcal{C}[\![\boldsymbol{v}\colon [\varphi, \psi]]\!]e & = & \textsf{Pres}_{R(\boldsymbol{v})}(\mathcal{P}[\![\varphi]\!]e, \mathcal{P}[\![\psi]\!]e) \\
\mathcal{C}[\![\textbf{con}\ i\colon \tau = E\ \textbf{in}\ C]\!]e & = & \textsf{Con}_{[\![\tau]\!]}(\mathcal{E}[\![E]\!]e, \lambda k \in [\![\tau]\!].\, \mathcal{C}[\![C]\!]e[i \mapsto k])
\end{array}$$

where $R(\boldsymbol{v})$ denotes the equivalence relation on states given by

$$x[R(\boldsymbol{v})]x' \iff \forall v \notin \boldsymbol{v}.\, x(v) = x'(v)$$

Interpretation of Guarded Commands

$$\begin{array}{rcl}
\mathcal{G}[\![\epsilon]\!]e & = & \textsf{Empty} \\
\mathcal{G}[\![E \to C]\!]e & = & \textsf{Guard}(\mathcal{E}[\![E]\!]e, \mathcal{C}[\![C]\!]e) \\
\mathcal{G}[\![G_1 \mathbin{[\,]} G_2]\!]e & = & \textsf{Bar}(\mathcal{G}[\![G_1]\!]e, \mathcal{G}[\![G_2]\!]e)
\end{array}$$

Table 3. Semantics of Refinement Calculus

We denote these semantic functions by $\mathcal{C}_{\mathsf{M}}$ and $\mathcal{G}_{\mathsf{M}}$ for commands and guarded commands respectively.

The fact that all the semantic algebra operations are monotonic implies that program contexts preserve refinement, i.e., $C \sqsubseteq C'$ implies $P\{C\} \sqsubseteq P\{C'\}$ for any program context $P\{\ \}$. This result is essential for program refinement because it allows one to refine whole programs by refining their components one at a time.

3 State Transformers and Predicate Transformers

Consider the set of states Σ. The set obtained by adding an element $\bot$ (for the undefined state) is denoted $\Sigma_\bot$. We make $\Sigma_\bot$ into a poset by defining the partial order $x \sqsubseteq y \iff x = \bot \vee x = y$. The Smyth powerdomain of $\Sigma_\bot$ is defined as follows:

$$\mathcal{P}_S(\Sigma_\bot) \;=\; \text{the set of nonempty finite subsets of } \Sigma \text{ and the infinite set } \Sigma_\bot, \text{ ordered by superset order.}$$

So, the least element of $\mathcal{P}_S(\Sigma_\bot)$ is $\Sigma_\bot$.

The domain of state transformers is

$$\mathsf{ST} = (\Sigma \to \mathcal{P}_S(\Sigma_\perp)), \quad \text{ordered pointwise}$$

The intuition is as follows. If $c \sqsubseteq c'$, then

1. c' terminates (possibly) more often than c, and
2. c' is (possibly) more deterministic than c.

We say that c' is "better" than c. Say that a state transformer c *satisfies* a specification $\langle a,\, a'\rangle$, written $c \models \langle a,\, a'\rangle$, if running c from a state in a gives a state in a'. Formally,

$$c \models \langle a,\, a'\rangle \iff \forall x \in a.\, c(x) \subseteq a'$$

Then, it is easy to see that $c \models \langle a,\, a'\rangle \wedge c \sqsubseteq c' \Longrightarrow c' \models \langle a,\, a'\rangle$. That is, better state transformers continue to satisfy all the old specifications.

By regarding a predicate transformer t as a collection of specifications $\{\langle t(a'), a'\rangle\}_{a' \in \mathcal{P}(\Sigma)}$, we have a notion of satisfaction for predicate transformers:

$$c \models t \iff \forall x. \forall a'. x \in t(a') \Rightarrow c(x) \subseteq a'$$

The strongest predicate transformer satisfied by c is denoted Tc:

$$Tc(a') = \{x \in \Sigma \mid c(x) \subseteq a'\}$$

Tc is nothing but the "weakest precondition" operator of c. It satisfies the following properties:

- **continuity**: $Tc(\bigcup_i a'_i) = \bigcup_i Tc(a'_i)$ for every ascending chain $\{a'_i\}_i$. The reason is that $Tc(\bigcup_i a'_i)$ includes all and only those initial states x whose results $c(x)$ are included in finite subsets of $\bigcup_i a'_i$.
- **positive multiplicativity**: $Tc(\bigcap_{i \in \mathcal{I}} a_i) = \bigcap_{i \in \mathcal{I}} Tc(a_i)$ for nonempty $\mathcal{I}$. The reason is that x is in $\bigcap_i Tc(a_i)$ only when for all i, $c(x)$ is a subset of a_i. This is equivalent to $x \in Tc(\bigcap_i a_i)$.
- **strictness**: $Tc(\emptyset) = \emptyset$. The reason is that $c(x)$ is always nonempty. So, $c(x) \subseteq \emptyset$ is impossible.

It is possible to recover c from Tc. For any predicate transformer t that satisfies these properties, let[2] $T^{-1}(t) = \lambda x.\, x \in t(\Sigma) \leadsto L_t(x); \Sigma_\perp$. It can be verified that $T^{-1}(t)$ is a state transformer.

Theorem 1 (Plotkin). *There is an order-isomorphism between* ST *and the poset of predicate transformers that are continuous, positively multiplicative and strict.*

Recall that the predicate transformers used in refinement calculus do not generally satisfy the properties mentioned above. We examine a series of state transformer concepts that correspond to wider classes of predicate transformers.

[2] We use the notation $p \leadsto x; y$ to mean "if p then x else y."

3.1 Guarded State Transformers

The idea of a guarded state transformer is similar to that of a partial function. A guarded state transformer is meant to be run only starting from certain initial states and not from others. Formally, a guarded state transformer is a pair

$$(p \subseteq \Sigma, c : p \to \mathcal{P}_S(\Sigma_\perp))$$

Note that c is only defined for states in p (which is called the "domain of definition") and undefined for others. This notion of "undefined" is different from nontermination. (The state transformer c might still map states in p to $\Sigma_\perp$.) A guarded state transformer is simply never meant to be used outside its domain of definition. The notion of satisfaction is:

$$(p, c) \models \langle a, a' \rangle \iff \forall x \in p.\, x \in a \Rightarrow c(x) \subseteq a'$$

So, we only worry about initial states within the domain of definition. As a result, the completely undefined state transformer satisfies every specification. In particular, $(\emptyset, \lambda x.\Sigma_\perp) \models \langle \Sigma, \emptyset \rangle$. Recall that there are no ordinary state transformers satisfying $\langle \Sigma, \emptyset \rangle$. But this is not the case for guarded state transformers. In refinement calculus literature, this (sneaky!) way of satisfying specifications is termed "miraculous" [19].

We define a partial order on guarded state transformers by

$$(p, c) \sqsubseteq (p', c') \iff p \supseteq p' \wedge (\forall x \in p'.\, c(x) \subseteq c'(x)).$$

This partial order may seem surprising. We get a better state transformer by *reducing* the domain of definition. However, this order is consistent with the notion of satisfaction:

$$(p, c) \sqsubseteq (p', c') \wedge (p, c) \models \langle a, a' \rangle \implies (p', c') \models \langle a, a' \rangle$$

Just as partial functions $A \rightharpoonup B$ can be regarded as total functions of type $A \to B_\perp$ with an adjoined $\perp$ element denoting the undefined result, guarded state transformers can be regarded as state transformers with an adjoined *top* element in the codomain: $\Sigma \to \mathcal{P}_S^\top(\Sigma_\perp)$. Here $\mathcal{P}_S^\top(\Sigma_\perp)$ is like the Smyth powerdomain but also includes the empty set $\emptyset$ (which serves as the top element under the superset order). A guarded state transformer (p, c) is represented under this representation as the function $\lambda x \in \Sigma.\, x \in p \leadsto c(x); \emptyset$. Conversely, a state transformer $d : \Sigma \to \mathcal{P}_S^\top(\Sigma_\perp)$ represents the guarded state transformer $(\mathrm{dom}(d), d \restriction \mathrm{dom}(d))$ where $\mathrm{dom}(d) = \overline{d^{-1}(\emptyset)}$. From here on, we will identify guarded state transformers with this alternative representation, which is technically convenient to work with.

Define GST as the poset:

$$\mathsf{GST} = \Sigma \to \mathcal{P}_S^\top(\Sigma_\perp), \quad \text{ordered pointwise}$$

For every guarded state transformer $d \in \mathsf{GST}$, we define a predicate transformer $Td : \mathcal{P}(\Sigma) \to \mathcal{P}(\Sigma)$ by

$$Td(a') = \{x \in \Sigma \mid d(x) \subseteq a'\}$$

This predicate transformer is *continuous* and *positively multiplicative* for the same reasons as before. But it is not strict. We have $Td(\emptyset) = \{x \in \Sigma \mid d(x) = \emptyset\} = \mathrm{dom}(d)$, which has no reason to be empty. There is an inverse to T:

$$T^{-1}(t) = \lambda x.\, x \in t(\Sigma) \rightsquigarrow L_t(x); \Sigma_\perp$$

Theorem 2. *There is an order-isomorphism between* GST *and the poset of predicate transformers that are continuous and positively multiplicative.*

3.2 State Transformer Sets

Given a specification $\langle \varphi, \psi \rangle$, we have a collection S of state transformers satisfying it. Any such collection is *closed under union* in the following sense: if c is a state transformer and, for every $x \in \Sigma$, there are $c_1, \ldots, c_n \in S$ such that $c(x) \subseteq c_1(x) \cup \ldots \cup c_n(x)$, then $c \in S$. There is a simpler statement of this. Let the "lower bound" map $\widehat{S} : \Sigma \to \mathcal{P}(\Sigma_\perp)$ be the pointwise union $\widehat{S}(x) = \bigcup\{c(x) \mid c \in S\}$ (which is not a state transformer). Closure under union says that any state transformer c such that $c(x) \subseteq \widehat{S}(x)$ is in S. The same idea can also be used for guarded state transformers. In this case, the collection S must be nonempty. If S is a nonempty set of guarded state transformers, we define its *closure under union* by $S^\dagger = \{c \mid \forall x.\, c(x) \subseteq \widehat{S}(x)\}$.

Remark 1. The lower bound maps $\widehat{S}$ can be regarded as maps of type $\Sigma \to \mathcal{P}_S^\infty(\Sigma_\perp)$ where $\mathcal{P}_S^\infty$ is the infinitely nondeterministic Smyth powerdomain [2], whose elements include $\Sigma_\perp$ and *all* subsets of Σ. Sets of state transformers closed under union are one-to-one with such infinitely nondeterministic maps. This is in fact an order-isomorphism.

Let PGST denote the poset with nonempty sets of guarded state transformers that are closed under union, ordered by superset order. We call the elements of PGST *state transformer sets.*

Lemma 5. PGST *is a complete lattice with the least upper bounds given by intersection:* $\bigsqcup_i S_i = \bigcap_i S_i$.

For any $S \in$ PGST, we define a predicate transformer $TS : \mathcal{P}(\Sigma) \to \mathcal{P}(\Sigma)$ by

$$TS(a') = \bigcap_{c \in S} Tc(a') = \{x \in \Sigma \mid \forall c \in S.\, c(x) \subseteq a'\}$$

This predicate transformer is *positively multiplicative:* $TS(\bigcap_{i \in \mathcal{I}} a_i) = \bigcap_{i \in \mathcal{I}} TS(a_i)$ for nonempty $\mathcal{I}$. But, it is not continuous. We have $TS(\bigcup_i a_i) = \{x \in \Sigma \mid \forall c \in S.\, c(x) \subseteq \bigcup_i a_i\}$. If S is the set of all terminating state transformers, then $TS(\Sigma) = \Sigma$, but $TS(a) = \emptyset$ for every finite $a \subseteq \Sigma$.

Conversely, every positively multiplicative predicate transformer corresponds to a state transformer set: $T^{-1}(t) = \{c \mid c \models t\}$.

Theorem 3. *There is an order-isomorphism between* PGST *and* PTM^+.

$$
\begin{array}{rcl}
\mathsf{Skip} & = & \{\lambda x.\,\{x\}\}^{\dagger} \\
\mathsf{Conv}(m) & = & \{\lambda x.\,\{m(x)\}\}^{\dagger} \\
\mathsf{Comp}(S_1, S_2) & = & \{\lambda x.\,\mathsf{App}(c_2, c_1(x)) \mid c_1 \in S_1,\ c_2 \in S_2\}^{\dagger} \\
\mathsf{Cond}(p, S) & = & \{\lambda x.\,p(x) \rightsquigarrow c(x); \Sigma_{\perp} \mid c \in S\}^{\dagger} \\
\mathsf{Do}(p, S) & = & \mathbf{fix}_{\mathsf{PGST}} \lambda S'.\,\{\lambda x.\,p(x) \rightsquigarrow \mathsf{App}(c', c(x)); \{x\} \mid c \in S,\ c' \in S'\}^{\dagger} \\
\mathsf{Empty} & = & (\lambda x.\,\mathsf{ff},\ \{\lambda x.\,\Sigma_{\perp}\}^{\dagger}) \\
\mathsf{Guard}(p, S) & = & (p, S) \\
\mathsf{Bar}((p_1, S_1), & = & (p_1 \vee p_2, \\
(p_2, S_2)) & & \{\lambda x.\,p_1(x) \rightsquigarrow (p_2(x) \rightsquigarrow c_1(x) \cup c_2(x); c_1(x)); (p_2(x) \rightsquigarrow c_2(x); \Sigma_{\perp}) \\
 & & \quad \mid c_1 \in S_1, c_2 \in S_2\}^{\dagger})
\end{array}
$$

where $\mathsf{App} : \mathsf{GST} \times \mathcal{P}_S^{\top}(\Sigma_{\perp}) \to \mathcal{P}_S^{\top}(\Sigma_{\perp})$ is defined by

$$\mathsf{App}(c, a') \quad = \quad (a' = \Sigma_{\perp}) \rightsquigarrow \Sigma_{\perp}; \textstyle\bigcup_{x' \in a'} c(x')$$

Table 4. Program Operations for PGST

4 State Transformer Semantics

We define a semantics of the refinement calculus using state transformer sets introduced in the previous section. We proceed as in Sec 2 by defining a semantic algebra over PGST. The operations for program statements are lifted versions of Plotkin's operations in [28]. They are shown in Table 4. The operations for specification statements are as follows:

1. **Prescription:** For any equivalence relation $R \subseteq \Sigma \times \Sigma$,

$$
\begin{array}{rcl}
\mathsf{Pres}_R & : & \mathcal{P}(\Sigma) \times \mathcal{P}(\Sigma) \to \mathsf{PGST} \\
\mathsf{Pres}_R(b, b') & = & \{c \in \mathsf{GST} \mid \forall x \in b.\, c(x) \subseteq b' \cap [x]_R\}
\end{array}
$$

   This defines our under-determinism semantics for specification statements. A specification statement stands for an arbitrary command that satisfies the specification.

2. **Constant introduction:**

$$
\begin{array}{rcl}
\mathsf{Con}_A & : & (\Sigma \to A) \times (A \to \mathsf{PGST}) \to \mathsf{PGST} \\
\mathsf{Con}_A(e, f) & = & \{c \in \mathsf{GST} \mid \forall x \in \Sigma.\, \exists c' \in f(e(x)).\, c(x) = c'(x)\}
\end{array}
$$

   This looks a bit intricate, but it is easier to see in terms of lower bound maps: $(\widehat{\mathsf{Con}_A(e, f)})(x) \;=\; \widehat{f(e(x))}(x)$.

Lemma 6. *The order-isomorphism* $T : \mathsf{PGST} \cong \mathsf{PTM}^{+}$ *is an isomorphism of the semantic algebra.*

The semantic equations in Table 4 now give a state transformer semantics for the refinement calculus. We denote these semantic functions by $\mathcal{C}_{\mathsf{S}}$ and $\mathcal{G}_{\mathsf{S}}$.

Theorem 4. *The isomorphism* $T : \mathsf{PGST} \cong \mathsf{PTM}^+$ *is an isomorphism of the semantics of refinement calculus in the sense that the following diagrams commute:*

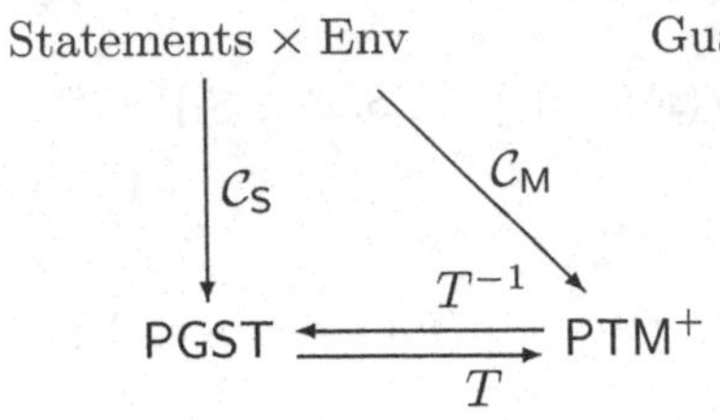

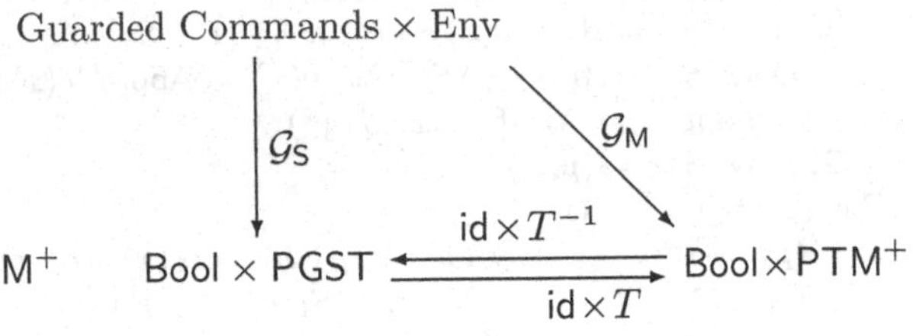

5 Beyond the Isomorphism

In the last section, we focused on giving a state transformer semantics to a refinement calculus in such a way that it matches the traditional predicate transformer semantics. The benefit of this exercise is that it gives an intuitive support for the traditional approach. However, we believe this semantics is not ideal. The state transformer set approach gives us a better handle on specifications which does not seem possible in the predicate transformer approach. In this section, we explore the new opportunities.

Consider the semantics of a **do** statement of the form **do** $B \to \boldsymbol{v}\colon [\varphi, \psi]$ **od**. The intent is that the specification $\boldsymbol{v}\colon [\varphi, \psi]$ will eventually be refined to a concrete program statement which will then be repeated during execution. If there are several possible refinements, one of them must be chosen before the execution ever begins. In contrast, the predicate transformer semantics as well as our matching state transformer semantics allow the statement of the loop body to be chosen each time the loop is repeated. In other words, they represent nondeterminism instead of under-determinism. To arrive at a better semantics, we redefine the Do operator as follows:

$$\begin{aligned} \mathsf{Do} &: \mathsf{Bool} \times \mathsf{PGST} \to \mathsf{PGST} \\ \mathsf{Do}(p, S) &= \{\mathsf{Do}_{\mathsf{GST}}(p, c) \mid c \in S\}^\dagger \\ \mathsf{Do}_{\mathsf{GST}}(p, c) &= \mathbf{fix}_{\mathsf{GST}} \lambda d.\, \lambda x.\, p(x) \rightsquigarrow \mathsf{App}(d, c(x)); \{x\} \end{aligned}$$

In this under-determinism semantics, a fixed command is chosen for the loop body which is then repeated during execution. It does not seem possible to express such an interpretation in the predicate transformer setting.

Morgan's refinement calculus contains a general constant-introduction operator of the form **con** $i\colon \tau.\, C(i)$, where there is no initialization of the constant identifier. This operator is termed "conjunction," and its meaning is explained as the worst program that is better than every $C(i)$. In other words, it is the least upper bound of all $C(i)$'s. Formally, the interpretation is

$$\mathcal{C}[\![\mathbf{con}\ i\colon \tau.\, C]\!]e \;=\; \bigsqcup_{k \in [\![\tau]\!]} \mathcal{C}[\![C]\!]e[i \to k]$$

Since, in PGST, least upper bounds are given by intersections, we obtain

$$\mathcal{C}_{\mathsf{S}}[\![\mathbf{con}\ i\colon\tau.\,C]\!]e \quad = \quad \bigcap_{k\in[\![\tau]\!]}\mathcal{C}_{\mathsf{S}}[\![C]\!]e[i\to k]$$

which says that a state transformer satisfying **con** $i\colon\tau.\,C(i)$ must satisfy $C(i)$ for every value of i. The semantics in PTM^+ amounts to:

$$\mathcal{C}_{\mathsf{M}}[\![\mathbf{con}\ i\colon\tau.\,C]\!]e \quad = \quad (\lambda a'.\,\bigcup_{k\in[\![\tau]\!]}\mathcal{C}_{\mathsf{M}}[\![C]\!]e[i\to k](a'))^*$$

Given that PGST and PTM^+ are order-isomorphic, these two interpretation match up in the sense of Theorem 4.

However, the traditional semantics [14] is given in PT where all monotone predicate transformers are present and least upper bounds are given pointwise. So, the interpretation of **con** amounts to

$$\mathcal{C}_{\mathsf{P}}[\![\mathbf{con}\ i\colon\tau.\,C]\!]e \quad = \quad \lambda a'.\,\bigcup_{k\in[\![\tau]\!]}\mathcal{C}_{\mathsf{P}}[\![C]\!]e[i\to k](a')$$

where the subscript P identifies the semantics in PT. This predicate transformer is not positively multiplicative even if every $\mathcal{C}_{\mathsf{P}}[\![C]\!]e[i\to k]$ is positively multiplicative.

What are the consequences of this mismatch? Since positively multiplicative predicate transformers form a proper subset of predicate transformers, our semantics identifies statements which would be semantically distinct in the traditional semantics. The following is an example. For convenience, we use a binary conjunction operator $C_1 \wedge C_2$, which can be regarded as a special case of the general one, for example as (**con** $i\colon\mathsf{bool}.$ **if** $i\to C_1 \,[\!]\, \neg i\to C_2$ **fi**). Consider the two statements:

$$C = [\text{true},\, n\geq 0]\wedge[\text{true},\, n\leq 0] \quad \text{and} \quad C' = [\text{true},\, n=0]$$

The collection of state transformers satisfying the two specifications is exactly the same. It is $\{\lambda x.\,\{0\}\}^{\dagger}$. (We are taking states to be the values of the variable n.) Hence, $C\equiv C'\equiv (n:=0)$ in our semantics. However, the traditional semantics interprets the two statements as the respective predicate transformers

$$\begin{aligned} t(a') &= ((a'\supseteq\mathbb{Z}^+\cup\{0\})\vee(a'\supseteq\mathbb{Z}^-\cup\{0\}))\leadsto\Sigma;\emptyset \\ t'(a') &= a'\supseteq\{0\}\leadsto\Sigma;\emptyset \end{aligned}$$

which are clearly distinct. Whereas t' is equivalent to $n:=0$, t is not equivalent to any program statement. Nevertheless, $n:=0$ is the only nontrivial statement that C can be refined to. These distinctions have nontrivial consequences under sequential composition. Consider

$$D = C;[n=0, n=9] \quad \text{and} \quad D' = C';[n=0,n=9].$$

The traditional semantics equates D to **abort**, whereas D' is equivalent to $n:=$ 9. The equivalence $D\equiv$ **abort** is surprising. We are hard put to find any intuitive explanation of why D should be equivalent to **abort**.

To pin down the difference between the traditional semantics and ours, we consider the following (hypothetical) $\wedge$-distributivity law:

$$(C_1 \wedge C_2); S \sqsubseteq (C_1; S) \wedge (C_2; S)$$

To us, this law seems unreasonable. Basically, it says that the requirements for a composite command $(C_1; S) \wedge (C_2; S)$ entail requirements for the component commands $(C_1 \wedge C_2)$. However, the law is validated by Morgan's semantics and the fact $D \sqsubseteq$ **abort** can be derived using it. This law is *not valid* in our semantics.

6 Conclusion

Refinement calculi have been proposed as integrated frameworks for combining programs and specifications and as vehicles for deriving programs from specifications. But their traditional semantics, defined in the predicate transformer setting, leaves several questions unanswered. The most important of these is what specification statements mean in terms of one's operational intuitions. By giving a semantics in terms of sets of state transformers, we hope to have answered these questions. We showed that the mysterious concept of "miracle" has a natural explanation in terms of partially defined state transformers. We also proposed that the non-multiplicative predicate transformers used in the traditional semantics may not be ideal, whereas a semantics based on positively multiplicative predicate transformers has a natural correspondence with the state transformer semantics.

We leave open the question of what it means for a semantics to be ideal. For programming languages, the ideal semantics is often taken to be a fully abstract semantics, i.e., one whose equality relation is the same as observational equivalence. For specification languages, it is not yet clear what observational equivalence might mean.

We have considered a very simple language here to focus on the main ideas. The extension of the ideas to cover procedures, abstract data types and object-oriented concepts remains to be addressed.

Acknowledgements We have benefited from discussions with David Naumann and Peter O'Hearn. This research was carried out as part of a joint US-Brazil project on refinement of object-oriented programs whose members include David Naumann, Ana Cavalcanti, Augusto Sampaio and Paulo Borba. It is supported by NSF grant INT-98-13845.

References

[1] K. Apt and G. Plotkin. A Cook's tour of countable non-determinism. In *8th ICALP*. Springer-Verlag, 1981.
[2] K. Apt and G. Plotkin. Countable nondeterminism and random assignment. *J. ACM*, 33(4):724–767, October 1986.

[3] R.-J. R. Back. On the correctness of refinement steps in program development. Report A-1978-4, Department of Computer Science, University of Helsinki, 1978.
[4] R.-J. R. Back. On the notion of correct refinement of programs. Technical report, University of Helsinki, 1979.
[5] R.-J. R. Back. A calculus of refinements for program derivations. *Acta Informatica*, 25:593–624, 1988.
[6] R.-J. R. Back and J. von Wright. *Refinement Calculus: A Systematic Introduction.* Springer-Verlag, Berlin, 1998.
[7] M. M. Bonsangue and J. N. Kok. Isomorphism between state and predicate transformers. In *Math. Foundations of Comput. Sci.*, volume 711 of *LNCS*, pages 301–310. Springer-Verlag, Berlin, 1993.
[8] M. M. Bonsangue and J. N. Kok. The weakest precondition calculus: Recursion and duality. *Formal Aspects of Computing*, 6, 1994.
[9] J. W. de Bakker. Recursive programs as predicate transformers. In E. J. Neuhold, editor, *Formal Description of Programming Concepts.* North-Holland, Amsterdam, 1978.
[10] E. Denney. *A Theory of Programm Refinement.* PhD thesis, Univ. of Edinburgh, 1999.
[11] E. W. Dijkstra. *A Discipline of Programming.* Prentice-Hall, Englewood Cliffs, 1976.
[12] P. H. B. Gardiner. Algebraic proofs of consistency and completeness. *Theoretical Comput. Sci.*, 150:161–191, 1995.
[13] P. H. B. Gardiner, C. E. Martin, and O. de Moor. An algebraic construction of predicate transformers. *Science of Computer Programming*, 22:21–44, 1994.
[14] P. H. B. Gardiner and C. C. Morgan. Data refinement of predicate transformers. *Theoretical Comput. Sci.*, 87:143–162, 1991. Reprinted in [23].
[15] C. A. Gunter. *Semantics of Programming Languages: Structures and Techniques.* MIT Press, 1992.
[16] E. C. R. Hehner. *The Logic of Programming.* Prentice-Hall, London, 1984.
[17] J. McCarthy. Towards a mathematical science of computation. In C. M. Popplewell, editor, *Information Processing 62: Proceedings of IFIP Congress 1962*, pages 21–28. North-Holland, Amsterdam, 1963.
[18] J. C. Mitchell. *Foundations of Programming Languages.* MIT Press, 1997.
[19] C. C. Morgan. The specification statement. *ACM Trans. Program. Lang. Syst.*, 10(3), Jul 1988. Reprinted in [23].
[20] C. C. Morgan. The cuppest capjunctive capping, and Galois. In A. W. Roscoe, editor, *A Classical Mind: Essays in Honor of C. A. R. Hoare.* Prentice-Hall International, 1994.
[21] C. C. Morgan. *Programming from Specifications, 2nd Edition.* Prentice-Hall, 1994.
[22] C. C. Morgan and P. H. B. Gardiner. Data refinement by calculation. *Acta Informatica*, 27, 1991. Reprinted in [23].
[23] C. C. Morgan and T. Vickers, editors. *On the Refinement Calculus.* Springer-Verlag, 1992.
[24] J. M. Morris. The theoretical basis for stepwise refinement and the programming calculus. *Science of Computer Programming*, 9(3):287–306, December 1987.
[25] D. Naumann. A categorical model for higher order imperative programming. *Math. Struct. Comput. Sci.*, 8(4):351–399, Aug 1998.
[26] D. Naumann. Predicate transformer semantics of a higher order imperative language with record subtypes. *Science of Computer Programming*, 1999. To appear.
[27] G. Nelson. A generalization of Dijkstra's calculus. *ACM Trans. Program. Lang. Syst.*, 11(4):517–561, October 1989.

[28] G. D. Plotkin. Dijkstra's predicate transformers and Smyth's power domains. In D. Bjorner, editor, *Abstract Software Specifications*, volume 86 of *LNCS*, pages 527–553. Springer-Verlag, 1980.
[29] M. B. Smyth. Powerdomains and predicate transformers: A topological view. In J. Diaz, editor, *Intern. Colloq. Aut., Lang. and Program.*, volume 154 of *LNCS*, pages 662–675. Springer-Verlag, 1983.
[30] J. E. Stoy. *Denotational Semantics: The Scott–Strachey Approach to Programming Language Theory.* MIT Press, 1977.
[31] M. Wand. A characterization of weakest preconditions. *J. Comput. Syst. Sci.*, 15(2):209–212, 1977.

Subtyping and Typing Algorithms for Mobile Ambients

Pascal Zimmer

Ecole Normale Supérieure de Lyon
Pascal.Zimmer@ens-lyon.fr

Abstract. The ambient calculus was designed to model mobile processes and study their properties. A first type system was proposed by Cardelli-Gordon-Ghelli to prevent run-time faults. We extend it by introducing subtyping and present a type-checking algorithm which returns a minimal type relatively to this system. By the way, we also add two new constructs to the language. Finally, we remove the type annotations from the syntax and give a type-inference algorithm for the original type system.

1 Introduction

With the growing development of the World-Wide-Web, it becomes interesting and fruitful to investigate the problems and properties of mobile code. The *ambient calculus* was designed to model within a single framework both *mobile computing*, that is to say computation in mobile devices like a laptop, and *mobile computation*, that is to say mobile code moving between different devices, like applets or agents. It also shows how the notions of administrative domains, their crossing, firewalls, authorizations... can be formalized in a calculus. In this sense, it is more appropriate than the π-calculus ([Mil91]), even if the bases are the same (for more discussion about the problems raised by mobility and computation over wide-area networks, see [Car99a, Car99b]).

Informally, an ambient is a bounded place, with an inside and an outside, where computation happens. Many ambients can be nested so that they form a hierarchy. Each of them has a name (not necessarily distinct from other ambient names), which will be used to control access. An ambient can be moved as a whole with all the computations and subambients it contains: it can enter another ambient or exit it. It can also be opened so that its contents get visible at the current level. For more intuitions motivating the ambient calculus or its graphical vision (the *folder calculus*), we recommend reading [CG97, CG98, Car99a].

In order to prove some specific properties concerning mobility, locking, communication... in the ambient calculus, Cardelli and Gordon proposed a simple type system, nondeterministic and without subtyping (see [CG99, CGG99]): some simple valid processes like $\langle 1\rangle \mid (x : Real).P$ were not typable. The aim of our work was to introduce a subtyping relation, deduce a typing algorithm and, in doing this, to make the type system more suitable for a treatment of mobile

J. Tiuryn (Ed.): FOSSACS 2000, LNCS 1784, pp. 375–390, 2000.

ambients as a "programming language for mobility" (departing thus from the "ambients as a specific language for reasoning on mobility" approach).

The rest of the paper is organized as follows. In Section 2, we will review briefly the ambient calculus and its semantics, by the way adding two new constructs to the original syntax. Then, in Section 3, we present our extension of the type system, introduce a subtyping ordering, and define a new typing system. In Section 4, we show that the set of derivable types for a term has got a minimum, and we give an algorithm to compute it efficiently. It is now possible to type-check a term of the ambient calculus automatically. The next step in Section 5 is to remove all type annotations from the term and try to find a type-inference algorithm. We give a complete solution for the original type system without subtyping.

This paper is a shortened version of an internship report [Zim99], which contains more explanations, further developments and all the proofs of the theorems enunciated in this paper.

2 Mobile Ambients: Syntax and Semantics

In this Section, we are going to briefly review the polyadic ambient calculus we will use throughout this paper. We will try to explain its main constructs and rules, but we recommend reading [CG98] (or any other paper presenting the calculus extensively) to have a more complete presentation. By the way, we are also going to extend the original calculus and introduce two new constructs.

The polyadic ambient calculus is mainly composed of processes. As in many other process calculi, we have an inactive process $\mathbf{0}$ which does nothing, we can compose processes in parallel ($P \mid Q$), we have a construct to replicate a process as many times as necessary ($!P$) and we have a restriction operator ($(\nu n)P$) which introduces a new name n and restricts its scope to the inside of P. In the π-calculus, those names represented channels; here they represent ambient names. In our calculus, we also declare the type of this ambient name ($(\nu n : Amb^Y[T_n, T'_n])P$), but we will not care about that until the next Section.

An ambient is composed of a name n and a process P which is running inside the ambient. We write it $n[P]$. Here we extend the syntax of the polyadic ambient calculus with a new construction. Up to now, the locking-unlocking of an ambient was defined only in the declaration of its name. So ambients with the same name had all the same locking annotation. We kept this possibility (extending it with ordering), but we changed the syntax of ambient constructions: $n[P]$ is an unlocked ambient and $n[\![P]\!]$ is a locked one. So we can now have an explicit construct which guarantees that an ambient will be locked. This can seem redundant with the locking annotation in the type declaration of n, but from a programming point of view, it just appears to be more flexible.

The process $M.P$ executes the action induced by the capability M and then continues with the process P. There are three kinds of capabilities: one to enter an other ambient ($in\ n$), one to exit ($out\ n$) and one to open up an ambient ($open\ n$). To build such a capability, a process must know the name n. It can also have received the capability via communication (see below). Implicitly, it is impossible to reconstruct the ambient name n out of one or all of these capabilities (this is important to prove the security of a firewall for example). (In the original calculus, we could also compose capabilities into paths ($M.M'$) where ε was the empty path; we do not use these constructs in this paper, but they are not difficult to handle; see [Zim99] for details.)

The use of these three capabilities is given by the following reduction rules:

$$\begin{array}{ll} n[in\ m.P \mid Q] \mid m[R] \ \rightarrow\ m[n[P \mid Q] \mid R] & \text{(Red In)} \\ m[n[out\ m.P \mid Q] \mid R] \ \rightarrow\ n[P \mid Q] \mid m[R] & \text{(Red Out)} \\ open\ n.P \mid n[Q] \ \rightarrow\ P \mid Q & \text{(Red Open)} \end{array}$$

with the convention that in (Red In) and (Red Out), each occurrence of $[.]$ can be replaced by $[\![.]\!]$ (the ambients can be locked or unlocked), whereas in (Red Open), the ambient n must be unlocked.

Here we add our second extension: the *imm* capability. A process containing it must be immobile. We added it, because also for immobility we want a language construct which obliges a process to be immobile, instead of delegating it to the types (an other reason is that, without it, no construct would introduce the mobility annotation $\veebar$ in our type system). The corresponding reduction rule

$$imm.P \ \rightarrow\ P \qquad \text{(Red Imm)}$$

is very simple and actually "ignores" the *imm* capability. In fact, *imm* is only useful when typing: if $imm.P$ is typable, then P cannot contain moving capabilities (even by receiving them). At run-time, only this guarantee is important and we can throw *imm* away.

Finally, we have two communication primitives: $(n_1 : W_1, \ldots, n_k : W_k).P$ and $\langle M_1 \times \cdots \times M_k \rangle$. The first waits for a tuple of values of respective types $W_1, \ldots, W_k$, and binds them to the variables $n_1, \ldots, n_k$ in the continuing process P. The second outputs a tuple of values. Note that the output is asynchronous (no continuing process). The corresponding reduction rule is:

$$\begin{array}{ll} (n_1 : W_1, \ldots, n_k : W_k).P \mid \langle M_1, \ldots, M_k \rangle & \\ \quad \rightarrow\ P\{n_1 \leftarrow M_1, \ldots, n_k \leftarrow M_k\} & \text{(Red Comm)} \end{array}$$

The five last rules just say that reduction (i.e. computation) can also occur beyond scope restrictions, inside ambients, or by using the structural congruence rewriting (which we will not detail here):

$$\begin{array}{ll} P \rightarrow Q \Rightarrow (\nu n : W)P \ \rightarrow\ (\nu n : W)Q & \text{(Red Res)} \\ P \rightarrow Q \Rightarrow n[P] \ \rightarrow\ n[Q] & \text{(Red Amb}_\circ\text{)} \\ P \rightarrow Q \Rightarrow n[\![P]\!] \ \rightarrow\ n[\![Q]\!] & \text{(Red Amb}_\bullet\text{)} \\ P \rightarrow Q \Rightarrow P \mid R \rightarrow Q \mid R & \text{(Red Par)} \\ P' \equiv P, P \ \rightarrow\ Q, Q \equiv Q' \ \Rightarrow\ P' \ \rightarrow\ Q' & \text{(Red } \equiv \text{)} \end{array}$$

Here is the complete syntax of our calculus. Note that it allows strange expressions like $(in\ n)[P]$ or $out\ (out\ n).P$. Rejecting those nonsense terms will be an automatic property of the type system.

$P, Q ::=$	processes		$M ::=$	expressions
$(\nu n : Amb^Y[T, T'])P$	restriction		n	name
$\mathbf{0}$	inactivity		$in\ M$	can enter into M
$P \mid Q$	composition		$out\ M$	can exit out of M
$!P$	replication		$open\ M$	can open M
$M[P]$	unlocked ambient		imm	immobility
$M[\![P]\!]$	locked ambient			
$M.P$	action			
$(n_1 : W_1, \ldots, n_k : W_k).P$	input			
$\langle M_1, \ldots, M_k \rangle$	async output			

Terms are also identified up to the consistent renaming of bound variables, in the restriction and input constructs. Thus, we can always suppose that all the ambient names and input variables are distinct.

3 A Type System with Subtyping

In order to verify some properties of processes in the ambient calculus, Cardelli and Gordon proposed a first type system in [CG99] and extended it with Ghelli in [CGG99]. It assured that a well-typed process could not cause certain kinds of run-time fault: exchanging values of the wrong type, moving or opening an ambient if it was not allowed to... We will always refer to this type system as "CGG".

In this Section, we will describe a new type system, extending (in some way) CGG. We will first introduce some new types and define an ordering relation on them (subtyping is essential to be able to write a typing algorithm). Then, we will give new typing rules and show some properties.

3.1 Type Definitions

We start by giving all the definitions of our types:

$Z ::=$	mobility annotations		$Y ::=$	locking annotations
$\bot^{\curvearrowright}$	mobility unknown		$\bot^{\circ}$	locking bottom
$\underline{\vee}$	immobile		$\bullet$	locked
$\curvearrowright$	mobile		$\circ$	unlocked
$\top^{\curvearrowright}$	mobile and immobile		$\top^{\circ}$	locking top

$O, I ::=$	input/output types		$T ::=$	process type
$\bot$		bottom value	${}^{Z}O \rightsquigarrow I$	
$W_1 \times \cdots \times W_k$	$(k \geq 0)$	tuple		
$\top$		top value		

$W ::=$	message types	
$Amb^Y[T, T']$	with $T \leq T'$ (see below)	ambient name
$Cap[T]$		capability

3.2 Intuitive Meanings and Ordering

The main intuition in defining the order is to always respect the subsumption rule: if P has got type T and $T \leq T'$, then P has also type T'. There are a few changes in the syntax of types compared to those of CGG. They were motivated by the introduction of subtyping: what seems "intuitive" is not always correct (this problem appeared clearly in the referee reports for a draft of this paper: whereas one referee found "may be mobile < immobile, may be opened < locked" as the "implicit" relation in CGG, an other one stated that "immobile < mobile and locked < unlocked" was the "obvious subtyping of CGG").

Mobility Annotations What is the "obvious" subtyping of CGG ? It depends on the point of view. If we consider that an immobile process can generate movements, we should define $\underline{\vee} < \curvearrowright$. For example, everybody would say that the process $\mathbf{0}$ is immobile, but in order to type $in\ n.\mathbf{0}$, we should also be able to say that $\mathbf{0}$ is mobile. On the other hand, with this definition, if we restrict a process to stay immobile, it can always remove this restriction with the subsumption rule, which speaks more in favour of $\curvearrowright < \underline{\vee}$.

The subtyping relation we need depends on the property we privilege: generation of movement or restriction of immobile processes. If we want to keep both results, we have to introduce a new symbol $\perp_{\curvearrowright}$, and keep $\curvearrowright$ and $\underline{\vee}$ incomparable. In order to have a complete lattice, we introduce also $\top^{\curvearrowright}$ (which will also be useful in the typing algorithm and for the ambient types), and we define $\perp_{\curvearrowright} < \underline{\vee}, \curvearrowright < \top^{\curvearrowright}$. Since this structure is a complete lattice (4 points with a lozenge-like ordering), there is no problem to define meet and join operations on it.

Process Type In the type system of CGG, there was only one single term representing the type of values exchanged in the ambient (Shh or a tuple). In presence of subtyping, we should now accept that outputs and inputs have different types. For example, the output of the integer 1 should be accepted by an input variable of type $Real$. So we decided to track the types of output and input values exchanged in the ambient. If a process is valid, it must then have type ${}^{Z}O \rightsquigarrow I$ with $O \leq I$ to ensure that any output can be read by any input instruction (note that this is not specified in the syntax of T, but will be a property of the type system; see also below). Later, it appeared that Yoshida and Hennessy used the same approach for a higher-order π-calculus with subtyping ([YH99]). Moreover, a valid process should not contain both mobile and immobile instructions; consequently the mobility annotation $\top^{\curvearrowright}$ is forbidden for processes.

Definition 1 (Validity). *A process type ${}^{Z}O \rightsquigarrow I$ is said to be* valid *if $Z \neq \top^{\curvearrowright}$ and $O \leq I$.*

For the process type, we define :

$$ {}^{Z}O \rightsquigarrow I \leq {}^{Z'}O' \rightsquigarrow I' \iff \begin{cases} Z \leq Z' \\ O \leq O' \\ I \geq I' \end{cases} $$

$$
\begin{aligned}
{}^{Z}O \rightsquigarrow I \wedge {}^{Z'}O' \rightsquigarrow I' &\triangleq {}^{Z\wedge Z'}O \wedge O' \rightsquigarrow I \vee I' \\
{}^{Z}O \rightsquigarrow I \vee {}^{Z'}O' \rightsquigarrow I' &\triangleq {}^{Z\vee Z'}O \vee O' \rightsquigarrow I \wedge I'
\end{aligned}
$$

The set of all process types has a complete lattice structure, with ${}^{\downarrow\!\rightarrow}\bot \rightsquigarrow \top$ as the minimal element and ${}^{\Rsh}\top \rightsquigarrow \bot$ as the maximal one. But, if we consider only valid processes, there are many maximal types: all ${}^{\curvearrowright}O \rightsquigarrow O$ and ${}^{\underline{\vee}}O \rightsquigarrow O$ for every input/output type O.

Input/Output Types Then, we have to define what are output and input types. As before, it can be a tuple. But we had to replace Shh by two different values, one for outputs ($Shh_{out} = \bot$) and one for inputs ($Shh_{in} = \top$). Then it appeared useful to consider that the meaning of these values was different for the input and output terms:

Value	Output term (O)	Input term (I)
$\bot$	No output Dumb process (Shh_{out})	There can be an input of any type
$\top$	There can be an output of any type	No input Deaf process (Shh_{in})

For example, if there are two outputs of different arities in parallel, the resulting process has type $\top$ for O. With the condition that $O \leq I$, the process is valid if and only if $I = \top$, i.e. if there are no input instruction (you can say anything only if nobody is listening). A similar argument holds by exchanging inputs and outputs. This is a different vision from [YH99] where $\top$ was forbidden as an output type and $\bot$ as an input type.

For the input/output types, we define the partial order:

$$
\begin{gathered}
\bot < W_1 \times \cdots \times W_k < \top \qquad \forall k\, \forall W_i \\
W_1 \times \cdots \times W_k \leq W_1' \times \cdots \times W_k' \iff W_i \leq W_i' \ \ \forall\, 1 \leq i \leq k
\end{gathered}
$$

This definition induces a complete lattice structure on input/output types, so that the meet and join operations are always defined (the obvious cases with $\bot$ and $\top$ are omitted for simplicity):

$$
W_1 \times \cdots \times W_k \wedge W_1' \times \cdots \times W_{k'}' \triangleq \begin{cases} W_1 \wedge W_1' \times \cdots \times W_1 \wedge W_k' & \text{if } k = k' \\ \quad \text{and } W_i \wedge W_i' \text{ is defined } \forall\, 1 \leq i \leq k \\ \\ \bot \quad \text{otherwise} \end{cases}
$$

$$
W_1 \times \cdots \times W_k \vee W_1' \times \cdots \times W_{k'}' \triangleq \begin{cases} W_1 \vee W_1' \times \cdots \times W_1 \vee W_k' & \text{if } k = k' \\ \quad \text{and } W_i \vee W_i' \text{ is defined } \forall\, 1 \leq i \leq k \\ \\ \top \quad \text{otherwise} \end{cases}
$$

Message Types Finally, we have a type for messages that can be exchanged in an ambient. It can be either an ambient name or a capability. It is safe to add here other common types like Int, $Bool$...

A capability $Cap[T]$ contains simply the effects T which will be released if the capability is executed. And the ordering is natural:

$$Cap[T] \leq Cap[T'] \iff T \leq T'$$

$$Cap[T] \wedge Cap[T'] \triangleq Cap[T \wedge T']$$
$$Cap[T] \vee Cap[T'] \triangleq Cap[T \vee T']$$

An ambient name is composed of a locking annotation and two types representing the processes running inside the ambient. Concerning the locking annotations, we can repeat the same discussion as for mobility annotations. Thus we add two new symbols $\bot_\circ$ and $\top^\circ$, and define $\bot_\circ < \bullet, \circ < \top^\circ$ with $\bullet$ and $\circ$ incomparable.

With $\bot_\circ$ all three constructions $n[P]$, $n[\![P]\!]$ and *open* n are allowed. With $\circ$ only $n[P]$ and *open* n are allowed, and with $\bullet$ only $n[\![P]\!]$ is allowed. With $\top^\circ$ none of them is allowed. However, note that all other constructions (like *in* n or $\langle n \rangle$) are valid with any locking annotation for n.

Concerning the process running inside an ambient, it seems that only one process type would be enough (it was in CGG). With subtyping, we would like to say that a process is allowed to run inside an ambient of type $Amb^Y[T]$ if and only if it has a type $T' \leq T$ (so that $\mathbf{0}$ is always accepted). T represents the maximal effects allowed in the ambient.

Now, what is the natural ordering for ambient names ? Suppose $Amb^Y[T] \leq Amb^Y[T']$ when $T \leq T'$. Then, if n has type $Amb^Y[T]$, it has type $Amb^Y[T']$ by the subsumption rule for any $T' \geq T$. Thus, $n[P]$ is typable for any process P of arbitrary type T', which is contrary to our requirements.

On the other hand, suppose $Amb^Y[T] \leq Amb^Y[T']$ when $T' \leq T$. Then, if n has type $Amb^Y[T]$, it has type $Amb^Y[T_{min}]$ where T_{min} is the minimal process type. *open* n has type $Cap[T_{min}]$, which is contrary to our intuition: n can contain processes with "stronger" effects.

This explains why we need two process types in the type of an ambient name, with two different orderings. In $Amb^Y[T, T']$, T represents the maximal type allowed for processes inside the ambient (i.e. all valid processes also have type T) (cf. rules (Proc Amb$_\circ$) and (Proc Amb$_\bullet$) in Section 3.3), whereas T' represents the maximal effect a valid process can produce (cf. rule (Exp Open)), thus the condition $T \leq T'$ to be coherent. We define:

$$Amb^Y[T_1, T_2] \leq Amb^{Y'}[T_1', T_2'] \iff \begin{cases} Y \leq Y' \\ T_1 \geq T_1' \\ T_2 \leq T_2' \end{cases}$$

At first sight, it could seem strange to declare a new ambient name with $T < T'$: if we specify the maximal allowed type T, why would we say that worse effects T' can appear when opening an ambient of that name ? In fact, we need them to be consistent with the rest of the calculus. Suppose we want to write the program $\langle n \rangle \mid \langle m \rangle \mid (x :?).P$ where n and m accept processes of type T_n and T_m respectively. What input type should we declare for x ? We can use the type of the parallel output $\langle n \rangle \mid \langle m \rangle$, which is with our ordering $Amb^Y[T_n \wedge T_m, T_n \vee T_m]$.

In general, there is no reason to have $T_n \wedge T_m = T_n \vee T_m$. This explains why we cannot replace T and T' by one single process type in an ambient name.

Note that the conditions $Z \neq \overset{\rightarrow}{\top}$ and $O \leq I$ are not required for an ambient name. For example, $Amb^Y[\overset{\rightarrow}{\top}\top \rightsquigarrow \bot, \overset{\rightarrow}{\top}\top \rightsquigarrow \bot]$ is the type of an ambient name allowing all processes, whereas the ambient name $Amb^Y[\overset{\rightarrow}{\bot}\bot \rightsquigarrow \top, \overset{\rightarrow}{\bot}\bot \rightsquigarrow \top]$ is the most restrictive one, allowing only processes which do not have inputs or outputs, i.e. only processes behaving like **0**.

We can only define partial meet and join operations, since there are some incomparable types (the other cases are undefined):

$$Amb^Y[T_1, T_2] \wedge Amb^{Y'}[T_1', T_2'] \triangleq Amb^{Y \wedge Y'}[T_1 \vee T_1', T_2 \wedge T_2']$$
$$\text{if } T_1 \vee T_1' \leq T_2 \wedge T_2' \text{ (or equivalently if } T_1 \leq T_2' \text{ and } T_1' \leq T_2)$$

$$Amb^Y[T_1, T_2] \vee Amb^{Y'}[T_1', T_2'] \triangleq Amb^{Y \vee Y'}[T_1 \wedge T_1', T_2 \vee T_2']$$

There is no comparability between ambient names and capabilities. It is safe to add other useful types here with their usual ordering (for example, $Int \leq Real$), with no comparability with ambient names and capabilities.

The set of capability types has a structure similar to the process types (i.e. a complete lattice). The set of ambient names has a maximal element ($Amb^{\top^\circ}[\overset{\rightarrow}{\bot}\bot \rightsquigarrow \top, \overset{\rightarrow}{\top}\top \rightsquigarrow \bot]$), but infinitely many minimal elements: all the types $Amb^{\bot^\circ}[T, T]$ for every process type T.

3.3 Typing Rules

Having defined the types and explained their ordering, we can now give the typing rules of this new type system. A feature of the present approach w.r.t. CGG is that we avoid to introduce arbitrary types in the conclusions of typing rules. However note that this derivation system is also not deterministic because of the subsumption rules and the shape of some rules (for example, in (Proc Par), the same type T appears in two premises).

Good Environment ($E \vdash \diamond$)

$$\text{(Env } \emptyset\text{)} \ \frac{}{\emptyset \vdash \diamond} \qquad \text{(Env } n\text{)} \ \frac{E \vdash \diamond \quad n \notin dom(E)}{E, n : W \vdash \diamond}$$

These two rules are exactly the same as in CGG.

Good Expression of Type W ($E \vdash M : W$)

$$\text{(Exp In)} \ \frac{E \vdash M : Amb^Y[T, T']}{E \vdash in\ M : Cap[\frown\bot \rightsquigarrow \top]} \qquad \text{(Exp Out)} \ \frac{E \vdash M : Amb^Y[T, T']}{E \vdash out\ M : Cap[\frown\bot \rightsquigarrow \top]}$$

$$\text{(Exp Open)} \ \frac{E \vdash M : Amb^\circ[T, T']}{E \vdash open\ M : Cap[T']} \qquad \text{(Exp Imm)} \ \frac{E \vdash \diamond}{E \vdash imm : Cap[\veebar\bot \rightsquigarrow \top]}$$

$$\text{(Exp } n\text{)} \ \frac{E', n : W, E'' \vdash \diamond}{E', n : W, E'' \vdash n : W} \qquad \text{(Exp Sub)} \ \frac{E \vdash M : W \quad W \leq W'}{E \vdash M : W'}$$

In (Exp In), (Exp Out) and (Exp Imm), the type in the conclusion of the rule is the minimal effect (or constraint) that the corresponding instruction produces. In (Exp Open), we use the maximal effect contained in the ambient name and we check that M is an unlocked ambient. In (Exp Sub), we allow to upgrade the type of an expression. The other rules are identical to those of CGG.

Good Process of Type T ($E \vdash P : T$)

$$\text{(Proc Par)}\ \frac{E \vdash P : T \quad E \vdash Q : T}{E \vdash P \mid Q : T} \qquad \text{(Proc Action)}\ \frac{E \vdash M : Cap[T] \quad E \vdash P : T}{E \vdash M.P : T}$$

$$\text{(Proc Zero)}\ \frac{E \vdash \diamond}{E \vdash \mathbf{0} : {}^{+}\!\bot \rightsquigarrow \top} \qquad \text{(Proc Repl)}\ \frac{E \vdash P : T}{E \vdash !P : T}$$

$$\text{(Proc Res)}\ \frac{E, n : Amb^{Y}[T_n, T_n'] \vdash P : T}{E \vdash (\nu n : Amb^{Y}[T_n, T_n'])P : T}$$

$$\text{(Proc Amb}_\circ\text{)}\ \frac{E \vdash M : Amb^{\circ}[T, T'] \quad E \vdash P : T}{E \vdash M[P] : {}^{+}\!\bot \rightsquigarrow \top}$$

$$\text{(Proc Amb}_\bullet\text{)}\ \frac{E \vdash M : Amb^{\bullet}[T, T'] \quad E \vdash P : T}{E \vdash M[\![P]\!] : {}^{+}\!\bot \rightsquigarrow \top}$$

$$\text{(Proc Input)}\ \frac{E, n_1 : W_1, \ldots, n_k : W_k \vdash P : {}^{Z}O \rightsquigarrow I \quad I \leq W_1 \times \cdots \times W_k}{E \vdash (n_1 : W_1, \ldots, n_k : W_k).P : {}^{Z}O \rightsquigarrow I}$$

$$\text{(Proc Output)}\ \frac{E \vdash M_1 : W_1 \quad \cdots \quad E \vdash M_k : W_k \quad (E \vdash \diamond \text{ if } k = 0)}{E \vdash \langle M_1, \ldots, M_k \rangle : {}^{+}W_1 \times \cdots \times W_k \rightsquigarrow \top}$$

$$\text{(Proc Sub)}\ \frac{E \vdash P : T \quad T \leq T' \quad T' \text{ valid}}{E \vdash P : T'}$$

(Proc Par), (Proc Action), (Proc Repl) and (Proc Res) are the same rules as those of CGG (with a syntax modification for (Proc Res)). In (Proc Zero), we use the minimal process type.

In (Proc Amb$_\circ$), we check that M is an unlocked ambient name and that P has the type of an allowed process inside M (with the subsumption rule, we can always upgrade it or decrease the type in the ambient name so that they match). Like for **0**, we use the minimal process type in the conclusion of the rule. (Proc Amb$_\bullet$) is similar.

In (Proc Input), we just need to check that the input type of the process P is below the type generated by the input (i.e. is more specific since the ordering for input types is contravariant). This is valid: every input type is accepted in the conclusion provided that it covers the input $W_1 \times \cdots \times W_k$. If P has a bigger input type ($\top$ for **0** for example), it must first be upgraded with the subsumption rule before applying (Proc Input).

In (Proc Output), we just give the minimal effect: the output of a type $W_1 \times \cdots \times W_k$. Since the output is asynchronous, there is no condition to check like in (Proc Input).

(Proc Sub) is the classical subsumption rule, with the additional condition that the new process type must be valid (we are explicitly typing a process here and not a capability or an ambient name).

3.4 Results

Theorem 2 (Subject reduction). *If* $E \vdash P : T$ *and* $P \rightarrow Q$*, then* $E \vdash Q : T$.

Theorem 3 (Validity). *If* $E \vdash P : T$*, then* T *is valid.*

By this last theorem, we are sure that a well-typed process will never cause run-time faults, i.e. there will never be an exchange of incompatible values during execution and it cannot contain instructions requiring both mobility and immobility (like in $imm.in\ n.P$). Another desired property is that we do not want an ambient to be opened if it is locked. This property is a direct result of the type system: the instructions $open\ n$ and $n[P]$ can be typed only if we can prove that n is unlocked.

4 A First Typing Algorithm

In this Section, we are going to deduce a typing algorithm from the type system we introduced in the previous one. Then, we will see that this algorithm returns exactly all the types (in a certain sense) that could be derived.

4.1 Typing Rules

Definition 4. *An environment is said to be* well-formed *if all the names it contains are different. This is of course equivalent to* $E \vdash \diamond$. *Algorithmically, it just consists in checking that all the names are different.*

For any well-formed environment E, we define an algorithm returning the type of expressions and processes by the following rules. For every undefined case, we will say that the algorithm *fails*. Note that even if we write it as derivation rules for simplicity, it can also be expressed directly in an algorithmic way. Note also that the algorithm can be implemented in a parallel way when there are several recursive calls (for instance in (Type Par)).

Type of an Expression M ($Type(E, M) = W$)

$$\text{(Type In)}\ \frac{Type(E, M) = Amb^{Y}[T, T']}{Type(E, in\ M) = Cap[{}^{\frown}\bot \rightsquigarrow \top]}$$

$$\text{(Type Out)}\ \frac{Type(E, M) = Amb^{Y}[T, T']}{Type(E, out\ M) = Cap[{}^{\frown}\bot \rightsquigarrow \top]}$$

$$\text{(Type Open)}\ \frac{Type(E, M) = Amb^{Y}[T, T'] \quad Y \leq \circ}{Type(E, open\ M) = Cap[T']}$$

$$\text{(Type Imm)}\ \frac{}{Type(E, imm) = Cap[{}^{\curlyvee}\bot \rightsquigarrow \top]}$$

$$\text{(Type } n\text{)}\ \frac{}{Type((E', n : W, E''), n) = W}$$

For each message type, we always return the minimal type required by this capability (for example, $Cap[{}^{\frown}\bot \rightsquigarrow \top]$ for $in\ M$). In (Type Open), we return the maximal effects T' which can appear when opening an ambient of that name and we check that this ambient is unlocked by $Y \leq \circ$.

Type of a Process P ($Type(E, P) = T$)

$$\text{(Type Par)}\ \frac{Type(E,P) = T \quad Type(E,Q) = T' \quad T \vee T' \ valid}{Type(E, P \mid Q) = T \vee T'}$$

$$\text{(Type Action)}\ \frac{Type(E,M) = Cap[T] \quad Type(E,P) = T' \quad T \vee T' \ valid}{Type(E, M.P) = T \vee T'}$$

$$\text{(Type Zero)}\ \frac{}{Type(E,\mathbf{0}) = {}^{\downarrow}\bot \rightsquigarrow \top} \qquad \text{(Type Repl)}\ \frac{Type(E,P) = T}{Type(E, !P) = T}$$

$$\text{(Type Res)}\ \frac{Type((E, n : Amb^Y[T_n, T_n']), P) = T}{Type(E, (\nu n : Amb^Y[T_n, T_n'])P) = T}$$

$$\text{(Type Amb}_\circ\text{)}\ \frac{Type(E,M) = Amb^Y[T,T'] \quad Type(E,P) = T'' \quad T'' \leq T \quad Y \leq \circ}{Type(E, M[P]) = {}^{\downarrow}\bot \rightsquigarrow \top}$$

$$\text{(Type Amb}_\bullet\text{)}\ \frac{Type(E,M) = Amb^Y[T,T'] \quad Type(E,P) = T'' \quad T'' \leq T \quad Y \leq \bullet}{Type(E, M[\![P]\!]) = {}^{\downarrow}\bot \rightsquigarrow \top}$$

$$\text{(Type Input)}\ \frac{Type((E, n_1 : W_1, \ldots, n_k : W_k), P) = {}^{Z}O \rightsquigarrow I \quad O \leq W_1 \times \cdots \times W_k}{Type(E, (n_1 : W_1, \ldots, n_k : W_k).P) = {}^{Z}O \rightsquigarrow I \wedge W_1 \times \cdots \times W_k}$$

$$\text{(Type Output)}\ \frac{Type(E, M_1) = W_1 \quad \cdots \quad Type(E, M_k) = W_k}{Type(E, \langle M_1, \ldots, M_k \rangle) = {}^{\downarrow}W_1 \times \cdots \times W_k \rightsquigarrow \top}$$

In (Type Par), we just take the join of the two sub-processes types, ensuring first that the resulting process is still valid.

In (Type Amb$_\circ$), we must check that the type T'' of P is accepted by this ambient ($T'' \leq T$) and that the ambient can be opened ($Y \leq \circ$).

In (Type Input), we add the information of the input instruction by returning the meet of I and $W_1 \times \cdots \times W_k$. We must also check that $O \leq W_1 \times \cdots \times W_k$ in P, to ensure that $O \leq I \wedge W_1 \times \cdots \times W_k$ in the resulting process.

In (Type Output), we just put the information of an output of type $W_1 \times \cdots \times W_k$. Since there is no continuation, there is nothing to check here.

The other rules are similar or (quite) natural.

4.2 Results

Theorem 5 (Soundness).

- *If $Type(E, M) = W$, then $E \vdash M : W$.*
- *If $Type(E, P) = T$, then $E \vdash P : T$.*

Theorem 6 (Completeness).

- *If $E \vdash M : W$, then the algorithm succeeds on M and $Type(E, M) \leq W$.*
- *If $E \vdash P : T$, then the algorithm succeeds on P and $Type(E, P) \leq T$.*

From those two theorems, we easily deduce the property of minimal type for our type system and that the algorithm is able to compute it efficiently.

Corollary 7 (Minimal Type). *The set of all possible types for a typable expression or process has a minimum and this minimum is precisely the type returned by the algorithm.*

5 Type Inference

In the previous Section, we described a deterministic typing algorithm. This is a satisfactory result, to be compared to the nondeterministic type system we had before. But, up to now, this algorithm performs only type-checking: the programmer must still annotate explicitly all ambient names and input variables with their types. To go one step further, the natural extension would be to remove these type annotations and try to design a type-inference algorithm. Unfortunately, even if at first sight this seems to require only minor modifications, some new and difficult problems appear if we want to keep the subtyping relation. So we will have to go a little back and restrict our problem to the original type system of CGG. For this system, we will show that it can be completely and efficiently solved with a Damas-Milner style algorithm.

5.1 Background

For the syntax, we will consider the calculus we studied since the beginning, that is with the two new constructs and the associated reduction rules (they do not bring any new difficulties). For the type system, we will nearly take the typing rules of CGG, as they are described in [CGG99]. We modify them only to handle the two new constructs.

Instead of simply removing the type annotations, we keep them but allow to write type variables instead. For this, we must extend the definitions of types by adding an infinite set of variables for each of them. More generally, for the same letter, the lower case one will denote a type variable and the upper case one will denote a metavariable (as before).

Now we can write expressions like $(x : w).P$ or $(\nu n : Amb^y[t])P$, or even $(x : Cap[\frown u]).P$. In fact, we allow to mix both type variables and explicit types in a same term or even in a same type expression. By this mean, we get a more generic algorithm, and this property can be useful in practice: for example, if you want to check an insecure code, you should be able to constraint some of its types by specifying them explicitly before applying the type-inference algorithm. Note also that one can express equality constraints between types just by using the same variable: in $(x : w).P \mid (y : w).Q$, the input variables x and y must have the same type.

5.2 The Algorithm

We first need some classical definitions and results: a *substitution* is a total map from the set of all type variables (of any kind) to types of the same kind. We will denote them by the letters σ, θ, ρ... The empty substitution is the identity function and will be noted **id**. Finally, the composition of substitutions is defined in exactly the same way as functions. We extend naturally substitutions to complex types (and not only type variables), to processes (by replacing type annotations in input and restriction constructions) and to environments.

An *unifier* of two types X_1 and X_2 is a substitution σ such that $\sigma(X_1) = \sigma(X_2)$. Since the types in our system are simple trees, we know that there is a sound and complete unification algorithm for those types. It returns the *principal unifier* of two types (when it exists; otherwise it fails). We will call it $mgu(.,.)$ (it is not difficult to write its rules explicitly).

We can know give the rules of the typing algorithm. They are used to infer judgments of the forms $Infer(E, M) = (W, \sigma)$ and $Infer(E, P) = (T, \sigma)$, where W or T is the most generic possible type for M or P (possibly containing type variables), σ is a substitution representing the constraints on the type variables in M or P, and E is a well-formed environment.

In the following rules, the premises must be read (and applied) from left to right. We do not detail how the algorithm gets *new* type variables. We will only consider that whenever a variable is declared **new**, it is different from all type variables previously used. In practice this can be achieved by using a global counter to number new type variables.

Type-Inference for an Expression M ($Infer(E,M)$)

$$\text{(Infer In)}\ \frac{Infer(E,M) = (W,\sigma) \quad y,t\ \mathbf{new} \quad mgu(W, Amb^y[t]) = \rho \quad u\ \mathbf{new}}{Infer(E, in\ M) = (Cap[{}^{\frown}u], \rho\sigma)}$$

$$\text{(Infer Out)}\ \frac{Infer(E,M) = (W,\sigma) \quad y,t\ \mathbf{new} \quad mgu(W, Amb^y[t]) = \rho \quad u\ \mathbf{new}}{Infer(E, out\ M) = (Cap[{}^{\frown}u], \rho\sigma)}$$

$$\text{(Infer Open)}\ \frac{Infer(E,M) = (W,\sigma) \quad t\ \mathbf{new} \quad mgu(W, Amb^{\circ}[t]) = \rho}{Infer(E, open\ M) = (Cap[\rho(t)], \rho\sigma)}$$

$$\text{(Infer Imm)}\ \frac{u\ \mathbf{new}}{Infer(E, imm) = (Cap[{}^{\underline{\vee}}u], \mathbf{id})}$$

$$\text{(Infer } n\text{)}\ \frac{}{Infer((E, n : W, E'), n) = (W, \mathbf{id})}$$

Type-Inference for a Process P ($Infer(E,P)$)

$$\text{(Infer Par)}\ \frac{Infer(E,P) = (T,\sigma) \quad Infer(\sigma(E), \sigma(Q)) = (T', \sigma') \quad mgu(\sigma'(T), T') = \rho}{Infer(E, P \mid Q) = (\rho(T'), \rho\sigma'\sigma)}$$

$$\text{(Infer Zero)}\ \frac{t\ \mathbf{new}}{Infer(E, \mathbf{0}) = (t, \mathbf{id})} \qquad \text{(Infer Repl)}\ \frac{Infer(E,P) = (T,\sigma)}{Infer(E, !P) = (T,\sigma)}$$

$$\text{(Infer Action)}\ \frac{Infer(E,M) = (W,\sigma) \quad Infer(\sigma(E), \sigma(P)) = (T, \sigma') \quad mgu(\sigma'(W), Cap[T]) = \rho}{Infer(E, M.P) = (\rho(T), \rho\sigma'\sigma)}$$

$$\text{(Infer Res)}\ \frac{Infer((E, n : Amb^Y[T]), P) = (T', \sigma)}{Infer(E, (\nu n : Amb^Y[T])P) = (T', \sigma)}$$

$$\text{(Infer Amb}_{\circ}\text{)}\ \frac{Infer(E,M) = (W,\sigma) \quad Infer(\sigma(E), \sigma(P)) = (T, \sigma') \quad mgu(\sigma'(W), Amb^{\circ}[T]) = \rho \quad t\ \mathbf{new}}{Infer(E, M[P]) = (t, \rho\sigma'\sigma)}$$

$$\text{(Infer Amb}_\bullet) \; \frac{Infer(E,M) = (W,\sigma) \quad Infer(\sigma(E),\sigma(P)) = (T,\sigma') \quad mgu(\sigma'(W), Amb^\bullet[T]) = \rho \quad t \textbf{ new}}{Infer(E, M[\![P]\!]) = (t, \rho\sigma'\sigma)}$$

$$\text{(Infer Input)} \; \frac{Infer((E, n_1 : W_1, \ldots, n_k : W_k), P) = (T,\sigma) \quad z \textbf{ new} \quad mgu(T, {}^z\sigma(W_1) \times \cdots \times \sigma(W_k)) = \rho}{Infer(E, (n_1 : W_1, \ldots, n_k : W_k).P) = (\rho(T), \rho\sigma)}$$

$$\text{(Infer Output)} \; \frac{Infer(E, M_1) = (W_1,\sigma_1) \quad Infer(\sigma_1(E), M_2) = (W_2,\sigma_2) \quad \cdots \quad Infer(\sigma_{k-1}\ldots\sigma_1(E), M_k) = (W_k,\sigma_k) \quad z \textbf{ new}}{Infer(E, \langle M_1, \ldots, M_k\rangle) = ({}^z\sigma_k \ldots \sigma_2(W_1) \times \cdots \times \sigma_k(W_{k-1}) \times W_k, \sigma_k \ldots \sigma_1)}$$

5.3 Results

Theorem 8 (Soundness). *If $Infer(E,P) = (T,\sigma)$, then $\sigma(E) \vdash_{CGG} \sigma(P) : T$. Moreover, $\sigma'\sigma(E) \vdash_{CGG} \sigma'\sigma(P) : \sigma'(T)$ for any substitution σ' (we will say that all these derivations are* solutions *returned by the inference algorithm).*

Theorem 9 (Completeness). *If there is a type T such that $\sigma(E) \vdash_{CGG} \sigma(P) : T$ (i.e. if the process P is typable in the environment E after performing some substitutions on type variables), the inference algorithm $Infer(E,P)$ succeeds and $\sigma(E) \vdash_{CGG} \sigma(P) : T$ is one of the returned solutions.*

5.4 Type Inference with Subtyping

Returning back to the original problem, can we do the same as above with the type system with subtyping ? Adding subtyping brings many problems, mainly because there is no minimal type for ambient names and because we get ordering constraints due to ambient names and valid processes. Some similar problems appeared in the type system of Abadi and Cardelli for object calculus. In this case, Jens Palsberg gave a solution in [Pal95], by building a graph of constraints and checking some properties on it. Maybe the same approach would be possible with the ambient calculus, but our attempts in this way failed. Up to now, all we could do is build a set of constraints that type variables should satisfy in order to get a solution. But solving it remains an open problem (see [Zim99] for more details and explanations).

6 Conclusion

We have extended the previous type system for mobile ambients with new types and with a subtyping relation. We gave the corresponding typing rules and deduced a type-checking algorithm. We also gave a type-inference algorithm for CGG, but the problem of solving the constraints set in the system with subtyping remains open.

These algorithms are efficient and could be implemented quite easily. To our knowledge, there are two "implementations" of ambients so far: a Java applet from L. Cardelli and a translation into the join-calculus in a modified version of Objective Caml ([FS99]). None of them use types for now.

An other primitive was introduced by Cardelli-Ghelli-Gordon in [CGG99]: the primitive *go*, which performs objective moves. To prevent some dangerous effects such moves can induce (entrapping of an ambient), they extended the type system so that the type of an ambient name says explicitly if the ambient allows them or not. We did not keep this primitive to simplify the notations for ambient names, but we checked that all our work and algorithms could be easily extended so as to include *go*.

In [LS00], Levi and Sangiorgi studied *plain and grave interferences* in the ambient calculus. They proposed a syntax extension along with a new type system to prevent grave interferences. Future work may be to extend our subtyping relation and algorithms to their system.

Acknowledgments

This work is the result of a two-months internship in the University of Turin, Italy. I would like to express my gratitude to Mariangiola Dezani, who supervised the internship and proposed the subject. Many thanks also to Paola Giannini, Ferruccio Damiani and Giorgio Ghelli for some useful suggestions and pointers. Last but not least, thanks to Daniel Hirschkoff for correcting the draft.

References

[Car99a] L. Cardelli. Abstractions for Mobile Computation. *Secure Internet Programming: Security Issues for Distributed and Mobile Objects*, 1999.

[Car99b] L. Cardelli. Wide Area Computation. In *ICALP'99*, April 1999.

[CG97] L. Cardelli and A. D. Gordon. A Calculus of mobile Ambients. 1997. Slides.

[CG98] L. Cardelli and A. D. Gordon. Mobile Ambients. In *Proceedings FoSSaCS'98*, volume LNCS 1378, pages 140–155. Springer, 1998.

[CG99] L. Cardelli and A. D. Gordon. Types for Mobile Ambients. In *Proceedings of the 26th ACM Symposium on Principles of Programming Languages*, pages 79–92. ACM, January 1999.

[CGG99] L. Cardelli, G. Ghelli, and A. D. Gordon. Mobility Types for Mobile Ambients. In *Proceedings of ICALP'99*, volume LNCS, April 1999.

[FS99] C. Fournet and A. Schmitt. An Implementation of Ambients in JoCaml. In *Proceedings MOS'99*, April 1999.

[LS00] F. Levi and D. Sangiorgi. Controlling Interference in Ambients. Draft of a paper to appear in the Proceedings of POPL'00, 2000.

[Mil91] R. Milner. The Polyadic π-Calculus: a Tutorial. Technical Report ECS-LFCS-91-180, University of Edinburgh, October 1991.

[Pal95] J. Palsberg. Efficient Inference of Object Types. *Information and Computation*, 1995.

[YH99] N. Yoshida and M. Hennessy. Subtyping and Locality in Distributed Higher Order Processes. Technical Report 01/99, University of Sussex, May 1999.

[Zim99] P. Zimmer. Subtyping and Typing Algorithms for Mobile Ambients. Internship Report – Ecole Normale Supérieure de Lyon, 1999. Available at `http://www.ens-lyon.fr/~pzimmer/`.

Author Index

Baier, Christel, 1
Barthe, Gilles, 17
Bérard, Beatrice, 35

Caucal, Didier, 48

Damiani, Ferruccio, 82
Di Cosmo, Roberto, 63
Drewes, Frank, 98

Engelhardt, Kai, 114

Hannay, Jo Erskine, 130
Herescu, Oltea Mihaela, 146
Hoffmann, Berthold, 98
Honsell, Furio , 161
Husson, Jean-François , 177

Kesner, Delia, 63

Labroue, Anne, 35
Laroussinie, François, 192
Lin, Huimin, 208
Longley, John, 161

Maietti, Maria Emilia, 223
Merro, Massimo, 238
Meyden, Ron van der, 114
Morin, Rémi , 177
Morvan, Christophe, 252
Moses, Yoram, 114

Paiva, Valeria de, 223
Palamidessi, Catuscia, 146
Pinto, Jorge Sousa, 267
Plump, Detlef, 98
Polonovski, Emmanuel, 63

Quaglia, Paola, 283

Raamsdonk, Femke van, 17
Reddy, Uday S., 359
Ritter, Eike, 223

Sannella, Donald , 161
Schnoebelen, Philippe, 35, 192
Schubert, Aleksy, 297
Stoelinga, Mariëlle, 1

Tarlecki, Andrzej, 161
Thiemann, Peter, 314
Treinen, Ralf, 329
Tsay, Yih-Kuen, 344

Walker, David, 283

Yang, Hongseok, 359
Yi, Wang, 208

Zimmer, Pascal, 375

Lecture Notes in Computer Science

For information about Vols. 1–1707
please contact your bookseller or Springer-Verlag

Vol. 1708: J.M. Wing, J. Woodcock, J. Davies (Eds.), FM'99 – Formal Methods. Proceedings Vol. I, 1999. XVIII, 937 pages. 1999.

Vol. 1709: J.M. Wing, J. Woodcock, J. Davies (Eds.), FM'99 – Formal Methods. Proceedings Vol. II, 1999. XVIII, 937 pages. 1999.

Vol. 1710: E.-R. Olderog, B. Steffen (Eds.), Correct System Design. XIV, 417 pages. 1999.

Vol. 1711: N. Zhong, A. Skowron, S. Ohsuga (Eds.), New Directions in Rough Sets, Data Mining, and Granular-Soft Computing. Proceedings, 1999. XIV, 558 pages. 1999. (Subseries LNAI).

Vol. 1712: H. Boley, A Tight, Practical Integration of Relations and Functions. XI, 169 pages. 1999. (Subseries LNAI).

Vol. 1713: J. Jaffar (Ed.), Principles and Practice of Constraint Programming – CP'99. Proceedings, 1999. XII, 493 pages. 1999.

Vol. 1714: M.T. Pazienza (Eds.), Information Extraction. IX, 165 pages. 1999. (Subseries LNAI).

Vol. 1715: P. Perner, M. Petrou (Eds.), Machine Learning and Data Mining in Pattern Recognition. Proceedings, 1999. VIII, 217 pages. 1999. (Subseries LNAI).

Vol. 1716: K.Y. Lam, E. Okamoto, C. Xing (Eds.), Advances in Cryptology – ASIACRYPT'99. Proceedings, 1999. XI, 414 pages. 1999.

Vol. 1717: Ç. K. Koç, C. Paar (Eds.), Cryptographic Hardware and Embedded Systems. Proceedings, 1999. XI, 353 pages. 1999.

Vol. 1718: M. Diaz, P. Owezarski, P. Sénac (Eds.), Interactive Distributed Multimedia Systems and Telecommunication Services. Proceedings, 1999. XI, 386 pages. 1999.

Vol. 1719: M. Fossorier, H. Imai, S. Lin, A. Poli (Eds.), Applied Algebra, Algebraic Algorithms and Error-Correcting Codes. Proceedings, 1999. XIII, 510 pages. 1999.

Vol. 1720: O. Watanabe, T. Yokomori (Eds.), Algorithmic Learning Theory. Proceedings, 1999. XI, 365 pages. 1999. (Subseries LNAI).

Vol. 1721: S. Arikawa, K. Furukawa (Eds.), Discovery Science. Proceedings, 1999. XI, 374 pages. 1999. (Subseries LNAI).

Vol. 1722: A. Middeldorp, T. Sato (Eds.), Functional and Logic Programming. Proceedings, 1999. X, 369 pages. 1999.

Vol. 1723: R. France, B. Rumpe (Eds.), UML'99 – The Unified Modeling Language. XVII, 724 pages. 1999.

Vol. 1724: H. I. Christensen, H. Bunke, H. Noltemeier (Eds.), Sensor Based Intelligent Robots. Proceedings, 1998. VIII, 327 pages. 1999 (Subseries LNAI).

Vol. 1725: J. Pavelka, G. Tel, M. Bartošek (Eds.), SOFSEM'99: Theory and Practice of Informatics. Proceedings, 1999. XIII, 498 pages. 1999.

Vol. 1726: V. Varadharajan, Y. Mu (Eds.), Information and Communication Security. Proceedings, 1999. XI, 325 pages. 1999.

Vol. 1727: P.P. Chen, D.W. Embley, J. Kouloumdjian, S.W. Liddle, J.F. Roddick (Eds.), Advances in Conceptual Modeling. Proceedings, 1999. XI, 389 pages. 1999.

Vol. 1728: J. Akoka, M. Bouzeghoub, I. Comyn-Wattiau, E. Métais (Eds.), Conceptual Modeling – ER '99. Proceedings, 1999. XIV, 540 pages. 1999.

Vol. 1729: M. Mambo, Y. Zheng (Eds.), Information Security. Proceedings, 1999. IX, 277 pages. 1999.

Vol. 1730: M. Gelfond, N. Leone, G. Pfeifer (Eds.), Logic Programming and Nonmonotonic Reasoning. Proceedings, 1999. XI, 391 pages. 1999. (Subseries LNAI).

Vol. 1731: J. Kratochvíl (Ed.), Graph Drawing. Proceedings, 1999. XIII, 422 pages. 1999.

Vol. 1732: S. Matsuoka, R.R. Oldehoeft, M. Tholburn (Eds.), Computing in Object-Oriented Parallel Environments. Proceedings, 1999. VIII, 205 pages. 1999.

Vol. 1733: H. Nakashima, C. Zhang (Eds.), Approaches to Intelligent Agents. Proceedings, 1999. XII, 241 pages. 1999. (Subseries LNAI).

Vol. 1734: H. Hellwagner, A. Reinefeld (Eds.), SCI: Scalable Coherent Interface. XXI, 490 pages. 1999.

Vol. 1564: M. Vazirgiannis, Interactive Multimedia Documents. XIII, 161 pages. 1999.

Vol. 1591: D.J. Duke, I. Herman, M.S. Marshall, PREMO: A Framework for Multimedia Middleware. XII, 254 pages. 1999.

Vol. 1624: J. A. Padget (Ed.), Collaboration between Human and Artificial Societies. XIV, 301 pages. 1999. (Subseries LNAI).

Vol. 1635: X. Tu, Artificial Animals for Computer Animation. XIV, 172 pages. 1999.

Vol. 1646: B. Westfechtel, Models and Tools for Managing Development Processes. XIV, 418 pages. 1999.

Vol. 1735: J.W. Amtrup, Incremental Speech Translation. XV, 200 pages. 1999. (Subseries LNAI).

Vol. 1736: L. Rizzo, S. Fdida (Eds.): Networked Group Communication. Proceedings, 1999. XIII, 339 pages. 1999.

Vol. 1737: P. Agouris, A. Stefanidis (Eds.), Integrated Spatial Databases. Proceedings, 1999. X, 317 pages. 1999.

Vol. 1738: C. Pandu Rangan, V. Raman, R. Ramanujam (Eds.), Foundations of Software Technology and Theoretical Computer Science. Proceedings, 1999. XII, 452 pages. 1999.

Vol. 1739: A. Braffort, R. Gherbi, S. Gibet, J. Richardson, D. Teil (Eds.), Gesture-Based Communication in Human-Computer Interaction. Proceedings, 1999. XI, 333 pages. 1999. (Subseries LNAI).

Vol. 1740: R. Baumgart (Ed.): Secure Networking – CQRE [Secure] '99. Proceedings, 1999. IX, 261 pages. 1999.

Vol. 1741: A. Aggarwal, C. Pandu Rangan (Eds.), Algorithms and Computation. Proceedings, 1999. XIII, 448 pages. 1999.

Vol. 1742: P.S. Thiagarajan, R. Yap (Eds.), Advances in Computing Science – ASIAN'99. Proceedings, 1999. XI, 397 pages. 1999.

Vol. 1743: A. Moreira, S. Demeyer (Eds.), Object-Oriented Technology. Proceedings, 1999. XVII, 389 pages. 1999.

Vol. 1744: S. Staab, Extracting Degree Information from Texts. X; 187 pages. 1999. (Subseries LNAI).

Vol. 1745: P. Banerjee, V.K. Prasanna, B.P. Sinha (Eds.), High Performance Computing – HiPC'99. Proceedings, 1999. XXII, 412 pages. 1999.

Vol. 1746: M. Walker (Ed.), Cryptography and Coding. Proceedings, 1999. IX, 313 pages. 1999.

Vol. 1747: N. Foo (Ed.), Adavanced Topics in Artificial Intelligence. Proceedings, 1999. XV, 500 pages. 1999. (Subseries LNAI).

Vol. 1748: H.V. Leong, W.-C. Lee, B. Li, L. Yin (Eds.), Mobile Data Access. Proceedings, 1999. X, 245 pages. 1999.

Vol. 1749: L. C.-K. Hui, D.L. Lee (Eds.), Internet Applications. Proceedings, 1999. XX, 518 pages. 1999.

Vol. 1750: D.E. Knuth, MMIXware. VIII, 550 pages. 1999.

Vol. 1751: H. Imai, Y. Zheng (Eds.), Public Key Cryptography. Proceedings, 2000. XI, 485 pages. 2000.

Vol. 1752: S. Krakowiak, S. Shrivastava (Eds.), Advances in Distributed Systems. VIII, 509 pages. 2000.

Vol. 1753: E. Pontelli, V. Santos Costa (Eds.), Practical Aspects of Declarative Languages. Proceedings, 2000. X, 327 pages. 2000.

Vol. 1754: J. Väänänen (Ed.), Generalized Quantifiers and Computation. Proceedings, 1997. VII, 139 pages. 1999.

Vol. 1755: D. Bjørner, M. Broy, A.V. Zamulin (Eds.), Perspectives of System Informatics. Proceedings, 1999. XII, 540 pages. 2000.

Vol. 1757: N.R. Jennings, Y. Lespérance (Eds.), Intelligent Agents VI. Proceedings, 1999. XII, 380 pages. 2000. (Subseries LNAI).

Vol. 1758: H. Heys, C. Adams (Eds.), Selected Areas in Cryptography. Proceedings, 1999. VIII, 243 pages. 2000.

Vol. 1759: M.J. Zaki, C.-T. Ho (Eds.), Large-Scale Parallel Data Mining. VIII, 261 pages. 2000. (Subseries LNAI).

Vol. 1760: J.-J. Ch. Meyer, P.-Y. Schobbens (Eds.), Formal Models of Agents. Poceedings. VIII, 253 pages. 1999. (Subseries LNAI).

Vol. 1761: R. Caferra, G. Salzer (Eds.), Automated Deduction in Classical and Non-Classical Logics. Proceedings. VIII, 299 pages. 2000. (Subseries LNAI).

Vol. 1762: K.-D. Schewe, B. Thalheim (Eds.), Foundations of Information and Knowledge Systems. Proceedings, 2000. X, 305 pages. 2000.

Vol. 1763: J. Akiyama, M. Kano, M. Urabe (Eds.), Discrete and Computational Geometry. Proceedings, 1998. VIII, 333 pages. 2000.

Vol. 1764: H. Ehrig, G. Engels, H.-J. Kreowski, G. Rozenberg (Eds.), Theory and Application of Graph Transformations. Proceedings, 1998. IX, 490 pages. 2000.

Vol. 1765: T. Ishida, K. Isbister (Eds.), Digital Cities. IX, 444 pages. 2000.

Vol. 1767: G. Bongiovanni, G. Gambosi, R. Petreschi (Eds.), Algorithms and Complexity. Proceedings, 2000. VIII, 317 pages. 2000.

Vol. 1768: A. Pfitzmann (Ed.), Information Hiding. Proceedings, 1999. IX, 492 pages. 2000.

Vol. 1769: G. Haring, C. Lindemann, M. Reiser (Eds.), Performance Evaluation: Origins and Directions. X, 529 pages. 2000.

Vol. 1770: H. Reichel, S. Tison (Eds.), STACS 2000. Proceedings, 2000. XIV, 662 pages. 2000.

Vol. 1771: P. Lambrix, Part-Whole Reasoning in an Object-Centered Framework. XII, 195 pages. 2000. (Subseries LNAI).

Vol. 1772: M. Beetz, Concurrent Ractive Plans. XVI, 213 pages. 2000. (Subseries LNAI).

Vol. 1773: G. Saake, K. Schwarz, C. Türker (Eds.), Transactions and Database Dynamics. Proceedings, 1999. VIII, 247 pages. 2000.

Vol. 1774: J. Delgado, G.D. Stamoulis, A. Mullery, D. Prevedourou, K. Start (Eds.), Telecommunications and IT Convergence Towards Service E-volution. Proceedings, 2000. XIII, 350 pages. 2000.

Vol. 1776: G.H. Gonnet, D. Panario, A. Viola (Eds.), LATIN 2000: Theoretical Informatics. Proceedings, 2000. XIV, 484 pages. 2000.

Vol. 1777: C. Zaniolo, P.C. Lockemann, M.H. Scholl, T. Grust (Eds.), Advances in Database Technology – EDBT 2000. Proceedings, 2000. XII, 540 pages. 2000.

Vol. 1780: R. Conradi (Ed.), Software Process Technology. Proceedings, 2000. IX, 249 pages. 2000.

Vol. 1781: D.A. Watt (Ed.), Compiler Construction. Proceedings, 2000. X, 295 pages. 2000.

Vol. 1782: G. Smolka (Ed.), Programming Languages and Systems. Proceedings, 2000. XIII, 429 pages. 2000.

Vol. 1783: T. Maibaum (Ed.), Fundamental Approaches to Software Engineering. Proceedings, 2000. XIII, 375 pages. 2000.

Vol. 1784: J. Tiuryn (Ed.), Foundations of Software Science and Computation Structures. Proceedings, 2000. X, 391 pages. 2000.

Vol. 1785: S. Graf, M. Schwartzbach (Eds.), Tools and Algorithms for the Construction and Analysis of Systems. Proceedings, 2000. XIV, 552 pages. 2000.

Vol. 1786: B.H. Haverkort, H.C. Bohnenkamp, C.U. Smith (Eds.), Computer Performance Evaluation. Proceedings, 2000. XIV, 383 pages. 2000.

Vol. 1790: N. Lynch, B.H. Krogh (Eds.), Hybrid Systems: Computation and Control. Proceedings, 2000. XII, 465 pages. 2000.

Vol. 1794: H. Kirchner, C. Ringeissen (Eds.), Frontiers of Combining Systems. Proceedings, 2000. X, 291 pages. 2000. (Subseries LNAI).